OZ CLARKE'S
WINE
GUIDE

1997

THIRTEENTH EDITION

Contributors to *Oz Clarke's Wine Guide 1997*

Stephen Brook is a contributor on wine to *Vogue* and many other magazines and the author of *Sauternes and the Sweet White Wines of Bordeaux* as well as numerous travel books. His latest book is *Opera: an Anthology*. **Dave Broom** is a freelance wine writer. **Bob Campbell MW** is New Zealand's first MW and a specialist on the wines of that country. **Rosemary George MW** is the author of many wine books including *Chablis*, *French Country Wines* and *Chianti*; her latest, *The Wines of New Zealand*, is published in 1996. **Alex Liddell** is the author of *Port Wine Quintas of the Douro*, and has an interest in Madeira and other fortified wines. **Jasper Morris MW** is a wine merchant and the author of *The White Wines of Burgundy* and *The Wines of the Loire*. **Angela Muir MW** is an international winemaker and consultant and specialises in Eastern Europe. **Richard Neill** writes about wine in *Esquire*, *The Daily Telegraph*, *Time Out* and other publications, and has a particular interest in South America. **John Radford** is a wine writer with a particular knowledge of Spain. **Tom Stevenson** is a specialist in Champagne and the author of *Champagne* and *The Wines of Alsace*. California-based wine writer **Larry Walker** is a contributor to many British publications as well as being US consultant editor for Microsoft Wine Guide CD-ROM and the author, with his wife, of numerous books including *A Season in Spain*, *The Best of California* and *Tequila: the Book*. **Stuart Walton** is a freelance wine and food writer with a monthly column in *BBC Good Food* magazine; his book, *The World Encyclopedia of Wine*, is published in 1996.

Reviews of previous editions

'…cram-full of the straightforward, practical info you really need to know. In other words, "Where from? How good? How much?"' *Manchester Evening News*

'Oz relentlessly pulls the cork on the old-fashioned wine snobs. This no-nonsense guide gives the amateur wine enthusiast the confidence to explore wine…in an informal yet informed way.' *Daily Mirror*

'Packed with insider information and opinion, and worth every penny.' Derek Cooper

'…the guide gets better with every vintage. Clarke writes with enthusiasm virtually steaming off the page. Here is someone who loves wine.' *The Guardian*

'If you haven't bought a copy, there is little hope for you.' *The Sunday Telegraph*

'An enthusiastic, opinionated and entertaining survey of the world's wines and a price guide to wines on the shelves of Britain.' *The Sunday Times*

'…typically up-to-date, irreverent but informative.' *The Independent*

'Scholarly, funny and thought-provoking.' Robert Parker

OZ CLARKE'S
WINE GUIDE

1997
THIRTEENTH EDITION

'WEBSTER'S'
THE COMPLETE WINE
BUYER'S HANDBOOK

WEBSTERS
MITCHELL BEAZLEY
LONDON

The information and prices contained in the guide were correct to the best of our knowledge when we went to press, and the impression of relative price and relative value is almost certainly still accurate, even if a particular price has changed.

Although every care has been taken in the preparation of the guide, neither the publishers nor the editors can accept any liability for any consequences arising from the use of information contained herein.

Oz Clarke's Wine Guide *is an annual publication. We welcome any suggestions you may have for the 1998 edition.*

General Editor Margaret Rand
Price Guides Editor Lorna Bateson
Sub-editor Pauline Savage
Editorial Assistants Julie Ross,
Emma Richards, Sophie Howard
Art Editor Christopher Howson
DTP Jonathan Harley
Database Consultant Alexandra Boyle
Indexer Naomi Good
Cover photograph James Merrell
Editorial Director Claire Harcup
Design Manager Nigel O'Gorman

Advertising Sales
Logie Bradshaw Media Limited,
Strathallan House, Fernville Lane,
Midland Road, Hemel Hempstead,
Herts HP2 4LS
tel 0144 2233331, fax 0144 2231131

Created and designed by
Websters International Publishers Limited,
Axe and Bottle Court, 70 Newcomen Street,
London SE1 1YT
in association with Mitchell Beazley, an imprint of
Reed Consumer Books Limited,
Michelin House,
81 Fulham Road,
London SW3 6RB

Oz Clarke's Wine Guide 1997 Edition
© Websters International Publishers
and Reed International Books Limited 1996

ISBN 1 85732 867 1

Printed and bound in the UK by
Cox & Wyman, Reading

CONTENTS

INTRODUCTION

There's a new Most Expensive Wine in the world: yippee!

How expensive? £290 a glass. And we're talking retail, not restaurant, prices here. On April 13th 1996 an anonymous bidder bought a case of 1982 le Pin in a New York auction for £24,371 ($36,800) – £2031 a bottle, £290 a glass, and about £30 for a reasonably restrained gulp. Crazy.

Pity, really. Sounds like rather a nice wine, and now I'll never taste it. I could have done, though. I have a friend who had a couple of cases which, in normal circs he'd have been happy to broach in the spirit of scholarship and research. He sold them and built a new kitchen instead.

But nice though it may be, no one has really suggested it's the best wine in the world. It's such a loony price because there's not much of it – the two-hectare site only produces a maximum of 1000 cases or so each year – and because such rarity and exclusivity appeals massively to a whole new breed of super-rich who are turning the world of fine wine on its head – the brand-conscious, icon-hungry, commercial and financial whizzkids of the Far East.

Pin money

The person who bought the le Pin 1982 was from Hong Kong. Four days later Sotheby's offered some le Pin 1983 and 1985, and these five cases were snapped up for £55,000 ($83,360) by a guy in Singapore bidding on his mobile telephone. He replaced the battery, and next day bought all ten cases of le Pin 1988, 1989 and 1990 offered at Christie's, for £68,000 ($103,408). My friend could have built a conservatory, too, if he'd held on to his cases for another few weeks.

The last time there was a massive incursion of new wine enthusiasts desperate to buy up as much of 'the best' as they could lay their hands on, regardless of price, was in 1983, when the 1982 Bordeaux vintage was first offered for sale and a smart young American lawyer-cum-wine writer, Robert Parker, sniffed the air and knew America was ready for this sumptuous, juicy type of red Bordeaux, so clearly high quality, so utterly easy to appreciate, that many old-timers gave it short shrift. They lived to regret their hauteur as prices soared, and Robert Parker became America's most influential wine critic.

And the prices stayed up. They may have been too cheap before 1982, but during the 1980s, as America bought and bought, and collecting wine became a fashionable pastime for the dentists and doctors, lawyers and Wall Street traders whose pockets were bulging with spare cash, no-one ever said they were too cheap again.

And prices? I actually bought a case of Pichon-Lalande 1982 early on for £110. I see it goes for about £1200 a case now at auction. If I wanted to buy the Pichon-Lalande 1995 it would cost me £330 ex-cellars, and it isn't even bottled yet.

In 1982, if you went to a wine lover's home, there's every chance he or she would rip open a mature red Bordeaux without a second thought. Claret was the British drink. We understood it, we supported it, and we could afford it. In 1996 I can't think of anyone of my acquaintance who still regards high-quality mature Bordeaux as their staple – we've been pushed out of the market to such an extent that we no longer understand it, we no longer support it, and we certainly can't afford it. Indeed, its absence is likely to become more and more marked, because the producers of the world's most expensive wines, though still eager for the approbation of British experts, are business people first and foremost. They create markets for their brands.

Britain used to be the most important market for Bordeaux. It had to get all the best wines. It doesn't anymore, just as it doesn't get the best Burgundy, the best Barolo or Rioja, or the best Napa Cabernet, because as demand for such wines has increased, prices have quite understandably soared, and we, price-conscious as ever, have called a halt. The business people in charge of the world's top wines have shifted their targets to where prestige and image are craved, regardless of price. Sometimes great flavours go hand in hand with the rustle of new banknotes glistening in the candlelight, sometimes they don't. If the promotion and the hype are good enough, it can be years before a brand is rumbled.

The Far East's fascination with fine wine may not be just a flash in the pan. Since these are the booming economies, these are the places where money is frantically earned and frantically spent, and in a very few years' time we could find the majority of the world's most visibly extravagant wines swishing around the Pacific Rim. Already the average value of a bottle of Bordeaux, red or white, imported into Singapore is 2.5 times that of the average British import. Hong Kong's bottle value is three times that of Britain. Taiwan's is 4.5 times Britain's. And that's taking red and white together. Divided up, the price of the less-chic white is FF22.50. The average for reds is FF75 – that's about £10 a bottle.

Where does that leave us? It leaves us in some danger of being marginalized as a so-called fine wine market. If we don't support the duff vintages – and by 'support' I mean persuade unwilling and wary customers that a patently unexciting vintage is a must buy even at a high price – then our allocation of good vintages is cut. The 1995 Bordeaux vintage is a case in point. Last spring merchants were rushing out their en primeur offers, gushing with enthusiasm for what is clearly an overpriced and only sporadically exciting vintage with far too many question marks against its eventual quality. One of their tactics was to say how

little of the wine there was to purchase. Well, there may not be that much on sale here, but there's no shortage of wine – 1995 is a massive vintage. It's just that we're not offered much any more. Our allocations are going to buyers in France itself, Germany and America, but above all to the Far East. All because we wouldn't buy the hardly thrilling vintages since 1991, at prices which increasingly make no sense.

Taste not waste
So are we missing out? No, not really. If it's merely the flavour of Bordeaux you want, not the cachet, there are a reasonable number of determined, unsung châteaux making excellent wine at a fair, if high, price.

But do we even have to go to these levels for fine wine? No. Not if we make our own definition of what fine wine is, rather than slavishly follow received wisdom about how it must be from long-established vineyards in marginal, cool climates using a tiny clutch of classic grape varieties. Increasingly it's becoming obvious that the warm-climate areas and their grapes are making the wines we actually prefer – and at far lower prices. If we do want classic grapes, then the Catena Chardonnay from Argentina or the Mulderbosch Chardonnay from South Africa, the top Reserve Cabernets of Errázuriz and Concha y Toro in Chile, or Chapel Hill's Cabernet from Australia will do me nicely – all at under a tenner, all from warm climates. But why stick to classic varieties? And why even pay as much as a tenner? What about the stunning Semillons of the Clare and Barossa valleys in Australia, the heady Viogniers of southern France, the gorgeous, throaty bush vine Grenaches and Mourvèdres and Carignans of France and Australia, the revivalist Negroamaros and Primitivos of southern Italy, the Malbecs of Argentina, the Zinfandels of California, the St Laurents of Austria and the Douro reds of Portugal. All stunning. All way under a tenner. All at a shop near you. All my kind of wine. And, I hope, yours too.

100 BEST BUYS

These are my favourite wines, selected from those listed by the merchants in this book, and representing all that's good in wine today. I'm as pleased as punch with them: there are wonderful flavours here, flavours for every occasion and for every palate. They're listed country by country, and in alphabetical order within each country.

MY 1997 TOP TEN

FRANCE
1993 Alsace Gewürztraminer Grand Cru Sonnenglanz Vieilles Vignes, Domaine Bott Geyl, £13.84 (SUM)
Everything I want Gewürz to be – rich, heady wine full of the scent of musk and Nivea Creme, and fat juiciness of super-ripe grapes.

1993 Alsace Gewürztraminer Reserve Personnelle, Henry Fuchs, £8.92 (PIP)
Another superb sultry Gewürz, thick syrupy fruit like sultanas and mincemeat that dominates the Nivea perfume and the crackle of freshly ground black pepper.

GERMANY
1994 Serriger Schloss Saarsteiner Riesling Spätlese, £12.84 (SUM)
Thrilling in its austerity, but irresistible for its mix of apple peel, lime, steely slate and honeysuckle.

PORTUGAL
1994 Quinta de la Rosa, Douro, £5.90 (AD, GE, LEA, MV, PLA)
Stunning red. Most of the Douro's best red gets turned into vintage port, but the Douro Valley is a brilliant place for red table wine too, with a marvellous climate and original grape varieties. Above all, Douro reds have a heart-stopping soft, warm core that highlights their silky mulberry fruit and warm spice.

AUSTRALIA
1994 Tim Adams The Fergus, Clare Valley, £8.99 (AUS)
Grenache doesn't come any better than this – mint and eucalyptus and liquorice, lording it over lean but juicy ripe red fruit. The first mouthful may shock you, but you'll be sorry when you've drained the bottle.

1992 Doonkuna Shiraz, £7.99 (AUS)
Less brawn, less thudding tannin and gooey-eyed fruit than most Aussie Shiraz, but instead a midweight red full of soft chewy fruit and bayleaf and peppercorn scent.

1994 Oscars Traditional Semillon, Basedow's, £5.99-6.50 (VIC, BIB)
Wonderful whacky mix of custard and lime and leather. Excellent example of how exciting whites not made from Chardonnay can be.

1993 Tyrrells Vat 8 Shiraz-Cabernet, £14.99 (UN)
What a pleasure to see one of the grand old names of Australian wine back on form after a few rocky years – and rebuilding its reputation with traditional palate-blasters, super-ripe fruit and not entirely up-to-date wine-making.

SOUTH AMERICA
1995 Errázuriz Merlot, Curicó Valley, Chile, £4.99 (OD)
Young, rumbustuous, a smell of grass and well-hung meat leading into crunchy cranberry and damson fruit that combines brilliantly with the pepper and radish roughness.

SOUTH AFRICA
1995 Avontuur Pinotage, Stellenbosch, £4.99 (WAI)
Where else can you get one hundred per cent tub-thumping red that packs a punch of damson sweetness and tannin and coal and mixes that with cream and toasted marshmallows?

These are still smashing wines, with seven of them almost squeezing into the top ten. Nice try, guys, but there's always next year.

Again the wines are listed country by country, and are given in alphabetical order within each country.

THE NEXT BEST

BORDEAUX
1994 Château Bauduc Bordeaux Blanc Sec, £6.16 (SUM)
Seductive, as soft as junket and cream.

1990 Château Granins Grand Poujeaux Cru Bourgeois, Moulis-en-Médoc, £11.95 (PIP)
Rustic fruit and earthy flavour, good ripeness.

1993 Château Paloumey Cru Bourgeois Haut-Médoc, £8.90 (MV)
Good mainstream claret that will age nicely.

1990 Château Sergant, Lalande de Pomerol, £9.95 (ROB)
Good chunky claret that ends up tasting a bit like cream of oxtail and chocolate.

BURGUNDY
1994 Bourgogne Les Bons Batons, Rion, £8.50 (MV)
Excellent basic perfume tasting of cherry and freshly baked almond slices.

1994 Chablis, £6.89 (ASD)
Good and honeyed, with a streak of lemon.

1994 Chablis Domaine des Marronniers, £8.75 (BIB)
Classic Chablis – lean and lemony now but showing signs of filling out and fattening up.

1994 Hautes-Côtes de Nuits, Domaine du Bois Guillaume, Devevey, £9.90 (MV)
Very good full, nutty Burgundy.

CHAMPAGNE
Champagne Brut Blanc de Noirs, £11.99 (SAI)
Classy soft-centred fizz with a puffed wheat yeastiness.

Champagne Deutz Classic Brut, £17.60 (FOR)
Dry foaming wine with a delicious soft cashew and yeast texture and Deutz's characteristic whiff of cedar.

RHONE
1993 Châteauneuf-du-Pape Domaine de Monpertuis, £10.56 (EL)
Solidly fruity red, nicely seasoned with bay leaf and thyme.

Clairette de Die Tradition Georges Aubert, £6.99 (UN)
Delightful crunchy grapiness and just a hint of elderflower.

1988 Cornas Chante Perdrix, Delas, £9.70 (FOR)
Beautiful smell of chocolate and grilled meat and deep, dark, loganberry and chocolate fruit.

1994 Domaine du Colombier Crozes-Hermitage, £8 (BIB)
Interesting round-hipped white that will age well to attractive baked apple and honeysuckle.

1994 Domaine la Renejeanne, les Arbousiers, Côtes du Rhône, £5.79 (OD)
Rich, juicy jumble of loganberry and cherry and the trailing scent of rosemary.

1992 Lirac les Queyrades, André Mejan, £6.50 (FOR, TAN)
Pleasant meaty southern Rhône red with a flicker of hillside herbs.

LOIRE
1993 Sancerre Lucien Crochet, £10.20 (BY)
Expensive but classy coffee bean and blackcurrant leaf Sauvignon.

1994 Sancerre le Manoir, André Neveu, £9.75 (BIB)
Ooh, these Sancerre prices. Still, this is good wine, full of ripe green fruit mingled with honey.

1993 Savennières Clos du Papillon, £8.35 (EL)
Curious but enticing mix of nuts and guava and lemon peel flavours that will happily age ten years.

1994 Vouvray Vieilles Vignes, Domaine Bourillon, £7.50 (MV)
Lovely quirky blend of lemon zest and apple peel in a dry yet rich wine.

ALSACE
1988 Alsace Gewürztraminer Reserve, Trimbach, £12.99 (BUT, UN)
Gentle crunchy grape flavour and haunting perfume of violet leaf.

1993 Alsace Muscat Riquewihr Domaine Bott Geyl, £8.06 (SUM)
Seductive fragrance of rose petals, orange blossom, Cox's orange pippins and green grapes.

1993 Alsace Pinot Blanc Henry Fuchs, £6.47 (PIP)
Soft honeyed white with a creamy texture.

SOUTHERN FRANCE
1993 Château Lamargue, Costières de Nîmes, £4.23 (EL)
Real come-hither glugger, damsons and loganberries and a hint of herbs.

1994 Minervois, Domaine des Murettes, £3.99 (MAJ)
Lovely juicy red, both gutsy and modern; the best of both worlds.

1994 Château Pech-Celeyran, La Clape Coteaux du Languedoc, £5.10 (AD, TAN)
Ferocious but fascinating wild-eyed red full of dark black fruit and the crunchy perfume of pine needles underfoot.

1993 Fitou Château de Segure, £5.99 (UN)
Good dusty red with bay leaf scent.

1994 Vin de Pays des Côtes de Gascogne, Domaine Loubadère, £4.82 (EL)
Excellent ripe white scythed through with lemon and lime zest.

1994 Vin de Pays d'Oc Sauvignon Blanc, £4.90 (TAN)
Full-bodied dry white pinging with green grass freshness.

GERMANY
1993 Ungsteiner Herrenberg Scheurebe Spätlese, Pfeffingen, £8.70 (SUM)
Unusual German white with gorgeous rich pink grapefruit flavour.

ITALY
1995 Langhe Arneis Alasia, £7.99 (ENO)
Unctuous yet dry white, redolent of white peaches in syrup and may blossom.

1991 Rocca Sveva Recioto della Valpolicella Classico Amarone, £9.69 (UN)
Disconcerting but delicious sweet-and-sour red packed with flavours of stewed cherries and plums.

SPAIN
1993 Dominio de Valdepusa Syrah Marqués de Griñon, £7.99 (TES)
Rather cooked fruit yet enough peppery attack to make it interesting.

1992 Viña Valoria Rioja Crianza, £6.15 (PE)
Big old custardy style with glimpses of orange and nuts and strawberry.

USA
1995 Bonny Doon Clos de Gilroy Grenache, California, £7.20 (MV)
The ultimate juicy-fruit, breezy glugger.

1995 Ca' del Solo Malvasia Bianca, Monterey, California, £7.60 (MV)
Soft, come-hither white tasting of Cox's apples, lychees, blood oranges and peach blossom. I mean it.

1994 Geyser Peak Chardonnay, Sonoma County, California, £6.99 (VIC)
Full, nutty, smoky Chardonnay.

1992 Mount Eden Vineyards Cabernet Sauvignon, California, £12.95 (RAE)
Deep, dark red redolent of the tastes of coconut and mint.

1994 Quady Elysium Black Muscat, California, £5.99 for 37.5mm (NO, ROB, UN)
Pungent concentrated sweet essence of cranberry, loganberry and damson in a red wine.

1994 Qupé Syrah, Central Coast, California, £9.90 (MV)
Exciting red overflowing with loganberry and bramble syrup sweetness.

1993 Terra Rosa, Laurel Glen Vineyard, California, £7.95 (NI)
Strong, plummy Bordeaux-style red.

AUSTRALIA
Australian Chardonnay, £4.49 (SAI)
Very good full style, peaches, nectarines and a pinch of spice.

1992 Australian Chardonnay-Pinot Noir, £9.75 (BER)
Classy Aussie fizz with a yeasty feel.

1994 Chapel Hill McLaren Vale Shiraz, £7.99 (AUS)
Lovely ripe texture, and gentle tannin that is quite restrained for an Aussie Shiraz – promising a future full of black fruit, chocolate and toffee flavours but not delivering them quite yet.

1995 Delatite Limited Release Victoria Chardonnay, £8 (ARM)
Gentle, delicate, perfumed Aussie Chardie, not as weighty as some.

1994 Dennis McLaren Vale Cabernet Sauvignon, £8.49 (PE)
Minty blackcurrant and soft, juicy mulberries with just a whiff of green leaf and a black cherry finish.

1993 Dennis McLaren Vale Shiraz, £8.49 (PE)
Not hefty, but a delicious warm-blooded blend of liquorice, chocolate, black plums and bacon smoke.

1994 Kingston Estate Murray Valley Mataro, Australia, £5.99 (TES)
Mataro is the southern Rhône's Mourvèdre grape, flying under different colours. This is chunky, ripe red flecked with cinnamon and nutmeg.

1995 Hanging Rock Jim Jim Sauvignon Blanc, £9.99 (PE)
Starkly beautiful splash of gooseberry and passion fruit and lime, with just a hint of sweet syrup.

1993 Ironstone Western Australian Cabernet-Shiraz, £5.99 (MAJ)
Deep old-fashioned chunky red balancing pepper and leather with horsehair.

1993 St Hallett Old Block Shiraz, £10.49 (AUS)
This is somewhat lighter and more restrained than usual, but it'll go to cocoa and toffee plums in time.

1995 Salisbury Estate Chardonnay, £5.99 (ENO)
Spot on traditional Aussie Chardie.

1993 Saltram Mamrebrook Chardonnay, £6.99 (WAI, UN)
Rich, syrupy wine balanced by biscuit and bacon smoke.

**Seaview Brut Pinot Noir-Chardonnay,
£7.99 (SAI, UN)**
Full, foaming soft fizz, nutty and with a touch of
puffed wheat yeastiness.

**1993 South Australian Cabernet
Sauvignon, £3.99 (ASD)**
Lovely soft-centred fruit soup of mint,
blackcurrant and a little raisin sweetness to
round it off.

1993 Stoniers Cabernet, £7.99 (WAT)
Deep, dry red with a captivating perfume of
eucalyptus and mint to spice up its good but
lean blackcurrant fruit.

**1995 Stoniers Pinot Noir, Mornington
Peninsula, £8.99 (WAT)**
Elegant cool-climate Pinot, strawberry with a
hint of chocolate.

**1994 Tatachilla Cabernet Sauvignon,
McLaren Vale & Langhorne Creek,
£5.99 (WAI)**
Ripe, sweet but balanced red with oodles of
blackcurrant skins and leaves.

**1994 Tyrrells Old Winery Semillon,
Australia, £6.69 (UN)**
Excellent traditional Hunter Semillon to drink
now or age – custard creams, leather and lime
now, and it can only get better.

**1990 Wakefield Cabernet Sauvignon,
Clare Valley, £5.99 (UN)**
Lovely gentle wine, full of blackcurrant and
butter and coconut cream.

**1995 Grenache, Whitmore Old
Vineyard, Yaldara, SE Australia, £5.75
(WAI)**
Ripe, soft, red fruit glugger perfumed with
rosehips.

NEW ZEALAND
**1995 Dry River Sauvignon Blanc,
Martinborough, £9.95 (RAE)**
Fragrant Sauvignon Blanc perfumed with kiwi
fruit, lime and freshly cut grass.

**1994 Lawsons Dry Hills Marlborough
Chardonnay, £8.75 (BIB)**
Rich, creamy Chardonnay with a savoury
nuttiness to fill it out and a streak of kiwi green
fruit to balance.

**1995 Mills Reef Hawkes Bay Reserve
Riesling, £6.10 (FOR)**
Delightful aromatic white, glycerine-soft and
marvellously scented with honeysuckle and
lemon leaf.

**1995 Matua Marlborough Sauvignon
Blanc, £8.29 (UN)**
Good, aggressive gooseberry and lemon peel
Sauvignon Blanc from the difficult 1995
vintage.

**1994 Mills Reef Hawkes Bay Reserve
Chardonnay, £7.50 (FOR)**
Syrupy fruit fattened out even further with
custard and nuts.

**1995 Mills Reef Sauvignon Blanc, £5.60
(FOR)**
Kiwi fruit and Cox's orange pippins streaked
with green grass.

**1995 Oyster Bay Marlborough
Sauvignon Blanc, £6.99 (MAJ)**
Earth and gooseberry pepped up with a squirt
of citrus fruit.

**1995 Palliser Estate Martinborough
Sauvignon Blanc, £7.95 (BY, CB)**
Rather rich style but pretty good green grass
and fresh earth too.

**1995 Waipara Chardonnay Mark
Rattray Vineyards, £9.15 (WAT)**
Perfumed, creamy Chardonnay that is
delicious now but that will nevertheless
improve with time.

**1994 Stoniers Chardonnay, £7.99
(WAT)**
Classy cool-climate Chardonnay, all, toffee and
hazelnut richness with a streak of cool green
leaf.

1995 Waipara Springs Riesling, £5.75 (WAT)
Pleasant limy Riesling, a little honey and flicker of spritz.

1995 Waipara West Sauvignon Blanc, £7.99 (WAT)
Light yet quite intense gooseberry and grass Sauvignon.

SOUTH AMERICA
1994 Alamos Ridge Malbec, Mendoza, Argentina, £5 (BIB)
Juicy red with a splash of cream and spice that manages to be both serious and easy-going at the same time.

Chilean Merlot, £3.99 (SAI)
Good crunchy blackcurrant leaf and fresh coffee bean aroma.

1995 Cono Sur Pinot Noir Selection Reserve, Chile, £6.49 (ASD, FUL, OD, VIC, WS)
Beautifully stylish Pinot with the intriguing mixture of fresh strawberry and the fig and date richness of a good Côte de Beaune.

1995 Errázuriz Chardonnay, Curicó Valley, Chile, £4.99 (HA, OD)
Rich tinned peaches in syrup; fat texture like the caramel on buttered brazils.

1988 Torreon del Paredes Cabernet Sauvignon Reserve, Chile, £4.80 (FOR)
Delicious mature Cabernet with in-yer-face blackcurrant and eucalyptus.

SOUTH AFRICA
1995 Beyerskloof Pinotage, Stellenbosch, £4.99 (OD)
Smashing aggressive brew of tannin and damson, cream and marshmallow.

1994 Neil Ellis Pinotage, Stellenbosch, £6.30 (FOR)
Strange Mortadella sausage nose, but lots of squashy black plum fruit and marshmallow softness.

1995 Neil Ellis Sauvignon Blanc, Elgin, £6 (FOR, FUL, ROB, SAI, UB)
Arresting aggressive blend of gooseberry, grapefruit, green grass and mint.

1994 Fairview Estate Cabernet Sauvigon, Paarl, £5.99 (VIC)
Powerful, gutsy red with rich, stewy fruit and a whiff of coal smoke.

1994 Grangehurst Pinotage, £8.95 (BIB)
Big bruiser of black cherry and plumskins, but the marshmallow comes through at the end.

1995 Hilltop Chardonnay, Paarl, £6.99 (PE)
Good mix of New World ripeness and that 'savage' character of traditional Burgundy.

1995 Klein Constantia Chardonnay, Constantia, £6.99 (CAP, UN)
Very elegant wine delicately balanced between smoky oak and ripe, dry fruit.

1995 Mulderbosch Chardonnay, Stellenbosch, £9 (ARM)
Splendid mix of oatmeal, grilled cashews and spice in classic Burgundian style.

1995 Steenberg Sauvignon Blanc, Constantia, £7 (ARM)
Strong, direct, zippy white full of grapefruit and lime.

Beyers Truter Pinotage, Stellenbosch, £4.99 (TES)
Another gutsy, brash but delicious young Pinotage.

1994 Uiterwyck Pinotage, £9.20 (LAY)
Powerful, almost too powerful, but there is rich, dark-hearted fruit in there that should develop well in a year or two.

1995 Vriesenhof Chardonnay, Stellenbosch, £5.20 (FOR)
Bright, youthful Chardonnay with an attractive layer of new oak warmth.

IDEAL CELLARS

This is one of my favourite parts of the book. Since the first edition in 1984, merchants have received imaginary cheques of £100, £500 and £1000 to produce, together with my own selections, a total of 402 cellars. For regular readers of this section, this has provided a unique collection of wine advice. Admittedly, the merchants have all chosen from their own lists, but then I assume their lists reflect their own tastes. And it does at least mean that you know where to get hold of their recommendations and hold them to account if you disagree.

ALLAN CHEESMAN

SAINSBURY

It is six years since I was last asked to submit my Ideal Cellars from Sainsbury's shelves, and I have to confess that some price points have changed. What hasn't changed, however, is the value and variety that are available from no fewer than 23 countries, so selecting the wines was quite tough.

£100

Four half-cases that prove that cheap doesn't have to mean poor quality. These wines give a good introduction to four classic, internationally famous grape varieties.

Bulgarian Reserve Cabernet Sauvignon
Good everyday drinking with varietal character. I still don't know how they do it for the price. **6 for £29.94**

South Bay Pinot Noir *From California, this blend gives clean fruit without any jamminess. It's cheaper than red Burgundy, by quite a lot, and it still has a remarkable touch of class.* **6 for £29.94**

Sauvignon Vin de Pays d'Oc, Domaine St-Marc *A touch of New World wine-making has delivered clean, fresh gooseberry fruit that was unheard of from this region even five years ago.* **6 for £23.94**

Santara Chardonnay, Conca de Barbera
This is real Hugh Ryman magic: he's turned his hand to a really stylish Chardonnay with a little oak. Again, it's from an unlikely corner of Europe. **6 for £23.94**

Total cost: £107.76

£500

For this amount I can have seven cases, which is a good start for any cellar.

1995 Sainsbury's Sancerre *Sauvignon from Sancerre cannot be beaten, and this one, newly sourced from Fouassier, is a perfect crisp, clean example.* **12 for £88.20**

1994/5 Sainsbury's Chardonnay, Altesino
From northern Italy, this barrique fermented and aged wine was made by Australian Geoff Merrill. **12 for £65.88**

1994 La Baume Chardonnay *From the south of France, this Chardonnay captures all the class, weight and power of a wine from a much loftier appellation. More Australian wine-making.* **12 for £53.40**

South Bay Pinot Noir *The same California Pinot that I had in my £100 cellar. Well, I like it.* **12 for £59.88**

Sainsbury's Chilean Cabernet-Merlot, Curicó *Rich, powerful fruit, a deep colour and a classic blend.* **12 for £45.48**

1994 Château Carsin, Premières Côtes de Bordeaux *Modern wine-making techniques have here produced an elegant, soft wine.* **12 for £71.40**

Sainsbury's Cava *No great pretensions, but a good bet for any party. I often serve it at home.* **12 for £59.88**

Muscat de St-Jean-de-Minervois *Ideal with puds, but also good with Roquefort and other blue cheeses.* **12 halves for £37.80**

Total cost: £481.92

£1000

This gives me no fewer than 12 cases.

Sainsbury's Chardonnay, Altesino *Yes, I know I've had it before. But I can't resist a bargain.* **12 for £65.88**

1994 Mâcon Blanc les Ecuyers *One of the best in its class, with all the characteristics of wines from the Côte d'Or.* **12 for £83.40**

1995 Firestone Sauvignon Blanc *Fine, clean, fresh Sauvignon with lovely tropical fruit flavours.* **12 for £55.09**

Gentil Hugel *Why is it that only the wine trade enjoys Alsace wines? This one is a real classic.* **12 for £63.00**

1995 Santa Rita Chardonnay Estate Reserve, Chile *Rich and full with some class and 'Old World' notes.* **12 for £69.00**

1996 Mount Hurtle Grenache Rosé, Australia *Rosé with 'A' levels. Rather full for light quaffing, but a superb food wine for salads, fish and spiced foods.* **12 for £59.40**

1990 Clos St-Georges, Graves Supérieures *We've been following this wine for years: it is benchmark sweet white Bordeaux.* **12 for £89.40**

Sainsbury's South African Cabernet-Merlot Reserve Selection *A stylish blend from near Stellenbosch. Ripe and rich with a good tannic backbone.* **12 for £51.00**

Sainsbury's Red Burgundy *We have worked with Antonin Rodet in Mercurey to emulate the finer Burgundy appellations, but at a more affordable price.* **12 for £65.40**

1993 Châteauneuf-du-Pape, Domaine André Brunel *There's no such thing as cheap Châteauneuf, but this is a stunner. It's already showing complexity.* **12 for £119.40**

1990 Château Vieille Cure, Fronsac *This small property makes better and better wine each year.* **12 for £88.20**

Sainsbury's Blanc de Noirs Champagne *Soft and ripe with a fine mousse, this can grace any table.* **12 for £143.40**

Total cost: £952.57

CLAUDE GIRET

ANTHONY BYRNE FINE WINES

Since I am of French origin, perhaps it is natural that I have a penchant for French wines – but the most important thing to me is that the wine I drink matches the food I eat. One of my favourite hobbies is cooking, and nothing can be more disastrous than a wine which dominates the food or, even worse, clashes with it. And, like most people, I am limited by the fact that I have no proper cellar.

£100

This is a modest budget, which means that quantity has to prevail. I've chosen the sort of wines that will be excellent with well-prepared, straightforward food.

1995 Sauvignon Vin de Pays d'Oc, Francisque Dumas *This is bottled in Beaujolais by the Cellier des Samsons, and it has achieved a miracle. Pristine and zippy Sauvignon with a good balance of fruit and acidity. I would drink this with grilled sardines, or with mussels.* **6 for £24.75**

1995 Viognier Vin de Pays d'Oc, Francisque Dumas *This comes from the same stable and I make no apology, because I simply love it. Dry, rich, honeyed, and with a peachy and apricot nose and palate. It would go nicely with trout meunière, grilled salmon steaks or even pasta and tuna in a light mayonnaise.* **6 for £34.69**

1995 Syrah, Vin de Pays de Vaucluse, Vignoble Chancel *This has a wonderful nose of violets and liquorice with lots of spice. Just the thing for spicy saussicon sec, barbecued meat, jambon de Bayonne and fairly strong cheeses.* **6 for £22.56**

1994 Vin de Pays du Gers Rouge, Producteurs de Plaimont *Textbook stuff from Gascony, light, fruity and easy to drink. A versatile wine for chicken dishes and meat salads. Superior daily plonk.* **6 for £20.72**

Total cost: £102.72

£500

This is a totally different exercise. I shall invest in a few of my favourite bottles, and set about planning 12 dinner parties.

Champagne Drappier Cuvée Speciale NV *One needs a good Champagne as an apéritif. Nothing is more stylish, and it does not spoil your palate. It is sufficiently versatile to go with any nibbles.* **12 for £150.45**

1994 Tokay Vieilles Vignes, Domaine Zind-Humbrecht *A world-class wine from a world-class winemaker. It's very intriguing, with a hint of exotic fruits, spices, rich and very complex. I would serve it with all sorts of terrines, salmon, shrimps, smoked chicken and, of course, cheese.* **12 for £187.25**

1994 Fleurie, Domaine de la Bouronière *I spent 16 years working with Georges Duboeuf, which gave me a terrific appetite for good Gamay. This is not one of Georges', but it is one of the best Beaujolais I have ever drunk. It has a powerful floral nose, and a supple, delightfully fragrant and vivacious palate with a silky finish. Excellent for drinking with saussison de Lyon en brioche or coq au vin, or with goat's cheese.* **12 for £100.95**

1993 Cabernet Sauvignon, Santa Carolina Estate, Chile *I've been extravagant, so I now have just £5 a bottle to spend. For that sort of price, I'll go to Chile. This is impressive, with weight and substance, and a lush flavour. It will go with roasts of any kind and most cheeses.* **12 for £58.93**

Total cost: £497.58

£1000

Having lavishly described two of my favourite bottles in my £500 cellar, I want them again in this cellar. Otherwise, I shall upgrade the Champagne and add three or four wines so that the whole cellar is better balanced. I will have to have a good white Burgundy, a good spicy Rhône and, say, a classic Bordeaux.

Champagne Henriot Blanc de Blancs NV *This makes a marvellous apéritif. It is thirst-quenching, light, elegant and stylish. I find that guests always love it – so one case may not be enough.* **12 for £205.86**

1994 Tokay Vieilles Vignes, Domaine Zind-Humbrecht *I chose this before, and I'll choose it again.* **12 for £187.25**

Vin de pays if you like it. Vin de don't pay if you don't.

Choosing a wine has never been easy. Who can remember the good years from the bad, the regions, the grapes, the soil types, and all the different crus?

The details can sloosh around like so much wine in a taster's glass.

Which is why we'll refund your money if the wine you choose doesn't meet your expectations.

It's as simple as that, no questions asked.

Of course, as Supermarket Wine Merchant of the Year four times in the past seven years, we're absolutely confident that you'll enjoy any bottle we sell.

So, even if you don't know your Pouilly Fuissé from your Pouilly Fumé, remember there's one word that will help. Sainsbury's

1994 Fleurie, Domaine de la Bouronière
If you like andouillettes, this is the wine that's best for them.   **12 for £100.95**

1993 St-Aubin les Pucelles, Domaine Lamy Pillot   *St-Aubin is supposed to be Chassagne's poor relation. Well, this one is anything but. It has a powerful, smoky aroma, and it's quite weighty with some maturity showing. Very racy. Best served with fish accompanied by sauce, or cheese like chaource with fresh walnuts.* **12 for £150.31**

1988 Châteauneuf-du-Pape Clos St-Jean
Young Vincent Maurel refuses to sell this wine unless it is fully mature. This wine is as colossal as the Palais des Papes in Avignon. Chunky, solid, spicy and generous. A wine for game – and to be served for only the most appreciative friends.   **12 for £127.46**

1992 Château Lady Langoa, Bordeaux
I am very keen on second wines of Bordeaux châteaux. This is the second wine of Langoa-Barton, and is a masterpiece. It's very stylish and it can be drunk now, but will improve considerably within the next five years or so. Drink it with all roast meats, game birds and with cheese.   **12 for £110.55**

1992 Savigny-lès-Beaune Les Bourgeots, Simon Bize, Burgundy   *A good cellar cannot be complete without some decent Burgundy, and this one is succulent, with fragrant fruit and good structure: a most seductive combination. Again, I'd drink it with game, boeuf Bourguignonne and various sorts of cheese. It is drinking very well now, too, so there's no need to wait.*   **12 for £144.80**

Total cost: £1027.18

MARGARET HARVEY MW

FINE WINES OF NEW ZEALAND

I have been shipping and selling New Zealand wines now for 11 years, and I think we are only seeing the start of what the country has to offer. New areas are coming into being all the time, and so are new varieties and new clones. My money is on Riesling, especially the sweet late harvest styles, and Pinot Noir and Merlot.

£100

New Zealand will never be a bulk producer, nor will we see many wines at less than £5 a bottle. So I've settled on just two wines for my cellar which will give me constant pleasure.

1994 Aotea Sauvignon Blanc   *This is my own label, blended specially. It has a nettly green pepper nose with a delicate herbaceous flavour and clean, fresh acidity.* **6 for £35.70**

1994 Redwood Valley Cabernet Sauvignon   *Classic blackcurrant nose and flavour, deep crimson-plum colour and rich fruit. This is benchmark cool-climate Cabernet Sauvignon.*   **6 for £48.00**

Total cost: £83.70

£500

I've opted here for wines for everyday drinking that also have development potential.

1995 Sauvignon Blanc, Hawkes Bay, Vidal   *Delicate, herbaceous and green pepper bouquet and flavour, with lots of gooseberries. Nice fresh acidity; it would be ideal with fish or smoked meat.*
12 for £83.40

1994 Dry Riesling, Nelson, Seifried Estate   *A first-class example of this grape variety. Dry on the palate with lime, floral and peach aromas and flavour.* **12 for £83.40**

1995 Sauvignon Blanc, Waipara,
Waipara West *This new vineyard is
producing passionfruit and wild gooseberry
flavours and good acidity.* **12 for £95.40**

1994 Merlot Rosé, Hawkes Bay, Vidal
*A personal favourite. Soft red berry fruit
character with clean, well-balanced acidity. An
ideal apéritif.* **12 for £81.00**

1994 Cabernet Sauvignon-Merlot,
Hawkes Bay, Vidal *Fresh berry fruit with
warm spicy overtones; a hint of redcurrant and
plenty of spicy plums.* **12 for £106.80**

Total cost: £450.00

£1000

This would provide some fascinating and
delicious wines for the serious collector.
Reds have often been regarded as second
best in New Zealand, but I think these are
tremendously exciting.

1994 Cabernet Sauvignon-Merlot,
Waiheke Island, Te Motu *A nose of rich,
succulent fruit; youthful tannins and a long
finish. It's drinking now.* **12 for £234.00**

1995 Pinot Noir, Martinborough, Ata
Rangi *A nose of succulent plums and black
cherries, and a hint of raspberries. It's drinking
well now, but will develop over the next three
to five years.* **12 for £192.00**

1995 Célèbre, Martinborough, Ata
Rangi *A classic blend of Cabernet
Sauvignon, Merlot and Syrah. The nose is
reminiscent of summer pudding, and the
palate is brimming with soft, spicy hints and
gentle oak.* **12 for £180.00**

1994 Pinot Noir, Wanaka, Rippon
Vineyards *These grapes are farmed
organically, and this is one of six vineyards in
one of the world's most southerly vineyard
areas. The nose is of raspberries, plums and
maraschino cherries; the palate has fresh fruit
and well integrated oak.* **12 for £180.00**

1994 Chardonnay, Nelson, Redwood
Valley *Burgundian in style, complex and
buttery-biscuity with firm acidity. It's drinking
beautifully now, but it will develop over the
next three to six years.* **12 for £108.00**

1995 Sauvignon Blanc, Nelson,
Redwood Valley *This is full of
gooseberries, green peppers and grassiness on
the nose, and the palate has well-balanced
fruit and acidity.* **12 for £99.00**

Total cost: £993.00

ZUBAIR MOHAMED

RAEBURN FINE WINES

Whether it is cheap or expensive, there is
not much point in drinking a wine unless it
has individuality. This is the deciding factor
in all my selections.

£100

Good everyday drinking which should not
bore anyone.

1992 Domaine de Paguy, Vin de Pays
Blanc des Landes, Albert Darzacq,
Betbezer d'Armagnac *This is the best of
the wines made at this domaine. Rich, dry,
concentrated Colombard with excellent
balance and acidity.* **6 for £28.20**

1992 Lago di Corbara Rosso Vino da
Tavola, Vinicola Barbi, Umbria *This has
the spicy, red cherry fruit of the Italian
Montepulciano d'Abruzzo grape, which here
produces a wine that is high-toned and
elegant.* **6 for £29.94**

£15 WINE VOUCHER IS <u>YOURS</u>

WHEN YOU BUY YOUR PERSONAL NUMBER

You have a phone, an office phone, a mobile phone, a fax machine - on Monday your in Peterborough, Tuesday London, Wednesday at the office and Friday your at home - working of course. So how on earth do you let people know where you are and on what number? Simple, just nip down to the printers and get yourself some nice A4 size business cards to hand out to your Friends, Colleagues, Partner and The Babysitter.

OR

You could pick up a phone **NOW** and get *yourself an* **07000** *phone* number - the phone number for life. Just redirect to any telephone you wish as many times as you like. Just one simple number - easy for everyone to remember too! **07000**, *your own* prestigious Personal Phone Number.

PHONE 07000 799 799

BUY AN 07000 NUMBER TODAY AND RECEIVE

A WINE VOUCHER WORTH £15 - FREE.

TO CELEBRATE OF COURSE!!

  CHEERS!

1994 Domaine l'Hortus, Coteaux du Languedoc, Jean Orliac, Pic St-Loup *Full-bodied, superbly made and with lots of personality, this excellent red is indicative of the fine quality currently coming from this region.* **6 for £39.00**

Total cost: £97.14

This cellar reflects my fondness for the Riesling grape: it is versatile and ages superbly. I've also chosen two characterful reds made from local grape varieties allied to the *terroirs* that suit them: so much more interesting than the ubiquitous Chardonnay and Cabernet.

1986 Erdener Treppchen Riesling Kabinett, Weingut Moenchof, Robert Eymael *From one of my favourite estates in Germany, here is a classic Mosel with some bottle age. Honeyed yet still fresh, with fine balance of fruit and acidity.* **12 for £71.88**

1985 Riesling (Recolte 15 Novembre), Rolly-Gassmann, Alsace *A late picked yet dry cuvée from an excellent year. Classy and concentrated.* **12 for £143.88**

1989 Deidesheimer Hohenmorgen Riesling Auslese, Bassermann-Jordan, Pfalz *This is a delicious, complex and wonderfully light pudding wine. It comes in a half-bottle size.* **12 halves for £119.88**

1991 Redoma, Douro Valley, Niepoort Vinhos *The first table wine from the excellent port house of Niepoort. This shows complexity, a fine balance, and should be even better in four or five years, although it is delicious now.* **12 for £95.88**

1992 Côtes du Roussillon Rouge, élève en fût, Domaine Gauby et Fils *Gauby is widely considered to be one of the finest estates in the Côtes du Roussillon. It makes stunning, highly individual cuvées of white as*

well as exciting reds. This has been aged in new oak and shows a fine harmony of fruit with wood. There is real depth and concentration of ripe blackcurrant, spicy fruit and excellent balancing acidity. This is the quality that can be achieved from well-situated old vines and, above all, low yields allied to thoughtful wine-making. **12 for £81.00**

Total cost: £512.52

Most of these wines could be termed classics, although the producers may be less familiar.

Fino Soto Sherry, José de Soto *This is possibly the best-value sherry I have ever come across. It is shipped in small quantities so the freshness is maintained, and it is light and beautifully crisp and clean. One of the world's great drinks.* **12 for £59.40**

Champagne Brut Cuvée de Reserve NV, Henri Billiot *There are very few substitutes for quality Champagne, and having tried lots of them this remains a favourite for its intensity of flavour, balance and personality.* **12 for £239.88**

1992 Meursault, François Jobard *This is one of the great domaines for white Burgundy. Stylish, elegant and superbly balanced, this is from an excellent vintage. Ideally needs another three years, and will go on improving after that.* **12 for £299.40**

1994 Vouvray le Mon Sec, Huet *One of my favourite domaines in France, making wine from one of my favourite grape varieties, Chenin Blanc. Only very small quantities were made in 1994, but they are stunning and have remarkable concentration. This has a deep yellow colour with an explosive bouquet of apples and honey balanced by crisp, refreshing acidity. It will age very well, although it is lovely now.* **12 for £129.60**

1992 Beaune Premier Cru Clos du Roi, Luc Camus-Bruchon   *This shows what is possible in a difficult vintage. It has a lovely youthful colour and a bouquet of ripe red fruits. On the palate there is a silky, creamy texture and a complex, superbly balanced finish.*   **12 for £179.88**

1991 Collioure La Coume Pascol, Domaine de la Rectorie, Parce Frères   *Lovely texture and great complexity, perhaps almost like a fine Rhône. It's drinking well now, but will improve.*   **12 for £107.88**

Total cost: £1016.04

JEREMY PLATT

TERRY PLATT

When I was asked to choose these three cellars I thought it would be easy. Little did I know…

£100

For this cellar I've opted for wines to go on holiday with.

1995 Sauvignon Blanc, Marlborough, Whitehaven Winery   *Grassy, aromatic New Zealand Sauvignon with a lovely tropical nose and intense fruit.*   **6 for £44.04**

1993 Cabernet Sauvignon, Paarl, Backsberg Estate   *Michael Back produces great South African wine. This red has a rich blackcurrant flavour, soft tannins and great length.*   **6 for £31.68**

Candidato Blanco, Martínez Bujanda   *This wine is a 50/50 blend of Viura and Macabeo from Rioja and Penedes, so doesn't have either appellation. It's light and delicate on the palate.*   **6 for £24.60**

Total cost: £100.32

£500

With this amount of money my cellar becomes a little more serious. They're still for drinking now, but a couple could be kept, as well.

1994 Clos de Gilroy Grenache, Bonny Doon, California   *I am a great fan of this innovative winery, which has never disappointed me. This Grenache has a dark ruby colour, lovely soft, ripe berry flavours and plenty of depth.*   **12 for £98.52**

1994 Côtes du Ventoux la Ciboise, Chapoutier, Rhône   *During the past few years the quality of Chapoutier wines has improved dramatically. This wine has superb flavours, plenty of ripe berry fruit, some spice and will last.*   **12 for £73.20**

1994 Viño Dulce de Moscatel, Bodegas Ochoa   *Javier Ochao is the most innovative winemaker in Navarra. This is delicious with great acidity and delicate Moscatel flavours. It comes in 50cl bottles.*   **12 for £100.08**

1994 Château Ducla, Entre-Deux-Mers   *This property is owned by the Mau family. The wine has a lovely fresh style.*   **12 for £70.32**

1991 Gewürztraminer, Trimbach, Alsace   *I am a great fan of Alsace wines, and I particularly love the style of Trimbach. This is spicy, quite pungent, and has huge amounts of fruit.*   **12 for £121.08**

1993 Pinot Noir, Carneros, Famous Gate   *With my remaining money, perhaps I can squeeze in three bottles of this superb wine. It is the finest Pinot Noir I have tasted from California. The only problem is that the quantity is very limited.*   **3 for £46.00**

Total cost: £509.20

£1000

This cellar is pure indulgence, and I make no apology.

1991 Amarone Classico Vigneto Monte San Urbano, Speri *From a single estate, this is delicious. It has powerful fruit flavours, great length of flavour and richness that is second to none.* **12 for £162.00**

1988 Taittinger Comtes de Champagne *My favourite of all the prestige cuvées of Champagne. Taittinger produces superb Chardonnay wines with a biscuity flavour that lingers forever.* **12 for £298.56**

1994 Puligny-Montrachet les Charmes, Domaine Gérard Chavy *When buying this I shall have to buy a padlock as well. It is magnificent now, so I shall have to force myself to wait until it's even better in five to ten years' time.* **12 for £218.52**

1992 Château Yon Figeac, St-Émilion Grand Cru Classé *Superbly put together wine, with ripe fruit and good tannin. It will certainly last for a good part of the rest of my lifetime. So perhaps I'd better make that two padlocks.* **12 for £183.12**

Total cost: £987.60

OZ CLARKE

Every year I hear people bleat on about how it has become virtually impossible to find decent wine at less than three quid. Well, it depends where you look. If you look into areas full of well-known names and well-known grape varieties, then no, you'll find nothing better than dishwater at such a price. But if you look to less trendy areas or grapes, there's still smashing stuff to be found – and I've found it.

£100

Nagyrede Pinot Blanc, Hungary *Aromatic grapes aren't that popular, but they make wonderful wines.* **6 for £18**

Asda Dry Muscat *A smashing wine at a bargain price.* **6 for £16.80**

Eagle Mountain Hungarian Harslevelu *All it needed was some good old new-fangled Down Under know-how.* **6 for £18**

Los Fundos red and white *Chile has been the best performer in either hemisphere during 1996.* **6 for £18**

Santa Carolina Dry White *A blend of various grapes that didn't quite make it into the top selections.* **6 for £18**

Remonte Navarra *Delicious juicy basic red from Spain.* **1 for £3**

Coniusa Cava *Now that some companies have begun adding Chardonnay to their blends, Cava is massively improved.* **1 for £5**

Waitrose Fino *Tip-top bone dry sherry. If you haven't drunk dry sherry for years, now's the time to start again.* **1 half for £3**

Total cost: £99.80

£500

I can really go to town now: loads of tasty, intense reds and whites. But I don't have to change the areas I'm going to pillage.

1995 Nagyrede Pinot Gris Reserve, Hungary *Wonderfully classy honeyed wine that will age happily.* **6 for £21**

Neszemely Barrel-fermented Sauvignon Blanc, Hungary *Brilliant combination of grassy green fruit and soft spice.* **6 for £30**

Mecsekalji Chardonnay Reserve Full Chardonnay, Hungary *Fruit and some light oak flavour.* **6 for £19.80**

I'm not deserting South America either. If I add a couple of quid to the price I get absolutely stonking wine, probably the best value for money available today.

Lurton Mendoza Malbec-Tempranillo *Inspired blending by Jacques Lurton with the Tempranillo grape of Rioja fame.* **6 for £30**

Alamos Ridge Malbec *Revelatory use of Argentina's top red grape.* **6 for £30**

Argentina may be catching up at the top end, but the vast majority of the most exciting wine is still coming from Chile.

1995 Carmen Chardonnay-Semillon *Australian blend with a uniquely Chilean richness of fruit.* **6 for £30**

1995 Cono Sur Pinot Noir *Beautiful, fragrant Pinot Noir,* **6 for £30**

1995 Concha y Toro Cabernet-Syrah *Another Australian blend but here showing thrilling juicy Chilean fruit and exotic sun soaked perfume.* **6 for £30**

And Spain? No question. Despite suffering a couple of years of heavy drought, the good wineries are still producing their best-ever wines at affordable prices.

1994 Viura-Chardonnay, Agramont, Navarra **6 for £28.80**

1993 CVNE Monopole Barrel-fermented white Rioja *Two examples of superb oaky dry whites from northern Spain.* **6 for £36**

1991 Raïmat Merlot Reserva *Gorgeous ripe fruit wrapped with coconut spice from the oak barrels.* **6 for £30**

Right: on to pastures new. Or at least the pastures that I would never have included in the past. But good wine is bursting out all over. Even in the most unlikely places.

1994 Winzerhaus Blauer Zweigelt *Crunchy red fruit blends with celery and pepper in a tart but delicious warm weather quaffer.* **6 for £42**

And England? Surely not. Yes – England, but not the old England of drab semi-sweet whites. This a brave new England of classic varieties grown in the nooks and crannies of south-facing slopes drawing in every last ray of our fleeting summer sun. Except that in 1995 the problem for once wasn't sun, but lack of rain.

Denbies Chardonnay *This wine could even be an oak-aged Chablis Premier Cru, it's that good.* **6 for £42**

So, back to more familiar ground. The south of France is still undergoing a revolution, and wines are popping up in Corbières, Minervois and the Roussillon that gladden the heart of modernist and old-timer alike. But the so-called Flying Winemakers are improving, too, as they understand their *terroir* better each year.

1995 James Herrick Cuvée Simone *Smashing first-try red full of bramble fruit and southern warmth.* **6 for £33**

Domaine la Baume Merlot-Syrah *Best red yet from the French offshoot of Aussie giant Hardys.* **6 for £33**

1995 Domaine de Rivoyre *Gorgeous creamy Chardonnay full of spice, from English tyro Hugh Ryman.* **6 for £33**

Aaargh. No fizz. Well, there's nothing decent at £4.60 a bottle, but if I borrow a quid and promise to order another half dozen later in the week, I can usually find the excellent New Zealand Lindauer on offer for as little as £5.50.

Lindauer Brut **1 for 5.50**

Total cost: £504.10

£1000

The temptation of having a cool thousand to spend on wine is to head straight to the old classics. But I look at their distinctly patchy quality record right now, and then I look at their scary prices, and I say, no way. There's got to be a better way to pack my cellar with thrilling wine – and there is. You may not have heard of all these wines. Some of the flavours may shock you, but there's a whole New World of fabulous quality out there – and it starts right here.

South Africa is still finding its feet in the premier league of wine, but there's already some super stuff appearing.

1995 Beyerskloof Pinotage *A riot of pungent damson and marshmallow and wood smoke.* **12 for £60**

1995 Springfield Chardonnay *Brilliant Chardonnay showing how exciting this variety can be in the Cape when they let themselves go a bit.* **12 for £60**

1995 Buitenverwachting Sauvignon Blanc *Fabulous snappy, tangy Sauvignon Blanc.* **6 for £45**

1991 Thelema Cabernet Sauvignon Reserve *Supremely classy red from the Cape's top estate.* **6 for £57**

1995 Plaisir de Merle Merlot *Amazing, sumptuous Bordeaux-style red from the genius behind Bordeaux's Château Margaux, Paul Pontallier.* **12 for £120**

California is producing some superb wines at the moment, especially from the less widely planted southern French varieties, but I'm going to choose from two other exciting areas of the States – Washington State and Long Island, New York.

1992 Columbia Thurston Wolfe Lemberger, Washington State *Exotic*

mix of liquorice, smoky black treacle and brambles from a vine variety you hardly ever see outside Central Europe. **6 for £48**

1994 Leonetti Merlot, Washington State *This is expensive, sure, but it's also one of the most luscious, spice-laden Merlots in America.* **12 for £240**

Long Island prides itself on having a climate very similar to that of Bordeaux. Well, it's certainly having a better time of it during the 1990s than Bordeaux is, and Hargrave Vineyard is showing that, 20 years after the first vines went in, world-class wine is possible here.

1993 Hargrave Merlot, Long Island *Possibly the best Merlot I had all last year. Irresistible fullness of fruit with a luscious texture and cedar fragrance.* **12 for £144**

1993 Hargrave Pinot Noir, Long Island *Wild, chaotic and gorgeously unusual red. This is risk-taking and imagination out on the edge.* **6 for £72**

I'm getting slight withdrawal symptoms for France – but if you wonder when the Burgundy and claret are going to appear – they're not. My pangs are for elsewhere: for the Rhône Valley and the South, to be precise.

1994 Graillot Crozes-Hermitage *Outstanding soft red with marshmallow texture and damson perfume from Crozes' best grower.* **6 for £51**

1990 Gigondas Domaine St-Gayan *Deeper, sturdier, thick-limbed meaty red, power before beauty.* **6 for £55**

1994 Mas de Daumas Gassac *The maestro here reckons this red is one of his best ever. It'll be at least five years before it will blossom, but I can wait.* **6 for £66**

Total cost: £1018

PRICE GUIDES

We've rearranged the price guides this year. Instead of being all together at the back of the book the price guides for each country or region now follow their respective chapters. This should make for easier reference.

But what are the price guides? Quite simply, they are pages on which we have collated the current retail prices of the thousands of wines we hold on our computer database. Just a glance at the price difference on the same wine from one merchant to another can show why this information is so valuable – and the size of the undertaking means that it's not available in this form anywhere else.

On expensive wines the price differences can be dramatic. On cheaper wines, the differences may be small but they're still worth knowing about. And, in addition, many wines are in limited distribution: it's therefore of crucial importance to find out where the wines are stocked, and whether they'll sell by mail order. By using these price guides judiciously, you should be able to drink better and more cheaply during the coming year.

● All prices listed are *per bottle inclusive of VAT*, unless otherwise stated. When comparing prices remember that some wine merchants sell only by the case. In this instance, we have arrived at a bottle price by dividing by 12 the VAT-inclusive price of a single case. Where merchants who sell by the case will sell cases of mixed bottles, we have used the bottle price that would apply in a mixed case.

● Wines are listed in price bands and by vintage. Price bands run from the lowest to the highest. Vintages run from the most recent to the oldest. Within these two categories the wines are listed in alphabetical order.

● Within the price bands, stockists are listed in brackets after each entry in ascending order of price. The same wine may fall into more than one price band, but before you get too agitated about variations in price, remember that wine warehouses, for example, often come out much cheaper than individual merchants because you have to buy by the case, they do not deliver, they do not have smart high street premises to maintain, and so on. Equally, there's no getting away from the fact that the price of a given wine sometimes varies wildly for no good reason.

● The claret prices are a special case. Specific prices are shown in ascending order by vintage. There *are* some dramatic price variations here – some are to do with keen pricing and the reverse; more often it will be because claret is now (for better or for worse) an investment medium and is therefore highly responsive to market pressures. A merchant buying wine en primeur in Bordeaux on Monday *afternoon* may pay 25 per cent more than the going rate that morning! Replacement stocks over the years will vary in cost, and currency movements will also be a factor. So – for the sake of clarity – the prices we list were valid in the late spring/early summer of 1996.

● In the claret guide, all châteaux are listed alphabetically regardless of class. A wine quoted EC or IB, is offered on an en primeur basis (in Bordeaux or at the châteaux) or in bond (in the UK). All EC and IB prices are per case. The EC price simply includes the price of the wine in the bottle and excludes shipping, duties and taxes such as VAT. The EC price is usually payable when the wine is offered in the summer following the vintage. Other costs (including VAT on both invoices) become payable when the wine is shipped. The *crus classés* and better *bourgeois* are shipped two years later, the *petits châteaux* and the lesser *bourgeois* after a year. You should check beforehand the exact terms of sale with your merchant who will give you a projection of the final 'duty paid delivered' price at current rates of shipping, duty and VAT.

● When clubs have both member and non-member prices we have used the *non-member* prices.

● For the key to the merchant codes used throughout, see below.

● The merchants included in this year's guides have been chosen on the basis of the quality and interest of their lists. More information about each can be found in the Merchant Directory (page 424). There is also a Regional Directory (page 423) to show who is listed in your part of the country.

● To get the most out of the lists in the book, please remember that *Webster's* is a price GUIDE not a price LIST. While it is an invaluable reference whenever you are ordering or buying wine, it is not meant to replace up-to-date merchants' lists. What it *does* do, however, is give you a unique opportunity to compare prices; to develop a sense of what you can expect to pay for any given wine; to spot a bargain; to work out exactly what you can afford – *and to find it.*

MERCHANT CODES

AD	Adnams	ENO	Enotria Winecellars
AME	Amey's Wines	EY	Philip Eyres
ARM	John Armit Wines	FA	Farr Vintners
AS	Ashley Scott	FIZ	Fine Wines of New Zealand
ASD	ASDA	FOR	Forth Wines Ltd
AUR	Stéphane Auriol Wines	FUL	Fuller's
AUS	Australian Wine Centre	GAL	Gallery Wines
AV	Averys of Bristol	GAU	Gauntleys of Nottingham
BEN	Bennetts	GE	Gelston Castle Fine Wines
BER	Berry Bros. & Rudd	GOE	Goedhuis & Co
BIB	Bibendum	HA	John Harvey & Sons
BO	Booths	HAH	Haynes Hanson & Clark
BOD	Bordeaux Direct	HAL	Halves
BOT	Bottoms Up	HAW	Roger Harris Wines
BU	Butlers Wine Cellar	HE	Douglas Henn-Macrae
BUT	Bute Wines	HIC	Hicks & Don
BY	Anthony Byrne	HIG	High Breck Vintners
CAP	Cape Province Wines	HOG	J E Hogg
CB	Corney & Barrow	KA	J C Karn & Son Ltd
CHA	Châteaux Wines	LAY	Lay & Wheeler
CO	CWS	LAYT	Laytons
CRO	Croque-en-Bouche	LEA	Lea & Sandeman
DAV	Davisons	MAJ	Majestic Wine Warehouses
DI	Direct Wine		
EL	Eldridge, Pope & Co	MAR	Marks & Spencer
ELL	Ben Ellis Wines	MOR	Moreno Wines

MV	Morris & Verdin	SOM	Sommelier Wine Co
NA	The Nadder Wine Co Ltd	SUM	Summerlee Wines
NEW	New London Wine	SUN	Sunday Times Wine Club
NEZ	Le Nez Rouge	TAN	Tanners
NI	James Nicholson	TES	Tesco
NO	The Nobody Inn	THR	Thresher
OD	Oddbins	TW	T & W Wines
PE	Thos. Peatling	UB	The Ubiquitous Chip
PEN	Penistone Court Wine Cellars	UN	Unwins
PIP	Christopher Piper Wines	VA	Valvona & Crolla
PLA	Terry Platt	VIC	Victoria Wine
POR	Portland Wine Co	VIG	La Vigneronne
QUE	Quellyn Roberts	VIN	Vintage Wines
RAE	Raeburn Fine Wines	WAI	Waitrose
REI	Reid Wines (1992) Ltd	WAT	Waterloo Wine Co
RES	La Reserve	WHI	Whitesides of Clitheroe
RIP	Howard Ripley	WIW	Wines of Westhorpe Ltd
ROB	Roberson	WR	Wine Rack
SAF	Safeway	WRI	Wright Wine Co
SAI	Sainsbury	WS	Wine Society
SAT	Satchells	WY	Peter Wylie Fine Wines
SEC	Seckford Wines	YAP	Yapp Brothers
SO	Somerfield/Gateway	YOU	Noel Young Wines

FRANCE

Will anything come of it, or will the French settle back into their complacency, saying that a nation that can't even work out how to feed cattle properly can hardly be expected to judge the finer points of French wine?

By 'it' I mean the rising tide of criticism of Appellation Contrôlée. Last year the Institut National des Appellations d'Origine (INAO), the governing body of French wine, actually came to London to hear what British wine critics thought of its wares. And what's more it didn't like what it heard. The Wine Standards Board in Britain volunteered to send INAO samples of some of the more unworthy examples of AC to be found on British shelves, and it has done so – and very nasty they were too, by all (British) accounts.

But will INAO take note? And more importantly, will it act? Alain Berger, until recently head of INAO, ceased to be head of INAO and was sent off to look after deep sea fishing instead, when he said in the French press that some AC wines on sale were of 'scandalous' standard. His successor, Jean-Daniel Bénard, will at least know what he's up against, if he is ever inspired to say anything similar.

But are we naïve in expecting so much of AC? The AC system was never intended to guarantee quality, only origin, grape variety and method of production. It was designed to protect producers as much as consumers, and in that respect it has been superlatively successful.

And, of course, it covers some of the finest wines of the world. Nobody would deny that. But why should Pomerol or Savennières be legally considered the equal of Anjou Blanc? Or basic Muscadet? Or, come to that, most Mâcon Blanc?

QUALITY CONTROL

The French have the most far-reaching system of wine control of any nation, even though its adequacy as a form of quality control is now in question. The key factors are the 'origin' of the wine, its historic method of production and the use of the correct grape types. There are three defined levels – AC, VDQS, and *Vin de Pays*.

Appellation d'Origine Contrôlée (AC, AOC) To qualify for AC a wine must meet seven requirements:
Land Suitable vineyard land is minutely defined. **Grape** Only those grapes traditionally regarded as suitable can be used. **Degree of alcohol** Wines must reach a minimum (or maximum) degree of natural alcohol. **Yield** A basic permitted yield is set for each AC, but the figure may be increased or decreased year by year after consultation between the growers of

each AC region and the Institut National des Appellations d'Origine (INAO). **Vineyard practice** AC wines must follow rules about pruning methods and density of planting. **Wine-making practice** Each AC wine has its own regulations as to what is allowed. Typically, chaptalization – adding sugar during fermentation to increase alcoholic strength – is accepted in the north, but not in the south. **Tasting and analysis** Since 1979 wines must pass a tasting panel.

Vin Délimité de Qualité Supérieure (VDQS) This second group is, in general, slightly less reliable in quality. It is in the process of being phased out. No more vins de pays are being upgraded to VDQS but there is still no news on when existing ones will be upgraded to AC (or downgraded to vin de pays).

Vin de Pays The third category gives a regional definition to France's basic blending wines. The rules are similar to AC, but allow a good deal more flexibility and some wonderful cheap wines can be found which may well surprise. Quality can be stunning, and expect fruit, value and competent wine-making. There are also one or two high priced superstars in this category.

Vin de Table 'Table wine' is the title for the rest. No quality control except as far as basic public health regulations demand. Vins de pays are always available for approximately the same price, and offer a far more interesting drink. Many Vins de Table here are dull and poorly made, and branded, heavily advertised ones are seldom good value.

BORDEAUX

With a good vintage finally under its belt, Bordeaux's current experiments in the cellar seem to be directed to making the wine taste more appealing, and therefore potentially more expensive, younger

The sigh of relief could be heard from the northern tip of the Médoc to the southern reaches of the Graves, from the lowliest petit château to the most ambitious would-be super-second: at last, a fine vintage in Bordeaux. Admittedly, for the fifth year in a row fine summer conditions were followed by September rain – but this time the rain did not really spoil things. On the one hand it may have taken the edge off a five-star vintage; on the other some water was badly needed after the drought conditions of a long, hot summer. Remember the plight of Yorkshire Water.

Not only was 1995 clearly the first really decent year since 1990, but the world economy was in much better shape than in the previous few years. Almost every country was interested in buying, and loins were being girded by merchants across the world to descend on Bordeaux to taste the new vintage on or after April 1st. In the heady days of the 1980s the powers-that-were in Bordeaux, worried about the tendency for journalists to pronounce earlier and earlier on the new vintage, each being keen to steal a march on his or her rivals, decreed that none should taste before All Fools' Day. This held good for the feeble vintages of the early 1990s, but, guess what, as soon as (a) a decent vintage arrived, and (b) Robert Parker declared his intention of visiting Bordeaux in March, the rule was forgotten.

The snag with selling wines en primeur is that judgements have to be made at an embryonic stage. Who can really assess wines as young as this? Is the playing field really level? Every wine is at a different stage of its development in March or April after the vintage. Mostly the final blend has been made, although sometimes the vin de presse (a harsh component of the final wine which has a useful stiffening effect but is otherwise nix on sex appeal) has not yet been included.

Viscous circle

Last year we reported on the debate between the technocrat and naturalist styles of wine-making. The debate continues. Although most leading Bordeaux producers will speak of the necessity to keep yields down and to 'make the wine in the vineyard', there is little evidence that this is actually the case, as many châteaux seem to be paying more attention to wine-making than to grape-growing. Part of the problem is that wines need to be made to look good when buyers and press come to Bordeaux each spring to taste the new vintage being offered en primeur. Ace wine-making guru at the moment is Michel Rolland, who rose to fame in the early 1980s by transforming the quality of his Pomerol château, le Bon Pasteur. Now you can see the Rolland effect all over Bordeaux – Léoville-Poyferré is the latest to take him on as consultant.

The Rolland trademark is wines which are black in colour with plenty of extract and plenty of alcohol, viscous numbers with immediate appeal. Whether the wines will be good when it is time to drink them depends on the quality of the raw material, which no amount of wine-making skill can improve. However, while the wines are in their infancy this 'black' style of wine-making tends to look more impressive than the more traditional 'red' wines.

This year's special vinification talking point is 'doing the malolactic in barrel'. This secondary fermentation, which softens the acidity in the wine, used to happen in vat before the wines were put into their

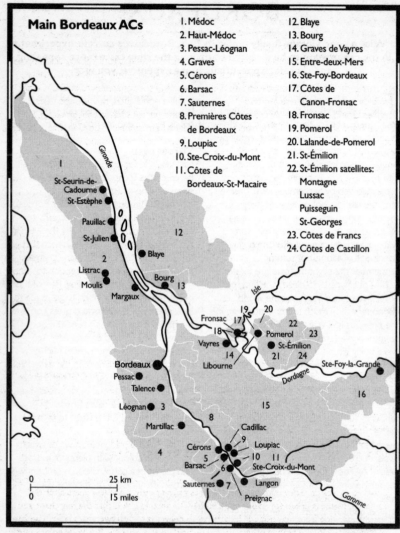

Main Bordeaux ACs

1. Médoc
2. Haut-Médoc
3. Pessac-Léognan
4. Graves
5. Cérons
6. Barsac
7. Sauternes
8. Premières Côtes de Bordeaux
9. Loupiac
10. Ste-Croix-du-Mont
11. Côtes de Bordeaux-St-Macaire
12. Blaye
13. Bourg
14. Graves de Vayres
15. Entre-deux-Mers
16. Ste-Foy-Bordeaux
17. Côtes de Canon-Fronsac
18. Fronsac
19. Pomerol
20. Lalande-de-Pomerol
21. St-Émilion
22. St-Émilion satellites:
   Montagne
   Lussac
   Puisseguin
   St-Georges
23. Côtes de Francs
24. Côtes de Castillon

Map labels: Gironde; St-Seurin-de-Cadourne; St-Estèphe; Pauillac; St-Julien; Blaye; Listrac; Moulis; Bourg; Margaux; Fronsac; Isle; Pomerol; St-Émilion; Vayres; Bordeaux; Pessac; Talence; Libourne; Dordogne; Ste-Foy-la-Grande; Léognan; Martillac; Cadillac; Cérons; Loupiac; Barsac; Ste-Croix-du-Mont; Sauternes; Langon; Preignac; Goronne

0 — 25 km
0 — 15 miles

barrels, perhaps in January. Now there is a move, especially with Merlot, to decant the wine into barrel much earlier, straight after the first fermentation, and let it do its malolactic in barrel. The result is wines which show much more seductively during the spring en primeur tastings, enabling the château to push for a higher opening price. However, it is far from clear that the

finished wine in bottle gains anything from this method.

Meanwhile, in St-Émilion, the armchair selectors have been out in force. Whereas the 1855 classification of the Médoc is more or less immutable, St-Émilion's version, first put together a century later, is reassessed periodically and is currently due for a revamp. Who will be promoted or relegated? Will Beau-Séjour-Bécot be reinstated as a Premier Grand Cru Classé? Will any of the trendy châteaux like Angélus or Troplong Mondot be promoted on the grounds of their current success, even though the location of their vineyards has not changed? The St-Émilion classification is unwieldy in any case. There are two Premier Grand Cru Classé 'A' châteaux, Cheval Blanc and Ausone, 11 (formerly 12) Premiers Grands Crus Classés, a horde of Grands Crus Classés and a sea of Grands Crus including lowly properties on the sandy soil down by the Dordogne. If it were up to me I would demote all Grands Crus to simple St-Émilion, and all Grands Crus Classés to Grands Crus.

Maybe Pomerol should have a classification, which at present it doesn't. But how would you do it? You couldn't do it on price, which was the rationale behind the 1855 classification, because the rarity value of some of the tiny Pomerol estates distorts the picture. Pétrus produces about 4000 cases a year, compared to Lafite's 30,000 or so; le Pin rarely exceeds 1000. However, without a classification the consumer needs to be pretty clued up to distinguish not only the relative quality levels of such châteaux as le Gay, Gazin, Lafleur and Pétrus, but also the various hybrid names such as Lafleur-Gazin, la Fleur-Pétrus, la Fleur-de-Gay, Croix-de-Gay, Vraye Croix-de-Pay, and so on.

The talking point in Sauternes is bottle sizes. There has been a definite move towards using the slim and elegant 50cl size, thus suppressing both 75cl bottles and halves. Several châteaux, including some of the better crus classés, were apparently planning to offer their '95s only in this new size, but have chickened out. Difficult times for this region look set to continue, especially when other parts of France can offer some marvellous sweet wines at more competitive prices. **JASPER MORRIS MW**

BUYING CLARET EN PRIMEUR

In the spring after the vintage the Bordeaux châteaux make their opening offers. This means that they do not have to sit on very expensive stock for a further two years until the wines are bottled and ready to ship. In theory this also means that you can buy the wine at a preferential price. Traditionally merchants would buy for stock while offering their customers the chance to take advantage of the opening prices as well. In the heady days of the 1980s, however, the market really took off.

There is a lot to be said for buying en primeur. For one thing, you may be able to find the finest and rarest wines far more cheaply than they will ever appear again. This was especially true of the 1982 and 1990 vintages.

But you should be aware of the risks: as they say in the investment world, prices can go down as well as up. They may easily not increase significantly in the few years after the campaign (witness prices for 1985s and 1989s). The second risk is that the merchant you bought the wine from may not still be around to deliver it to you two years later. The fate of Hungerford Wines among others should be held up as a warning. Buy your en primeur clarets from a merchant you can trust, one with a solid trading base in other wines. Once the wines are shipped you may want your merchant to store the wine for you. If so, you should insist that (1) you receive a stock certificate; (2) your wines are stored separately from the merchant's own stocks, and (3) your cases are identifiable as your property and are labelled accordingly. All good merchants will offer these safeguards as a minimum service. Of course, in an ideal world your house is equipped with its own temperature controlled cellar, because the best solution is certainly to take possession of your cases yourself.

GRAPES AND FLAVOURS

Fine claret has the most tantalizing and unlikely combination of flavours of any red wine. There's the blast of pure, fragrant blackcurrant essence of the basic fruit, and then the exotic, dry perfumes of lead pencil shavings, fresh-wrapped cigars and the intense smell of cedar resin to weave an endlessly fascinating balance of sweet and dry tastes with, increasingly, the buttery overlay of new oak barrels.

Bordeaux's vineyards are so poised on the knife-edge of being able to ripen their grapes or failing to do so that every vintage is fascinatingly, absorbingly different. The relatively temperate air in this coastal region is a crucial factor in the quality of the wine. In all but the very hottest years, the sunshine is tempered by cool breezes off the Atlantic. If the year nevertheless gets too hot, as in 1959 and 1976, and in some cases 1982, 1989 and 1990, the flavour can be rich, strong and burnt, more like the Californian or Italian attempts at claret. If the summer rains and autumn gales roll in off the Bay of Biscay and the grapes can't ripen, then the taste may be thin and green, resembling the Cabernets of the Loire Valley. But in the years of balance, like 1966, '70, '78, '83, '85, '86, '88, '89 and '90, those astonishing sweet and dry, fruity and tannic flavours mix to produce the glory that is claret.

As for the whites – well, for years the sweet, botrytized wines of Sauternes and Barsac were the only ones which could compete in quality with the reds, and not always successfully. But recent years have seen a revolution. The sweet whites have improved beyond measure, helped by massive investment and a run of excellent vintages in the 1980s, but so have the dry ones. Inexpensive Bordeaux Blanc, based on Sauvignon, is increasingly crisp and grassy, while fine oak-aged white Graves has taken its place among the great dry whites of France.

CABERNET FRANC (red) The lesser of the two Cabernets, giving lighter-coloured, softer wines than Cabernet Sauvignon, often slightly earthy but with good, blackcurranty fruit. It's always blended in Bordeaux. In St-Émilion and Pomerol it can give fine flavours and is widely planted. Château Cheval-Blanc in St-Émilion is two-thirds Cabernet Franc.

CABERNET SAUVIGNON (red) It comes as a surprise that this world-famous Bordeaux grape covers only a fifth of the vineyard area. In the Médoc and Pessac-Léognan, however, more than half the vines are Cabernet Sauvignon, and the grape has a greater influence on flavour here than elsewhere in Bordeaux. Crucially, a wine built to age needs tannin and acidity, and the fruit and extract to keep up with them. Cabernet Sauvignon has all these in abundance. It gives dark, tannic wine with a strong initial acid attack, and stark, pure blackcurrant fruit. When aged in new oak, it can be stunning. It's the main grape of the Haut-Médoc, but other varieties soften it and add complexity.

MALBEC (red) A rather bloated, juicy grape, little seen nowadays in Bordeaux, though it appears in some blends, especially in Bourg and Blaye. In Bordeaux it tastes rather like a feeble version of Merlot, soft and low in acidity. Upriver in Cahors it has real style, which probably explains why there's lots of it in Cahors and little in Bordeaux.

MERLOT (red) Bordeaux has more Merlot than Cabernet Sauvignon. It covers almost a third of the vineyard, and is the main grape in St-Émilion and Pomerol, whereas in the Médoc and Graves it's used to soften and enrich the Cabernet. It ripens early and gives a gorgeous, succulent, minty, blackcurrant or plummy wine, which explains why Pomerols and St-Émilions are easier to enjoy than Médocs. It also makes less long-lived wine than Cabernet, and tends to peak and fade sooner.

MUSCADELLE (white) A very little (up to five per cent) of this headily perfumed grape often goes into the Sauternes blend and has proved particularly good in Loupiac and Ste-Croix-du-Mont. In dry white blends a few per cent can add a very welcome honeyed softness. It is now being produced in small quantities as a varietal: dry, lean, but perfumed.

PETIT VERDOT (red) A dark, tough grape with a liquorice-and-plums taste, and a violet perfume, used for colour. Little planted in the past but on the increase now because it adds quality in a late, ripe year.

SAUVIGNON BLANC (white) There has been a rush to plant more of this fashionable grape in Bordeaux in recent years, but with a couple of exceptions – such as Malartic-Lagravière, Couhins-Lurton and Smith-Haut-Lafitte – Sauvignon by itself here often gives rather muddy, tough wine. Even so, many dry white Bordeaux are entirely Sauvignon, particularly at the cheaper end, and can be fresh and flowery if from careful winemakers like Mau, Dourthe, Ginestet and Coste. The best are almost always blended with Sémillon. A little Sauvignon adds acidity to Sauternes and the other sweet whites of the region, too.

SÉMILLON (white) The most important grape of Sauternes, and very susceptible to noble rot. Sémillon is vital to the best dry wines, too, though it has become sadly unfashionable. With modern techniques one can hardly tell a good dry Sémillon from a Sauvignon, except that it's a little fuller. But ideally they should be blended, with Sémillon the main variety. It gives a big, round dry wine, slightly creamy but with an exciting aroma of fresh apples and leaving a lanolin smoothness in the mouth. From the top estates, fermented cool and aged in oak barrels, the result is a wonderful, soft, nutty dry white, often going honeyed and smoky as it ages for seven to 15 years. Like this it produces one of France's great white wines, and is an antidote to anyone getting just a little tired of varietals.

WINES & WINE REGIONS

BARSAC, AC (sweet white) The only one of the five Sauternes villages with the right to use its own name as an official appellation (it may also call itself Sauternes – or Sauternes-Barsac for that matter). Barsac has chalkier soils than the other Sauternes villages, and tends to make lighter wines. Wines from good properties combine marvellous richness with a certain delicacy of texture.

BORDEAUX BLANC, AC (dry white) This AC covers a multitude of sins. It is the catch-all name for all white Bordeaux, and as such is the label on some of France's dullest medium-to-dry whites, as well as on many fresh, simple, well-made wines. With the sudden surge of interest in Bordeaux's dry whites spurred on by the idiotic pricing shenanigans of its rivals in the Loire and Burgundy, there is simply no excuse for the – happily decreasing – amounts of over-sulphured sludge still coming on to the market. Thank goodness every year sees another surge of good guys beating back the bad. Château wines are usually the best and should generally be drunk as young as possible. Recommended names include: *Birot, Grand-Mouëys, du Juge, Lamothe, Reynon*. Good blends are possible from the following merchants: *Coste, Dourthe, Dubroca, Ginestet, Joanne, Lurton, Mau, Sichel* and *Univitis*.

Some classy properties in red areas make good, dry white which is only allowed the AC Bordeaux in spite of often being excellent quality. *Château Margaux*'s white, for instance, is a simple AC Bordeaux. Many great Sauternes châteaux have started to make a dry wine from the grapes deemed unsuitable for Sauternes. These use the Bordeaux Blanc AC and often their initial letter – as in 'G' of *Guiraud*, 'R' of *Rieussec* and 'Y' of *Yquem*. 'Y' can really be spectacular.

BORDEAUX BLANC SUPÉRIEUR, AC

(dry white) Rarely used, but requires higher basic strength and lower vineyard yield than Bordeaux Blanc AC.

BORDEAUX ROUGE, AC (red) Unless

qualified by one of the other ACs below, this is the everyday red wine of Bordeaux, either from co-ops, from properties in undistinguished localities, or wine disqualified from one of the better ACs. It can come from anywhere in Bordeaux. Still reasonably priced, for drinking young, it is a delicious, appetizing meal-time red when good, and a palate-puckering disappointment when bad.

BORDEAUX SUPÉRIEUR, AC (red)

Similar to Bordeaux Rouge but, in theory, a bit more interesting. It must have more alcohol and be produced from a slightly lower yield. The same comments on quality apply, but from a good estate the wines can be delicious – and age for a number of years. Best results increasingly are from properties producing white Entre-Deux-Mers and from the Premières Côtes on the right bank of the Garonne river. Best châteaux: *Brethous, Cayla, Domaine de Terrefort, Fayau, la Gabory, le Gay, Grand-Moüeys, Gromel Bel-Air, Jalousie-Beaulieu, Jonqueyres, du Juge, Lacombe, Méaume, Peyrat, Pierredon, Reynon, la Roche, Tanesse, Thieuley, de Toutigeac, de la Vieille Tour.*

CADILLAC, AC (sweet white) In the south

of the Premières Côtes de Bordeaux, just across the river from Barsac; can produce attractive sweet whites, but since the price is low, many properties now produce dry white and red – which do *not* qualify for the AC Cadillac. The AC is in any case so involved that few growers bother with it.

CÉRONS, AC (sweet white) Enclave in the

Graves butting on to Barsac, making good, fairly sweet whites, but many growers now prefer to produce dry whites, which can sell as Graves. *Château Archambeau* is typical, producing tiny amounts of very good Cérons and larger amounts of good, fresh dry Graves.

Château Cérons makes splendidly complex sweet whites worthy of the AC of Barsac. Other good names: *Grand Enclos du Château Cérons, Haura.*

CÔTES DE BOURG, AC (red) The rather

full, savoury style of these reds from the east bank of the Gironde is backed up by sweet Merlot fruit and occasionally a touch of new oak. As Médoc and St-Émilion prices spiral, Bourg wines are slowly coming into their own. Best châteaux: *de Barbe, du Bousquet, Brûle-Sécaille, la Croix, Dupeyrat, Grolet, Guionne, Haut-Guiraud, Haut-Rousset, de Millorit* and wines from the co-op at *Tauriac.*

CÔTES DE CASTILLON, AC (red) and

CÔTES DE FRANCS, AC (red) Two

small regions east of St-Émilion on the road towards Bergerac, which are turning out an increasing number of exciting wines. They can be a little too earthy, but at their best they combine a grassy Cabernet Franc freshness with a gorgeous, juicy, minty Merlot sweetness, even honeyed in the best examples. Best châteaux: *Beau-Séjour, Belcier, Brisson, Canon-Monségur, Ferrasses, Fonds Rondes, Grand Taillac, les Hauts-de-Grange, Lessacques, Moulin-Rouge, Parenchère, Pitray, Rocher-Bellevue.* On the extreme eastern edge of the Gironde is the *département's* latest rising star, the Côtes de Francs. The scions of a number of well-known wine-making families are producing fruity, light, delicious wines to drink early, using a lot of Cabernet Franc. Best châteaux: *la Claverie, de Francs, Lauriol, du Moulin-la-Pitié, la Prade, Puygueraud.*

CÔTES DE FRONSAC, AC (red) with

the (in theory) superior **CANON-FRONSAC, AC** (red) A small area just west of Pomerol. The wines can be a bit grassy and tannic, but they can also be excellent, often having the sweet fruit of St-Émilion, the mineral depth of Pomerol, and a slightly cedary perfume. Nevertheless the general standard has been increasing, greatly helped by the interest shown by the firm and family of Jean-Pierre Moueix, the best merchants in Libourne.

Best châteaux: *Canon-de-Brem, Canon-Moueix, Cassagne Haut-Canon, Dalem, de la Dauphine, Fonteuil, Mayne-Vieil, Mazeris, Moulin Haut-Laroque, Plain Point, la Rivière, la Truffière* (super since 1985), *Toumalin, la Valade.*

ENTRE-DEUX-MERS, AC (dry white) Large Bordeaux area between the Garonne and Dordogne rivers. The AC is for dry whites, which are of varying quality, but every vintage produces more good, fresh, grassy ones. Many properties make red, which take the AC of Bordeaux or Bordeaux Supérieur. Best: *Bonnet, Ducla, de Florin, Fondarzac, Moulin-de-Launay, Tertre du Moulin, Thieuley, Union des Producteurs de Rauzan.*

GRAVES, AC (red, dry white) Since 1987 the Graves, the vast region south of Bordeaux town, has been deprived of its most prestigious properties, the ones nearest the city, which are now grouped in a separate AC, Pessac-Léognan. The southern two-thirds had a bad reputation as a semi-sweet white area, which it has taken a decade to overcome. These efforts have been intensified by the lopping off of Pessac-Léognan.

Red Graves run the gamut of claret flavours, and are less easy to sum up than others. There are various soils, and though the Cabernet Sauvignon is the dominant grape in the North, as in the Médoc, there's less stress here on Cabernet, more on Merlot, so slightly softer wines. They tend to have some of the blackcurrant and cedar of the Médoc, but without the sheer size of, say, Pauillac; they have some of the full, plummy richness of St-Émilion, yet it never dominates; and there is a slightly gravelly quality in many of them, too. The less well-known châteaux are cheapish, and pretty good. Local merchant Pierre Coste has developed a style of young-drinking Graves which is deliciously drinkable (available in Britain at Adnams, Haynes, Hanson & Clark, Tanners and others).

Modern white Graves is a dramatic improvement. Even at the level of commercial blends it can be sharply fruity and full in style, while at the best properties, with some oak aging employed, the wines are some of the most delicious dry whites in France. Best châteaux: *Archambeau, Bouscaut, Cabannieux, Carbonnieux, Domaine de Chevalier, Couhins-Lurton, de Cruzeau, Domaine la Grave, de Fieuzal, la Garance, la Garde, Haut-Brion, Landiras, Laville-Haut-Brion, la Louvière, Malartic-Lagravière, Montalivet, Rahoul, Respide, Rochemorin, Roquetaillade-la-Grange, Smith-Haut-Lafitte and la Tour-Martillac.*

GRAVES SUPÉRIEURES, AC (sweet or dry white) Graves with a minimum natural alcohol of 12 degrees. Often made sweet. Best property: *Clos St-Georges.*

HAUT-MÉDOC, AC (red) Geographically, the prestigious southern part of the Médoc, nearest Bordeaux – from Blanquefort in the South to St-Seurin de Cadourne in the North. The AC, however, covers the less exciting vineyards because there are six separate ACs within the region where the really juicy business gets done. These are Margaux, St-Julien, Pauillac, St-Estèphe, Listrac and Moulis. Even so, the AC Haut-Médoc has five Classed Growths including two superb ones – *Cantemerle* and *la Lagune* – and an increasing number of fine *bourgeois* properties like *Beaumont, de Castillon, Cissac, Hanteillan, Lamarque, Lanessan, Liversan, Pichon, Sociando-Mallet* and *la Tour-du-Haut-Moulin* – plus lots of lesser properties, such as châteaux *Bernadotte, Cambon-la-Pelouse, Coufran, le Fournas, Grandis, du Junca, Larose-Trintaudon, Malescasse, Maucamps, Moulin de Labarde, Quimper, Sénéjac* and *Verdignan.*

LALANDE-DE-POMEROL, AC (red) Pomerol's northern neighbour, a region as tiny as Pomerol itself, is often accused of being overpriced, but since it can produce rich, plummy wines with a distinct resemblance to those of Pomerol at a distinctly less painful price, this criticism is not entirely justified. The best châteaux are *Annereaux, Bel-Air, Belles-Graves, Bertineau-St-Vincent, Clos des Moines, Clos des Templiers, la Croix Bellevue, la Fleur St-Georges, Grand Ormeau, Haut-Ballet,* *les Hauts-Tuileries, Lavaud-la-Maréchaude, Siaurac, les Templiers, Tournefeuille.*

LISTRAC, AC (red) One of the less prestigious communes of the Haut-Médoc, just to the west of Margaux. Grown on clay-dominated soils, the wines contain a higher proportion of Merlot than elsewhere. They are rather tough and charmless, only lightly perfumed wines, lacking the complexity of the best villages, but the meteoric rise in quality amongst the *bourgeois* wines since the 1982 and '83 vintages has made its mark, though without quite the same show of fireworks. But some properties rise above this such as *la Bécade, Cap-Léon-Veyrin, Clarke, Fonréaud* (since 1988), *Fourcas-Dupré, Fourcas-Hosten, Fourcaud, Lestage* and the *Grand Listrac* co-op.

LOUPIAC, AC (sweet white) These wines from the lovely area looking across the Garonne to Barsac are not as sweet as Sauternes, and many properties until recently made dry white and red without the Loupiac AC because of difficulties in selling sweet whites. With rising prices has come a welcome flood of lemony, honeyed Barsac styles. Best châteaux: *Domaine du Noble, Loupiac-Gaudiet, Ricaud.*

MARGAUX, AC (red) This is the nearest of the famous Haut-Médoc communes to Bordeaux, covering various villages making rather sludgy, solid wines at one extreme, and the most fragrant, perfumed red wines France has yet dreamed up at the other. The great wines come from around the village of Margaux itself. People pay high prices for them and still get a bargain. The best châteaux include: *d'Angludet, la Gurgue, d'Issan, Labégorce-Zédé, Margaux, Monbrison, Palmer, Prieuré-Lichine, Rauzan-Ségla, du Tertre.* Among the next best are châteaux *Durfort-Vivens, Giscours, Lascombes, Marquis d'Alesme-Becker, Marquis de Terme, Siran* and *la Tour-de-Mons.*

MÉDOC, AC (red) This name covers the whole of the long (80km) tongue of land north of Bordeaux town, between the

Gironde river and the sea, including the Haut-Médoc and all its famous communes. As an AC it refers to the less-regarded but important lower-lying northern part of the area, traditionally known as the Bas-Médoc. AC Médoc reds, with a high proportion of Merlot grapes, are drinkable more quickly than Haut-Médocs and the best have a refreshing, grassy, juicy fruit, backed up by just enough tannin and acidity. Easily the best property is *Potensac*, where Michel Delon of *Léoville-Las-Cases* makes wine of Classed Growth standard. Other good wines are *le Bernadot, Cardonne, Cassan d'Estevil, David, d'Escot, la Gorce, Greysac, Grivière, Haut-Canteloup, Lacombe-Noaillac, Noaillac, Ormes-Sorbet, Patache d'Aux, la Tour-de-By, la Tour-St-Bonnet, Loudenne, Vieux-Château-Landon.* Most of the co-ops – especially *Bégadan, Ordornac* and *St-Yzans* – make good fruity stuff.

MOULIS, AC (red) Another lesser commune of the Haut-Médoc next door to, and similar to, Listrac, but with more potentially outstanding properties and a softer, more perfumed style in the best which can equal Classed Growths. Best are *Bel-Air-Lagrave, Brillette, Chasse-Spleen, Duplessis-Fabre, Dutruch-Grand-Poujeaux, Grand-Poujeaux, Gressier-Grand-Poujeaux, Maucaillou, Moulin-à-Vent, Poujeaux.*

PAUILLAC, AC (red) The most famous of the Haut-Médoc communes, Pauillac has three of the world's greatest red wines sitting inside its boundaries: *Latour, Lafite* and *Mouton-Rothschild.* This is where the blackcurrant really comes into its own. The best wines are almost painfully intense, a celestial mixture of blackcurrant and lead pencil sharpenings that sends well-heeled cognoscenti leaping for their cheque books. Best: *d'Armailhac* (formerly known as *Mouton-Baronne-Philippe*), *Grand-Puy-Lacoste, Haut-Bages-Avérous, Haut-Bages-Libéral, Lafite-Rothschild, Latour, Lynch-Bages, Mouton-Rothschild, Pichon-Baron, Pichon-Lalande.* Next best: *Batailley, Clerc-Milon-Rothschild, Duhart-Milon, Grand-Puy-Ducasse, Haut-Bages-Monpelou.*

PESSAC-LÉOGNAN, AC (red, dry white)
An AC in its own right since September 1987 for the area traditionally the Graves' best and containing all the *crus classés*. The AC covers ten communes but only 55 châteaux. In recent years the growers have fought back with increasing success against the tide of suburbia, replanting and improving their wines, above all the whites which, at their best, offer a depth surpassed only by the best Burgundies. Yields are lower than for white Graves and the percentage of Sauvignon is higher (at least a quarter of the grapes used). The best wines start out with a blast of apricot, peach and cream ripeness and slowly mature to a superb nutty richness with a dry savoury finish. The reds have a biscuity, bricky warmth. Best reds include those from: *Carbonnieux, Carmes-Haut-Brion, Cruzeau, Domaine de Chevalier, Domaine de Gaillat, Domaine la Grave, Ferrande, de Fieuzal, Haut-Bailly, Haut-Brion, Haut-Portets, la Louvière, Malartic-Lagravière, la Mission-Haut-Brion, Pape-Clément* (since 1985), *Rahoul, Rochemorin, de St-Pierre, Smith-Haut-Lafitte* (since 1988), *Roquetaillade-la-Grange, la Tour Martillac, Tourteau-Chollet.* Best whites: *Bouscaut, Carbonnieux* (from 1988), *Couhins-Lurton, Domaine de Chevalier, de Fieuzal, Haut-Brion, la Louvière, Malartic-Lagravière, Rochemorin, Smith-Haut-Lafitte, la Tour Martillac.*

POMEROL, AC (red) Tiny top-class area inland from Bordeaux, clustered round the town of Libourne. The Merlot grape is even more dominant in Pomerol than in St-Émilion, and most Pomerols have a deeper, rounder flavour, the plummy fruit going as dark as prunes in great years, but with the mineral backbone of toughness preserving it for a very long time. Pomerol has no classification, but it harbours the world's greatest red wine, *Château Pétrus.* Any vineyard that has been picked out by Jean-Pierre Moueix or influenced by oenologist Michel Rolland can be regarded as being of good Classed Growth standard. Best châteaux: *le Bon Pasteur, Bourgneuf-Vayron, Certan-de-May, Certan-Giraud, Clinet, Clos René, Clos du Clocher, Clos*

l'Église, la Conseillante, la Croix de Gay, l'Église Clinet, l'Évangile, le Gay, la Grave-Trigant-de-Boisset, Lafleur, Lafleur-Gazin, la Fleur-Pétrus, Lagrange-à-Pomerol, Latour-à-Pomerol, Petit-Village, Pétrus, le Pin, Trotanoy, Vieux-Château-Certan.

PREMIÈRES CÔTES DE BLAYE, AC
(red, dry white) There is a shift to red in this historically white area across the river from the Médoc. The reds are too often a little 'cooked' in taste and slightly jammy-sweet. They're cheap, but have a lot more improving to do. Good names: *Bas Vallon, Bourdieu, Charron, Crusquet-Sabourin, l'Escadre, Fontblanche, Grand Barail, Haut-Sociondo, Jonqueyres, Peybonhomme.*

PREMIÈRES CÔTES DE BORDEAUX, AC (red, white) Some very attractive reds and excellent dry whites from the right bank of the Garonne in the bang-up-to-date, fruit-all-the-way style, as well as some reasonable sweetish wines. The sweet wines can be sold as AC Cadillac, but you still get some under the Premières Côtes mantle, sometimes with their village name added, as in *Château de Berbec*, Premières-Côtes-Gabarnac. The 1988 and '89 vintages produced numerous reds with a surprising amount of soft fruit and durability. Best châteaux include: *de Berbec, Brethous, Cayla, Fayau, Grands-Moüeys, du Juge, Lamothe, de Lucat, Peyrat, la Roche, Reynon, Tanesse.*

ST-ÉMILION, AC (red) Soft, round and rather generous wines, because the main grape is the Merlot, aided by Cabernet Franc and Malbec, and only slightly by Cabernet Sauvignon. St-Émilions don't always have Pomerol's minerally backbone, and the sweetness is usually less plummy and more buttery, toffeed or raisiny. Top wines add to this a blackcurranty, minty depth. It's a well-known name, yet with few famous châteaux. It has its own classification, but is very sprawling, and has two top châteaux, *Cheval-Blanc* and *Ausone*, plus a dozen excellent ones. Some areas also annex the name, like St-Georges-St-

Émilion or Puisseguin-St-Émilion. They're often OK, but would be better value if they didn't trade greedily on the St-Émilion handle. Best in satellites: *St-Georges, Montaiguillon, Tour du Pas St-Georges* (St-Georges-St-Émilion); *Haut-Gillet, de Maison Neuve* (Montagne-St-Émilion); *Bel Air, la Croix-de-Berny* (Puisseguin-St-Émilion); *Lyonnat* (since 1983) (Lussac-St-Émilion). Best châteaux include: *l'Angélus, l'Arrosée, Ausone, Balestard-la-Tonnelle, Beauséjour-Duffau-Lagarosse, Canon, Canon-la-Gaffelière, Cheval-Blanc, Clos des Jacobins, la Dominique, Figeac, Fonroque, Larmande, Magdelaine, Pavie, Pavie-Decesse, Soutard, Tertre-Rôteboeuf, Troplong-Mondot*. Next best: *Belair, Cadet-Piola, Berliquet, Cap de Mourlin, Cardinal Villemaurine, Carteau, Clos Fourtet, Corbin-Michotte, Côtes Daugay, Corbin-Michotte, Couvent des Jacobins, Destieux, de Ferrand, Fombrauge, Franc-Mayne, la Gaffelière, Grand-Mayne, Gravet, Magnan-la-Gaffelière, Mauvezin, Monbousquet, Pavie-Macquin, Rolland-Maillet, Tour-des-Combes, la-Tour-du-Pin-Figeac, Trappaud, Trottevieille, Villemaurine*.

ST-ESTÈPHE, AC (red) The northernmost of the great Haut-Médoc communes is a more everyday performer. There aren't many famous names, and most are relatively cheap. Best: *Calon-Ségur, Chambert-Marbuzet, Cos d'Estournel, Haut-Marbuzet, Lafon-Rochet, Marbuzet, Meyney, Montrose, les Ormes-de-Pez, de Pez*. Next best: *Andron-Blanquet, Beausite, du Boscq, Cos Labory, le Crock, Lavillotte, Phélan-Ségur*.

ST-JULIEN, AC (red) There are two main styles of wine. One is almost honeyed, a rather gentle, round, wonderfully easy-to-love claret. The other has glorious cedar-cigar-box fragrance, mixed with just enough fruit to make it satisfying as well as exciting. Best châteaux to look for: *Beychevelle, Ducru-Beaucaillou, Gruaud-Larose, Lagrange* (in recent vintages especially), *Lalande-Borie, Langoa-Barton, Léoville-Barton, Léoville-Las-Cases, St-Pierre, Talbot*. Next best: *Branaire-Ducru, Gloria, Hortevie, Léoville-Poyferré* and *Terrey-Gros-Caillou*.

STE-CROIX-DU-MONT, AC (sweet white) The leading sweet white AC of the Premières Côtes de Bordeaux. The wines can be very attractive when properly made. *Château Loubens* is the best-known wine, but *Château Lousteau-Vieil* is producing better wine every year, and *Domaine du Tich, la Grave, la Rame, des Tours*, and the minuscule *de Tastes* are also good.

SAUTERNES, AC (sweet white) The overall appellation for a group of five villages in the south of the Graves: Sauternes, Bommes, Fargues, Preignac and Barsac. (Barsac wines may use their own village name if they wish.) Concentrated by noble rot, the Sémillon, along with a little Sauvignon and Muscadelle, produces at its glorious best a wine that is brilliantly rich and glyceriny. It combines honey and cream, pineapple and nuts when young, and becomes oily and penetrating as it ages. The sweetness begins to have an intensity of volatile flavours, rather like a peach, bruised and browned in the sun, then steeped in the sweetest of syrups. These are the fine wines. Sadly, owing to economic pressures, much Sauternes outside the top Growths used to be made sweet simply by sugaring the juice and stopping the fermentation with a massive slug of sulphur. In recent years the average quality has soared, and the wines are infinitely better, as indeed they ought to be given their rising prices. And in bad years those châteaux that can afford it can now practise cryoextraction – which isn't some ingenious form of torture but a method of freezing the grapes before fermentation which can increase the richness of the juice pressed out. Best châteaux: *Bastor-Lamontagne, Climens, Doisy-Daëne, Doisy-Védrines, de Fargues, Gilette, Guiraud, Lafaurie-Peyraguey, Lamothe-Guignard, Rabaud-Promis, Raymond-Lafon, Rayne-Vigneau, Rieussec, St-Amand, Suduiraut, la Tour Blanche, d'Yquem*.

The price guides for this section begin on page 63.

THE 1855 CLASSIFICATION

This is the most famous and enduring wine classification in the world – but it was never intended as such, merely as a one-off guide to the different Bordeaux wines entered for the Great Paris Exhibition of 1855, made up by various local brokers and based on the prices the wines had obtained over the previous century or so. Those brokers would be dumbfounded if they returned today to find we still revered their rather impromptu classification.

Since this classification applies only to the Médoc and one château, Haut-Brion, in the Graves, all the wines are red. The Graves has its own classification, for reds and whites, and Sauternes and St-Émilion are also classified. Of the great Bordeaux regions, only Pomerol proudly steers clear of any official hierarchy.

An interesting point to note is that in this 1855 classication it was the wine name that was classified, not the vineyard it came from. Some of the vineyards that make up a wine are now completely different from those of 1855, yet, because the name got into the lists, the level of classification remains. The only change so far occurred in 1973, when Mouton-Rothschild got promoted from Second to First Growth level after 50 years of lobbying by its late owner. In general, those properties which are classified do deserve their status, but that's never yet stopped anyone from arguing about it.

First Growths (1ers Crus)
Latour, *Pauillac*; Lafite-Rothschild, *Pauillac*; Margaux, *Margaux*; Haut-Brion, *Pessac-Léognan* (formerly *Graves*); Mouton-Rothschild, *Pauillac* (promoted in 1973).

Second Growths (2èmes Crus)
Rauzan-Ségla, *Margaux*; Rauzan-Gassies, *Margaux*; Léoville-Las-Cases, *St-Julien*; Léoville-Poyferré, *St-Julien*; Léoville-Barton, *St-Julien*; Durfort-Vivens, *Margaux*; Lascombes, *Margaux*; Gruaud-Larose, *St-Julien*; Brane-Cantenac, *Cantenac-Margaux*; Pichon-Longueville, *Pauillac*; Pichon-Longueville-Lalande (formerly Pichon-Lalande), *Pauillac*; Ducru-Beaucaillou, *St-Julien*; Cos d'Estournel, *St-Estèphe*; Montrose, *St-Estèphe*.

Third Growths (3èmes Crus)
Giscours, *Labarde-Margaux*; Kirwan, *Cantenac-Margaux*; d'Issan, *Cantenac-Margaux*; Lagrange, *St-Julien*; Langoa-Barton, *St-Julien*; Malescot-St-Exupéry, *Margaux*; Cantenac-Brown, *Cantenac-Margaux*; Palmer, *Cantenac-Margaux*; la Lagune, *Ludon-Haut-Médoc*; Desmirail, *Margaux*; Calon-Ségur, *St-Estèphe*; Ferrière, *Margaux*; Marquis d'Alesme-Becker, *Margaux*; Boyd-Cantenac, *Cantenac-Margaux*.

Fourth Growths (4èmes Crus)
St-Pierre, *St-Julien*; Branaire-Ducru, *St-Julien*; Talbot, *St-Julien*; Duhart-Milon-Rothschild, *Pauillac*; Pouget, *Cantenac-Margaux*; la Tour-Carnet, *St-Laurent-Haut-Médoc*; Lafon-Rochet, *St-Estèphe*; Beychevelle, *St-Julien*; Prieuré-Lichine, *Cantenac-Margaux*; Marquis-de-Terme, *Margaux*.

Fifth Growths (5èmes Crus)
Pontet-Canet, *Pauillac*; Batailley, *Pauillac*; Grand-Puy-Lacoste, *Pauillac*; Grand-Puy-Ducasse, *Pauillac*; Haut-Batailley, *Pauillac*; Lynch-Bages, *Pauillac*; Lynch-Moussas, *Pauillac*; Dauzac, *Labarde-Margaux*; d'Armailhac (formerly Mouton-Baronne-Philippe), *Pauillac*; du Tertre, *Arsac-Margaux*; Haut-Bages-Libéral, *Pauillac*; Pédesclaux, *Pauillac*; Belgrave, *St-Laurent-Haut-Médoc*; de Camensac, *St-Laurent-Haut-Médoc*; Cos Labory, *St-Estèphe*; Clerc-Milon-Rothschild, *Pauillac*; Croizet-Bages, *Pauillac*; Cantemerle, *Macau-Haut-Médoc*.

CHATEAU PROFILES

These properties are valued according to how they are currently performing; a five-star rating means you are getting a top-line taste – not just a well-known label. Some big names have been downgraded, some lesser-known properties are promoted – solely on the quality of the wine inside the bottle. A star in brackets shows that the wine can achieve the higher rating but does not always do so.

The £ sign shows which are offering particularly good value – that does not mean any of these wines will be cheap but look for occasional price reductions.

L'ANGÉLUS *grand cru classé St-Émilion* ★★★★(★) One of the biggest and best-known *grands crus classés*. A lot of Cabernet in the vineyard makes for a reasonably gutsy red, although rich and soft. Since 1979 new barrels have helped the flavour. The 1985 and '86 are the finest yet, with superb '87, '88 and '89. Excellent in the difficult years of the 1990s.

D'ANGLUDET *cru bourgeois Margaux* ★★★ £ *Bourgeois* red easily attaining Classed Growth standards. Owned by Englishman Peter Allan Sichel, the wine has much of the perfume of good Margaux without ever going through the traditional lean period. Fairly priced. Tremendous value. The 1980s have seen Angludet on a hot streak. The '83 and '90 are the finest ever, and the '85, '86, '88 and '89 are big and classy.

D'ARCHE *2ème cru Sauternes* ★★★(★) A little-known Sauternes property now increasingly highly thought of after a long period of mediocrity. 1983, '86, '88, '89 and '90 are good but I don't think they're that good. A little over-alcoholic, perhaps.

D'ARMAILHAC *5ème cru classé Pauillac* ★★★ (formerly known as Mouton-Baronne-Philippe) A red of very good balance for a Fifth Growth, with the perfume particularly marked, this obviously benefits from having the same ownership as Mouton-Rothschild. 1986 and '83 are very good, with '82 not bad either.

AUSONE *1er grand cru classé St-Émilion* ★★★★(★) The phoenix rises from the ashes. Between 1976 and 1994 the wines were made by Pascal Delbeck, proclaimed as a brilliant young genius, although his very fine, understated style of wine-making has slipped out of fashion recently. A new winemaker was appointed for the 1995. Potentially great red at its best. The 1985, '86, '89 and above all the '90, are especially good.

BASTOR-LAMONTAGNE *cru bourgeois Sauternes* ★★★ £ Unclassified property making marvellous, widely available and easily affordable sweet whites, as rich as many Classed Growths. 1983, '86, '88, '89 and '90 epitomize high-quality Sauternes.

BATAILLEY *5ème cru classé Pauillac* ★★★ £ Batailley's reputation has been of the squat, solid sort rather than elegant and refined, but now the wines have performed that extremely difficult Pauillac magician's trick – they've been getting a lot better, and the price has remained reasonable. Drinkable young, they age well too. The 1983, '85, '86, '88, '89 and '90 are excellent, and relatively affordable.

BELAIR *1er cru classé St-Émilion* ★★★ The arrival of Pascal Delbeck at Ausone had a dramatic effect on Belair too, since it's under the same ownership. It looked as though it was rapidly returning to a top position as a finely balanced, stylish St-Émilion red, but some recent bottles have been strangely unconvincing.

BEYCHEVELLE *4ème cru classé St-Julien* ★★★★ Certainly the most expensive Fourth Growth, but deservedly so, since traditional quality puts it alongside the top Seconds. It takes time to mature to a scented, blackcurranty, beautifully balanced – and expensive – red. At the end of the 1970s and beginning of the 1980s the wines were rather unconvincing, but the sale of the château (to a civil servants' pension fund) in 1985 dramatically improved matters. 1989 and 1990 are sublime, but there is still sometimes a tendency to overproduce.

BRANAIRE-DUCRU *4ème cru classé St-Julien* ★★★ Used to be soft, smooth red with a flavour of plums and chocolate, achieving a classic, cedary St-Julien perfume in maturity. The 1981, '82, '85 and '86 are good. But the 1980s were erratic, with dilute flavours and unclean fruit. 1982, '85 and '86 were clean and fruity, but '83, '87 and '88 were strangely insubstantial. 1989 and '90 saw a welcome return to form, thanks to a change of ownership, with wine of sturdy fruit and backbone. The cellar was rebuilt in 1991, and the improvements are showing in the wine.

BRANE-CANTENAC *2ème cru classé Margaux* ★★ A big and famous property which has been underachieving when most of the other Second Growths have been shooting ahead. It has had chances in the last few years to prove itself, but remains behind the rest of the field. Even its supposedly inferior stable-mate Durfort-Vivens has produced better wine recently.

BROUSTET *2ème cru classé Barsac* ★★★ A reliable, fairly rich sweet white not often seen, but worth trying. The 1988 and '90 are especially good, the dry white disappointing.

CABANNIEUX *Graves* ★★★ £ One of the new wave of non-classified Graves which is radically improving its white wine by the use of new oak barrels. The red is good, too. 1986, '88, '89 and '90 show the way.

CALON-SÉGUR *3ème cru classé St-Estèphe* ★★★(★) The château with the heart on its label. This is because the former owner, Marquis de Ségur, though he owned such estates as Lafite and Latour, declared 'my heart belongs to Calon'. An intensely traditional claret, it's certainly good on present showing, but doesn't set many hearts a-flutter. 1986 and '88 look good, '90 is fine and '94 promising. 1995 is superb.

CANON *1er grand cru classé St-Émilion* ★★★★(★) Mature Canon reeks of the soft, buttery Merlot grape as only a top St-Émilion can. Recently, it has been getting deeper and tougher, and although we'll probably miss that juicy, sweet mouthful of young Merlot, the end result will be even deeper and more exciting. The wines seem to get better and better; marvellous 1982s and '83s were followed by a stunning '85 and a thoroughly impressive '86. 1988 was excellent. 1989 and '90 are keeping up this high standard.

CANTEMERLE *5ème cru classé Haut-Médoc* ★★★(★) For some years after 1983 the Cordier company controlled this Fifth Growth red and the wine is now often up to Second Growth standards, although sometimes a little light. The 1988 and '89 are the best recent vintages by a long way, and the '83 was really good, but though the '85, '86 and '90 are beautifully perfumed, they are a little loose-knit. Interestingly, the perfumed style quite suits the '87.

CARBONNIEUX *cru classé Pessac-Léognan* ★★★(★) This large property has been using 50 per cent new oak for its whites since 1988 – and you can taste the difference. The 1990 is the best yet, and '92 and '93 are good. The red is increasingly complex.

CHASSE-SPLEEN *cru bourgeois Moulis* ★★★(★) A tremendously consistent wine, at the top of the *bourgeois* tree, and a prime candidate for elevation. It already sells above the price of many Classed Growths. The wines were impressive, chunky and beautifully made right through the 1980s, except for a rather over-elegant 1985. Choose 1982 and '86, followed by lovely '87 and tip-top '88. The 1989 is a bit fierce, but the '90 is first class, with lots of blackberry fruit backed by a firm structure. Even the '91 and '92 are impressive.

CHEVAL-BLANC *1er grand cru classé St-Émilion* ★★★★★ The property stands on an outcrop right next to Pomerol, and seems to share some of its sturdy richness, but adds extra spice and fruit that is unique, perhaps due to the very high proportion of Cabernet Franc. Good years are succulent. Lesser years like 1980 can be successes too, and only '84 and '87 haven't worked. The 1982 is unbelievably good, and the '81, '83, '85 and '86 are not far behind. 1988 and '90 are among the best of the vintage, but '89 is not quite of the intensity I want. 1995 is very promising, thanks to the ripeness of the Cabernet Franc.

CISSAC *cru grand bourgeois Haut-Médoc* ★★★ £ Traditionalists' delight! This is one of the best-known *bourgeois* reds, dark, dry and slow to mature with lots of oak influence, too – the oak perhaps a little more apparent than the fruit. It is best in richly ripe years like 1982 and '85, but can be a little lean in years like '86. 1988, '89 and '90 were very good indeed.

CLIMENS *1er cru Barsac* ★★★★★ Undoubtedly the best property in Barsac, making some of the most consistently fine sweet wines in France. 1980, '83, '86, '88, '89 and '90 are all excellent. It also makes a delicious second wine called les Cyprès that is well worth seeking out.

COS D'ESTOURNEL *2ème cru classé St-Estèphe* ★★★★★ £ The undoubted leader of St-Estèphe, this has much of the fame of the top Pauillacs. The wines are dark, tannic and oaky: classically made for long aging despite a high percentage of Merlot. The quality was so good in '85, '88 and '90 that they are probably undervalued, but the price has risen more recently. The '91 is decent. A new second label is being launched, now that Marbuzet has been a château in its own right from 1994.

COUHINS-LURTON *cru classé Pessac-Léognan* ★★★★ 100 per cent Sauvignon dry

white fermented in new oak barrels, producing a blend of grassy fruit and oaky spice. Recent vintages have been excellent.

COUTET *1er cru Barsac* ★★(★) A great sweet wine property which in recent years has not been living up to its previous exacting standards.

DOISY-DAËNE *2ème cru Barsac* ★★★(★) A very good, consistent property providing relatively light, but extremely attractive sweet wine. Doisy-Daëne Sec is a particularly good dry white.

DOISY-VÉDRINES *2ème cru Barsac* ★★★★ £ A rich, concentrated sweet white which is usually good value. 1980, '83, '86 and '89 are very good.

DOMAINE DE CHEVALIER *cru classé Pessac-Léognan* ★★★★(★) The red and white are equally brilliant. The red has a superb balance of fruit and oak, and the white is simply one of France's greatest. You have to book ahead even to see a bottle of the white

---

1855 CLASSIFICATION OF SAUTERNES

Grand premier cru   d'Yquem (Sauternes).

Premiers crus   Climens (Barsac); Coutet (Barsac); Guiraud (Sauternes); Haut-Peyraguey (Bommes); Lafaurie-Peyraguey (Bommes); Rabaud-Promis (Bommes); Rayne-Vigneau (Bommes); Rieussec (Fargues); Sigalas-Rabaud (Bommes); Suduiraut (Preignac); la Tour-Blanche (Bommes).

Deuxièmes crus   d'Arche (Sauternes); Broustet (Barsac); Caillou (Barsac); Doisy-Daëne (Barsac); Doisy-Dubroca (Barsac); Doisy-Védrines (Barsac); Filhot (Sauternes); Lamothe (Sauternes); Lamothe-Guignard (Sauternes); de Myrat (Barsac); Nairac (Barsac); Romer-du-Hayot (Fargues); Suau (Barsac); de Malle (Preignac).

but you might find some red. Buy it. It's expensive and worth every penny. The hottest years are not always the best here: 1982 is looking disappointing and the '81, '83, '85, '86 and '88 may yet turn out better. 1987 is a resounding success in a light vintage, as is the '84. 1989 and '90 were classy in an area of Bordeaux where results seem uneven in these vintages.

DUCRU-BEAUCAILLOU 2ème cru classé St-Julien ★★★(★) Potentially one of the glories of the Médoc. It initially distanced itself from most other Second Growths in price and quality, with a flavour so deep and warm, and balance so good, it was worth the money. With its relatively high yields, it has a less startling quality when young than its near rivals Léoville-Las-Cases and Pichon-Longueville-Lalande. The mid- to late 1980s saw problems with the barrels, so while '82 and '85 are top drawer, and '81, '79 and '78 fit for the long haul, other '80s vintages must be approached with caution. There may have been a problem with the élevage which is now under control. The 1995 should be excellent.

L'ÉVANGILE Pomerol ★★★(★) Top-line Pomerol, lacking the sheer intensity of its neighbour Pétrus, but perfumed and rich in a most irresistible way. Output isn't excessive, demand is. 1982, '85, and '88 are delicious, with first-rate '87 too. 1989 is packed with multi-layered, firm, luscious fruit, and '90 is another blockbuster.

DE FARGUES cru bourgeois Sauternes ★★★★(★) Small property owned by Yquem, capable of producing stunning, rich wines in the best years.

DE FIEUZAL cru classé Pessac-Léognan ★★★★(★) One of the stars of Pessac-Léognan, the white only just behind Domaine de Chevalier, the red well ahead. The red starts plum-rich and buttery, but develops earthiness and cedar scent allied to lovely fruit. It made one of the finest 1984s, outstanding '85s and '86s as well as lovely '87s and thrilling '88s.

1989 was top-notch, the '90 very good. The white, though unclassified, is scented, complex, deep and exciting. Even the '92 is worth buying.

FIGEAC 1er grand cru classé St-Émilion ★★★★ Figeac shares many of the qualities of Cheval Blanc (rare gravelly soil, for a start) but it's always ranked as the ever-reliable star of the second team. A pity, because the wine has a beauty and a blackcurranty, minty scent uncommon in St-Émilion. High quality. High(ish) price. Figeac is always easy to drink young, but deserves proper aging. The excellent 1978 is just opening out, and the lovely '82, '85 and '86 wines will all take at least as long. 1989 and '90 are already seductive.

FILHOT 2ème cru Sauternes ★★(★) Well-known Sauternes property producing pleasant but hardly memorable sweet whites, though the 1988 looks a bit more hopeful.

LA FLEUR-PÉTRUS Pomerol ★★★★ This red is in the top flight, having some of the mineral roughness of much Pomerol, but also tremendous perfume and length. Real class. We don't see much of this in the UK since the Americans got their teeth into it, but the 1982 and '89 are without doubt the best recent wines; the '85 and '86 seem to lack that little 'extra' class.

GAZIN Pomerol ★★★★ This can produce the extra sweetness and perfume Nenin usually lacks. Although fairly common on the British market, it wasn't that great up to about 1985. Now controlled by Moueix, '87 and '88 are an improvement, and '89 and '90 are really very fine, so we can all start buying it again. 1995 is first rate.

GILETTE cru bourgeois Sauternes ★★★★ Remarkable property which ages its sweet whites in concrete tanks for 20 to 30 years before releasing them. Usually delicious, with a dry richness unique in Sauternes thanks to long maturation and absence of wood. The 1970 is heavenly, and is the current vintage. Seriously! The wines come in different quality levels (not all of which are made every year), of which Crème de tête is the top.

GISCOURS *3ème cru classé Margaux* ★★★ This property excelled right through the 1970s and into the '80s, and made some of Bordeaux's best reds in years like '75, '78 and '80. But something's gone wrong since 1982. Although '86 is good, and '87 reasonable for the year, '83, '85 and '88 are not up to par. 1989 and '90 showed a return to form.

GLORIA *cru bourgeois St-Julien* ★★★ Owing to the high-profile lobbying of its late owner, Henri Martin, Gloria became expensive and renowned. The quality of this quick-maturing red has not always been faithful to the quality of the rhetoric. 1986, '88 and '89 show some signs that the wine is finally becoming worthy of the price.

GRAND-PUY-DUCASSE *5ème cru classé Pauillac* ★★★ £ With a price that is not excessive, its slightly gentle but tasty Pauillac style is one to buy. The 1979 is lovely now, and the '82 and '83 are very nice without causing the hand to tremble in anticipation. Since 1984 there has been a discernible rise in tempo, and '85 and '86 look to be the best wines yet, but little exciting wine was made in the late 1980s.

GRAND-PUY-LACOSTE *5ème cru classé Pauillac* ★★★★ £ This combines perfume, power and consistency in a way that shows Pauillac at its brilliant best. Blackcurrant and cigar-box perfumes are rarely in better harmony than here. Not cheap but worth it for a classic. The 1978 is sheer class, the '82, '83, '86 and '88 top wines, and the '84, though very light, is gentle and delicious. 1989 is deliciously perfumed with robust fruit – a real star, as is the super '90.

GRUAUD-LAROSE *2ème cru classé St-Julien* ★★★★(★) Another St-Julien that often starts rich, chunky and sweetish but will achieve its full cedary glory if given time, while still retaining a lovely sweet centre, typical of the wines (like Talbot) formerly owned by the Cordier family. The remarkable run of 1982, '83, '84 and '85 continued with a great '86, an attractive '87, an exceptionally impressive '88 and '89 and, keeping up the standards, an almost unnervingly juicy, ripe '90.

GUIRAUD *1er cru Sauternes* ★★★★(★) Fine sweet wine property owned since 1981 by a Canadian who has revolutionized the estate and brought the wines back to peak, and pricy, form. The wines are difficult to taste when young but are very special, and the 1983, '86, '88, '89 and '90 are going to be outstanding.

HAUT-BAILLY *cru classé Pessac-Léognan* ★★★★ Haut-Bailly red (there is no white) tastes sweet, rich and perfumed from its earliest youth, and the high percentage of new oak adds to this impression even further. But the wines do age well and, though expensive, are of a high class. 1981, '82, '85, '86, '88, '89 and '93 are the best recently.

HAUT-BATAILLEY *5ème cru classé Pauillac* ★★★ Once dark, plummy and slow to sweeten, this is now a somewhat lighter, more charming wine. In some years this has meant it was somehow less satisfying, but 1989 is the best yet, marvellously concentrated. 1986 and '88 are the best of earlier wines, with '82, '83 and '85 all good, but just a touch too diffuse and soft. The vineyard is now coming of age, so look for some very good wines in the mid-1990s.

HAUT-BRION *1er cru classé Pessac-Léognan* ★★★★★ The only non-Médoc red to be classified in 1855. The wines are not big, but are almost creamy in their gorgeous ripe taste, deliciously so. If anything, they slightly resemble the great Médocs. Although 1982 is strangely insubstantial, the next four vintages are all very fine, and '88 and '89 are outstanding, while the 1990, although worthy enough, could not quite compete with its predecessors. There are also small quantities of fine, long-lived white, also appealing when young. The 1985 and 1994 are both spectacular.

D'ISSAN *3ème cru classé Margaux* ★★★★ One of the truest Margaux wines, hard when young (though more use of new oak recently has sweetened things up a bit), but perfumed and deep-flavoured after ten to 12 years. Fabulous in 1983, '88 and '90, first rate in '85 and '86, with a good '87 too. 1989 has excellent fruit, while '90 is a star, rich and concentrated, with lots of liquorice fruit on the palate.

LAFAURIE-PEYRAGUEY *1er cru Sauternes* ★★★★(★) Fine sweet wine property, currently returning to top form after a dull period in the 1960s and '70s. Produced remarkably good wines in the difficult years of '82, '84 and '85, and it was stunning in '83, '86, '88 and '90.

LAFITE-ROTHSCHILD *1er cru classé Pauillac* ★★★★★ The most difficult of all the great Médocs to get to know. It doesn't stand for power like Latour, or perfume like Mouton. No, instead it stands for balance, for the elegant, restrained balance that is the perfection of great claret. And yet, till its day comes, Lafite can seem curiously unsatisfying. I keep looking for that day; at last I am finding satisfaction. 1990, '89, '88 and '86 are undoubtedly the best recent vintages, followed by '82, and this fabled estate at last seems to be dishing up fewer fairy tales and more of the real stuff that dreams are made on. Let's hope it lasts.

LAFLEUR *Pomerol* ★★★★★ This tiny property is regarded as the only Pomerol with the potential to be as great as Pétrus. So far, they couldn't be further apart in style, and Lafleur is marked out by an astonishing austere concentration of dark fruit and an intense tobacco spice perfume. The 1982 almost knocks you sideways with its naked power, and the '83 and '85 are also remarkable. 1989

is superbly fruity and displays tremendous finesse.

LAFON-ROCHET *4ème cru classé St-Estèphe* ★★★(★) An improving St-Estèphe, with as much body and a little more perfume than most. 1982, '83 and '85 are all good, though not stunning, while '86, '87, '88, '89 and '90 show real class and a welcome consistency of style. It looks set to move another gear upwards in the 1990s; 1994 and 1995, indeed, are most impressive.

LAGRANGE *3ème cru classé St-Julien* ★★★(★) Until its purchase by the Japanese Suntory whisky group in 1984, Lagrange had always missed real class, though '82 and '83 were reasonable. But investment is making its presence felt; '85, '86, '88, '89 and '90 are impressive and '87 was good too. Not great, though: the vineyard is not one of St-Julien's best, and in a way the current technical expertise underlines this, because the wine lacks heart. Make sure you concentrate on more recent vintages.

LA LAGUNE *3ème cru classé Haut-Médoc* ★★★★ Certainly making Second Growth-standard red, with a rich, soft intensity. It is now becoming more expensive, but the wine was consistently good, until the disappointing 1994. The 1982 is wonderfully rich and juicy, with '85 and '88 not far behind, and '83 not far behind that. 1986 is burly but brilliant stuff, as is '89. 1987 is more delicate but good.

LAMOTHE-GUIGNARD *2ème cru Sauternes* ★★★ Since 1981 this previously undistinguished sweet white has dramatically improved. 1983, '86 and '88 show the improvement, as will '89 and '90.

LANESSAN *cru bourgeois Haut-Médoc* ★★★ 'Grand Cru Hors Classe' is how Lanessan describes itself. This could be a reminder of the fact that a previous owner felt it unnecessary to submit samples for the 1855 Classification, so its traditional ranking as a Fourth Growth was never ratified. Nowadays, the wine is always correct, if not distinguished. But this may be because the owner resolutely refuses to use new oak and therefore his wines are more discreet when young. The 1982 and '83 are exhibiting classic claret flavours now, '88 looks set for the same path and '90 is a wine of balance and depth.

LANGOA-BARTON 3ème cru classé St-Julien ★★★★ £ This wine is very good, in the dry, cedary style, and is sometimes regarded as a lesser version of Léoville-Barton. The wine has character and style, and is reasonably priced. 1982 and '85 are exciting, '86 and '87 very typical, but the '88 may be the best for 30 years. The '89 vintage almost matched Léoville-Barton for elegance and the '90 was fully its equal.

LASCOMBES 2ème cru classé Margaux ★★★ Lascombes made its reputation in America, and that's where it still likes to be drunk. Very attractive early on, but the wine can gain flesh and character as it ages. It's been a little inconsistent recently, but the 1985 and '83 are good, and the '86 is the most serious effort for a long time. 1987 is also good, but '88 is so light you'd think they'd included every grape on the property. 1989, '90 and '91 are more hopeful.

LATOUR 1er cru classé Pauillac ★★★★★ This is the easiest of all the First Growths to comprehend. You may not always like it, but you understand it because it is a huge, dark, hard brute when young, calming down as it ages and eventually spreading out to a superb, blackcurrant and cedar flavour. It used to take ages to come round, but some recent vintages have seemed a little softer and lighter, whilst retaining their tremendous core of fruit. Let's hope they age as well as the previous ones, because the 1984 was more true to type than the '85. And though the '82 is a classic, both '83 and '81 are very definitely not. 1986 and '88 seem to be back on course, and '89 looks splendidly powerful. With the '89 and '90 the new management showed that power and richness were part of their inheritance. The '91

and '92 are the best wines of their years. The second wine, called les Forts-de-Latour, is getting better and better, while the third wine, Pauillac de Latour, is now made in most years to preserve the quality of the two greater wines.

LAVILLE-HAUT-BRION cru classé Pessac-Léognan ★★★★ This should be one of the greatest of all white Pessac-Léognan, since it is owned by Haut-Brion, but despite some great successes, the general effect is patchy – especially given the crazy prices.

LÉOVILLE-BARTON 2ème cru classé St-Julien ★★★★★ £ The traditionalist's dream. Whoever described claret as a dry, demanding wine must have been thinking of Léoville-Barton. Despite all the new fashions and trends in Bordeaux, Anthony Barton simply goes on making superlative, old-fashioned wine for long aging, and resolutely charging a non-inflated price for it. All the vintages of the 1980s have been attractive, but the '82, '83, '85 and '86 are outstanding, the '87 delicious, and the '88 and '90 are two of the best wines of the Médoc. 1989 keeps up the high standard. All the wines are *wonderfully* fairly priced.

LÉOVILLE-LAS-CASES 2ème cru classé St-Julien ★★★★★ Because of the owner's super-selectivity, this is the most brilliant of the St-Juliens, combining all the sweet, honeyed St-Julien ripeness with strong, dry, cedary perfume. The wine is justly famous, and despite a large production, the whole crop is snapped up at some of the Médoc's highest prices. The 1982 is more exciting every time a bottle is broached, and all the vintages of the 1980s are top examples of their year. The second wine, Clos du Marquis, is better than the majority of Classed Growths, if only because Michel Delon puts into it wines which any other owner would put into his *grand vin*.

LÉOVILLE-POYFERRÉ 2ème cru classé St-Julien ★★★★ The Léoville that got left behind, not only in its unfashionable reputation, but also in the quality of the wine, which until recently had a dull, indistinct flavour and an unbalancing dryness compared with other top St-Juliens. Things should now be looking up with new investment and renewed commitment, and every vintage shows progress. The 1982, '85, '86 and even the '87 are better, and '88, '89 and '90 continue the good work. Oenologist Michel Rolland now consults, and the '94 is remarkably good.

LOUDENNE *cru bourgeois Médoc* ★(★) The château is owned by Gilbey's and the wine is seen a lot in high street chains. Both red and white are fruity and agreeable, and best drunk young.

LA LOUVIÈRE *cru bourgeois Pessac-Léognan* ★★★★ This property has been making lovely, modern, oak-aged whites since the mid-1970s, and since 1987 the quality has climbed even higher. Reds are also good, and quite earthy.

LYNCH-BAGES *5ème cru classé Pauillac* ★★★★★ This château is so well known that its familiarity can breed contempt, causing its considerable quality to be underestimated. It is astonishingly soft and drinkable when very young, yet ages brilliantly, and has one of the most beautiful scents of minty blackcurrant in all Bordeaux. The most likely to show that character are the 1986, '83 and, remarkably, the '87, but for sheer exuberant starry-eyed brilliance the '88, '85 and particularly the '82 are the ones. The '89 is unusually big and powerful, while the '90 is more marginally restrained and classic.

MAGDELAINE *1er grand cru classé St-Émilion* ★★★★ This is a fine producer of St-Émilion, the wines combining the soft richness of Merlot with the sturdiness needed to age. They pick very late to maximize ripeness, and the wine is made with the usual care by Jean-Pierre Moueix of Libourne. Expensive, but one of the best. 1982 and '85 are both classics, '88 and '89 tremendously good.

MALARTIC-LAGRAVIÈRE *cru classé Pessac-Léognan* ★★★ £ While its near neighbour, Domaine de Chevalier, hardly ever produces its allowed crop, this property frequently has to declassify its excess. Even so, the quality is good, sometimes excellent, and while the white is very attractive young, the red is capable of long aging. 1987, '86, '85, '83 and '82 are all successful, with '88 and '89 the finest yet, but the '90s are disappointing. The red, in particular, is rather wishy-washy.

MALESCOT-ST-EXUPÉRY *3ème cru classé Margaux* ★★(★) This seemed to have lost its way. Traditionally it started lean and hard, but after ten years or so it began to display the perfume and delicate fruit only bettered by such wines as Palmer and Margaux. Yet after tasting and re-tasting the wines of the 1980s, the conclusion is that they were made too light and lacking in depth for this thrilling scent ever to develop. So thank goodness for the massive improvement in '88, '89 and '90.

DE MALLE *2ème cru Sauternes* ★★★ Good, relatively light sweet white from a very beautiful property set partly in the Graves and partly in Sauternes. It went through a bad patch in the early and mid-1980s when the owner died after a long illness, but since '88 his widow has been making wines fully worthy of the name.

MARGAUX *1er cru classé Margaux* ★★★★★ A succession of great wines under its new owners have set Margaux back on the pedestal of refinement and sheer, ravishing perfume from which it had slipped some years ago. The new Margaux is weightier and more consistent than before, yet with all its beauty intact. 1978 and '79 were the harbingers of this 'Mentzelopoulos era', the '80 was startlingly good in a tricky vintage, and '82, '83 and '86 are just about as brilliant as claret can be, while the '88 may well be the wine of the vintage. The deep, concentrated '89 doesn't seem to match up to the '88, but the '90 is as fragrant and powerful as the '86 – which is saying a lot.

In '91 and '92 the wines, though not up to Latour's level, were better than most of the First Growths.

MEYNEY *cru bourgeois St-Estèphe* ★★★(★) **£** This epitomizes St-Estèphe reliability, yet is better than that. It is big, meaty and strong, but never harsh. Vintages in the 1970s lacked personality, but recent wines are increasingly impressive, and although the wine is difficult to taste young, the '82, '83, '85, '86, '88 and '89 are all remarkable, and the '84, '87 and '90 are good.

LA MISSION-HAUT-BRION *cru classé Pessac-Léognan* ★★★(★) La Mission likes to put itself in a class apart, between Haut-Brion and the rest. Yet one often feels this red relies more on weight and massive, dark fruit and oak flavours than on any great subtleties. For those, you go to Haut-Brion or Domaine de Chevalier. 1982, '85 or '86 are recommendable of recent vintages.

MONTROSE *2ème cru classé St-Estèphe* ★★★★ Traditionally famous for its dark, tannic character, and its slow, ponderous march to maturity. For a wine with such a sturdy reputation, some recent vintages have seemed faintly hollow. 1986 made amends with a really chewy, long-distance number, and '87 was densely structured, if hardly classic, but it's taken until '89 and '90 vintages for the wine really to return to form. The château, which tends to pick rather early, came into its own in '89 and '90, and even made a decent '91 and a better '92. The second wine, Dame de Montrose, has been a bargain lately.

MOUTON-ROTHSCHILD *1er cru classé Pauillac* ★★★★★ After years of lobbying, Baron Philippe de Rothschild managed to raise Mouton to First Growth status in 1973. Of course it should be a First Growth. But then several Fifths should probably be Seconds. The wine has an astonishing flavour, piling intense cigar-box and lead-pencil perfume on to the rich blackcurrant fruit. The 1982 is already a legend, the '86 and '89 are likely to join '82,

and the '85, '84 and '83 are well worth the asking price. The 1988 and '90, though, are below par for the property, though the '95 is fabulous.

NENIN *Pomerol* ★★ A thoroughly old-fashioned red. It quite rightly pleases the royal family, who order rather a lot of it. But in fact it is rather chunky and solid and has quite a tough core for a Pomerol, which doesn't always disperse into mellow fruitfulness. The 1985 and '86 aren't bad, but, really, the '82, the '83 and the '88, all good vintages, were pretty feeble.

PALMER *3ème cru classé Margaux* ★★★★ 'Most expensive of the Third Growths?' asks one of Palmer's owners. 'No. Cheapest of the Firsts.' There's (some) truth in that. Until 1978 Palmer used to out-Margaux Margaux for sheer beauty and perfume. And it still can occasionally out-perform some of the First Growths in tastings. It was consistently brilliant in the 1960s and 1970s (excepting '64), but the 1980s have seen it lose some of its sure touch, and the '83 lacks some of its neighbours' class. 1987 and '88 are very good too, but are closer in style to out-Beychevelling Beychevelle. 1989 is cedary and elegant, rich but tannic, in a year when not all Margaux wines had great depth of fruit. In 1990 Palmer was better than most, but not all, of its neighbours.

PAPE-CLÉMENT *grand cru classé de Graves* ★★★★(★) One of the top properties in Pessac-Léognan, capable of mixing a considerable sweetness from ripe fruit and new oak with a good deal of tough structure. 1975 was great, but then we had a very poor decade until 1985. The last five vintages are outstanding, with the 1990 an example of Pessac-Léognan at its best.

PAVIE *1er grand cru St-Émilion* ★★★★ The biggest major property in St-Émilion, with high yields, too. Until recently good without being wonderful, stylish without being grand. Still, Pavie does have the true gentle flavours of good St-Émilion and recent releases are showing a deeper, more passionate style which puts it into the top flight. 1990, '89, '88, '87, '86 and '85 are good examples of the new, '82 of the old.

PETIT-VILLAGE *Pomerol* ★★★★ A fairly pricy red, it is not one of the soft, plummy Pomerols, and until recently there was a fair amount of Cabernet giving backbone. The wine is worth laying down, but the price is always high. 1985, '83 and the juicy '82 are all very good, but the '88, '89 and '90 look likely to be the best yet.

PÉTRUS *Pomerol* ★★★★★ One of the world's most expensive reds, and often one of the greatest. Astonishingly, its fame, though surfacing briefly in 1878, has only been acquired since 1945, and in particular since 1962, when the firm of Jean-Pierre Moueix took a half-share in the property. This firm has given the kiss of life to many Pomerol properties, turning potential into achievement, and with Pétrus it has a supreme creation. Christian Moueix says his intention is to ensure no bottle of Pétrus ever disappoints. 1982 and '89 were stupendously great. 1985 isn't far off it, nor is '81, and the only example from the last 20 years which seemed atypical is the rather Médoc-like 1978.

DE PEZ *cru bourgeois St-Estèphe* ★★★ One of the most famous *bourgeois* châteaux, the wine is almost always of Classed Growth standard, big, reliable, rather plummy and not too harsh. 1982 and '83 were both very attractive, though some prefer the more unashamedly St-Estèphe wines of the 1970s, which saw a bit of a comeback with the excellent '86.

PICHON-LONGUEVILLE *2ème cru classé Pauillac* ★★★★ Often described as more masculine than its 'sister', Pichon-Longueville-Lalande, this tremendously correct but diffident Pauillac (formerly Pichon-Longueville-Baron) was until 1987 only hinting at its potential. In 1987 the property was bought by the AXA insurance company and Jean-Michel Cazes of Lynch-Bages was brought in to run it. The '87 was very good, the '88 superb, the '89 *tremendous*, broodingly intense, while the '90 is one of the Médoc's greatest reds. However, the difficult vintages since have not been mastered so well.

PICHON-LONGUEVILLE-LALANDE *2ème cru classé Pauillac* ★★★★(★) Pichon-Longueville-Lalande (formerly Pichon-Lalande) produced a stunning 1970, and since then has been making a rich, oaky, concentrated red of tremendous quality. Its price has climbed inexorably and it wishes to be seen as the equal partner of St-Julien's leading pair, Léoville-Las-Cases and Ducru-Beaucaillou. 1982, '83 and '85 all brim with exciting flavours, and '86 may be even better. Nothing since then reaches the same standards, though '87 and '88 are good. Both '89 and '90 are below par, and easily outclassed by rival estate Pichon-Longueville over the road. But since then Lalande has been clearly back on form, especially with its brilliant '95.

PONTET-CANET *5ème cru classé Pauillac* ★★★ The biggest Classed Growth of them all. Famous but unpredictable, and still trying to find its traditionally reliable form. 1985 and '86 are hopeful, '87 and '88 less so, '90 hopeful again, and a new cellarmaster made a much better '94.

POTENSAC *cru bourgeois Médoc* ★★★(★) £ The most exciting red wine château in the Bas-Médoc. It is owned by Michel Delon of Léoville-Las-Cases, and a broadly similar style of wine-making is pursued. This gives wines with a delicious, blackcurrant fruit, greatly improved by a strong taste of oak from once-used Las-Cases barrels. Not expensive for the quality. Beats many *crus classés* every year for sheer flavour.

PRIEURÉ-LICHINE *4ème cru classé Margaux* ★★★ One of the more reliable Margaux wines, and in 1970, '71 and '75 it excelled. Recently it has been fairly priced and, although not that perfumed, good and sound. 1983, '86, '88 and '89 are all good, but the '90 was the first really exciting wine to have been made for some time, and '91 and '92 continued the improvement.

RABAUD-PROMIS *1er cru Sauternes* ★★★(★) At last! The 1986, '88, '89 and '90 are excellent and show a long-awaited return to First Growth sweet wine quality.

RAHOUL *cru bourgeois Graves* ★★(★) A leader of the new wave of cool-fermented, oak-aged whites among the Graves properties. Also generally good red. Ownership changes are worrying, though, and the 1988, '89 and '90 were not as special as previous vintages, though they are still good. Domaine Benoit and Château Constantin are also good in the same stable.

RAUZAN-SÉGLA *2ème cru classé Margaux* ★★★★(★) Up to and including the 1982 vintage this lovely property, rated second only to Mouton-Rothschild in the 1855 Second Growths, had been woefully underachieving

for a couple of generations. But a change of ownership in 1983 saw a return to quality – in the very first year. 1983, '85 and '86 were triumphs. 1987 was declassified as Château Lamouroux but is still delicious. The '88, '89, '90, '93 and '94 are all very good. The older spelling of the name, with a z, is now being used again.

RAUZAN-GASSIES *2ème cru classé Margaux* ★★ Leagues below most Second and Third Growth reds in quality, and so far hasn't taken the hint from Ségla that quality pays in the end.

RAYMOND LAFON *cru bourgeois Sauternes* ★★★★ Owned by the former manager of neighbouring d'Yquem, this is fine wine but not quite as fine as the increasingly daunting price would imply.

RIEUSSEC *1er cru Sauternes* ★★★★(★) One of the richest, most exotic Sauternes, and particularly good wines during the 1980s. The 1982 is good, the '83, '86 and '88 really special, the '89 and '90 wonderful.

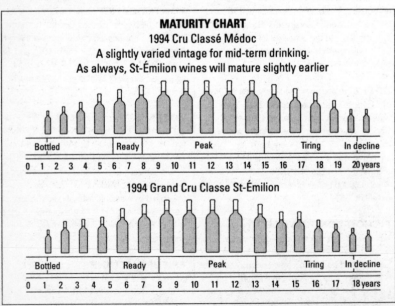

MATURITY CHART
1994 Cru Classé Médoc
A slightly varied vintage for mid-term drinking.
As always, St-Émilion wines will mature slightly earlier

| Bottled | Ready | Peak | Tiring | In decline |

0 1 2 3 4 5 6 7 8 9 10 11 12 13 14 15 16 17 18 19 20 years

1994 Grand Cru Classe St-Émilion

| Bottled | Ready | Peak | Tiring | In decline |

0 1 2 3 4 5 6 7 8 9 10 11 12 13 14 15 16 17 18 years

ST-AMAND *cru bourgeois Sauternes*
★★★(★) £ Splendid property making truly
rich wines that age well, at an affordable price.
Also seen as Château de la Chartreuse. Since
the 1970s each decent vintage has produced a
delicious example.

ST-PIERRE *4ème cru classé Médoc* ★★★★
Small St-Julien property producing superb,
underrated, old-fashioned red. Once under-
priced, but the image-conscious Henri Martin
of Gloria stopped that when he took over in
1982. Still, the quality has been worth it. While
the 1970 and '75 were stars, the wines of the
1980s are possibly even better. Martin died in
1991, and the family are carrying on the
tradition.

DE SALES *Pomerol* ★★★ £ An enormous
estate, the biggest in Pomerol by a mile. This
vastness shows in a wine which, though it is
good round claret, doesn't often seem to
excite. The 1985 is nice, the '83 and '82 are
very nice.

SIRAN *cru bourgeois Margaux* ★★★
Sometimes mistaken for a Classed Growth in
blind tastings, this property is indeed mostly
made up from the land of Châteaux Dauzac
and Giscours, both of which are Classed
Growths. The 1985 and '83 are the most
successful wines of recent years, but all
vintages have been good lately. The '88 was a
bit clumsy, but the '89 and '90 vintages are
both showing well.

SMITH-HAUT-LAFITTE *cru classé
Pessac-Léognan* ★★★★ A late convert to cool
fermentation and oak-aging, but since 1985
making superb wines. Also increasingly good,
and better-known, reds.

SUDUIRAUT *1er cru Sauternes* ★★★(★)
Rich, exciting wines, frequently deeper and
more intensely perfumed than any other
Sauternes – except for its neighbour, d'Yquem
– but unfortunately not as reliable as it should
be. A remarkable 1982 was followed by a fine
'83, a very good '85 but disappointing '86 and

ditto in 1988. 1989 was a leap up again,
though.

TALBOT *4ème cru classé St-Julien*
★★★ This used to be one of the most
carefully made and reliable of the fleshier St-
Juliens, suffering only in comparison with its
sister château in the former Cordier stable,
Gruaud-Larose. In more recent years, though,
it has seemed to be lagging way behind
Gruaud-Larose in quality. The vintages of the
mid- to late 1980s haven't shaped up as well
as they should have done, with the 1988 in
particular showing poorly (though the '82, '83
and '84 were very good). The '90 seems to
lack something in the way of concentration.

DU TERTRE *5ème cru classé Margaux*
★★★(★) This wine is unusually good, with a
lot of body for a Margaux, but that weight is all
ripe, strong fruit and the flavour is direct and
pure. Funnily enough, it's not cheap for a
relative unknown but neither is it expensive
for the quality. The 1985 is rich and dense and
yet keeps its perfume intact, while the '86, '83
and '82 are rich and blackcurranty – already
good and sure to improve for ten years more.
1988 was not quite so good, for some reason,
but '89 was back to normal.

TROTANOY *Pomerol* ★★★★ If you didn't
know Pétrus existed, you'd say this had to be
the perfect Pomerol – rich, plummy, chocolaty
fruit, some mineral hardness, and tremendous
fat perfume. It's very, very good, and makes
Pétrus' achievement in eclipsing it all the more
amazing. The 1982 is brilliant, and although the
'85 is also wonderfully good, the vintages of
the mid- and late 1980s haven't been quite as
thrilling as the previous examples of this
château.

D'YQUEM *grand 1er cru classé Sauternes*
★★★★★ This is the pinnacle of achievement
in great sweet wines. Almost every vintage of
d'Yquem is a masterpiece and its outlandish
price is almost justified, since d'Yquem at its
best is undoubtedly the greatest sweet wine in
the world.

CLARETS OUT OF THEIR CLASS

One of the most exciting things for a wine devotee is to catch a château at the beginning of a revival in its fortunes. While a reputation is being built or re-built, the quality will keep ahead of the price – for a while.

There are also some wines, notably Cos d'Estournel and Léoville-Barton, which have kept quality up and prices (relatively) down, though Cos has recently raised its prices. This is my assessment of some of Bordeaux's current best buys.

Médoc

Minor châteaux performing like top bourgeois: Grands Chênes, Malescasse, Moulin Rouge, Potensac, Tour Haut-Caussan, Tour du Haut-Moulin, Tour-de-By, Tour-St-Bonnet.

Top bourgeois performing like Classed Growths: d'Angludet, Chambert-Marbuzet, Chasse-Spleen, Citran, Haut-Marbuzet, Labégorce-Zédé, Lanessan, Meyney, Monbrison, Ormes-de-Pez, Phélan-Ségur, Pibran, Poujeaux, Siran, Sociando-Mallet, Tour-de-Mons.

Classed Growths performing above their station: Clerc-Milon-Rothschild, Grand-Puy-Lacoste, la Lagune, Léoville-Barton, Léoville-Las-Cases, Montrose, Pichon-Lalande, Pontet-Canet (from '94), Rauzan-Ségla.

Graves and Pessac-Léognan

Outperformers: White: Cabannieux, Carbonnieux, Couhins-Lurton, de Fieuzal, Montalivet, Olivier, Smith-Haut-Lafitte. *Red:* de Fieuzal, Haut-Bailly, Pape-Clément, Roquetaillade la Grange, la Tour-Martillac.

Pomerol

Outperformers: Beauregard, Bon-Pasteur, Certan-de-May, Clinet, l'Église-Clinet, l'Évangile, Gazin.

St-Émilion

Outperformers: l'Angélus, l'Arrosée, Beau-Séjour-Bécot, Bellefont-Belcier, la Dominique, Grand-Mayne, Larmande, Pavie-Macquin, Tertre Rôteboeuf, Troplong-Mondot, Valandraud.

Satellites

Outperformers: Canon-de-Brem, Canon Moueix, Charlemagne, Cassagne-Haut-Truffière (Canon-Fronsac); Lyonnat (Lussac-St-Émilion); Tour-du-Pas-St-Georges (St-Georges-St-Émilion); la Prade, de Francs (both Côte de Francs); des Annereaux, Bertineau-St-Vincent (both Lalande-de-Pomerol).

Sauternes

Outperformers: Bastor-Lamontagne, Chartreuse, Climens, Doisy-Daëne, de Fargues, Gilette, Liot, de Malle, Nairac, Roumieu Lacoste, St-Amand.

MERCHANTS SPECIALISING IN BORDEAUX
see Merchant Directory (page 424) for details

Virtually all merchants have some Bordeaux. Adnams (AD), John Armit (ARM), Averys of Bristol (AV), Bennetts (BEN), Berry Bros. & Rudd (BER), Bibendum (BIB), Bute Wines (BUT), Butlers Wine Cellar (BU), Anthony Byrne (BY), Châteaux Wines (CHA), Corney & Barrow (CB), Croque-en-Bouche (CRO), Davisons (DAV), Direct Wine (DI), Eldridge Pope (EL), Enotria

Winecellars (ENO), Farr Vintners (FA), Forth Wines (FOR), Gelston Castle (GE), Goedhuis (GOE), Harveys (HAR), High Breck (HIG), Lay & Wheeler (LAY), Oddbins (OD), Thos. Peatling (PE), Christopher Piper (PIP), Raeburn Fine Wines (RAE), Reid Wines (REI), T&W Wines (TW), Tanners (TAN), Thresher (THR), The Ubiquitous Chip (UB), Wine Society (WS), Peter Wylie (WY)

BORDEAUX VINTAGES

Claret vintages are accorded more importance than those of any other wine; so much so that good wine from a less popular vintage can get swamped under all the brouhaha. We have had a parade of 'vintages of the century' in recent years, although the fuss and hype more usually starts in Bordeaux itself or on the volatile American market than in more cynical Britain.

Wines age at different rates according to their vintage. They may get more delicious or less so as they mature; some may be at their best before they are fully mature, because, although their balance may not be terribly impressive, at least they've got a good splash of young fruit. Wines also mature differently according to the quality of the property.

The generic appellations – like Bordeaux Supérieur – rarely need any aging. A 1985, for instance, from a *premier cru*, might take 20 years to be at its best, a good *bourgeois* might take ten, and a *petit château* might take five.

The grape variety is also important. Wines based on Cabernet (many of the Médocs and the Graves) will mature more slowly than wines based on Merlot (most Pomerols and St-Émilions).

In these pages, **A** = quality; **B** = value for money; **C** = drink now; **D** = lay down.

1995 (AD) The vintage is not perfect: summer drought and vintage rain have made it unlikely that another 1990 has been produced. But the wines have both charm and structure, similar to 1985 only based on the successful Cabernet Sauvignon and Cabernet Franc, rather than the Merlot. Overall, 1995 should prove to be superior to 1985, and will provide a handful of truly great wines at the top end of the scale.

A warm spring gave rise to fears of frost damage which the vineyards mostly escaped, despite a few near misses. An early flowering promised an early vintage. All good signs, but the three preceding vintages had flattered to deceive. A marvellous summer followed: perhaps too good because it scarcely rained from mid-June to the end of August, apart from isolated storms in the latter month. Drought conditions began to cause anxiety, and the vines started to shut down their ripening cycle, although some showers around the 21st–24th August eased the situation.

Then the (seemingly) inevitable rain fell intermittently from 7th to 19th September, having both good and bad effects. It slightly diluted the Merlot which was ready to pick, but provided a much-needed drink for the Cabernets, which were still a fortnight or so away from ripening. The rest of the month was fine and dry if not especially warm: conditions which helped the grapes to finish off ripening nicely yet did not encourage any dangerous rot. Showers returned in early October, by which time most of the crop had been picked.

The red wines are deep in colour (thick skins on small berries) and the fruit is certainly ripe. Tannin indices are high (thick skins, small berries, ripe pips) and acidity low (hot summer, full ripeness) yet in most cases the fruit envelops the tannins in a balanced and harmonious fashion. In some instances, where the gravel banks of the Médoc, for example, dried out too much in the drought, the tannins seem unacceptably dry. Equally, a few wines are a little dilute because of the rain. Overall, though, this is clearly a very fine vintage.

The growers in Sauternes have had an even worse time of it since 1990 than the rest of the Bordelais. At least in 1995 there is a vintage to consider, though it will not compete with the great years of 1988 to 1990. The grapes ripened well to give good natural sugar levels, but not everybody achieved significant noble rot. One or two wines showed some distinctly dubious flavours, perhaps including a touch of grey rot.

The dry white wines of Bordeaux look good – they are rich and fat, but perhaps lack the zest of the '94s, which will prove superior in the long run.

1994 (AD) Sadly, the pattern of 1993 was broadly reproduced in 1994: great potential wrecked by rain. It cheered up in October, but the crop was in by then.

Nonetheless the 1994 clarets are more concentrated than the '93s, with deeper colours and more fruit. They also show greater tannins, though happily less green ones. The key questions to be asked are whether or not the fruit carries all the way through to the tannins at the end, and whether or not those tannins are in balance.

The most successful region was Pomerol, where most châteaux increased the usual percentage of Merlot, which ripened better than the Cabernets. However, in the Médoc producers were split between those who preferred the earlier-picked Merlot to their Cabernet, and those who played the Cabernet card, actually increasing the percentage of Cabernet in the final wine. Lafite, for example, excluded all Merlot apart from some press wine and made an almost 100 per cent Cabernet Sauvignon.

The vineyards closer to the river, with a tendency to ripen earlier, seem to have done better in 1994 than those in the colder soils found further inland. It is less easy to find a pattern commune by commune, but there seem to be a high proportion of successes in St-Estèphe and some very good wines in St-Julien. Pauillac is perhaps a little less dominant than in most years, and Margaux is its usual variable self.

A tiny crop of fair quality was made in Sauternes, a relief after three wipe-out years, but nothing like the great trio of 1988-'89-'90. Dry whites were better, especially in Pessac-Léognan.

1993 (D) This was the vintage which might have been. Until ten days before the harvest in the third week of September, there was promise of excellent quality. But then the rain started. It rained regularly and relentlessly; the only consolation was that the grapes were in very good condition after a dry summer, and ripe enough to permit fairly good wine to be made in spite of the weather.

In general, the Merlot-based wines have come out better than those based on Cabernet Sauvignon or Cabernet Franc, both of which lack power. But unlike in most wet years, there was very little rot.

Leaving aside the major appellations, the best reds were made by those who took account of the dilution of the juice and aimed for well-balanced wines with fruit and charm rather than wines for the long haul.

The Médocs are quite varied in style. The best, including most of the top châteaux, are good, though without the power or longevity of a great vintage. Below the top level the picture becomes more uneven, with wines that range from attractive but short to unattractive and even shorter.

The reds of the Graves and particularly of Pessac-Léognan are, at their best, elegant, delicate and subtle. The less successful ones are thin, but the general level of quality is pretty high.

The most successful wines of the vintage are from St-Émilion and Pomerol. The best here have excellent colour and above all a power and concentration not seen elsewhere. If any 1993 clarets keep, it will be these. The less good Pomerols are very deep coloured but rustic, and the less good St-Émilions lack personality.

It wasn't a year for fine Sauternes. The best wines are the semi-sweet ones made by sensible but unimaginative growers. These are perfectly sound wines but lack character and, above all, they lack botrytis.

The rain also stopped the dry whites from being outstanding, but the general level of quality is more uniform than among the red. Overall the wines are well-balanced and without aggressive acidity. The wines from the top châteaux of Pessac-Léognan are sound, but appear to outstrip their humbler neighbours in the Graves rather less convincingly than usual.

MATURITY CHART

1990 Cru Classé Médoc

The third great vintage in a row; and another one for the next millennium

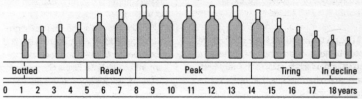

Bottled		Ready		Peak		Tiring	In decline

0   5   10   15   20   25 years

1990 Good Cru Bourgeois Médoc

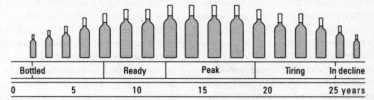

Bottled		Ready		Peak		Tiring	In decline

0 1 2 3 4 5 6 7 8 9 10 11 12 13 14 15 16 17 18 years

1989 Cru Classé Médoc

Rich fruit combines with ripe tannins, mainly for the long term

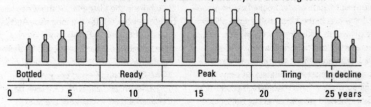

Bottled		Ready		Peak		Tiring	In decline

0   5   10   15   20   25 years

1989 Good Cru Bourgeois Médoc

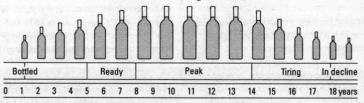

Bottled		Ready		Peak		Tiring	In decline

0 1 2 3 4 5 6 7 8 9 10 11 12 13 14 15 16 17 18 years

1992 (C) This was the wettest summer for at least 50 years and Bordeaux had less sunshine than in any year since 1980. Many of the grapes did not ripen, reaching only a miserable seven or eight degrees of potential alcohol, a mere two-thirds of the level they had reached in 1990. Even in the best estates the wines risk dilution – most obviously with the Merlot, where some of the grapes were as bloated as small plums.

In Sauternes, a handful of châteaux managed to harvest some botrytized grapes in September, but quantities are small. The best dry whites from the Graves are well-structured, but most whites are merely pleasant.

1991 (C) A small and wildly variable vintage, spoiled by heavy September and October rain. It is a year in which to stick to the very best estates, stars like Margaux, Latour, Pichon-Longueville and Léoville-Las-Cases. Montrose also stood out: Jean-Louis Charmolüe is famous for picking early, so he got his grapes in before the onset of the rains. Even his second wine (Dame de Montrose) is good value. Among the *crus bourgeois* reliable estates like Chasse-Spleen and Sociando-Mallet came up to scratch. In the Graves a few estates like Smith-Haut-Lafitte and la Tour-Martillac made decent wines. In the Libournais the situation was still worse, with nine-tenths of most crops simply wiped out by spring frosts.

It was a very difficult year in Sauternes. The impact of the frost was greatest on the Sémillon, making for an overly high proportion of Sauvignon. Most are correct or better, but only Climens seems to have produced a stunner. Quantities of dry whites were also well down, though what there is is good.

1990 (AD) For the third consecutive year and for the eighth time in a decade, the harvest was excellent if not superlative.

It was generally the old vines with deep roots which coped best with the extreme heat, and a water-collecting, clay-based subsoil proved an advantage: those vines grown on well-drained pebbles (chiefly Cabernet Sauvignon) had a hard time. With some notable exceptions, the Merlot-based wines did better than those made from Cabernet Sauvignon. Some Médoc properties (Latour is unusual in this) have a subsoil of clay.

The quality now looks the most even of the three great years of 1990, '88 and '89. Of the three it now seems clear that anyone looking for a classic Bordeaux vintage (albeit a tough and tannic one) should opt for the 1988; the last two vintages having been too unusual to produce wines in the old claret mould, though many were splendid, if richer and fruitier than old-style claret buffs would like. Modern drinkers, immersed in rich Australian reds, will lap them up.

In Sauternes it was the most extraordinary year since 1893. The wines are huge, and should be the treat (though not, alas, the bargain) of a lifetime. Dry whites were less successful, especially in the Graves. Be very selective here.

1989 (AD) For those who like to designate a Bordeaux vintage as either a Merlot year or a Cabernet year, this was one in which the Cabernet Sauvignon couldn't fail to ripen well. Merlot was more of a problem

Overall it may not be a Margaux year. Elsewhere in the Haut-Médoc the wines seem better constructed for the long haul. And over on the right bank, St-Émilion and Pomerol defied a Cabernet year with Merlots of charm and richness.

The Graves and Pessac-Léognan were more uneven, and although Domaine de Chevalier and Pape-Clément are as classy as you would hope, only de Fieuzal, la Louvière and Haut-Bailly stood out.

In Sauternes the wines are turning out to be wildly inconsistent. So stick to the stars – apart from Lafaurie-Peyraguey, which had an off-year. The dry whites suffered from overripe grapes and were much less successful than the sweet ones.

1988 (ABD) A difficult year, saved by a long warm summer – a vintage which could be the most classically balanced of the 1980s.

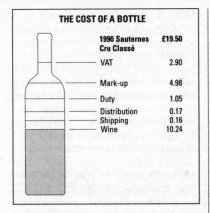

THE COST OF A BOTTLE

1990 Sauternes Cru Classé	**£19.50**
VAT	2.90
Mark-up	4.98
Duty	1.05
Distribution	0.17
Shipping	0.16
Wine	10.24

Graves/Pessac-Léognan yielded a remarkable range of wines. Margaux was less exciting. Chasse-Spleen and Poujeaux were the best of the Moulis, while St-Julien had beautiful wines from Beychevelle, Gloria, St-Pierre, Talbot, Gruaud, Langoa-Barton and Léoville-Barton. Pauillac did very well, with Lafite, Grand-Puy-Lacoste, Haut-Bages-Libéral and Pichon-Longueville-Lalande all excellent, tip-top Lynch-Bages and the triumphantly reborn Pichon-Longueville. St-Estèphe made its best vintage for years. The northern Médoc was a success too, in particular at Cissac, Hanteillan, Sociando-Mallet, la Tour-de-By and Potensac.

Pomerol made some excellent wines, and should have made more, but overproduction diluted the quality in many cases. Best are Clinet, Beauregard, Évangile, Moulinet, l'Enclos, Vieux-Château-Certan, with improved efforts from la Croix-de-Gay and la Pointe. St-Émilion was superb, as good as 1985 and '82.

In 1988 every Sauternes and Barsac château and many in Cadillac, Loupiac and Ste-Croix-du-Mont, had the chance to make the greatest wine for a generation. Many are destined to be classics. Some of the dry whites lack a little oomph, though most of those from good producers are delicious.

1987 (BC) There *are* lean, unbalanced edgy wines from 1987 – often made by the same uninspired proprietors who made mediocre '88s. But the overall style of the vintage is wonderfully soft and drinkable, the soft Merlot fruit combining with good new oak to produce light but positively lush reds. You should start drinking these now: the green unripeness is beginning to surface.

In Sauternes some pleasant, light wines were made, especially by those properties who used the cryoextraction method of freezing the grapes to concentrate what sugar there was. But some estates bottled no wine from this vintage. Dry whites were a safer bet, and the top wines are drinking well.

1986 (AD) These wines incline to the austere in style, but the fruit is rather thick and jammy, with a slight rasp. That said, the wines are good, sometimes very good, and mostly for the ten to 20 year haul, though some will be attractive earlier. I think you should have some in your cellar, but if I had only one fistful of £5 notes and '86 and '88 to choose between, I'd choose '88.

It was another marvellous year in Sauternes, when noble rot swept through the vineyards, and any proprietor who cared to could make great sweet wines. At the moment the best wines seem to be even better than the 1983s and '88s.

1985 (ACD) These are so delicious you can drink them now. The top wines will age as long as any sensible person wants to age them – but like, I'm told, 1953, they'll *always* be good to drink. The *petits châteaux* are still gorgeous, the *bourgeois* probably the best ever at many properties and most of the Classed Growths and Graves/Pessac-Léognans are ravishing.

Sauternes made some quite pleasant lightish wines, but only a handful are outstanding, from estates with the courage to wait for botrytis in a very dry year.

1984 The cheaper wines have deservedly sunk unloved into their fruitless grave. But the best Classed Growths from the Médoc are showing some surprising lean but fragrant Cabernet class.

1983 (ABCD) A true Bordeaux classic, still relatively well-priced. Though tannic now, the wines will flower into a lovely dry cedar and blackcurrant maturity – but it'll take another year or two. AC Margaux made its best wines for a generation.

In Sauternes there were superbly rich, exciting wines to be ranked alongside 1986 and '88, '89 and '90.

1982 (ACD) A fabulous year, with unbelievably ripe, fat, juicy and rich wines. They're going to make great drinking right to their peak in five or so years' time, although some of the lesser wines, while marvellous now, are not likely to last much longer than this. Sauternes was mixed in quality.

1981 (BC) Good but not spectacular. Quite light, but classic flavours from top properties which could still age a bit. A slightly graceless year in Sauternes.

1980 (BC) Nice light, grassy claret, which should have been drunk by now. The best Sauternes are still drinking well.

1979 (ABCD) Many of these wines demand another couple of years at least. You can keep your top wines, but hurry up and drink the lesser ones. There was attractive, mid-weight Sauternes.

1978 (AC) Virtually all the Classed Growths are lovely now, and lesser wines are beginning to dry out. Graves and St-Émilion are delicious and won't improve.

1976 (C) Rather soft and sweet on the whole. Not inspiring, apart from a few exceptions in St-Émilion and Pomerol. Drink it up. The best Sauternes are still fat and rich.

1975 (A) A difficult vintage. The very harsh tannins frequently didn't have fruit ripe enough to mesh with, and the flavour went stale and brown before the wine had time to soften. The best may yet bloom; I'm not sure when. Nice, well-balanced Sauternes.

1970 (ACD) Now re-emerging with the fruit intact to make lovely current drinking – but the very top wines will age a few more years yet, if you can bear to wait.

1966 (AC) All the wines are ready, with most at their peak. Yet some lesser wines which seemed to be dying out have taken on a new lease of life.

1961 (AC) Still wonderful wines. I marvel at how great claret can match richness and perfume with a bone-dry structure of tannin and acidity.

Most other vintages of the 1960s will now be risks; '69 and '67 are basically past it, '64 can still be good, rather big, solid wines, and '62, one of the most gorgeous, fragrant vintages since the war, is just beginning to show the ladders in its stockings. If your godfather's treating you, and offers '59, '55 or '53, accept with enthusiasm. If he offers you '49, '47 or '45, get it in writing before he begins to change his mind.

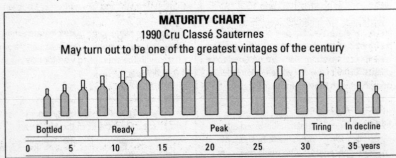

MATURITY CHART
1990 Cru Classé Sauternes
May turn out to be one of the greatest vintages of the century

| Bottled | Ready | Peak | Tiring | In decline |

| 0 | 5 | 10 | 15 | 20 | 25 | 30 | 35 years |

RED BORDEAUX

l'Abbaye *Puisseguin-St-Émilion*
1989 £6.56 (FOR)

d'Agassac *cru grand bourgeois
exceptionnel Haut-Médoc*
1990 £10.65 (NI)
1989 £9.06 (FOR)
1985 £11.50 (GE)

Amiral-de-Beychevelle *St-Julien*
1992 £12.50 (BU)
1990 £14.95 (ROB)
1988 £18.25 (WRI)

Andron-Blanquet *cru grand bourgeois
exceptionnel St-Estèphe*
1990 £10.65 (EL)
1989 £13.50 (PIP)

l'Angélus *grand cru classé St-Émilion*
1993 £26.00 (BER)
1989 £26.14 (BUT)
1988 IB £350.00 (FA)

d'Angludet *cru bourgeois supérieur
exceptionnel Margaux*
1994 EC £92.04 (TAN) £93.00 (LAY)
1993 £11.95 (LAY) £11.98 (QUE) £12.42 (HA)
1991 £10.85 (BER) £12.55 (HAH) £13.41 (EY)
1990 £16.30 (NEZ) £17.30 (BER) £19.00 (PIP)
1990 IB £150.00 (GOE)
1989 £17.99 (NI) £18.40 (TAN) £19.50 (POR)
1985 £29.00 (UB) £29.50 (ROB)
1983 £16.50 (REI) £22.82 (BY) £30.00 (ROB)
1978 £18.74 (BUT) £33.00 (CRO)

des Annereaux *Lalande-de-Pomerol*
1990 £10.95 (ROB)
1989 £10.49 (AME) £10.79 (KA) £16.85 (UB)

Anthonic *cru bourgeois supérieur Moulis*
1994 EC £99.00 (CB)
1992 £9.37 (CB)
1990 £17.50 (CRO)
1989 £10.92 (FOR)
1986 £12.33 (PLA)

Archambeau *Graves*
1991 £9.95 (SAT)

d'Arche *Graves*
1986 £9.00 (GOE)

**d'Armailhac (was Mouton-Baronne-
Philippe)** *5ème cru classé Pauillac*
1992 £13.49 (BOT) £13.49 (WR)
1990 £12.37 (BUT) £27.40 (EY)
1989 £13.27 (BUT) £13.95 (BO) £15.20 (NO)
£15.57 (PLA) £19.50 (POR) £25.50 (ROB)
1986 £15.24 (BUT) £17.55 (WAT)
1985 £25.95 (ROB)
1975 £26.04 (PEN)
1961 £111.63 (WY)

Arnauld *Haut-Médoc*
1990 £10.38 (HA)
1987 £8.25 (GE)

l'Arrosée *grand cru classé St-Émilion*
1994 £18.39 (LAY)
1994 IB £159.00 (RAE)
1994 EC £171.00 (LAY)
1989 IB £220.00 (GOE)
1985 £45.00 (CRO)

Ausone *1er grand cru classé St-Émilion*
1990 £88.32 (BUT)
1990 IB £950.00 (BIB)
1989 IB £800.00 (BIB)
1986 £58.26 (FA)
1985 £64.82 (BUT) £98.50 (ROB)
1983 £78.00 (CRO) £83.35 (UB)
1982 IB £1,450.00 (FA)
1979 £62.00 (CRO) £120.00 (ROB)
1961 £223.25 (FA)
1961 IB £2,650.00 (WY)

Bahans-Haut-Brion *Graves*
1990 ½ bottle £12.99 (OD) £13.50 (ROB)
1990 ½ bottle IB £190.00 (FA)
1989 £16.54 (BUT) £24.99 (OD) £29.96 (LEA)
1989 IB £260.00 (FA)
1985 £21.95 (BO)

de Barbe *Côtes de Bourg*
1993 £5.99 (DAV)

Baret *Pessac-Léognan*
1993 £8.44 (EL) £9.99 (HIG)
1991 £8.25 (BER)
1990 £8.80 (BER) £12.49 (DAV)
1989 £8.95 (BER)

Barreyres *cru bourgeois Haut-Médoc*
1959 £35.00 (REI)

Batailley *5ème cru classé Pauillac*
1994 IB £112.50 (ELL)
1993 £12.75 (BER) £14.00 (HIG)
1992 £13.75 (DI)
1991 £11.95 (DI)
1990 magnum £35.25 (HIG)
1989 £14.10 (BUT) £14.75 (DI) £16.50 (BER)
   £16.99 (AUR) £19.95 (DAV) £26.99 (MAJ)
1989 IB £150.00 (BIB)
1989 magnum £28.98 (BUT) £35.25 (HIG)
1989 double magnum £78.33 (HIG)
1988 £16.99 (AUR) £18.75 (DAV)
1988 magnum £35.25 (HIG)
1988 double magnum £78.33 (HIG)
1985 £18.99 (YOU) £19.25 (REI) £28.50
   (ROB)
1985 IB £180.00 (GOE)
1983 IB £130.00 (FA)
1982 £25.95 (ELL) £48.75 (UB)
1978 magnum £45.00 (BU)
1970 £23.00 (WY) £38.00 (CRO) £56.35 (UB)
1961 £38.50 (REI) £70.50 (WY) £95.00 (RES)

Beau-Rivage *Bordeaux*
1994 £4.95 (DI)

Beau-Séjour-Bécot *grand cru classé St-
   Émilion*
1994 £19.27 (LAY)
1994 EC £154.00 (MV) £164.04 (TAN)
1990 £19.81 (BY)

Beau-Site *cru grand bourgeois
   exceptionnel St-Estèphe*
1993 £10.55 (HAH)
1991 £8.95 (BU)
1990 £8.81 (HIG) £11.09 (SUM)
1989 £8.43 (BUT) £15.75 (BY)
1971 £13.75 (BU) £29.38 (WY)

Beau-Site-Haut-Vignoble *cru bourgeois
   St-Estèphe*
1989 £12.35 (UB)

Beaumont *cru grand bourgeois Haut-Médoc*
1994 £9.01 (FOR)
1993 £8.53 (EL) £9.01 (FOR) £9.45 (DAV)
1990 £8.40 (WS) £10.50 (WRI) £14.95 (BU)
1989 £12.35 (WRI) £12.95 (ROB) £14.10 (AV)
1989 IB £140.00 (GOE)

Beauséjour-Duffau-Lagarrosse *1er
   grand cru classé St-Émilion*
1992 £6.75 (WHI)
1985 £20.30 (NO)

Bédats-Bois-Montet *1ères Côtes de
   Bordeaux*
1990 £5.75 (GAL)
1988 £5.25 (GAL)

Bel-Air *Puisseguin-St-Émilion*
1993 £7.99 (SAT)

Bel-Orme-Tronquoy-de-Lalande *cru
   grand bourgeois Haut-Médoc*
1988 £9.75 (DAV)
1978 £29.00 (CRO)

Belair *1ères Côtes de Blaye*
1986 £19.50 (BU)
1982 £29.50 (BU)

Belair *1er grand cru classé St-Émilion*
1994 £18.33 (ARM) £20.16 (LAY)
1994 EC £189.00 (LAY)
1985 £16.64 (BUT) £18.25 (REI)
1985 IB £210.00 (GOE)
1983 £18.50 (REI)

de Belcier *Côtes de Castillon*
1992 £7.99 (AME)
1990 £6.99 (POR)
1989 £7.25 (DAV)

Belgrave *5ème cru classé Haut-Médoc*
1989 £12.25 (NI)
1970 £34.49 (TW)

Bertin *Montagne-St-Émilion*
1989 £8.95 (SAT)
1988 £6.72 (BUT)

Bertineau-St-Vincent *Lalande-de-Pomerol*
1992 £9.85 (UB)

Beychevelle *4ème cru classé St-Julien*
1991 £16.95 (WRI) £18.95 (SAI) £19.60 (BY)
1990 £25.78 (BY)
1990 IB £220.00 (BIB) £225.00 (SEC)
1989 £21.74 (BUT) £23.65 (FOR) £25.99
   (OD) £26.00 (UN) £26.69 (BOT)
1989 IB £250.00 (BIB) £250.00 (FA)
1989 ½ bottle IB £295.00 (WY)
1988 £28.00 (WS)

> *All châteaux are listed
> alphabetically
> regardless of class.*

1988 IB £195.00 (BIB) £260.00 (WY)
1986 £35.90 (PIP) £37.50 (ROB)
1985 £26.20 (GAL) £32.50 (RES) £40.75
(UB)
1985 ½ bottle £22.50 (ROB)
1985 magnum £70.00 (ROB)
1983 £22.99 (OD) £28.95 (POR)
1983 IB £205.00 (FA) £240.00 (GOE)
1983 magnum £95.00 (VIG)
1982 £35.25 (LEA) £40.00 (WY) £45.04
(FA) £65.00 (ROB)

1982 IB £460.00 (GOE)
1981 £18.00 (WY) £22.50 (GAL)
1981 IB £215.00 (WY)
1980 ½ bottle £7.75 (BU)
1979 £24.50 (REI) £30.50 (ROB)
1978 magnum £60.00 (WY)
1975 £30.00 (ROB)
1970 £35.00 (REI) £54.50 (ROB) £56.80 (AD)
1966 £40.00 (YOU) £62.50 (ROB)
1966 ½ bottle £32.90 (WY)
1961 £100.00 (WY) £115.00 (BU)
1928 IB £2,900.00 (FA)
1924 £75.00 (REI)

le Bon-Pasteur *Pomerol*
1994 £18.98 (LAY)
1994 EC £159.96 (TAN) £177.00 (LAY)
1993 £17.75 (BER)
1986 £24.48 (ELL)
1985 £22.05 (BUT) £39.95 (UB)

Bonnet *Bordeaux Supérieur*
1994 £6.29 (EL)
1993 £6.85 (NI) £6.99 (WR) £6.99 (THR)
1992 £6.08 (FOR)

Bourgneuf-Vayron *Pomerol*
1989 £14.60 (BUT) £21.91 (BY) £23.50 (LAY)
1988 £20.95 (LAY)

de Bourgueneuf *Pomerol*
1990 £18.05 (NEZ)
1987 £13.58 (ARM)

Bouscaut *cru classé Pessac-Léognan*
1990 £11.49 (PE)
1989 £12.95 (RAE) £15.00 (UN)
1988 £13.50 (PLA)
1985 £10.79 (YOU)
1982 IB £150.00 (FA)

Boyd-Cantenac *3ème cru classé Margaux*
1985 £23.75 (ROB)
1983 IB £170.00 (BIB)
1982 £31.65 (ROB)

Branaire-Ducru *4ème cru classé St-Julien*
1994 EC £118.00 (MV) £155.00 (CB)
1990 £18.50 (HOG) £22.00 (WS)
1989 £16.74 (BUT) £19.95 (ROB) £21.17
(FOR) £21.74 (HOG) £24.68 (LEA)
1989 IB £200.00 (BIB)
1986 £18.50 (GAL) £18.80 (TAN) £19.99
(FUL)
1986 IB £155.00 (FA)
1985 £23.50 (ROB) £24.68 (LEA) £25.50 (RES)
1983 £15.85 (REI) £23.50 (ROB)
1982 £27.91 (ELL) £28.00 (WY)
1982 IB £320.00 (FA)
1981 £27.50 (VIG)
1979 £27.50 (RES)
1979 double magnum £99.87 (TW)
1978 £20.00 (WY) £20.07 (ELL) £21.40 (BEN)
1978 IB £210.00 (FA)
1970 £24.00 (WY) £39.00 (CRO)
1967 £14.75 (BU)
1959 IB £700.00 (FA)
1928 £160.00 (CRO)

Brane-Cantenac *2ème cru classé Margaux*
1994 IB £153.00 (RAE)
1990 £23.03 (FOR)
1989 £19.85 (RAE) £25.00 (UN)
1989 IB £190.00 (GOE)
1988 £16.99 (RAE) £21.50 (NI)
1986 IB £220.00 (BIB)
1985 magnum IB £240.00 (FA)
1983 IB £200.00 (BIB) £220.00 (GOE)
1982 £29.95 (DAV) £29.99 (OD) £33.00
(WS) £35.95 (ROB) £45.50 (DI)
1982 IB £270.00 (FA) £295.00 (WY)
1982 magnum IB £290.00 (WY)
1978 £17.00 (WY) £19.50 (REI) £31.00 (ROB)
1978 IB £210.00 (FA) £220.00 (BIB)
1978 magnum IB £210.00 (FA)
1975 magnum IB £260.00 (FA)
1970 £23.00 (WY) £24.50 (REI)
1970 IB £240.00 (WY)
1970 magnum £57.50 (BU) £75.00 (ROB)

1966 £41.13 (WY)
1955 £58.50 (REI)
1928 £210.00 (CRO)
1928 IB £2,600.00 (FA)

du Breuil *cru bourgeois supérieur Haut-Médoc*
1990 £11.95 (DI)

Brulesecaille *Côtes de Bourg*
1991 £6.39 (WR)

Cabannieux *Graves*
1993 £9.46 (CB)
1990 £8.99 (NEW)
1989 £7.43 (FOR)

Calon-Ségur *3ème cru classé St-Estèphe*
1991 £18.93 (BY)
1990 £26.50 (NA) £28.00 (BER)
1989 £19.39 (ELL) £19.92 (LEA) £23.00 (UN) £23.95 (ROB) £24.85 (CB)
1989 IB £175.00 (BIB)
1988 £15.86 (BUT) £18.95 (NI) £23.50 (BER)
1988 IB £190.00 (FA)
1986 £19.00 (GAL) £19.09 (FA) £23.50 (LEA) £27.50 (ROB) £34.00 (CRO)
1986 IB £185.00 (BIB)
1985 £21.66 (BY) £23.50 (ROB) £24.50 (RES)
1984 £12.50 (ROB) £13.99 (BO)
1982 £37.66 (NO) £41.50 (ROB)
1973 £14.95 (BU)
1970 £25.00 (WY) £35.00 (BU)
1955 £75.00 (REI)
1947 £210.00 (CRO)
1947 IB £2,700.00 (FA)

de Camensac *5ème cru classé Haut-Médoc*
1991 £9.95 (DI)
1990 £9.85 (BER)
1988 IB £120.00 (GOE)
1986 £12.50 (GAL)
1983 £13.15 (PLA) £14.50 (BU)
1982 £18.50 (REI) £25.00 (RES)
1970 £19.50 (REI) £22.50 (BU) £29.50 (WRI)

Canon *1er grand cru classé St-Émilion*
1993 IB £150.00 (GOE)
1992 £19.15 (BY)
1990 £24.19 (BUT)
1990 IB £295.00 (SEC)
1989 £27.61 (BUT) £29.00 (RAE) £35.72 (AV)
1989 IB £275.00 (GOE)
1988 £12.46 (BUT) £24.50 (RAE)
1988 IB £260.00 (BIB)

1986 £22.72 (BUT) £24.95 (RAE)
1986 IB £280.00 (FA)
1985 £29.47 (BUT) £38.00 (RES) £39.00 (PIP)
1985 IB £300.00 (BIB)

Canon de Brem *Canon-Fronsac*
1994 EC £69.00 (MV)
1992 £9.83 (ARM)
1990 £10.95 (POR)
1988 £8.58 (ARM) £8.80 (MV)
1983 £11.95 (WS)

Canon-la-Gaffelière *grand cru classé St-Émilion*
1989 £14.77 (BUT) £15.49 (BO)
1985 £25.50 (RES)

Cantemerle *5ème cru classé Haut-Médoc*
1990 £17.90 (HOG) £17.99 (MAJ) £19.95 (BEN)
1989 £13.90 (BUT) £15.36 (FOR) £15.49 (BO) £16.89 (HOG) £19.99 (PE)
1989 IB £200.00 (FA)
1988 £15.57 (ELL) £17.00 (GE) £17.50 (REI)
1986 £19.99 (PE)
1985 £19.99 (PE) £22.91 (LEA) £27.50 (ROB)
1985 IB £160.00 (FA) £185.00 (BIB)
1982 £28.75 (PE) £38.50 (ROB)
1978 £7.50 (REI) £16.00 (WY) £20.00 (BU)
1978 IB £175.00 (WY)
1975 £17.75 (NA)
1970 £18.50 (REI) £42.50 (UB)

Cantenac-Brown *3ème cru classé Margaux*
1991 £18.70 (BY)
1990 IB £200.00 (GOE)
1989 £26.50 (ROB)
1988 £18.99 (FUL)
1970 £22.33 (BUT)
1966 £27.50 (BU) £28.50 (REI)
1959 £85.00 (VIG)
1950 £48.50 (REI)

Cap-de-Mourlin *grand cru classé St-Émilion*
1992 £11.95 (BY)

Carbonnieux *cru classé Pessac-Léognan*
1993 £14.95 (DI)
1988 £13.50 (BU) £18.50 (DI)
1988 IB £110.00 (GOE)
1985 £19.00 (CRO)
1975 £16.00 (CRO)
1959 IB £70.00 (WY)
1929 £85.00 (RES)

de Cardaillan *Graves*
1990 £8.99 (DAV)
1989 £11.20 (HIC)
1988 £8.49 (DAV)
1970 £18.50 (BU)

Cardeneau *Fronsac*
1990 £9.49 (LAY)

la Cardonne *cru grand bourgeois Médoc*
1992 £8.25 (FOR)
1991 £7.99 (HOG) £10.19 (AV)
1989 £14.32 (AV)
1988 £12.90 (PIP)

les Carmes-Haut-Brion *Pessac-Léognan*
1989 £16.50 (BUT)

Caronne-Ste-Gemme *cru grand bourgeois exceptionnel Haut-Médoc*
1990 £7.97 (NO) £9.48 (EL) £9.50 (WS)
1989 ½ bottle £4.25 (REI)
1988 £9.44 (HOG) £9.44 (EL)
1986 £9.95 (AME) £10.79 (HA) £12.79 (AUR)
1986 ½ bottle £6.95 (ROB)
1985 £18.50 (CRO)

Carruades de Lafite (Moulin des Carruades until 1987) *Pauillac*
1992 £14.06 (BY)
1989 £16.55 (BUT) £20.92 (PLA)
1980 £18.56 (TW)
1967 £25.00 (BU)
1955 £95.00 (REI)
1934 IB £80.00 (WY)

Carteau-Côtes-Daugay *grand cru St-Émilion*
1990 £10.00 (WS)
1989 £9.99 (NEW)

Castéra *cru bourgeois Médoc*
1994 £4.35 (SAF)

Cazebonne *Graves*
1992 £7.83 (LAY)

Certan-de-May *Pomerol*
1992 £26.67 (ARM) £31.50 (REI)
1991 £16.00 (MV)
1989 £30.06 (BUT)
1988 £37.90 (GAU) £40.80 (BUT)
1986 £65.00 (RES)
1986 IB £360.00 (GOE)
1985 £36.66 (GOE) £37.95 (BUT)

1985 IB £360.00 (GOE)
1983 £32.50 (REI)
1983 IB £350.00 (FA)
1982 IB £1,500.00 (FA)

Certan-Giraud *Pomerol*
1989 £18.48 (BUT)
1988 £21.99 (NA)
1985 £19.00 (REI)

Charron *1ères Côtes de Blaye*
1993 £7.39 (PLA)

Chasse-Spleen *cru grand bourgeois exceptionnel Moulis*
1993 £13.90 (TAN) £15.95 (BER)
1990 £15.96 (ELL) £17.95 (SAI)
1989 £17.82 (BUT) £24.80 (NO)
1989 IB £190.00 (FA) £210.00 (WY)
1988 £14.74 (CHA) £17.50 (REI) £21.95 (LAY)
1986 £11.61 (BUT) £19.78 (EY) £25.00 (ROB) £25.44 (NO) £31.00 (CRO)
1986 magnum £49.74 (NO)
1982 £17.63 (BUT) £23.50 (EY) £25.50 (WRI) £37.50 (ROB)
1978 £32.00 (ROB) £36.00 (CRO)
1966 magnum £60.00 (REI)

le Châtelet *grand cru classé St-Émilion*
1990 £13.99 (MAJ)

Chauvin *grand cru classé St-Émilion*
1990 IB £140.00 (GOE)
1986 £10.74 (BUT)

Cheret-Pitres *Graves*
1994 £7.39 (CHA)
1993 £7.39 (CHA)

Cheval-Blanc *1er grand cru classé St-Émilion*
1993 £44.74 (LAY) £45.00 (BER)
1992 £37.50 (ARM)
1989 £52.39 (BUT) £75.00 (ROB) £94.75 (BEN)
1989 IB £820.00 (BIB) £850.00 (WY)
1989 magnum £104.77 (BUT)
1988 £82.50 (ROB)
1985 £85.23 (NO) £97.10 (UB)
1985 IB £890.00 (GOE) £1,160.00 (FA)
1984 £38.50 (BER) £53.00 (UN)
1983 £117.50 (FA)
1983 IB £1,200.00 (FA) £1,260.00 (WY)
1983 ½ bottle IB £1,250.00 (FA)
1982 IB £3,000.00 (FA) £3,200.00 (BIB)

1982 magnum IB £3,200.00 (FA)
1981 IB £720.00 (FA)
1981 ½ bottle £49.50 (ROB)
1980 £65.00 (VIG)
1978 £65.00 (REI) £98.00 (BER)
1978 IB £900.00 (FA)
1970 £129.25 (FA) £157.00 (ROB)
1970 IB £1,350.00 (BIB)
1967 £75.00 (RES)
1966 £145.00 (REI) £199.75 (WY)
1962 £65.00 (REI)
1959 £245.00 (REI)
1953 £165.00 (WY)
1953 magnum £520.00 (WY)
1952 £180.00 (CRO)
1950 £75.00 (REI)
1950 ½ bottle £45.00 (WY)
1949 ½ bottle £125.00 (WY)
1947 magnum £4,230.00 (FA)
1943 £75.00 (WY)

Chicane *Graves*
1994 EC £49.92 (TAN)
1991 £9.95 (VIG)

Cissac *cru grand bourgeois exceptionnel
Haut-Médoc*
1994 EC £81.96 (TAN)
1990 £9.45 (HAH) £11.49 (HA) £12.01 (EY)
    £12.16 (SUM) £12.23 (ELL) £12.33 (PLA)
1989 £11.67 (FOR) £11.75 (AV) £12.15
    (EL) £12.16 (SUM) £13.50 (WRI)
1988 £11.20 (GAL) £12.08 (EL) £12.16 (SUM)
    £12.90 (TAN) £13.34 (HA) £13.75 (AV)
1987 £9.25 (CO) £9.30 (ELL) £9.95 (POR)
1987 magnum £20.27 (ELL)
1986 £10.75 (BUT) £11.50 (WS) £14.10
    (TAN) £15.50 (WRI) £17.95 (ROB)
1985 £13.25 (WRI) £14.10 (EL) £18.95 (ROB)
1983 £10.85 (CO) £13.50 (REI)
1982 £28.00 (ROB)
1981 £14.50 (REI)
1978 £24.50 (ROB) £29.00 (CRO)
1976 magnum £29.50 (BU)
1970 £20.25 (BUT)
1970 magnum £48.07 (EL) £65.00 (ROB)
1961 £32.31 (EL)

Citran *cru grand bourgeois exceptionnel
Haut-Médoc*
1990 £16.43 (PEN)
1988 £13.50 (WS)

la Clare *cru bourgeois Médoc*
1989 £6.44 (FOR) £6.82 (HOG)

Clarke *cru bourgeois Listrac*
1992 £12.50 (ROB)
1988 £11.63 (PEN)

la Claverie *Côtes de Francs*
1990 £9.10 (PIP)

Clerc-Milon *5ème cru classé Pauillac*
1994 £15.16 (LAY)
1994 EC £138.00 (LAY)
1992 £13.99 (WR) £13.99 (BOT)
1990 £21.99 (YOU)
1989 £15.75 (BUT) £21.50 (ROB)

Clinet *Pomerol*
1994 IB £490.00 (WY) £500.00 (GOE)
    £520.00 (FA)
1990 £40.00 (WY)
1989 IB £1,400.00 (FA)
1985 £39.50 (RES)

Clos Beauregard *Pomerol*
1992 £8.99 (BOT) £8.99 (WR) £8.99 (THR)
1982 £16.70 (BUT)
1970 £22.50 (BU)

Clos de l'Eglise *Lalande-de-Pomerol*
1991 £14.50 (BY)
1987 £13.99 (MAR)

Clos des Jacobins *grand cru classé St-
Émilion*
1989 £19.49 (BO) £20.24 (BUT)
1988 £22.91 (LEA) £29.99 (PE)
1985 £20.75 (PE) £21.50 (RES)

Clos du Clocher *Pomerol*
1994 £14.87 (LAY)
1994 EC £135.00 (LAY)
1986 £22.25 (ROB)

Clos du Marquis *St-Julien*
1994 £15.16 (LAY)
1994 EC £138.00 (LAY)
1992 IB £85.00 (SEC)
1991 £15.99 (WR) £15.99 (BOT)
1990 £11.71 (BUT) £22.95 (DAV)
1988 £11.20 (BUT) £16.50 (GAL)
1985 £19.25 (REI)

Clos Fourtet *1er grand cru classé St-
Émilion*
1994 IB £182.50 (ELL)
1993 £17.14 (LAY) £18.15 (BER)
1989 £22.67 (FOR) £27.10 (BER)

1988 £24.80 (PIP)
1985 £16.75 (REI) £30.55 (UB)
1982 £37.50 (RES)
1970 £22.50 (BU)
1945 £185.00 (WY)

Clos René Pomerol
1978 £36.00 (CRO)
1975 £15.75 (REI)

la Clotte grand cru classé St-Émilion
1989 £19.90 (BUT)
1982 £27.50 (RES)

la Commanderie cru bourgeois St-Estèphe
1990 £9.92 (ARM) £9.95 (BU)

Connétable Talbot St-Julien
1993 £12.24 (LAY)
1992 £10.52 (BY)
1987 £10.99 (PE)

la Conseillante Pomerol
1994 IB £290.00 (GOE)
1993 IB £275.00 (RES)
1990 IB £800.00 (BIB)
1989 £48.18 (BUT)
1989 IB £720.00 (FA)
1988 £45.17 (AV)
1986 £30.61 (GOE) £31.86 (AV) £39.50 (RES)
1985 £60.00 (CRO)
1967 £26.75 (REI)
1953 £175.00 (CRO)

Corbin grand cru classé St-Émilion
1989 £11.16 (BUT)

Cos d'Estournel 2ème cru classé St-Estèphe
1994 IB £192.50 (ELL)
1993 £22.38 (BER)
1993 IB £190.00 (GOE)
1992 £21.54 (LAY) £25.57 (BY)
1991 IB £150.00 (GOE)
1990 £29.99 (PE) £30.00 (WY) £43.00
　(BER) £50.50 (TAN)
1990 IB £370.00 (FA) £400.00 (WY)
1989 £26.73 (BUT) £29.48 (FOR) £29.50
　(UN) £36.25 (CB)
1989 IB £310.00 (BIB) £340.00 (FA)
1989 magnum £55.95 (BUT)
1989 double magnum IB £300.00 (FA)
1988 magnum £54.44 (BUT)
1986 £26.44 (BUT) £31.90 (GAU)
1986 IB £440.00 (BIB)
1986 jeroboam IB £260.00 (FA)

1985 £47.00 (REI) £54.05 (WY)
1985 IB £500.00 (WY)
1984 £19.50 (UN)
1983 £25.00 (SOM) £25.75 (REI) £32.90 (LEA)
1983 IB £350.00 (GOE)
1983 magnum £50.82 (ELL) £75.00 (ROB)
1982 £85.19 (LEA) £94.00 (WY)
1982 IB £850.00 (GOE) £850.00 (FA)
1981 £29.38 (LEA)
1981 IB £260.00 (FA)
1979 £32.80 (ELL)
1978 £66.00 (BER)
1978 imperial £295.00 (REI)
1975 £29.50 (BU)
1975 magnum £65.00 (REI)
1971 £27.50 (REI) £36.99 (YOU)
1970 £45.00 (WY) £47.00 (FA) £48.00 (CRO)
　£52.88 (BUT)
1962 £69.00 (YOU)
1959 £98.00 (CRO) £140.00 (WY)
1943 £95.00 (REI)

Cos Labory 5ème cru classé St-Estèphe
1990 £17.53 (ELL) £21.99 (YOU)
1989 £13.99 (PE) £16.50 (GAL)
1988 £11.99 (PE) £14.95 (BU) £19.25 (PIP)
1970 £16.50 (REI)

Coufran cru grand bourgeois Haut-Médoc
1990 £10.30 (NEZ)
1988 £9.75 (WS) £12.99 (WW)
1988 ½ bottle £7.78 (HAL)
1983 ½ bottle £8.50 (CRO)
1973 £7.50 (REI)
1937 £70.00 (ROB)

la Couspaude grand cru St-Émilion
1992 £14.21 (NEZ)

Couvent-des-Jacobins grand cru classé
　St-Émilion
1993 £16.75 (BER)
1988 £19.20 (PIP)

le Crock cru grand bourgeois exceptionnel
　St-Estèphe
1994 IB £99.00 (RAE)
1993 £10.80 (PLA)
1991 £9.50 (BER)
1990 IB £140.00 (GOE)

la Croix-de-Gay Pomerol
1990 £15.65 (BUT)
1989 £16.64 (BUT)
1985 £21.50 (ROB)

la Croix-de-Pez *St-Estèphe*
1990 £10.89 (HA)

la Croix-des-Moines *Lalande-de-Pomerol*
1990 £9.95 (REI) £10.99 (BO) £11.30 (RAE)
£15.40 (UB)

la Croix-du-Casse *Pomerol*
1994 £16.92 (LAY)
1994 IB £130.00 (FA) £175.00 (RES)
1994 EC £156.00 (LAY)
1990 £17.25 (NEZ)

Croizet-Bages *5ème cru classé Pauillac*
1988 £14.75 (BU)
1982 £33.06 (BY)
1970 £17.05 (BUT)
1961 £75.00 (ROB)

de Cruzeau *Pessac-Léognan*
1988 £7.17 (FOR)

la Dame de Montrose *St-Estèphe*
1990 £23.95 (POR)
1989 £11.26 (BUT) £16.99 (PIP)
1985 £19.67 (BUT)

de la Dauphine *Fronsac*
1989 £8.71 (BUT)

Dauzac *5ème cru classé Margaux*
1988 £15.50 (WRI)

Desmirail *3ème cru classé Margaux*
1990 £16.99 (HIG)
1989 £13.95 (RAE) £16.99 (HIG)

Domaine Cheval-Blanc *1ères Côtes de Bordeaux*
1994 £5.99 (NA)
1993 £5.99 (NA)

Domaine de Chevalier *cru classé Pessac-Léognan*
1993 IB £162.00 (RAE)
1991 £16.95 (RAE) £29.80 (UB)
1990 £25.99 (OD)
1990 ½ bottle £17.67 (HAL)
1989 £24.85 (REI) £26.99 (OD) £29.00 (RAE) £30.99 (BUT) £36.60 (CB)
1989 IB £240.00 (FA) £300.00 (GOE)
1988 £24.99 (OD)
1985 £25.50 (REI) £32.99 (OD) £35.50 (NA) £37.50 (BER)
1985 IB £290.00 (FA)
1982 £28.91 (NO) £31.33 (FA) £32.50 (BU) £32.84 (BUT) £45.00 (AD) £63.45 (TW)
1982 IB £320.00 (FA)£400.00 (GOE)
1981 £23.50 (REI) £26.95 (RAE)
1980 IB £120.00 (BIB)
1979 IB £260.00 (FA)
1978 £33.90 (BUT) £38.19 (LEA) £58.75 (TW)
1975 £24.50 (REI) £35.00 (BU) £45.00 (RES)
1970 £60.00 (REI)
1970 IB £650.00 (FA)
1966 £66.00 (CRO)

Domaine de Curebourse *Margaux*
1989 £15.28 (NO)
1979 £9.95 (RAE)

Domaine de Dupeyrat *1ères Côtes de Blaye*
1993 £6.95 (SAT)

Domaine de l'Eglise *Pomerol*
1991 £13.25 (BER)
1990 £15.66 (HIG)
1989 £16.71 (BUT)
1989 magnum £33.45 (BUT)
1986 £18.75 (DAV)
1982 £27.50 (RES)

Domaine la Grave *Graves*
1989 £90.00 (GOE)

la Dominique *grand cru classé St-Émilion*
1994 £20.74 (LAY)
1994 EC £195.00 (LAY)
1989 £17.77 (BUT)
1985 £16.85 (BUT) £33.00 (ROB)
1982 IB £340.00 (FA)

Ducluzeau *cru bourgeois Listrac*
1990 £10.30 (NI)
1989 £11.75 (LAY)
1988 £11.67 (ARM)

Ducru-Beaucaillou *2ème cru classé St-Julien*
1994 IB £180.00 (RAE)
1992 £19.19 (LAY) £20.93 (BY)
1989 £25.65 (BUT) £34.49 (PE)

1988 £23.50 (BUT) £25.50 (RAE) £33.50 (LAY) £34.00 (BER)
1988 double magnum IB £220.00 (FA)
1988 imperial IB £175.00 (FA)
1987 £19.95 (VIG)
1986 IB £310.00 (WY) £320.00 (BIB)
1985 £30.06 (BUT) £35.00 (RES) £38.50 (BEN) £41.61 (ELL) £42.00 (BER) £65.70 (UB)
1985 IB £340.00 (FA) £350.00 (GOE)
1985 magnum £48.24 (BUT)
1984 £18.99 (PE) £27.00 (UN)
1983 £27.61 (BUT) £29.75 (NI) £32.99 (OD) £39.00 (PIP) £39.75 (ROB)
1983 IB £285.00 (GOE) £300.00 (FA)
1983 magnum £65.00 (RES)
1983 imperial IB £200.00 (FA)
1982 £59.00 (BEN) £60.00 (RES) £62.09 (NO) £62.99 (OD) £68.15 (WY) £69.50 (LAY)
1982 double magnum £230.00 (WY)
1982 imperial IB £520.00 (FA)
1981 £29.38 (LEA) £31.50 (REI) £33.50 (DAV)
1981 magnum £63.00 (REI)
1970 £73.50 (BEN) £79.00 (CRO)
1966 £95.00 (RES)
1966 ½ bottle £46.00 (CRO)
1961 £125.00 (REI) £193.88 (LEA) £210.00 (CRO) £223.25 (FA)
1924 £95.00 (WY)

Duhart-Milon-Rothschild *4ème cru classé Pauillac*
1990 £28.95 (BEN)
1989 £16.16 (BUT) £17.57 (LEA) £20.50 (LAY) £25.07 (FOR)
1986 £14.10 (BUT) £21.02 (PEN)
1985 £29.00 (PIP)
1985 IB £240.00 (GOE)
1981 £13.50 (REI)
1970 £21.50 (REI)

Durand-Laplagne *Puisseguin-St-Émilion*
1993 £10.25 (NI)

Durfort-Vivens *2ème cru classé Margaux*
1989 £20.15 (FOR)
1978 £22.99 (YOU)
1970 £25.99 (RAE)

Dutruch-Grand-Poujeaux *cru grand bourgeois exceptionnel Moulis*
1993 £12.91 (CB)
1962 £16.50 (REI)

l'Église-Clinet *Pomerol*
1993 £22.60 (MER)
1990 £48.96 (FA)
1989 £23.39 (BUT) £45.04 (FA)
1988 IB £420.00 (FA)
1985 £80.00 (RES)

l'Enclos *Pomerol*
1994 EC £105.96 (TAN)
1992 £15.20 (PIP)
1990 £18.95 (ROB)
1985 £17.75 (BUT) £32.50 (RES)

l'Éperon *Bordeaux*
1991 £5.90 (CB)
1990 £6.45 (BER)

l'Ermitage de Chasse-Spleen *Haut-Médoc*
1993 £8.52 (FOR)
1990 £12.81 (NO)

l'Escadre *1ères Côtes de Blaye*
1993 £6.95 (ROB)
1991 £6.95 (ROB)

l'Etoile *Graves*
1994 EC £35.40 (TAN)
1993 £6.35 (AD) £7.23 (CB)
1988 £7.95 (BU)

l'Évangile *Pomerol*
1994 IB £450.00 (GOE) £450.00 (FA)
1993 IB £375.00 (RES)
1992 £22.81 (BY)
1990 £66.08 (AV)
1986 £50.00 (RES)
1985 £46.04 (BUT)
1983 £41.13 (LEA) £41.75 (TAN)
1983 IB £390.00 (FA)
1982 £115.00 (RES)
1975 IB £1,700.00 (FA)

Feytit-Clinet *Pomerol*
1989 £17.45 (AD)
1986 £14.20 (AD)
1959 £40.00 (ROB)

Les Fiefs-de-Lagrange *St-Julien*
1994 £8.70 (LAY)
1994 EC £72.00 (LAY)
1993 £11.23 (FOR) £13.50 (BU)
1992 £10.99 (MAR)
1990 £13.98 (HOG) £14.95 (BU)
1989 £13.98 (HOG) £15.11 (NEZ)
1985 £16.85 (BUT)

de Fieuzal *cru classé Pessac-Léognan*
1994 EC £146.04 (TAN)
1993 £13.20 (TAN)
1991 £14.24 (AV)
1990 £18.51 (ELL)
1990 IB £180.00 (GOE) £190.00 (WY)
1989 £16.84 (BUT) £18.75 (PE) £19.50
1989 IB £180.00 (GOE)
1988 £13.99 (PE) £16.65 (ELL) £17.50 (REI)
1986 £13.75 (PE) £16.16 (ELL)
1985 £14.69 (BUT) £16.16 (ELL) £22.25 (AD)
1983 £16.16 (ELL)
1975 £14.85 (REI)

Figeac *1er grand cru classé St-Émilion*
1989 £25.85 (BUT) £31.39 (FOR)
1989 IB £290.00 (BIB)
1988 £33.50 (DI)
1988 IB £255.00 (BIB)
1985 £20.07 (BUT)
1985 IB £370.00 (FA)
1983 £35.98 (ELL)
1983 IB £380.00 (FA)
1982 £81.50 (ROB)
1982 IB £780.00 (GOE) £880.00 (FA)
1978 £60.00 (ROB) £72.00 (BER)
1970 £90.00 (ROB)
1959 £152.75 (FA)
1905 £85.00 (REI)

la Fleur-Milon *cru grand bourgeois Pauillac*
1990 £13.55 (NI)

la Fleur-Pétrus *Pomerol*
1993 £32.72 (CB)
1992 £21.95 (CB)
1989 £41.65 (BUT)
1988 £32.98 (BUT)
1986 £34.08 (LEA)
1985 £32.80 (BUT)
1983 £88.00 (WY)

1982 IB £950.00 (FA)
1970 £85.00 (REI) £105.00 (ROB)
1966 £82.25 (FA)
1947 £225.00 (ROB)

Fombrauge *grand cru St-Émilion*
1993 £13.50 (BER)
1989 £12.40 (BEN) £12.45 (BER)
1988 £21.95 (UB)
1985 £13.23 (BUT)
1983 IB £90.00 (FA)
1966 £14.50 (REI) £21.50 (YOU)

Fonbadet *cru bourgeois supérieur Pauillac*
1991 £12.00 (BER)
1983 £12.50 (HOG)

Fonpiqueyre *cru bourgeois Haut-Médoc*
1978 £19.50 (CRO)

Fonplégade *grand cru classé St-Émilion*
1988 £19.75 (SAT)
1987 £17.60 (VIN)

Fonréaud *cru bourgeois Listrac*
1993 £8.48 (HA)

Fonroque *grand cru classé St-Émilion*
1990 £18.99 (YOU)
1989 £14.58 (ARM) £17.99 (AV)
1986 £14.99 (WW)
1982 £17.21 (BUT)

les Forts-de-Latour *Pauillac*
1992 £21.05 (LAY)
1991 £14.96 (HA) £17.85 (RAE) £19.20
 (PIP) £22.75 (ROB) £24.46 (BY)
1990 £19.78 (BUT)
1989 £21.54 (FOR) £30.80 (NI)
1988 £21.54 (FOR) £23.60 (HOG) £26.90
 (BY) £27.99 (WR) £27.99 (BOT)
1988 IB £320.00 (WY)
1987 £16.95 (SAI) £21.95 (NEZ) £22.81 (BY)
1986 £35.35 (HAH)
1983 £23.50 (PEN)
1979 £29.00 (CRO) £33.95 (ROB) £45.45
 (UB)

Fourcas-Dupré *cru grand bourgeois
 exceptionnel Listrac*
1990 £8.28 (FOR) £11.95 (BEN)
1989 £13.40 (PIP)
1988 £11.70 (DI) £11.95 (BEN)
1986 £11.50 (GE)
1983 £18.00 (CRO)

Fourcas-Hosten *cru grand bourgeois
exceptionnel Listrac*
1993 £9.50 (HIG)
1990 £9.60 (DI) £11.00 (HIG) £11.95 (WRI)
1989 £11.00 (BER) £11.50 (TAN) £12.85
  (AV) £14.95 (ROB)
1986 £13.51 (LAY)
1985 £11.95 (DI) £16.50 (RES)

Franc-Mayne *grand cru classé St-Émilion*
1990 £18.99 (MAJ)

de Francs *Côtes de Francs*
1993 £7.49 (THR) £7.49 (WR) £7.49 (BOT)
1990 £12.95 (ROB)

la Gaffelière *1er grand cru classé St-Émilion*
1994 IB £155.00 (GOE) £156.00 (RAE)
1976 £17.50 (REI)
1970 £40.00 (RES)

la Garde *Pessac-Léognan*
1989 £8.40 (NEZ)
1982 £12.50 (BU)

le Gardera *1ères Côtes de Bordeaux*
1992 £6.95 (BEN)

le Gay *Pomerol*
1994 £5.95 (AD)
1994 EC £135.00 (MV)
1993 £13.71 (MV)
1992 £16.00 (ARM)
1989 IB £250.00 (FA)
1986 £25.85 (TAN)
1985 £20.00 (WY) £20.93 (BUT)

Gazin *Pomerol*
1994 EC £230.00 (CB)
1993 £16.16 (MV)
1992 £15.30 (HAH) £17.99 (FUL)
1989 £6.10 (HA) £19.36 (BUT)
1982 £32.90 (AV)
1982 magnum £69.50 (RES)
1976 £35.00 (UB)
1970 £37.50 (BU)

Giscours *3ème cru classé Margaux*
1988 £18.99 (HIG)
1986 £21.96 (PEN)
1985 £36.75 (ROB)
1983 IB £160.00 (FA)
1981 £28.00 (CRO)
1975 £34.01 (LEA) £41.50 (ROB)
1975 IB £340.00 (GOE)

1970 £35.00 (RES) £45.00 (REI) £55.00
  (ROB) £79.31 (LEA)
1970 IB £550.00 (GOE) £780.00 (FA)
1966 £65.60 (WY)

du Glana *cru grand bourgeois exceptionnel
St-Julien*
1990 £11.75 (BER)
1975 £14.09 (PLA)
1942 £35.00 (BU)

Gloria *cru bourgeois St-Julien*
1990 £14.20 (BUT) £14.70 (NEZ) £14.85
  (CHA) £15.00 (HOG) £25.00 (ROB)
1989 £29.90 (UB)
1988 £17.80 (PIP) £21.50 (RES)

Grand-Corbin *grand cru classé St-Émilion*
1990 £17.99 (AME)

Grand-Lartigue *St-Émilion*
1992 £7.35 (REI) £9.99 (UN)

Grand-Mayne *grand cru classé St-Émilion*
1994 EC £155.04 (TAN)
1993 £13.70 (TAN) £16.65 (HIG)
1990 £23.99 (OD)
1985 £16.50 (WS)

Grand-Pontet *grand cru classé St-Émilion*
1990 £12.99 (BO) £21.50 (ROB)
1985 £15.50 (REI)

Grand-Puy-Ducasse *5ème cru classé
Pauillac*
1989 £16.62 (HOG)
1989 IB £160.00 (GOE)
1988 £13.50 (QUE)
1985 £25.50 (ROB)
1979 £16.85 (REI)
1966 £37.50 (BU)
1961 £52.88 (WY) £77.00 (CRO)

Grand-Puy-Lacoste 5ème cru classé
Pauillac
1992 £16.95 (LEA)
1991 £18.61 (BY)
1990 £32.95 (LAY)
1989 £18.60 (BUT) £19.92 (LEA) £21.54
(FA) £25.75 (DAV) £41.24 (NO)
1989 IB £220.00 (GOE)
1989 magnum £38.14 (BUT)
1988 £16.30 (RAE) £17.72 (ELL)
1988 IB £220.00 (GOE)
1987 £12.95 (BU)
1986 £15.99 (BUT) £18.60 (FA) £26.67 (EL)
1986 IB £240.00 (GOE)
1985 £23.11 (BUT) £26.25 (PE) £32.92 (HA)
1983 £20.99 (YOU) £21.74 (BUT)
1983 IB £170.00 (FA)
1982 £52.00 (CRO)
1982 IB £480.00 (GOE) £520.00 (FA)
1980 £16.00 (CRO)
1978 £29.50 (BU) £45.00 (CRO)
1975 IB £235.00 (BIB)
1970 £59.35 (UB) £60.00 (CRO)
1961 £85.00 (REI) £88.13 (WY)

★ **Granin-Grand-Poujeaux** cru bourgeois
Moulis-en-Médoc
1990 £11.95 (PIP)

la Grave-Trigant-de-Boisset Pomerol
1992 £15.59 (CB)
1989 £22.72 (BUT)
1985 £31.00 (WS)
1978 £100.00 (AD)

Gravet grand cru St-Émilion
1990 £7.70 (FOR)
1989 £7.70 (FOR)

Gressier-Grand-Poujeaux cru
bourgeois supérieur Moulis
1993 £12.55 (DI)
1989 £12.90 (HOG)
1985 £11.99 (PE)
1970 £24.27 (BUT)

> *EC (ex-cellar) price per*
> *dozen, excl shipping,*
> *duty and VAT. IB (in*
> *bond) price per dozen,*
> *excl duty and VAT.*
> *All other prices,*
> *per bottle incl VAT.*

Greysac cru grand bourgeois Médoc
1993 £8.95 (ROB)
1991 £6.37 (HOG) £6.95 (POR)
1987 £7.32 (BUT)

Gros-Caillou St-Estèphe
1994 £7.29 (NEW)
1989 £7.40 (BUT)

Gros-Moulin Côtes de Bourg
1993 £6.26 (NEZ)

Gruaud-Larose 2ème cru classé St-Julien
1991 £19.00 (BER)
1990 £31.73 (PEN) £32.50 (PE) £32.95 (WR)
£32.95 (BOT) £43.71 (TW)
1989 £27.92 (BUT) £29.00 (UN) £29.99 (MAJ)
£29.99 (PE) £31.95 (WR) £31.95 (BOT)
1989 IB £200.00 (FA) £230.00 (GOE)
1989 magnum £58.33 (BUT)
1989 double magnum £78.33 (BUT)
1989 double magnum IB £165.00 (FA)
1988 £18.60 (FA) £18.80 (BUT) £24.62
(LEA) £24.99 (FUL) £27.49 (PE)
1988 IB £200.00 (GOE)
1988 double magnum IB £200.00 (FA)
1987 £15.75 (PE) £22.95 (RES) £25.95
(BOT) £25.95 (WR)
1986 £36.99 (PE) £37.50 (RES) £38.78
(LEA) £42.50 (LAY) £43.50 (ROB)
1986 IB £320.00 (GOE) £340.00 (FA)
1985 £23.01 (ELL) £25.65 (BUT) £30.00
(WY) £34.95 (BEN) £34.99 (OD)
1985 IB £320.00 (FA) £330.00 (BIB)
1985 ½ bottle £11.99 (ELL) £13.99 (YOU)
£23.00 (CRO)
1985 jeroboam IB £205.00 (FA)
1984 £19.50 (UN)
1983 £24.99 (PE) £32.00 (WY) £33.50
(GAL) £37.00 (PIP) £45.00 (RES)
1983 IB £300.00 (GOE) £330.00 (BIB)
1983 ½ bottle £16.00 (WY)
1983 double magnum £145.00 (WY)
1983 jeroboam £250.00 (WY)
1983 jeroboam IB £200.00 (FA)
1982 £50.00 (WY) £60.00 (RES) £62.50 (BEN)
1982 IB £620.00 (GOE) £650.00 (FA)
1981 £19.99 (YOU) £22.91 (ELL) £23.99
(PE) £30.00 (WS) £39.00 (POR)
1981 magnum £65.00 (ROB)
1978 £23.50 (FA) £34.08 (LEA) £35.00 (PE)
1976 £27.08 (PEN)
1976 IB £235.00 (WY)
1976 double magnum IB £160.00 (FA)
1975 £23.50 (FA) £24.50 (REI) £29.50 (BU)

1975 jeroboam IB £180.00 (FA)
1970 £47.20 (TAN) £50.00 (VIG)
1961 £252.63 (WY) £275.00 (RES)
1961 IB £2,300.00 (WY)
1949 £205.62 (TW)

Guillot *Pomerol*
1990 £20.00 (WS)
1986 £16.05 (HIC)
1981 £13.50 (GE)

Guionne *Côtes de Bourg*
1994 £4.88 (HOG)
1993 £5.50 (ARM) £5.88 (QUE)

la Gurgue *cru bourgeois supérieur Margaux*
1990 £9.95 (SAI)

Hanteillan *cru grand bourgeois Haut-Médoc*
1988 £8.91 (ELL) £10.20 (PIP)

Haut-Bages-Avérous *cru bourgeois
  Pauillac*
1992 £11.99 (MAJ)
1991 £13.56 (HA) £15.83 (BY)
1989 £12.59 (BUT) £15.75 (BER) £17.63 (LEA)
1988 £14.99 (BOT) £14.99 (THR)

Haut-Bages-Libéral *5ème cru classé
  Pauillac*
1993 £13.05 (BER)
1988 £15.00 (GAL)
1986 £11.30 (BUT) £20.77 (NEZ)
1979 £18.20 (PLA)

Haut-Bages-Monpelou *cru bourgeois
  Pauillac*
1992 £8.99 (FUL)

Haut-Bailly *cru classé Pessac-Léognan*
1994 £16.34 (LAY)
1994 IB £157.50 (ELL) £159.00 (RAE)
1994 EC £150.00 (LAY)
1993 £12.93 (LEA)
1989 £17.49 (PE)
1988 £14.95 (RAE) £22.95 (ROB)
1988 IB £180.00 (GOE)
1985 £18.98 (BUT)
1979 £17.50 (REI)

Haut-Batailley *5ème cru classé Pauillac*
1992 £14.59 (LAY)
1991 £13.84 (BY)
1990 IB £210.00 (GOE)
1989 £15.18 (BUT)

1989 IB £160.00 (BIB)
1989 magnum £31.33 (BUT)
1987 £15.50 (ROB)
1986 £12.20 (BUT) £16.22 (HOG)
1985 £20.75 (REI) £29.50 (RES) £32.45 (UB)
1983 £21.50 (RES)
1982 £39.16 (EY)
1982 magnum £75.00 (VIG)
1979 magnum £26.00 (WY)
1978 £20.50 (REI)
1978 IB £220.00 (GOE)
1975 £19.25 (REI)
1975 magnum £38.50 (REI)

Haut-Brion *1er cru classé Pessac-Léognan*
1994 IB £425.00 (SEC) £450.00 (FA)
  £490.00 (RES)
1993 £45.00 (BER) £48.30 (DI)
1992 £44.84 (BY) £49.95 (BOT) £49.95 (WR)
1991 £40.25 (BER)
1990 £56.00 (BUT) £73.50 (ROB) £78.00
  (WS)
1990 IB £750.00 (FA) £770.00 (WY)
1990 magnum £98.99 (BUT)
1990 double magnum IB £750.00 (FA)
1990 imperial IB £620.00 (FA)
1989 magnum £138.98 (BUT)
1989 double magnum £251.52 (BUT)
1988 £64.00 (BEN) £72.95 (WR)
1988 IB £500.00 (BIB) £500.00 (FA)
1986 £45.24 (BUT) £69.99 (PE) £82.03 (BY)
1986 imperial IB £450.00 (FA)
1985 £50.13 (BUT) £58.30 (UN) £60.71
  (FA) £65.25 (PE) £69.95 (RES)
1984 £37.50 (BER) £41.00 (UN)
1983 £49.00 (UN) £54.99 (LEA) £54.99
  (OD) £62.00 (BER) £65.00 (BU)
1983 IB £520.00 (FA) £565.00 (WY)
1982 £66.08 (BUT) £99.88 (PEN) £120.00
  (BER) £120.00 (WY) £130.00 (BEN)
1982 IB £1,350.00 (FA)
1982 double magnum £587.50 (FA)
1982 imperial IB £1,250.00 (FA)
1981 £53.00 (BER) £60.00 (ROB)
1979 £75.00 (ROB) £75.50 (BEN)
1979 IB £850.00 (BIB)
1978 £59.39 (BUT) £70.50 (FA) £78.00
  (BEN) £89.75 (ROB) £126.00 (UB)
1976 £62.00 (BER) £65.00 (BU)
1974 £37.50 (BU)
1974 magnum £65.00 (BU)
1970 £85.00 (WY) £85.00 (CRO) £95.00
  (REI) £110.00 (ROB)
1970 IB £890.00 (WY) £1,180.00 (BIB)
1969 £35.63 (BUT)

1966 £97.80 (BUT) £182.13 (WY)
1966 IB £1,450.00 (FA) £1,535.00 (WY)
1966 magnum £399.50 (WY)
1961 £430.83 (FA) £495.00 (RES)
1959 £295.00 (CRO)
1955 £125.00 (BUT)
1948 £155.00 (WY)
1928 £385.00 (WY) £495.00 (ROB)
1924 double magnum £1,800.00 (WY)

Haut-Gardère *Pessac-Léognan*
1990 £8.85 (WAT)
1989 £8.36 (BUT)

Haut-Marbuzet *cru grand bourgeois exceptionnel St-Estèphe*
1992 £16.99 (AME)
1989 £16.60 (ELL) £16.61 (NO) £19.50 (POR)
1989 IB £195.00 (BIB)
1988 £16.75 (WRI)
1986 £15.95 (RES)

Haut-Pontet *grand cru St-Émilion*
1989 £15.28 (AV)

de Haut-Sociondo *lères Côtes de Blaye*
1989 £7.86 (NO)
1988 £7.86 (NO)

Hortevie *cru bourgeois St-Julien*
1990 £9.99 (PE)
1988 £11.00 (WS)

Houissant *cru bourgeois supérieur St-Estèphe*
1989 £11.61 (NEZ)
1978 £15.00 (VIG)

d'Issan *3ème cru classé Margaux*
1991 £12.62 (CHA)
1990 £16.95 (DI)
1989 £17.20 (NI)
1989 IB £160.00 (GOE)
1986 £13.34 (BUT) £16.85 (REI) £29.95 (UB)
1983 £18.73 (BY) £19.18 (AV) £33.00 (CRO)
1983 magnum £55.00 (ROB)
1982 £25.00 (RES)
1982 IB £235.00 (FA)
1982 magnum £52.50 (BU) £67.95 (ROB)
1979 £20.00 (BU) £23.00 (CRO)
1978 £15.67 (FA) £28.00 (YOU)
1970 £22.50 (REI) £39.95 (RES)

du Juge *lères Côtes de Bordeaux*
1993 £6.75 (AV)

Kirwan *3ème cru classé Margaux*
1994 £14.87 (LAY)
1994 IB £130.00 (WY)
1994 EC £135.00 (LAY)
1993 £12.99 (FUL)
1989 £22.95 (DI)
1988 £18.45 (HAH) £19.18 (AV)

Labégorce *cru bourgeois supérieur Margaux*
1989 £16.00 (NEZ)

Labégorce-Zédé *cru bourgeois supérieur Margaux*
1993 IB £95.00 (GOE)
1992 £9.95 (REI) £10.95 (RAE)
1989 £14.54 (BUT) £22.75 (DAV)
1986 IB £150.00 (BIB)
1985 £19.50 (CRO)

Lacombe *Bordeaux Supérieur*
1993 £5.99 (SAT)

Lacoste-Borie *Pauillac*
1993 £10.79 (EL)
1990 £10.00 (WS) £12.49 (DAV) £14.75 (AD)
1989 £12.49 (DAV)
1989 IB £120.00 (GOE)
1988 £11.35 (REI)

Lafite-Rothschild *ler cru classé Pauillac*
1994 £41.99 (LAY)
1994 IB £385.00 (GOE) £490.00 (ELL)
1994 EC £395.00 (MV) £411.96 (LAY)
1993 £32.25 (ARM) £39.50 (LAY)
1991 £46.25 (BER) £49.66 (BY)
1990 £76.50 (DI)
1990 IB £780.00 (BIB) £800.00 (FA)
£850.00 (GOE)
1987 ½ bottle £29.50 (ROB)
1986 £62.37 (BUT)
1986 IB £850.00 (GOE) £1,050.00 (FA)
£1,100.00 (BIB) £1,150.00 (WY)
1985 £50.13 (BUT) £60.00 (WY) £69.99 (PE)
1985 IB £750.00 (FA) £750.00 (BIB)
£780.00 (GOE)
1983 £63.90 (BEN) £68.15 (LEA)

1983 IB £540.00 (GOE)
1983 magnum IB £640.00 (FA)
1982 £115.00 (DI) £142.11 (BUT) £160.00 (CRO) £220.90 (WY)
1982 IB £1,800.00 (GOE) £1,800.00 (FA)
1982 magnum IB £1,800.00 (FA)
1981 £53.85 (FA) £75.00 (CRO)
1981 IB £665.00 (WY)
1981 magnum IB £570.00 (FA)
1979 £65.80 (FA) £75.50 (BEN)
1979 IB £740.00 (GOE)
1978 £83.75 (BEN) £107.71 (ELL)
1978 magnum IB £780.00 (FA)
1976 IB £1,150.00 (FA)
1975 £103.99 (BUT)
1975 IB £1,150.00 (BIB)
1971 £65.00 (REI)
1970 £115.00 (WY) £125.00 (REI) £175.00 (ROB)
1970 magnum £150.00 (REI)
1966 £130.00 (BEN) £154.17 (NO)
1966 magnum £245.00 (BEN)
1964 £55.00 (WY) £65.00 (REI) £95.00 (BU)
1962 £120.00 (ROB)
1961 £450.00 (PE) £452.38 (WY)
1961 ½ bottle £164.50 (WY)
1959 £195.00 (RES) £452.38 (FA)
1956 £376.00 (WY)
1956 magnum £781.38 (WY)
1953 £220.00 (WY) £225.00 (REI) £411.25 (FA)
1953 magnum £435.00 (WY)
1952 £90.00 (WY)
1950 £135.00 (REI)
1948 ½ bottle £70.00 (WY)
1947 £175.00 (WY)
1945 £620.00 (WY)
1934 £145.00 (WY)
1929 £360.00 (WY)
1929 magnum £1,325.00 (WY)
1914 £175.00 (WY)

Lafleur *Pomerol*
1993 IB £900.00 (FA)
1992 £21.67 (ARM)
1992 IB £780.00 (FA)
1989 £103.87 (BUT)
1989 IB £1,800.00 (FA)
1988 £96.64 (BUT)
1988 IB £1,200.00 (FA) £1,400.00 (WY)
1986 £250.00 (RES)
1986 IB £1,600.00 (FA)
1984 £35.00 (REI)
1982 £362.29 (FA)
1971 IB £1,850.00 (FA)

Lafleur-Gazin *Pomerol*
1989 £5.88 (BY)
1982 £15.50 (REI) £21.07 (AV)
1979 £18.50 (REI)

Lafon-Rochet *4ème cru classé St-Estèphe*
1992 £13.61 (LAY)
1989 £13.80 (GAL)
1986 £13.50 (GAL)
1982 £21.50 (WRI) £25.00 (RES)
1978 £18.50 (CRO)
1975 £19.95 (ROB)

Lagrange *Pomerol*
1993 £10.42 (ARM) £14.50 (LAY)
1992 £11.40 (TAN)
1989 £13.90 (BUT) £21.57 (HOG)
1988 £22.50 (LAY)
1982 £25.00 (BU)

Lagrange *3ème cru classé St-Julien*
1994 £14.28 (LAY)
1994 EC £129.00 (LAY)
1993 £6.95 (DI)
1988 £26.50 (BER)
1985 £24.00 (GAL) £24.01 (HA) £32.50 (ROB)
1983 £23.50 (ROB)
1981 IB £180.00 (WY)
1975 £22.50 (BU)

la Lagune *3ème cru classé Haut-Médoc*
1994 EC £117.96 (TAN)
1993 £15.00 (HIG) £15.20 (DI)
1990 £19.95 (ROB) £21.99 (YOU)
1990 IB £220.00 (GOE) £220.00 (BIB)
1989 £21.15 (NI) £23.50 (ROB) £23.77 (NEZ) £24.75 (BEN) £27.20 (PIP)
1989 magnum IB £240.00 (FA)
1988 £19.99 (HIG) £21.50 (DAV)
1988 IB £175.00 (BIB) £200.00 (GOE)
1986 £18.60 (BUT) £19.50 (GAL) £25.50 (DAV)
1985 £15.86 (BUT) £22.56 (CHA) £23.50 (FA) £26.41 (HA) £26.85 (REI)

EC (ex-cellar) price per dozen, excl shipping, duty and VAT. IB (in bond) price per dozen, excl duty and VAT. All other prices, per bottle incl VAT.

1984 £17.50 (UN)
1983 £22.50 (REI) £27.00 (CRO)
1983 IB £175.00 (FA) £265.00 (WY)
1983 magnum IB £240.00 (GOE)
1982 £41.51 (NO) £42.30 (LEA) £45.00
  (CRO) £47.50 (DAV) £67.50 (ROB)
1982 IB £420.00 (FA) £440.00 (GOE)
1982 double magnum IB £450.00 (FA)
1981 £21.95 (REI) £31.66 (TW)
1981 IB £195.00 (FA)
1981 magnum £43.85 (REI)
1979 £32.00 (CRO)
1978 £26.93 (BUT) £31.95 (DAV) £34.99
  (OD) £36.00 (CRO) £46.00 (BER)
1978 IB £260.00 (FA)
1978 magnum IB £260.00 (FA)
1977 £9.50 (REI)
1976 £24.00 (CRO) £32.66 (TW)
1976 ½ bottle £12.00 (CRO)
1975 £18.50 (REI) £22.80 (BUT)
1975 IB £225.00 (GOE)
1975 magnum £48.48 (BUT)
1973 £19.00 (CRO)
1971 magnum £49.50 (BU)
1970 £48.00 (ROB) £55.00 (CRO)
1970 magnum £45.00 (BU)
1962 £47.50 (BEN)
1928 £28.20 (WY)

Lalande d'Auvion *Médoc*
1990 £6.15 (SAI)

Lalande-Borie *cru bourgeois supérieur St-Julien*
1989 £16.85 (BY) £16.85 (BY)
1989 IB £125.00 (GOE)
1988 £11.85 (REI)
1988 IB £125.00 (GOE)
1987 £12.40 (BY)
1986 £10.79 (BUT) £11.35 (REI)
1983 magnum £29.50 (BU)
1981 £16.00 (CRO)

de Lamarque *cru grand bourgeois Haut-Médoc*
1993 £9.87 (CB)
1990 £12.69 (CB)
1989 £12.40 (CB)
1988 £12.69 (CB)

Lamothe-Bergeron *cru bourgeois Haut-Médoc*
1993 £9.44 (AV) £9.45 (DAV)
1990 £10.53 (EL)
1989 £10.60 (UB)

Lamothe-Cissac *Haut-Médoc*
1992 £7.99 (DI)
1990 £8.90 (GAL)
1989 £8.25 (GAL) £9.50 (DI)

Lanessan *cru bourgeois supérieur Haut-Médoc*
1992 £11.86 (CHA)
1990 £16.99 (BOT) £16.99 (WR)
1989 £10.25 (BUT) £14.65 (BER) £15.95 (RES)
1988 £14.50 (BER) £14.95 (RES)
1985 £13.80 (NEZ) £15.12 (HA) £18.50
  (RES) £19.20 (PIP)

Langoa-Barton *3ème cru classé St-Julien*
1994 £15.46 (LAY)
1994 IB £136.00 (GOE) £140.00 (WY)
1994 EC £135.96 (TAN) £141.00 (LAY)
1994 magnum IB £140.00 (GOE)
1993 £16.15 (BER) £17.99 (DI)
1993 IB £120.00 (GOE)
1992 £15.39 (BY)
1990 £13.67 (BUT) £31.20 (EY) £39.95 (NI)
1989 IB £155.00 (BIB) £160.00 (GOE)
1988 £15.25 (WRI) £19.39 (LAY) £26.46 (BY)
1988 magnum £40.73 (LAY)
1986 £16.25 (BUT) £33.10 (BY)
1985 £32.00 (BY) £34.80 (UB)
1985 magnum £46.95 (ROB)
1978 £27.32 (BY) £29.00 (CRO) £31.73 (LEA)
1970 £30.00 (VIG)

Larcis-Ducasse *grand cru classé St-Émilion*
1983 £15.95 (RES)
1982 £22.95 (ROB)

Larmande *grand cru classé St-Émilion*
1994 IB £125.00 (GOE)
1994 EC £129.96 (TAN)
1989 £15.37 (BUT) £21.00 (BER)
1986 £16.50 (WS)
1985 £14.39 (BUT) £14.85 (REI)

Larose-Trintaudon *cru grand bourgeois Haut-Médoc*
1989 £12.03 (HA)

Laroze *grand cru classé St-Émilion*
1990 £19.80 (LAY)

Larrivet-Haut-Brion *Pessac-Léognan*
1989 £14.25 (BUT)
1985 £12.73 (BUT)
1982 £24.09 (PLA)

Lascombes *2ème cru classé Margaux*
1991 £17.99 (WR) £17.99 (BOT)
1990 £11.79 (BUD) £17.98 (QUE) £19.23
  (NO) £25.00 (ROB)
1989 £15.99 (PE) £18.76 (VIN) £19.95
  (ROB) £20.99 (BOT) £20.99 (WR)
1988 £15.00 (WY) £20.17 (NO)
1986 £23.50 (NO) £36.75 (ROB)
1983 £21.95 (RAE) £26.00 (WS)
1978 magnum £52.50 (BU)

Latour *1er cru classé Pauillac*
1994 IB £490.00 (ELL)
1993 £38.30 (HAH) £44.00 (BER)
1993 IB £350.00 (GOE) £385.00 (SEC)
1992 £43.51 (BY)
1992 IB £310.00 (RAE)
1991 £43.00 (DI) £45.25 (BER)
1990 IB £1,800.00 (FA) £2,000.00 (GOE)
  £2,000.00 (BIB) £2,250.00 (SEC)
1989 £65.00 (DI) £65.00 (UN) £98.00 (ROB)
1989 IB £675.00 (GOE) £680.00 (FA)
1989 magnum £105.75 (BUT)
1989 magnum IB £680.00 (FA)
1988 £44.00 (NI) £45.00 (RAE) £48.81 (BUT)
1988 IB £500.00 (GOE) £520.00 (BIB)
1987 £33.29 (FA) £51.92 (BY) £55.00 (RES)
1986 IB £600.00 (FA) £670.00 (BIB)
  £700.00 (GOE)
1986 magnum IB £620.00 (FA)
1986 imperial £425.00 (WY)
1985 £59.51 (NO) £68.54 (FA) £69.99 (PE)
1985 IB £550.00 (GOE) £770.00 (WY)
1985 imperial IB £500.00 (FA)
1984 £35.99 (FUL) £44.00 (UN) £49.75 (ROB)
1983 £55.00 (UN) £57.00 (HOG) £59.00
  (SOM) £65.00 (BER) £68.15 (PEN)
1983 IB £500.00 (FA) £520.00 (GOE)

1982 £120.00 (DI) £180.00 (WY)
1982 IB £2,400.00 (FA)
1982 double magnum £800.00 (WY)
1981 £47.00 (BUT) £49.00 (SOM)
1980 £50.16 (HA)
1979 £63.65 (ELL) £66.50 (ROB) £79.90 (PEN)
1979 IB £495.00 (BIB) £550.00 (FA)

1978 £88.00 (HOG) £93.03 (LEA) £118.00
  (ROB) £125.00 (RES)
1978 IB £800.00 (GOE) £1,100.00 (FA)
1976 £65.00 (BU) £75.44 (FOR) £77.39
  (BY) £80.00 (RES) £80.00 (ROB)
1976 double magnum £287.88 (WY)
1975 £84.40 (BUT) £90.00 (WY) £95.96
  (FA) £96.35 (LEA) £142.45 (UB)
1973 £45.00 (BU)
1971 £90.00 (ROB)
1970 £122.50 (BUT) £190.00 (WY) £220.00
  (CRO) £235.00 (FA) £252.50 (REI)
1970 magnum IB £2,350.00 (WY)
1969 £35.00 (REI) £35.63 (BUT)
1967 £65.50 (RES)
1966 £167.50 (REI) £240.00 (CRO)
1966 IB £2,400.00 (GOE) £2,600.00 (FA)
1965 £45.00 (REI)
1964 IB £1,950.00 (FA)
1962 £164.50 (FA) £165.00 (CRO)
1961 £499.38 (WY) £595.00 (ROB)
1959 £300.00 (RES) £340.75 (WY) £395.00
  (REI) £395.00 (ROB)
1956 £175.00 (RES) £511.13 (WY)
1955 £295.00 (BEN)
1955 IB £3,900.00 (FA)
1953 £145.00 (REI)
1953 IB £2,800.00 (FA)
1953 magnum £490.00 (WY)
1952 £85.00 (WY)
1950 £140.00 (BEN) £155.00 (REI)
1947 £495.00 (ROB)
1945 £1,468.75 (WY)
1944 £175.00 (REI)
1937 £135.00 (REI) £180.00 (RES)
1918 £255.00 (WY)

Latour-à-Pomerol *Pomerol*
1993 £23.03 (CB)
1992 £18.77 (CB)
1990 IB £285.00 (WY)
1989 £30.43 (CB)
1988 £27.50 (BO) £28.80 (TAN) £29.79
  (BUT)
1982 IB £1,250.00 (FA)
1981 £26.14 (BUT) £32.50 (RES) £35.00 (WY)

Laujac *cru grand bourgeois Médoc*
1993 £9.86 (AV)

Lavillotte *cru bourgeois Médoc*
1993 £10.95 (GE)
1991 £10.95 (GE)
1986 £11.95 (GE)
1983 £12.50 (GE)

Léoville-Barton *2ème cru classé St-Julien*
1994 IB £189.00 (RAE) £240.00 (WY)
1994 EC £210.00 (CB)
1993 £18.80 (DI)
1993 IB £180.00 (GOE)
1992 £17.60 (BY) £23.99 (BOT) £23.99 (WR)
1991 £14.95 (DI) £16.95 (ROB) £17.55 (BER)
1990 IB £300.00 (GOE) £320.00 (BIB)
1989 £22.00 (SOM) £27.12 (NEZ)
1989 IB £240.00 (GOE) £265.00 (BIB)
   £270.00 (FA) £300.00 (WY)
1989 magnum IB £270.00 (FA)
1988 £19.09 (FA) £25.00 (GAL) £25.00
   (CRO) £26.24 (LAY) £29.99 (MAJ)
1988 IB £220.00 (GOE)
1988 magnum £54.44 (LAY)
1986 £20.27 (BUT) £22.00 (HOG) £26.44
   (FA) £34.50 (LAY)
1986 IB £240.00 (GOE) £270.00 (FA)
1986 magnum £50.00 (WY)
1985 £22.09 (SUM) £31.25 (DAV)
1985 IB £240.00 (FA) £300.00 (GOE)
1983 £19.58 (FA) £20.01 (BUT) £26.26
   (HA) £27.57 (BY) £28.75 (ROB)
1983 IB £250.00 (GOE) £270.00 (WY)
1982 £46.50 (DI) £55.00 (LAY) £59.95 (DAV)
1982 IB £460.00 (GOE) £495.00 (FA)
1982 magnum £96.94 (FA)
1982 magnum IB £460.00 (GOE)
1982 double magnum £205.63 (FA)
1981 £27.50 (DAV)
1981 IB £200.00 (GOE)
1979 £17.53 (ELL) £26.95 (DAV)
1979 magnum £33.00 (WY)
1978 £23.50 (FA) £31.95 (DAV) £33.50 (ROB)
1976 £32.31 (TW)
1975 £21.50 (REI) £31.60 (TAN) £40.00 (VIG)
1970 £33.00 (WY)
1970 magnum IB £360.00 (WY)
1961 £95.00 (CRO) £129.25 (WY)
1961 magnum £270.25 (WY)
1929 £150.00 (REI)

Léoville-Las-Cases *2ème cru classé St-Julien*
1994 £26.32 (LAY)
1994 IB £225.00 (GOE) £330.00 (RAE)
1994 EC £252.00 (LAY)
1993 £24.15 (DI)
1993 IB £200.00 (GOE) £225.00 (SEC)
1992 £21.36 (BY)
1991 £22.00 (BER)
1990 IB £460.00 (FA) £495.00 (GOE)
1989 £26.50 (PIP) £39.00 (ROB) £39.70
   (FOR) £45.00 (VIG) £51.76 (NEZ)

1989 IB £410.00 (GOE) £420.00 (FA)
   £560.00 (WY)
1989 double magnum £199.75 (FA)
1989 imperial IB £300.00 (FA)
1988 IB £295.00 (BIB) £320.00 (GOE)
1986 £27.41 (BUT) £94.95 (BOT) £94.95
   (WR)
1986 IB £540.00 (GOE) £600.00 (BIB)
1986 magnum £55.54 (BUT)
1986 imperial IB £460.00 (FA)
1985 £32.51 (BUT) £38.53 (SUM) £39.99
   (PE) £40.00 (BER) £46.41 (LEA)
1985 IB £420.00 (FA) £445.00 (WY)
1985 magnum IB £420.00 (FA)
1985 double magnum £190.95 (FA)
1985 imperial IB £350.00 (FA)
1984 £18.99 (PE) £20.00 (WS) £27.00 (UN)
1983 £30.60 (GAL) £32.00 (WS) £36.40
   (AD) £39.50 (LAY) £45.00 (VIG)
1983 IB £350.00 (GOE)
1983 magnum £80.00 (ROB)
1983 magnum IB £320.00 (FA)
1983 imperial IB £230.00 (FA)
1982 £115.00 (BEN) £115.00 (RES)
1982 IB £1,200.00 (FA) £1,225.00 (GOE)
1982 double magnum £528.75 (FA)
1982 imperial £1,020.00 (REI)
1982 imperial IB £950.00 (FA)
1981 £28.79 (AV) £45.00 (VIG)
1981 IB £300.00 (GOE) £400.00 (WY)
1981 magnum £58.00 (REI) £65.00 (ROB)
1981 magnum IB £360.00 (WY)
1979 £26.30 (TAN) £48.50 (BOT) £48.50
   (WR) £55.00 (VIG)
1979 magnum £74.99 (OD)
1979 magnum IB £290.00 (FA)
1979 double magnum £117.50 (FA)
1979 imperial IB £200.00 (FA)
1978 £45.72 (LEA) £58.85 (UB) £65.95
   (WR) £65.95 (BOT)
1978 IB £450.00 (FA) £510.00 (WY)
1978 magnum IB £450.00 (FA)
1978 double magnum £199.75 (FA)
1978 imperial IB £325.00 (FA)
1975 £29.50 (REI) £35.00 (WY) £46.88
   (LEA) £48.25 (ROB)
1975 magnum £82.25 (FA)
1970 £41.13 (FA) £58.75 (AV) £65.00 (VIG)
1970 magnum £157.20 (UB)
1967 ½ bottle £8.50 (REI)
1966 £95.00 (RES) £95.00 (VIG)
1961 £94.00 (FA) £135.00 (REI) £170.38
   (WY)
1959 magnum £105.75 (FA)
1934 £110.00 (REI)

Léoville-Poyferré 2ème cru classé St-Julien
1994 £19.00 (GE)
1994 IB £159.00 (RAE)
1992 £14.95 (RAE)
1990 £17.63 (BUT) £23.95 (ROB) £25.99 (OD) £35.00 (GAL)
1989 £21.49 (NA) £30.20 (BER)
1989 IB £180.00 (GOE)
1987 magnum £39.00 (RAE)
1986 £23.50 (ROB) £28.00 (BER)
1985 £17.53 (ELL) £29.95 (ROB)
1983 £29.95 (ROB)
1983 IB £240.00 (GOE)
1982 £32.00 (WRI) £32.99 (OD) £33.50 (TAN) £42.50 (ROB) £49.95 (NI)

Lestage cru bourgeois supérieur Listrac
1991 £7.67 (WAT)

Liversan cru grand bourgeois Haut-Médoc
1990 £9.42 (FOR) £9.52 (HOG) £13.25 (BER) £13.95 (LEA)
1989 £11.50 (GAL)
1986 £10.85 (REI)
1985 £15.65 (UB) £24.00 (CRO)

Livran cru bourgeois Médoc
1990 £6.99 (HOG)

Loudenne cru grand bourgeois Médoc
1990 £9.95 (ROB)
1989 £8.68 (HOG)

la Louvière Pessac-Léognan
1989 £12.50 (BUT) £15.55 (NI)

Lynch-Bages 5ème cru classé Pauillac
1994 IB £192.50 (ELL)
1994 jeroboam IB £390.00 (WY)
1992 £19.99 (MAJ) £23.13 (BY)
1991 £24.00 (BER) £25.57 (BY)
1990 £35.00 (WY) £38.99 (OD) £39.97 (HA) £42.00 (BER) £45.00 (GAL)
1990 IB £360.00 (HA) £385.00 (GOE) £395.00 (SEC) £430.00 (WY)
1989 £32.51 (BUT) £42.30 (LEA) £46.85 (AV) £49.99 (POR) £50.41 (NO) £56.00 (ROB)
1989 IB £475.00 (FA) £475.00 (GOE) £530.00 (WY)
1989 magnum £65.02 (BUT) £95.18 (LEA)
1988 £30.60 (NI) £31.33 (FA) £33.49 (LEA)
1988 IB £320.00 (FA) £385.00 (WY)
1987 £23.14 (BY)
1986 £25.46 (BUT) £45.00 (REI)

1986 IB £390.00 (FA) £425.00 (BIB)
1985 £36.23 (BUT) £42.51 (NO) £55.00 (RES)
1985 IB £550.00 (BIB) £580.00 (FA)
1983 £37.50 (DAV)
1983 IB £400.00 (BIB) £400.00 (FA)
1983 jeroboam IB £200.00 (FA)
1982 £65.00 (WY) £95.00 (RES) £99.00 (UB)
1982 IB £750.00 (BIB) £750.00 (GOE)
1981 £35.95 (DAV) £47.50 (ROB)

1981 IB £295.00 (FA)
1979 £26.44 (FA) £32.50 (DAV) £35.25 (WY) £45.00 (PIP)
1979 IB £320.00 (WY)
1979 jeroboam IB £195.00 (FA)
1978 £30.00 (WY) £33.29 (FA) £40.95 (DAV) £52.50 (ROB) £60.00 (RES)
1978 IB £370.00 (WY)
1978 jeroboam £129.25 (FA)
1975 £28.95 (BEN) £44.65 (LEA) £54.05 (WY)
1970 £69.52 (BUT) £85.00 (REI) £108.10 (WY) £110.00 (RES) £112.60 (FA)
1966 £76.38 (FA) £95.00 (VIG)
1962 £55.00 (REI) £67.99 (YOU)
1961 £165.00 (RES) £205.63 (FA)

Lynch-Moussas 5ème cru classé Pauillac
1991 £9.95 (BER)
1990 £11.45 (NI)
1988 £15.17 (BY)
1980 £15.69 (BUT)

du Lyonnat Lussac-St-Émilion
1993 £8.15 (HIC) £9.95 (DAV)
1990 £7.65 (FOR) £8.68 (EL) £9.95 (ROB)
1989 £8.51 (HOG)

Macquin-St-Georges St-Georges-St-Émilion
1993 £5.99 (FUL) £7.20 (AD) £7.45 (HAH)
1990 £6.74 (EY) £7.78 (AV) £7.87 (CB) £14.00 (CRO)
1989 £8.35 (SAT)
1988 £6.99 (DAV)

la Madeleine Pomerol
1987 £21.50 (RES)

Magdelaine *1er grand cru classé St-Émilion*
1994 £18.75 (ARM)
1993 £16.17 (ARM) £22.50 (CB)
1992 £18.77 (CB)
1990 £29.38 (AV)
1989 £30.02 (BUT)
1981 £19.29 (BUT) £22.00 (WY)
1978 £59.00 (UB)

Malartic-Lagravière *cru classé Pessac-Léognan*
1985 £15.03 (BUT)

Malescasse *cru bourgeois Haut-Médoc*
1993 £12.00 (HIG)
1990 £9.95 (SEC) £9.99 (MAJ)
1985 £18.00 (CRO)

Malescot-St-Exupéry *3ème cru classé Margaux*
1990 £18.60 (ROB) £19.50 (POR)
1990 magnum £37.95 (POR)
1987 £16.85 (BO)
1983 £17.64 (AV)
1982 £25.00 (BU) £29.95 (DAV) £29.99 (MAJ) £37.95 (WR) £37.95 (BOT)
1979 magnum £37.50 (BU)
1970 £27.50 (BU)
1961 £59.00 (BEN)

de Marbuzet *cru grand bourgeois exceptionnel St-Estèphe*
1990 £10.28 (BUT) £13.51 (LEA)
1990 IB £120.00 (GOE)
1989 £14.85 (BER) £14.98 (LEA)
1989 IB £120.00 (GOE)
1986 £17.95 (RES)

Margaux *1er cru classé Margaux*
1994 IB £400.00 (GOE)
1993 £38.35 (HAH) £45.00 (BER) £54.05 (PEN)
1993 IB £350.00 (GOE) £395.00 (SEC)
1992 £45.27 (BY)
1991 £46.25 (BER)
1990 £120.00 (DI)
1989 £75.00 (UN) £81.76 (FOR)
1989 magnum IB £880.00 (BIB)
1988 IB £570.00 (FA) £660.00 (WY)
1987 £79.75 (UB)
1986 £176.00 (ROB)
1986 IB £1,250.00 (FA)
1986 magnum IB £1,250.00 (FA)
1985 £135.00 (ROB)

1985 IB £1,000.00 (FA) £1,090.00 (WY)
1984 £42.00 (BER) £44.00 (UN)
1983 £56.51 (BUT) £100.00 (WY) £104.58 (LEA) £117.50 (ELL) £147.00 (ROB)
1983 IB £1,120.00 (FA) £1,300.00 (BIB)
1983 magnum IB £1,120.00 (FA)
1982 £90.00 (GAU)
1982 IB £2,250.00 (FA) £2,350.00 (WY)
1982 magnum IB £2,250.00 (FA)
1981 £43.34 (BUT) £68.54 (FA) £88.00 (CRO) £95.00 (ROB)
1979 £125.00 (ROB)
1979 IB £820.00 (FA)
1979 magnum £195.00 (UB)
1978 £85.00 (BO) £98.50 (BEN) £111.63 (LEA) £117.50 (REI) £140.00 (ROB)
1978 IB £1,100.00 (FA)
1975 £73.14 (BUT) £95.00 (VIG)
1973 £39.50 (BU)
1971 £95.00 (VIG)
1970 £50.00 (SOM) £85.00 (BU)
1970 IB £815.00 (WY) £950.00 (BIB)
1970 magnum IB £860.00 (FA)
1966 £135.13 (WY)
1962 £85.00 (REI)
1959 £279.06 (FA)
1955 £135.00 (REI) £146.88 (WY)
1953 magnum £800.00 (WY)
1945 £620.00 (WY)
1940 £95.00 (BU)

Marquis d'Alesme-Becker *3ème cru classé Margaux*
1989 £16.21 (HOG)
1988 £11.99 (PE) £15.40 (HIC) £15.50 (NI)

Marquis de Ségur *St-Estèphe*
1985 £19.67 (BUT)

Marquis-de-Terme *4ème cru classé Margaux*
1992 £12.95 (SAI)
1990 ½ bottle £11.97 (HAL)
1989 £14.99 (YOU) £17.63 (LEA)
1985 £14.36 (BUT)

Marsau *Côtes de Francs*
1994 £5.45 (SAI)

Martinet *grand cru St-Émilion*
1989 £10.50 (GE)
1988 £10.50 (GE)

de Martouret *Bordeaux*
1994 £5.69 (AME)

Maucaillou *cru bourgeois Moulis*
1990 £12.59 (NI)
1989 £12.25 (SAI) £14.90 (HA) £15.25 (DAV)

Mayne-Vieil *Fronsac*
1990 £7.10 (HA)
1989 £7.49 (YOU)

Mazeris *Canon-Fronsac*
1994 £6.67 (ARM)
1990 £10.06 (CB) £11.50 (AD)
1989 £8.75 (ARM) £11.89 (CB)
1988 £8.50 (MV) £9.90 (BUT) £9.93 (CB)

Méaume *Bordeaux Supérieur*
1992 £5.49 (MAJ)
1991 £5.99 (NA) £6.20 (HA)

le Menaudat *1ères Côtes de Blaye*
1993 £6.46 (AV)

Mendoce *Côtes de Bourg*
1992 £5.75 (DAV)
1990 £7.45 (BER)

Meyney *cru grand bourgeois exceptionnel St-Estèphe*
1992 £9.99 (MAJ)
1991 £13.95 (LEA) £13.98 (QUE) £14.99 (WHI)
1990 £14.59 (HOG) £15.67 (FA) £19.50 (RES) £21.95 (DAV)
1990 magnum £31.33 (FA)
1989 £12.99 (PE) £15.67 (FA) £17.59 (NI) £24.50 (ROB)
1988 £12.24 (ELL) £14.99 (FUL) £15.50 (GAL) £19.50 (RES)

de Mirefleurs *1ères Côtes de Bordeaux*
1992 £4.99 (VIC)

la Mission-Haut-Brion *cru classé Pessac-Léognan*
1994 IB £350.00 (RES)
1993 £32.00 (BER)
1991 £25.00 (BU)
1990 IB £500.00 (FA)
1989 £64.82 (BUT)
1989 magnum £130.62 (BUT)
1989 double magnum £225.52 (BUT)
1988 £48.00 (BER)
1988 double magnum IB £300.00 (FA)
1987 £33.21 (BY)
1986 £32.51 (BUT) £44.99 (OD) £45.00 (WY) £49.99 (PE) £56.00 (BER)

1986 IB £420.00 (FA) £515.00 (WY)
1985 £39.85 (BUT) £45.00 (REI) £49.35 (LEA) £52.00 (CRO) £58.00 (BER) £150.00 (UB)
1985 IB £460.00 (FA)
1985 magnum £83.23 (BUT)
1984 £36.00 (BER) £39.50 (UN)
1983 £34.00 (HOG) £50.00 (WY)
1983 IB £285.00 (GOE)
1981 £38.19 (FA) £40.00 (WY) £49.50 (RES)
1981 magnum £70.00 (WY)
1981 magnum IB £400.00 (WY)
1979 £45.00 (BER) £50.00 (RES)
1978 £89.50 (RES)
1976 £35.00 (REI) £45.00 (BU) £47.00 (WY)
1976 magnum £105.75 (WY)
1970 £95.96 (FA)
1970 IB £820.00 (GOE)
1966 £139.25 (UB) £145.00 (WY)
1953 £260.00 (CRO)
1945 £640.00 (WY)

des Moines *Lalande-de-Pomerol*
1988 £11.99 (SAT)

Monbousquet *grand cru St-Émilion*
1959 £48.00 (ROB)

Monbrison *cru bourgeois Margaux*
1990 £13.61 (BUT)
1985 £11.32 (BUT)

Monconseil-Gazin *1ères Côtes de Blaye*
1993 £6.20 (AD)

Montaiguillon *Montagne-St-Émilion*
1993 £9.20 (PIP) £9.95 (LEA)
1992 £8.10 (NEZ)
1990 £9.85 (UB)

Montalivet *Graves*
1990 £9.23 (EL)

Montbrun *cru bourgeois Margaux*
1988 £10.49 (DAV)

du Monthil *cru bourgeois Médoc*
1986 £9.75 (NA)

Montrose *2ème cru classé St-Estèphe*
1994 EC £175.00 (MV)
1993 £17.99 (OD) £20.40 (BER)
1993 IB £160.00 (GOE)
1986 £22.50 (WRI)
1986 IB £280.00 (FA) £330.00 (BIB)
1985 £24.99 (PE) £32.00 (UB)

1983 £29.38 (AV) £32.25 (ROB)
1983 IB £250.00 (BIB)
1982 £33.50 (WRI) £37.00 (PIP) £57.50
(RES) £60.00 (ROB)
1982 IB £390.00 (GOE) £395.00 (FA)
1981 £20.00 (WY) £30.90 (PIP)
1981 IB £190.00 (WY)
1978 £25.00 (WY) £29.50 (BU)
1976 ½ bottle £12.00 (CRO)
1975 £27.95 (BEN)
1970 £59.50 (REI) £70.00 (WY)
1966 £47.00 (PEN) £64.63 (WY)
1966 ½ bottle £23.00 (WY)
1957 £45.99 (YOU)
1928 £225.00 (WY)

Moulinet *Pomerol*
1988 £14.99 (BOT) £14.99 (THR) £14.99
(WR) £18.75 (WHI) £19.49 (SAT)
1986 £21.70 (VIN)
1973 £19.39 (TW)

Mouton-Rothschild *1er cru classé Pauillac*
1994 IB £385.00 (GOE) £435.00 (WY)
£490.00 (ELL)
1994 imperial IB £502.50 (WY)
1993 £80.00 (BER)
1993 IB £340.00 (GOE)
1992 £53.03 (BY)
1991 IB £425.00 (BIB) £425.00 (SEC)
1990 £71.50 (DI) £111.63 (PEN)
1990 IB £750.00 (FA) £820.00 (BIB)
1990 imperial IB £550.00 (FA)
1989 £61.88 (BUT) £78.78 (NO) £102.50
(BEN)
1989 IB £810.00 (FA) £920.00 (BIB)
1988 £73.32 (NO) £75.50 (BEN)
1988 IB £680.00 (FA) £740.00 (WY)
1987 £50.00 (WY)
1986 £108.88 (BUT)
1986 imperial IB £1,650.00 (FA)
1985 £79.99 (PE) £91.50 (BEN) £105.00
(ROB)
1985 IB £950.00 (GOE)£980.00 (FA)
£1,000.00 (BIB) £1,120.00 (WY)
1985 double magnum IB £930.00 (FA)
1985 jeroboam IB £500.00 (FA)
1984 £40.00 (BER) £49.95 (WR) £49.95
(BOT) £55.60 (HAH) £70.00 (WY)
1984 jeroboam IB £180.00 (FA)
1983 £70.01 (ELL) £72.00 (BER) £77.50
(POR) £79.50 (LAY) £89.50 (RES)
1983 IB £740.00 (FA) £750.00 (GOE)
1983 magnum £145.00 (BEN) £163.33
(LEA)

1983 jeroboam IB £320.00 (FA)
1982 IB £3,000.00 (FA) £3,000.00 (GOE)
£3,200.00 (BIB)
1982 magnum IB £3,400.00 (FA)
1982 double magnum £1,386.50 (FA)
1982 jeroboam £1,100.00 (WY)

1981 £61.75 (PE) £66.40 (DAV) £74.95 (BOT)
£74.95 (WR) £85.00 (RES) £95.00 (VIG)
1981 IB £595.00 (BIB) £600.00 (WY)
1980 £70.00 (VIG)
1979 £48.96 (FA) £79.50 (BEN) £82.85 (DAV)
1979 jeroboam £370.00 (WY) £500.00
(ROB)
1978 £65.00 (WY) £95.60 (DAV) £110.00
(VIG) £110.00 (BER) £130.00 (ROB)
1978 IB £750.00 (FA) £850.00 (GOE)
1978 double magnum £250.00 (WY)
1976 £56.79 (FA) £65.00 (BU)
1975 £73.44 (FA) £74.61 (BUT) £89.00
(GAU) £99.88 (WY) £125.00 (ROB)
1975 magnum IB £800.00 (FA)
1975 imperial IB £720.00 (FA)
1975 jeroboam IB £520.00 (FA)
1973 double magnum £325.00 (WY)
1972 £57.00 (WY) £65.00 (REI)
1971 £57.50 (BU) £120.00 (VIG)
1970 £120.00 (WY) £125.00 (REI) £135.00
(CRO) £186.25 (ROB)
1970 imperial £1,700.00 (REI)
1968 £195.00 (WY)
1966 £175.00 (REI) £217.38 (WY) £250.00
(VIG)
1966 magnum £195.00 (UB) £464.13 (WY)
1961 £450.00 (SOM) £553.00 (REI)
£580.00 (WY) £611.00 (FA)
1955 £334.88 (FA)
1948 magnum £1,325.00 (WY)
1937 £345.00 (WY)
1929 £275.00 (REI)
1909 ½ bottle £75.00 (WY)

Nenin *Pomerol*
1982 £26.50 (BU)
1981 £38.85 (UB)
1966 £40.00 (RES)
1959 £85.00 (WY)

d'Olivier *cru classé Pessac-Léognan*
1986 £16.27 (BY)

Les Ormes-de-Pez *cru grand bourgeois*
St-Estèphe
1992 £15.17 (BY)
1990 £13.38 (BUT) £22.50 (DAV) £26.46
   (BY) £26.50 (PIP)
1989 £12.63 (BUT) £14.99 (PE) £21.00 (ROB)
1985 £19.94 (LEA) £31.70 (UB)
1985 IB £130.00 (FA)

Les Ormes-Sorbet *cru grand bourgeois*
Médoc
1988 IB £100.00 (GOE)

Palmer *3ème cru classé Margaux*
1993 £23.00 (BER)
1992 £15.99 (FUL) £26.95 (DI)
1991 £24.95 (BER)
1990 £37.75 (NI) £48.60 (BY) £48.95 (LAY)
1990 IB £395.00 (FA) £395.00 (BIB)
1989 £35.45 (BUT) £44.25 (ROB) £47.50
   (UN) £55.00 (BU) £69.95 (BOT)
1989 IB £520.00 (FA)
1989 magnum £72.07 (BUT)
1988 £29.00 (FUL) £34.79 (EY) £34.99 (PE)
   £38.00 (BEN) £42.00 (WS) £46.85 (NI)
1987 IB £200.00 (BIB)
1986 £26.95 (DI) £28.10 (BUT) £46.85 (NI)
   £47.20 (TAN) £60.79 (BY)
1986 IB £340.00 (GOE) £380.00 (FA)
1986 magnum £75.00 (ROB)
1985 £30.04 (BUT) £35.00 (WY) £37.80
   (GAL) £39.90 (BEN) £44.00 (BER)
1985 IB £385.00 (FA) £400.00 (BIB)
   £420.00 (GOE)
1983 £74.00 (BEN)
1983 IB £780.00 (FA)
1982 £44.00 (WY) £47.98 (FA) £55.23 (LEA)
1981 £32.31 (BUT) £33.50 (REI) £38.95
   (BEN) £42.75 (ROB) £44.65 (TW)
1979 £36.25 (REI)
1978 £54.00 (BEN) £65.00 (DI) £85.00 (UB)
1978 IB £560.00 (FA)
1976 £36.50 (REI)
1975 £95.00 (ROB)
1975 magnum £101.83 (FA)
1973 £44.65 (TW)

1971 £55.00 (CRO)
1970 £69.00 (BO) £89.00 (CRO) £90.00
   (WY) £95.00 (REI) £99.50 (BEN)
1970 IB £990.00 (WY) £1,050.00 (FA)
1970 magnum IB £1,050.00 (FA)
1967 £32.50 (REI) £37.00 (BO)
1966 IB £2,150.00 (FA)
1964 £75.00 (RES)
1955 magnum £200.00 (REI)

★ **Paloumey** *cru bourgeois Haut-Médoc*
1993 £8.90 (MV)

Panigon *cru bourgeois Médoc*
1990 £8.65 (HA)

Pape-Clément *cru classé Pessac-Léognan*
1994 IB £172.20 (RAE)
1992 £19.00 (LAY)
1989 £24.50 (RAE) £27.50 (BU)
1988 £19.87 (BUT)
1986 IB £210.00 (FA)
1985 £18.11 (BUT)
1982 £14.69 (FA) £25.11 (HA) £38.85 (UB)
1970 £25.00 (WY)

Patache d'Aux *cru grand bourgeois Médoc*
1993 £8.30 (TAN)
1992 £8.95 (ROB)
1990 £9.05 (EY) £9.77 (HA) £9.89 (YOU)
1989 £9.75 (GAL) £10.85 (REI) £11.40 (PIP)
   £17.00 (CRO)
1982 £10.20 (BUT)

Pauillac de Château Latour *Pauillac*
1992 £11.85 (AD)
1990 £16.95 (BEN)

Paveil-de-Luze *cru bourgeois Margaux*
1993 £12.32 (EL)

Pavie *1er grand cru classé St-Émilion*
1994 IB £189.00 (RAE)
1993 IB £160.00 (GOE)
1991 £18.75 (BER)
1990 £45.90 (ROB)
1989 £18.95 (BO) £19.29 (BUT) £26.44
   (LEA) £29.75 (ROB) £29.99 (MAJ)
1988 £20.85 (REI) £29.50 (PIP)
1985 £21.61 (BUT) £35.00 (RES)
1983 £20.50 (BUT) £32.00 (WS)
1983 magnum £84.05 (UB)
1982 £56.00 (BER)
1975 £25.80 (BUT) £34.25 (ROB)
1955 £85.00 (REI)

Pavie-Decesse *grand cru classé St-Émilion*
1993 IB £120.00 (GOE)
1990 £18.95 (RAE)
1989 £13.22 (FA) £14.20 (BUT)
1989 IB £160.00 (GOE)
1988 £23.24 (PIP)
1986 £14.20 (FA)

Pavie-Macquin *grand cru classé St-Émilion*
1961 £50.00 (SOM)

Pavillon-Rouge-du-Château
  Margaux *Margaux*
1994 £16.34 (LAY)
1994 EC £150.00 (LAY)
1993 £17.40 (DI)
1989 £29.50 (ROB)
1988 £29.95 (DAV)
1987 £19.85 (PEN)
1986 £32.00 (WY) £36.00 (CRO)

Péconnet *Bordeaux Supérieur*
1975 £7.75 (BU)

Pédesclaux *5ème cru classé Pauillac*
1988 £14.50 (BU)
1985 £18.00 (BU) £22.17 (BUT)

Pérenne *1ères Côtes de Blaye*
1990 £6.66 (NEZ)

Petit-Village *Pomerol*
1994 £26.62 (LAY)
1994 IB £225.00 (GOE)
1994 EC £255.00 (LAY)
1990 £28.67 (BUT)
1990 IB £350.00 (GOE)
1989 £29.80 (BUT) £49.50 (BER)
1989 IB £350.00 (GOE)
1982 IB £465.00 (FA)
1966 £38.50 (REI)

les Petits Arnauds *Côtes de Blaye*
1991 £5.90 (HOG)

Pétrus *Pomerol*
1994 EC £1,368.00 (HAH)
1992 IB £1,950.00 (WY)
1990 £558.13 (WY)
1990 IB £4,600.00 (FA) £5,400.00 (WY)
1989 £569.88 (WY)
1989 IB £5,000.00 (BIB) £5,400.00 (WY)
1988 £270.00 (BEN)
1988 IB £2,800.00 (FA) £3,000.00 (WY)
1987 £188.00 (TW) £201.71 (ELL)

1987 IB £1,700.00 (WY)
1986 IB £2,750.00 (WY)
1986 magnum £479.79 (FA)
1986 magnum IB £2,400.00 (WY)
1985 £275.34 (BUT)

1983 IB £2,500.00 (BIB) £2,500.00 (FA)
1983 magnum IB £2,100.00 (FA)
1982 £435.00 (BUT) £793.13 (WY)
1982 IB £6,500.00 (GOE) £7,700.00 (WY)
1982 magnum £971.73 (BUT)
1981 £264.38 (WY) £295.00 (RES)
1981 IB £2,250.00 (FA)
1981 magnum IB £2,100.00 (FA)
1980 magnum £420.00 (ROB)
1978 magnum £675.00 (REI)
1976 £195.00 (REI) £223.25 (FA)
1976 IB £2,600.00 (BIB)
1970 £500.00 (WY) £540.00 (CRO)
1970 IB £6,500.00 (FA) £6,650.00 (WY)

Peybonhomme-Les-Tours *1ères Côtes*
  de Blaye
1993 £7.30 (HIC)

du Peyrat *1ères Côtes de Bordeaux*
1989 £4.95 (SAI)

de Pez *cru bourgeois supérieur St-Estèphe*
1989 £13.52 (HOG)
1988 £13.60 (WRI) £14.50 (AD)
1985 £22.50 (RES)
1983 £17.56 (BUT)
1982 £32.50 (RES)
1975 £18.00 (BU)

Phélan-Ségur *cru grand bourgeois*
  exceptionnel St-Estèphe
1994 EC £96.00 (MV)
1990 £16.20 (HOG) £16.95 (DI)
1989 £17.04 (LEA) £29.00 (UB)
1975 £12.50 (REI)
1959 £45.00 (ROB)

Pibran *cru bourgeois Pauillac*
1990 £14.06 (BUT) £15.00 (BER)
1989 £14.69 (BUT) £15.99 (CB)
1989 IB £150.00 (GOE)
1988 £15.00 (GE)
1987 £17.47 (BY)

Picard *cru bourgeois St-Estèphe*
1986 £10.49 (DAV)
1985 £10.49 (DAV)

Pichon-Longueville (called Pichon-Baron until 1988) *2ème cru classé Pauillac*
1993 £22.25 (NI)
1992 £24.99 (WR) £24.99 (BOT)
1990 £49.95 (DI)
1990 IB £450.00 (FA) £465.00 (BIB)
1989 £35.45 (BUT) £38.85 (AV)
1988 £20.76 (BUT)
1987 £24.26 (BY)
1986 £18.51 (ELL) £37.50 (ROB)
1985 £21.73 (ELL) £43.00 (BER)
1983 £36.75 (ROB)
1982 £100.00 (WY)
1959 £59.93 (LEA)

Pichon-Longueville-Lalande (called Pichon-Lalande until 1993) *2ème cru classé Pauillac*
1993 £21.10 (BER) £21.75 (DI) £22.25 (NI) £23.10 (HIG)
1991 £25.00 (ROB)
1990 £31.50 (REI) £32.50 (ROB) £34.99 (OD) £38.59 (FOR)
1990 IB £350.00 (FA) £360.00 (BIB)
1990 imperial IB £280.00 (FA)
1989 £36.99 (OD) £39.50 (ROB)
1989 IB £350.00 (FA) £385.00 (BIB)
1988 £34.00 (BER) £35.00 (GAL) £37.55 (NI) £39.50 (LAY)
1988 IB £290.00 (FA)
1987 £18.05 (BUT) £22.50 (RES)
1986 £41.96 (BY) £43.75 (BUT) £55.23 (LEA) £73.80 (TAN) £81.50 (ROB)
1986 IB £550.00 (GOE) £580.00 (FA)
1986 magnum £87.73 (BUT)
1985 £34.99 (OD) £35.00 (WY) £35.23 (HA) £39.00 (PIP) £45.00 (RES)
1985 IB £350.00 (GOE) £400.00 (BIB)
1985 imperial IB £320.00 (FA)
1984 £17.75 (PE) £20.00 (WS)
1983 £39.99 (OD) £42.00 (WY) £42.70 (NI) £45.00 (RES) £45.00 (LAY)
1983 IB £440.00 (FA) £500.00 (WY)

1983 magnum £99.00 (LEA)
1983 jeroboam IB £240.00 (FA)
1983 imperial IB £340.00 (FA)
1982 £104.58 (LEA)
1982 IB £1,300.00 (GOE) £1,300.00 (FA)
1981 £22.68 (BUT) £23.00 (YOU) £33.50 (REI) £34.66 (LEA) £37.00 (CRO)
1979 £30.00 (YOU) £47.00 (CRO) £48.00 (WS)
1979 IB £440.00 (FA)
1978 £42.59 (BUT) £58.75 (FA) £64.50 (LAY) £69.00 (CRO) £73.00 (EY)
1978 imperial IB £520.00 (FA)
1975 £54.64 (LEA)
1970 £89.00 (CRO) £125.00 (VIG)
1970 IB £820.00 (FA)
1966 £125.00 (VIG)
1964 £105.00 (ROB)

le Pin *Pomerol*
1994 IB £2,200.00 (GOE)
1993 IB £2,000.00 (GOE)
1992 IB £1,380.00 (FA)
1991 £90.00 (BER)
1991 IB £2,500.00 (FA)
1990 £182.13 (BUT)
1990 IB £4,500.00 (GOE) £5,300.00 (BIB)
1989 IB £4,600.00 (FA)
1988 £97.17 (BUT) £575.00 (RES)
1988 IB £4,000.00 (FA) £4,400.00 (BIB)
1987 IB £2,850.00 (FA) £2,995.00 (BIB)
1986 IB £4,800.00 (GOE) £4,850.00 (WY)
1985 £509.17 (FA) £538.54 (WY)
1985 IB £5,200.00 (BIB) £5,500.00 (GOE)

Pitray *Bordeaux Supérieur Côtes de Castillon*
1990 £6.60 (WS) £6.95 (REI) £7.85 (SEC) £8.58 (NO)

Plagnac *cru bourgeois Médoc*
1992 £8.25 (WHI) £9.04 (PLA)
1983 £10.75 (BU)

Plaisance *Montagne-St-Émilion*
1991 £8.65 (BER)

> *EC (ex-cellar) price per dozen, excl shipping, duty and VAT. IB (in bond) price per dozen, excl duty and VAT. All other prices, per bottle incl VAT.*

Plince *Pomerol*
1991 £11.40 (BY)
1988 £13.99 (SAT)
1986 £16.75 (ROB) £16.99 (MAJ)

la Pointe *Pomerol*
1982 £25.00 (BU)
1980 £18.21 (TW)

Pontet-Canet *5ème cru classé Pauillac*
1994 IB £137.50 (ELL) £138.00 (RAE)
1994 EC £120.00 (MV)
1990 £21.26 (BY) £23.50 (BER)
1989 £14.25 (BUT) £18.60 (HIG) £22.69 (BY)
1989 magnum £28.51 (BUT) £38.00 (HIG)
1988 £16.99 (HIG) £19.70 (BY)
1985 £16.90 (HOG) £19.95 (RES)
1982 £21.54 (FA) £34.20 (BY) £35.95 (ROB)
1981 IB £115.00 (FA)

Potensac *cru grand bourgeois Médoc*
1994 IB £72.00 (GOE)
1994 EC £62.00 (MV)
1993 £5.00 (ARM) £9.50 (HIG)
1992 £9.77 (CHA)
1989 £9.89 (BUT) £13.40 (PIP) £14.95
 (ROB) £18.99 (WR) £18.99 (BOT)

1988 £9.50 (RAE) £13.22 (ELL) £16.95 (RES)
1986 IB £140.00 (GOE)
1985 £20.00 (CRO)
1983 £17.95 (ROB) £17.95 (RES)

Poujeaux *cru grand bourgeois exceptionnel Moulis*
1994 EC £102.00 (MV) £105.96 (TAN)
1993 £13.95 (BER) £15.20 (DI)
1990 £17.50 (WS)
1989 £12.63 (BUT) £15.00 (TAN)
1989 IB £140.00 (GOE)
1988 £14.85 (WS)

de Prade *Bordeaux Supérieur Côtes de Castillon*
1990 £7.39 (YOU)

la Prade *Côtes de Francs*
1992 £7.20 (AD)

Prieur de Meyney *St-Estèphe*
1992 £8.75 (WHI)
1991 £8.23 (HOG)
1988 £9.99 (PE)

le Prieuré *grand cru classé St-Émilion*
1990 £17.50 (AD)
1985 £18.93 (BY)

Prieuré-Lichine *4ème cru classé Margaux*
1994 EC £120.00 (TAN)
1993 IB £120.00 (GOE)
1990 £19.81 (BY)
1988 £14.74 (CHA) £16.99 (HIG) £27.29 (HA)
1986 £11.75 (BUT) £26.00 (CRO)

Puygueraud *Côtes de Francs*
1993 £8.50 (DI)
1990 £7.93 (ELL)
1989 £7.34 (BUT) £8.95 (SEC)
1988 £10.70 (TAN)

Puylazat *Côtes de Castillon*
1994 EC £32.04 (TAN)

Rahoul *Graves*
1990 £11.75 (NI)
1985 £10.95 (BU)

Ramage-la-Bâtisse *cru bourgeois Haut-Médoc*
1991 £9.95 (THR) £9.95 (BOT) £9.95 (WR)
1990 £10.99 (POR) £11.99 (AME)
1989 £8.46 (FOR) £12.89 (KA)

Rauzan-Ségla *2ème cru classé Margaux*
1994 £19.27 (LAY)
1994 EC £156.00 (MV) £180.00 (LAY)
1990 £27.48 (NO) £41.75 (BOT)
1990 IB £280.00 (FA) £325.00 (WY)
1989 £30.00 (WS) £43.69 (WR) £43.69 (BOT)
1988 £24.11 (BUT) £31.95 (NO)
1985 £28.78 (TW) £33.18 (BY) £34.12 (NO)
1982 £27.50 (GAL)
1975 £13.50 (REI)
1970 £39.95 (RES)

Rauzan-Gassies *2ème cru classé Margaux*
1986 £22.50 (DAV)
1970 £25.00 (BU)
1966 £22.50 (REI) £32.90 (WY)
1961 £38.50 (REI) £100.00 (RES)
1940 £95.00 (VIG)
1937 £95.00 (ROB)

Réserve de la Comtesse *Pauillac*
1992 £10.50 (TAN)
1990 £39.95 (NI)
1989 £15.75 (WS) £20.00 (BU)
1988 £10.98 (BUT)
1984 £13.51 (BY)

Respide-Médeville *Graves*
1986 £13.80 (TW)
1961 £29.50 (BU)

Reynon *1ères Côtes de Bordeaux*
1994 £8.74 (BY)

Reysson *cru bourgeois Haut-Médoc*
1990 £10.95 (LEA)
1989 £7.12 (FOR)

Richotey *Fronsac*
1990 £6.70 (CB)
1989 £7.99 (SAT)

la Rivière *Fronsac*
1992 £7.99 (BOT) £7.99 (THR) £7.99 (WR)
1990 £12.49 (AUR) £12.95 (SAT)
1989 £12.49 (AME) £13.95 (VIG) £14.29 (SAT)
1988 £12.49 (AUR) £13.99 (SAT)
1987 £10.99 (SAT) £11.49 (AUR) £19.50 (UB)

de Rochemorin *Pessac-Léognan*
1988 £7.17 (FOR)

de Roquetaillade-la-Grange *Graves*
1989 £8.49 (DAV)
1988 £6.95 (SAI) £8.49 (DAV)

Roquevieille *Côtes de Castillon*
1988 £5.58 (PEN)

Rouget *Pomerol*
1990 £14.75 (CB)
1985 £16.94 (BUT)
1982 £21.81 (BY)
1978 £22.50 (BU)

Rousset *Côtes de Bourg*
1991 £6.20 (AD)

St-Bonnet *cru bourgeois Médoc*
1990 £7.95 (SAI)
1985 £8.43 (BUT)

St-Pierre *4ème cru classé St-Julien*
1989 £16.93 (BUT)
1987 £11.95 (BU)
1986 £22.17 (BY) £22.50 (LEA)
1983 £22.00 (GAL) £23.00 (CRO)
1982 £25.80 (GAL) £31.50 (AD)

de Sales *Pomerol*
1992 £12.95 (BY)
1990 £18.05 (BY)
1983 £16.60 (BUT) £19.25 (NEZ)

Sarget de Gruaud-Larose *St-Julien*
1992 £9.50 (BU) £11.75 (WHI) £12.99
    (SAF) £17.00 (CRO)
1989 £15.94 (LEA) £17.92 (PLA)
1986 £15.75 (PE)
1985 £15.75 (DAV) £15.95 (POR)

Sauman *Côtes de Bourg*
1993 £5.95 (DI)

Segonzac *1ères Côtes de Blaye*
1994 £5.85 (DI)
1993 £5.25 (WAI) £5.65 (AS)
1991 £6.25 (SAI)

Sénéjac *cru bourgeois supérieur Haut-
Médoc*
1991 £7.85 (BER) £9.40 (TAN)
1990 £10.99 (TAN) £11.25 (PIP)
1989 £10.80 (MV) £11.50 (GE)

Sénilhac *cru bourgeois Haut-Médoc*
1990 £9.45 (HAH)

la Serre *grand cru classé St-Émilion*
1989 £13.95 (RAE) £13.99 (PE)
1988 £11.49 (PE)

★ **Sergant** *Lalande-de-Pomerol*
1990 £9.95 (ROB)

Siaurac *Lalande-de-Pomerol*
1990 £9.99 (FUL) £11.32 (BY)

Siran *cru bourgeois supérieur Margaux*
1989 £14.50 (GAL) £16.45 (ELL) £23.60 (PIP)
1988 £11.60 (NI) £17.50 (SOM) £22.79
  (KA) £23.30 (PIP)
1986 £17.14 (ELL)
1962 £21.50 (REI)

Sirius *Bordeaux*
1993 £6.39 (WR) £6.39 (THR) £6.39 (BOT)

Smith-Haut-Lafitte *cru classé Pessac-Léognan*
1986 £18.75 (NA)
1983 £11.99 (YOU)
1982 £25.50 (TW)
1978 £24.50 (ROB)
1959 £28.50 (REI)

Sociando-Mallet *cru grand bourgeois Haut-Médoc*
1991 £10.99 (RAE)
1989 £13.71 (BUT) £13.95 (RAE)
1989 IB £140.00 (GOE) £185.00 (BIB)
1987 £19.95 (RES)
1986 IB £185.00 (GOE)
1983 £18.00 (CRO)
1982 £29.50 (BU)

de Sours *Bordeaux Supérieur*
1993 £5.99 (MAJ)
1989 £6.51 (BUT)

Soutard *grand cru classé St-Émilion*
1994 IB £130.00 (ELL)
1990 £15.96 (ELL)
1981 £14.00 (GE)

de Tabuteau *Lussac-St-Émilion*
1993 £8.79 (VIN)

du Tailhas *Pomerol*
1992 £11.84 (BY)

---

*Stars (★) indicate wines
selected by Oz Clarke in the
100 Best Buys section which
begins on page 8.*

Talbot *4ème cru classé St-Julien*
1994 EC £155.00 (CB)
1990 £20.56 (FA) £22.99 (PE)
1990 IB £195.00 (BIB)
1990 magnum £41.13 (FA)
1989 £14.70 (BUT) £18.00 (BO) £18.60
  (FA) £22.20 (PLA) £22.45 (PEN)
1989 IB £240.00 (WY)
1989 ½ bottle £8.00 (WY)
1989 ½ bottle IB £240.00 (WY)
1989 magnum £29.77 (BUT) £37.21 (FA)
1988 £15.67 (FA) £19.99 (FUL) £19.99 (PE)
1988 IB £220.00 (WY)
1987 £16.99 (NI)
1986 £23.49 (BO) £27.99 (PE) £28.75 (NI)
  £29.95 (DI) £32.31 (FA) £33.50 (GAL)
1986 double magnum IB £345.00 (FA)
1985 £17.75 (BUT) £22.03 (ELL)
1985 IB £285.00 (GOE) £285.00 (BIB)
1983 £25.46 (FA) £25.99 (PE) £37.75 (ROB)
1982 £50.00 (WY) £55.95 (DAV)
1982 IB £500.00 (FA)
1982 ½ bottle IB £500.00 (FA)
1981 £15.66 (BUT) £21.00 (RES) £27.50
  (DAV)
1981 IB £225.00 (BIB)
1981 magnum £55.00 (ROB)

1979 £26.95 (DAV)
1979 IB £220.00 (FA)
1978 £21.33 (BUT) £31.95 (DAV)
1978 IB £240.00 (FA) £340.00 (GOE)
1970 £25.00 (WY) £28.50 (REI) £47.50 (RES)
1970 magnum £52.00 (WY)
1966 £58.75 (WY)
1966 double magnum £235.00 (WY)
1961 £66.58 (FA) £105.00 (CRO)
1959 £89.00 (CRO) £90.00 (WY)
1952 £75.00 (REI)
1947 £140.00 (ROB)

Terre Rouge *Médoc*
1993 £7.60 (AD) £7.65 (LAY) £8.05 (HAH)
1988 £7.16 (BUT) £7.74 (ARM)

de Terrefort-Quancard *Bordeaux Supérieur*
1992 £5.95 (POR)

Terrey-Gros-Cailloux *cru bourgeois St-Julien*
1988 £10.52 (NEZ) £12.90 (PIP)
1988 IB £110.00 (GOE)

du Tertre *5ème cru classé Margaux*
1989 £18.50 (BER)
1988 £18.13 (BY)
1986 £15.80 (GAL)
1985 £26.50 (RES)
1970 £24.50 (BU)

Tertre-Daugay *grand cru classé St-Émilion*
1949 £35.00 (REI)

Tertre Rôteboeuf *St-Émilion*
1992 £25.97 (CB)
1990 £30.85 (BUT)
1989 £58.00 (CRO)
1988 £30.55 (BUT)
1986 £28.20 (BUT) £42.95 (RES)

Timberlay *Bordeaux Supérieur*
1993 £5.95 (NA)
1992 £5.99 (DAV)

la Tonnelle *St-Émilion*
1990 £7.48 (NO)
1988 £7.48 (NO)

Toumalin *Canon-Fronsac*
1988 £7.25 (GE)
1986 £7.25 (GE)

la Tour-Carnet *4ème cru classé Haut-Médoc*
1989 £17.50 (BY)
1982 £22.50 (ROB)
1978 £19.00 (CRO)
1975 £17.95 (WRI)

> *EC (ex-cellar) price per dozen, excl shipping, duty and VAT. IB (in bond) price per dozen, excl duty and VAT. All other prices, per bottle incl VAT.*

la Tour-de-By *cru grand bourgeois Médoc*
1994 IB £69.00 (ELL)
1993 £9.20 (TAN) £9.99 (HIG)
1991 £9.76 (PIP) £9.95 (POR)
1990 £9.99 (HIG) £11.65 (ELL) £14.79 (KA)
1989 £10.20 (GAL)
1982 £18.00 (CRO)

Tour de l'Espérance *Bordeaux Supérieur*
1993 £5.09 (BY)
1990 £5.48 (BY)

la Tour-de-Mons *cru bourgeois supérieur Margaux*
1991 £11.45 (BER)
1924 £95.00 (CRO)

Tour-des-Combes *grand cru St-Émilion*
1990 £9.00 (WAT)

Tour-du-Haut-Moulin *cru grand bourgeois Haut-Médoc*
1993 £12.25 (DI)
1991 £11.55 (DI)
1990 £12.50 (WS) £13.89 (DI)
1990 IB £120.00 (GOE)
1988 £12.99 (DI)
1985 £9.32 (BUT)

Tour-du-Pas-St-Georges *St-Georges-St-Émilion*
1994 EC £54.00 (MV) £57.96 (TAN)
1993 £10.00 (MV)
1990 £8.91 (ELL) £9.99 (YOU)
1988 £10.75 (BU)

la Tour-du-Pin-Figeac *grand cru classé St-Émilion*
1986 £19.95 (SAT)
1975 £12.50 (REI)
1959 £39.00 (ROB)

la Tour-Figeac *grand cru classé St-Émilion*
1989 £12.99 (PE)
1988 £15.18 (ELL) £16.99 (NI)
1986 £18.60 (BY)
1983 £12.75 (REI)

la Tour-Haut-Brion *cru classé Pessac-Léognan*
1982 IB £480.00 (FA)

la Tour-Martillac *cru classé Pessac-Léognan*
1990 £16.95 (VIG)

la Tour-St-Bonnet *cru bourgeois Médoc*
1992 £6.81 (FOR) £6.95 (POR)
1991 £6.45 (BER) £7.95 (BU)
1990 £8.95 (REI) £9.49 (DAV) £13.95 (ROB)
1989 £7.75 (REI) £11.35 (WRI)
1982 £20.62 (NO)

Les Tourelles de Longueville *Pauillac*
1992 £10.99 (VIC)
1991 £15.83 (BY)
1990 £13.38 (BUT) £14.95 (RAE) £21.15
(LEA)
1989 £14.95 (RAE)
1988 IB £140.00 (GOE)
1987 £15.83 (BY)

Tournefeuille *Lalande-de-Pomerol*
1993 £7.95 (LEA)

Tourteau-Chollet *Graves*
1990 £8.99 (BO)

Troplong-Mondot *grand cru classé St-Émilion*
1994 IB £225.00 (GOE)
1990 £15.01 (BUT)
1989 £17.14 (BUT) £24.75 (DAV)
1989 IB £240.00 (GOE)
1987 £12.00 (GE)
1971 £14.50 (REI)

Trotanoy *Pomerol*
1994 IB £290.00 (FA)
1993 £29.95 (CB)
1992 £24.88 (CB)
1990 £50.89 (AV)
1990 IB £470.00 (BIB)
1989 £39.36 (BUT)
1988 £32.50 (REI) £37.89 (BUT) £39.00 (BO)
1986 £27.91 (BUT)
1985 £65.00 (RES)
1983 IB £320.00 (FA)
1983 jeroboam IB £160.00 (FA)
1982 £315.00 (ROB)
1982 IB £1,325.00 (BIB) £1,920.00 (WY)
1981 IB £440.00 (WY)
1978 £70.00 (REI) £85.00 (ROB) £95.00 (BU)
1976 £69.95 (UB)

Trottevieille *1er grand cru classé St-Émilion*
1990 £23.95 (DI)
1989 £20.07 (BUT) £21.54 (HIG)
1983 £26.50 (DAV)
1979 £27.50 (RES)

la Valade *Fronsac*
1992 £7.30 (UB)

Verdignan *cru grand bourgeois Haut-Médoc*
1989 £12.14 (NEZ) £14.25 (PIP)
1985 £14.50 (ROB)

Vieux-Château-Certan *Pomerol*
1994 IB £290.00 (GOE) £294.96 (RAE)
1994 EC £288.48 (TAN)
1993 £27.30 (BER) £35.90 (DI)
1993 IB £210.00 (RAE)
1992 IB £140.00 (BIB) £150.00 (GOE)
1990 £29.96 (BUT) £29.99 (PE) £36.50 (ROB)
1990 magnum £62.08 (BUT) £70.00 (REI)
1989 £28.50 (BUT) £37.50 (REI) £38.99 (PE)
1989 magnum £57.38 (BUT)
1988 £30.06 (BUT) £34.64 (TAN)
1988 IB £320.00 (GOE)
1986 £29.57 (BUT) £45.00 (CRO)
1986 IB £400.00 (GOE) £410.00 (BIB)
1985 £34.99 (PE) £35.30 (UN) £45.00 (RES)
£49.00 (PIP) £54.50 (DI)
1985 IB £350.00 (FA) £350.00 (BIB)

Vieux-Château-Landon *cru bourgeois Médoc*
1990 £8.95 (SAI)
1988 £10.00 (SOM)

Villars *Fronsac*
1988 £9.95 (DAV)

Villegeorge *cru bourgeois supérieur exceptionnel Haut-Médoc*
1992 £9.95 (SEC)
1992 IB £9.49 (VIC)
1989 £11.26 (ELL)
1982 £13.95 (RAE)
1979 £14.00 (CRO)
1978 £13.99 (RAE) £18.35 (UB)

Villemaurine *grand cru classé St-Émilion*
1992 £16.99 (NA)
1990 £18.50 (NA) £18.99 (QUE)
1988 £18.75 (NA)
1986 £18.95 (NA)

Villeneuve de Cantemerle *Haut-Médoc*
1993 £11.29 (WHI)

Vraye-Croix-de-Gay *Pomerol*
1989 £16.71 (BUT)
1983 £23.81 (BY)
1982 £13.14 (BUT) £13.71 (FA)

WHITE BORDEAUX

DRY

Under £5.00
1995
Thieuley (SOM)
1994
les Bouhets (SAI)
l'Ortelan (SAI)
1993
Baduc (SUM)
de Sours (FUL)
Tertre du Moulin (SAI)
1992
Moulin de Launay (EY)

£5.00 → £6.99
1995
Bonnet (NI)
de Ricaud (HAH)
1994
Bonnet (ELL, EL)
Carsin (SAI)
Ducla (HIC, PLA)
de l'Étoile (AD, TAN)
Mouton-Cadet (SAI)
Thieuley (MAJ, AD, HAH)
1993
Bauduc les Trois Hectares (SUM)
Bonnet (WR, THR, BOT)
de l'Étoile (EL)
Moulin de Launay (TAN)
Sirius (BOT, THR, WR)
Thieuley (HIC)
1992
de Sours (PLA)
Thieuley (EY)
1991
Cabannieux (FOR)

£7.00 → £8.99
1995
Reynon Vieilles Vignes (OD)
1994
Cabannieux (CB)
Reynon Vieilles Vignes (WS)
1993
'L' de la Louvière (VIC)
1992
Bonnet (WR, THR, BOT)
Cruzeau (EL)
la Grave (GE)
de Rochemorin (NI)

1990
Cabannieux (ROB)
1989
Bauduc les Trois Hectares (PIP)
Guiraud 'G' (BUT)

Montalivet (REI)
1985
la Tour Martillac (RAE)

£9.00 → £11.99
1993
Couhins-Lurton (SEC)
1992
Couhins-Lurton (REI)
Thieuley (ARM)
1990
la Louvière (BUT)
1989
Bouscaut (RAE, BIB)
Doisy-Daëne Grand Vin Sec (TAN)
1988
Bouscaut (RAE, GE)
1985
Rieussec 'R' (BUT)

£12.00 → £14.99
1993
Olivier (BER)
1992
Couhins-Lurton (GE)
la Garde (LAYT)
1991
Couhins-Lurton (RAE, NI)
1990
Couhins-Lurton (AD, TAN, BIB)
1989
la Louvière (BUT)
1988
la Grave (BUT)
1985
Smith-Haut-Lafitte (BUT)
1981
Couhins-Lurton (RAE)

£15.00 → £19.99

1993
Carbonnieux (GE)
1992
Carbonnieux (HAH, BOT, WR)
Laville-Haut-Brion (OD)
1991
Couhins-Lurton (UB)
1990
la Tour Martillac (NI)
1989
de Fieuzal (OD)
la Tour Martillac (ENO)
1988
la Tour Martillac (BUT)
1987
'L' de la Louvière (RAE)
1983
de Fieuzal (EY)
1982
Malartic-Lagravière (BUT)

£20.00 → £29.99

1994
Pavillon Blanc du Château Margaux (CB, HAH)
1993
Laville-Haut-Brion (FA)
Pavillon Blanc du Château Margaux (ARM)
1992
la Louvière (FOR)
Pavillon Blanc du Château Margaux (FOR)
1990
Laville-Haut-Brion (FA)
1989
de Fieuzal (REI, TAN, ELL, BUT)
1988
de Fieuzal (OD)
Pavillon Blanc du Château Margaux (CRO)
1987
de Fieuzal (REI)
1986
Pavillon Blanc du Château Margaux (UB)
1980
'Y' d'Yquem (REI)
1979
Laville-Haut-Brion (FA)

£30.00 → £39.99

1994
Laville-Haut-Brion (FA)
1993
Domaine de Chevalier (RAE)
1992
Domaine de Chevalier (RAE)

1991
Domaine de Chevalier (RAE)
1990
de Fieuzal (BEN, AD)
1988
Laville-Haut-Brion (BUT)
Pavillon Blanc du Château Margaux (TW)
'Y' d'Yquem (BUT)
1986
Domaine de Chevalier (BU)
1985
'Y' d'Yquem (REI, CRO, BEN)
1984
Haut-Brion Blanc (BU)
1983
Laville-Haut-Brion (FA)
1982
Laville-Haut-Brion (REI, FA)
1981
Laville-Haut-Brion (REI)

£40.00 → £49.99

1989
Domaine de Chevalier (BUT)
1988
Haut-Brion Blanc (BUT, RAE)
1986
Domaine de Chevalier (BUT)
1985
Domaine de Chevalier (BER)
1978
Laville-Haut-Brion (REI)
'Y' d'Yquem (WY)

£50.00 → £69.99

1993
Haut-Brion Blanc (SEC)
1988
Laville-Haut-Brion (ROB)
'Y' d'Yquem (UB)
1983
Domaine de Chevalier (TW, TW)
Laville-Haut-Brion (BER)
1982
Haut-Brion Blanc (FA)
1967
Laville-Haut-Brion (WY)
1964
'Y' d'Yquem (WY)

£70.00 → £80.00

1989
Laville-Haut-Brion (BUT)
1960
'Y' d'Yquem (BEN)

£85.00 → £89.99

1994
Haut-Brion Blanc (FA)
1983
Haut-Brion Blanc (NO)

c. £95.00
1990
Haut-Brion Blanc (BUT)

SWEET

Under £7.00
1993
Marquis de Beausoleil St Croix du Mont
   (UN)
1992
des Arroucats (REI)
1990
de Berbec (OD, VIC, THR, WR, BOT)
Lousteau-Vieil (NO)
1988
Bastor-Lamontagne ½ bottle
   (BUT)
Doisy-Védrines ½ bottle (CRO)
1984
Coutet ½ bottle (NI)

£7.00 → £8.99
1993
des Arroucats (QUE)
Domaine du Noble (PLA, BIB)
du Juge (GAL)
des Tours (AD)
1992
Fayau (MV)
des Tours (HIC)
1990
Clos St-Georges (SAI)
Guiraud ½ bottle (BUT)
Loupiac Gaudiet (HOG)
Rayne-Vigneau ½ bottle (BUT)
1989
Coutet ½ bottle (BUT)
Filhot ½ bottle (REI)
Liot ½ bottle (HAL)
1988
Filhot ½ bottle (QUE)
Liot ½ bottle (HAL)
Nairac ½ bottle (REI)
Rabaud-Promis ½ bottle (BUT)
Rayne-Vigneau ½ bottle (QUE)
1986
Bastor-Lamontagne ½ bottle (HOG)
Rabaud-Promis ½ bottle (BUT)

1985
Filhot ½ bottle (DAV)
1981
Broustet (BU)
Doisy-Dubroca ½ bottle (REI)

£9.00 → £11.99
1993
la Rame (NI)
1991
Climens ½ bottle (THR, BOT, WR)
Doisy-Dubroca ½ bottle (LAYT)
1990
Bastor-Lamontagne ½ bottle (SAI, BUT)
la Chartreuse ½ bottle (WS)
Guiraud (BUT)
Liot (REI)
Rabaud-Promis ½ bottle (BIB)
1989
la Chartreuse ½ bottle (WAI, HAH)
1988
Broustet (BUT)
la Chartreuse ½ bottle (TAN)
Guiraud ½ bottle (BUT)
Guiteronde du Hayot (HOG)
les Justices ½ bottle (TW)
de Malle (DAV)
1986
Coutet ½ bottle (NI, HOG)
les Justices ½ bottle (TW)
de Ricaud (CRO)
Rieussec ½ bottle (CRO)
1985
Coutet ½ bottle (DAV)
1983
Nairac ½ bottle (CRO)
Rayne-Vigneau ½ bottle (WY)
1981
Filhot ½ bottle (SAT)
1979
Coutet ½ bottle (WY)
Doisy-Védrines (WY)
Suduiraut ½ bottle (CRO)
1978
Doisy-Daëne (WY)
1975
d'Arricaud (RAE)

£12.00 → £14.99
1994
Les Cyprès de Climens (LAYT)
1992
Les Cyprès de Climens (RAE)
1991
Fayau (UB)

1990
Climens ½ bottle (BUT)
Guiraud ½ bottle (MV)
Rieussec ½ bottle (WY)
Suduiraut ½ bottle (SAI)
1989
la Chartreuse (FUL)
Nairac ½ bottle (ROB)
Rabaud-Promis ½ bottle (RAE, HAL)
Rieussec ½ bottle (REI, BUT)
Suduiraut ½ bottle (WY)
1988
Coutet ½ bottle (WY)
Filhot (BIB)
Rayne-Vigneau ½ bottle (WY, NO)
St-Amand (AUR)
1986
Climens ½ bottle (BUT)
Filhot ½ bottle (HAH, RES)
Liot (EY)
St-Amand (GE)
1985
Filhot (DAV)
1984
Coutet (VIG)
Rieussec (DAV)
Rieussec ½ bottle (RES)
1983
Liot (SAT)
Loupiac Gaudiet (SAT)
de Malle (SAT, DAV)
Rieussec ½ bottle (CRO)
1982
Climens ½ bottle (RAE)
1981
Rieussec ½ bottle (REI)
1976
Filhot ½ bottle (WY)

£15.00 → £19.99
1992
Pascaud-Villefranche (THR, WR, BOT)
1990
de Cérons (EL)
Doisy-Daëne (BUT)
Loubens (LAY)
de Malle (BUT)
Rayne-Vigneau (BUT)

> *Stars (★) indicate wines*
> *selected by Oz Clarke in the*
> *100 Best Buys section which*
> *begins on page 8.*

1989
Broustet (BUT)
Climens ½ bottle (REI, RAE)
Coutet (BUT, BIB, BO, HOG)
Coutet ½ bottle (WY, UB)
Doisy-Daëne (GE, TAN)
Filhot (HA)
Guiraud ½ bottle (WS)
Loubens (LAY)
de Malle (ELL)
Nairac (TAN, TAN)
Suduiraut ½ bottle (BO, NO)
1988
d'Arche (TAN)
Broustet (RES)
Cantegril (AD)
la Chartreuse (HIC)
Climens ½ bottle (BUT)
Filhot (RAE, WAT)
Guiraud (BUT)
Guiraud ½ bottle (NO)
Lamothe-Guignard (AD)
Liot (WS)
Rabaud-Promis (RAE)
Suduiraut ½ bottle (RES)
la Tour Blanche (FA)
1986
d'Arche (GE)
Cantegril (AD)
Coutet ½ bottle (ROB)
Filhot (DI)
Lamothe-Guignard (EY)
Nairac (BUT)
Rabaud-Promis (BUT)
Suduiraut (TAN)
1985
Coutet (DAV)
1984
Coutet (DI)
1983
Filhot (DAV, REI, SAT)
Lamothe-Guignard (GE)
Rayne-Vigneau (HOG)
Suduiraut ½ bottle (ROB)
la Tour Blanche (REI, EY)
1981
Guiraud (TAN)
Lafaurie-Peyraguey (YOU)
1979
Filhot (SAT)
1978
Climens (FA)
Filhot (BU)
1977
Climens (REI)

1976
Climens ½ bottle (CRO)
Rieussec ½ bottle (EY)
1974
Climens (REI)

£20.00 → £29.99

1992
Coutet (WR, BOT)
1991
Climens (BOT, WR, THR, RAE, BIB)
Doisy-Dubroca (LAYT)
1990
Bastor-Lamontagne (BUT)
la Chartreuse (HAH)
Coutet (TAN, CB, WS)
Doisy-Védrines (BER)
Filhot (NI)
Guiraud (MV)
Lafaurie-Peyraguey (PE)
Nairac (MV)
Rabaud-Promis (BIB)
Rieussec (NI, TAN)
la Tour Blanche (BUT, NI)
1989
Broustet (PIP)
Coutet (WAT, ELL, WS)
Doisy-Daëne (EY, BER, EL, AD)
Lafaurie-Peyraguey (BUT, PE)
Rabaud-Promis (RAE)
Rayne-Vigneau (FOR, AD)
Rieussec (REI)
Romer du Hayot (AD)
Suduiraut (BEN)
1988
Broustet (PIP, ROB)
Coutet (FA, FA, NI, WY, RES)
Guiraud (GOE, HIC)
Lafaurie-Peyraguey (REI, BUT)
de Malle (PIP, ROB)
Rayne-Vigneau (PIP, EL)
Rieussec (REI)
Rieussec ½ bottle (WY, ELL)
Suduiraut (FA, BO, BUT)
la Tour Blanche (GOE, BUT, PIP)
1987
Rabaud-Promis (AD)
1986
Climens (BUT)
Coutet (BEN, EY)
Guiraud (TAN)
les Justices (TW)
Rieussec (BUT, FA, REI)
Rieussec ½ bottle (NO)
Sigalas-Rabaud (PIP)

1985
Climens (HA)
de Fargues (REI)
Rieussec (DAV)
Suduiraut (HOG, AD)
1983
Coutet (DI, RES)
Doisy-Védrines (RES)
Filhot (WY, ROB)
Guiraud (FA)
de Malle (NO)
Nairac (CRO, TW)
Suduiraut (FA, BUT, BU)
1982
Coutet (ROB)
Rieussec (UN)
Suduiraut (REI)
1980
Climens (RAE, SEC, TAN, DI, RES)
Raymond-Lafon (CRO)
1979
Guiraud (VIG)
1976
Filhot (BEN)
1975
Climens (EY)
Coutet (REI)
Filhot (BEN)
Guiraud (PLA)
1971
Suduiraut (FA)
1970
Rayne-Vigneau (PLA)
Suduiraut (REI)
1966
Coutet (BU)
Sigalas-Rabaud (BU)
1960
Rieussec (REI)

£30.00 → £39.99

1990
Climens (RAE)
Lafaurie-Peyraguey (HOG, VIG)
1989
Climens (REI, RAE, HAH)
Rieussec (RAE, AD)
Suduiraut (FOR, PIP, TAN, BO)
la Tour Blanche (AD, BER)
1988
Climens (BUT, RES)
Lafaurie-Peyraguey (RES)
Rieussec (BUT, RES)
Rieussec ½ bottle (NO)
Suduiraut (BER)

1986
Coutet (ROB)
de Fargues (GOE)
Rieussec (WY, PIP)
1983
Climens (WY, REI, BUT, VIG, BEN)
Coutet (HA)
Lafaurie-Peyraguey (REI)
Raymond-Lafon (FA)
Rieussec (EY, WY, BUT, FA)
Rieussec ½ bottle (UB)
Sigalas-Rabaud (VIG)
1982
Suduiraut (ROB)
1980
Climens (UB)
1976
Doisy-Védrines (AUR)
Rayne-Vigneau (VIG)
1975
Coutet (TAN)
Doisy-Védrines (RES)
Filhot (WY)
1971
Coutet (CRO)
1964
Suduiraut (BU)
1961
Rieussec ½ bottle (VIG)
la Tour Blanche (REI)

£40.00 → £59.99
1990
Climens (BER)
1989
Climens (BER)
Rieussec (HAH)
Sigalas-Rabaud (BER)
1988
Rieussec (ELL)
1986
Rieussec (MV, BOT, WR, NO)
1985
de Fargues (BUT)
d'Yquem ½ bottle (BUT)
1983
Climens (RES, ROB)
de Fargues (WY)
Rieussec (NI, DAV, RES)
1982
Suduiraut (UB)
1979
de Fargues (REI)
1976
Climens (WY)

1975
Coutet (RES)
Filhot (ROB)
Rieussec (CRO)
1970
Suduiraut (VIG)
1966
Climens (REI)
1962
Coutet (YOU, FA)
Gilette (CRO)
1961
Coutet (YOU)
Doisy-Daëne (FA)
Doisy-Védrines (YOU)
Guiraud (BIB)

£60.00 → £89.99
1989
d'Yquem ½ bottle (OD, RES)
1988
d'Yquem (EL)
d'Yquem ½ bottle (WY, BIB)
1987
d'Yquem (REI)
1986
d'Yquem ½ bottle (WY)
1983
d'Yquem ½ bottle (BUT, WY, ELL)
1982
d'Yquem ½ bottle (WY, REI)
1981
d'Yquem ½ bottle (BER, WY)
1970
Gilette Crème de Tête (TW)
1969
d'Yquem (FA)
1968
d'Yquem (FA)
1966
Climens (WY)
1965
d'Yquem (FA)
1962
Rieussec (REI)
Sigalas-Rabaud (WY)
la Tour Blanche (CRO)
1961
Coutet (WY)
Doisy-Daëne (WY)
Rieussec (WY)
1959
Doisy-Daëne (REI)
1953
Gilette Crème de Tête (CRO)

1952
Filhot (REI)
1939
Rayne-Vigneau (WY)
1924
Coutet (WY, WY)
1923
Rayne-Vigneau (BU)
la Tour Blanche (WY)
1919
Sigalas-Rabaud (WY)

£90.00 → £119.99

1989
d'Yquem (FA, GOE)
1988
d'Yquem (WY, BUT)
1987
d'Yquem (YOU)
1982
d'Yquem ½ bottle (UB)
1981
d'Yquem (WY)
1976
d'Yquem ½ bottle (NO)
1961
Climens (WY)
1959
Coutet (BEN)
Guiraud (REI)
Rieussec (BEN)
1956
Gilette (BU)
1949
Filhot (REI)
1943
Caillou (CRO)
Rieussec (WY)
1934
Filhot (WY)
1929
Filhot (SEC)

£120.00 → £149.99

1989
d'Yquem (WY, OD, LAY)
1988
Coutet ½ bottle (BER)
d'Yquem (BIB, TAN, LAY)
1986
d'Yquem (WY, FA, BUT, GOE, TAN)
1985
d'Yquem (BUT, REI, DI)
1983
d'Yquem (BUT, WY, FA)

1982
d'Yquem (ELL)
1981
d'Yquem (BEN, BU)
1979
d'Yquem (BU)
1978
d'Yquem (REI)
1971
de Fargues (WY)
1969
d'Yquem (BU, REI)
1965
d'Yquem (SEC)
1961
Rieussec (WY)
1959
Coutet (REI)
Suduiraut (REI)
1949
la Tour Blanche (REI)
1945
Doisy-Daëne (FA)
1937
Filhot (REI)
1928
Climens (WY)
1927
Climens (WY)
1926
Rayne-Vigneau (WY)

£150.00 → £199.99

1989
d'Yquem (WS, RES)
1988
d'Yquem (RES)
1986
d'Yquem (AD, BER, EL, CB, TW)
1983
d'Yquem (HA, ROB, BER)
1982
d'Yquem (BER, ROB)
1981
d'Yquem (RES, ROB)
1980
d'Yquem (TW)
1976
d'Yquem (FA)
1975
d'Yquem (BUT)
1969
d'Yquem (BUT)
1966
d'Yquem (FA)

1960
d'Yquem (FA, REI)
1953
Climens (BEN)
1949
Climens (FA)
Suduiraut (BEN)
1941
Rayne-Vigneau (WY)
1934
Filhot (ROB)

£200.00 → £249.99

1976
d'Yquem (WY, BEN)
1957
d'Yquem (FA, YOU, SEC)
1954
d'Yquem (REI)
1949
Gilette Crème de Tête (TW)
1947
Climens (WY)
1936
Suduiraut (WY)
1934
Gilette Crème de Tête (TW)
1924
d'Yquem (FA)
1921
Filhot (WY)

£250.00 → £299.99

1976
d'Yquem (RES)
1975
d'Yquem (FA)
1971
d'Yquem (BEN)
1962
d'Yquem (FA)
1945
Suduiraut (REI)
1938
d'Yquem (WY)
1921
Coutet (CRO)

£300.00 → £399.99

1967
d'Yquem (WY)
1962
d'Yquem (ROB)
1959
d'Yquem (NO)

1956
d'Yquem (WY)
1955
d'Yquem (FA)
1950
d'Yquem (BEN)

£400.00 → £499.99

1959
d'Yquem (REI)
1955
d'Yquem (REI, ROB, BEN)
1953
d'Yquem (WY)
1949
d'Yquem (FA)
1947
d'Yquem (FA)
1919
d'Yquem (WY)
1918
d'Yquem (WY)

£550.00 → £560.00

1967
d'Yquem (BEN)
1924
d'Yquem (WY)
1918
d'Yquem (REI)

c. £635.00

1959
d'Yquem (BEN)

c. £850.00

1945
d'Yquem (FA)

c. £1,000.00

1921
d'Yquem (FA)

ROSÉ

Under £6.00

1994
de Sours Rosé (MAJ)

> **Webster's** is an annual publication. We welcome your suggestions for next year's edition.

BURGUNDY

British Burgundy lovers seek ways to beat the *franc fort*, while the growers themselves increasingly look to the moon for guidance. And the wines? They're better than ever

Burgundy is not, by its nature, a region of dramatic alterations. Land is so expensive that it rarely changes hands except when whole domaines are put up for sale. The monopole *grand cru* Clos des Lambrays in Morey-St-Denis was on the market for years, and in spring 1996 it was finally sold. For FF48m the new owner has acquired over eight hectares of prime vineyard and stock estimated at 120,000 bottles. The Saier family never made money from the Clos, but let's hope the new proprietor has more luck.

The venerable négociant house of Bouchard Père et Fils, its cellars built into the very defences of Beaune itself, was also sold, to the Champagne magnate Joseph Henriot. The takeover took place just after the wines, after years in the doldrums, were showing signs of improvement, and after immense investment in a new *cuverie* had been completed. The humiliation of the Bouchard family was complete when Henriot declassified many of the top wines. Bottles previously marketed under *grand cru* labels were demoted a level or two, and in some cases removed from sale entirely. This public assertion that the wines were frequently unworthy of their official status (and price) cost Henriot huge sums of money. But it attracted publicity (as Henriot must have calculated) and demonstrated with one blow that when it came to wine, he would not accept second best.

Another famous négociant house, Joseph Drouhin, also suffered a blow, though to its pride more than to its viability, when Snow Brand Milk Products of Tokyo purchased 51 per cent of the business. No-one could accuse Drouhin of producing poor quality wines. Possibly its problems lay in the difficulty Drouhin, like many other négociants, found in balancing the production of meticulous show-stopping wines such as Montrachet Laguiche and le Musigny, which win acclaim but make no fortunes, with the production of the workaday wines which provide the volume.

Guy Accad, the influential oenologist of a few years ago, seems to have vanished. He was a controversial figure, especially for his methods of extracting colour and fruit often, critics affirm, at the expense of Burgundian typicity. Many of his disciples have returned to more traditional ways, retaining some Accadian principles and discarding others, and emerging, like Etienne Grivot in Vosne, purified and making better wines than ever.

Bio-Burgundy

Accad may no longer be casting spells in the cellar (literally, it has been claimed), but there is a new mysticism on the loose: bio-dynamism. Its dictates baffle the more rational-minded among us, but it can be defined as a method of viticulture related to the phases of the moon, a kind of grape-growing with the aid of astrology and potions. We could afford to laugh at it were it not that some of France's most illustrious estates, such as Coulée de Serrant in the Loire and Chapoutier in the Rhône, have adopted it. In Burgundy, so has Domaine Leroy, whose owner, Lalou Bize-Leroy, produces some of the most costly wines in the region. Insofar as bio-dynamism is based on an essentially organic viticulture, I am all for it. And although its zodiacal excesses strike one as somewhat ludicrous, a thorough cask tasting of Leroy's awesome 1995s persuaded me that Mme Bize-Leroy must know what she is doing. There may be greater wines than these in Burgundy, but if so I haven't encountered them. (Of course,

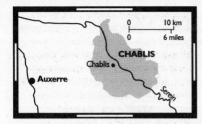

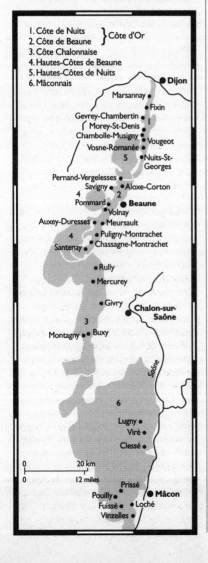

CLASSIFICATIONS

Burgundy has five different levels of classification:

Non-specific regional appellations with no geographical definition, e.g. Bourgogne, which may come from inferior land or young vines.

Specific regional appellations, e.g. Côte de Beaune-Villages, generally a blend from one or more villages. Côte de Nuits-Villages is usually better.

Village commune wines   Each village has its vineyards legally defined. Vineyards with no special reputation are usually blended together under the village name. But there is a growing move towards even relatively unknown vineyards appearing on the label. These unclassified vineyards are called *lieux-dits* or 'stated places'. They can only appear on the label in letters half the size of the village name.

Premier cru   It's typical of Burgundy that *premier cru* or 'First Growth' actually means 'Second Growth', because these are the second-best vineyard sites. Even so, they contain some of Burgundy's finest wines. They are classified by both village and vineyard names, e.g. Gevrey-Chambertin, Combe-aux-Moines. The vineyard name must follow the village name on the label, and it may be in the same size print. Confusingly, some growers use smaller print, but the appellation should make it clear whether it is a *premier cru* or a *lieu-dit*.

Grand cru   These are the real top growths. Not every village has one. The reds are mostly in the Côte de Nuits, the whites in the Côte de Beaune. A *grand cru* vineyard name can stand alone on the label without the village – for example, Chambertin from the village of Gevrey-Chambertin. (By long tradition, a Burgundy village is allowed to tack on the name of its *grand cru* vineyard, and use the compound name for wines that have nothing to do with *grand cru*, for instance Puligny-Montrachet.)

at about FF900 for a bottle of *grand cru* they need to be good.)

Most Burgundy lovers, however, will be looking not at the stars but at their bank accounts. But there is no cheery news here. The price of Burgundy has never been related to the quality of the wine. The fabulous 1990s were mostly cheaper than the 1989s, for the simple reason that much of Europe was in recession. At present prices seem stable. But a combination of the British devaluation of sterling and the *franc fort* means that, even buying at the cellar door, there is little wine of character to be found beneath £10. Fine Burgundy is rare and has always been expensive, but that is little comfort. Nevertheless, although a few producers have seen the back of their British importers, we remain the largest export market for Burgundy. Prices may well rise, but not significantly.

Ironically, the quality of wine-making has rarely been better. Visiting rising stars such as Sylvie Esmonin and Denis Mortet in Gevrey-Chambertin, Bruno Clavelier in Vosne-Romanée, and the Chandon de Briailles estate in Savigny, one is struck by their dedication to quality at every stage, from choosing a rootstock to taking the decision whether or not to filter. Their wines are superb, even in modest vintages, but the price tags are daunting.

Down with the franc

Until a devaluation of the franc, for which British winelovers pray daily, takes place, we must seek out other sources of dependable Burgundy. There's a snobbery to Burgundy. We like to have a Volnay or Gevrey-Chambertin on the table; an Auxey-Duresses or St-Aubin doesn't make the same impression. But there are excellent wines to be found in these lesser villages.

For red wines, Monthelie seems an unjustly neglected village. Decades ago its wines were sold as Pommard, even though they resemble Volnay far more; the soils lack the clay that gives Pommard its body. The Monthelie-Duhairet estate is now producing some exquisite wines from a range of vineyards here. They are extremely stylish, and not that expensive. Auxey-Duresses is quite a good source, too, though the wines are more rustic and tannic, especially the basic village wines. But *premiers crus* such as Clos de Val can be delicious, though the wines need some bottle age. Mercurey is more reliable, especially from dedicated growers like Michel Juillot, Faiveley and Yves Suremain.

Whites are more problematic. The underrated 1993s can be quite acidic, though the best wines are beginning to show tremendous class; most 1994s are decidedly flabby. It's the 1995s, very ripe, some with a touch of botrytis (like 1986), yet with good acidity, that should be worth waiting for. There's attractive white Savigny (sometimes Pinot Blanc rather than Chardonnay, but none the worse for that) from Pavelot, and delicious delicate Pernand-Vergelesses Île de Vergelesses from Chandon de Briailles.

Auxey-Duresses can be patchy, but there are reliable whites from the likes of Michel and Pascal Prunier and Jean-Pierre Diconne. More interesting are the whites from St-Aubin, where some vineyards creep towards Montrachet. Marc Colin makes some excellent wines, and so does Olivier Leflaive, at very attractive prices. These aren't wines for the long haul, but they can be delicious short-term white Burgundies.

As for Beaujolais, although its Nouveau manifestation no longer seduces British palates, the growers still manage to dispose of about 60 million bottles a year, mostly within France and to Germany, where drinkers crave anything red. In Britain, where we take wine seriously, we ought to be drinking lovely wines like the 1991 *crus*, and sticking a few 1994 and 1995 *cru* wines in our cellars for the year 2000. By and large we don't. That's because Beaujolais has exhibited symptons of split personality: simple glugging wines, often poorly made, and stylish *cru* wines, almost always overpriced.   **STEPHEN BROOK**

GRAPES & FLAVOURS

ALIGOTÉ (white) Not planted in the best sites – though there are a few vines in Corton-Charlemagne. Aligoté used to be merely sharp, spritzy café wine, but from old vines it can produce a lovely, refreshing wine, scented like buttermilk soap yet as sharp and palate-cleansing as a squeeze of lemon juice. A few producers such as *Dujac* barrique-ferment Aligoté with surprising success.

CHARDONNAY (white) In a world panting for Chardonnay, Burgundy makes the most famous Chardonnay of all. Even in the decidedly dicky Burgundian climate, it produces a fair to considerable amount of good to excellent wine almost every year. Its flavour depends on where it is grown, and how the wine is made. Chardonnays made without the use of oak barrels for aging will taste very different from barrel-aged wines. A Mâcon produced in stainless steel will have rather appley fruit as well as something slightly fat and yeasty or, in a hot year, a slightly exotic peachiness. Côte Chalonnaise Chardonnay is generally rather taut and chalky-dry, but given some oak, it can become delicately nutty. In the north of the Beaujolais region Chardonnay has a stony dryness; in the South it is nearer to the fatter, softer, wines of southern Burgundy. Chablis generally produces lean wine, but in riper years and with some oak aging it can get much rounder. The Côte d'Or is the peak of achievement for Chardonnay, and a top wine from the Côte de Beaune manages to be luscious, creamy, honeyed yet totally dry, the rich, ripe fruit entwined with the scents of new oak in a memorable and surprisingly powerful wine – from the right producer, the world's greatest dry white. It is this that has so enticed the New World wineries – and quite a few in the Old World, too, outside France – into trying to mimic Burgundian Chardonnay.

GAMAY (red) The Gamay grape produces pretty dull or tart stuff in most places. But somehow, on the granite slopes of Beaujolais, it has the ability to give one of the juiciest, most gulpable, gurgling wines the world has to offer. The Gamay has no pretensions. Ideally Beaujolais is simple, cherry-sharp, with candy-like fruit, sometimes with hints of raspberry or strawberry. The wines from the *crus* go further, but in the main their similarity from the grape is greater than the differences in the places they come from. All but the wines of the top villages should be drunk as young as you can find them, although years like 1991 and 1993 produced *cru* wines that are now drinking well. The *cru* wines from 1994 and 1995 will also repay keeping. A proportion of Gamay from nine out of the ten Beaujolais *cru* villages (not Regnié) can also be used in wines labelled 'Burgundy' or 'Bourgogne', or, if from elsewhere in Burgundy in wines labelled 'Bourgogne Passe-Tout-Grains', 'Bourgogne Grand Ordinaire' or 'Mâcon'.

PINOT BEUROT (white) Known elsewhere as Pinot Gris. Very rare in Burgundy, but it produces rich, buttery wine usually blended in to soften the Chardonnay. There is a little unblended Pinot Beurot in the Hautes-Côtes and Aloxe-Corton.

PINOT BLANC (white) There is a little of this about in the Côte d'Or – in Aloxe-Corton, for instance, where it makes a soft, rather unctuous, quick-maturing wine. Rully in the Côte Chalonnaise has a good deal and it ripens well in the Hautes-Côtes. There is also an odd white mutation of Pinot Noir – as in Nuits-St-Georges where the *premier cru* la Perrière produces a very savoury white, and in the Monts Luisants vineyard in Morey-St-Denis.

PINOT NOIR (red) The sulkiest, trickiest fine wine grape in the world is the exclusive grape in almost all red Burgundies. It needs a more delicate balance of spring, summer and autumn climate than any other variety to achieve greatness.

It used to be true to say that no other part of the world could produce a Pinot Noir to match those of Burgundy. But isolated growers in Oregon, California, New Zealand, Australia and South Africa are now making very fine examples. Even so, Burgundy is still the only place on earth where fine Pinot Noirs are made in any great quantity. The problem is, there are still some awful Pinot Noirs, too: heavy, chewy and sweet-fruited or thin and pallid. But there are fewer of these than there were. Thirty years ago much Burgundy imported into Britain was thick and soupy, because it had been doctored with heavier wines from the Midi or Algeria. This distortion has now been rectified and from a good producer Burgundian Pinot Noir should be light, elegant, intense, and perfumed with raspberry or strawberry fruit and a hint of violets. Oak will add spicier, complex notes. Except for wine from top vineyards, Burgundy can be drunk young with pleasure. But a great cru from a great vintage undoubtedly benefits from a decade or more in bottle.

WINES & WINE REGIONS

ALOXE-CORTON, AC (Côte de Beaune; red, white) The production of this village at the northern end of the Côte de Beaune is overwhelmingly red, and it has the only red *grand cru* in the Côte de Beaune, le Corton. This is also sold under various subdivisions like Corton-Bressandes, Corton Clos du Roi and so forth, and is more widely available than the other *grands crus* of Burgundy. If we're talking about village wines, then the reds of Savigny are at least as good, and you're not paying a premium there for the hyphenated Corton. Go for *Jadot, Drouhin, Jaffelin, Chandon de Briailles, Daniel Senard,* and *Tollot-Beaut.* Also good are the following: *Faiveley, Dubreuil-Fontaine, Juillot, Michel Voarick, Bouzereau-Gruère.*

The village also has one of the Côte's most famous white *grands crus,* Corton-Charlemagne. This can be a magnificent, blasting wall of flavour, not big on nuance, but strong, buttery and ripe, which traditionally is supposed to require long aging to show its full potential. Except from a handful of producers, Corton-Charlemagne rarely matches the quality of Burgundy's other white Grands Crus. Some argue that the *cru,* like Clos de Vougeot, is simply too large; others that the temptation to overproduce is not always resisted.

AUXEY-DURESSES, AC (Côte de Beaune; red, white) One of the villages behind the Côte d'Or itself, with a deservedly high reputation for full, but fairly gentle, nicely fruity reds. After a slump in the early '80s there have been excellent wines made recently by a handful of good growers, especially in the years from 1987 to 1990. Look for *Ampeau, Diconne, Alain Gras, Duc de Magenta, Leroy, Roy, Pascal Prunier* and *Thévenin.*

Too many of the whites recently have been disappointingly soft and flabby, but new confidence is evident and 1992, '90, '89 and '88 have all produced good wine. Producers like *Ampeau, Diconne, Duc de Magenta, Jadot, Leroy* and *Pascal Prunier* are still producing pretty decent stuff.

BÂTARD-MONTRACHET, AC (Côte de Beaune; white) *Grand cru* of Chassagne and Puligny lying just below le Montrachet and, from a good producer, displaying a good deal of its dramatic flavour, almost thick in the mouth, all roast nuts, butter, toast and honey. Can be exciting, if inevitably expensive. Good names: *Blain-Gagnard, Jean-Noël Gagnard, Leflaive, Bernard Morey, Pierre Morey, Michel Niellon, Pernot, Poirier, Ramonet* and *Sauzet.*

BEAUJOLAIS, AC (red) This covers all the basic wines, the produce of the flatter, southern part of Beaujolais. Most of the best is now sold as Nouveau. Run-of-the-mill Beaujolais, apart from Nouveau, is likely to be pretty thin stuff, or beefed up illegally with something altogether different. In fact, since you're allowed to re-label Nouveau as 'Beaujolais', some of the best wine in the new year (much appreciated by those who scoff at Nouveau) will be none other than re-labelled Nouveau. Best: *Blaise, Carron, Charmet, Ch. de la Plume,* co-op at *Bully, Duboeuf Bouteille Cristal, Garlon, Labruyère, Loron, Domaine des Vissoux.*

BEAUJOLAIS BLANC, AC (white) To be honest, Beaujolais Blanc is usually quite expensive and in its rather firm, stony-dry way is rarely as enjoyable as a good Mâcon-Villages. Most of the examples we see come from the North, often bordering on St-Véran in the Mâconnais, so despite being rather closed in, you expect it to blossom sometimes – but it doesn't. I'd plant Gamay instead if I were them. *Charmet* is the most interesting producer, but his vineyards are in the South. *Tête* is good.

BEAUJOLAIS ROSÉ, AC (rosé) Usually an apology for a wine, although the co-op at *Bois d'Oingt* can make good stuff. But it's usually too expensive.

BEAUJOLAIS NOUVEAU (or PRIMEUR) (red) The new vintage wine of Beaujolais, released in the same year as the grapes are gathered, at midnight on the third Thursday in November. It is usually the best of the simple wine, and will normally improve for several months in bottle, but in good Nouveau vintages like 1991 it can improve for years. I always keep a bottle or two to fool my wine-buff friends – and it always does: they're usually in the Côte de Beaune at about £12 a bottle. I'm sniggering in the kitchen.

BEAUJOLAIS SUPÉRIEUR, AC (red) *Supérieur* means that the basic alcoholic degree is higher. It doesn't ensure a better wine, and is in any case rarely even seen on the label.

BEAUJOLAIS-VILLAGES, AC (red) Thirty-nine villages can use this title. They're mostly in the north of the region, and in fact there are quite major soil differences that account for the demarcation of Beaujolais and the generally better Beaujolais-Villages. The wines are certainly better than basic Beaujolais, a little fuller and deeper, and the cherry-sharp fruit of the Gamay is usually more marked. However, always look for a wine bottled in the region, and preferably one from a single vineyard, because an anonymous blend of Beaujolais-Villages may simply mean a heftier version of an ordinary Beaujolais. And ordinary Beaujolais can be very ordinary. *Noël Aucoeur, Domaine de la Brasse, Domaine de la Chapelle de Vatre (Sarrau), Jacques Dépagneux, de Flammerécourt, Château Gaillard, Gutty Père et Fils, André Large, Château des Loges, Jean-Charles Pivot, Jean-Luc Tissier, Trichard* and *Château des Vergers* are good and local, but most domaines are bottled by one of the merchants in the region. Labelling by the domaine is on the increase.

BEAUNE, AC (Côte de Beaune; red, white) One of the few reliable commune wines, usually quite light, with a soft, 'red fruits' sweetness and a flicker of something minerally to smarten it up nicely. The wines are nearly all red. Beaune has the largest acreage of vines of any Côte d'Or commune, and they are mostly owned by merchants. It has no *grands crus* but many excellent *premiers crus*, for example Grèves, Marconnets, Teurons, Boucherottes, Vignes Franches and Cent Vignes. Prices tend to be reasonable, as Beaune is less fashionable than many other communes. Among the best producers are *Morot, Drouhin, Jadot* and *Tollot-Beaut,* but reliable wines are also made by *Lafarge, Besancenot-Mathouillet, Bouley, Germain, Jaffelin* and *Morey.*

BIENVENUES-BÂTARD-MONTRACHET, AC (Côte de Beaune; white) A tiny *grand cru* situated in Puligny below le Montrachet, and within the larger Bâtard-Montrachet AC, whose wines are similar. The Bienvenues wines, however, are often lighter and more elegant, although they may lack a tiny bit of Bâtard's drive. Best producers: *Carillon, Clerc, Leflaive, Pernot, Ramonet.*

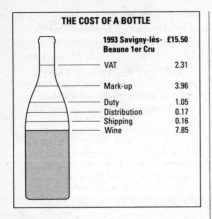

THE COST OF A BOTTLE

1993 Savigny-lès-Beaune 1er Cru	£15.50
VAT	2.31
Mark-up	3.96
Duty	1.05
Distribution	0.17
Shipping	0.16
Wine	7.85

BLAGNY, AC (Côte de Beaune; red) Tiny hamlet on the boundary between Meursault and Puligny-Montrachet. The red wine is usually a bit fierce, but then this is the white wine heartland of Burgundy, so I'm a bit surprised they grow any red at all. Best producers: *Leflaive, Matrot.*

BONNES-MARES, AC (Côte de Nuits; red) *Grand cru* of 15.54 hectares mostly in Chambolle-Musigny, with a little in Morey-St-Denis. Usually one of the most – or should I say one of the very few – reliable *grands crus*, which ages extremely well over ten to 20 years to a lovely smoky, chocolate-and-prunes richness. Best names: *Domaine des Varoilles, Drouhin, Dujac, Groffier, Jadot, Roumier, de Vogüé.*

BOURGOGNE ALIGOTÉ, AC (white) Usually rather sharp and green except for sites near Pernand-Vergelesses where old vines can make exciting wine, but the locals add crème de cassis to it to make kir – which tells you quite a lot about it. Look out for *Coche-Dury, Confuron, Devevey, Diconne, Jobard, Rion, Rollin.*

BOURGOGNE ALIGOTÉ DE BOUZERON, AC (Côte Chalonnaise; white) The white wine pride of the Côte Chalonnaise is made not from Chardonnay but from the Aligoté grape in the village of Bouzeron. The vines are frequently old – this

seems to be more crucial for Aligoté than for most other wines – and the buttermilk soap nose is followed by a very dry, slightly lemony, pepper-sharp wine, too good to mix with cassis. It got its own AC in 1979. It owes its sudden fame to the interest of the *de Villaine* family, who own a substantial estate there making the best of all Aligotés, rich and oaky. Those from *Chanzy* and *Bouchard Père et Fils* are also good.

BOURGOGNE BLANC, AC (white) This can mean almost anything – from a basic Burgundy grown in the less good spots anywhere between Chablis and the Mâconnais to a carefully matured wine from a serious producer, either from young vines or from parts of his vineyard that just miss a superior AC, especially on the borders of Meursault. Best producers: *Boisson-Vadot, Michel Bouzereau, Boyer-Martenot, Boisson-Morey, Coche-Dury, Dussort, Jadot, Javillier, Jobard, Labouré-Roi, René Manuel, Millot-Battault* and the *Buxy* co-operative (look for *Clos de Chenoves*).

BOURGOGNE GRAND ORDINAIRE, AC (red) Très Ordinaire. Pas Très Grand. Rarely seen outside Burgundy, this is the bottom of the Burgundy barrel. It may be made from Pinot Noir and Gamay, and even a couple of obscure grapes, the Tressot and César, as well.

BOURGOGNE PASSE-TOUT-GRAINS, AC (red) Often excellent value, lightish wine made usually in the Côte d'Or or the Côte Chalonnaise from Gamay blended with a minimum of one-third Pinot Noir. In some years it may well be mostly Pinot. *Rodet* and *Chanson* make it well, but as usual, the growers make it best, particularly in the less famous Côte d'Or and Hautes-Côtes villages; *Rion* in Nuits-St-Georges, *Léni-Volpato* in Chambolle-Musigny, *Henri Jayer* in Vosne-Romanée, *Thomas* in St-Aubin, *Chaley* or *Cornu* in the Hautes-Côtes, and many others like them. But even at its absolute best, true Burgundy it ain't.

BOURGOGNE ROUGE, AC (red) The basic red AC from Chablis in the North to the Beaujolais *crus* in the South. Unknown Bourgogne Rouge is best avoided – much of it is very basic indeed. Most Bourgogne Rouge is made exclusively from Pinot Noir, but Gamay can be used in the Beaujolais (if declassified from one of nine of the ten *crus*), and the César and Tressot are permitted in the Yonne around Chablis. Domaine-bottled Bourgogne Rouge from good growers – and a handful of merchants – can be excellent value. The best wines come from those vineyards that are situated just outside the village appellations. Look for *Bourgeon, Coche-Dury, Germain, d'Heuilly-Huberdeau, Henri Jayer, Juillot, Lafarge, Mortet, Parent, Pousse d'Or, Rion* and *Rossignol*. Good merchants include *Drouhin, Faiveley, Jadot, Jaffelin, Labouré-Roi, Latour, Olivier Leflaive, Leroy, Rodet, Vallet*. The co-ops at *Buxy* and *Igé* are also good as is the *Caves des Hautes-Côtes*. Some 1988s, '90s and '93s can be aged a bit longer, but wines from '89, '91, '92 and '94 should all be drunk soon.

BROUILLY, AC (Beaujolais; red) Southernmost and largest of the Beaujolais crus, Brouilly has the flattest of the *cru* vineyards, and usually makes one of the lightest *cru* wines. There is some variation in style between the more northerly villages of Beaujolais and those in the South where granite produces a deeper, fuller wine, but in general Brouilly rarely improves much with keeping. In fact, it makes a very good Nouveau. A few properties make a bigger wine to age – but even then, nine months to a year is quite enough. Good names include *Château de la Chaize, Domaine Crêt des Garanches, Château de Fouilloux, Hospices de Belleville, Château de Pierreux, Domaine de Combillaty (Duboeuf), Domaine de Garanches, André Large* and *Château de Nevers*. *Château des Tours*, although lovely young, can age longer.

CHABLIS, AC (white) Simple Chablis, mostly soft, sometimes acidic, covers the widest area of the appellation. Well it would,

CHABLIS VINEYARDS

Grands Crus
Blanchots, Bougros, les Clos, Grenouilles, Preuses, Valmur, Vaudésir. la Moutonne, considered a Grand Cru, is from a parcel in Preuses and Vaudésir.

Premiers Crus
Fourchaume (including Fourchaume, Vaupulent, Côte de Fontenay, Vaulorent, l'Homme Mort); Montée de Tonnerre (including Montée de Tonnerre, Chapelot, Pied d'Aloup); Monts de Milieu; Vaucoupin; les Fourneaux (including les Fourneaux, Morein, Côte des Prés-Girots); Beauroy (including Beauroy, Troesmes); Côte de Léchet; Vaillons (including Vaillons, Châtains, Séché, Beugnons, les Lys); Mélinots (including Mélinots, Roncières, les Epinottes); Montmains (including Montmains, Forêts, Butteaux); Vosgros (including Vosgros and Vaugiraut); Vaudevey.

wouldn't it? They've included most of what used to be Petit Chablis for a start. But at the rate they're now extending the *premier cru* status to virtually anything that grows, maybe *premiers crus* will soon overtake Chablis in acreage. Chablis covers a multitude of sins, with a lot of wine going under négociants' labels, and a lot being sold by the co-op – they make most of the négociants' stuff too. Some of the co-op's best *cuvées* are outstandingly good, but many of the cheaper *cuvées* are too bland and soft. New oak, which is lavishly used by growers such as Fèvre and Droin, often smothers the steely and minerally qualities that make top Chablis such an exciting wine. Expect high prices this year. Good producers: *Adhémar-Boudin, Christian Adine, Jean-Claude, Pascal Bouchard, Jean-Marc Brocard, la Chablisienne co-op, Jean Collet, René Dauvissat, Defaix, Jean-Paul Droin, Joseph Drouhin, William Fèvre, Alain Geoffroy, Jean-Pierre Grossot, Michel Laroche, Bernard Légland, Long Depaquit, Louis Michel, Dom. des Milandes, Moreau, Guy Mothe, Raveneau, Regnard, Savary, Simmonet-Fèbvre, Robert Vocoret*.

CHABLIS GRAND CRU, AC (white)
The seven *grands crus* (Blanchots, Preuses, Bougros, Grenouilles, Valmur, Vaudésir and les Clos) come from a small patch of land just outside the town of Chablis, on a single slope rising from the banks of the river Serein. The wines *can* be outstanding, though still unlikely to rival the *grands crus* of the Côte de Beaune. To get the best out of them, you need to age them, preferably after oaking, although *Louis Michel*'s oak-free wines age superbly. Recent vintages have seen a growing use of oak by producers, sometimes giving deeper, richer wines which will benefit from bottle-aging, but some wines are marred by clumsy or excessive use of new oak.

CHABLIS PREMIER CRU, AC (white)
There are some 30 names in this category, but they have been rationalized into 12 main vineyards. Once upon a time, this used to be a very reliable classification for good, characterful dry white, if less intense than *grand cru*, but again, there has been this expansion mania, meaning that many hardly suitable pieces of vineyard are now accorded *premier cru* status. Given that there is a price difference of £3 to £4 a bottle between Chablis and Premier Cru Chablis, the quality difference should be plain as a pikestaff. Sadly it rarely is. However, in the 1990s there has been a definite move towards quality by the better growers and *la Chablisienne* co-op.

CHAMBERTIN, AC (Côte de Nuits; red)
Most famous of the eight *grands crus* of Gevrey-Chambertin, this 13-hectare vineyard should make wines that are big, strong and intense in their youth, mellowing to a complex, perfumed, plummy richness as they mature. Good ones (those that match the description, in other words) need ten to 15 years' aging. Best producers: *Drouhin, Faiveley, Leroy, Denis Mortet, Ponsot, Rebourseau, Rousseau, Tortochot.*

CHAMBERTIN CLOS-DE-BÈZE, AC
(Côte de Nuits; red) *Grand cru* in the village of Gevrey-Chambertin next to Chambertin both geographically and in quality. Like Chambertin,

it benefits from seven to ten years in bottle. The wines may also be sold as Chambertin. Best names: *Drouhin, Bruno Clair, Faiveley, Gelin, Mugneret-Gibourg, Rousseau, Thomas-Moillard* and *Damoy* from 1992.

CHAMBOLLE-MUSIGNY, AC (Côte de Nuits; red) This village near the south of the Côte de Nuits can make light, cherry-sweet, intensely perfumed, 'beautiful' Burgundy, but sadly most commercial Chambolle will be too sweet and gooey to retain much perfume. The best producer is *Georges Roumier*, with wonderful wines in every vintage from 1985. The best *premier cru* is les Amoureuses, which deserves to be *grand cru* and is priced accordingly. Best producers: *Barthod-Noëllat, Château de Chambolle-Musigny, Drouhin, Dujac, Groffier, Hudelot-Noëllat, Rion, Serveau* and *de Vogüé.*

CHAPELLE-CHAMBERTIN, AC (Côte de Nuits; red) Small *grand cru* vineyard (5.4 hectares) just south of the Clos-de-Bèze in Gevrey-Chambertin. They are typically lighter and more delicate than the other *grands crus*. But over-lightness – resulting from over-production – is their curse. The best producers are *Damoy* (since 1993), *Louis Jadot* and *Rossignol-Trapet.*

CHARMES-CHAMBERTIN, AC (Côte de Nuits; red) At 31.6 hectares, this is the biggest of the *grands crus* of Gevrey-Chambertin. It can be fine, strong, sensuous wine, but as with all the Gevrey-Chambertin *grands crus*, it can also be disgracefully light. Best producers: *Bachelet, Charlopin-Parisot, Drouhin, Dugat, Dujac, Rebourseau, Roty, Rousseau, Tortochot.*

CHASSAGNE-MONTRACHET, AC
(Côte de Beaune; red, white) About half the wine Chassagne-Montrachet produces is red, even though its fame lies in its large share of the white *grand cru* vineyard of le Montrachet. The reds are a puzzle. At their best they're good value, if a bit heavy, plummy and earthy. The best names for red are *Amiot-Bonfils,*

Carillon, Colin, Jean-Noël Gagnard, Duc de Magenta, Gagnard-Delagrange, René Lamy, Albert Morey, Moreau, Jean Pillot, Ramonet. Of the whites, the *grands crus* are excellent, but the *premiers crus* rarely dazzle quite like those of nearby Puligny-Montrachet. The Chassagne '86s are mostly at their best now, and should be drunk; the '89s are wonderfully ripe and concentrated and can be drunk now or kept for years. The '90s and '92s will be magic. Best producers of white in Chassagne include: *Blain-Gagnard, Carillon, Colin, Duc de Magenta, Fontaine-Gagnard, Jean-Noël Gagnard, Gagnard-Delagrange, Lamy-Pillot, Laguiche, Château de la Maltroye, Moreau, Albert Morey, Bernard Morey, Niellon, Fernand Pillot* and *Ramonet. Jaffelin* is the best merchant in the commune.

CHÉNAS, AC (Beaujolais; red) This second-smallest Beaujolais *cru* makes strong, dark wines, sometimes a bit tough, that can be drunk a year after the harvest, or aged to take on a Pinot Noir-like flavour. Chénas is exceedingly fashionable in France. Look out for the wines of *Louis Champagnon, Charvet, Château de Chénas, Domaines des Brureaux, Domaine Chassignon, Domaine de la Combe Remont (Duboeuf), Pierre Perrachon* and *Émile Robin.*

CHEVALIER-MONTRACHET, AC (Côte de Beaune; white) A *grand cru* vineyard of the village of Puligny, situated directly above the ultra-famous le Montrachet. The higher elevation of Chevalier-Montrachet gives a leaner wine, but one with a deep flavour as rich and satisfying as a dry white wine can get. Good examples will last for 20 years. Best: *Bouchard Père et Fils, Clerc, Jadot, Latour, Leflaive, Niellon.*

CHIROUBLES, AC (Beaujolais; red) Another *cru* for early drinking, grown on hillsides towards the south of the Beaujolais *crus.* The wines are naturally light, similar to Beaujolais-Villages in weight, but with a cherry scent that makes this France's favourite Beaujolais *cru.* Good names include *Georges Boulon, René Brouillard, Cheysson, Château*

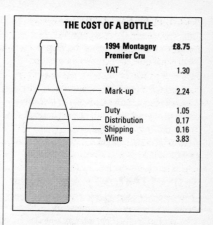

THE COST OF A BOTTLE

	1994 Montagny Premier Cru	£8.75
VAT		1.30
Mark-up		2.24
Duty		1.05
Distribution		0.17
Shipping		0.16
Wine		3.83

Javernand, Château de Raousset, Jean-Pierre Desvignes, Duboeuf, Méziat and *Georges Passot.*

CHOREY-LÈS-BEAUNE, AC (Côte de Beaune; red) This is a good lesser commune near Beaune, producing good value soft, fruity reds. Because the village isn't popular or hyped, these are some of the few affordable wines Burgundy can offer in top vintages such as 1988, '89 and '90. *Drouhin, Germain* and *Tollot-Beaut* are the best producers.

CLOS DES LAMBRAYS, AC (Côte de Nuits; red) A *grand cru* only since 1981, this nine-hectare vineyard in Morey-St-Denis belongs to a single owner, and has recently been sold. In the 1970s the estate became very run down and the wines were not only very rare but also not very tasty. The Clos has ample potential, but as yet it has not been realised, and the wines, while sound, are not of *grand cru* quality.

CLOS DE LA ROCHE, AC (Côte de Nuits; red) Largest and finest *grand cru* of Morey-St-Denis, on the border with Gevrey-Chambertin. When not made too lightweight, this can be splendid wine, full of redcurrant-and-strawberry richness when young, but coming to resemble pretty good Chambertin after ten years or so. Best names: *Amiot, Dujac, Leroy,* both *Hubert* and *Georges Lignier, Ponsot, Rousseau.*

CLOS ST-DENIS, AC (Côte de Nuits; red) The village of Morey-St-Denis gets its name from this *grand cru* but the villagers probably should have chosen another one – like the much better known Clos de la Roche – because this small 6.5-hectare vineyard has rarely achieved great heights and is probably the least famous of all the *grands crus*. Dujac's is the best known, but look out too for *Charlopin-Parisot, Georges* or *Hubert Lignier*, and *Ponsot*.

CLOS DE TART, AC (Côte de Nuits; red) *Grand cru* of Morey-St-Denis owned by Beaujolais merchants *Mommessin*. At its best Clos de Tart is a light but intense wine which lasts a surprisingly long time.

CLOS DE VOUGEOT, AC (Côte de Nuits; red) This 50-hectare vineyard dominates the village of Vougeot. Over 80 growers share the enclosure and, while the land at the top is very fine, the land by the road is not. That rare thing, a good bottle of Clos de Vougeot, is fat, rich, strong and thick with the sweetness of perfumed plums and honey, unsubtle but exciting. It is only found in top vintages, like 1988 and '90, and then only from the best producers. Best names: *Arnoux, Ch. de la Tour, Jacky Confuron, Drouhin-Laroze, Engel, Grivot, Gros, Hudelot-Noëllat, Jadot, Lamarche, Leroy, Meo-Camuzet, Mugneret, Raphet.*

CORTON, AC (Côte de Beaune; red, white) This is the only red *grand cru* vineyard in the Côte de Beaune, situated on the upper slopes of the famous dome-shaped hill of Corton. The Corton *grand cru* vineyards do grow a little Chardonnay and Pinot Blanc, but this does not have the *grand cru*. The finest white is the *Hospices de Beaune*'s Corton-Vergennes, and *Chandon de Briailles* makes Corton-Bressandes that is half Pinot Blanc. Ideally, red Corton should have something of the richness and strength of Clos de Vougeot, but it tends to be four-square and unrewarding until it is mature, and then only the top wines are good. Best producers include: *Chandon de Briailles, Dubreuil-Fontaine,* *Faiveley, Gaunoux, Laleur-Piot, Maldant, Prince de Mérode, Rapet, Daniel Senard, Tollot-Beaut.*

CORTON-CHARLEMAGNE, AC (Côte de Beaune; white) This famous *grand cru* of Aloxe-Corton and Pernand-Vergelesses occupies the upper half of the dome-shaped hill of Corton. It is planted almost entirely with Chardonnay, but a little Pinot Blanc or Pinot Beurot can add intriguing fatness to the wine. Good names: *Bitouzet, Bonneau du Martray, Chandon de Briailles, Chapuis, Dubreuil-Fontaine, M Juillot, Hospices de Beaune, Jadot, Laleure-Piot, Latour, Rapet.*

CÔTE CHALONNAISE, AC (red, white) As the ordered vines of the Côte de Beaune swing away and dwindle to the west, the higgledy-piggledy vineyards of the Côte Chalonnaise hiccup and splutter into life as a patchwork of south- and east-facing outcrops. Light, usually clean-tasting Chardonnay predominates among the whites – although at long last the idea of oak-aging is catching on. But the Côte Chalonnaise has one star that cannot be overshadowed by the famous Côte d'Or: the village of Bouzeron makes the finest and the most famous Aligoté in all France. The top three villages of Rully, Mercurey and Givry all produce good reds, too, with a lovely, simple strawberry-and-cherry fruit.

CÔTE DE BEAUNE (red, white) The southern part of the Côte d'Or, fairly evenly divided between red and white wines. The tiny AC Côte de Beaune can produce light but tasty reds in warm years. Best producers: *Bouchard Père et Fils, René Manuel, J Allexant.*

CÔTE DE BEAUNE-VILLAGES, AC (red) Catch-all red wine appellation for 16 villages on the Côte de Beaune. Only Aloxe-Corton, Beaune, Volnay and Pommard cannot use the appellation. Rarely seen nowadays and rarely exciting, it used to be the source of much excellent soft red, as many lesser-known but good villages would blend their wines together. Still, it *is* worth checking out the wines of *Jaffelin, Lequin-Roussot* and *Bachelet.*

CÔTE DE BROUILLY, AC (red) The
Mont de Brouilly, a pyramid-shaped hill in the
middle of the *cru* of Brouilly, makes quite
different wine to Brouilly itself. The soil is of
volcanic origin, and the slopes lap up the sun.
Best: *Château Thivin, Conroy, Domaine de la
Pierre Bleue, Jean Sanvers, Lucien Verger,
Chanrion.*

CÔTE DE NUITS (red, white) The
northern part of the Côte d'Or, theoretically
producing the biggest wines. Frequently it
doesn't and many of Burgundy's most
disappointing bottles come from the top Côte
de Nuits communes. It is almost entirely
devoted to Pinot Noir.

CÔTE DE NUITS-VILLAGES, AC (red)
Covers the three southernmost villages of
Prissey, Comblanchien and Corgoloin, plus
Fixin and Brochon in the North. Usually fairly
light and dry, they can have good cherry fruit
and the delicious vegetal decay flavour of good
Côte de Nuits red. Often good value. Look
out for *Durand, Rion, Rossignol* and *Tollot-
Voarick*, and especially *Chopin-Groffier* and
Domaine de l'Arlot.

CÔTE D'OR (red, white) The source of
Burgundy's fame – a thin sliver of land worth
its weight in gold. It's only 30 miles long, and
often less than a mile wide, and it runs from
Dijon to Chagny. It has two halves, the Côte
de Nuits in the North and the Côte de
Beaune in the South. There is a fine crop of
illustrious whites in the southern portion.

CRÉMANT DE BOURGOGNE, AC
(white, rosé) Excellent, eminently affordable
sparkling wine, made by the Champagne
method, from the same grapes they grow in
Champagne: Chardonnay and Pinot Noir.
Caves de Lugny and *Caves de Bailly* are the two
we see most often. The first is better for
white, the second for lovely fresh,
strawberryish pink.

**CRIOTS-BÂTARD-MONTRACHET,
AC** (Côte de Beaune; white) Tiny 1.6 hectare
grand cru in the village of Chassagne-
Montrachet nuzzled up against the edge of
Bâtard-Montrachet itself. In fact it's hardly ever
seen; the wines resemble Bâtard in power and
concentration but are leaner and more
minerally in style. Best producers: *Blain-
Gagnard, Fontaine-Gagnard.*

CRU The ten Beaujolais *crus* or growths
(Fleurie, Moulin-à-Vent, Brouilly, Chénas, Côte
de Brouilly, Chiroubles, Juliénas, St-Amour,
Morgon, Regnié) are the top villages in the
steeply hilly, northern part of Beaujolais. All
should have definable characteristics, but the
produce of different vineyards and growers is
all too often blended to a mean by merchants
elsewhere. Always buy either a single-estate
wine, or one from a good local merchant like
*Chanut Frères, Duboeuf, Dépagneux, Ferraud,
Loron, Sarrau, Thomas la Chevalière, Louis Tête,*
and *Trenel.*
    Elsewhere in Burgundy the best vineyards
are labelled *grand cru*, and the second-best
premier cru.

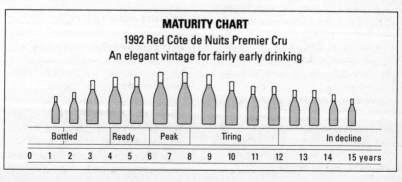

MATURITY CHART
1992 Red Côte de Nuits Premier Cru
An elegant vintage for fairly early drinking

Bottled	Ready	Peak	Tiring		In decline

0   1   2   3   4   5   6   7   8   9   10   11   12   13   14   15 years

ÉCHÉZEAUX, AC (Côte de Nuits; red)
This is a large, slightly second-line *grand cru* vineyard in the village of Vosne-Romanée. Best producers: *Domaine de la Romanée-Conti, Engel, Faiveley, Forey, Louis Gouroux, Grivot, Henri Jayer, Mongeard-Mugneret, Mugneret-Gibourg*.

EPINEUIL, AC (red) Tiny region near Tonnerre, right in the north of Burgundy, producing light but fragrant styles of Pinot Noir.

FIXIN, AC (Côte de Nuits; red) A suburb of Dijon, Fixin can make some of Burgundy's sturdiest reds: deep, strong, tough but plummy when young, but capable of mellowing with age. Such wines are slowly reappearing. If you want to feel you're drinking Gevrey-Chambertin without shouldering the cost, Fixin from the following producers could fit the bill: *Bordet, Charlopin-Parizot, Bruno Clair, Fougeray, Roger Fournier, Gelin, Guyard, Joliet, Jadot, Moillard, Philippe Rossignol*.

FLAGEY-ÉCHÉZEAUX, AC (Côte de Nuits; red) A commune that sells its basic wines as Vosne-Romanée but, in Échézeaux and Grands-Échézeaux, has two *grands crus*.

FLEURIE, AC (Beaujolais; red) Often the most delicious of the *crus*, gentle and round, its sweet cherry-and-chocolate fruit just held firm by a touch of tannin and acid. Its deserved popularity in Britain and the US has led to high prices, so Fleurie is no bargain. Try *Château de Fleurie (Loron), Chauvet, Chignard, Colonge, Domaine de la Grand, Grand Pré (Sarrau), Domaine de la Presle, Domaine des Quatre Vents, Duboeuf's la Madone, Bernard Paul, Verpoix*, the Fleurie co-op's *cuvées, Cuvée Presidente Marguerite* and *Cuvée Cardinale*.

GEVREY-CHAMBERTIN, AC (Côte de Nuits; red) The start of the big time for reds. Gevrey-Chambertin has eight *grands crus*, and two of them, Chambertin and Chambertin Clos-de-Bèze can be some of the world's greatest wines. They should have rough, plumskins and damson strength, fierce when young, but assuming a brilliant, wafting perfume and intense, plummy richness when mature. Many of the best wines are made by young growers who do not own as much land in the top vineyards as the larger, old-established estates, but whose commitment to quality shines through. *Bachelet, Boillot, Burguet, Dugat, Michel Esmonin, Philippe Leclerc, Mortet, Naddef* and *Rossignol-Trapet* are the names to look out for. Of the old estates, *Rousseau* is best but *Domaine des Varoilles* is also good. Also look out for *Frédéric Esmonin, René Leclerc, Maume* and *Roty*, and for the merchants' bottlings from *Drouhin, Jadot, Faiveley* and *Jaffelin*. But there are still some overpriced horrors bearing the sacred name.

GIVRY, AC (Côte Chalonnaise; red) Small but important red wine village. At their best, the wines are deliciously warm and cherry-chewy with a slightly smoky fragrance to them, but there are too many mediocre bottles around, especially from négociants. *Baron Thénard* is the best estate, but *Chofflet, Clos Salomon, Joblot, Laborbe, Lespinasse, Mouton* and *Ragot* are also worth investigating.

LA GRANDE RUE, AC (Côte de Nuits; red) This vineyard is wholly owned by the Lamarche family. Elevated to *grand cru* status in 1990, more because of its potential – it is situated between la Tâche and la Romanée-Conti, the two greatest vineyards in Burgundy – than because of the wines it has recently produced.

GRANDS-ÉCHÉZEAUX, AC (Côte de Nuits; red) A *grand cru* capable of delicately scented, plum-and-wood-smoke flavoured wine which will go rich and chocolaty with age. Best names: *Domaine de la Romanée-Conti, Drouhin, Engel, Mongeard-Mugneret*.

GRIOTTE-CHAMBERTIN, AC (Côte de Nuits; red) One of the smallest *grands crus* of Gevrey-Chambertin at just 5.58 hectares. Best producers: *Drouhin, Claude Dugat, F Esmonin, Ponsot, Roty*.

HAUTES-CÔTES DE BEAUNE and HAUTES-CÔTES DE NUITS (red,

white) A happy hunting ground, this hilly backwater behind the line of famous villages and vineyards on the Côte d'Or. The 28 Hautes-Côtes villages make fairly good, light, strawberry-like Pinot and a lot of reasonably good, light, dry Chardonnay at a decent price. The red grapes do not always ripen fully every year, but they had no problems in 1988, '89 or '90. Look out for the red Hautes-Côtes de Nuits wines of Cornu, Domaine des Mouchottes, Jayer-Gilles, Thévenet and Verdet and the red Hautes-Côtes de Beaunes of Bouley, Capron Manieux, Chalet, Guillemard, Joliot, Mazilly and Plait. The Caves des Hautes-Côtes is beginning to produce some of the best value wines in the whole of Burgundy. Good whites come from Chaley, Cornu, Devevey, Goubard, Jayer-Gilles, Thevenot-Lebrun, Alain Verdet (organic).

IRANCY, AC (red) Mostly Pinot Noir from

vineyards just to the south-west of Chablis, sometimes with a little of the darker, tougher local grape, the César. Rarely deep in colour, but always perfumed, slightly plummy and attractive. Cool years can provide disappointingly thin wines. Best drunk while young and fresh. It must legally be labelled 'Bourgogne Irancy'. Good producers: Léon & Serge Bienvenu, Bernard Cantin, André & Roger Delaloge, Gabriel Delaloge, Jean Renaud, Simmonet-Febvre.

JULIÉNAS, AC (Beaujolais; red) Juliénas can

be big wine, with tannin and acidity, but many of the best more closely resemble the mixture of fresh red fruit and soft, chocolaty warmth that makes for good Fleurie. Good ones include Château du Bois de la Salle, Domaine des Bucherats, Château des Capitans, Château de Juliénas, Domaine de la Dîme, René Monnet and Domaine de la Vieille Église. Also good: Pelletier and Duboeuf.

LADOIX-SERRIGNY, AC (Côte de

Beaune; red) An obscure village, overshadowed by the far more famous village of Aloxe-Corton next door. It's worth looking out for though, as Capitain, Cornu, Prince de Mérode, Chevalier and Ravaut all make decent, crisp wines at very fair prices.

LATRICIÈRES-CHAMBERTIN, AC

(Côte de Nuits; red) Small grand cru vineyard in Gevrey-Chambertin and very similar in style to Chambertin though without the power. So long as the producer hasn't pushed the yields too high, it is at its best at ten to 15 years. Best producers: Ponsot, Leroy, Rossignol-Trapet.

MÂCON BLANC, AC (Mâconnais; white)

It seemed, some years ago, that the spiralling price of Pouilly-Fuissé, the region's only white star, was spurring the producers to improve quality. As Pouilly-Fuissé came spinning back to earth – a wiser but better, and cheaper, wine – upping the price of Mâcon seemed to have been the only effect. Now prices are back down again, and quality has yet to improve. Most Mâcon simply cannot compete with the best-value New World wines.

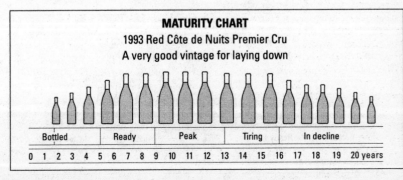

MATURITY CHART
1993 Red Côte de Nuits Premier Cru
A very good vintage for laying down

Bottled	Ready	Peak	Tiring	In decline

0 1 2 3 4 5 6 7 8 9 10 11 12 13 14 15 16 17 18 19 20 years

MÂCON BLANC-VILLAGES, AC

(Mâconnais; white) One step up from basic Mâcon Blanc, this must come from the 43 Mâcon communes with the best land. The rare good ones show the signs of honey and fresh apples and some of the nutty, yeasty depth associated with fine Chardonnay. These come from those villages, notably Viré, Clessé, Prissé and Lugny, that add their own village names (Mâcon-Viré, etc). Full, buttery yet fresh, sometimes spicy: look for that and, if you find it, don't mind too much about the price. There is a handful of growers making serious, oak-aged wine from low-yielding vines. *Merlin* and *Guffens Heynen* are names to look for, plus the unique wines of *Jean Thevenet*. Other good ones include: *Bicheron, Bonhomme, Danauchet, Goyard, Guillemot-Michel, Josserand, Lassarat, Manciat-Poncet, Signoret, Talmard* and *Thévenet-Wicart*.

MÂCON ROUGE, AC (Mâconnais; red)

There's a lot of red wine made in the Mâconnais but it's usually fairly lean, earthy Gamay without the spark of Beaujolais' fruit. If you like that sort of thing, try the wines of Igé and Mancey, or *Lafarge*'s wine from Bray. *Lassarat* is improving things by using new oak, and I'm sure more will follow.

MARANGES, AC (Côte de Beaune; red)

An AC created in 1989 to cover Dezize, Sampigny and Cheilly, each hyphenated with Maranges, the best vineyard, straddling all three villages. Previously the wines were usually sold as Côte de Beaune-Villages but now these sturdy, rustic reds are coming into their own. *Drouhin*'s is good.

MARSANNAY, AC (Côte de Nuits; red, rosé)

Used to produce mostly rosé under the name Bourgogne Rosé de Marsannay, but the introduction of an appellation for reds in 1987 has encouraged growers to switch. The first results of this new seriousness are most encouraging and some lovely wines are already emerging, usually quite dry and cherry-perfumed, sometimes more full-blown and exciting. One to watch. Best: *Bouvier, Charlopin-Parizot, Roty, Bruno Clair, Collotte, Fougeray, Fournier, Geantet-Pansiot, Huguenot, Jadot, Naddef*.

MAZIS-CHAMBERTIN, AC (Côte de Nuits; red)

12.5-hectare *grand cru* in Gevrey-Chambertin, far more reliable than most of the neighbouring *grands crus*. Mazis can have a superb deep blackberry-pip, damson-skin and blackcurrant fruit which gets more exciting after six to 12 years. Best: *Faiveley, Gelin, Hospices de Beaune, Maume, Rebourseau, Roty, Rousseau, Tortochot*.

MAZOYÈRES-CHAMBERTIN, AC

(Côte de Nuits; red) *Grand cru* of Gevrey-Chambertin, rarely seen since producers generally take up the option of using the *grand cru* Charmes-Chambertin instead. *Perrot-Minot* produces a fine example.

MERCUREY, AC (Côte Chalonnaise; red, white)

The biggest Chalonnais village,

MATURITY CHART
1993 White Côte de Beaune Premier Cru
Good fruit, but not a vintage for long aging

Bottled	Ready	Peak	Tiring	In decline

0   1   2   3   4   5   6   7   8   9   10   11   12 years

producing half the region's wines. Indeed many call the Côte Chalonnaise the 'Région de Mercurey'. It's mostly red wines, and they are often fairly full, with attractive strawberry fruit and a little smoky fragrance. As with the other Chalonnais reds, Mercurey's problems are infuriating inconsistency of quality, allied to callous exploitation of the name by some négociants. *Faiveley* and *Juillot* make a fine range of red Mercureys, but look out also for *Ch. de Chamirey, Chandesais, Chanzy, Domaine la Marche, Dufouleur, Jacqueson, de Launay, Meix-Foulot, Monette, Saier* and *de Suremain*. Whites have been improving, as rising prices in the Côte de Beaune have spurred producers to greater efforts. Good examples come from *Château de Chamirey, Faiveley, M Juillot, Protheau, Rodet.*

MEURSAULT, AC (Côte de Beaune; white) Situated halfway down the Côte de Beaune, this village is the first, working southwards, of the great white wine villages. It has by far the largest white production of any commune in the Côte d'Or, and this is one of several reasons why its traditionally high overall standard is gradually being eroded. The wines should be big and nutty and have a delicious, gentle lusciousness, and sometimes even peachy, honeyed flavours. But there are too many bland, flabby wines that don't come even close to what Meursault should be. Meursault has more producers bottling their own wine than any other village. These are some of the best: *Ampeau, Pierre Boillot, Boisson-Vadot, Boyer-Martenot, Michel Bouzereau, Buisson-Battault, Coche-Debord, Coche-Dury, Comtes Lafon, Fichet, Gauffroy, Henry Germain, Jean Germain, Grivault, Patrick Javillier, François Jobard, René Manuel, Matrot, Michelot-Buisson, Millot-Battault, Pierre Morey, Prieur, Roulot.*

MONTAGNY, AC (Côte Chalonnaise; white) A white-only AC in the south of the Côte Chalonnaise. In general the wines are a bit lean and chalky-dry, but now that the use of new oak barrels for aging the wine is creeping in, some much more interesting wines are appearing. Best: *Arnoux*, co-op at *Buxy, Latour, B Michel, de Montorge, Alain Roy, Vachet.* Best merchants: *Olivier Leflaive* and *Rodet.*

MONTHELIE, AC (Côte de Beaune; red) Monthelie shares borders with Volnay and Meursault, but shares the fame of neither village. It's a red wine-only village, and the wines deserve recognition, because they're full, dry, rather herby or piney, but with a satisfying rough fruit. They're often a good buy but beware the insidious growth of négociants' labels from firms who traditionally never noticed the AC. Best producers: *Boussey, Caves des Hautes-Côtes, Deschamps, Doreau, Garaudet, Château de Monthelie, Monthelie-Douhairet, Potinet-Ampeau, de Suremain, Thévenin-Monthelie.*

LE MONTRACHET, AC (Côte de Beaune; white) This is white Burgundy at its absolute greatest, the finest of fine white *grands crus* in the villages of Puligny and Chassagne. Does it mean most enjoyable, most happy-making? Not really. In fact the flavours can be so intense it's difficult sometimes to know if you're having fun drinking it or merely giving your wine vocabulary an end of term examination. So be brave if someone opens a bottle of Montrachet for you and let the incredible blend of spice and smoke, honey and ripeness flow over your senses and your palate. Good producers of le Montrachet include the following: *Amiot-Bonfils Père et Fils, Domaine de la Romanée-Conti, Jadot, Comtes Lafon, Drouhin Laguiche, Pierre Morey, Prieur, Thénard* and, since 1991, *Leflaive.*

MOREY-ST-DENIS, AC (Côte de Nuits; red) Once obscure and good value, the wines of Morey-St-Denis are now expensive and often suffer from overproduction. At their best they blend the perfume of Chambolle-

The price guides for this section begin on page 124.

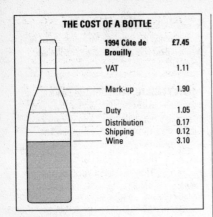

THE COST OF A BOTTLE

1994 Côte de Brouilly	£7.45
VAT	1.11
Mark-up	1.90
Duty	1.05
Distribution	0.17
Shipping	0.12
Wine	3.10

Musigny with the body of Gevrey-Chambertin, and exhibit a slight savouriness that mellows into a rich chocolaty mouthful. Many are too light to be successful, but you'll find sound and sometimes exciting bottles from *Pierre Amiot, Bryczek, Dujac, Georges* and *Hubert Lignier, Marchand, Ponsot, Serveau, Charloppin, Perrot-Minot* and *Vadey-Castagnier.*

MORGON, AC (Beaujolais; red) The wines of this *cru* can be glorious. They can start thick and dark, and age to a chocolaty, plummy depth with an amazing cherries smell. A sort of reserve category called Morgon Age has to be kept for at least 18 months before release. *Jacky Janodet's* Morgon is intense. Look also for *Aucoeur, Château de Pizay, Château de Raousset, Descombes, Desvignes, Domaine de la Chanaise, Domaine Roche-St-Jean, Domaine de Ruyère, Drouhin, Gobet, Lapierre, Félix Longepierre* and *Georges Vincent.*

MOULIN-À-VENT, AC (Beaujolais; red) Enter the heavy brigade. These *cru* wines should be solid, and should age for three to five years and more from years like 1991. The best of them have a big, plummy, Burgundian style, and their toughness doesn't give you much option but to wait for them to mellow. At the opposite end of the spectrum to straight Beaujolais, this is one of the few *crus* that can respond well to discreet oak aging. *Louis Champagnon's* is good, as is *Brugne,*

Charvet, Duboeuf, Château des Jacques, Château du Moulin-à-Vent, Château Portier, Domaine de la Tour de Bief, Jacky Janodet, Raymond Siffert and *Héritiers Maillard* (formerly *Héritiers Tagent*).

MUSIGNY, AC (Côte de Nuits; red, white) Extremely fine *grand cru* which gave its name to Chambolle-Musigny. All but a third of a hectare of the 10.65-hectare vineyard is planted to the red Pinot Noir, capable of producing Burgundy's most heavenly scented wine, and there have been some great recent offerings: 1989 and 1993 from *Château de Chambolle-Musigny*, all vintages since 1990 from *de Vogüé* (which also makes white) as well as tiny amounts from *Roumier*. Best names include: *Château de Chambolle-Musigny, Jadot, Leroy, Jacques Prieur, Georges Roumier, de Vogüé.*

NUITS-ST-GEORGES, AC (Côte de Nuits; red) When it's good, this has an enthralling decayed – rotting even – brown richness of chocolate and prunes rising out of a fairly light, plum-sweet fruit – quite gorgeous, whatever it sounds like. It used to be one of the most abused of all Burgundy's names and virtually disappeared from the export markets, but is now fairly common, expensive but immeasurably better, and increasingly reliable. From companies such as *Jadot, Jaffelin, Labouré-Roi* and *Moillard*, it's even becoming possible to buy good merchants' Nuits once more. *Labouré-Roi* is the most consistent merchant for Nuits, although *Moillard* and *Jadot* are increasingly good particularly at *premier cru* level. The most famous growers are *Robert Chevillon, Gouges, Michelot* and *Daniel Rion*, but excellent wines are also made by *Domaine de l'Arlot, Ambroise, Jean Chauvenet, Chicotot, Jean-Jacques Confuron* and the amazingly deep (and amazingly expensive) *Leroy*. There were problems with rot in 1986 and with hail in 1987 so stick to top years such as 1989, '90 and '93.

PERNAND-VERGELESSES, AC (Côte de Beaune; red, white) The village whites can be good, with some of the best Aligoté in Burgundy. The Chardonnays are generally fairly lean and need time to soften, but can be gently nutty and very enjoyable from a good producer. Can also be very good value. Best names in white: *Dubreuil-Fontaine, Germain, Laleure-Piot, Pavelot, Rapet, Rollin*. Some quite attractive, softly earthy reds, mostly on the lean side. Look for the *premier cru* Île de Vergelesses. Best reds: *Besancenot-Mathouillet, Caves des Hautes-Côtes, Chandon des Briailles, Delarche, Dubreuil-Fontaine, Laleure-Piot, Pavelot, Rapet* and *Rollin*.

PETIT CHABLIS, AC (Chablis; white) There used to be lots of this grown on the least-good slopes. But the growers objected that it made it sound as though their wine was a lesser form of Chablis. Nowadays, of course, pretty well the whole lot is called 'Chablis' – so we can't tell what's what, *they're* all richer, they're happy, we're not… I give up.

POMMARD, AC (Côte de Beaune; red) From good producers, Pommard can have a strong, meaty sturdiness, backed by slightly jammy but attractively plummy fruit. Not subtle, but many people's idea of what red Burgundy should be. They need ten years to show their class. The most consistently fine wines are made by *de Courcel, Comte Armand* and *de Montille*, but also look out for the wines of *Boillot, Château de Pommard, Girardin, Lahaye, Lejeune, Jean Monnier, Parent, Pothier* and *Pousse d'Or*.

POUILLY-FUISSÉ, AC (Mâconnais; white) Like Chablis, this is an appellation whose price yo-yos unacceptably according to supply and demand. It is sometimes best in years which are not too rich. Best producers: *Barraud, Béranger, Cordier, Corsin, Duboeuf*'s top selections, *Ferret, M Forest, Guffens-Heynen, Leger-Plumet, Loron*'s *les Vieux Murs, Manciat-Poncet, Noblet, Roger Saumaize, Valette, Vincent* at *Château Fuissé*. Adjoining villages Pouilly-Loché, AC and Pouilly-Vinzelles, AC have borrowed the name and make similar wines at half the price.

PULIGNY-MONTRACHET, AC (Côte de Beaune; white) The peak of great white pleasure is to be found in the various Montrachet *grands crus*. Le Montrachet is peerless, showing how humble words like honey, nuts, cream, smoke, perfume and all the rest do no honest service to a wine that seems to combine every memory of ripe fruit and scent with a dry, penetrating savouriness. There are several other *grands crus* less intense, but which offer the same unrivalled mix. There are *premiers crus* as well. While 'village' Meursault may be good, it's always worth buying a single-vineyard wine in Puligny-Montrachet. Much of the wine that's produced is sold in bulk to négociants whose offerings vary between the delicious and the disgraceful, but look for *Amiot-Bonfils, Jean-Marc Boillot, Boyer-Devèze, Carillon, Gérard Chavy, Drouhin, Jadot, Labouré-Roi, Laguiche*, both *Domaine Leflaive* and *Olivier Leflaive, Pernot, Ramonet-Prudhon, Antonin Rodet, Sauzet, Thénard*.

RÉGNIÉ, AC (Beaujolais; red) Since the 1988 vintage, Beaujolais' tenth *cru*. Makes wine quite similar to Brouilly in ripe vintages but a bit weedy when the sun doesn't shine. *Duboeuf Bouteille Cristal* is the best from this village so far.

RICHEBOURG, AC (Côte de Nuits; red) Exceptional *grand cru* at the northern end of Vosne-Romanée. It's a wonderful name for a wine – Richebourg – and, at its best, it manages to be fleshy yet filled with spice and perfume and the clinging richness of chocolate and figs. Best producers: *Grivot, Domaine de la Romanée-Conti, Gros, Henri Jayer, Leroy, Méo-Camuzet*.

LA ROMANÉE, AC (Côte de Nuits; red) This *grand cru* is the smallest AC in France, solely owned by the Liger-Belair family and sold by *Bouchard Père et Fils*. Now that Bouchard has been acquired by the more rigorous Joseph Henriot, we may see whether Romanée, solid but never sensational hitherto, deserves the same status as its neighbouring *grands crus* at the Dom. de la Romanée-Conti.

LA ROMANÉE-CONTI, AC (Côte de Nuits; red) This tiny *grand cru* of almost two hectares is capable of a more startling brilliance than any other Burgundy. The 7000 or so bottles it produces per year are instantly seized on by the super-rich before we mere mortals can even get our tasting sheets out. It is wholly owned by the *Domaine de la Romanée-Conti*.

LA ROMANÉE-ST-VIVANT, AC (Côte de Nuits; red) 9.54-hectare *grand cru* in the village of Vosne-Romanée. Far less easy to taste young than its neighbouring *grands crus* and needs a good 12 years to show what can be a delicious, savoury yet sweet personality. Best names: *Arnoux, Domaine de la Romanée-Conti, Latour, Leroy*.

RUCHOTTES-CHAMBERTIN, AC (Côte de Nuits; red) This is the smallest Gevrey-Chambertin *grand cru* at 3.1 hectares, with wines of deeper colour and longer-lasting perfumed richness than most of the village's other *grands crus*. Best producers: *F Esmonin, Georges Mugneret, Roumier, Rousseau*.

RULLY, AC (Côte Chalonnaise; red white) This village gets my vote for the most improved white AC in Burgundy. It was originally known for fizz, and then for pale, nutty, dull Chardonnay, but the use of new oak to ferment and age the wine has turned a lot into wonderfully soft, spicy Burgundies of good quality – and, surprisingly, still low prices. Best producers for white: *Bêtes, Chanzy, Cogny, Delorme, Drouhin, Dury, Duvernay, Domaine de la Folie, Jacqueson, Jaffelin, Olivier Leflaive, Rodet*. Best for red: *Chanzy, Ch. de Rully, Delorme, Domaine de la Folie, Duvernay, Faiveley, Jacqueson, Jaffelin*.

ST-AMOUR, AC (Beaujolais; red) Among the most perfect Beaujolais, this pink-red wine from one of the least spoilt villages usually has freshness and peachy perfume and good, ripe fruit all at once. It isn't that common here (though the French love it), and yet it is frequently the most reliable and most enjoyable *cru*. Sadly, the news has leaked out and prices are leaping up. The perfect Valentine's Day gift, as wine merchants are well aware. Look out for *Château de St-Amour, Domaine des Billards* (Loron), *Buis, Domaine des Ducs, Domaine du Paradis, Patissier, André Poitevin, Francis Saillant, Paul Spay*.

ST-AUBIN, AC (Côte de Beaune; red, white) This large commune offers some of Burgundy's best-value wines, though the reds are a touch earthy. But they are reliable, and give real pleasure after a few years of aging. Best: *Bachelet, Clergy, Lamy, Prudhon, Gérard Thomas* and *Roux*, but wines from négociants *Jadot* and *Olivier Leflaive* are their equal. Good whites come from *Bachelet, Clerget, Lamy, Olivier Leflaive, Prudhon, Thomas* and *Roux*.

ST-ROMAIN, AC (Côte de Beaune; red, white) Even more out of the way than St-Aubin. Full, rather broad-flavoured, cherry-stone dry reds, that perform best in very warm years. On the whole sold cheaper than they deserve. Look for *Bazenet, Buisson, Gras, Thévenin* and *Thévenin-Monthelie*. The flinty, dry whites are often of decent quality and pretty good value. Beware cooler vintages, when the grapes sometimes don't ripen properly. Best are: *Bazenet, Buisson, Germain, Gras, Thévenin, Thévenin-Monthelie*.

ST-VÉRAN, AC (Mâconnais; white) Pouilly-Fuissé's understudy, capable of simple, soft, quick-maturing but attractive, rather honeyed white Burgundy. There are some great 1989s and '90s but '92 produced high quality across the board. Best producers: *Corsin, Dépardon, Dom. des Deux Roches, Duboeuf, Grégoire, Lassarat, de Montferrand, Saumaize, Thibert, Vincent* – and, above all, *Drouhin*.

SANTENAY, AC (Côte de Beaune; red) Rough and ready red. At its best, with a strong, savoury flavour and good strawberry fruit, though nowadays frequently rather lean and mean. Best: *Belland, Drouhin, Girardin, Lequin-Roussot, Morey, Pousse d'Or, Prieur-Bonnet, Roux*. Even here, there can be variation.

SAVIGNY-LÈS-BEAUNE, AC (Côte de Beaune; red)
Gaining in reputation at the expense of Beaune. Light, attractive earthiness and strawberry fruit. Try *Bize, Camus-Bruchon, Capron-Manieux, Chandon de Briailles, Écard-Guyot, Girard-Vollot, Guillemot, Pavelot, Tollot-Beaut.*

SAUVIGNON DE ST-BRIS, VDQS
(white) Wine of AC quality grown south-west of Chablis that languishes as a VDQS because Sauvignon Blanc is not an AC grape in the area. Often one of the most nettly, most greeny-gooseberryish of all, but recent ones have been more expensive and less exciting. It has not really faced up to the competition from New Zealand – and Bordeaux. Best: *Louis Bersan, Jean-Marc Brocard, Robert & Philippe Defrance, Michel Esclavy, Goisot, André Sorin.*

LA TÂCHE, AC (Côte de Nuits; red)
Another *grand cru* monopoly of the *Domaine de la Romanée-Conti*. As famous as Romanée-Conti, but not so totally unobtainable, since the 6.06-hectare vineyard can produce all of 24,000 bottles a year. The wine is heavenly, so rich and heady that the perfumes are sometimes closer to age-old brandy than table wine and the flavour loaded with spice and dark fruits and the acrid richness of chocolate.

VOLNAY, AC (Côte de Beaune; red)
Volnay is one of the most perfumed red Burgundies, with a memorable cherry-and-strawberry spice, but also, in its *premiers crus*, able to turn on a big, meaty style without losing the perfume. The best are *Lafarge,*

Comte Lafon, Marquis d'Angerville, de Montille and *Pousse d'Or,* Other good names: *Ampeau, Blain-Gagnard, Boillot, Bouley, Clerget, Delagrange, Vaudoisey-Mutin, Voillot.* Volnay did very well in 1989, '90, '91 and '93.

VOSNE-ROMANÉE, AC (Côte de Nuits; red)
The greatest Côte de Nuits village. Its *grands crus* cost more than any red on earth, and, remarkably for Burgundy, they are dominated by a single estate, *Domaine de la Romanée Conti.* These vineyards make wines capable of more startling brilliance than any other, with flavours as disparate yet as intense as the overpowering, creamy savouriness of fresh *foie gras* and the deep, sweet scent of ripe plums and prunes in brandy. You may need to re-mortgage your house in order to experience this, though. There are also fine *premiers crus,* and the village wines, though not as reliable as they were, can sometimes reflect their leaders. The 1987s and '89s are good; the '85s, '88s and '90s unutterably great. Apart from the DRC, look for *Arnoux, Sylvain Cathiard, Confuron-Coteditot, Engel, Grivot, Jean Gros, Hudelot-Noëllat, Georges Jayer, Henri Jayer, Henri Lamarche, Leroy, Méo-Camuzet, Mongeard-Mugneret, Georges Mugneret, Pernin-Rossin, Rouget, Daniel Rion* and *Jean Tardy.*

VOUGEOT, AC (Côte de Nuits; red)
A village famous only because of its *grand cru,* Clos de Vougeot, which at its best is plummy and broad. However, there are some decent wines made outside the Clos – most notably from *Bertagna* and *Clerget.*

MERCHANTS SPECIALISING IN BURGUNDY
see Merchant Directory (page 424) for details

These are exceptionally good. Adnams (AD) John Armit (ARM), Averys (AV), Bennetts (BEN), Berry Bros. & Rudd (BER), Bibendum (BIB), Bute Wines (BUT), Butlers Wine Cellar (BU), Anthony Byrne (BY), Châteaux Wines (CHA), Corney & Barrow (CB), Davisons (DAV), Direct Wine (DI), Eldridge Pope (EL), Enotria Winecellars (ENO), Farr Vintners (FA), Gelston Castle Fine Wines (GE), Goedhuis (GOE), Roger Harris (HAW), John Harvey & Sons (HAR), Haynes Hanson & Clark (HAH), Lay & Wheeler (LAY), Lea & Sandeman (LEA), Le Nez Rouge (NEZ), Morris & Verdin (MV), James Nicholson (NI), Oddbins (OD), Thos. Peatling (PE), Raeburn (RAE), Reid Wines (REI), T&W Wines (TW), Tanners (TAN), Howard Ripley (RIP), Wine Society (WS), Peter Wylie (WY)

BURGUNDY AND BEAUJOLAIS VINTAGES

Red Burgundy is more subject to vintage fluctuation than white; with the latter, most years can produce a fair amount of pretty good wine. The rule for Beaujolais, drink as young as possible. Only top wines from the best villages will benefit much from aging, although Nouveau may improve with a month or two's rest.

1995   The summer was magnificent, but September proved cool. However, the sunshine returned, and an early October harvest took place in warm, dry conditions. A year of low yields, ripe tannins and good concentration in the reds . For once, there is little to choose in quality between the Côte de Beaune and the Côte de Nuits. Growers compare the potential to that of 1993. Among the whites, the greatest excitement is found in Chablis, where the quality is first-rate. There was no frost, so quantity is up on 1994. In the Côte d'Or, the whites are balanced, but yields are below average, so prices are likely to rise. Quality is good, but few growers are claiming greatness. Beaujolais also had a hot summer, and for once no hailstorms. It was even sunnier than 1994, although the harvest period was interrupted by rain. In general it is a very good rather than an exceptional year for Beaujolais, offering soft, fruity wines, but there will be considerable variations depending on harvesting dates and location. Some of the *cru* wines could prove well-structured and, like the 1991s, suitable for aging.

1994   Yet again September rain took the gilt off the gingerbread. Instead of a great vintage we have lighter wines with attractive, reasonable colours and lowish acidity. However, some reds are over-extracted and show harsh tannins without sufficient fruit to support them. Buy cautiously. The whites are proving an unexpected surprise. Initially they were lean and a bit mean, but the best wines are showing a raciness and vigour that contrasts nicely with the plumper, richer 1992s, which have always overshadowed them. Beaujolais had an early, ripe vintage, with some very attractive wines, although quality varies.

1993   September rain appeared to prevent the reds from being great. But those from the best producers have a depth of colour, power of fruit and well-constructed tannins that bespeak greatness after all. Some wines are a little too tannic or underripe. The whites have turned out far better than at first seemed likely. They have plumped up nicely and have plenty of fruit, but don't count on them making old Beaunes. Beaujolais, like most of France, suffered from rain at the vintage. However, August had been hot, so most of the grapes were ripe and picked before the heavens really opened on 20 September. There are some good wines among the *crus*.

1992   A large vintage, affected by storms. Acidity is low among the reds, and only those who kept yields low will have made exciting wines. A good year to choose in restaurants, as the wines are fast developers. Comparable to 1982. The whites were far better, with masses of exuberant fruit and seemingly better acidity than their 1991 counterparts. The best white vintage since 1989, but in a less alcoholic, more elegantly balanced style than most 1989s. Beaujolais was below average in quality, with thin, light wines. Buy only from quality-conscious producers.

1991   A small crop of reds, partly because of hail damage, and spoilt by rain at vintage time. Even so, there were some very good reds made – and with some yields as low as ten hectolitres per hectare, they can have extraordinary concentration. It's a very patchy vintage, but the good wines will be ones to keep, because of that concentration. The whites are also patchy in quality, though without the reds' occasional brilliance. That vintage-time rain did more damage to the Chardonnay than to the Pinot Noir, in terms of rot, and some of the picking had to be pretty hasty. The whites don't match up to the previous three vintages in quality, but the Mâconnais wines are drinking well now. Beaujolais was excellent, with good colour and relatively high tannin levels.

1990 The long, warm summer produced yet another large crop. The 1990 reds are brilliantly fruity, naturally high in sugars. Most producers now consider this the best of the great trio of 1988, 1989 and 1990. Lesser wines will be ready early; the best are sumptuously rich. The Chardonnay crop was very large, so the whites are proving to be inferior to the reds. A good rather than a great vintage for white Burgundy. In Beaujolais it was a corker of a vintage – very good quality and plenty of it. The *crus* are drinking beautifully now.

1989 A lot of good reds were made in this warm year, but only a few exceptional ones. They are softer than the 1988s, though some are superbly concentrated, particularly in the Côte de Beaune. Some may prove better than the '88s. it was an outstanding year for white Burgundy, at least in the hands of competent winemakers. Hailed as the best white vintage of the 1980s, almost all the best growers' wines are beautifully balanced, despite their richness. However, a number of wines have worryingly low acidity levels, and some are already showing signs of premature aging. Beaujolais had wonderful colour and pungent fruit, and prices shot up.

1988 Hardly a textbook year, but many growers produced firm, concentrated reds. High tannins have so far kept the pleasure factor low, but they are beginning to emerge from their shells. Some superb wines, but quite a few dour ones, too. Among the whites, Mâconnais wines had a bright, fresh fruit not seen down that way for a few years. Chablis prices went up by ten to 15 per cent, but you couldn't honestly say that its quality went up by the same degree. Beaujolais was exceptional, with marvellous luscious, clear, ripe fruit. The best are now on their second wind.

1987 The best 1987 reds are very good indeed, Côte de Beaune having the edge over Côte de Nuits. The lesser wines aren't as good as those of 1985, but are better than those of 1986. Drink now.

1986 Over the last year the reds have been shedding toughness, and now exhibit their best feature, perfume. Stick to decent producers, because there was some rot. Drink up. The good whites have proved to be much better balanced than previously thought, and whilst a few '86s have closed up somewhat, others have suddenly started to tire. Chablis had that classic blend of leanness and restrained ripeness which can make it the logical, if not the emotional choice for so many fish dishes. *Grands crus* are drinking well, but there's no hurry to drink up.

1985 When the 1985 reds were young, they were terrific. Some have gone from strength to strength. Some seem stuck in a 'dumb' phase. Some shot their bolt early. The whites have proper acid balance and an outstanding concentration of fruit. Pity nobody waited to find out because most '85s were consumed long ago. If you do see one from a good producer, go for it – well, perhaps not, I've just remembered the price it'll be. Chablis started out with a lesser reputation, but wines from good producers can still improve. Some Beaujolais are still excellent.

1983 The best reds display impressive flavour. If you can wait another few years you may have the most impressive old-style Burgundies made in the last two decades, but I'd avoid Vosne-Romanée, Chambolle-Musigny and Morey-Saint-Denis. The whites are frequently heavy, rather unrefreshing, soggy-flavoured wines (made, all too often, from overripe, rot-affected grapes) which rapidly lost their fruit. Some rare examples may turn out to be wonderful, but if that is the case I have yet to discover them. Even the best should be ready by now, though.

1982 The best reds are from the Côte de Beaune and are delicate, perfumed, nicely balanced and need drinking up.

BASIC BURGUNDY

RED

Under £7.00
1993
Bourgogne Coteaux de St-Bris, Brocard (AD)
Bourgogne Rouge, Cave de Buxy (BOT, WR, THR)
1992
Bourgogne Passe-Tout-Grains, Rion (MV)
1987
Bourgogne Passe-Tout-Grains, Lejeune (RAE)
1986
Bourgogne Passe-Tout-Grains, Lejeune (RAE)

£7.00 → £7.99
1994
Bourgogne Rouge, Jadot (WR, BOT, THR)
1993
Bourgogne Rouge, Faiveley (DI)
Bourgogne Rouge Tasteviné, Bichot (UN)
1988
Bourgogne Passe-Tout-Grains, Henri Jayer (RAE)

£8.00 → £11.50
1993
Bourgogne Rouge, Michel Lafarge (GAU, HAH)
Bourgogne Rouge, Parent (NEZ)
1992
Bourgogne la Digoine, Villaine (CRO)
Bourgogne Rouge, Georges Roumier (SEC)
1991
Bourgogne la Digoine, Villaine (AD)
Bourgogne Passe-Tout-Grains, Henri Jayer (REI)
1990
Bourgogne Passe-Tout-Grains, Rion (CRO)
1988
Bourgogne Rouge, Chevillon (YOU)

c. £24.50
1988
Bourgogne Rouge, Henri Jayer (REI)

c. £38.00
1985
Bourgogne Rouge, Henri Jayer (BUT)

WHITE

Under £6.00
1993
Bourgogne Aligoté, Cave de Buxy (BO)
Bourgogne Chardonnay, A Bichot (UN)

£6.00 → £7.99
1994
Bourgogne Aligoté de Bouzeron, Ancien Domaine Carnot Bouchard (DAV)
Bourgogne Aligoté, Larousse (LAYT)
Bourgogne Aligoté, Rion (MV)
Bourgogne Aligoté, Rollin (BIB)
Bourgogne Blanc, Latour (SEC, MAJ, PEN)
1993
Bourgogne Chardonnay, Jadot (VIC)

£8.00 → £9.99
1994
Bourgogne Aligoté de Bouzeron, Villaine (AD, BY, TAN, ARM, CB)
★ Bourgogne les Bons Batons, Rion (MV)
1993
Bourgogne Aligoté, Rion (CRO)
Bourgogne Blanc, Jobard (LEA)
Bourgogne Blanc les Clous, Villaine (BY)
1990
Bourgogne Blanc, Leroy (RIP)
1989
Bourgogne Aligoté de Bouzeron, Villaine (BUT)

£10.00 → £15.99
1994
Bourgogne Blanc, Jobard (LEA, RAE)
1993
Bourgogne Blanc, Domaine Leflaive (ARM)
Bourgogne Blanc, Jobard (RAE)
1992
Bourgogne Blanc, Jobard (RAE)
1991
Bourgogne Blanc, Domaine Leflaive (ARM)
Bourgogne Blanc, Jobard (RAE)
1990
Bourgogne Blanc, Jobard (RAE)
Bourgogne Blanc, Leroy (BUT, GOE)
1989
Bourgogne Blanc, Domaine Leflaive (DI)
1986
Bourgogne Blanc, Domaine Leflaive (BUT)
Bourgogne Blanc, Jobard (BUT)

CÔTE D'OR

RED

Under £7.00

1993
Hautes-Côtes de Beaune, Caves des
   Hautes-Côtes (DI)
1992
Hautes-Côtes de Beaune, Caves des
   Hautes-Côtes (WAI)
Hautes-Côtes de Nuits, Caves des
   Hautes-Côtes (TES, VIC)

£7.00 → £7.99

1993
Hautes-Côtes de Nuits, Domaine Guy
   Dufouleur (DAV)
1992
Savigny-lès-Beaune Latour (FOR)
1989
Hautes-Côtes de Nuits aux Dames
   Huguettes, Barolet (SAI)

£8.00 → £8.99

1994
Chorey-lès-Beaune Labouré-Roi (PIP)
1993
Chorey-lès-Beaune Maillard (WAI)
Côte de Beaune-Villages Drouhin (NI)
Savigny-lès-Beaune Latour (NEW)
1992
Santenay Latour (KA)

£9.00 → £9.99

1994
★ Hautes-Côtes de Nuits Domaine du Bois
   Guillaume, Devevey (MV)
1993
Nuits-St-Georges, Paul Dugenais (SAI)
Santenay Latour (PEN)
1992
Chorey-lès-Beaune Château de Chorey-
   lès-Beaune, Jacques Germain (SAF)
Meursault les Forges, Prieur-Brunet (EL)
Nuits-St-Georges Caves des Hautes
   Côtes (FUL)

£10.00 → £10.99

1994
Chorey-lès-Beaune Tollot-Beaut (AD)
1993
Gevrey-Chambertin Labouré-Roi (EL)
St-Aubin les Frionnes, Prudhon (TAN)

1992
Chassagne-Montrachet Latour (PLA)
Chorey-lès-Beaune Tollot-Beaut (YOU, WR)
Marsannay Monchenevoy, Philippe
   Charlopin-Parizot (YOU)
1991
Aloxe-Corton Latour (FOR)
St-Aubin les Argillières, Lamy-Pillot (ARM)
St-Aubin Sentier du Clou, Prudhon (BIB)
1990
Hautes-Côtes de Nuits, Michel Gros (BY)
Santenay Adrien Belland (SOM)
1989
St-Aubin les Argillières, Lamy-Pillot (ARM)
Savigny-lès-Beaune Pavelot (GE)

£11.00 → £11.99

1993
Chorey-lès-Beaune Tollot-Beaut (NEZ, DI)
Pernand-Vergelesses Dubreuil-Fontaine
   (BY)
Santenay Drouhin (NI)

Savigny-lès-Beaune les Lavières, Camus-
   Bruchon (RAE)
1992
Fixin Fougeray (BER)
Fixin Gelin (PLA)
Monthélie Garaudet (PIP)
Monthélie Monthélie-Douhairet (MV)
Santenay la Maladière, Girardin (NEZ)
Savigny-lès-Beaune Pavelot (LEA)
1991
Aloxe-Corton les Chaillots, Latour (NEW,
   FOR)
1990
St-Aubin Sentier du Clou, Prudhon (EY)
1989
Ladoix Drouhin (PEN)
St-Aubin les Frionnes, Prudhon (CRO)
Santenay 1er Cru, Armand Rousseau (SAI)
1987
Santenay Clos du Haut Village, Lequin-
   Roussot (PLA)

1985
Hautes-Côtes de Nuits, Michel Gros (BUT)
1982
Beaune Teurons, Michel Rossignol (CHA)

£12.00 → £12.99

1994
Savigny-lès-Beaune les Lavières, Camus-Bruchon (RAE)
1993
Chassagne-Montrachet Henri Germain (TAN)
Chorey-lès-Beaune Maillard (ENO)
Gevrey-Chambertin Trapet (OD)
Marsannay Philippe Naddef (ROB)
Nuits-St-Georges les Damodes, Laboiré-Roi (SAI)
1992
Aloxe-Corton Latour (GAL, WHI)
Beaune Vignes Franches, Latour (FOR)
Savigny-lès-Beaune Faiveley (DI)
Savigny-lès-Beaune Pavelot (DAV)
1991
Beaune Vignes Franches, Latour (KA)
1990
Gevrey-Chambertin Rossignol-Trapet (SAF)
1989
Savigny-lès-Beaune Henri de Villamont (ROB)
Vosne-Romanée Georges Noëllat (SAI)
1988
Santenay la Maladière, Prieur (EL)
Savigny-lès-Beaune Bize (RIP)
Savigny-lès-Beaune Girard-Vollot (MV)

£13.00 → £13.99

1994
Hautes-Côtes de Nuits Jayer-Gilles (AD)
Marsannay Monchenevoy, Philippe Charlopin-Parizot (MV)
1993
Auxey-Duresses Michel Prunier (TAN)
Pommard les Cras, Belland (WAT)
Savigny-lès-Beaune Aux Grands Liards, Bize (RIP)
1992
Chassagne-Montrachet Fontaine-Gagnard (LAYT)
Côte de Nuits-Villages Clos du Chapeau, Domaine de l'Arlot (BY)
Gevrey-Chambertin Rossignol-Trapet (BY)
Monthélie Château de Monthélie, Suremain (NEZ)
Pernand-Vergelesses Île de Vergelesses, Chandon de Briailles (CRO)

1991
Monthelie Garaudet (LAYT)
Nuits-St-Georges Rion (BER)
Savigny-lès-Beaune les Guettes, Doudet-Naudin (BER)
1990
Beaune Cent Vignes, Monnier (ELL)
Pernand-Vergelesses Rollin (PLA)
Savigny-lès-Beaune les Lavières, Camus-Bruchon (WRI)
1987
Aloxe-Corton Rollin (RAE)
Savigny-lès-Beaune Ampeau (REI)
1983
Gevrey-Chambertin Chanson (BUT)

£14.00 → £14.99

1993
Chassagne-Montrachet Ramonet (RIP)
Côte de Nuits-Villages Clos du Chapeau, Domaine de l'Arlot (THR, WR, BOT)
Gevrey-Chambertin Rossignol-Trapet (PIP)
Monthelie Château de Monthelie, Suremain (RAE)
Nuits-St-Georges Rodet (WHI)
1992
Aloxe-Corton Rollin (RAE)
Gevrey-Chambertin Latour (FOR)
Gevrey-Chambertin Rebourseau (MV)
1991
Chassagne-Montrachet Gagnard-Delagrange (BY)
Côte de Nuits-Villages Jayer-Gilles (WS)
Nuits-St-Georges Champy (HOG)
1990
Savigny-lès-Beaune Girard-Vollot (ROB)
1989
Beaune Teurons, Domaines du Château de Beaune (HOG)
1984
Volnay Santenots Lafon (MV, ELL)
1983
Chambolle-Musigny Georges Roumier (RAE)
Chassagne-Montrachet Colin (CRO)
1982
Auxey-Duresses Ampeau (CHA)

£15.00 → £15.99

1993
Aloxe-Corton Rollin (RAE)
Beaune Bressandes, Henri Germain (AD)
Chambolle-Musigny Alain Hudelot-Noëllat (RIP)
Gevrey-Chambertin Latour (PEN)
Gevrey-Chambertin Rodet (WHI)

1992
Beaune Bressandes, Henri Germain (TAN)
Beaune Vignes Franches, Latour (PLA)
Chambolle-Musigny Georges Roumier (EL)
Nuits-St-Georges Faiveley (DI)
1991
Santenay Clos Tavannes, Domaine de la
    Pousse d'Or (DI)
Vosne-Romanée Rion (BER)
1990
Aloxe-Corton Champy (HOG)
Beaune Clos du Roi, Chanson (POR)
Chassagne-Montrachet Gagnard-
    Delagrange (BY)
Vosne-Romanée les Violettes, Georges
    Clerget (BY)
1989
Pernand-Vergelesses Île de Vergelesses,
    Chandon de Briailles (HAH)
Volnay Drouhin (REI)
1986
Chambolle-Musigny Faiveley (DI)
1983
Beaune Bressandes, Henri Germain (EY)
Corton Chanson (BUT)

£16.00 → £16.99
1993
Beaune Marconnets, Bouchard Père (LAYT)
Chambolle-Musigny la Combe d'Orvaux,
    Grivot (REI)
Savigny-lès-Beaune les Vergelesses, Bize
    (RIP)
Vosne-Romanée Engel (GAU)
1992
Beaune Toussaints, Albert Morot (GE)
Chambolle-Musigny Latour (HA)
Nuits-St-Georges Michelot (NEZ)
Vosne-Romanée Georges Mugneret (SAI)
1991
Gevrey-Chambertin Armand Rousseau
    (GOE)
Savigny-lès-Beaune les Vergelesses, Bize (DI)
Volnay Frémiets, Marquis d'Angerville (CB)
Vosne-Romanée Jean Gros (DI)
1990
Santenay Clos Tavannes, Domaine de la
    Pousse d'Or (DI)
Santenay les Gravières, Domaine de la
    Pousse d'Or (WS)
1989
Beaune Teurons, Jadot (MAR)
Chambolle-Musigny Dujac (BUT, RIP)
Nuits-St-Georges Robert Chevillon (YOU)
Volnay Drouhin (BO)

1988
Beaune Marconnets, Chanson (QUE)
Chambolle-Musigny Dujac (BUT)
1985
Beaune Clos de la Mousse, Bouchard Père
    (REI)
Côte de Nuits-Villages Jayer-Gilles (REI)
1983
Beaune Teurons, Domaines du Château
    de Beaune (PEN)

£17.00 → £17.99
1993
Chambolle-Musigny Dujac (RIP)
Chassagne-Montrachet Gagnard-
    Delagrange (LAYT)
1992
Chambolle-Musigny Georges Roumier
    (RES, MV)
Gevrey-Chambertin Armand Rousseau
    (TAN)
Vosne-Romanée Confuron-Cotétidot
    (GE)
1991
Aloxe-Corton Rollin (BIB)
Beaune Clos des Ursules, Jadot (POR)
Corton Latour (GAL)
Vosne-Romanée Georges Mugneret (LEA)
1990
Nuits-St-Georges Robert Chevillon
    (GAU)
Volnay Santenots Brunet (EL)
1989
Beaune Chouacheux, Machard de
    Gramont (DAV)
Nuits-St-Georges Faiveley (DI)
Nuits-St-Georges Rion (CO)
Vosne-Romanée Rion (CO)
1988
Savigny-lès-Beaune les Vergelesses, Bize
    (HAH, RIP)
1987
Corton Tollot-Beaut (NEZ)
Gevrey-Chambertin Vieilles Vignes, Alain
    Burguet (RIP)
Pommard les Saussilles, Jean-Marc Boillot
    (RIP)
1984
Griotte-Chambertin Ponsot (GOE)
Latricières-Chambertin Ponsot (GOE)
1983
Aloxe-Corton Tollot-Beaut (BUT)
Chambolle-Musigny Alain Hudelot-
    Noëllat (REI)
Charmes-Chambertin Roty (REI)

£18.00 → £19.99

1994
Fixin Charlopin-Parizot (LEA)
Morey-St-Denis Clos de la Bussière,
   Georges Roumier (TAN)
Volnay Michel Lafarge (RAE)

1993
Aloxe-Corton Tollot-Beaut (EY)
Chassagne-Montrachet les Embrazées,
   Bernard Morey (OD)
Gevrey-Chambertin Armand Rousseau
   (TAN, AD)
Gevrey-Chambertin Bachelet (RIP)
Gevrey-Chambertin Drouhin (NI)
Morey-St-Denis Dujac (RIP)
Pernand-Vergelesses Île de Vergelesses,
   Chandon de Briailles (LEA)
Savigny-lès-Beaune la Dominode, Pavelot
   (LEA)
Vosne-Romanée les Suchots, Alain
   Hudelot-Noëllat (RIP)

1992
Chassagne-Montrachet Champs-Gains,
   Jean Marc Morey (PIP)
Gevrey-Chambertin Cazetiers, Armand
   Rousseau (RIP)

1991
Beaune Clos du Roi, Tollot-Beaut (DI)
Beaune Teurons, Jadot (HA)
Morey-St-Denis Dujac (DI)
Nuits-St-Georges Méo-Camuzet (GOE)
Vosne-Romanée Georges Mugneret (LEA)

1990
Beaune Bressandes, Morot (RES)
Corton Clos de la Vigne au Saint, Latour
   (HA)
Gevrey-Chambertin Rossignol-Trapet
   (TW, BEN)
Meursault Clos de Mazaray, Prieur (BER)
Volnay Drouhin (NI)

1989
Beaune Grèves Vigne de l'Enfant Jesus,
   Bouchard Père (REI)
Nuits-St-Georges Jadot (ELL)
Savigny-lès-Beaune la Dominode, Bruno
   Clair (BEN)
Volnay Santenots Drouhin (BO)
Vosne-Romanée Rion (SOM)

> *In each price band wines*
> *are listed in vintage order.*
> *Within each vintage they*
> *are listed in A–Z order.*

1988
Beaune les Montrevenots, Jean-Marc
   Boillot (RIP, LEA)
Gevrey-Chambertin Bachelet (GAU)
Savigny-lès-Beaune les Lavières, Tollot-
   Beaut (RES)

1987
Beaune Teurons, Jacques Germain (WHI)
Clos de Vougeot Noëllat (NEZ)

1986
Clos de la Roche Armand Rousseau (GOE)
Nuits-St-Georges les Porets St-Georges,
   Gouges (REI)
Pommard les Épenots, Armand (REI)

1985
Nuits-St-Georges Doudet-Naudin (BER)

1983
Aloxe-Corton Latour (PEN)
Beaune Clos des Ursules, Jadot (BUT)
Morey-St-Denis Clos des Ormes, Lignier
   (BUT)
Pernand-Vergelesses Île de Vergelesses,
   Chandon de Briailles (CRO)
Volnay Clos des Ducs, Marquis
   d'Angerville (REI)

1982
Corton-Grancey Latour (SEC)

1980
Volnay Santenots Ampeau (RIP)

1979
Chambolle-Musigny Latour (FOR)

£20.00 → £22.49

1994
Nuits-St-Georges les Pruliers, Grivot (RAE)

1993
Nuits-St-Georges Rion (MV, YOU)
Pommard les Bertins, Lescure (PIP)
Pommard les Saussilles, Jean-Marc Boillot
   (RAE)
Pommard Rugiens, Domaine Courcel (RIP)
Volnay les Caillerets, Domaine de la
   Pousse d'Or (LAY)
Vosne-Romanée Georges Mugneret (LEA)
Vosne-Romanée Rion (MV)

1992
Gevrey-Chambertin Vieilles Vignes, Alain
   Burguet (RIP)
Morey-St-Denis Clos des Ormes, Lignier
   (VIG)
Morey-St-Denis Dujac (LAY)
Volnay Champans, Marquis d'Angerville
   (RES)
Volnay les Caillerets, Domaine de la
   Pousse d'Or (WR)

1991

Volnay les Caillerets, Clos des 60 Ouvrées, Domaine de la Pousse d'Or (MV)

Volnay les Caillerets, Marquis d'Angerville (EL)

Volnay Santenots-du-Millieu, Tête de Cuvée, Lafon (TAN)

1990

Beaune les Montrevenots, Jean-Marc Boillot (LEA)

1989

Morey-St-Denis Clos de la Bussière, Georges Roumier (WS)

Nuits-St-Georges Clos de la Maréchale, Faiveley (HOG)

Volnay Michel Lafarge (WS)

Vosne-Romanée Jean Gros (WR, BOT)

Vosne-Romanée Rion (MV)

1988

Corton Latour (WY)

1987

Clos de Vougeot Drouhin (SOM)

1986

Latricières-Chambertin Trapet (BY)

Nuits-St-Georges Vignes Rondes, Rion (FOR)

Volnay Clos des Ducs, Marquis d'Angerville (CB)

1985

Chambolle-Musigny Lignier (BUT)

1983

Clos St-Denis Lignier (GOE)

Nuits-St-Georges Clos de Thorey, Moillard (PEN)

1982

Beaune Dames Hospitalières, Hospices de Beaune (VIG)

Volnay les Caillerets, Clos des 60 Ouvrées, Domaine de la Pousse d'Or (BU)

Volnay Santenots Ampeau (CHA)

1980

Bonnes-Mares Domaine des Varoilles (CRO)

1978

Volnay Caillerets Cuvée Carnot, Bouchard Père (YOU)

£22.50 → £24.99

1993

Chambolle-Musigny Dujac (LAYT)

Échézeaux Engel (RIP)

Gevrey-Chambertin Vieilles Vignes, Alain Burguet (RIP)

Nuits-St-Georges les Pruliers, Gouges (EY)

Vosne-Romanée les Chaumes, Jean Tardy (RES)

1992

Échézeaux Mongeard-Mugneret (GOE)

Mazis-Chambertin Armand Rousseau (RIP)

Nuits-St-Georges Clos des Forets St-Georges, Domaine de l'Arlot (GOE, LAY)

Pommard Domaine de la Pousse d'Or (OD)

1991

Charmes-Chambertin Armand Rousseau (GOE)

Nuits-St-Georges les Porets St-Georges, Gouges (LAYT)

Pommard Rugiens, Domaine Courcel (EL)

Volnay Santenots Latour (AD)

1990

Chambolle-Musigny Dujac (RES, BUT, RIP)

Corton Clos de la Vigne au Saint, Latour (SEC)

Morey-St-Denis Dujac (DI)

Nuits-St-Georges Faiveley (TAN)

Vosne-Romanée les Orveaux, Mongeard-Mugneret (GOE)

1989

Clos St-Denis Lignier (SOM)

Corton-Grancey Latour (PEN)

Gevrey-Chambertin Vieilles Vignes, Alain Burguet (REI)

Volnay de Montille (HAH)

1988

Chambolle-Musigny Faiveley (WRI)

Nuits-St-Georges Méo-Camuzet (RAE)

Savigny-lès-Beaune les Lavières, Tollot-Beaut (UB)

Volnay Champans, Marquis d'Angerville (BEN)

Volnay Santenots Matrot (CB)

Vosne-Romanée les Chaumes, Méo-Camuzet (REI)

1987

Clos de la Roche Armand Rousseau (BUT)

Gevrey-Chambertin Clos St-Jacques, Armand Rousseau (BUT)

Grands-Échézeaux Drouhin (SOM)

Nuits-St-Georges Richemone, Pernin-Rossin (RAE)

Nuits-St-Georges Rion (ROB)

1986

Beaune Grèves Vigne de l'Enfant Jesus, Bouchard Père (REI)

Vosne-Romanée les Beaumonts, Domaine Rion (GAU)

1985

Nuits-St-Georges Clos de Thorey, Moillard (BER)

£25.00 → £27.49

1993
Beaune Clos des Mouches, Drouhin (NI)
Chassagne-Montrachet Clos de la
  Boudriotte, Ramonet-Prudhon (RIP)
Corton Pougets, Jadot (GOE)
Nuits-St-Georges Clos des Forets St-
  Georges, Domaine de l'Arlot (RIP)
Vosne-Romanée les Orveaux, Mongeard-
  Mugneret (GOE)
1992
Pommard Rugiens, Domaine Courcel (RES)
Volnay Santenots Lafon (MV, YOU)
1991
Mazis-Chambertin Armand Rousseau (RIP)
Pommard les Épenots, Armand (ELL)
Pommard les Épenots, Mme de Courcel
  (EL)
Vosne-Romanée les Chaumes, Méo-
  Camuzet (GOE)
1990
Charmes-Chambertin Armand Rousseau
  (SOM)
Corton Cuvée Charlotte Dumay,
  Hospices de Beaune (BY)
Grands-Échézeaux Thénard (FA)
Nuits-St-Georges Méo-Camuzet (GOE)
Pommard les Saussilles, Jean-Marc Boillot
  (RIP)
1989
Corton Clos du Roi, Chandon de Briailles
  (RIP)
Nuits-St-Georges Clos des Forets St-
  Georges, Domaine de l'Arlot (GOE)
Volnay Clos des Santenots, Prieur (BER)
1988
Gevrey-Chambertin Drouhin (UB)
Volnay Santenots-du-Millieu, Tête de
  Cuvée, Lafon (GAU)
Vosne-Romanée Beaux Monts, Thomas-
  Moillard (BER)

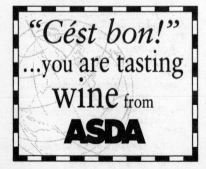

1987
Gevrey-Chambertin Combottes, Dujac
  (BUT, GOE)
1986
Charmes-Chambertin Dujac (RIP)
Clos St-Denis Dujac (BUT, RIP)
Griotte-Chambertin Ponsot (BU)
Vosne-Romanée Cros Parantoux, Méo-
  Camuzet (REI)
1983
Chambolle-Musigny Lignier (CRO)
1980
Vosne-Romanée les Malconsorts,
  Lamarche (BU)

£27.50 → £29.99

1993
Mazis-Chambertin Armand Rousseau (RIP)
Nuits-St-Georges les St-Georges, Faiveley
  (SEC)
Volnay 1er Cru, Michel Lafarge (RIP)
Vosne-Romanée les Suchots, Alain
  Hudelot-Noëllat (RES)
1992
Charmes-Chambertin Armand Rousseau
  (TAN, EL)
Latricières-Chambertin Trapet (OD)
1991
Charmes-Chambertin Bachelet (RIP)
Corton-Bressandes Dubreuil-Fontaine (RES)
Corton-Bressandes Tollot-Beaut (TAN, DI)
Nuits-St-Georges les Boudots, Méo-
  Camuzet (GOE)
Ruchottes-Chambertin Armand Rousseau
  (GOE, FA)
Volnay Clos d'Audignac, Domaine de la
  Pousse d'Or (ROB)
Volnay les Caillerets, Clos des 60 Ouvrées,
  Domaine de la Pousse d'Or (GAU)
1990
Corton-Bressandes Drouhin (REI)
Corton-Grancey Latour (PEN)
Volnay les Caillerets, Clos des 60 Ouvrées,
  Domaine de la Pousse d'Or (MV, DI)
Vosne-Romanée les Chaumes, Rion (GAU)
1989
Clos de Vougeot Mongeard-Mugneret
  (GOE)
Corton Pougets, Jadot (WR, BOT, THR)
Gevrey-Chambertin Combottes, Dujac
  (BUT)
Volnay Frémiets, Marquis d'Angerville
  (GE)
Vosne-Romanée les Chaumes, Méo-
  Camuzet (NO)

1988

Beaune Clos des Mouches, Drouhin (TW)

Beaune Cuvée Brunet Hospices de
Beaune, Patriarche (BER)

Clos de Vougeot Noëllat (NEZ)

Nuits-St-Georges Clos des Argillières,
Rion (GAU)

Nuits-St-Georges Vignes Rondes, Rion
(GAU)

Volnay les Caillerets, Domaine de la
Pousse d'Or (RES)

1987

Charmes-Chambertin Dujac (BUT, RIP,
GOE)

1986

Clos de la Roche Dujac (RIP, BUT)

Clos de la Roche Vieilles Vignes, Ponsot
(GOE)

Clos St-Denis Dujac (GOE)

Gevrey-Chambertin Clos St-Jacques,
Armand Rousseau (BUT)

Latricières-Chambertin Ponsot (GOE)

Romanée-St-Vivant Michel Voarick (RES)

1985

Aloxe-Corton Tollot-Beaut (CRO)

Beaune Grèves Vigne de l'Enfant Jesus,
Bouchard Père (REI)

Chambolle-Musigny Jadot (GOE)

Gevrey-Chambertin Clos des Varoilles,
Domaine des Varoilles (REI)

Nuits-St-Georges Doudet-Naudin (ROB)

Nuits-St-Georges les Damodes, Machard
de Gramont (REI)

Volnay Santenots Lafon (BUT)

1983

Bonnes-Mares de Vogüé (REI)

Bonnes-Mares Domaine des Varoilles (REI)

Chambertin Clos-de-Bèze, Damoy (BUT)

Clos St-Denis Lignier (BUT)

Ruchottes-Chambertin Domaine
Mugneret (REI)

1982

Chambertin Clos-de-Bèze, Faiveley (REI)

1978

Gevrey-Chambertin Rossignol-Trapet (BY)

£30.00 → £34.99

1994

Clos de Vougeot Méo-Camuzet (GOE)

Volnay Clos des Chênes, Michel Lafarge
(RAE)

1993

Chapelle-Chambertin Jadot (GOE)

Charmes-Chambertin Armand Rousseau
(AD)

Clos de la Roche Armand Rousseau (RIP)

Clos de Vougeot Grivot (REI)

Gevrey-Chambertin Combottes, Dujac (RIP)

Volnay Clos des Chênes, Michel Lafarge
(RAE)

Volnay Santenots Lafon (REI)

Vosne-Romanée les Beaumonts, Domaine
Rion (MV)

Vosne-Romanée les Chaumes, Méo-
Camuzet (RAE)

1992

Bonnes-Mares Roumier (RIP)

Chambertin Trapet (OD)

Chambolle-Musigny les Amoureuses,
Roumier (RIP)

Charmes-Chambertin Bachelet (YOU)

Clos de la Roche Armand Rousseau (TAN)

Clos St-Denis Dujac (RIP)

Gevrey-Chambertin Clos St-Jacques,
Armand Rousseau (GOE)

1991

Charmes-Chambertin Armand Rousseau
(RES, ROB)

Corton Clos du Roi, Chandon de Briailles
(REI)

Nuits-St-Georges les St-Georges, Faiveley
(DI)

Volnay Clos de la Bousse d'Or, Domaine
de la Pousse d'Or (DI)

Volnay Clos des Chênes, Michel Lafarge
(RIP, HAH, RAE)

1990

Beaune Clos des Mouches, Drouhin (BEN)

Charmes-Chambertin Armand Rousseau
(GOE)

Clos de Vougeot Château de la Tour (BER)

Corton Bouchard Père (HOG)

Nuits-St-Georges Clos des Forets St-
Georges, Domaine de l'Arlot (BOT, GOE)

Volnay Santenots Matrot (TW)

Vosne-Romanée Rion (CRO)

1989

Beaune Clos des Mouches, Drouhin (NO)

Bonnes-Mares de Vogüé (CRO)

Bonnes-Mares Jadot (FA)

Charmes-Chambertin Dujac (BUT, GOE)

Corton Clos du Roi, Dubreuil-Fontaine (BY)

Échézeaux Mongeard-Mugneret (GOE)

Grands-Échézeaux Mongeard-Mugneret
(FA, GOE)

Nuits-St-Georges les Chaignots, Michelot
(NO)

Nuits-St-Georges Vignes Rondes, Rion (MV)

Ruchottes-Chambertin Armand Rousseau
(FA)

1988
Corton-Grancey Latour (WY)
Gevrey-Chambertin Combottes, Dujac
 (GOE, BUT)
Latricières-Chambertin Trapet (BY)
Mazis-Chambertin Armand Rousseau (GAU)
Nuits-St-Georges les Pruliers, Gouges (UB)
Nuits-St-Georges Soeurs Hospitalières,
 Hospice de Nuits (FA)
1987
Bonnes-Mares Jadot (HA)
Corton Clos des Cortons, Faiveley (DI)
1986
Chambertin Ponsot (GOE)
Chambolle-Musigny de Vogüé (CRO)
Clos de Vougeot Méo-Camuzet (REI)
Corton Maréchaudes, Chandon de
 Briailles (TW)
Échézeaux Dujac (RIP)
1985
Corton les Renardes, Michel Voarick (BUT)

Corton Pougets, Jadot (REI)
1983
Clos de Vougeot Moillard (PEN)
Romanée-St-Vivant les Quatres Journaux,
 Latour (REI)
1978
Gevrey-Chambertin Clos des Varoilles,
 Domaine des Varoilles (CRO)
Gevrey-Chambertin Faiveley (BUT)

£35.00 → £39.99

1993
Charmes-Chambertin Bachelet (ELL)
Gevrey-Chambertin Clos St-Jacques,
 Armand Rousseau (FA)
Grands-Échézeaux Engel (RIP)
Ruchottes-Chambertin Armand Rousseau
 (RES)
Volnay Clos des Chênes, Michel Lafarge
 (GAU, RIP)
Volnay Santenots Lafon (BEN)
1992
Bonnes-Mares de Vogüé (REI)
Échézeaux Henri Jayer (RAE)

Gevrey-Chambertin Clos St-Jacques,
 Armand Rousseau (EL)
Nuits-St-Georges Clos des Forets St-
 Georges, Domaine de l'Arlot (BY)
Ruchottes-Chambertin Domaine
 Mugneret (LEA)
1991
Bonnes-Mares Lignier (SOM)
Clos de la Roche Armand Rousseau (RES)
Clos de la Roche Dujac (RIP, DI)
Gevrey-Chambertin Clos des Ruchottes,
 Armand Rousseau (RES)
1990
Clos de la Roche Armand Rousseau (BUT)
Clos de Vougeot Château de la Tour (EL)
Gevrey-Chambertin Combottes, Dujac
 (BUT)
Pommard les Épenots, Mme de Courcel
 (RES)
1989
Bonnes-Mares Dujac (BUT)
Clos de la Roche Dujac (BUT)
Gevrey-Chambertin Clos St-Jacques,
 Armand Rousseau (BUT)
1988
Clos de Vougeot Moillard (BER)
Clos St-Denis Dujac (BUT, RIP)
Corton-Bressandes Tollot-Beaut (AD)
Échézeaux Faiveley (DI)
Savigny-lès-Beaune les Guettes, Bize (FA)
Vosne-Romanée les Beaux Monts,
 Domaine Jean Grivot (CRO)
1987
Bonnes-Mares Roumier (BUT)
Chambertin Clos-de-Bèze, Armand
 Rousseau (ELL)
Clos de la Roche Vieilles Vignes, Ponsot
 (GOE)
Clos de Vougeot Arnoux (WHI)
Clos de Vougeot Méo-Camuzet (ELL)
Échézeaux Drouhin (RES)
Échézeaux Jacqueline Jayer (BUT)
Pommard les Épenots, Mme de Courcel
 (UB)
1986
Bonnes-Mares Dujac (RIP)
1985
Chambolle-Musigny les Charmes, Michel
 Clerget (RES)
Corton Pougets, Jadot (FA)
Volnay Champans, Marquis d'Angerville
 (UB)
1982
Corton Clos des Cortons, Faiveley (TW)
Volnay Santenots Ampeau (YOU, LEA, WS)

1970
Charmes-Chambertin Armand Rousseau (RES)
Échézeaux Domaine de la Romanée-Conti (FA)
1969
Gevrey-Chambertin Clos des Varoilles, Domaine des Varoilles (REI)

£40.00 ➜ £49.99

1994
Bonnes-Mares Roumier (TAN)
Échézeaux Henri Jayer (RAE)
Vosne-Romanée Cros Parantoux, Méo-Camuzet (GOE, RAE)
1993
Bonnes-Mares Jadot (ELL, VIG, FA)
Chambertin Clos-de-Bèze, Damoy (RES)
Charmes-Chambertin Bachelet (RIP)
Clos de Vougeot Méo-Camuzet (RES)
Clos St-Denis Dujac (RIP)
Grands-Échézeaux Mongeard-Mugneret (GOE)
Latricières-Chambertin Faiveley (SEC)
Mazis-Chambertin Faiveley (RIP)
Ruchottes-Chambertin Domaine Mugneret (LEA)
1992
Chambertin Clos-de-Bèze, Armand Rousseau (RIP, GOE, EL, TAN)
Chambertin Ponsot (GOE)
Clos de la Roche Vieilles Vignes, Ponsot (GOE, LAY, YOU)
Clos St-Denis Dujac (BY)
Échézeaux Domaine de la Romanée-Conti (EL)
Griotte-Chambertin Ponsot (MV)
Latricières-Chambertin Ponsot (MV)
1991
Chambertin Clos-de-Bèze, Bruno Clair (REI)
Clos de Vougeot Méo-Camuzet (RES)
1990
Charmes-Chambertin Dujac (BUT)
Grands-Échézeaux Mongeard-Mugneret (GOE)
1989
Chambolle-Musigny les Amoureuses, de Vogüé (NO)
Charmes-Chambertin Armand Rousseau (UB)
1988
Bonnes-Mares de Vogüé (FA)
Clos de la Roche Dujac (BUT)
Clos de Vougeot Grivot (GOE)
Échézeaux Engel (CRO)

1987
Clos de la Roche Ponsot (YOU)
Clos de Vougeot Château de la Tour (RES)
1986
Échézeaux Georges Jayer (REI)
1985
Corton Pougets, Jadot (GOE)
Nuits-St-Georges Henri Jayer (BUT)
Nuits-St-Georges Richemone, Pernin-Rossin (CRO)
Vosne-Romanée les Beaumonts, Domaine Rion (CRO)
1982
Musigny Vieilles Vignes, de Vogüé (WY)
1978
Clos de Vougeot Clos de la Perrière, Bertagna (CRO)
1976
Chambertin Clos-de-Bèze, Faiveley (REI)
Nuits-St-Georges Clos de la Maréchale, Faiveley (TW)

£50.00 ➜ £59.99

1993
Chambertin Clos-de-Bèze, Armand Rousseau (FA)
Gevrey-Chambertin Clos St-Jacques, Armand Rousseau (RES)
1992
Musigny Vieilles Vignes, de Vogüé (REI)
1989
Clos de la Roche Vieilles Vignes, Ponsot (GOE)
Musigny Vieilles Vignes, de Vogüé (FA)
1988
Clos de Vougeot Méo-Camuzet (RIP)
Griotte-Chambertin Ponsot (GOE)
1987
Chambolle-Musigny les Amoureuses, de Vogüé (TW)
Échézeaux Domaine de la Romanée-Conti (GOE, BUT)
1985
Clos St-Denis Lignier (CRO)
1984
Richebourg Domaine Gros (BUT)
1982
Romanée-St-Vivant Domaine de la Romanée-Conti (FA)
1979
Clos de Vougeot Faiveley (TW)
Latricières-Chambertin Faiveley (TW)
Mazis-Chambertin Faiveley (TW)
Pommard Pezerolles, Domaine de Montille (RES)

1978
Volnay de Montille (RES)
Volnay Santenots Ampeau (LEA)
1976
Chambertin Trapet (BY)

£60.00 → £79.99

1993
Chambertin Armand Rousseau (RIP, RES)
Chambertin Clos-de-Bèze, Faiveley (RIP)
Griotte-Chambertin Ponsot (FA)
Mazis-Chambertin Faiveley (BER)
Vosne-Romanée aux Brulées, Méo-
    Camuzet (RES)
1992
Clos de Vougeot Leroy (FA)
Grands-Échézeaux Domaine de la
    Romanée-Conti (BER)
Richebourg Domaine de la Romanée-
    Conti (LAY)
1991
Échézeaux Domaine de la Romanée-
    Conti (BER)
Musigny Vieilles Vignes, de Vogüé (NO,
    REI)
Richebourg Domaine Gros (DI, REI)
Romanée-Conti Domaine de la Romanée-
    Conti (EL)
1990
Bonnes-Mares Dujac (BUT)
Gevrey-Chambertin Clos St-Jacques,
    Armand Rousseau (BER)
Ruchottes-Chambertin Armand Rousseau
    (BER)
1988
Clos de la Roche Vieilles Vignes, Ponsot
    (GOE)
1987
Romanée-St-Vivant Domaine de la
    Romanée-Conti (BUT)
1986
Vosne-Romanée Cros Parantoux, Henri
    Jayer (FA)
1985
Chambertin Clos-de-Bèze, Armand
    Rousseau (WS)
Clos St-Denis Dujac (BY)
Échézeaux Domaine de la Romanée-
    Conti (BUT)
1983
Chambertin Trapet (UB)
Échézeaux Domaine de la Romanée-
    Conti (TW)
1982
Mazis-Chambertin Cave Roty (RES)

1978
Corton Clos des Cortons, Faiveley (CRO)
Pommard Clos Micault, Parent (CRO)
1976
Musigny Faiveley (TW)
Musigny Prieur (RES)
1974
Richebourg Domaine de la Romanée-
    Conti (REI)
1965
Grands-Échézeaux Domaine de la
    Romanée-Conti (VIG)

£80.00 → £99.99

1992
Romanée-St-Vivant Domaine de la
    Romanée-Conti (BER)
1991
Grands-Échézeaux Domaine de la
    Romanée-Conti (FA, BER)
Richebourg Méo-Camuzet (GOE)
1989
la Romanée Domaines du Château de
    Vosne-Romanée, Bouchard Père (HOG)
1987
La Tâche Domaine de la Romanée-Conti
    (BUT)
1986
Échézeaux Henri Jayer (BUT)
Grands-Échézeaux Domaine de la
    Romanée-Conti (TW, UB)
1985
Musigny Vieilles Vignes, de Vogüé (BEN)
Romanée-St-Vivant Cuvée Marey Monge,
    Domaine de la Romanée-Conti (BUT)
1978
Musigny de Vogüé (RES)
1972
Grands-Échézeaux Domaine de la
    Romanée-Conti (BUT)
1961
Richebourg Domaine de la Romanée-
    Conti (FA)

£100.00 → £149.99

1993
Clos de la Roche Ponsot (FA)
1992
Richebourg Leroy (FA)
Romanée-St-Vivant Leroy (FA)
1990
Échézeaux Domaine de la Romanée-
    Conti (FA)
Romanée-St-Vivant Domaine de la
    Romanée-Conti (EL)

1989
Grands-Échézeaux Domaine de la
Romanée-Conti (BER)
1987
Richebourg Domaine de la Romanée-
Conti (BUT, TW, GOE)
1985
Chambertin Ponsot (FA)
Clos de la Roche Vieilles Vignes, Ponsot (FA)
Latricières-Chambertin Ponsot (FA)
1983
Échézeaux Henri Jayer (FA, REI)
La Tâche Domaine de la Romanée-Conti
(FA)

£150.00 ➜ £199.99

1992
Chambertin Leroy (FA)
1991
La Tâche Domaine de la Romanée-Conti
(FA, WY, EL)
1990
Richebourg Domaine de la Romanée-
Conti (FA, BER)
1989
La Tâche Domaine de la Romanée-Conti
(FA)

1985
Romanée-St-Vivant Domaine de la
Romanée-Conti (GOE)
1976
Échézeaux Domaine de la Romanée-
Conti (REI)
1969
Grands-Échézeaux Domaine de la
Romanée-Conti (BEN)
1964
Griotte-Chambertin Drouhin (RES)

£200.00 ➜ £299.99

1992
La Tâche Domaine de la Romanée-Conti
(BER)
1990
La Tâche Domaine de la Romanée-Conti
(BER, FA)

£300.00 ➜ £499.99

1992
Romanée-Conti Domaine de la Romanée-
Conti (BER)
1987
Romanée-Conti Domaine de la Romanée-
Conti (BUT)

1985
La Tâche Domaine de la Romanée-Conti
(BUT, WY)
1978
La Tâche Domaine de la Romanée-Conti
(SEC, BEN)

c. £1,150.00
1959
Romanée-Conti Domaine de la Romanée-
Conti (FA)

WHITE

Under £10.00
1993
St-Aubin le Charmois, Olivier Leflaive (POR)
St-Romain Domaine Leflaive (DI)

£10.00 → £11.99
1994
Pernand-Vergelesses Olivier Leflaive (CB)
1993
Auxey-Duresses Labouré-Roi (PIP)
Marsannay Jadot (BOT, WR)
St-Aubin la Chatenière, Roux Père et Fils
(EL)
1992
St-Aubin Jadot (VIC)
St-Aubin Jaffelin (BER)
1991
St-Aubin Prudhon (BIB)
1988
Puligny-Montrachet Jean Germain (CRO)

£12.00 → £13.99
1994
Meursault Latour (FA)
Pernand-Vergelesses Rollin (RAE)
St-Aubin le Charmois, Olivier Leflaive (LAY)
1993
Meursault Chanson (POR)
Meursault Michelot (OD)
Meursault Michelot-Buisson (OD)
Puligny-Montrachet Labouré-Roi (EL)

1992
Pernand-Vergelesses Dubreuil-Fontaine (BY)
1991
Puligny-Montrachet Latour (HOG)
1990
St-Aubin Jadot (ELL, REI)

£14.00 → £15.99
1994
Meursault Boisson-Vadot (BY)
Meursault Michelot (AD)
Puligny-Montrachet Drouhin (NI)
St-Aubin la Chatenière, Chartron et
Trébuchet (LAYT)
1993
Meursault Latour (HOG, MAJ, NEW, GAL)
Monthelie le Champ Fulliot, Garaudet (PIP)
Puligny-Montrachet Carillon (OD)
Puligny-Montrachet Domaine Leflaive (DI)
1992
Chassagne-Montrachet Domaine Leflaive
(SOM)
Pernand-Vergelesses Rollin (BIB)
1991
Meursault-Blagny, Latour (MAJ)
Meursault Genevrières, Latour (HOG)
Meursault Jobard (LEA)
1987
Meursault les Luchets, Roulot (BUT)

£16.00 → £17.99
1994
Meursault Charmes, Latour (FA)
Puligny-Montrachet Carillon (GOE)
Puligny-Montrachet Clerc (FUL)
1993
Chassagne-Montrachet Latour (MAJ, WY)
Meursault-Blagny, Latour (HOG)
Puligny-Montrachet les Folatières,
Drouhin (SOM)
1992
Meursault Jadot (MAR, ELL)
Meursault Michelot-Buisson (NEZ)
1991
Meursault Matrot (CB)
Puligny-Montrachet Clavoillon, Domaine
Leflaive (SOM)
1990
Meursault Bouchard Père (BU)
Meursault l'Ormeau, Coche (RAE)
Puligny-Montrachet Bouchard Père (QUE)
1989
Chassagne-Montrachet Niellon (BUT)
1988
Meursault Clos du Cromin, Javillier (SUM)

£18.00 → £19.99

1995
Puligny-Montrachet Carillon (NEZ)
1994
Chassagne-Montrachet Sauzet (FA)
Puligny-Montrachet Drouhin (MAJ)
Puligny-Montrachet les Folatières, Latour (FA)
St-Aubin Albert Morey (DAV)
1993
Chassagne-Montrachet Drouhin (WY)
Chassagne-Montrachet Fontaine-Gagnard (OD)
Puligny-Montrachet Chartron et Trébuchet (LAYT)
Puligny-Montrachet les Folatières, Latour (GAL)
Puligny-Montrachet Sauzet (EY)
1992
Chassagne-Montrachet Latour (WY)
Chassagne-Montrachet Morgeot, Henri Germain (TAN)
Meursault Charmes, Brunet (EL)
Meursault Clos de Mazeray, Prieur (BER)
Puligny-Montrachet les Folatières, Boisson-Vadot (BY)
1991
Chassagne-Montrachet Lamy-Pillot (BY)
Chassagne-Montrachet Morgeot, Gagnard Delagrange (BY)
Puligny-Montrachet Carillon (YOU, BOT)
Puligny-Montrachet Sauzet (FA)
1990
Chassagne-Montrachet Drouhin (CRO)
Meursault Jobard (SOM)
Puligny-Montrachet Grands Champs, Jean Germain (DAV)
Puligny-Montrachet Jadot (ELL)
Puligny-Montrachet Latour (PEN)
1989
Chassagne-Montrachet Albert Morey (DAV)
1988
Puligny-Montrachet Domaine Leflaive (BUT)
1986
Meursault Genevrières, Jobard (BUT)
1985
Chassagne-Montrachet Roux (PE)

£20.00 → £24.99

1994
Chassagne-Montrachet les Vergers, Colin (RAE)
Meursault Jobard (RAE)
Puligny-Montrachet les Champs Gains, Clerc (FUL)

1993
Chassagne-Montrachet la Maltroie, Fontaine-Gagnard (OD)
Chassagne-Montrachet les Chaumes, Jean-Marc Morey (PIP)
Meursault Charmes, Henri Germain (TAN)
Meursault Clos de Mazeray, Prieur (BER)
Meursault Genevrières, Jobard (LEA)
Meursault Jobard (MV, RAE)
Meursault les Luchets, Roulot (ARM)
Puligny-Montrachet Olivier Leflaive (TW)
Puligny-Montrachet les Folatières, Drouhin (WY)
Puligny-Montrachet les Referts, Sauzet (FA)
Puligny-Montrachet Monnier (EL)
1992
Chassagne-Montrachet Drouhin (WY)
Chassagne-Montrachet Marquis de Laguiche (BER)
Meursault-Blagny, Jadot (FA)
Meursault-Blagny, Latour (BEN)
Meursault-Blagny, Matrot (CB)
Meursault Genevrières, Latour (BER)
Puligny-Montrachet Carillon (REI, ROB, GOE)
Puligny-Montrachet Jadot (ELL)
Puligny-Montrachet Latour (WHI)
Puligny-Montrachet les Perrières, Sauzet (TAN)
1991
Chassagne-Montrachet la Boudriotte, Gagnard-Delagrange (HAH)
Meursault Genevrières, Jobard (LEA)
Meursault Perrières, Domaine Leflaive (DI)
Puligny-Montrachet Domaine Leflaive (ARM)
1990
Chassagne-Montrachet Fontaine-Gagnard (YOU)
Chassagne-Montrachet Gagnard (GOE)
Chassagne-Montrachet Marquis de Laguiche (CRO)
Puligny-Montrachet les Folatières, Latour (REI)
1989
Chassagne-Montrachet Jadot (REI, WR, BOT)
Chassagne-Montrachet les Vergers, Colin (EY)

> *Please remember that* **Webster's** *is a price GUIDE and not a price LIST. It is not meant to replace up-to-date merchants' lists.*

Chassagne-Montrachet Morgeot, Gagnard
  Delagrange (BY)
Chassagne-Montrachet Morgeot, Henri
  Germain (RIP)
Meursault Charmes, Henri Germain (BEN)
Puligny-Montrachet Drouhin (BO)
Puligny-Montrachet les Perrières, Sauzet
  (PE)
1988
Meursault-Blagny, Jadot (FA)
Puligny-Montrachet Latour (PEN)
Puligny-Montrachet les Folatières,
  Drouhin (WY)
1987
Puligny-Montrachet Clerc (TW)
Puligny-Montrachet les Folatières, Clerc
  (PE)
1986
Puligny-Montrachet Domaine Leflaive (BUT)

£25.00 → £29.99
1994
Chassagne-Montrachet Morgeot, Gagnard
  Delagrange (LAYT)
Puligny-Montrachet les Referts, Sauzet
  (FA)
1993
Beaune Clos des Mouches, Drouhin (WY)
Chassagne-Montrachet Morgeot, Henri
  Germain (LEA)
Corton-Charlemagne Latour (FA)
Meursault Genevrières, Jobard (RAE)
Puligny-Montrachet Champ Canet, Sauzet
  (FA)
Puligny-Montrachet Clavoillon, Domaine
  Leflaive (TAN, AD, FA)
Puligny-Montrachet les Perrières, Sauzet
  (EY, TAN)
1992
Chassagne-Montrachet la Maltroie,
  Fontaine-Gagnard (LAYT)
Chassagne-Montrachet les Caillerets,
  Bachelet-Ramonet (RES)
Chassagne-Montrachet Niellon (BER)
Meursault Charmes, Brunet (GAU)
Meursault Charmes, Matrot (CB)
Puligny-Montrachet les Champs Gains,
  Clerc (BY)
Puligny-Montrachet les Combettes, Prieur
  (BER)
Puligny-Montrachet les Referts, Sauzet (FA)
Puligny-Montrachet Mouchère, Boillot (DAV)
1991
Chassagne-Montrachet Ramonet (BER)
Corton-Charlemagne Latour (MAJ)

Puligny-Montrachet Clavoillon, Domaine
  Leflaive (PE, FA)
Puligny-Montrachet les Combettes, Clerc
  (CRO)
1990
Chassagne-Montrachet les Caillerets,
  Albert Morey (DAV)
Meursault-Blagny, Jadot (BOT, WR)
Meursault-Blagny, Matrot (CB)
Meursault Clos de la Barre, Lafon (GAU)
Puligny-Montrachet Domaine Leflaive
  (CRO)
Puligny-Montrachet Olivier Leflaive (AD)
Puligny-Montrachet les Folatières,
  Drouhin (RES)
1989
Meursault-Blagny, Jadot (FA)
Meursault Charmes, Michelot (RIP)
Puligny-Montrachet Clos de la Garenne,
  Drouhin (WY)
Puligny-Montrachet Domaine Leflaive (DI)
1988
Chassagne-Montrachet les Vergers, Colin
  (GOE)
Chassagne-Montrachet Marquis de
  Laguiche (WY)
Meursault Charmes, Henri Germain (AD)
Puligny-Montrachet les Pucelles, Domaine
  Leflaive (FA)
Puligny-Montrachet Sauzet (CRO)
1987
Puligny-Montrachet Clavoillon, Domaine
  Leflaive (REI)
1986
Chassagne-Montrachet les Vergers, Colin
  (GOE)
Meursault Poruzots, Jobard (BUT)
Puligny-Montrachet Carillon (REI)
Puligny-Montrachet Clavoillon, Domaine
  Leflaive (REI)
Puligny-Montrachet les Folatières,
  Bouchard Père (PEN)
1985
Meursault Charmes, Matrot (REI)
Meursault Charmes, Michelot (RIP)
1984
Corton-Charlemagne Bonneau du
  Martray (REI)
1983
Meursault Ampeau (CHA)
1981
Bienvenues-Bâtard-Montrachet Bachelet-
  Ramonet (RIP)
1980
Meursault Charmes, Ampeau (CHA)

£30.00 → £39.99

1994
Corton-Charlemagne Latour (FA)
Corton-Charlemagne Olivier Leflaive (HAH)
Corton-Charlemagne Rollin (RAE)
Meursault Genevrières, Jobard (RAE)
Meursault Poruzots, Jobard (RAE)
Puligny-Montrachet Champ Canet, Sauzet (FA)
Puligny-Montrachet les Caillerets, Domaine Chartron (LAYT)
Puligny-Montrachet les Perrières, Sauzet (FA)

1993
Corton-Charlemagne Bonneau du Martray (GOE)
Corton-Charlemagne Jadot (FA)
Meursault Clos de la Barre, Lafon (BEN)
Puligny-Montrachet les Combettes, Sauzet (FA)
Puligny-Montrachet les Pucelles, Domaine Leflaive (AD)

1992
Chassagne-Montrachet Ramonet (BER)
Corton-Charlemagne Drouhin (WY, NI)
Corton-Charlemagne Rollin (RAE)
Meursault Charmes, Michelot (WS)
Meursault Clos de la Barre, Lafon (ELL)
Puligny-Montrachet Champ Canet, Sauzet (FA)

1991
Puligny-Montrachet les Combettes, Domaine Leflaive (ARM)
Puligny-Montrachet les Pucelles, Domaine Leflaive (FA, ARM, RES)

1990
Bâtard-Montrachet Latour (WY)
Corton-Charlemagne Bonneau du Martray (GOE)
Corton-Charlemagne Drouhin (RES)
Meursault Charmes, Matrot (TW)
Puligny-Montrachet Clavoillon, Domaine Leflaive (FA, WS)

1989
Chassagne-Montrachet Marquis de Laguiche (WY)
Corton-Charlemagne Chapuis (GOE)
Puligny-Montrachet Champ Canet, Sauzet (AD)
Puligny-Montrachet les Folatières, Drouhin (BEN)
Puligny-Montrachet les Pucelles, Domaine Leflaive (BUT)
Puligny-Montrachet les Referts, Jadot (FA)

1988
Corton-Charlemagne Bonneau du Martray (BUT)
Corton-Charlemagne Jadot (FA)
Corton-Charlemagne Latour (PLA)
Corton-Charlemagne Olivier Leflaive (AD)
Corton-Charlemagne Michel Voarick (BEN)
Corton-Charlemagne Rollin (RAE)
Puligny-Montrachet Clavoillon, Domaine Leflaive (PE)
Puligny-Montrachet les Folatières, Latour (GOE)
Puligny-Montrachet les Referts, Sauzet (GAU)

1987
Corton-Charlemagne Bonneau du Martray (RIP)
Puligny-Montrachet les Pucelles, Domaine Leflaive (REI)

1986
Chassagne-Montrachet Morgeot, Henri Germain (AD)
Chevalier-Montrachet Chartron (REI)
Corton-Charlemagne Bonneau du Martray (BUT)
Corton-Charlemagne Bouchard Père (PEN)
Corton-Charlemagne Olivier Leflaive (REI)
Meursault Charmes, Brunet (GAU)

1985
Beaune Clos des Mouches, Drouhin (FA)

1984
Corton-Charlemagne Bonneau du Martray (RIP)

1980
Puligny-Montrachet les Combettes, Ampeau (CHA)

£40.00 → £49.99

1994
Bâtard-Montrachet Latour (FA)

1992
Corton-Charlemagne Latour (BER, FA)
Puligny-Montrachet les Combettes, Sauzet (FA)

1991
Bâtard-Montrachet Domaine Leflaive (AD, GOE)
Bâtard-Montrachet Sauzet (FA)
Bienvenues-Bâtard-Montrachet Louis Carillon (ELL)
Bienvenues-Bâtard-Montrachet Domaine Leflaive (GOE, FA)
Bienvenues-Bâtard-Montrachet Sauzet (REI)
Corton-Charlemagne Rollin (BIB)
Meursault Clos de la Barre, Lafon (RES)

1990
Chevalier-Montrachet Bouchard Père
    (HOG)
Corton-Charlemagne Jadot (FA, GOE)
1989
Chevalier-Montrachet Chartron (REI)
Corton-Charlemagne Drouhin (BO)
Corton-Charlemagne Jadot (GOE)
Corton-Charlemagne Olivier Leflaive (CRO)
Puligny-Montrachet les Combettes,
    Sauzet (FA)
Puligny-Montrachet les Pucelles, Domaine
    Leflaive (RIP)
1988
Bienvenues-Bâtard-Montrachet Clerc (TW)
Puligny-Montrachet Domaine Leflaive (BO)
1986
Corton-Charlemagne Bonneau du
    Martray (GOE, FA, RIP)
Puligny-Montrachet les Pucelles, Domaine
    Leflaive (FA)
1985
Corton-Charlemagne Bonneau du
    Martray (RIP, BUT, REI)
Corton-Charlemagne Jadot (REI)
Puligny-Montrachet Clavoillon, Domaine
    Leflaive (REI)
Puligny-Montrachet les Folatières, Clerc
    (RES)
1984
Bâtard-Montrachet Domaine Leflaive (REI)

£50.00 → £69.99
1994
Bâtard-Montrachet Gagnard (FA)
Bâtard-Montrachet Gagnard-Delagrange
    (LAYT)
Bienvenues-Bâtard-Montrachet Sauzet (FA)
Chevalier-Montrachet les Desmoiselles,
    Latour (FA)
1993
Bâtard-Montrachet Domaine Leflaive (FA,
    GOE, RES)
Bâtard-Montrachet Drouhin (WY)
Bâtard-Montrachet Olivier Leflaive (ARM)
Bâtard-Montrachet Sauzet (FA, RES)
Bâtard-Montrachet Domaine Ramonet (FA)
Bienvenues-Bâtard-Montrachet Domaine
    Ramonet (FA)
Chevalier-Montrachet Domaine Leflaive
    (GOE)
Chevalier-Montrachet Prieur (FA)
Meursault Charmes, Lafon (BEN)
Meursault Perrières, Lafon (BEN)
le Montrachet Jadot (FA)

1992
Bâtard-Montrachet Latour (BER)
Chevalier-Montrachet Bouchard Père (BER)
Corton-Charlemagne Michel Voarick (WY)
1991
Bâtard-Montrachet Domaine Ramonet (FA)
Bienvenues-Bâtard-Montrachet Domaine
    Ramonet (RIP)
Chevalier-Montrachet Domaine Leflaive
    (GOE, FA, ARM)
Criots-Bâtard-Montrachet Blain-Gagnard
    (BIB)
le Montrachet Thénard (CRO)
1990
Bâtard-Montrachet Albert Morey (DAV)
Bâtard-Montrachet Pierre Morey (FA)
Bienvenues-Bâtard-Montrachet Domaine
    Leflaive (FA)
Chassagne-Montrachet Jadot (FA)
Chevalier-Montrachet les Desmoiselles,
    Latour (WY)
Puligny-Montrachet les Combettes,
    Sauzet (BER)
1989
Bâtard-Montrachet Domaine Leflaive (EY)
Bâtard-Montrachet Olivier Leflaive (WS,
    DI)
Beaune Clos des Mouches, Drouhin (RES)
Corton-Charlemagne Drouhin (WY)
Corton-Charlemagne Latour (BEN)
1988
Bienvenues-Bâtard-Montrachet Domaine
    Leflaive (FA)
Chevalier-Montrachet Domaine Leflaive
    (CB)
Meursault Perrières, Lafon (FA)
1987
Bâtard-Montrachet Olivier Leflaive (TW)
Chevalier-Montrachet Domaine Leflaive
    (REI)
1986
Bâtard-Montrachet Latour (BUT, WY, GOE)
Bienvenues-Bâtard-Montrachet
    Remoissenet (CRO)
Chevalier-Montrachet Bouchard Père (PEN)
Corton-Charlemagne Latour (PE)
le Montrachet Thénard (BUT)
Puligny-Montrachet les Perrières, Sauzet
    (FA)
1985
Bâtard-Montrachet Domaine Leflaive (BUT)
Bâtard-Montrachet Latour (WY)
Corton-Charlemagne Latour (BUT, WY)
1983
Corton-Charlemagne Latour (FA)

le Montrachet Château Herbeux (BUT)
le Montrachet Prieur (WY)
1978
Chevalier-Montrachet Bouchard Père (REI)
1969
Meursault Leroy (FA)

£70.00 → £99.99

1994
Bâtard-Montrachet Sauzet (FA)
Chevalier-Montrachet Domaine Leflaive
  (LAY)
le Montrachet Jadot (FA)
le Montrachet Latour (FA)
1993
Bâtard-Montrachet Pierre Morey (RES)
le Montrachet Latour (WY)
le Montrachet Prieur (FA)
Musigny Comte de Vogüé (GOE)
1992
Bâtard-Montrachet Sauzet (FA)
Chevalier-Montrachet Domaine Leflaive
  (TW)

Chevalier-Montrachet Niellon (BER)
Meursault Charmes, Lafon (FA)
Meursault Perrières, Lafon (FA)
le Montrachet Marquis de Laguiche (WY)
Musigny Comte de Vogüé (FA, GOE)
1991
Chevalier-Montrachet Niellon (BER)
le Montrachet Marquis de Laguiche (NI)
Musigny Comte de Vogüé (WY)
1989
Chevalier-Montrachet Domaine Leflaive
  (DI)
1988
Bâtard-Montrachet Latour (VIN)
Chevalier-Montrachet Domaine Henri
  Clerc (RES)
1986
Chevalier-Montrachet Domaine Leflaive
  (BUT)
le Montrachet Bouchard Père (PEN)
le Montrachet Latour (BUT)
Puligny-Montrachet la Truffière, Sauzet
  (RES)

1985
Chevalier-Montrachet Domaine Leflaive
  (FA)
Chevalier-Montrachet les Desmoiselles,
  Latour (TW)
Corton-Charlemagne Latour (FA)
1982
Bienvenues-Bâtard-Montrachet Domaine
  Leflaive (RES)
1964
Puligny-Montrachet les Pucelles, Domaine
  Leflaive (REI)

£100.00 → £199.99

1994
le Montrachet Gagnard-Delagrange (LAYT)
1990
le Montrachet Bouchard Père (HOG)
1989
le Montrachet Marquis de Laguiche (WY)
le Montrachet Thénard (WS)
1987
le Montrachet Marquis de Laguiche (BUT)
1986
le Montrachet Jadot (NO)
1983
Bienvenues-Bâtard-Montrachet Domaine
  Leflaive (RES)
1977
le Montrachet Domaine de la Romanée-
  Conti (BUT)
1971
Bâtard-Montrachet Domaine Leflaive (RES)
le Montrachet Marquis de Laguiche (FA)

£300.00 → £399.99

1993
le Montrachet Leflaive (FA)
1983
le Montrachet Domaine de la Romanée-
  Conti (WY, FA)

£400.00 → £499.99

1991
le Montrachet Domaine de la Romanée-
  Conti (EL)
1987
le Montrachet Domaine de la Romanée-
  Conti (TW, BUT)
1985
le Montrachet Domaine de la Romanée-
  Conti (FA)
1982
le Montrachet Domaine de la Romanée-
  Conti (TW)

CÔTE CHALONNAISE

RED

Under £9.00

1994
Givry Clos du Cellier aux Moines, Delorme (WAT)
1993
Rully Drouhin (OD)
1992
Mercurey les Mauvarennes, Faiveley (DI)
1990
Givry Gérard Mouton (REI)
1987
Rully Clos de Bellecroix, Domaine de la Folie (BUT)

£9.00 → £10.99

1993
Mercurey Domaine de la Croix Jacquelet, Faiveley (BEN)
Mercurey Latour (PEN)
Mercurey les Mauvarennes, Faiveley (DI)
1991
Mercurey Château de Chamirey (EL)
Mercurey les Mauvarennes, Faiveley (BEN)
Rully Faiveley (BEN)
1990
Mercurey Château de Chamirey (WHI)
Mercurey Maréchal (PIP)
1983
Rully Domaine de l'Hermitage, Chanzy (BUT)

£11.00 → £14.99

1993
Mercurey Clos du Roy, Faiveley (HAH, BEN)
Mercurey Domaine du Meix-Foulot (PLA, ROB)
1992
Givry Gérard Mouton (RES)
1991
Mercurey Clos du Roy, Faiveley (HAH)
1989
Mercurey Domaine de la Croix Jacquelet, Faiveley (ROB)
1988
Givry Remmoissenet (CRO)
Rully Clos de Bellecroix, Domaine de la Folie (BUT)
1985
Mercurey Clos des Barraults, Juillot (BUT)
Mercurey Juillot (BUT)

WHITE

Under £6.50

1993
Montagny 1er Cru, Cave de Buxy (MAR)

£6.50 → £7.99

1993
Montagny Latour (NEW)
1992
Montagny 1er Cru, Cave de Buxy (VIC)
Montagny Château de Davenay, Picard (SAI)
Montagny Latour (HOG)

£8.00 → £8.99

1994
Montagny 1er Cru, Olivier Leflaive (AD)
1992
Montagny Arnoux (SUM)
1991
Rully la Chaume, Dury (SEC)

£9.00 → £10.99

1994
Montagny 1er Cru, Bernard Michel (DAV)
Montagny Roy (WRI)
1993
Montagny Roy (POR, PLA)
Rully les St-Jacques, Chandesais (WR)
1992
Givry Chofflet (NEZ)
Givry Thénard (HOG)
Rully Château de Rully Rodet (WHI)
Rully la Chaume, Dury (EY)
Rully Marissou, Dury (RAE)
1991
Mercurey Château de Chamirey, Rodet (MAR)
Mercurey Émile Voarick (WRI)

£11.00 → £12.99

1994
Rully la Chaume, Chartron et Trébuchet (LAYT)
1993
Rully Château de Rully Rodet (BER)
Rully Faiveley (ROB)
Rully Grésigny, Cogny (AD)
Rully Olivier Leflaive (CRO)
1992
Mercurey Clos Rochette, Faiveley (WS)

MÂCONNAIS

WHITE

Under £5.00
1994
Mâcon-Villages Cave Co-op. de Viré (CO)

£5.00 → £5.99
1994
Mâcon-Lugny Duboeuf (NEZ)
Mâcon-Villages Loron (TAN)
Mâcon-Villages Rodet (MAR)
1993
Mâcon-Lugny les Genièvres, Latour (POR)
Mâcon-Prissé Duboeuf (NI)

£6.00 → £6.99
1994
Macon Chardonnay les Ecuyers (SAI)
Mâcon Chardonnay Talmard (EY)
Mâcon-Lugny les Genièvres, Latour (HOG)
Mâcon-Prissé Cave Co-op. Prissé (HAH)
St-Véran Domaine Deux Roches (POR)
St-Véran Domaine St-Martin, Duboeuf
    (NEZ)
1993
Mâcon-Villages Cave Co-op. Prissé (ARM)
1992
Mâcon Blanc Clos de Condemine, Luquet
    (REI)

£7.00 → £7.99
1994
St-Véran Château Fuissé, Vincent (AD)
1993
Mâcon la Roche Vineuse, Merlin (BIB)
St-Véran Domaine de la Batie, Duboeuf
    (AV)
1992
Mâcon-Clessé Signoret (HAW)
Mâcon-Viré Clos du Chapitre, Dépagneux
    (WS)
Pouilly-Loché Cave des Crus Blancs (HAW)

£8.00 → £9.99
1995
Pouilly-Vinzelles Mathias (PIP)
1994
Mâcon-Clessé Guillemot (TAN)
Mâcon la Roche Vineuse, Merlin (MV)
Mâcon-Viré André Bonhomme (DAV)
Pouilly-Vinzelles Château de Pouilly-
    Vinzelles, Loron (AV)

1993
Mâcon-Charnay Blanc Manciat-Poncet
    (ENO)
Mâcon-Viré Cuvée Spéciale, Bonhomme
    (GE)
Pouilly-Loché Cave des Crus Blancs (PLA)
St-Véran Château Fuissé, Vincent (DI)

£10.00 → £12.49
1994
Pouilly-Fuissé Domaine Béranger,
    Duboeuf (NEZ)
Pouilly-Fuissé Latour (HOG, WY)
1993
Mâcon Monbellet, Goyard (BIB)
1992
Mâcon-Clessé Domaine de la Bon Gran,
    Thévenet (TAN)
Pouilly-Fuissé Manciat-Poncet (HAW)
1991
Mâcon-Viré Goyard (EY)

£12.50 → £15.99
1994
Pouilly-Fuissé Château Fuissé, Vincent (TAN)
Pouilly-Fuissé Corsin (REI)
Pouilly-Fuissé les Crays, Forest (NI)
1993
Pouilly-Fuissé Vieilles Vignes, Daniel
    Barraud (LEA)
1992
Mâcon-Clessé Thévenet (DAV)
Mâcon-Viré Goyard (UB)
1986
Pouilly-Fuissé Domaine de l'Arillière (BUT)

£16.00 → £19.99
1993
Mâcon-Clessé Domaine de la Bon Gran,
    Thévenet (LEA)
Pouilly-Fuissé Château Fuissé, Vincent (DI)
1988
Pouilly-Fuissé Château Fuissé, Vincent
    (RAE, CRO)

£20.00 → £29.99
1993
Pouilly-Fuissé Château Fuissé Vieilles
    Vignes, Vincent (EL, DI, TAN)
1988
Pouilly-Fuissé Château Fuissé Vieilles
    Vignes, Sourice (NO)

CHABLIS

WHITE

Under £6.00

1994
Sauvignon de St-Bris, Brocard (FOR)
1992
Sauvignon de St-Bris, Defrance (EL)

£6.00 → £6.99

1994
Chablis la Chablisienne (WAI)
Sauvignon de St-Bris, Domaine des
  Remparts (HIG)
1993
Sauvignon de St-Bris, Goisot (YOU)
Sauvignon de St-Bris, Sorin-Defrance (WRI)
Sauvignon de St-Bris, Verret (CRO)

£7.00 → £7.99

1994
Chablis Domaine de Vauroux (FUL)
Chablis la Chablisienne (VIC)
Chablis Laroche (BO)
Chablis Pautré (SAF)
Chardonnay Domaine des Remparts,
  Sorin (HIG)

£8.00 → £9.99

1995
Chablis Christian Adine (LAYT)
Chablis J Moreau (DAV)
Chablis Laroche (PLA)
Chablis Simonnet-Febvre (DAV)
Chablis Vocoret (MAJ)
1994
Chablis Bernard Defaix (SEC, PE)
Chablis Daniel Defaix (WR, THR, BOT)
Chablis Domaine de Biéville, J Moreau (WHI)
Chablis Domaine de l'Églantière (PE, AME)
Chablis Domaine des Manants, Brocard
  (AD)
Chablis Domaine des Marronniers (BIB)
Chablis Domaine du Valéry, Durup (TAN)
Chablis Drouhin (NI)
Chablis Durup (HAH)
Chablis Fourchaume, J Moreau (FOR)
Chablis Grossot (LAY)
Chablis Hamelin (ELL)
Chablis Vaillons, J Moreau (BOT, WR, THR)
1993
Chablis Bonard (POR)
Chablis Château de Maligny, Durup (BY)

Chablis Domaine de Colombier, Mothe
  (POR)
Chablis Domaine de Vauroux (NI)
Chablis Gautheron (UN)
Chablis Grossot (LAY)
Chablis Légland (BIB)
Chablis Vocoret (UB)
1992
Chablis Brocard (HIC)
Chablis Château de Maligny, Durup (THR)
Chablis Montmains, Brocard (SAI)

£10.00 → £11.99

1995
Chablis Adhémar Boudin (LEA)
Chablis Pic (MV)
1994
Chablis 1er Cru, Laroche (PLA)
Chablis Domaine Servin (WRI)
Chablis Fourchaume, Domaine de Valéry
  (TAN)
Chablis Montmains, Brocard (EY, AD)
Chablis Montmains, Domaine Adine (LAYT)
Chablis Montmains, Filippi (QUE)
Chablis Vau Ligneau, Hamelin (NEZ)
Chablis Vocoret (VIN)
1993
Chablis Fourchaume, la Chablisienne (HOG)
Chablis Fourchaume, Domaine de
  Colombier, Mothe (ASD)
Chablis Long-Depaquit (VIN)
Chablis Montée de Tonnerre, Durup (EL)
Chablis Montée de Tonnerre, Louis
  Michel (OD)
Chablis Montmains, Domaine de la Tour
  Vaubourg (NI)
Chablis Montmains, Louis Michel (OD)
Chablis Vaillons, Simonnet-Febvre (CHA)
Chablis Vaudevey, Laroche (PLA)
1992
Chablis Mont de Milieu, Pinson (BIB)
Chablis Séchet, René Dauvissat (TAN)
1990
Chablis 1er Cru Grand Cuvée, la
  Chablisienne (SO, MAR)

£12.00 → £13.99

1994
Chablis Fourchaume, Laroche (PLA)
Chablis Montée de Tonnerre, Droin (GOE)
Chablis Montmains, Domaine Pico Race
  (MV)

Chablis Montmains, Droin (GOE)
Chablis Montmains, Laroche (PLA)
Chablis Vaillons, Long-Depaquit (PEN)
Chablis Vaillons, Simonnet-Febvre (DAV)
1993
Chablis 1er Cru, Drouhin (NI)
Chablis 1er Cru, Laroche (DI)
Chablis Drouhin (BEN)
Chablis la Forêt, Pinson (PIP)
Chablis Mont de Milieu, Grossot (LAY)
Chablis Mont de Milieu, Pinson (PIP)
Chablis Montée de Tonnerre, Droin (BIB)
Chablis Vaillons, Droin (BIB)
Chablis Vaillons, Laroche (PLA)
Chablis Vaillons, Servin (WRI)
1991
Chablis Vaillons, Collet (LAYT)
1990
Chablis Latour (FOR)
Chablis Montée de Tonnerre, Régnard
   (HOG)
1986
Chablis Montée de Tonnerre, Louis
   Michel (BUT)
Chablis Régnard (BUT)

£14.00 ➡ £16.99
1994
Chablis Séchet, René Dauvissat (LEA)
1993
Chablis Vaillons, Raveneau (HAH)
1992
Chablis Bougros, Ancien Domaine Auffray
   (MAJ)
Chablis Fourchaume, Laroche (POR)
Chablis Vaudésir, J Moreau (HOG)
Chablis Vaulorent, Fèvre (BEN)
1991
Chablis Bougros, Fèvre (REI)
1990
Chablis Grand Cru les Preuses, Filippi
   (SAI)
Chablis la Forêt, René Dauvissat (BUT)
Chablis les Lys, Daniel Defaix (TAN, LAY)
Chablis Vaillons, Daniel Defaix (LAY, VIG)
Chablis Vaudésir, Gautherin (SOM)

£17.00 ➡ £19.99
1993
Chablis Beauroy, Verret (CRO)
Chablis Bougros, Domaine de Colombier,
   Mothe (POR)
Chablis les Clos, Servin (EL)
Chablis Vaudésir, Long-Depaquit (PEN)
Chablis Vaudésir, Louis Michel (OD)

1992
Chablis Bougerots, Laroche (BO)
Chablis les Clos des Hospices, Moreau
   (HOG)
1991
Chablis les Clos, Pinson (BIB)
1990
Chablis Grenouilles, Domaine de Château
   Grenouille (MAR)
Chablis la Moutonne, Long-Depaquit (FUL)
1989
Chablis Valmur, J Moreau (HA)

£20.00 ➡ £24.99
1994
Chablis Grenouilles, Droin (RAE)
Chablis les Clos, René Dauvissat (TAN)
Chablis Valmur, Droin (RAE, EY)
1992
Chablis les Clos, Drouhin (NO)
Chablis les Clos, Pinson (PIP, NO)
Chablis les Clos, Vocoret (VIN)
1991
Chablis Blanchots, Laroche (PLA)
Chablis Valmur, Droin (BIB)
Chablis Vaudésir, Droin (BIB)
1989
Chablis Bougerots, Laroche (NO)
1988
Chablis Blanchots, Laroche (DI)
Chablis les Clos, Drouhin (REI)
1986
Chablis Vaudésir, Fèvre (BUT)
1983
Chablis Vaulorent, Fèvre (CRO)

£25.00 ➡ £34.99
1994
Chablis les Clos, René Dauvissat (LEA)
1992
Chablis les Clos, Laroche (PLA, DI)
Chablis Vaillons, Raveneau (ROB)
1990
Chablis les Clos, Laroche (DI)
1988
Chablis Vaudésir, Louis Michel (CRO)
1984
Chablis les Lys, Daniel Defaix (VIG, ROB)
1976
Chablis Vaudésir, Long-Depaquit (REI)

c. £45.00
1983
Chablis les Clos, René Dauvissat (CRO)
Chablis Vaudésir, Louis Michel (CRO)

BEAUJOLAIS

RED

Under £5.00

1995
Beaujolais-Villages Château du Basty (OD)
1994
Beaujolais-Villages Domaine de la Ronze (ASD)
Beaujolais-Villages Duboeuf (FUL)
1993
Beaujolais-Villages Duboeuf (TES)
1992
Beaujolais-Villages Château du Bluizard (TES)

£5.00 → £5.99

1995
Beaujolais-Villages Château de Lacarelle (WS)
Beaujolais-Villages Château des Vierres, Duboeuf (NI)
Beaujolais-Villages Jaffre (WHI)
Régnié Duboeuf (SAF)
1994
Beaujolais Loron (TAN, DI)
Beaujolais-Villages Château de Néty (EL)
Beaujolais-Villages Colonge (ELL)
Beaujolais-Villages Loron (UN)
Régnié Duboeuf (SAF)
1993
Beaujolais Cave Beaujolais de St-Verand (HAW)
Beaujolais Château de Tanay (HAW)
Morgon Jambon (ASD)

£6.00 → £6.49

1995
Beaujolais-Villages Domaine Aucoeur (HIC)
1994
Juliénas Domaine Joubert (EY)
1993
Beaujolais Blaise Carron (HAW)
Beaujolais Garlon (HAW)
Beaujolais-Villages Cave des Producteurs Juliénas (HAW)
Chénas Château de Chénas (HAW)
1992
Juliénas les Envaux, Pelletier (HIG)
Morgon le Clachet, Brun (HIG)

£6.50 → £6.99

1995
Brouilly de Pierreux, Duboeuf (FUL)

1994
Beaujolais Lantignié, Domaine Joubert (AD)
Côte de Brouilly Domaine de Chavannes (EL)
Fleurie Duboeuf (TES)
Fleurie Verpoix (ASD)
Juliénas Loron (UN)
Juliénas Pelletier (EL)
Morgon Duboeuf (WR, THR, BOT)

Morgon le Clachet, Brun (EL)
Morgon Loron (UN)
1993
Chénas Léspinasse (HAW)
Chiroubles Méziat (OD)
Juliénas Château des Capitans, Sarrau (SAI)
Juliénas Domaine de la Seigneurie (NEZ)
Morgon Domaine des Arcades (AS)
Moulin-à-Vent le Vivier, Brugne (WHI)
Régnié Noël (HAW)

£7.00 → £7.49

1995
Brouilly Domaine de Combillaty, Duboeuf (NEZ)
1994
Brouilly Duboeuf (POR)
Chénas Château Bonnet (AV)
Morgon Domaine des Vieux Cèdres, Loron (PEN)
Morgon Domaine Jean Descombes, Duboeuf (NEZ)
1993
Chiroubles la Maison des Vignerons (HAW)
Côte de Brouilly Château du Grand Vernay (HAW)
Morgon Côte de Py, Gaget (ELL)
Morgon Fontcraine, Loron (UB)
Régnié Roux (HAW)
St-Amour Domaine du Paradis (NEZ)
1992
Fleurie Cave Co-op. de Fleurie (HAW)
Morgon Aucoeur (HAW)

£7.50 → £7.99

1995
Brouilly Château Thivin (AD)
Chiroubles Loron (TAN)
Fleurie Château des Deduits, Duboeuf (WAI)
Fleurie la Madone, Celliers des Samsons (SAI)
1994
Brouilly Large (PLA)
Brouilly Latour (HOG)
Côte de Brouilly Joubert (TAN)
Fleurie Domaine Paul Bernard (OD)
Juliénas Domaine de la Vieille Église, Loron (DI)
Juliénas les Capitains, Louis Tête (HOG)
Morgon Jambon (AUR)
Moulin-à-Vent Domaine de la Tour du Bief, Duboeuf (BOT, WR, THR)
Moulin-à-Vent le Vivier, Brugne (EL)
Moulin-à-Vent Loron (UN)
St-Amour Domaine des Pins, Echallier (ELL)
1993
Beaujolais Cuvée Centenaire, Charmet (HAW)
Brouilly Geoffray (HAW)
Brouilly Jean Lathuilière (HAW)
Juliénas Duboeuf (QUE)
Moulin-à-Vent Duboeuf (NI)

£8.00 → £8.99

1995
Brouilly Château des Tours (PIP)
Fleurie Domaine des Quatre Vents, Duboeuf (NEZ)
Fleurie Sélection Éventail, Domaine de Montgénas (PLA)
1994
Brouilly Domaine de Saburin (WY)
Brouilly Loron (CRO)
Brouilly Michaud (MV)
Chénas Domaine Louis Champagnon (PIP)
Chiroubles Château de Raousset (PIP)
Fleurie Château de Fleurie, Loron (EL, TAN, PEN, PE, WRI)
Fleurie Colonge (TAN, AME)
Fleurie la Madone, Louis Tête (HOG)
Fleurie les Garans, Latour (WY, HOG)
Juliénas Domaine de Berthets, Dépagneux (ROB)
Juliénas Drouhin (REI)
Moulin-à-Vent Caves Kuhnel (SAI)
Moulin-à-Vent Château Bonnet (AV)
Moulin-à-Vent Château des Jacques (AS)
St-Amour les Bonnets, Bernard Patissier (PLA)

1993
Côte de Brouilly Château Thivin (HAW)
Moulin-à-Vent Janin (PIP)
1992
Juliénas Condemine (HAW)

£9.00 → £11.49

1995
Fleurie Domaine de la Grand' Cour (DAV)
Fleurie Michel Chignard (MV)
1994
Chiroubles Loron (ROB)
Fleurie Drouhin (REI)
Fleurie Verpoix (BEN)
Juliénas Clos des Poulettes, Loron (UB)
Morgon Marcel Lapierre (BIB)
Moulin-à-Vent Domaine Charvet (TAN)
Moulin-à-Vent Drouhin (REI)
1993
St-Amour Domaine des Billards, Loron (UB)
1992
Morgon Charmes Domaine Princesse Lieven, Duboeuf (LAYT)
1991
Moulin-à-Vent les Hospices, Collin & Bourisset (POR)
1989
Moulin-à-Vent Château du Moulin-à-Vent (HAW)

£11.50 → £19.99

1994
Fleurie Domaine des Quatre Vents, Duboeuf (CRO)
1988
Moulin-à-Vent Lafond (CRO)

WHITE

Under £6.00
1994
Beaujolais Blanc Bully (TES)

£8.00 → £8.50
1995
Beaujolais Blanc Château des Tours (PIP)
1992
Beaujolais Blanc Charmet (HAW)

ROSÉ

c. £6.00
1993
Beaujolais Supérieur Rosé, Cave Beaujolais du Bois d'Oingt (HAW)

CHAMPAGNE

**If you want to buy Champagne, now is the time: it is unlikely to be this
cheap again this side of the millennium. And now that the Champenois have
got their act together, quality is brilliant**

Champagne is not going out of fashion,
even though we are all buying it as
though it were. More bottles were sold in
1995 than in any year since 1989, and sales
in the earlier year had been not so much a
sign of Champagne's success as its stupidity.

In 1989 nearly everything that could be
wrong with Champagne, was. It was the
most successful year in Champagne's
history, but it was also the year in which the
industry managed to get itself caught in a
cleft stick. In 1989 the bad old contract
between the houses and the growers still
existed: it determined the amount of grapes
a house could buy, and based that amount
on the house's previous year's sales of
Champagne. This kept the big houses big
and the little houses in their place, but
something happened in the mid- to late
1980s that threatened this status quo. The
growers refused to sell sufficient grapes to
cover the needs of the houses, which
owned just 12 per cent of the vineyards,
but accounted for more than 70 per cent of
Champagne sales. The only way a particular
house could guarantee a bigger slice of the
shrinking cake of grapes was to sell more
Champagne, but as the very nature of the
problem meant that it was desperately
short of grapes to make Champagne in the
first place, it was a vicious circle. There were
two ways out, neither of them good.

One was for houses to sell progressively
younger wines, but this would deplete
stocks essential for the future of the
industry. The other was for the houses to
buy wines *sur-lattes* (that is, wines that had
been made by other producers and
undergone their second fermentation in
bottle but that had not yet been disgorged.
Growers, co-ops and houses all participated
in this trade). Wines bought *sur-lattes*

would then have the label of the buyer
slapped on and sold to faithful consumers.
Astonishingly, this was perfectly legal.

Green is the answer
With these as the two alternatives, it was
not surprising that we went through a
period of young, green sometimes dire
quality Champagnes. Not all was bad or
young, of course: some houses depended
heavily on grapes they grew themselves,
and some managed to buy better wines *sur-
lattes* than they ever made themselves.

The point is that the peak in sales in 1989
was for the worst possible reasons, whereas
the second-highest year on record was
achieved in 1995 under much healthier
conditions. The old contract was torn up in
1990, and it is this that has been responsible
for raising the quality of the Champagne
we're drinking today, rather than any new
quality criteria that have been introduced
since. Unfortunately it was also responsible
for the financial difficulties most Champagne
houses endured in the meantime, as free
market conditions were introduced when
the demand for grapes was most frenzied,
so prices soared and the grape-starved
houses purchased unprecedented
quantities, often using bank loans to do so.
When the Champagnes produced from
these grapes hit the market it was in the
depths of a recession. Sales plunged and
prices plummeted, but repayments still had
to be made to the banks. The houses were
thus forced to sell off their most expensive
stocks at whatever prices they could get, to
create the cash-flow they needed. Prices
thus sunk even further, and the industry's
losses reached record levels. For a number
of houses these losses proved too great to
bear. Deutz has been taken over by

Roederer, and Joseph Perrier by Laurent-Perrier. Some lesser-known houses have also been swallowed up, and other more famous names could also go in the next 18 months, despite the better market conditions that now prevail.

Sales in the sunset

While sales bottomed out in 1992, prices did not begin to recover until 1995. For consumers this meant that Champagnes were at their cheapest between 1992 and 1994, when the Champenois were experiencing their greatest difficulties. The Champagne market has always been cyclical, going from boom to bust and back again, and prices are currently hardening. We'll be unlikely to see Champagne as cheap again until well into the next century.

Now, however, is the time to buy, because in the past there was so much dross about, particularly in 1991, that Champagne was only a bargain if you managed to buy good quality in the first place. The quality of Champagne today is brilliant, and the price, although increasing, has a long way to go before it gets back up to its 1991 level. Prices will probably rise by six per cent in 1996, as the Champenois try and claw back their losses, but the best advice is to buy in the run-up to Christmas. Why? Because about 40 per cent of all Champagne sales occur then. One would think it was a seller's market, and yet for some strange reason prices almost always drop. When I once tried to discover why, all the merchants said that it is traditional; everyone else does it, and so they have to do it too, to keep pace. As they're all locked into this annual marketing folly, and as all good Champagne improves with extra bottle age, anyone with his or her head screwed on, and some spare cash to spend, would buy their entire year's supply of Champagne every Christmas, at bargain prices. **TOM STEVENSON**

GRAPES & FLAVOURS

CHARDONNAY The grape of white Burgundy fame here tends to produce a lighter, fresher juice, and the resulting Champagnes are certainly the most perfumed and honeyed. They have been criticized for lacking depth and aging potential. Not true. Good Blancs de Blancs have a superb, exciting flavour that is improved by aging, especially those from the southern end of the Côte des Blancs.

PINOT MEUNIER The other black grape, making a softer, fruitier style of wine, important for producing simple wines for drinking young, and useful for lightening the assertive weight of Pinot Noir. That being said, Krug uses Pinot Meunier in its very long-lived Grande Cuvée.

The price guides for this section begin on page 157.

PINOT NOIR The grape that makes all the finest red Burgundies further south also makes white Champagne. Pinot Noir has enough difficulty in ripening in Burgundy, and further north in Champagne it almost never attains any great depth and strength of colour or alcohol, which is fair enough since the general idea here is to produce a *white* wine. Very careful pressing of the grapes in traditional vertical presses is the best way to draw off the juice with as little colour from the skins as possible, and what reddish tinge there is (and there's always some) generally precipitates out naturally during fermentation. Even so, the juice does feel quite big: a Champagne relying largely on Pinot Noir is certain to be heavier and take longer to mature. It can also go with food rather better. And yes, Champagne does make a very little still red wine from Pinot Noir, but it takes a hot year to make it attractive. Most Pinot made as red wine is used to colour rosé.

WINES & WINE STYLES

BLANC DE BLANCS Champagne made only from Chardonnay. Has become more fashionable as drinkers look for a lighter style. Should not only be fresh but creamy and bright as well, and should get deeper and richer as it ages. Some firms, notably *Henriot, Mumm, Joseph Perrier* and *Bruno Paillard* make excellent NV Blanc de Blancs, and the *Union* co-operatives at Avize and le Mesnil make the most of their positions at the heart of the Côte des Blancs. Most firms sell vintage Blanc de Blancs (watch out for *Billecart-Salmon, Drappier, Jacquesson, Pol Roger, Roederer*) and a couple also make luxury *cuvées. Taittinger's Comtes de Champagne, Dom Ruinart, Salon* and *Krug's Clos de Mesnil* are the benchmarks.

BLANC DE NOIRS This white style is made from black grapes only and is common throughout the Marne Valley. Few have the quality and longevity of *Bollinger's Vieilles Vignes*, but none are even half as expensive. Most are rather solid. *Pierre Vaudon* is an elegant exception; *H Billiot* is fine, and *de Venoge* is rich and ripe. *Sainsbury's* version is good value. *Serge Mathieu* does not indicate on the label that it is Blanc des Noirs, and you would never guess it from its fresh, light, zesty style.

BRUT Very dry.

BUYER'S OWN BRAND (BOB) A wine blended to a buyer's specification, or more probably, to a price limit. The grapes are of lesser quality, the wines usually younger, and cheaper. *Sainsbury* and *Waitrose* are consistent, M&S less so but good when it's on song.

CM This means *co-opérative-manipulant* and shows that the wine comes from a co-operative, whatever the brand name implies.

COTEAUX CHAMPENOIS Still wines, red, rosé or white. Overpriced and generally rather acid. A village name, such as Cramant (white) or Bouzy (red) may appear. *Alain Vesselle's* Bouzy and *René Geoffroy's* Cumiéres have produced exciting reds, but all producers are as variable as the climate.

DE LUXE/CUVÉE DE PRESTIGE/ CUVÉE DE LUXE A special highly prized blend, mostly vintage. Some undeniably great wines and some gaudy coat-trailers. At these prices one's looking for immense complexity and refinement. In general these wines are drunk *far* too young. Most need a good ten years to shine. Some of the best: *Bollinger RD, Charles Heidsieck Cuvée de Millenaires, Dom Pérignon, Dom Ruinart, Krug Grande Cuvée, Laurent Perrier Grand Siècle, Pol Roger Cuvée Sir Winston Churchill, Roederer Cristal, Taittinger Comtes de Champagne, Cuvée NF Billecart, Cattier Clos du Moulin, Philipponnat Clos des Goisses, Perrier-Jouët Belle Epoque, Veuve Clicquot la Grande Dame.*

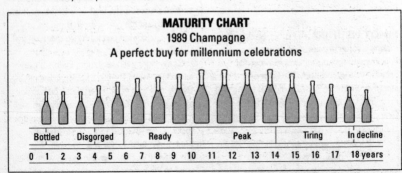

MATURITY CHART
1989 Champagne
A perfect buy for millennium celebrations

Bottled	Disgorged	Ready	Peak	Tiring	In decline

0 1 2 3 4 5 6 7 8 9 10 11 12 13 14 15 16 17 18 years

DEMI-SEC Medium-sweet. Rarely very nice, but *Louis Roederer* can be outstanding, and *Veuve Clicquot* is usually the most consistent.

DOUX Sweet. *Louis Roederer* is excellent.

EXTRA DRY Confusingly, this is less dry than 'Brut', but drier than 'Sec'.

GRANDE MARQUE Ambiguous term meaning 'great brand'. It is a self-styled group of 24 houses, including the 15 or so best known. The term *should* be synonymous with quality – better grapes, older reserve wines and more rigid selection. It might be in future, if they ever get around to agreeing anything.

NM In the code on the label, this means *négociant-manipulant* (merchant-handler) and shows that the producer is one of the 265 Champagne houses in the region.

NON-DOSAGE Most Champagne has a little sweetness – a 'dosage' – added just before the final cork is put in. A few are sold absolutely bone-dry and will have names like Brut Zero. Best are *Laurent-Perrier, Piper-Heidsieck*. They're designed to show that it's the wine, not the dosage that provides the quality. Do they prove their point? Well, they're uncompromising. And I'm not sure that I'd choose to drink one for pure pleasure.

NON-VINTAGE The flagship of most houses, and the one by which a producer should be judged. Until the early 1990s many reputable firms were not making a wine of consistent quality, let alone a recognizable house style. But now they are. The wines are generally based on one vintage and usually aged for three years. But many of the best provide greater depth and age, and ensure consistency by using up to 40 per cent of *vins de réserve*, still wines from previous years, and thus giving more depth and maturity to the blend, and a few producers reduce their output of vintage wines to ensure NV quality. Best: *Alfred Gratien, Henriot, Jacquesson, Bruno Paillard, Pol Roger, Billecart-Salmon, Mailly Grand Cru, Charles Heidsieck, Veuve Clicquot* and *Bollinger*. All, especially the lighter wines, gain from a few months in bottle after purchase.

RC A new designation of *récoltant-co-opérateur* – for a grower selling wine produced at a co-op. It should stop growers who've carted their grapes along to the co-op and collect the bottles afterwards, pretending they've made it themselves. Should. So far we haven't seen any of the 11 million bottles under this heading.

CLASSIFICATIONS

The classification system in Champagne is based on vineyards. The approved areas for vineyards are strictly demarcated and the vineyard land graded according to suitability for black and white grapes, going from 100 per cent for the finest Grand Cru villages through 90–99 per cent for the 38 Premier Cru villages and on to 80 per cent for the least favoured.

If the guideline price is 20 francs per kilo of grapes, a 100 per cent village grower receives the full 20 francs. An 80 per cent grower will receive only 80 per cent – 16 francs – and so on; it's all quite simple. The whole system is now less rigorous than it was 50 years ago, when percentages ranged from 50 to 100.

Champagne houses boast about how high their 'average percentage' of grapes is. Some Champagne labels will say either '100 per cent Grand Cru' or 'Premier Cru' and even a village name as well, Avize, for example, if the wine comes entirely from one single top village.

Hardly surprisingly, no one ever bothers to declare on the label percentages in the 80s or lower 90s, but in actual fact many of the best value Champagnes on the UK market come from these so-called 'lowly' villages. There is no reason why careful vineyard managment and vinification should not produce good results.

A LITTLE INSIDE INFORMATION...

Not so many years ago, the subject of wine was an area which many people avoided. Having little or no knowledge of wine, they mistakenly believed it to be far too complex. Of course, the situation has changed considerably since then, partly thanks to guides such as this one.

But, to many people, Scotch whisky is equally as daunting and as complicated as wine used to be. Faced with a shelf full of unfamiliar names, many will opt for a well-advertised brand simply because of the reassurance that advertising provides. However, as readers of this book well know, the exploration of an unknown field can be intensely rewarding. And as far as Scotch whisky goes, a little rudimentary knowledge goes a long way.

Malt whisky is a subject which has been dissected in hundreds of books and there are always a few tomes in any bookshop. Most are good quality and easy to understand. However, blended whisky is considerably more popular than malt whisky but has yet to receive the same amount of attention.

Although there are considerably more varieties of blended whisky than there are malts, choosing a quality blend is not quite as complicated as it looks.

The art of blending whisky originated in about 1865, when it was discovered that blending malt whisky with its lighter counterpart, grain whisky, resulted in a much lighter spirit. It had all the benefits of its constituent parts but none of the heaviness that some people found off-putting. It was this development that launched what is now the world's number one spirit.

However, as with any boom industry, unscrupulous traders sought to exploit it. Without any legal standardisation, 'blended whiskies' were appearing which were no more than ethyl alcohol with colour added. A famous one in particular was known as N.S.S., popularly translated as 'Never Seen Scotland'!

Thankfully, the definition of Scotch whisky is now legally enshrined. Leaving aside the technical jargon, it is spirit that has been distilled in Scotland from a mash of cereals (either malted barley or grain), and matured in Scotland in oak casks for a minimum of three years. Once bottled for consumption, its strength can be no less than 40% alc./vol.

If you have ever visited a distillery and seen freshly distilled spirit coming off the still, you will have noted that it is the same colour as vodka. It is only after the mandatory three years mellowing in oak casks that it loses some of the harshness of new spirit and takes on the colour of whisky as we know it. However, few malt distillers would consider their product ready for drinking at htree years of age, even though it is legally Scotch whisky. A quick look at any supermarket shelf will show that most will wait up to eight, ten or sixteen years, or even longer; the maturation period will vary from malt to malt. What you can be certain of is that the distiller will have matured his malt for as long as it takes to reach perfection.

The question of age for blend drinkers is a little more complex. In addition to the grain which lightens it, a blend can contain anything from ten to thirty different malts. But what is not divulged is the age of these malts. Theoretically, they could all be the legal minimum of three years old. The question is, how do you know? The simple answer is you don't – unless there is an age statement on the label, e.g. 8 years old, etc.

Yet, with up to thirty or more whiskies in the blend, what does the age statement on the label actually mean? Quite simply, it is the age of the *youngest* whisky in the blend. The number of malts doesn't matter, nor does the average age. It is only the youngest whisky that is relevant, as this tells you the *minimum* maturity the blender considered suitable for his blend.

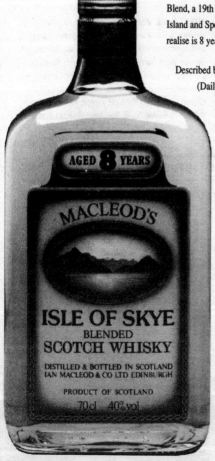

Now that we've established a few relevant whisky facts, here's the advert. We'd like to introduce you to Isle of Skye 8-Year-Old Blend, a 19th century recipe containing a high proportion of mature Island and Speyside malts (the youngest of which you will now realise is 8 years old).

Described by the author of the book as "...extremely good..." (Daily Telegraph 5/3/93), Isle of Skye is available in the stockists listed below *for the price of an ordinary blend.* So if your preference is a dram with the elegance and harmony that only maturity can bestow – you know now what to ask for. Unless, of course, you prefer something a little younger. In which case, you have plenty of choice.

...FOR THOSE IN THE KNOW!

STOCKISTS

UK	SCOTLAND
Savacentre	Tesco
Major Sainsburys	Scotmid
Major Budgens	Selected Oddbins
Stewarts Wine Barrels	Selected Threshers

and independent stockists
throughout the country

Ian Macleod & Co 01506 852205

RECENTLY DISGORGED A term for Champagnes that have been left in the cellars, drawing flavour from their yeast deposits, for much longer than usual before disgorging. The wines can rest for 20–30 years on the lees but are usually released after seven to ten. *Bollinger RD* is the most famous and still the best; also good are *Deutz*, *Alfred Gratien* and *Laurent-Perrier*.

RICH The sweetest Champagne. *Roederer* can be superbly balanced. *Veuve Clicquot* has just released a great vintage version.

RM Indicates that a grower, a *récoltant-manipulant*, made it himself, rather than taking it to the co-op. Try: *Bara, Billiot, Bonnaire, Clouet, René Geoffroy, Michel Gonet, André Jacquart, Lassalle, Legras, Vesselle, Vilmart*.

ROSÉ Traditionally, the pink colour is gained by a short maceration of the black grapeskins with the juice, as practised by *Laurent-Perrier* Most producers add a little still red Bouzy to white wine before bottling. Ideally rosés are aromatic, fruity wines, with a delicious strawberry or cherry flavour. Sadly, many are indistinguishable from white. Most should be drunk young. Best: *Billecart-Salmon, Bollinger, Dom Ruinart, Alfred Gratien, Jacquart Mosaïque, Lassalle, Laurent-Perrier, Moët et Chandon, Pol Roger, Louise Pommery, Roederer and Roederer Cristal. Krug rosé* is in a class of its own, and at that price so it should be.

SEC Literally 'dry', but any Champagne so labelled will actually be medium dry.

SR Société de Récoltants. Label code for a family company of growers.

VINTAGE Wine of a single, good year, generally fuller and deeper than non-vintage, but almost always nowadays released too young. Best names: *Billecart-Salmon, Bollinger, Charles Heidsieck, Devaux, Drappier, Gosset Grande Millésime, Henriot, Krug, Lanson, Mailly Grand Cru, Bruno Paillard, Joseph Perrier, Perrier-Jouët, Pol Roger, Louis Roederer, Ruinart and Veuve Clicquot.*

CHAMPAGNE HOUSE PROFILES

BILLECART-SALMON ★★★★(★) Terrifically elegant Champagne from a family-owned house. Very refined, mature wines and a delicate rosé. Its vintage, Cuvée NF Billecart, is also excellent.

BOLLINGER ★★★★(★) Like Krug, makes 'English-style' Champagnes: rich, oaky, but more steely and almost half the price. RD, its luxury cuvée, is kept on its lees until just before sale.

F BONNET ★★ Inexpensive offshoot of Piper Heidsieck and Charles Heidsieck, with mature and biscuity non-vintage.

DEUTZ ★★★ This house is back on form again with creamy-rich, biscuity non-vintage and an excellent quality prestige cuvée called William Deutz.

DRAPPIER ★★(★) Consistent quality, although the style appears to bounce between ultra-fruity and rich and biscuity according to how much landed age the wine has.

DUVAL-LEROY ★★ Fresh, fragrant style in a Chardonnay-dominated Champagne. Good value and consistent.

ALFRED GRATIEN ★★★★ Serious, oak-fermented wine at a much lower price than Krug. Very long-lived vintage.

CHARLES HEIDSIECK ★★★★ Probably the best value Grande Marque NV around at the moment; sensuously rich, full style and great vanilla finesse.

HENRIOT ★★(★) Good bottle age and unrelenting quality.

KRUG ★★★★★ Classic, mellow, rich. Oak-fermented Grande Cuvée is outstanding. The expensive rosé has incomparable Pinot Noir cherry fruit. Even more expensive Clos de Mesnil is a rich, single-vineyard Blanc de Blancs.

JACQUESSON ★★★★ Always great quality and finesse, whether the elegant, flowery non-vintage or the rich, well-extracted vintage.

LANSON ★★(★) Until recently had a (well-deserved) reputation for excessive acidity, but has always produced classic, long-maturing vintage.

BRUNO PAILLARD ★★★ Fresh, elegant and satisfying Champagne from one of the most consistent producers.

LAURENT-PERRIER ★★★★ One of the most reliable of non-vintages, with excellent rosé. Prestige brand Grand Siècle is (sensibly) a blend of several vintages, but there is now also a much more expensive vintage version.

MOËT & CHANDON ★★★ Brut Imperial has been reliable of late. Vintages usually show well but are released too young.

MUMM ★★ Traditionally rich (I'm told), but all too frequently unimpressive. Delicate, creamy Mumm de Cramant, when you catch it freshly disgorged.

JOSEPH PERRIER ★★★ The non-vintage is extremely rich and well aged, with biscuity complexity and wonderfully high acidity.

PERRIER-JOUËT ★★★ Able to make light, classic Champagne. Best known for Belle Époque in a pretty bottle, all flowery elegance, echoed in the fresh, slightly unripe-cherry feel of the wine, which always mellows with age.

POL ROGER ★★★★ Model family firm, producer of Churchill's favourite fizz. Delicious, delicate Blanc de Blancs. NV, vintage and Cuvée Sir Winston Churchill are all top class. New are vintage Blanc de Chardonnay, vintage rosé and a Demi-sec.

POMMERY ★★★ This house is currently on good form, with wines of light, flowery elegance. The prestige cuvée, Louise Pommery, is superb.

LOUIS ROEDERER ★★★★★ Most famous for Cristal, invented for sweet-toothed Russian Tsars. Now the most natural of all the prestige cuvées, reflecting the quality of each vintage. NV can be one of the best. Good Demi-sec.

TAITTINGER ★★★(★) Splendidly light, modern, Chardonnayish style, though its Blanc de Blancs Comtes de Champagne goes sumptuously rich with age.

VEUVE CLICQUOT ★★★★ For a century and a half greatly loved by the British. The NV can still have the rich, warm style first made famous by the formidable Madame Veuve Clicquot-Ponsardin. Prestige cuvée la Grande Dame almost chocolate-rich – its 1985 was a classic.

MERCHANTS SPECIALISING IN CHAMPAGNE
see Merchant Directory (page 424) for details

Most good merchants have a fair variety of Champagnes, and generally list the most popular of the Grandes Marques, plus one or two cheaper ones. Most, too, have a pretty varied list of sparkling wines from other countries, and it is quite hard to single out merchants with exceptionally good lists of Champagne. Nevertheless, for

a wider than average choice, try especially: Adnams (AD), Averys of Bristol (AV), Bennetts (BEN), Bibendum (BIB), Eldridge Pope (EL), Farr Vintners (FA), Lea & Sandeman (LEA), Majestic (MAJ), Oddbins (OD), Roberson (ROB), T&W Wines (TW), Tanners (TAN), Peter Wylie (WY) a few old vintages – back to 1947

CHAMPAGNE VINTAGES

In theory Champagne firms only make single-vintage wines in especially fine years. But only a few firms, like Bollinger and Laurent-Perrier, follow the theory. Most either opt too readily for vintage wines in marginal years or, increasingly common, release wines after only five years in bottle, which may be okay for French tastes but leaves the average Brit with an acid stomach. Nevertheless, most firms come up with decent vintage.

1995 Although it rained before the harvest, the wines are significantly superior to those of the previous four years, and this will be the first widely declared vintage since the outstanding 1990.

1994 The fourth and worst in a string of four vintages spoiled by rain, 1994 was potentially a great year until the downpour ruined it. Of the few reputable producers likely to declare this a vintage, Vilmart's Grand Cellier d'Or will probably be the best.

1993 Another year of great summer, shame about the harvest. 1993 probably ranks slightly below 1992, but Roederer managed to produce a vintage Champagne after rejecting no less than half its own crop. Others who will declare this year include Vilmart, Jacquesson, Gosset and Gardet, with Cattier, Drappier and Jacquart also possible.

1992 No-one seriously expected any house to declare 1992 a vintage. But after the drenching debacle of 1993 all hopes were pinned on 1994, and when that suffered the same damp fate, the Champagne trade suddenly found itself staring at a four year gap between vintage years. It is hard not to be cynical, but even as the 1994 crop was being harvested, a number of houses had already re-evaluated 1992 and – surprise, surprise – they decided that 1992 would be the vintage to follow 1990. Well, it has the edge over 1991, 1993 and 1994, but whether the quality is really good enough is another matter.

1991 Possibly a dark horse of a vintage. Alain de Polignac of Pommery rates this year as better than 1989 and 1988. Generally speaking it is the second-worst year between 1991 and 1994, but individual wines can have great potential: try Philipponnat's Clos des Goisses, Vilmart's Coeur de Vucée and De Nauroy. Roederer declared a rosé.

1990 There'll be plenty of vintage Champagnes, many of them superb, although because grapes reached record prices that year the wines are likely to be expensive.

1989 A vintage year with wines which could be ready after a mere five years, like the '82s of blessed memory.

1988 The wines have bite, backbone and fruit, but will be drunk too young. Try and buck the trend and put some aside for a few more years.

1987 A lot of wine, but even the Champenois are not enthusiastic about its quality. Only Pommery declared a vintage. Why, we ask ourselves?

1986 Useful wines, despite some rot. They would have made a decent, if slightly hard vintage, but got sold far too young.

1985 Fine wines, without any of the hardness of some vintages.

1983 The second of the record-breaking vintages, and still high-grade, if a little lean.

1982 A year when Nature was generous, allowing Champagne to make luscious wines which were virtually all ready within five years but are still on song – if you can get them.

CHAMPAGNE

SPARKLING WHITE

Under £10.00
Non-vintage
Moët & Chandon ½ bottle (FOR)
Veuve Clicquot ½ bottle (FOR, REI)

£10.00 → £11.99
Non-vintage
Bollinger ½ bottle (FOR)
Bruno Paillard ½ bottle (HAL)
Georges Gardet (SOM)
Heidsieck Dry Monopole (NEW)
Moët & Chandon ½ bottle (TAN, PLA, WAT, POR, ROB, WHI, TES, BO, CO, FUL)
Veuve Clicquot ½ bottle (BO, ROB, FUL)
1988
Veuve Clicquot ½ bottle (REI)

£12.00 → £13.99
Non-vintage
Bauget-Jouette (HIG)
Blin (OD)
Bollinger ½ bottle (PLA, DI, BUT, BO, BEN, ROB)
Camuset Réserve (BIB)
Canard-Duchêne (HOG, CRO, NEW)
Duchâtel (UN)
Ellner (DAV)
Heidsieck Dry Monopole (OD)
Piper Heidsieck (FOR)
Salon (FA)
Salon Blanc de Blancs (EY, THR, BOT, WR)
de Telmont (MAJ)
Veuve Clicquot ½ bottle (BEN)
1988
Veuve Clicquot ½ bottle (CRO)

£14.00 → £15.99
Non-vintage
Ayala (MAJ)
Beerens (BIB)
Canard-Duchêne (UN, MAJ, ROB)
Drappier Carte d'Or (BOT, THR, WR, BY)
Ellner (LAY)
George Goulet (REI)
Joseph Perrier (FUL, PE)
Joseph Perrier Cuvée Royal (ROB)
Mercier (FOR, ASD, WAI, BOT, SAI, VIC, DAV, TES, UN, THR, FUL, WR)
Mumm Cordon Rouge (THR, BOT, WR)
Pierre Vaudon 1er Cru (HAH)

Piper Heidsieck (SO, BO, SAI, TES, ASD)
Pol Roger (SOM)
Pol Roger White Foil (SOM)
1988
Duchâtel (UN)
Veuve Clicquot ½ bottle (ROB)

£16.00 → £17.99
Non-vintage
Billecart-Salmon (ELL, NI)
Bruno Paillard (WHI)
Charles Heidsieck (HOG)
★ Deutz (FOR)
Duval Leroy Fleur de Champagne (PLA)
George Goulet (PIP, BEN)
Georges Gardet (VIN)
Henriot Blanc de Blancs (PEN, BY)
Henriot Souverain (BY)
Joseph Perrier Cuvée Royal (HIC) (TAN)
Lanson (HOG, SO, BO, SAI, VIC, TES, UN, FOR)
Laurent-Perrier (BIB)
Louis Roederer (REI)
Mercier (SUM, PE, ROB, LAY)
Moët & Chandon Brut Impérial (HOG, POR)
Mumm Cordon Rouge (VIC, ROB, UN, OD)
Perrier-Jouët (MAJ, FUL, WR, THR, BOT, OD)
Piper Heidsieck (BOT, WR, THR, SAF, FUL, CO)
Pol Roger White Foil (REI)
Pommery (ROB)
The Society's Champagne (WS)
de Venoge Cordon Bleu (EL)
Veuve Clicquot (WY, REI)
1989
Canard-Duchêne (NEW)
Drappier Carte d'Or (BY)

£18.00 → £19.99
Non-vintage
Billecart-Salmon (WW, LEA, CB, OD, AD, AD)
Bollinger (REI)
Bruno Paillard (BUT)
Charles Heidsieck (FOR, ROB, WR, BOT, TES)
Gosset Brut Reserve (YOU)
Joseph Perrier Cuvée Royal (HAH)
Lanson (WAI, THR, ASD, BOT, CO, WR, SAF, HA, PLA, DAV, WHI)
Laurent-Perrier (EL, BO, UN, PE, WR, THR, BOT, CB, ARM, LAY, CHA, MAJ, DAV, OD)
Moët & Chandon Brut Impérial (FOR, PLA, BO, ROB, UN, TAN, WRI, SUM, WR, SAI, THR, VIC, BOT, MAJ, FUL, TES, DAV, ELL, HIC, WHI)
Piper Heidsieck (UB)

Pol Roger (FOR)
Pol Roger White Foil (HOG, GE, MAJ, VIC)
'R' de Ruinart (BIB, LEA)
Taittinger (PLA, FOR, HOG)
de Venoge (ROB)
Veuve Clicquot (FOR, NEW, HOG, PLA, GE)
1990
Pierre Vaudon 1er Cru (HAH)
1988
Canard-Duchêne (ROB)
Duval Leroy Fleur de Champagne (TAN)
Perrier-Jouët (FUL)
Pol Roger (SOM)

£20.00 → £21.99
Non-vintage
Bollinger (HOG, PLA, TAN, FOR)
Bruno Paillard Blanc de Blancs (NEZ, GAU)
Charles Heidsieck (PIP, UN, ELL)
Joseph Perrier (CRO)
Laurent-Perrier (MV)
Louis Roederer (HOG, PLA, AD, UN, TES, ELL)
Louis Roederer Rich (PLA, MAJ)
Moët & Chandon Brut Impérial (PE, CB, LAY)
Perrier-Jouët (PIP)
Pol Roger (ROB, WS, POR)
Pol Roger White Foil (PEN, LEA, WR, BOT,
    OD, THR, ELL, TAN, UN, WRI, QUE, DAV)
Taittinger (ARM, POR, FUL, DAV, UN, LEA, LAY)
Veuve Clicquot (BIB, LEA, TES, BO, ENO, MAJ,
    YOU, UN, TAN, CB, PEN, WHI, ARM, ELL, LAY)
Veuve Clicquot White Label Demi-Sec
    (ENO, FUL, VIC)
1990
Jacquesson Blanc de Blancs (YAP)
1989
Joseph Perrier Cuvée Royal (NEW)
Perrier-Jouët (OD)
Pommery (FUL)
1988
Henriot (BY)
Mercier (AME)
Moët & Chandon (FOR, HOG, PLA)
Veuve Clicquot (REI, FOR)
1983
Bauget-Jouette (HIG)
Lanson (REI)

£22.00 → £23.99
Non-vintage
Bollinger (ELL, GAU, BUT, PEN, UN, ENO, POR,
    DI, BO, ASD, CRO, WAT, LEA, PIP, SAT, ARM)
Louis Roederer (ARM, BIB, TAN, PE, WRI,
    BEN, ROB, WAI, OD, LAY, EL, QUE)
Louis Roederer Rich (PEN, WRI, ROB, BEN)
1990
Deutz Blanc de Blancs (FOR)
Moët & Chandon (FUL)
1989
Bruno Paillard (YAP)
Charles Heidsieck (PIP)
Lanson (HOG, VIC, HA)
1988
Deutz (ARM)
Drappier (SAT)
Lanson (PLA)
Laurent-Perrier (NEW, ROB)
Perrier-Jouët (ROB)
Pol Roger (REI)
Pol Roger Blanc de Chardonnay (SOM)

Veuve Clicquot Gold Label (PLA)
1986
Moët & Chandon (WAT)

£24.00 → £25.99
Non-vintage
Bollinger (WRI, WHI, PE, BEN, LAY, EL, CB, MV)
Laurent-Perrier Ultra Brut (LEA, AD)
1990
Deutz (LAYT)
Moët & Chandon (WHI, DAV)
1989
Pommery (OD)
Taittinger (POR)
1988
Laurent-Perrier (BO, ARM, LEA, CB)
Moët & Chandon (HAH, THR, BOT, WR, VIC)
Pol Roger (GOE)
'R' de Ruinart (LEA)
Veuve Clicquot (BIB, ENO, FUL)
Veuve Clicquot Gold Label (GE)
1986
Moët & Chandon (WRI, QUE, TES, OD)
Pol Roger (HOG)

£26.00 → £29.99

Non-vintage
Duval Leroy Fleur de Champagne
magnum (SAI)
Jacquesson Blanc de Blancs (CRO)
Perrier-Jouët Blason de France (PIP)
1990
Louis Roederer Blanc de Blancs (PLA)
Taittinger (OD)
1989
Louis Roederer (GOE, FUL)
Perrier-Jouët (PIP)
Taittinger (ARM, LEA, FUL, DI)
Veuve Clicquot (OD)
Veuve Clicquot Gold Label (PIP)
1988
Billecart-Salmon Cuvée N.F. Billecart (ELL)
Laurent-Perrier (LAY, AD, CHA)
Louis Roederer (HOG, ENO)
Pol Roger (HAH, TAN, MV, BEN, ROB)
Veuve Clicquot (WHI, ARM, CB, WRI, LEA,
UN, ROB, MAJ, PE, HAH, EL, SAI, CRO)
Veuve Clicquot Rich (LEA)
1986
Louis Roederer Blanc de Blancs (NI)
Pol Roger (PEN)
Pol Roger Blanc de Chardonnay (REI)

£30.00 → £39.99

Non-vintage
Krug Grande Cuvée ½ bottle (CRO, BEN,
THR, BOT, WR)
Lanson magnum (WR, BOT)
Laurent-Perrier magnum (MAJ, CHA)
Moët & Chandon magnum (FOR, TAN, POR,
WRI, TES, CO, BO)
Perrier-Jouët magnum (ROB)
Pol Roger White Foil magnum (REI)
1990
Louis Roederer Blanc de Blancs (LAY)
1989
Bollinger (PIP)
Bollinger Grande Année Vintage (HIC)
Deutz Blanc de Blancs (LAYT)
Louis Roederer (TAN, LEA, LAY, CB, HAH)
1988
Bollinger (HOG, GOE, ARM, WAT, POR, WRI,
CB, AD, BEN, PE, MV, HAH, EL)
Bollinger Grande Année Vintage (SAI, DI,
ELL, CRO, QUE, VIC, MAJ, FUL, LEA)
Deutz Cuvée de William Deutz (FOR, LAYT)
Dom Ruinart Blanc de Blancs (LEA)
Louis Roederer Blanc de Blancs (YOU, BEN)
Pol Roger Blanc de Chardonnay (PEN, WRI)
Veuve Clicquot Rich (HAH, BOT, WR)

1986
Billecart-Salmon Blanc de Blancs (ELL)
Pol Roger Blanc de Chardonnay (MV, BEN)
Pol Roger Cuvée Sir Winston Churchill
(SOM)
'R' de Ruinart (HA)
1985
Bollinger (ENO)
Bollinger Année Rare RD (BUT)
Dom Ruinart Blanc de Blancs (PEN)
Heidsieck Diamant Bleu (OD)
Perrier-Jouët Belle Époque (YOU)
Pol Roger (VIN)
1983
Billecart-Salmon Blanc de Blancs (NI)
Gosset Grande Millésime (LEA, YOU, WRI)
Louis Roederer (PEN)

£40.00 → £49.99

Non-vintage
Bollinger magnum (PLA, DI, LAY, BO)
Laurent-Perrier Cuvée Grande Siècle (EL)
Moët & Chandon magnum (WHI, LAY, ROB)
Pol Roger White Foil magnum (PEN, UB,
ROB, WRI, QUE)
Veuve Clicquot magnum (WR, BOT, THR)
1989
Veuve Clicquot la Grande Dame (GE)
1988
Perrier-Jouët Belle Époque (WRI, OD)
Veuve Clicquot la Grande Dame (WY, NEW)
1986
Dom Ruinart Blanc de Blancs (BIB)
Moët & Chandon magnum (UN)
Pol Roger Cuvée Sir Winston Churchill
(REI, FA)
1985
Perrier-Jouët Belle Époque (PIP)
Taittinger Comtes de Champagne Blanc
de Blancs (FA)
Veuve Clicquot la Grande Dame (POR)
1982
Alfred Gratien (CRO)
Bollinger RD (ENO, PEN, BO, FA, HOG, PLA, DI)
Taittinger Comtes de Champagne Blanc
de Blancs (DI)

£50.00 → £59.99

Non-vintage
Bollinger magnum (TAN, BEN)
Krug Grande Cuvée (FOR, FA, ELL, CB, VIC)
Laurent-Perrier Cuvée Grande Siècle
(PEN, AD, CHA)
1989
Louis Roederer Cristal (PEN)

1988
Dom Pérignon (FUL, WHI, UN)
Louis Roederer Cristal (REI, FOR)
Moët & Chandon magnum (ROB)
Veuve Clicquot la Grande Dame (HAH, ROB, FUL, RES, LEA, VIC, UN)
1986
Dom Pérignon (BIB, POR)
Louis Roederer Cristal (NO)
Pol Roger Cuvée Sir Winston Churchill (HOG, RES, WRI, TAN, BEN)
Taittinger Comtes de Champagne Blanc de Blancs (LEA, ROB)
1985
Dom Pérignon (WY, HOG, FOR, PLA, ELL, BO, REI, GOE, FUL, WAT, WRI, FA, ROB, TAN, CB)
Louis Roederer Cristal (NI)
Pol Roger Cuvée Sir Winston Churchill (PEN)
1982
Bollinger (MV)
Bollinger RD (TAN, YOU, BEN, LEA, CB, ROB)
Dom Pérignon (TES)

£60.00 → £74.99

Non-vintage
Krug Grande Cuvée (POR, WHI, ARM, HOG, WAT, EL, PEN, BIB, BEN, CRO, AD, PIP, TAN, AUR, PE, WR, BOT, THR, LAY, ROB, QUE, LEA)

1989
Louis Roederer Cristal (PLA, FA, TAN, BIB, EL, LAY, CB)
1988
Bollinger magnum (BEN)
Dom Pérignon (DAV)
Louis Roederer Cristal (ELL, HOG, NO, FA, ENO, WRI, BEN)
Veuve Clicquot la Grande Dame (WR, BOT)
1985
Dom Pérignon (OD, VIC, LEA, VIN, HAH, YOU)
Krug (FA, ARM, HOG, GOE, BIB, BEN, AD, PIP)
1983
Dom Pérignon (WY)
Louis Roederer Cristal (NO)
Salon (CB)

1982
Bollinger RD (VIN)
Krug (BO)
Salon (FA, CB)
Taittinger Comtes de Champagne Blanc de Blancs (BUT)
1981
Louis Roederer Cristal (NO)
1975
Bollinger Année Rare RD (BUT)

£75.00 → £99.99

Non-vintage
Moët & Chandon jeroboam (HOG)
Veuve Clicquot jeroboam (MAJ)
1989
Louis Roederer Cristal (LEA, NO, HAH, MAJ)
1988
Louis Roederer Cristal (QUE, LEA, AD, WR)
1986
Pol Roger Cuvée Sir Winston Churchill magnum (REI)
1985
Krug (LEA, OD, HAH, CB, ROB)
1982
Louis Roederer Cristal (NO)
1980
Dom Pérignon (REI)
1978
Dom Pérignon (YOU)
Louis Roederer Cristal (YOU)
1975
Krug (PEN)
1953
Charles Heidsieck (REI)

£100.00 → £129.99

Non-vintage
Bollinger jeroboam (LAY, TAN)
Laurent-Perrier Cuvée Grande Siècle magnum (CHA)
Pol Roger White Foil jeroboam (QUE, WRI)
Veuve Clicquot jeroboam (WR, BOT)
1988
Bollinger Vieilles Vignes Françaises, Blanc de Noirs (BEN)
Louis Roederer Cristal magnum (REI)
1986
Bollinger Vieilles Vignes Françaises, Blanc de Noirs (RES)
1985
Dom Pérignon magnum (FA, BO)
Krug magnum (FA)
1973
Dom Pérignon (FA)

£130.00 → £199.99

Non-vintage
Moët & Chandon methuselah (HOG)
1985
Krug Clos du Mesnil Blanc de Blancs (FA)
1983
Krug Clos du Mesnil Blanc de Blancs (BEN)
1982
Bollinger Vieilles Vignes Françaises, Blanc
   de Noirs (CRO)
1976
Krug (BO)
Krug Collection (REI)

£200.00 → £299.99

Non-vintage
Moët & Chandon methuselah (ROB)
Pol Roger White Foil methuselah (PEN, WRI)
Veuve Clicquot methuselah (MAJ)

SPARKLING ROSÉ

Under £15.00

Non-vintage
Bruno Paillard ½ bottle (HAL)
Mercier (FOR)

£15.00 → £19.99

Non-vintage
Bauget-Jouette (HIG)
Bruno Paillard (YAP, NEZ)
Canard-Duchêne (NEW, HOG, CRO)
Jacquart (MV)
Pommery (ROB)
1988
Pol Roger (SOM)

£20.00 → £29.99

Non-vintage
Ayala (BEN)
Billecart-Salmon (NI, ELL, LEA, OD)
Bruno Paillard (WHI)
Lanson (HOG, HA, VIC, PE, BOT, THR, UN, WR)
Laurent-Perrier (NEW, EL, UN, BIB, FUL, ARM,
   SAI, CHA, CB, ROB, BO, MAJ, LEA, WRI, TAN)
Joseph Perrier Cuvée Royale (NEW)
Pommery (BIB)
Louis Roederer (NI)
1988
Deutz (LAYT)
Moët & Chandon (UN, ROB)
1985
Charles Heidsieck (PIP)
Veuve Clicquot (FA, KA, BOT, THR, WR)

£30.00 → £39.99

Non-vintage
Billecart-Salmon (CRO)
Laurent-Perrier magnum (REI)
Pol Roger (QUE)
1989
Louis Roederer (HAH, ROB)
1988
Bollinger (BEN)
1986
Pol Roger (ROB, PEN)
1985
Bollinger (DI, TAN)

£40.00 → £54.99

Non-vintage
Krug (BO)
1986
Dom Ruinart (BIB)
Perrier-Jouët Belle Époque (ROB)
1985
Dom Pérignon (PEN)
1983
Taittinger Comtes de Champagne (FA)

£80.00 → £99.99

Non-vintage
Krug (LEA, HAH)
1983
Louis Roederer Cristal Rosé (FA)

£125.00 → £149.99

1982
Dom Pérignon (FA, ROB, HAH)

STILL WHITE

Under £17.00

Non-vintage
Coteaux Champenois Blanc de
   Chardonnay, Laurent-Perrier (CHA)

STILL RED

Under £17.50

Non-vintage
Coteaux Champenois Pinot Franc Cuvée
   de Pinot Noir, Laurent-Perrier (CHA)

Webster's is an annual
publication. We welcome
your suggestions for next
year's edition.

RHÔNE

Polarised between North and South, between innovation and tradition, and between top quality and relentless mediocrity, the Rhône is still trying to find its way

What do we expect from the Rhône? If it's not easy for wine lovers to answer that question, it's even harder for the producers. In the past we consumers were given outstanding value. Today we are offered rising standards of quality, but it sometimes seems that prices, pegged ever higher by the weakness of sterling, have increased more than the quality justifies.

The producers, too, seem confused. In the North there is a continuing battle between traditionalists and innovators. In the South, there is a growing recognition that the mediocrity of most Côtes du Rhône is no longer acceptable in an international market where Australian and even South African quaffing wines are offering greater reliability. But reducing yields and opting for higher concentration and quality – as many estates in the south are now doing – inevitably leads to higher prices. Is Gigondas at £10 a bottle, only a tad less than the price of Châteauneuf-du-Pape, good value? It's certainly debatable.

For the traditionalists in the North, their wines are an expression of *terroir*, the complex soils of the great hills of Hermitage and Côte-Rôtie and the steep terraces of the best parts of St Joseph and Cornas, all giving different expressions of the sublime Syrah grape. The traditionalists vinify as their fathers did: macerating the grapes, stalks and all, at fairly high temperatures, and aging the wines in large oak casks for two years or more. In their youth such wines are exceedingly tough. After considerable bottle age they might transform themselves into memorably aromatic and profound wines. Then again they might not.

The innovators destem all the grapes, monitor the maceration period carefully, and age part or all of the wine in small oak

casks. Guigal, famously, uses 100 per cent new oak for his fabulous single-vineyard Côte-Rôties. Most innovators are more cautious, but nevertheless their wines have a sheen and sophistication that is initially more appealing than the tannic rusticity of some of the traditionalists' bottlings.

The crusading oenologist and winemaker Jean-Luc Colombo in Cornas observes: 'Most growers in the northern Rhône only taste their own wines. You can be sure that Guigal constantly tastes wines from all over the world, and so would any Californian winemaker. But here it's the exception rather than the rule. So most producers have no idea how remote their wines still are from changing public taste.'

The abrasive but highly skilled Bernard Burgaud in Côte-Rôtie likes to point out that the techniques he uses, such as destemming and barrique-aging, are not innovatory, but reflect the true tradition of wine-making in the region, and cites historical sources to back his view.

Que Syrah Syrah

Well, you pays your money and you takes your choice. If you want old-fashioned Syrah at its most austere, try a bottle from Robert Michel in Cornas. Similar in style but more consistent in quality are the wines from Clape or Noël Verset. For a more international style, oaky, majestic and concentrated, look to examples from Colombo and Jean Lionnet in Cornas, and Gerin in Côte-Rôtie.

I myself prefer the middle path. I accept the innovators' criticism that most traditionalists' wines are too tough and raw for their own good, but I also find that the rich, glossy wines of Colombo and his disciples can lack typicity. Devotees of the middle way should look to producers such as Burgaud, Gaillard and Rostaing in Côte-Rôtie, and to de Barjac and Juge in Cornas. Look out too for the new St-Pierre estate bottling from Jaboulet; cask samples I tasted were highly promising.

The best entertainment of the year was provided by the distinguished négociant house of Chapoutier. Under young Michel Chapoutier, quality has improved beyond recognition. But Michel's cockiness got up everybody's nose, and when Robert Parker hailed Chapoutier's 1993 Hermitage as fabulous, those noses smelt rats.

Let me remind you how awful the 1993 vintage in the North was. Jean-Michel Gerin says that during the harvest in Côte-Rôtie as much rain fell in three weeks as usually falls in six months. He doubled his team of pickers, but there was so much rot that the daily crop was one-tenth of the usual.

I've tasted many 1993s, some dire, some adequate, none great. So how come Chapoutier transcended the malignancy of nature? The answer is that he didn't. Tasted by many experienced British palates, his Hermitage showed poorly, though Chapoutier courageously encouraged comparisons between the three different bottlings of the wine. Robert Parker has also revised his opinion, downwards.

Perhaps Parker had an off-day when he originally tasted the 1993s; perhaps what he was offered to taste was not the same as what was eventually bottled. Speculation is idle. But it does remind us of the dangers of making any definitive assessments of wines before they are bottled.

Wars of the Crozes

The much heralded improvement in white wines from the Rhône still has some way to go. Chave's white Hermitage has always been magnificent, Condrieu can be an exquisite wine (am I alone in finding those from Cuilleron and Rostaing superior to the celebrated wines from Georges Vernay?), and the best white Châteauneufs (from Clos des Papes, Beaucastel and Mont

Redon) are irresistible. But all these wines are expensive. At a more affordable level, the splendid white Crozes-Hermitage of Graillot shows what can be done with the inscrutable Marsanne variety.

I tasted, blind, some 40 white wines from Crozes, St-Joseph and St-Péray, and the results were uninspiring, though there were honourable exceptions. From Crozes, Château Curson, the Tain co-op, Entrefaux's Le Dessus, and Combier; from St-Joseph, the Désirat co-op's Domaine Rochevine, Cuilleron, Philippe Faury and Didier Morion; from St-Péray, Voge.

In the South, standards continue to rise. Gigondas can be great, but Vacqueyras, from top estates such as Clos des Cazaux and La Garrigue, can often offer better value for a similarly styled wine. Elsewhere in the Côtes du Rhône improvements are patchy. Cairanne shows promise, with good cuvées from Marcel Richaud and characterful if earthy wines from Rabasse-Charavin. Domaine les Gouberts makes fine Gigondas but the red Beaumes-de-Venise is almost as good and considerably cheaper. Jean-March Antran makes concentrated reds and whites at Sablet, and André Romero of Domaine La Soumade is making blockbuster reds at Rasteau.

Another subregion on the move is the Costières de Nîmes. Here the soil is stony, the climate relentlessly hot, the grape mix the usual Midi blend. Yet the Costières is no longer a viticultural backwater and there are impressive wines emerging at reasonable prices from Paul Blanc, Mas de Bressades and, best of all, Mourgues du Grés.

Unlike the Languedoc, increasingly infatuated with varietal wines, the Rhône remains a conservative region, the North faithful (as AC laws require) to Syrah, the South still dominated by gutsy Grenache. Dynamic estates proliferate in the South, but they are surrounded by mediocrity. Yet at the top level, whether in Hermitage or Côte-Rôtie, or at Châteauneuf and Gigondas, the standards of wine-making have never been better. **STEPHEN BROOK**

GRAPES & FLAVOURS

CARIGNAN (red) This grape is much maligned because in the far South it used to, and often still does, produce raw, fruitless wines that are the mainstay of the cheapest bulk wines. But old Carignan vines can produce strong, tasty, flavoursome wines that age well, and the variety's toughness is brilliantly moderated by the use of carbonic maceration.

CINSAUT (red) Widely planted in the 1960s to reduce the aggressiveness of the red Grenache, it's now out of favour because of its inability to age. But it can add pepperiness and acidity to the blend, as at Château Rayas. Cinsaut often makes a successful contribution to rosé blends.

CLAIRETTE (white) Makes sparkling Crémant de Die, but is a bit dull unless livened up with the aromatic Muscat. In the South it makes rather big, strong whites, sometimes creamy, but more often dull and nutty. Needs careful handling and early drinking.

COUNOISE (red) Rich, spicy, floral flavours, and highly regarded at Beaucastel and Durieu in Châteauneuf. Could be promising.

GRENACHE (red) The most important red grape in the southern Rhône, with loads of alcohol and a gentle, juicy, spicy fruit perked up by a whiff of pepper, ideal for rosés and easy-going reds. Grenache achieves its greatest power and longevity at Châteauneuf. But it's not good at flowering successfully.

GRENACHE BLANC (white) A widely planted variety in the southern Rhône producing rich, appley wines with a strong whiff of aniseed. Good, but soft, so drink young.

MARSANNE (white) The dominant of the two grapes that go to make white Hermitage and Crozes-Hermitage, as well as white St-Joseph and St-Péray. Marsanne is weighty and can be flabby, but at its best it is rich and scented. Further south it makes burly, lanoliny wine, but is capable of rich, exotic peach and toffee flavours, too.

MOURVÈDRE (red) This late-ripening variety only really works in sites with ample warmth and sunshine and, ideally, some maritime influence. Highly resistant to oxidation, it contributes backbone and tannin to blended wines, and on its own, as in Bandol, it develops wonderful smoky, leathery, meaty flavours as it ages.

MUSCAT (white) Used to great effect blended with Clairette to make the sparkling Clairette de Die, but more famous for Muscat de Beaumes-de-Venise.

SYRAH (red) The whole of the northern Rhône is dominated by this one red grape variety. The Syrah makes some of the blackest, most startling, pungent red wine in France, and, although it is grown elsewhere, it is here that it is at its most brilliant. From Hermitage and Cornas, it rasps with tannin and tar and woodsmoke, backed by the deep, ungainly sweetness of black treacle. But give it five or ten years, and those raw fumes will have become sweet, pungent, full of raspberries, brambles and cassis. Syrah is less common than the Grenache in the southern Rhône, but as more is planted, the standard of southern Rhône reds is sure to rise.

ROUSSANNE (white) Altogether more delicate and fragrant than the Marsanne, but it is inconveniently prone to disease and oxidation. Being a low yielder, it is increasingly losing ground to the latter grape. Found chiefly in Hermitage and St-Péray in the North, though it also makes light, fragrant wines further south in Châteauneuf. Look out for *Beaucastel's* Roussanne *Vieilles Vignes* – pricy but superb.

UGNI BLANC (white) Boring workhorse grape planted all over the South to produce basic gulping stuff. The same as the Trebbiano of Italy, where it is hardly any more exciting.

VIOGNIER (white) The grape of Condrieu and Château-Grillet. It has one of the most memorable flavours of any white grape, blending the rich, musky scent of overripe apricots with that of spring flowers. The wine is made dry, but it is so rich you hardly believe it. Sweet versions are making a comeback. Viognier is becoming a bit of a cult, with plantings increasing in the southern Rhône, in California and even Australia. It is permitted in the blend authorized for Côte-Rôtie, although it is rare that more than five to eight per cent is used. It contributes perfume and alcohol, but growers have differences over whether it should be added to this Syrah-based wine.

WINES & WINE REGIONS

CHÂTEAU-GRILLET, AC (white; north) A single property in the far north-west of the northern Rhône, and the smallest AC in France at only 3.8 hectares, excepting a couple of Vosne-Romanée *Grands Crus* in Burgundy. Wildly expensive, this 100 per cent Viognier wine is often surpassed in freshness and quality by top Condrieus. But unlike Condrieu, it can age interestingly.

CHÂTEAUNEUF-DU-PAPE, AC (red, white; south) This can be delicious, deep, dusty red, almost sweet and fat, low in acidity, but kept appetizing by back-room tannin. *Can* be. It can also be fruit-pastilly and pointless, or dark, tough and stringy. Thirteen different red and white grapes are permitted, and the resulting flavour is usually slightly indistinct, varying from one property to another. Great vintages such as 1978, '81, '89 and '90 give wines that will improve for 15 or more. Around one-third of the growers make good wine – and as much as two-thirds of the wine sold probably exceeds the permitted yields. So it makes sense always to go for a domaine wine and certainly not one bottled away from the region. The most consistently reliable wine comes from *Château de Beaucastel*, the most celebrated (and expensive) from *Château Rayas*. Also recommended are *Clos du Mont Olivet*, *Château Fortia*, *Château St-André*, *La Nerthe*, *Chante-Cigale*, *Clos des Papes*, *Chante-Perdrix*, *le Vieux Donjon*, *Font de Michelle*, *Font du Loup*, *les Cailloux*, *la Gardine*, *la Janasse*, *Quiot*, *Domaine du Grand Tinel*, *Domaine de Mont Redon*, *Domaine du Vieux Télégraphe*, *Domaine Durieu*, *Bosquet des Papes*, *Lucien Gabriel Barrot*, *les Clefs d'Or*, *Chapoutier's la Bernadine* and *Henri Bonneau*.

Only three per cent of the AC is white, but the wines can be outstandingly perfumed with a delicious nip of acidity, leaving you wondering how on earth such aromatic wines could come from such a hot, arid region. Magic or technology; or it might be such delights as the Roussanne and Picpoul varieties adding something to the base of Grenache Blanc, Clairette and Bourboulenc. Wonderful wines can be produced in the most unlikely places – and this is one of them. In its youth, the wine has a perfumed rush of springtime madness. Then it closes up for a few years, emerging at seven years as a rich, succulent, nutty mouthful. Best: *Château de Beaucastel* (its pure Roussanne *Vieilles Vignes* – and the new Viognier white), *Clefs d'Or*, *Clos des Papes*, *Font de Michelle*, *Grand Tinel*, *Mont Redon*, *Nalys*, *Rayas*, *Vieux Télégraphe*.

CLAIRETTE DE DIE, AC (sparkling; south) New rules mean that the dull Champagne-method wine (which used to be called Clairette de Die) is now called Crémant de Die, and what used to be called Clairette de Die Tradition, made by the ancient *méthode dioise ancestrale*, is now the only wine allowed to be called Clairette de Die. Made half from Clairette, half from Muscat, it's delicious, light and off dry. The still wine is Coteaux Diois.

CONDRIEU, AC (white; north) Wonderful when made properly, with apricot scent that leaps out of the glass, and an exciting balance of succulent fruit and gentle acidity. But its sudden popularity has led to great replanting, sometimes by people concerned more with high prices than high quality. Yet the potential quality is so stunning that with luck the *arrivistes* will realize that the real thing is worth striving for. The potential area is 100 hectares, and about 80 are planted. There is some *cépage* Viognier, which will show what the fuss is about – at half the Condrieu price. (Yapp has one.) Despite its high price, Condrieu is best young, but beware its high alcohol. Top names: *Château du Rozay, Chapoutier, Cuilleron, Delas, Dumazet, Guigal, Multier,* (who, like some others, is using new oak), *Niero Pinchon, Jean Pinchon* and *Georges Vernay.*

CORNAS, AC (red; north) Black and tarry tooth-stainers, from the right bank of the Rhône, opposite Valence. Usually rather hefty, jammy even, and lacking some of the fresh fruit that makes Hermitage so remarkable, yet at ten years old it's impressive. There have been quite big price rises in recent years, but then quality seems to improve year by year, too. Excellent blockbusters are made by *Auguste Clape, Robert Michel* and *Noël Verset.* It's also worth looking for *René Balthazar, Colombo* (*Domaine des Ruchets*), *Courbis, Delas, Jaboulet, Juge, Leménicier, Allemand, Jean Lionnet* (especially *Cuvée Rochepertuis*), *Alain Voge.*

COSTIÈRES DE NÎMES, AC (red, rosé; south) The growers here have opted for being in the Rhône, even though the wines are more Languedoc in style: decent rosés and meaty, smoky reds. They're improving: try *Ch. la Tuilerie, Dom. de l'Amarine, Ch. de Campuget, Mas Carlot* (especially its top wines under the *Ch. Paul Blanc* label), *Ch. Mourgues du Grès.*

COTEAUX DU TRICASTIN, AC (red, white; south) Fast-improving, good-value, spicy, fruity reds, and fresh, fruity and quite full-flavoured whites, not as exciting as the reds. Best producers (reds): *Dom. de Grangeneuve,*

Tour d'Elyssas (its 100 per cent Syrah), *Prods. Réunis Ardéchois* (co-op; also good white), *Dom. Saint-Luc, Dom. du Vieux Micocoulier.*

CÔTE-RÔTIE, AC (red; north) Together with Hermitage, the greatest wine of the northern Rhône. It can have exceptional finesse, thanks to the occasional addition of a dash of Viognier. The vineyard area has been expanded on to the plateau above the steep slope that gives the wine its name, and this can only damage its reputation. The increasing use of new oak has also proved controversial. Some exceptional single sites are cited on the label, notably La Landonne. The greatest growers are *Guigal, Rostaing* and *Burgaud.* Look also for *Barge, Champet, Chapoutier, Clusel-Roch, Delas, Gaillard, Gerin, Jaboulet* and *Jasmin.*

CÔTES DU LUBÉRON, AC (red, white; south) Upgraded from VDQS in 1987, Lubéron makes decent reds, usually rather light, but capable of stronger personality. The *Val Joanis* rosé is one of the best in the South. Try also *Château de Canorgue, Château de l'Isolette, Mas du Peyroulet, Val Joanis* (also to be seen under the names of *Domaines Chancel* or *Domaine de la Panisse*), *Vieille Ferme.* The whites are usually pleasant and light southern wine but little more, though recent innovations have started to produce much more fragrant, interesting styles at such properties as *Château de l'Isolette, Mas du Peyroulet, Val Joanis* and *la Vieille Ferme.*

CÔTES DU RHÔNE, AC (red, white) This huge AC covers 80 per cent of all Rhône wines. Well-made basic Côtes du Rhône reds are delicious when young, wonderfully fresh and fruity, like a soft Beaujolais. Or they can be fierce, black, grapeskins-and-alcohol monsters. Many of the weightiest are made by Châteauneuf growers (*Cru de Coudoulet* from Beaucastel, *Château de Fonsalette* from Rayas) or northern Rhône producers like *Guigal* and *Clape. Château du Grand Moulas* is spicy and attractive, with plenty of body. Also good: *Château de Ruth, Château de Goudray, Clos du Père Clément, Dom. de Bel Air, Dom. de la*

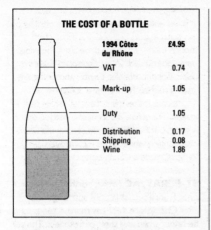

THE COST OF A BOTTLE

1994 Côtes du Rhône	**£4.95**
VAT	0.74
Mark-up	1.05
Duty	1.05
Distribution	0.17
Shipping	0.08
Wine	1.86

Cantharide, Dom. de St-Estève, Dom. des Aussellons, Jean Lionnet and *Chapoutier's* rosé. Whites are generally fresh and fruity.

CÔTES DU RHÔNE-VILLAGES, AC

(red, white; south) One of the best areas for good, full reds that can also age, combining earthy, dusty southern heat with spicy, raspberry fruit. They come from higher quality villages, 17 of which can add their names on the label, including Cairanne, Chusclan, Valréas, Beaumes-de-Venise and Rasteau. These wines often offer excellent value. Best: *Dom. Pelaquié* (Laudun); *Dom. de Grangeneuve* (Rasteau); *Jean-Pierre Cartier, Château de Trignon, Dom. de Boisson, Dom. St-Antoine, Dom. de Verquière* (Sablet); *Dom. de l'Ameillaud, Dom. Brusset, Dom. l'Oratoire St-Martin, Dom. de la Présidente, Dom. Rabasse-Charavin* (Cairanne); *Dom. Ste-Anne* (St-Gervais); *Dom. Courançonne, Dom. de Cabasse* (Séguret); *Roger Combe, Dom. des Grands Devers, le Val des Rois* (Valréas). The whites are increasingly fresh, fruity and gulpable, especially from the villages of Laudun and Chusclan. *Dom. Pelaquié* is the leading estate, and *Dom. Ste-Anne* is good.

CÔTES DU VENTOUX, AC

(red, white, rosé; south) Good area producing lots of fresh, juicy wine; the red is the best. Can even be quite special. Best: *Dom. des Anges, Jaboulet, Pascal, la Vieille Ferme, Vieux Lazaret.*

CROZES-HERMITAGE, AC

(red, white; north) This large AC produces red wine that varies from the light and juicy to a well-structured smoky wine recognizable as a lesser cousin of the great Hermitage. Sadly, prices of the best wines are rising fast. *Etienne Pochon* (Château de Curson), *Chapoutier's les Meysonniers* and *Varonniers, Graillot's Guiraude, Jaboulet's Thalabert* are tops. Also good are *Albert Belle, Bernard Chave, Cave des Clairmonts, Domaine des Entrefaux, Cave de Tain, Fayolle, Laurent Combier, Stephane Cornu, Pradelle* and *Vidal-Fleury.* The white is generally rather dull and strong, but there are good ones from *Graillot, Fayolle, Jaboulet* and *Pradelle.*

GIGONDAS, AC

(red; south) Big, chunky, plummy wines that can be short on finesse. This is Grenache country, and proud of it. *Dom. de St-Gayan* is very good, as are the following: *Clos des Cazaux, Dom. de Cayron, Dom. les Goubelts, Dom. de Longue-Toque, Dom. l'Oustau Fauquet, Dom. les Pallières, Dom. Raspail-Ay, Dom. de Santa Duc.*

HERMITAGE, AC

(red, white; north) Grand, burly red from a small, precipitous area around the hill of Hermitage. Strong and fierily tough when young, it matures to a rich, brooding magnificence. There is always a stern, vaguely medicinal or smoky edge, and an unmatchable depth of raspberry and blackcurrant fruit. Although many people produce Hermitage of sorts, there have traditionally been only two stars, the marvellously good *Chave*, who produces small amounts of impeccable wine, and the ebullient, export-orientated *Paul Jaboulet Aîné*, who produces larger amounts of more variable wine. To them should be added *Chapoutier's le Pavillon.* Also good: *Delas Cuvée Marquise de la Tourette, Desmeure, B Faurie, Guigal, Sorrel, Belle, Faurie* and *Jean-Louis Grippat.* The white is often heavy and dull, but it ages tremendously well to a soft, rich nuttiness. *Chave* makes magnificent white Hermitage even in modest vintages, and other good producers include *Chapoutier, Desmeure, Ferraton, Guigal, Grippat* and *Marc Sorrel.*

LIRAC, AC (red, white, rosé; south) A good, often underrated area producing light, attractive wines. Reds are packed with fruit, often tinged with a mineral edge. The rosés are remarkably fresh for so far south. Whites can be first-class if caught young, resembling a less exotic Châteauneuf: less exotic flavour; less exotic price. Best: *Ch. d'Aquéria, Dom. de Ch. St-Roch, Dom. des Causses et St-Eymes, Dom. les Garrigues, Dom. la Fermade, Maby, Dom. de la Tour.*

MUSCAT DE BEAUMES-DE-VENISE, AC (fortified white; south) This Côtes du Rhône village is the only place in the Rhône to grow Muscat grapes. The golden sweet wine – a *vin doux naturel* – was briefly a real fad drink, but for once the fad was a good one, because it's supremely delicious. Grapy, fresh, rich but not cloying. Look for *Dom. de Coyeux, Dom. Durban, Jaboulet, Beaumes-de-Venise co-op.*

RASTEAU, AC (fortified red, fortified white; south) The Côtes du Rhône village of Rasteau also makes a few big, port-like fortified wines – *vins doux naturels* – both red and off-white. Young ones can have a delightful raspberry scent from the Grenache Noir. The whites are made from Grenache Blanc and can be frankly unpleasant. Production is pretty small. Try *Dom. de la Soumade, Rasteau co-op.*

ST-JOSEPH, AC (red; north) Almost smooth and sweet compared to their tougher neighbours, these reds, especially those from the hills between Condrieu and Cornas, can be fairly big, fine wines, stacked with blackcurrant in good years. There has been some planting on less suitable land, but quality is mostly high, and though there have been price rises, the wines *were* undervalued. *Chave, Coursodon, Cuilleron, Gripa, Grippat, Jaboulet, Courbis* and *Trollat* are leading names. The co-op at *St-Désirat Champagne* makes lovely Beaujolais-type St-Joseph. The white is decent and nutty. *Grippat* is good, but *Florentin*, an old-style oxidative, headbanging white, is more controversial. White Crozes is usually better value.

ST-PÉRAY, AC (white; north) This was once France's most famous sparkling wine after Champagne. Not any more. It tends to be rather stolid and short of freshness. The still whites are often dull, but quality is improving from the likes of *Chaboud, Grippat, Domaine de Fauterie,* and Cornas estates such as *Clape, Lionnet* and *Voge.*

TAVEL, AC (rosé; south) The AC only applies to one colour of wine – pink. The wines are quite expensive, certainly tasty, but too big and alcoholic to be very refreshing. Any of the Rhône grapes will do, but generally it's Grenache-dominated, with the addition of a little Cinsaut. Best producers: *Château d'Aquéria, Château de Trinquevedel, Domaine de la Forcadière, Domaine de la Genestière.*

VACQUEYRAS, AC (red, white, rosé; south) Reds and rosés of character and structure, the best being from the Garrigue plateau, 300ft above the village. Some white

MATURITY CHART
1991 Côte-Rôtie
A very good vintage for this appellation and one to keep

Bottled	Ready	Peak	Tiring	In decline

0	5	10	15	20	25 years

wine is also produced, but it tends to be heavy. Cinsaut fanatic *Ch. de Montmirail* is good, as are *Clos des Cazau, Dom. de la Fourmone, Dom. la Garrigue, le Sang des Cailloux.*

VIN DE PAYS DES COLLINES RHODANIENNES (red; north) A usually impressive and expanding northern Rhône area, particularly for inexpensive, tasty Syrah reds, though Gamay can also be good.

VIN DE PAYS DES COTEAUX DE L'ARDÈCHE (red, white; south) What vins de pays should be doing. A mixture of go-ahead co-ops and outside influences decided to plant grapes to make wine that would *sell*: delicious Nouveau-style Gamay, first-class Syrah, good Cabernet, plus Sauvignon, Pinot Noir – and Chardonnay, both for *Louis Latour's* Chardonnay de l'Ardèche and the local co-ops (higher quality, far lower prices).

MERCHANTS SPECIALISING IN THE RHÔNE
see Merchant Directory (page 424) for details

Adnams (AD), John Armit (ARM), Bennetts (BEN), Bibendum (BIB), Anthony Byrne (BY), Direct Wine (DI), Eldridge Pope (EL), Ben Ellis (ELL), Enotria Winecellars (ENO), Farr Vintners (FA), Gelston Castle (GE), Lay & Wheeler (LAY), Oddbins (ODD), James Nicholson (NI), Nobody Inn (NO), Raeburn Fine Wines (RAE), Reid (REI), T&W Wines (TW), Tanners (TAN), Ubiquitous Chip (UB), Wine Society (WS), Yapp Bros (YAP)

RHÔNE VINTAGES

1995 A dry summer reduced yields and promised a great vintage, but rain in September marred the harvest. Top growers made very good wines, and there will be great wines in the North from those who, like Chapoutier and Chave, picked late.

1994 Despite a rainy harvest, this exceptionally early vintage delivered good fruit, resulting in succulent reds and lively, flowery whites. Very good but not great.

1993 Châteauneuf and Côtes du Rhône escaped much of the worst weather. In the North attractive whites but raw and rather dilute reds from Hermitage, Crozes and Cornas.

1992 A poor year; buy only from top growers and drink up quickly.

1991 Côte-Rôtie is generally better than in 1990. The South was only moderately good.

1990 The North survived the drought best though rain affected picking in Côte-Rôtie. Choose 1990 for the North (though Côte-Rôtie is dodgy); 1989 for the South.

1989 Drought, and some poor Hermitage and Cornas. Concentrated Châteauneuf.

1988 Best in Côte-Rôtie, Hermitage and Châteauneuf-du-Pape. Some is too tannic.

1987 The few good wines should have been drunk by now, though Côte-Rôtie and Hermitage provided some very good bottles, now drinking well.

1986 A rather joyless vintage for reds. Some very good Châteauneuf and Hermitage.

1985 Brilliant Côte-Rôtie, St-Joseph and Cornas. Châteauneuf is delicious and juicy.

1983 Outstanding dark, rich, complex Hermitage and very good Côte-Rôtie for keeping. Southern reds are good, though some are a bit tough. In general, drink 1982 before 1983.

NORTHERN RHÔNE

RED

Under £6.00
1991
Crozes-Hermitage Jaboulet (BY)

£6.00 → £6.99
1993
Crozes-Hermitage Domaine des
Entrefaux (BY)
1992
Crozes-Hermitage Cave de Vins Fins à
Tain-Hermitage (POR, AME)
Crozes-Hermitage Cave des Clairmonts,
Borja (WAI)
1985
Crozes-Hermitage Domaine des
Entrefaux (BUT)

£7.00 → £8.99
1994
Crozes-Hermitage Cave des Clairmonts,
Borja (YAP)
Crozes-Hermitage Domaine des
Entrefaux (TAN, PIP)
Crozes-Hermitage Graillot (BY, OD)
Crozes-Hermitage Jaboulet (HAH)
Crozes-Hermitage les Meysonniers,
Chapoutier (REI, OD)
St-Joseph Deschants, Chapoutier (OD)
St-Joseph le Grand Pompée, Jaboulet
(OD)
1993
Crozes-Hermitage Domaine des
Remizières, Desmeure (RAE)
Crozes-Hermitage les Meysonniers,
Chapoutier (DI)
1992
Crozes-Hermitage Jaboulet (WHI)
St-Joseph Cave de St-Désirat (YAP)
1991
Crozes-Hermitage les Meysonniers,
Chapoutier (HOG)

> *Please remember that*
> **Webster's** *is a price*
> *GUIDE and not a price*
> *LIST. It is not meant to*
> *replace up-to-date*
> *merchants' lists.*

1990
Crozes-Hermitage Cave des Clairmonts,
Borja (HIC)
Crozes-Hermitage Domaine des
Remizières, Desmeure (RAE)
St-Joseph Cave de St-Désirat (SO)
1989
Côte-Rôtie Delas (BO)
1985
Crozes-Hermitage les Meysonniers,
Chapoutier (BUT)

£9.00 → £10.99
1994
Crozes-Hermitage Chapoutier (BEN)
Crozes-Hermitage Domaine de
Thalabert, Jaboulet (OD, NI)
Crozes-Hermitage la Guiraude, Graillot (BY)
St-Joseph le Grand Pompée, Jaboulet (HAH)
1993
St-Joseph Deschants, Chapoutier (DI)
1992
Crozes-Hermitage Domaine de
Thalabert, Jaboulet (TAN)
St-Joseph le Grand Pompée, Jaboulet (PLA)
1991
Crozes-Hermitage Graillot (GAU)
St-Joseph Larmes du Père, Paret (PIP)
1990
St-Joseph Larmes du Père, Paret (AME)
1989
St-Joseph Deschants, Chapoutier (GAU)
1988
★ Cornas Chante Perdrix, Delas (FOR)
St-Joseph le Grand Pompée, Jaboulet (HOG)
1987
Cornas Jaboulet (NI)
1986
Cornas Noël Verset (CRO)
Hermitage Domaine des Remizières (PE)
1985
St-Joseph Deschants, Chapoutier (BUT)
1982
Hermitage la Sizeranne, Chapoutier (CRO)

£11.00 → £12.99
1994
St-Joseph Chave (YAP)
St-Joseph Grippat (YAP)
1993
Cornas Juge (EL)
St-Joseph Coursodon (EL)

1991
Cornas Coteau, Michel (TAN)
St-Joseph Clos de l'Arbalestrier, Florentin
(GAU)
1990
Cornas Jaboulet (HOG)
Crozes-Hermitage Domaine de
Thalabert, Jaboulet (HOG, BUT)
Crozes-Hermitage les Meysonniers,
Chapoutier (AV)
St-Joseph le Grand Pompée, Jaboulet (UB)
1989
Crozes-Hermitage Domaine de
Thalabert, Jaboulet (CRO)
1988
Côte-Rôtie les Jumelles, Jaboulet (HOG)
1987
Cornas Delas (PEN)
Cornas Jean Lionnet (GE)
1986
Cornas Jaboulet (HOG, WS)
Côte-Rôtie Gentaz-Dervieux (CRO)
1985
Crozes-Hermitage Domaine de
Thalabert, Jaboulet (BUT)
1984
Cornas Clape (FA)
Cornas Jaboulet (REI)
Côte-Rôtie Jasmin (FA)
1983
Cornas Delas (REI)
1982
Côte-Rôtie Barge (CRO)

£13.00 → £14.99
1993
Cornas Clape (YAP)
1992
Cornas Noël Verset (GAU, RAE)
1991
Cornas Noël Verset (RAE)
1989
Cornas Noël Verset (RAE)
St-Joseph Clos de l'Arbalestrier, Florentin
(AD, WS)
1988
Cornas Michel (YAP)
Cornas Noël Verset (RAE)
Côte-Rôtie Seigneur de Maugiron, Delas
(FOR)
Hermitage Marquise de la Tourette, Delas
(FOR)
1987
Cornas Noël Verset (YOU)
Cornas Rochepertuis, Jean Lionnet (GE)

1986
Côte-Rôtie les Jumelles, Jaboulet (HOG)
Hermitage Domaine des Remizières (BUT)
St-Joseph Grippat (CRO)
St-Joseph le Grand Pompée, Jaboulet (REI)
1985
Cornas Jaboulet (HOG)
Cornas Michel (CRO)
Hermitage Cuvée des Miaux, Ferraton
(GOE)
Hermitage Sorrel (BUT)
St-Joseph Réserve Personnelle, Jaboulet
(CRO)
1984
Cornas Michel (GAU)
Hermitage Chave (CRO)
Hermitage la Chapelle, Jaboulet (CRO)
1983
Côte-Rôtie Chapoutier (GOE)
Côte-Rôtie Delas (REI)
Hermitage Domaine des Remizières (BUT)
1982
Crozes-Hermitage Domaine de
Thalabert, Jaboulet (CRO)
1980
Côte-Rôtie de Vallouit (CRO)

£15.00 → £16.99
1994
Cornas Clape (YAP)
1993
Côte-Rôtie Burgaud (YAP)
Côte-Rôtie Champet (YAP)
Côte-Rôtie Jamet (BIB)
1992
Cornas Clape (YAP, DI)
Côte-Rôtie Burgaud (YAP)
Côte-Rôtie Champet (YAP)
Côte-Rôtie Jamet (BIB)
1991
Cornas Clape (GAU)
Cornas de Barjac (LAY)
Côte-Rôtie Barge (FUL)
Côte-Rôtie Champet (DAV)
1988
Hermitage la Chapelle, Jaboulet (HAH)
1987
Côte-Rôtie Barge (GE)
Côte-Rôtie Côte Brune, Gentaz-
Dervieux (EY)
1986
Côte-Rôtie la Viaillère, Dervieux-Thaize
(PIP)
1985
Côte-Rôtie Chapoutier (BUT)

Crozes-Hermitage Domaine de
Thalabert, Jaboulet (CRO)
1983
Côte-Rôtie les Jumelles, Jaboulet (GAU)
Hermitage Jaboulet (HOG)
Hermitage la Sizeranne, Chapoutier (CRO,
YOU)
1982
St-Joseph le Grand Pompée, Jaboulet (REI)
1978
Côte-Rôtie Chapoutier (YOU)

£17.00 → £19.99

1994
Côte-Rôtie Champet (YAP)
Côte-Rôtie Jasmin (YAP)
Hermitage la Sizeranne, Chapoutier (TAN,
OD)
1993
Côte-Rôtie Jasmin (YAP)
Côte-Rôtie René Rostaing (ELL, NI)
Hermitage Bernard Faurie (HAH)
1992
Côte-Rôtie Barge (TAN)
Côte-Rôtie Brune et Blonde, Guigal (BY)
Côte-Rôtie Gérin (BOT)
Côte-Rôtie Jasmin (YAP)
Côte-Rôtie René Rostaing (CRO, AD, LAY)
Hermitage la Sizeranne, Chapoutier (GAU)
1991
Côte-Rôtie Brune et Blonde, Guigal (SOM)
Côte-Rôtie Burgaud (LAY)
Côte-Rôtie Champet (YAP)
Côte-Rôtie Chapoutier (CRO)
Côte-Rôtie René Rostaing (SEC)
Hermitage Domaine des Remizières (BIB)
Hermitage Guigal (SOM)
Hermitage Marquise de la Tourette, Delas
(LAYT)
1990
Côte-Rôtie Brune et Blonde, Guigal (CRO)
Côte-Rôtie Chapoutier (AV)
Côte-Rôtie Guigal (VIC)
Côte-Rôtie René Rostaing (BUT)
Hermitage Guigal (POR)
1989
Cornas les Ruchottes, Colombo (GAU)
Côte-Rôtie Barge (GE)

Webster's is an annual
publication. We welcome
your suggestions for next
year's edition.

Côte-Rôtie Champet (YAP)
Côte-Rôtie Chapoutier (DI)
Côte-Rôtie Jamet (BUT)
Côte-Rôtie la Viaillère, Dervieux-Thaize
(REI)
Côte-Rôtie Seigneur de Maugiron, Delas
(LAYT, PEN)
Hermitage la Sizeranne, Chapoutier (GAU)
1988
Cornas Clape (BUT, GAU, CRO)
Côte-Rôtie Barge (GAU)

Côte-Rôtie Brune et Blonde, Guigal (NI)
Côte-Rôtie la Viaillère, Dervieux-Thaize
(GAU)
Côte-Rôtie Seigneur de Maugiron, Delas
(PEN)
Hermitage Desmeure (GAU)
1987
Hermitage Chave (WS)
Hermitage Guigal (BY)
Hermitage la Chapelle, Jaboulet (CRO, PLA)
1986
Cornas Clape (BUT)
Côte-Rôtie Côte Brune, Gentaz-
Dervieux (RAE)
Côte-Rôtie Gentaz-Dervieux (GOE)
1985
Cornas de Barjac (BUT)
Cornas Voge (CRO)
Côte-Rôtie les Jumelles, Jaboulet (RAE)
Hermitage Domaine Ferraton (CRO)
Hermitage la Sizeranne, Chapoutier (BUT)
St-Joseph le Grand Pompée, Jaboulet (REI)
1984
Hermitage la Chapelle, Jaboulet (BUT)
1983
Cornas Clape (SAT)
Côte-Rôtie Chapoutier (BUT)
Côte-Rôtie de Vallouit (CRO)
Crozes-Hermitage Domaine de
Thalabert, Jaboulet (BUT)
1982
Côte-Rôtie Champet (SAT)
Côte-Rôtie les Jumelles, Jaboulet (REI)
1981
Hermitage Guigal (BUT)

1980
Côte-Rôtie les Jumelles, Jaboulet (WHI)
1978
Crozes-Hermitage Jaboulet (CRO)

£20.00 → £24.99
1994
Hermitage la Chapelle, Jaboulet (REI, OD)
1993
Côte-Rôtie Côte Blonde, René Rostaing
(ELL, NI)
Hermitage Grippat (YAP)
1992
Côte-Rôtie Côte Brune, Gentaz-
Dervieux (RAE)
Côte-Rôtie Gentaz-Dervieux (GAU)
1991
Côte-Rôtie Brune et Blonde, Guigal (EL)
Côte-Rôtie Côte Brune, Gentaz-
Dervieux (RAE)
Côte-Rôtie Gentaz-Dervieux (CRO)
Côte-Rôtie Guigal (SUM)
Hermitage Chave (SEC, MAJ)
Hermitage la Sizeranne, Chapoutier (CRO)
1990
Côte-Rôtie Brune et Blonde, Vidal-Fleury
(NO)
Côte-Rôtie Côte Blonde, René Rostaing
(BUT)
Côte-Rôtie Côte Brune, Gentaz-
Dervieux (RAE)
Hermitage Albert Belle (GAU)
1989
Côte-Rôtie Gentaz-Dervieux (WS)
Côte-Rôtie Guigal (DI)
Côte-Rôtie les Jumelles, Jaboulet (PLA)
Hermitage Guigal (DI)
Hermitage Marquise de la Tourette, Delas
(PEN)
1988
Côte-Rôtie Burgaud (GAU)
Côte-Rôtie Champet (NO)
Côte-Rôtie Chapoutier (GAU)
Côte-Rôtie Guigal (WS)
Côte-Rôtie Jamet (CRO, BUT)
Hermitage la Chapelle, Jaboulet (GAU, HOG)
1986
Hermitage Chave (WS)
Hermitage la Chapelle, Jaboulet (LAY, HOG)
1985
Cornas Clape (BUT, CRO)
Côte-Rôtie Brune et Blonde, Guigal (EY,
BUT, CRO, REI)
Côte-Rôtie la Viaillère, Dervieux-Thaize
(CRO)

Hermitage Bernard Faurie (ELL)
Hermitage Chave (BUT)
Hermitage Guigal (EY, REI)
Hermitage la Chapelle, Jaboulet (DI)
1984
Côte-Rôtie Brune et Blonde, Guigal (REI)
1983
Côte-Rôtie Barge (CRO)
Côte-Rôtie Brune et Blonde, Guigal (REI)
Côte-Rôtie Jamet (CRO)
Hermitage Guigal (EY, REI)
Hermitage le Gréal, Sorrel (CRO)
1981
Côte-Rôtie Gentaz-Dervieux (CRO)
1980
Hermitage la Chapelle, Jaboulet (ROB)
1979
Côte-Rôtie Jasmin (CRO)
Hermitage Guigal (CRO)
Hermitage la Sizeranne, Chapoutier (CRO)
1978
St-Joseph Jaboulet (CRO)
1974
Hermitage la Sizeranne, Chapoutier (CRO)

£25.00 → £29.99
1994
Hermitage Chave (YAP)
1993
Hermitage Chave (YAP)
1992
Hermitage Chave (YAP)
1991
Hermitage Guigal (TW)
Hermitage la Chapelle, Jaboulet (TAN)
1990
Hermitage la Sizeranne, Chapoutier (EL, DI)
1989
Cornas Clape (UB)
1988
Côte-Rôtie Gentaz-Dervieux (CRO)
Côte-Rôtie Jasmin (CRO)
Hermitage Chave (DI)
1986
Côte-Rôtie Gentaz-Dervieux (WS)
1985
Côte-Rôtie Burgaud (BUT)
Hermitage la Chapelle, Jaboulet (PE)
1984
Hermitage Guigal (CB)
1983
Côte-Rôtie la Viaillère, Dervieux-Thaize
(CRO)
Hermitage Marquise de la Tourette, Delas
(CRO)

1982
Côte-Rôtie Brune et Blonde, Guigal (CRO)
Hermitage Guigal (CRO)
1980
Côte-Rôtie Gentaz-Dervieux (CRO)
1979
Hermitage Chave (CRO)
1976
Côte-Rôtie les Jumelles, Jaboulet (CRO)
Hermitage Guigal (CRO)
Hermitage Jaboulet (CRO)

£30.00 → £39.99
1991
Côte-Rôtie la Landonne, René Rostaing
   (CRO)
1989
Hermitage Chave (FA)
Hermitage la Chapelle, Jaboulet (FA)
1988
Côte-Rôtie la Landonne, René Rostaing
   (CRO)
1986
Côte-Rôtie Jasmin (AD)
1985
Côte-Rôtie Jasmin (CRO)
Hermitage la Chapelle, Jaboulet (CRO, BUT,
   WS, AD)
1984
Côte-Rôtie la Landonne, Guigal (CRO)
1983
Cornas Clape (CRO)
Côte-Rôtie Brune et Blonde, Guigal (CRO)
Côte-Rôtie Gentaz-Dervieux (CRO)
Côte-Rôtie Jasmin (CRO)
Hermitage la Chapelle, Jaboulet (BUT)
1982
Hermitage Chave (DI, CRO)
Hermitage la Chapelle, Jaboulet (CRO)
1979
Hermitage la Chapelle, Jaboulet (PIP, CRO)

1978
Cornas Jaboulet (WS)
Crozes-Hermitage Domaine de
   Thalabert, Jaboulet (CRO)
Hermitage la Sizeranne, Chapoutier (CRO)
1976
Cornas Jaboulet (CRO)
Côte-Rôtie de Vallouit (CRO)
1974
Hermitage Chave (REI)
1971
Hermitage Marquise de la Tourette, Delas
   (CRO)

£40.00 → £65.00
1992
Ermitage le Pavillon, Chapoutier (FA)
1991
Ermitage le Pavillon, Chapoutier (FA)
1989
Hermitage la Chapelle, Jaboulet (REI, NO)
1987
Côte-Rôtie la Landonne, Guigal (CRO)
Côte-Rôtie la Mouline Côte Blonde,
   Guigal (CRO)
1986
Côte-Rôtie la Landonne, Guigal (CRO)
1985
Côte-Rôtie Gentaz-Dervieux (CRO)
Hermitage Chave (GOE, NO)
1984
Côte-Rôtie la Landonne, Guigal (REI)
Côte-Rôtie la Mouline Côte Blonde,
   Guigal (CRO, BUT, REI)
1983
Hermitage Chave (CRO)
1982
Côte-Rôtie Gentaz-Dervieux (CRO)
Côte-Rôtie la Landonne, René Rostaing
   (CRO)
1981
Côte-Rôtie la Landonne, Guigal (CRO)
Côte-Rôtie la Mouline Côte Blonde,
   Guigal (CRO)
1978
Côte-Rôtie Brune et Blonde, Guigal (CRO)
Côte-Rôtie Champet (REI)
Hermitage Guigal (CRO)
Hermitage Marquise de la Tourette, Delas
   (CRO)
1976
Côte-Rôtie la Chevalière d'Ampuis,
   Jasmin (REI)
Hermitage Chave (REI)
Hermitage la Chapelle, Jaboulet (REI)

1970
Crozes-Hermitage Domaine de
Thalabert, Jaboulet (CRO)
1962
Côte-Rôtie les Jumelles, Jaboulet (FA)
Hermitage Chapoutier (CRO)

£70.00 → £99.99

1992
Ermitage le Pavillon, Chapoutier (BEN)
1990
Hermitage la Chapelle, Jaboulet (FA)
1986
Côte-Rôtie la Landonne, Guigal (SEC, FA,
BUT)
Côte-Rôtie la Mouline Côte Blonde,
Guigal (SEC, FA, BUT)
1982
Côte-Rôtie la Landonne, Guigal (CRO, FA,
BUT)
Côte-Rôtie la Mouline Côte Blonde,
Guigal (CRO, BUT)
1980
Côte-Rôtie la Landonne, Guigal (CRO)
Côte-Rôtie la Mouline Côte Blonde,
Guigal (CRO)
1979
Côte-Rôtie la Landonne, Guigal (CRO)
Côte-Rôtie la Mouline Côte Blonde,
Guigal (CRO, FA)
1978
Côte-Rôtie Jasmin (REI)
Hermitage Chave (NO, FA)
1976
Côte-Rôtie la Chevalière d'Ampuis,
Jasmin (CRO)
1970
Hermitage Chave (FA)
Hermitage la Chapelle, Jaboulet (CRO)
1962
Côte-Rôtie les Jumelles, Jaboulet (TW)
1959
Côte-Rôtie les Jumelles, Jaboulet (CRO)

£110.00 → £174.99

1991
Côte-Rôtie la Mouline Côte Blonde,
Guigal (FA)
1989
Côte-Rôtie la Mouline Côte Blonde,
Guigal (SEC)
1985
Côte-Rôtie la Landonne, Guigal (NO, CRO)
Côte-Rôtie la Mouline Côte Blonde,
Guigal (BUT, CRO)

1983
Côte-Rôtie la Landonne, Guigal (AD, NO)
Côte-Rôtie la Mouline Côte Blonde,
Guigal (BUT)
1978
Hermitage Chave (AD, ROB, CRO)
Hermitage la Chapelle, Jaboulet (BUT, CRO,
FA)
1976
Côte-Rôtie la Mouline Côte Blonde,
Guigal (CRO)
1971
Hermitage la Chapelle, Jaboulet (REI)
1966
Hermitage Chave (CRO)

c. £205.00

1983
Côte-Rôtie la Landonne, Guigal (CRO)
Côte-Rôtie la Mouline Côte Blonde,
Guigal (CRO)

WHITE

Under £7.00

1994
Crozes-Hermitage Domaine des
Entrefaux (BY)
1993
Crozes-Hermitage Delas (FOR)

£7.00 → £8.99

1994
Crozes-Hermitage Cave des Clairmonts,
Borja (YAP)
★ Crozes-Hermitage Domaine du
Colombier (BIB)
Crozes-Hermitage la Mule Blanche,
Jaboulet (OD)
1993
Crozes-Hermitage Domaine des
Remizières (RAE)
1990
St-Joseph Courbis (BUT)

£9.00 → £11.99

1994
St-Joseph Chapoutier (TAN, DI)
St-Joseph Grippat (YAP)
1993
Crozes-Hermitage la Mule Blanche,
Jaboulet (TAN)
1991
St-Joseph Clos de l'Arbalestrier, Florentin
(GAU)

1989
Hermitage Chante-Alouette, Chapoutier
(BER)
1986
St-Joseph Clos de l'Arbalestrier, Florentin
(RAE)
1984
St-Joseph Clos de l'Arbalestrier, Florentin
(BUT)

£12.00 → £15.99

1991
Hermitage Chante-Alouette, Chapoutier
(BER)
Hermitage Guigal (WR, BOT)
Hermitage la Tourette, Delas (FOR)
1986
Hermitage Domaine des Remizières (RAE)
St-Joseph Clos de l'Arbalestrier, Florentin
(GAU, UB)
1985
Hermitage Chante-Alouette, Chapoutier
(BUT)

£16.00 → £19.99

1994
Condrieu Coteaux de Chéry, Perret (AD)
Condrieu les Cepes du Nebadon, Paret
(AD, REI)
Hermitage Chevalier de Stérimberg,
Jaboulet (NI)
1993
Condrieu Dumazet (BIB)
Hermitage Chante-Alouette, Chapoutier
(AD)
1992
Condrieu Coteaux de Chéry, Perret (NI)
Condrieu Delas (PEN)
Condrieu Pinchon (RAE)
Hermitage Chevalier de Stérimberg,
Jaboulet (PLA)
Hermitage Grippat (YAP)
Hermitage Guigal (BY)
Hermitage la Tourette, Delas (PEN)
1990
Hermitage Domaine des Remizières (RAE)
Hermitage la Tourette, Delas (PEN)
1988
Hermitage Chante-Alouette, Chapoutier
(CRO)
1986
Condrieu Barge (BUT)
Hermitage Domaine des Remizières (UB)
1985
Hermitage les Rocoules, Sorrel (BUT)

£20.00 → £24.99

1995
Condrieu Barge (TAN)
1994
Condrieu Château du Rozay (YAP)
Condrieu Vernay (YAP)
1993
Condrieu Delas (PE)
Condrieu Guigal (SOM, CRO)
Hermitage Chave (YAP)
1992
Condrieu Guigal (BY)
1991
Condrieu Coteaux de Chéry, Perret (NO)
Condrieu Pinchon (GAU)
1990
Hermitage Chante-Alouette, Chapoutier
(GAU, EL)
1989
Hermitage Grippat (BO)
1988
Condrieu Guigal (GOE, BUT)
1986
Hermitage Grippat (BEN)
1983
Hermitage Chevalier de Stérimberg,
Jaboulet (CRO)

£25.00 → £34.99

1994
Château Grillet (YAP)
Hermitage Chave (YAP)
1993
Condrieu Coteau de Vernon, Vernay (YAP)
1992
Château Grillet (YAP)
Hermitage Chave (YAP)
1991
Château Grillet (REI, LEA)
Condrieu Vernay (UB)
Hermitage Chave (WS)
1989
Condrieu Guigal (TW)
1987
Condrieu Coteau de Vernon, Vernay
(ROB)
1985
Condrieu Guigal (TW)
Hermitage Chave (BUT)
1983
Hermitage Chave (CRO)

c. £60.00

1989
Château Grillet (UB)

SOUTHERN RHÔNE

RED

Under £4.00

Non-vintage
Côtes du Rhône Meffre (VIC)

£4.00 → £4.99

1995
Côtes du Rhône-Villages Cairanne,
Domaine de l'Ameillaud (HAH)
1994
Coteaux du Tricastin Domaine de
Grangeneuve (ASD)
Côtes du Rhône Château St-Estève (SOM)
Côtes du Rhône Domaine de la
Renjardière (EL)
Côtes du Vivarais Domaine de Belvezet
(FUL)
1993
Côtes du Rhône-Villages Cairanne,
Domaine Brusset (PE)
Côtes du Rhône-Villages Château la
Courançonne (SAI)
Côtes du Ventoux la Vieille Ferme (ELL, SEC)
Côtes du Vivarais Domaine de Belvezet
(TAN)
Lirac Domaine les Garrigues (CHA)
1992
Coteaux du Tricastin Syrah, Domaine de
Grangeneuve (POR)
Côtes du Ventoux Jaboulet (OD)

£5.00 → £5.99

1995
Côtes du Rhône Château du Grand
Moulas (AD, TAN, HAH)
Côtes du Rhône Domaine des Moulins
(NEZ)
1994
Côtes du Rhône Caves des Vignerons de
Vacqueyras (TAN)
★ Côtes du Rhône Domaine la Renejeanne,
les Arbousiers (OD)
Côtes du Rhône Domaine St-Gayan,
Roger Meffre (YAP)
Côtes du Rhône-Villages Château du
Grand Moulas (EY)
1993
Côtes du Rhône Parallèle 45, Jaboulet (OD)
Côtes du Rhône-Villages Comté de
Signargues (SAI)
Côtes du Ventoux la Vieille Ferme (ROB)

1992
Côtes du Rhône Parallèle 45, Jaboulet (HOG)
Côtes du Rhône-Villages Cairanne,
Château de Gallifet (SAI)
Lirac les Queyrades, Mejan (FOR)
1991
Coteaux du Tricastin Domaine de Vieux
Micocoulier (CHA, AV)
Côtes du Rhône Guigal (REI)
Côtes du Rhône Laudun Rouge, Domaine
Pélaquié (SUM)
1988
Côtes du Rhône Cuvée Personnelle,
Pascal (NEW)

£6.00 → £6.99

1994
Côtes du Rhône-Villages Château du
Grand Moulas (AD)
1993
Côtes du Rhône-Villages Cairanne,
Domaine de l'Ameillaud (AD, HAH, ROB)
Vacqueyras Caves Bessac (EL)
1992
Côtes du Rhône Guigal (SOM, BY)
Lirac les Queyrades, Mejan (TAN)
1991
Côtes du Rhône Guigal (NI)
Côtes du Rhône-Villages Rasteau,
Domaine la Soumade (ELL)
Lirac la Fermade, Domaine Maby (YAP)
Lirac les Queyrades, Mejan (AD)
1990
Coteaux du Tricastin Domaine de Vieux
Micocoulier (POR)
Côtes du Rhône-Villages Jaboulet (NI)
1988
Côtes du Rhône Cuvée Personnelle,
Pascal (GAL)
Côtes du Rhône Rascasses, Berard (WAT)

£7.00 → £7.99

1995
Côtes du Rhône-Villages Château du
Grand Moulas (TAN)
1994
Côtes du Rhône-Villages Sablet, Château
du Trignon (PLA, AD)
Vacqueyras Domaine le Clos des Cazaux
(TAN)
Vacqueyras Domaine le Sang des Cailloux
(PIP)

1993
Châteauneuf-du-Pape Delas (WAI)
Châteauneuf-du-Pape les Galets Blancs (SAI)
Côtes du Rhône Coudoulet de Beaucastel (MAJ)
Côtes du Rhône Guigal (LAY)
Gigondas Tour de Queyron (SAI)
Vacqueyras Domaine du Clos du Caveau (YOU)
1992
Côtes du Rhône Château Redortier (PE)
Côtes du Rhône Guigal (UB, CRO, QUE)
Côtes du Rhône-Villages Rasteau, Domaine la Soumade (WS)
Vacqueyras Domaine le Clos des Cazaux (AD)
1991
Côtes du Rhône Coudoulet de Beaucastel (OD)
Côtes du Rhône Guigal (ROB)
Gigondas Domaine Raspail (HA)
Lirac les Queyrades, Mejan (LAY)
1990
Vacqueyras Domaine le Couroulu (ELL, AME)
Vacqueyras Jaboulet (WS)
Vacqueyras Jaboulet-Isnard (SAI)
Vacqueyras Pascal (YAP)
1989
Gigondas Domaine du Grand Montmirail (NEW)
Vacqueyras Domaine la Garrigue (HIC)

£8.00 → £9.99
1994
Côtes du Rhône-Villages Cuvée de l'Ecu, Château du Grand Moulas (AD)
Côtes du Rhône-Villages Domaine Ste-Anne (TAN)
Gigondas Côtes de la Tour, Sarrazine (TAN)
1993
Châteauneuf-du-Pape Domaine Brunel (SAI)
Châteauneuf-du-Pape Domaine de la Solitude (SO)
Châteauneuf-du-Pape Domaine de Nalys (HOG)
Châteauneuf-du-Pape Domaine du Père Caboche (OD)
Châteauneuf-du-Pape Domaine du Vieux Télégraphe (TAN)
Côtes du Rhône-Villages Rasteau, Domaine la Soumade (PIP)
Lirac Sabon (PIP)
Vacqueyras Sélection Maître de Chais, Combe (TAN)

1992
Châteauneuf-du-Pape Château des Fines Roches (ASD)
Châteauneuf-du-Pape Quiot (TES)
Côtes du Rhône Coudoulet de Beaucastel (BOT, WR, BY, ROB)
Lirac Domaine de Castel Oualou (UB)
Vacqueyras Domaine le Sang des Cailloux (NO)
1991
Côtes du Rhône Guigal (HIC)
Gigondas Domaine de Gour de Chaulé (EL)
Gigondas Domaine St-Gayan, Roger Meffre (YAP)
Gigondas Guigal (SOM, BY)
1990
Côtes du Rhône Coudoulet de Beaucastel (GOE)
Gigondas Jaboulet (NI)
Vacqueyras Domaine la Fourmone, Combe (EY)
1989
Gigondas Domaine de Gour de Chaulé (HOG)
Gigondas Domaine du Grand Montmirail (YAP)
1988
Gigondas Domaine du Cayron (BUT)

£10.00 → £11.99
1994
Châteauneuf-du-Pape la Bernardine, Chapoutier (REI, OD)
Châteauneuf-du-Pape Vieux Donjon (YAP)
1993
Châteauneuf-du-Pape Chante-Cigale (YAP)

Châteauneuf-du-Pape Domaine de Beaurenard (NEZ)
Châteauneuf-du-Pape Domaine de Montpertuis (EL)
Châteauneuf-du-Pape Domaine la Roquette (LAY)
Châteauneuf-du-Pape les Cailloux, Brunel (POR, YOU)
Gigondas Château du Trignon (PLA)

1992
Châteauneuf-du-Pape Domaine de
Beaurenard (ELL)
Châteauneuf-du-Pape Domaine du Vieux
Télégraphe (REI, LAY)
Châteauneuf-du-Pape Domaine Font de
Michelle (BOT, THR, WR, AME)
1991
Châteauneuf-du-Pape Château de
Beaucastel (NI, FA)
Gigondas Domaine du Cayron (AD)
Gigondas Domaine Raspail (LAY)
1990
Châteauneuf-du-Pape Chante-Cigale (KA)
Châteauneuf-du-Pape Domaine du Père
Caboche (YAP)
Châteauneuf-du-Pape Domaine du Vieux
Télégraphe (EY)
Châteauneuf-du-Pape les Cèdres, Jaboulet
(NI)
Gigondas Guigal (CRO, QUE)
1989
Châteauneuf-du-Pape Lucien Barrot (MV,
YOU)
Châteauneuf-du-Pape Château de la Font
du Loup (HOG)
Châteauneuf-du-Pape Château Fortia (POR)
Châteauneuf-du-Pape Domaine Grand
Tinel (HAH)
1988
Châteauneuf-du-Pape Clos des Papes,
Avril (BUT)
1986
Gigondas Domaine les Gouberts (CRO)
1979
Châteauneuf-du-Pape Delas (REI)
1978
Coteaux du Tricastin Cru de Meynas (CRO)

£12.00 → £14.99

1994
Châteauneuf-du-Pape Delas (PEN)
Châteauneuf-du-Pape Domaine de
Beaurenard (NI)
Châteauneuf-du-Pape Domaine Font de
Michelle (DAV)
Châteauneuf-du-Pape la Bernardine,
Chapoutier (GAU)
1993
Châteauneuf-du-Pape Château de
Beaucastel (FA, NI, GOE, GAU)
Châteauneuf-du-Pape Clos des Papes,
Avril (GAU, GE, RAE)
Châteauneuf-du-Pape Domaine Bosquet
des Papes (LAYT)

Châteauneuf-du-Pape Domaine du Vieux
Télégraphe (DI, ELL)
Châteauneuf-du-Pape Domaine la
Roquette (PIP)
Châteauneuf-du-Pape la Bernardine,
Chapoutier (DI)
1992
Châteauneuf-du-Pape Château de
Beaucastel (SEC, GOE, OD, YOU, GAU, NI)
Châteauneuf-du-Pape Domaine du Vieux
Télégraphe (TAN, SOM, POR, HAH, PIP, LAYT)
Châteauneuf-du-Pape Domaine Font de
Michelle (ARM)
Châteauneuf-du-Pape la Bernardine,
Chapoutier (PLA)
Côtes du Rhône Château de Fonsalette (DI)
1991
Châteauneuf-du-Pape Château de
Beaucastel (REI, BO, SEC, GOE, MAJ, LAY,
EY, TAN, MV, BY, BOT)
Côtes du Rhône Château de Fonsalette
(GAU)
Gigondas Guigal (UB)
1990
Châteauneuf-du-Pape Chante-Cigale (BEN)
Châteauneuf-du-Pape Château Fortia (QUE)
Châteauneuf-du-Pape Domaine du Vieux
Télégraphe (ELL)
Côtes du Rhône Guigal (CRO)
Gigondas Domaine les Pallières (PIP)
1988
Châteauneuf-du-Pape Château Fortia (CRO)
Châteauneuf-du-Pape Clos Pignan,
Reynaud (BUT)
1986
Châteauneuf-du-Pape Clos des Papes,
Avril (BUT)
Côtes du Rhône Château de Fonsalette
(CRO, BUT)
1985
Châteauneuf-du-Pape Clos Pignan,
Reynaud (BUT)
Gigondas Domaine les Pallières (CRO)
1983
Châteauneuf-du-Pape les Cèdres, Jaboulet
(BUT)
1974
Côtes du Rhône Jaboulet (CRO)

£15.00 → £19.99

1994
Châteauneuf-du-Pape Château de
Beaucastel (FA, GOE)
Châteauneuf-du-Pape la Bernardine,
Chapoutier (BEN)

1993
Châteauneuf-du-Pape Château de
Beaucastel (TAN, ROB)
Châteauneuf-du-Pape Clos des Papes,
Avril (ROB)
Châteauneuf-du-Pape Clos Pignan,
Reynaud (DI, GAU)
1992
Châteauneuf-du-Pape Domaine du Vieux
Télégraphe (ROB)
1991
Côtes du Rhône Château de Fonsalette
(WS, UB)
1990
Châteauneuf-du-Pape Château de
Beaucastel (BUT, SEC)
Châteauneuf-du-Pape Clos des Papes,
Avril (GE)
Châteauneuf-du-Pape Domaine Bosquet
des Papes (NO, CRO)
Côtes du Rhône Château de Fonsalette
(HOG)
1989
Châteauneuf-du-Pape Clos Pignan,
Reynaud (BUT)
Châteauneuf-du-Pape les Cailloux, Brunel
(CRO)
1988
Châteauneuf-du-Pape Château de
Beaucastel (FA)
Châteauneuf-du-Pape Clos Pignan,
Reynaud (HOG)
1986
Châteauneuf-du-Pape Château de
Beaucastel (CRO, REI)
1985
Châteauneuf-du-Pape les Cèdres, Jaboulet
(REI)
1984
Châteauneuf-du-Pape Château Rayas
(RAE)
1983
Châteauneuf-du-Pape Domaine Grand
Tinel (ROB)
Gigondas Domaine les Pallières (CRO)
1979
Gigondas Jaboulet (CRO)

£20.00 → £29.99
1990
Châteauneuf-du-Pape Château de
Beaucastel (CRO, FA, GOE, MV, TAN)
1988
Châteauneuf-du-Pape Château de
Beaucastel (GOE, MV, ROB, TAN)

1986
Châteauneuf-du-Pape Château Rayas (CRO)
1985
Châteauneuf-du-Pape Château de
Beaucastel (BUT)
Châteauneuf-du-Pape Château Rayas (BUT)
Châteauneuf-du-Pape Domaine Bosquet
des Papes (CRO)
Châteauneuf-du-Pape Domaine du Vieux
Télégraphe (DI)
Châteauneuf-du-Pape Vieux Donjon (CRO)
1981
Châteauneuf-du-Pape Domaine du Vieux
Télégraphe (CRO)
Gigondas Domaine les Gouberts (CRO)
Gigondas Domaine les Pallières (CRO)
1979
Châteauneuf-du-Pape Château Fortia (REI)
1976
Châteauneuf-du-Pape Domaine du Vieux
Télégraphe (CRO)
1969
Châteauneuf-du-Pape la Grappe des
Papes, Jaboulet (CRO)

£30.00 → £39.99
1993
Châteauneuf-du-Pape Château Rayas (DI,
GAU)
1989
Châteauneuf-du-Pape Château de
Beaucastel (CRO, SEC, MV, FA)
1988
Châteauneuf-du-Pape Château Rayas (CRO,
BUT)
Châteauneuf-du-Pape Clos Pignan,
Reynaud (REI)
1985
Châteauneuf-du-Pape Château de
Beaucastel (CRO, FA)
1981
Châteauneuf-du-Pape Domaine Grand
Tinel (CRO)
1978
Châteauneuf-du-Pape Clos du Mont
Olivet (CRO)

> Please remember that
> **Webster's** is a price
> GUIDE and not a price
> LIST. It is not meant to
> replace up-to-date
> merchants' lists.

Châteauneuf-du-Pape Domaine du Vieux
Télégraphe (CRO)
Châteauneuf-du-Pape les Cèdres, Jaboulet
(WS)
1970
Châteauneuf-du-Pape les Cèdres, Jaboulet
(CRO)
Gigondas Jaboulet (CRO)
1969
Châteauneuf-du-Pape Château Fortia (REI)
Châteauneuf-du-Pape la Grappe des
Papes, Jaboulet (REI)

£40.00 → £54.99

1989
Châteauneuf-du-Pape Château de
Beaucastel (GOE)
1983
Châteauneuf-du-Pape Château Rayas (CRO)
1981
Châteauneuf-du-Pape Château de
Beaucastel (CRO, FA, REI)
Châteauneuf-du-Pape Château Rayas (CRO)
1979
Châteauneuf-du-Pape Château de
Beaucastel (FA)
1978
Châteauneuf-du-Pape Château Fortia (CRO)
1974
Châteauneuf-du-Pape Château Rayas (CRO)
1967
Châteauneuf-du-Pape les Cèdres, Jaboulet
(CRO)
1962
Châteauneuf-du-Pape les Cèdres, Jaboulet
(REI)

£70.00 → £84.99

1989
Châteauneuf-du-Pape Château Rayas (UB)
1985
Châteauneuf-du-Pape Château de
Beaucastel (UB)
1961
Châteauneuf-du-Pape Domaine de Mont-
Redon (CRO)

c. £104.00

1967
Châteauneuf-du-Pape Château de
Beaucastel (CRO)

c. £128.00

1978
Châteauneuf-du-Pape Château Rayas (FA)

WHITE

Under £6.00

1994
VdP des Coteaux de l'Ardèche
Chardonnay, Latour (HOG, FOR, ELL)
1993
VdP des Coteaux de l'Ardèche
Chardonnay, Latour (EY, ELL)

£6.00 → £9.99

1995
Côtes du Rhône Domaine St-Gayan,
Roger Meffre (YAP)
1994
Côtes du Rhône Coudoulet de Beaucastel
(FA, REI, CRO, GOE)
Côtes du Rhône Domaine Pélaquié (BIB)
Lirac la Fermade, Domaine Maby (YAP)
1993
Côtes du Rhône Guigal (SOM, EY)
1992
Côtes du Rhône Guigal (ARM)

£10.00 → £12.99

1995
Châteauneuf-du-Pape Domaine de Mont-
Redon (WS)
1994
Châteauneuf-du-Pape Domaine de Mont-
Redon (UB)
Châteauneuf-du-Pape Domaine du Père
Caboche (YAP)
Châteauneuf-du-Pape les Cèdres, Jaboulet
(AD)
1993
Côtes du Rhône Coudoulet de Beaucastel
(GAU)
1992
Châteauneuf-du-Pape Domaine du Vieux
Télégraphe (REI)
Côtes du Rhône Coudoulet de Beaucastel
(BU)

£13.00 → £15.99

1995
Châteauneuf-du-Pape Domaine du Vieux
Télégraphe (TAN)
Châteauneuf-du-Pape Domaine Font de
Michelle (DAV)
1994
Châteauneuf-du-Pape Domaine du Vieux
Télégraphe (REI, AD)
Châteauneuf-du-Pape Domaine Font de
Michelle (LAY)

1993
Châteauneuf-du-Pape Domaine du Vieux
  Télégraphe (LAY)
1992
Côtes du Rhône Château de Fonsalette
  (WS)
1989
Côtes du Rhône Château de Fonsalette
  (GAU)
1987
Châteauneuf-du-Pape Château de
  Beaucastel (BUT)

£16.00 → £20.00
1994
Châteauneuf-du-Pape Domaine du Vieux
  Télégraphe (SOM)
1993
Châteauneuf-du-Pape Château de
  Beaucastel (FA, GOE)
1991
Châteauneuf-du-Pape Château de
  Beaucastel (TAN)
1988
Châteauneuf-du-Pape Château de
  Beaucastel (BU)
1986
Châteauneuf-du-Pape Château Rayas (HOG)

£25.00 → £34.99
1992
Châteauneuf-du-Pape Château Rayas (WS)
Châteauneuf-du-Pape Roussanne Vieilles
  Vignes, Château de Beaucastel (REI, FA)
1990
Châteauneuf-du-Pape Roussanne Vieilles
  Vignes, Château de Beaucastel (AD)
1989
Châteauneuf-du-Pape Château Rayas
  (BUT, AD, GAU)
1988
Châteauneuf-du-Pape Château Rayas (BUT)

ROSÉ

Under £6.50
1992
Tavel Château de Trinquevedel (EL, HOG)

£6.50 → £7.99
1995
Tavel la Forcadière, Domaine Maby (YAP)
1994
Lirac Rosé la Fermade, Domaine Maby (YAP)
Tavel la Forcadière, Domaine Maby (PE)

1992
Tavel l'Espiègle, Jaboulet (HOG)

c. £10.00
1994
Tavel l'Espiègle, Jaboulet (UB)

SPARKLING

Under £10.00
Non-vintage
Clairette de Die Brut Archard-Vincent (YAP)
Clairette de Die Georges Aubert (UN)
Clairette de Die Tradition Demi-sec
  Archard-Vincent (YAP)

FORTIFIED

Under £7.00
1992
Muscat de Beaumes-de-Venise Domaine
  de Coyeux ½ bottle (AD)
1987
Muscat de Beaumes-de-Venise Domaine
  de Coyeux ½ bottle (NO)

£7.00 → £9.99
Non-vintage
Muscat de Beaumes-de-Venise Cave Co-
  op. de Beaumes-de-Venise (WHI)
Muscat de Beaumes-de-Venise Cuvée
  Pontificale, Pascal (DAV)
1993
Muscat de Beaumes-de-Venise Cave Co-
  op. de Beaumes-de-Venise (OD)
1991
Muscat de Beaumes-de-Venise Domaine
  de Coyeux (POR)

£10.00 → £12.99
Non-vintage
Muscat de Beaumes-de-Venise Perrin (PE)
1995
Muscat de Beaumes-de-Venise Domaine
  de Durban (YAP)
1993
Muscat de Beaumes-de-Venise Domaine
  de Durban (EL, SOM, ELL)

c. £14.00
1994
Muscat de Beaumes-de-Venise Domaine
  de Durban (PIP)
Muscat de Beaumes-de-Venise Domaine
  des Bernardins (PIP)

LOIRE

Are we watching a river turning into a backwater? The growers of the Loire are threatened by competition on all sides, particularly from the New World. And are they worried?

Consider the most common wines of the Loire Valley, the Sauvignons of Sancerre and Pouilly-Fumé, Muscadets, sparkling Saumur and Chenin Blanc in its various manifestations. Competitors from the New World immediately come to mind. It is really only the red wines, plummy Cabernet Franc from Chinon and Bourgueil and the rare sweet wines of Bonnezeaux and Quarts de Chaume that do not have an obvious New World rival.

With such fierce competition, you might expect the producers of the Loire to be a bit edgy. If I were making Sancerre, I would be nervous about New Zealand Sauvignon, with its ripe fruit and upfront flavours, and its price, which is often a little lower than that of Sancerre. Yet M. Vacheron of Sancerre seems unconcerned. New Zealand is a problem for the négociants, he says, not for the individual producers; accordingly, the outside world seems to pass him by. The director of the co-op of Sancerre believes that as long as quality is maintained all will be well, especially as prices of Sancerre are for the moment stable. However, on the other side of the world Allan Clarke of the New Zealand Vine Improvement Group says that so far they have been unable to obtain Sauvignon cuttings from the Loire. From Bordeaux, yes, but not the Loire. It seems that for all that they claim not to be, the French are, after all, a little prickly about the competition.

If I grew Chenin Blanc in Anjou, I would be concerned about South Africa, where the grapes at least ripen regularly every year. It is true that the Cape does not have the same potential for noble rot, and could only rarely produce dessert wines with the concentration and aging potential of fine Vouvray or Bonnezeauz. However, year in,

year out, it can provide vast quantities of fruity dry Chenin Blanc, not spoiled by the searing acidity that can make basic Anjou Blanc one of the least desirable flavours around. With cheap labour costs, Cape Chenin Blanc reaches our shelves at an affordable £2.99 a bottle.

Flat fizz
The producers of Saumur Brut and Crémant de Loire are probably the most aware of competition. Ten years ago, if we looked for an alternative to Champagne, we generally ended up in the Loire. Now, we are more likely to look to Australia, California and New Zealand. Sparkling Loire continues to be drunk in France, but it is not in demand across the Channel, and the producers of Saumur realise that they need to take action. Many have family and business links with Champagne, which give them broader horizons and a more professional approach to marketing. As a result they have grouped together to initiate a marketing effort.

As for Muscadet it is, with rare exceptions, nondescript. So it sells on price, which fluctuates according to demand and the size of the crop. And with the average Muscadel currently costing about £3.69 and the better ones a pound or two more, there is plenty of choice elsewhere.

In spite of all this competition, the Loire growers give the impression of being content with their own horizons. Few see further than the far side of the river. Meanwhile sales stagnate and it is only the better growers who can transcend the reputations of their regions. It may be that things will have to get much worse before the producers are galvanised into making them better. **ROSEMARY GEORGE MW**

GRAPES AND FLAVOURS

CABERNET FRANC (red) The great quality grape of Anjou and Touraine. All the best reds are based on Cabernet Franc, and the styles go from the palest, most fleeting of reds to deep, strong and often austerely tannic wines of character and longevity.

CABERNET SAUVIGNON (red) This doesn't always ripen very well in the Loire, but even so it adds some backbone to the wines. It is really at its best in the warmest, ripest years.

CHARDONNAY (white) Increasingly widespread in the Loire and producing lean, light but tangy results in Haut-Poitou, in Anjou as Vin de Pays du Jardin de la France and in Orléans as Vin de l'Orléanais (where it's called Auvernat) *Clos St-Fiacre* is terrific. It also occurs in Muscadet (*le Chouan* and *Domaine Couillaud* are good) and adds character and softness to Anjou Blanc.

CHASSELAS (white) Makes adequate but dull wine at Pouilly-sur-Loire; it's actually best as a table grape, in a fruit salad.

CHENIN BLANC (white) A grape that cries out for sun and ripens (if that's the word) long after the other varieties. Experiments with allowing the skins to steep in the juice before fermentation, and the quiet addition of a bit of Chardonnay, are beginning to produce outstanding peachy whites.

It also performs superbly in the Loire in a few warm and misty mesoclimates (especially Quarts de Chaume and Bonnezeaux), where noble rot strikes the Chenin with enough frequency to make it worthwhile going through all the pain and passion of producing great sweet wine, with steely acidity and honeyed, ripe-apple fruit. These wines can seem curiously disappointing when young, but fine sweet Chenin manages to put on weight and become sweeter for perhaps 20 years before bursting out into a richness as exciting as all but the very best from Germany or Bordeaux. And then it lasts and lasts… Because Chenin Blanc is unfashionable, these wines can be remarkably undervalued; but you have to be prepared to tuck them away for a long time.

GAMAY (red) In the Loire this rarely achieves the lovely, juicy glugginess of Beaujolais, but when made by a careful modern winemaker it can have a fair amount of fruit, though it always seems to have a tough edge.

MELON DE BOURGOGNE (white) The grape of Muscadet, light and neutral. It's good at producing fresh white, usually quite biting, but sometimes fairly soft, slightly peppery and dry with a salty tang. It's usually for drinking young though a good domaine-bottled *sur lie* can mature surprisingly well.

PINOT NOIR (red) In and around Sancerre this can, in warm years, produce a lovely, light, cherry-fragrant wine that will be either a rosé or a light red. But really interesting examples are rare in the Loire, where it's usually too chilly to ripen the Pinot properly.

SAUVIGNON BLANC (white) The grape of Sancerre and Pouilly, and the main white grape of Touraine, with a whole range of fresh, green, tangy flavours that might remind you of anything from gooseberries to nettles and fresh-cut grass, and there's sometimes even a whiff of newly roasted coffee. The wines are usually quite tart – but thirst-quenching rather than gum-searing – and have loads of fruit. Sauvignon can age interestingly in bottle, but the odds are against it, except for the high-priced oak-aged cuvées.

The price guides for this section begin on page 190.

WINES & WINE REGIONS

ANJOU BLANC SEC, AC (white)
France's cheapest AC dry white made from the hard-to-ripen Chenin Blanc, grown anywhere in Anjou upriver from the Muscadet region, often tart, sulphured and sour. But it *can* be good, steely and honeyed, especially from Savennières with its two tiny special ACs, Coulée-de-Serrant and la Roche-aux-Moines, and from names such as *Domaine Richou* which mixes Chardonnay with the Chenin, for extra flavour and fruit. They are allowed up to 20 per cent Chardonnay or Sauvignon. Some have planted a bit more, and it's no bad thing. Other good names: *Mark Angelli (Cuvée Christine), Baranger, Château de Valliennes, Domaine de la Haute Perche, Jaudeau.*

ANJOU ROUGE CABERNET, AC (red)
Until a few years ago Anjou Rouge was a byword for raw, rasping red fit to drive a chap to Liebfraumilch. Now it's mostly light and dry from the co-ops, and spicy, strong and capable of aging from the best estates. It can rival Bourgueil. Best: *Mark Angeli (Cuvée Martial), Ch. d'Avrille, Ch. de Chamboureau (Soulez), Clos de Coulaine, Dom. de la Petite Croix, Dom. du Petit Val, Dom. des Rochettes (Chauvin), Logis de la Giraudière (Baumard), Richou, Roussier.*

ANJOU ROUGE GAMAY, AC (red)
Rarely more than adequate, but in the hands of someone like *Richou*, the 'rooty' character is replaced by a fresh, creamy fruit that is sharp and soft all at once, and *very* good. *Domaine des Quarres* is also worth a try.

ANJOU-VILLAGES, AC (red) Cabernets Franc and Sauvignon from the 46 best villages in Anjou. Some are labelled Anjou-Villages Val-de-Loire. *Domaine de Montgilet, J-Y & H Lebreton, Domaine Ogereau* and *Richou* are good. Go for the concentrated 1990s or fresh 1993s.

BONNEZEAUX, AC (white) One of the most unfairly forgotten great sweet wines of France. After a long period of decline, this small AC inside the Coteaux du Layon is on the up again. The vineyard area has grown from 42 hectares in 1975 to 157 hectares in 1985, and prices for the lovely noble-rot-affected wines are rising fast. So much the better; they were far too cheap before, and if you don't make it profitable for the growers to make great sweet wine, they'll give up and plant apples. Look out for the outstanding wines of *Mark Angeli* (from old vines), *Château de Fesles, Goizil, Renou* and *Denéchère.*

BOURGUEIL, AC (red) Some of the best reds of the Loire come from this AC in Touraine. When they are young they can taste a bit harsh and edgy, but give them a few years and they will have a piercing blackcurrant fruit, sharp and thirst-quenching. They can age remarkably well, developing complex leathery, meaty flavours. Best: *Audebert* (estate wines), *Pierre Breton, Caslot-Galbrun, J-F Demont, Domaine des Forges, Domaine des Ouches, Pierre-Jacques Druet, Lamé-Delille-Boucard.*

CABERNET D'ANJOU, AC (rosé) There is a reasonable chance of a pleasant drink here, because the Cabernets – mostly Franc, but often with Cabernet Sauvignon too – do give pretty tasty wine, usually less sweet than simple Rosé d'Anjou. Best: *Dom. Baranger, Dom. de Hardières, Dom. de Richou, Château de Valliennes.*

CHEVERNY, AC (red, white) This Touraine region is improving fast. Its claim to fame is the teeth-grittingly dry white Romorantin grape, but there is also Chardonnay, Sauvignon Blanc and Chenin. *Dom. des Huards* is delicate and fine, and the *confrérie* at Oisly-et-Thésée is reliable. Others: *Cazin, Gendrier, Gueritte* and *Tessier.* Red Cheverny tends to be light and crisp, with a healthy dollop of Gamay perhaps beefed up with Cabernet Franc. *Oisly-et-Thésée's* is strawberryish with a fair bit of Pinot Noir in it.

CHINON, AC (red) In a ripe year (1988, '89, '90, '95), Chinon can be delicious, exhibiting a great gush of blackcurrant and raspberry flavours. There's earthiness too, but it is soft and cooling, and after a few years it seems to dissolve into mouthwatering fruit. In the poorer vintages, it can be unpalatably bitter with surprising levels of green tannin. Domaine wines are *far* better than négociant wines, which can be thin. Best: *Bernard Baudry, Jean Baudry, Domaine du Colombier, Couly-Dutheil, Druet, Gatien Ferrand, René Gouron, Charles Joguet, Alain Lorieux, Pierre Manzagol, Jean-François Olek, Jean-Maurice Raffault, Raymond Raffault, Domaine du Roncée, Domaine de la Tour.*

COTEAUX DE L'AUBANCE, AC (white) Quite cheap, pleasant semi-sweet whites. Best: *Dom. des Rochettes, Jean-Yves Lebreton* and *Dom. Richou.*

COTEAUX DU LAYON, AC (white) A large AC producing varying qualities of sweet white wine, at its best rich and tasty with a taut acidity that allows the wine to age for a long time. *Dom. Ambinois, Ch. du Breuil* (from very old vines), *Ch. de la Guimonière, Ogereau, Dom. du Petit Val, Dom. de la Pierre St-Maurille, Dom. des Quarres, Ch. de la Roulerie, Clos Ste-Catherine* and *Dom. de la Soucherie* are worth trying. There are also six Coteaux du Layon-Villages ACs that usually offer higher quality. Some Anjou growers are now making *sélection de grains nobles*, very sweet, concentrated wines made from only botrytized grapes.

CRÉMANT DE LOIRE, AC (white) Sparkling wine AC intended to denote higher quality but not much used. Compared with Saumur AC fizz, the yield must be lower (50 rather than 60 hectolitres per hectare), the juice extract less (150kg of grapes as against 130kg for one hectolitre of juice), and the wine must lie on its lees after its second fermentation for 12 months rather than nine. The result is usually softer and nicer than the frequently harsh wines of Saumur, but the merchants have built up Saumur and don't seem inclined to put much effort into Crémant de Loire. Laudable exceptions are the first-rate house of *Gratien & Meyer, Langlois-Château, St-Cyr-en-Bourg* co-op and the small *Cave des Liards.*

GROS PLANT, VDQS (white) Gros Plant rejoices in being one of the rawest wines in France, and the prosperity of dentists in Nantes is thanks in no small measure to the locals' predilection for the stuff. That said, it *does* go amazingly well with seafood and seems to suit oysters. *Bossard's* is soft and honeyed. *Métaireau* and *Sauvion* have also tamed its fury. *Clos de la Sénaigerie* and *Clos de la Fine* from *Dom. d'Herbauges* are good.

HAUT-POITOU, VDQS (red, white) Produced in an isolated area south of the main Loire vineyards. Chardonnay and Sauvignon from the *Cave Co-opérative du Haut-Poitou* are good but tending to the lean side, for the whites; the reds are fairly 'green' but reasonably enjoyable, and are usually made from Gamay.

MENETOU-SALON, AC (red, white, rosé) Small AC west of Sancerre making equally good Sauvignon (and some fair reds and rosés). The *Vignerons Jacques Coeur* co-op produces about half the Sauvignon. *Henry Pellé* makes the best in Menetou, followed by *Jean-Max Roger* and *Dom. de Chatenoy.*

MONTLOUIS, AC (white) Chenin area south of Vouvray. Makes similar wines, but often more robust – which, when it comes to the Chenin grape, isn't always a good idea. *Dominique Moyer, Domaine des Liards* and *Jean-Pierre Trouvé* are good, but lots are short on fruit, long on sulphur.

MUSCADET, AC (white) Simple, light, neutral wine from the area around Nantes. Straight Muscadet, without any further regional title, is usually flat and boring. But at least it's light – the Muscadet ACs are the only ones in France to impose a *maximum* alcohol level (12.3 per cent).

MUSCADET COTES DE GRANDLIEU, AC (white) Demarcated in 1994, this latest Muscadet sub-region covers a large area south-east of Nantes. It accounts for nearly half of the area that was basic Muscadet, and quality is variable. Wines of slightly better concentration come from the sandier southern part, from communes such as Corcoués/Logne and St-Philbert-de-Bouaine. The good news is that most of the wine is bottled *sur lie*.

MUSCADET DE SÈVRE-ET-MAINE, AC (white) The biggest Muscadet area, making the most but also the best wine. A good one may taste slightly nutty, peppery or salty, even honeyed, sometimes with creaminess from being left on the lees, sometimes a chewy apricot-skin taste and sometimes with a slight prickle. It should always have a lemony acidity, and should feel light. Buy domaine-bottled wine only, and check the address, looking out for St-Fiacre and le Pallet, two of the best villages.

MUSCADET DES COTEAUX DE LA LOIRE, AC (white) A small area east of Nantes. Quality isn't bad though the wines tend to lack the distinction of Muscadet de Sèvre-et-Maine. *Pierre Luneau* is good.

MUSCADET SUR LIE (white) This is the most important thing to look for on a Muscadet label. It indicates that the wine has been bottled straight off the lees (the yeast sediment from fermentation), thus having more character than usual and a slight prickle. The law has now been tightened up, and from the 1994 vintage any wine labelled *sur lie* must have been bottled at the property where the wine was made. Bottling is in two designated periods in spring and autumn. Some merchants, like *Sauvion*, have portable bottling lines, and have always bottled *sur lie* at the grower's cellar. Its *Ch. du Cléray* and *Découvertes* range are very good. *Guy Bossard* makes good organic *sur lie*. Others: *Dom. de Coursay-Villages*, *Dom. du Grand Mouton*, *Pierre Luneau*, *Dom. de la Montaine*, *Ch. de Chasseloir*,

Clos de la Sénaigerie, *Jean-Louis Hervouet*, *Dom. du 'Perd-son-pain'*, any from *Louis Métaireau* including *Dom. du Grand Mouton*, *Cuvée LM*, *Cuvée One*, unfiltered *Huissier*, both *Michel* and *Donatien Bahuaud*'s single-domaine wines, *Bonhomme* and *Guilbaud*.

POUILLY-FUMÉ, AC (white) Just over the river from Sancerre and very similar. They can be fuller than Sancerre, and the best have a mineral complexity, but given the prices, there are still too many under-achievers. Best: *J C Châtelain*, *Didier Dagueneau* (Pouilly's most brilliant winemaker), *Serge Dagueneau*, *Château Favray*, *André Figeat* and the too-expensive *Baron de L.*

POUILLY-SUR-LOIRE, AC (white) Made from the dull Chasselas grape which makes good eating but not memorable drinking. *Serge Dagueneau* makes a good example.

QUARTS DE CHAUME, AC (white) A tiny 38-hectare AC with a perfect mesoclimate for nobly-rotten sweet wines. They are rare and expensive, not as sweet as Sauternes, but can be even more intense, with high acid stalking the rich apricot and honey fruit. *Jean Baumard* is superb; also *Ch. de Bellerive* and *Ch. de l'Echarderie*.

QUINCY, AC (white) Crisp Sauvignon Blanc, grown west of Sancerre though usually lighter in style. *Dom. de Maison Blanche*, *Pierre Mardon*, *Jacques Rouzé* and the *Jacques Coeur* co-op make good examples.

REUILLY, AC (white) Light, fragrant Sauvignon Blanc from near Quincy. *Gérard Cordier* and *Claude Lafond* are the main growers here. (There is also some tasty red and rosé.)

ROSÉ D'ANJOU, AC (rosé) The omnipresent and frequently omnihorrid French rosé. It is based on a pretty feeble grape, the Groslot, and suffers in the main from lack of fruit and excess of sulphur. A few like the co-op at *Brissac* can make it fresh.

ROSÉ DE LOIRE, AC (rosé) A little-made dry rosé from Anjou or Touraine.

ST-NICOLAS-DE-BOURGUEIL, AC (red) These Cabernet reds from an AC within Touraine AC are grown on gravelly soil, so they tend to be lighter and more forward than the reds of nearby Bourgueil. They can be good, but stick to warm years. The wines of *Claude Ammeux, Caslot-Jarnet, Jean-Paul Mabileau* and *Joël Taluau* seem best.

SANCERRE, AC (white) Green, smoky, tangy wine from the Sauvignon Blanc grape grown at the eastern end of the Loire. At its best young, it should be super-fresh and fruity, tasting and smelling of gooseberries or cut grass. But too often it smells meaty or sulphurous, and tastes flabby and fruitless. Look for single-domaine wines – especially from *Archambault, Balland-Chapuis, Henri Bourgeois, Francis and Paul Cotat, Lucien Crochet, Pierre and Alain Dézat, Gitton, Dom. Laporte, Alphonse Mellot, Paul Millérioux, Henri Natter, Reverdy, Jean-Max Roger, Pierre Riffault, Vacheron* and *André Vatan.*

SANCERRE ROUGE, AC (red) Pinot Noir, and in general overrated, but occasionally you can find a fleeting cherry fragrance and sweetness of strawberries that can survive a year or two in bottle. Silly prices, though. *Henri Bourgeois, Domaine Vacheron, Pierre & André Dezat* and *Domaine de Chatenoy* at the nearby Menetou-Salon AC are good and worth a try.

SAUMUR, AC (white) Champagne-method fizz from Chenin Blanc, perhaps with the welcome addition of Chardonnay, Sauvignon or even Cabernet Franc to round out the acid Chenin. Well-made sparkling Saumur (there is a little rosé) is lively and appley but too many are just too rough to revel with. Best: *Ackerman-Laurance, Bouvet-Ladubay, Gratien & Meyer, Langlois-Château.*

SAUMUR BLANC, AC (white) Usually ultra-dry, though it can occasionally be sweet, similar to Anjou Blanc.

SAUMUR-CHAMPIGNY, AC (red) Cabernet from the best villages in Saumur. It is way above other Loire reds thanks to a firm structure and velvety softness, fruit that is slightly raw and rasping, yet succulent and rich at the same time. Although the term 'vieilles vignes' is open to interpretation it is always the best bet for quality. *Domaine Filliatreau* makes an outstanding one, as well as *Primeur*, for immediate drinking. Also good: *Château de Chaintres, Château du Hureau, Château de Targé, Domaine Dubois, Domaine Lavigne, Domaine Sauzay-Legrand, Denis Duveau, Domaine de Nerleux, Domaine des Roches Neuves, Domaine du Val Brun.*

SAUMUR ROUGE, AC (red) Usually very light and dry Cabernet Franc from 38 villages round Saumur. Although it's light the fruit is often marked and attractively blackcurranty. The co-op at *St-Cyr-en-Bourg* is good, as is *Château Fouquet* from Paul Filliatreau.

SAVENNIÈRES, AC (white) Some of the world's steeliest, longest-living, diamond-dry white wines come from this tiny Anjou AC where the Chenin grape comes into its own. One vineyard, Savennières Coulée-de-Serrant, has its own AC within Savennières, and *Nicolas Joly's Clos de la Coulée-de-Serrant* is excellent. Also: *Yves Soulez* from the *Ch. de Chamboreau, Clos du Papillon, Jean Baumard (Clos Ste-Catherine), Dom. de la Bizolière* and the *Dom. aux Moines.*

TOURAINE, AC (red, white) Everybody sees Touraine Sauvignon, with some justification, as a Sancerre substitute. The *Confrérie des Vignerons de Oisly-et-Thésée* is good, as are *Paul Buisse, Ch. de l'Aulée, Dom. de la Charmoise (Marionnet), Ch. de Chenonceau, Dom. des Corbillières, Dom. Joël Delaunay* and *Dom. Octavie.* The reds aren't usually very exciting, being rather green and stalky. They are often Gamay-based but may be made from a variety of grapes, including Cabernet. The *Domaine de la Charmoise (Marionnet),* and the co-op of *Oisly-et-Thésée* produce fair Gamays. *Château de Chenonceau* is also good.

VIN DE PAYS DU JARDIN DE LA FRANCE (white) The general vin de pays of the Loire. Usually pleasant but unmemorable, but those based on Sauvignon Blanc and Chardonnay can be considerably better. Biotteau's *Château d'Avrille* Chardonnay and *Domaine des Hauts de Saulière*'s Chardonnay have lovely fruit.

VIN DE PAYS DES MARCHES DE BRETAGNE (red, white) These wines from the mouth of the Loire are usually fairly flimsy, lightweight numbers, but a good innovative grower can use the denomination to produce something unusual and exciting. *Guy Bossard*, for instance, a leading Muscadet producer,

makes an amazingly fragrant and fruity red from Cabernet Franc.

VOUVRAY, AC (white) Sparkling and still whites from tangily dry to richly sweet, though usually caught in the middle. In fact Vouvray is best at producing the off-dry demi-sec style, and from a good producer this Chenin wine, initially all searing acidity and rasping dryness, over many years develops a deep, nutty, honey-and-cream flavour. Most commercial Vouvray is poor. Best: *Daniel Allias, Domaine des Aubuisières, Brédif, Chamalou, Château Gaudrelle, Pierre Mabille, Château Moncontour, Foreau, Huet, Prince Poniatowski* and *Domaine de Vaugoudy.*

MERCHANTS SPECIALISING IN THE LOIRE
see Merchant Directory (page 424) for details

Most merchants have some, though the choice is not always tremendously wide. Unusually imaginative lists can be found at: Adnams (AD), Averys of Bristol (AV), Bennetts (BEN), Anthony Byrne (BY),

Eldridge Pope (EL), Lay & Wheeler (LAY), The Nobody Inn (NO), Terry Platt (PLA), Raeburn Fine Wines (RAE), T&W Wines (TW), Tanners (TAN), Ubiquitous Chip (UB), Waterloo Wine (WAT), Wine Society (WS)

LOIRE VINTAGES

Loire vintages are very important, and can be radically different along the river length. In poor vintages, Muscadet is most likely to be OK, while in hot vintages Sauvignon goes dull, but the Chenin finally ripens. The red grapes need the warm years.

1995 September was cold and wet, and some growers panicked and picked too early. Those who waited have produced some luscious dessert wines as well as fine reds.

1994 Sancerre and Pouilly-Fumé were picked after the rain and are fair, but there are only a few decent Vouvrays. Coteaux du Layon should be best of all. Reds are lightweight.

1993 Good, flinty Sauvignon from Touraine and the upper Loire, and crisp Anjou Chenin. Reds look capable of aging. The best Coteaux du Layon is botrytized and concentrated.

1992 A large crop of wines that generally lack concentration. The reds are very light.

1991 Sancerre and Pouilly-Fumé were down by half. Quality was average.

1990 Sweet Chenins, built to last, may beat the '89s. Great reds too. Sancerre and Pouilly can be low in acidity, but late-harvest Sauvignon is back.

1989 An exceptional year, particularly for sweet Chenin Blancs, which are comparable with the legendary '47s. The reds were ripe, but some dry whites lack acidity.

LOIRE

DRY WHITE

Under £4.00

1995
Sauvignon du Haut Poitou, Cave Co-op.
du Haut Poitou (SO, NEW)
1994
Sauvignon de Touraine Comte d'Ormont,
Saget (MAJ)
Sauvignon de Touraine Confrérie d'Oisly
et Thésée (OD)
1993
Saumur Cave des Vignerons de Saumur
(TES)

£4.00 → £4.99

1995
Chardonnay du Haut Poitou Cave Co-op
(NEW)
Muscadet de Sèvre-et-Maine Domaine de
la Roche (SAT)
Saumur Cave des Vignerons de Saumur
(YAP)
Sauvignon de Touraine Domaine Guy
Mardon (VIC)
1994
Muscadet de Sèvre-et-Maine sur lie
Château de la Ferronière (EL)
Muscadet de Sèvre-et-Maine sur lie la
Goélette (SAI)
1993
Muscadet de Sèvre-et-Maine Moreau (FOR)
1992
Saumur Domaine des Hauts de Sanziers
(SAI)

£5.00 → £5.99

1995
Muscadet de Sèvre-et-Maine sur lie Carte
d'Or, Sauvion (NEZ)
Muscadet de Sèvre-et-Maine sur lie
Château de Cléray (PIP)
Muscadet sur lie Chéreau, Domaine de la
Mortaine (YAP)
Vin de Thouarsais, Gigon (YAP)
1994
Chardonnay du Haut Poitou Cave Co-op
(FOR)
Muscadet de Sèvre-et-Maine Fief de la
Brie, Bonhomme (TAN)
Muscadet de Sèvre-et-Maine sur lie
Domaine de la Bretonnière (NI)

Muscadet des Coteaux de la Loire
Guindon (BIB)
Muscadet sur lie Château de la
Galissonière (DI)
Sauvignon de Touraine Domaine des
Corbillières (HIC)
Sauvignon du Haut Poitou, Cave Co-op.
du Haut Poitou (FOR)
1993
Muscadet de Sèvre-et-Maine sur lie
Domaine de la Loge (ELL)
Muscadet de Sèvre-et-Maine sur lie
Domaine des Hauts Pemions (EY)
Muscadet de Sèvre-et-Maine sur lie
Thuaud (CHA)
Muscadet de Sèvre-et-Maine sur lie
Première, Jean Douillard (SAI)
1992
Muscadet de Sèvre-et-Maine sur lie
Château de Chasseloir (AME)
Saumur Blanc Domaine Langlois (DI)

£6.00 → £6.99

1995
Menetou-Salon Moroges, Pellé (WS)
Menetou-Salon Pellé (OD)
Reuilly Beurdin (AD)
Sauvignon de Touraine Domaine de la
Charmoise, Marionnet (BIB)
Sauvignon de Touraine Domaine de la
Preslé (PIP)
Vouvray Jarry (YAP)
1994
Muscadet de Sèvre-et-Maine sur lie Clos
des Bourguignons (HAH)
Muscadet sur lie Château l'Oiselinière,
Carré (WS)
Pouilly-Fumé Figeat (SAI)
Pouilly-Fumé les Loges, Saget (MAJ)
Sauvignon de Touraine Confrérie d'Oisly
et Thésée (HAH)
Vouvray Château Moncontour (NI)
1993
Cheverny Domaine Gendrier (HAH)
Menetou-Salon les Thureaux, Mellot (HOG)
Menetou-Salon Pellé (SAI)
Muscadet de Sèvre-et-Maine sur lie Cuvée
LM, Louis Métaireau (NI)
Sancerre les Garennes, Brochard (WAT)
1992
Sauvignon de Touraine Domaine des
Corbillières (BUT)

£7.00 → £7.99

1995

Montlouis Domaine des Liards, Berger (YAP)

Quincy Jaumier (YAP)

Quincy Rouze (HAH)

Reuilly Robert & Gérard Cordier (YAP)

Touraine Azay-le-Rideau la Basse
Chevrière, Pavy (YAP)

1994

Menetou-Salon Domaine de Chatenoy
(VIG)

Menetou-Salon Pellé (BOT, THR, WR)

Muscadet de Sèvre-et-Maine sur lie
Château de la Ragotière Black Label (VIN)

Pouilly-Fumé Bailly (WS)

Pouilly-Fumé les Loges, Saget (SAT)

Reuilly Beurdin (BER)

Sancerre Daulny (GAL)

Sancerre Domaine des Trois Piessons
(BOT, THR, WR)

Savennières Domaine de la Bizolière (YAP)

★ Vouvray Vieilles Vignes, Domaine
Bourillon (MV)

1993

Coteaux du Giennois Balland-Chapuis (SUM)

Menetou-Salon Morogues, Pellé (WHI, YOU)

Pouilly-Fumé Domaine Coulbois (ASD)

Pouilly-Fumé Jean Pabiot (YOU)

Savennières Domaine du Closel, Mme de
Jessey (WAT)

VdP du Jardin de la France Chardonnay,
Domaine Couillaud (FUL)

Vouvray Château Moncontour (BEN, ROB)

1990

Vouvray Domaine Peu de la Moriette (PIP)

£8.00 → £9.99

1995

Menetou-Salon Domaine de Chatenoy (DI)

Menetou-Salon Pellé (MV, HAH)

Menetou-Salon Teiller (YAP)

Sancerre la Reine Blanche (WS)

Sancerre les Perriers, Vatan (YAP)

Sancerre Michel Thomas (BOD, SUN)

Sancerre Roger (MV)

1994

Pouilly-Fumé André Dezat (NI)

Pouilly-Fumé Château Fauray (ENO)

Pouilly-Fumé Domaine des Rabichattes
(RAE, PE)

Pouilly-Fumé Domaine Thibault (EY, ELL)

Pouilly-Fumé Jean Pabiot (HAH)

Pouilly-Fumé les Griottes, Bailly (KA)

Pouilly-Fumé les Loges, Jean-Claude
Guyot (YAP)

Pouilly-Fumé les Loges, Saget (VIN)

Pouilly-Fumé Seguin Père et Fils (RAE)

Sancerre André Dézat (EY, TAN, POR)

Sancerre Chavignol, Delaporte (LEA)

Sancerre Clos de la Crêle, Lucien Thomas
(EL)

Sancerre Clos des Roches, Vacheron (KA)

Sancerre Clos du Chêne Marchand,
Roger (TAN)

Sancerre Clos du Roy, Millérioux (ARM)

Sancerre Daulny (WHI, HAH)

Sancerre Domaine de Montigny, Natter
(RAE, LAY)

Sancerre Laporte (PIP)

Sancerre Paul Prieur (HA)

Sancerre Vacheron (MAJ)

Savennières Château de Chamboureau,
Soulez (YAP)

1993

Menetou-Salon Domaine de Chatenoy
(WRI)

Menetou-Salon Roger (TAN)

Pouilly-Fumé Domaine des Berthiers,
Jean-Claude Dagueneau (GAL)

Pouilly-Fumé Domaine Thibault (POR)

Sancerre Clos du Roy, Millérioux (CB)

Sancerre Domaine du Nozay, de Benoist
(CB)

Savennières Clos du Papillon, Baumard
(HOG, EL)

Savennières Domaine du Closel, Mme de
Jessey (YAP)

Vouvray Clos du Bourg, Huet (WS)

Vouvray Clos Naudin, Foreau (GAU, DI)

Vouvray le Haut Lieu, Huet (AV)

1992

Menetou-Salon Morogues, Pellé (HIC)

Pouilly-Fumé Redde (QUE)

Sancerre Domaine de Montigny, Natter
(GAU)

Sancerre les Creux, Gitton (HIG)

Savennières Clos du Papillon, Baumard
(POR)

Savennières Clos du Papillon, Domaine du
Closel (AD)

1991
Savennières Clos de Coulaine (RAE)
Savennières Clos du Papillon, Baumard (SOM)
Vouvray Clos Naudin, Foreau (GAU)
1990
Muscadet Vieilles Vignes, Château de Chasseloir (WHI)
Vouvray Brédif (POR, CRO, QUE)
1989
Muscadet de Sèvre-et-Maine sur lie Château de Chasseloir (PEN)
Vouvray Château de Vaudenuits (UN)
1988
Savennières Clos de Coulaine (REI)
Vouvray le Haut Lieu, Huet (GAU)
1985
Vouvray Aigle Blanc, Poniatowski (VIG)
1984
Vouvray le Haut Lieu, Huet (RAE)

£10.00 → £14.99
1994
Menetou-Salon Domaine de Chatenoy (ROB)
Pouilly-Fumé Château de Tracy (AD, WS, LAY, LAYT, CB)
Pouilly-Fumé Domaine des Berthiers, Jean-Claude Dagueneau (WRI)
Pouilly-Fumé Domaine Thibault (BER)
Sancerre Balland-Chapuis (BER)
Sancerre Chavignol la Grande Côte, Cotat (LAYT, RAE, VIG)
Sancerre Chavignol les Monts Damnés, Cotat (LAYT)
Sancerre Clos des Roches, Vacheron (BEN, ROB)
Sancerre Laporte (DI)
Savennières Roche-aux-Moines, Soulez (YAP)
Vouvray le Mont, Huet (RAE)
1993
Pouilly-Fumé de Ladoucette, Château du Nozet (HOG, FOR, HAH, ROB)
Sancerre Chavignol la Grande Côte, Cotat (GAU, AD, GE, RAE)
Savennières Clos du Papillon, Baumard (LAY, UB, TAN)
Vouvray Clos du Bourg, Huet (EY)
1992
Pouilly-Fumé Château de Tracy (AV)
Pouilly-Fumé Cuvée Prestige, Châtelain (NEZ)
Pouilly-Fumé de Ladoucette, Château du Nozet (WHI)

Sancerre Comte Lafond, Château du Nozet (HOG)
Sancerre les Romains, Gitton (HIG)
1991
Pouilly-Fumé de Ladoucette, Château du Nozet (BER)
Pouilly-Fumé les Pechignolles (HIG)
Savennières Baumard (NO)
Savennières Clos St-Yves (AV)
1989
Vouvray Domaine Peu de la Moriette (CRO)
1987
Vouvray Brédif (CRO)
1986
Vouvray Aigle Blanc, Poniatowski (UB)

£15.00 → £19.99
1994
Pouilly-Fumé Clos du Chailloux, Didier Dagueneau (FA)
Pouilly-Fumé Didier Dagueneau (TAN)
1992
Savennières Coulée-de-Serrant, Nicolas Joly (DI)
1976
Vouvray Aigle Blanc, Poniatowski (VIG)
1973
Vouvray Clos Naudin, Foreau (CRO)

£20.00 → £29.99
1994
Pouilly-Fumé Clos du Chailloux, Didier Dagueneau (UB)
Pouilly-Fumé Pur Sang, Didier Dagueneau (FA)
1993
Pouilly-Fumé Pur Sang, Didier Dagueneau (FA, UB)
Pouilly-Fumé Silex, Didier Dagueneau (YOU, FA)
Savennières Coulée-de-Serrant, Nicolas Joly (WS)
1991
Savennières Coulée-de-Serrant, Nicolas Joly (BIB)
1990
Pouilly-Fumé Baron de L Château du Nozet (BEN, WRI)
Savennières Coulée-de-Serrant, Nicolas Joly (WAT, NO, YAP)
1989
Pouilly-Fumé Silex, Didier Dagueneau (BUT)
1979
Savennières Coulée-de-Serrant, Nicolas Joly (CRO)

1975
Vouvray Aigle Blanc, Poniatowski (CRO)
1971
Vouvray Clos du Bourg, Huet (RAE)

£30.00 → £44.99
1992
Pouilly-Fumé Baron de L Château du
  Nozet (HAH, ROB)
1973
Savennières Coulée-de-Serrant, Nicolas
  Joly (CRO)
1971
Vouvray Clos du Bourg, Huet (REI)
1969
Savennières Coulée-de-Serrant, Nicolas
  Joly (CRO)
1952
Vouvray le Mont, Huet (REI)

SPARKLING

Under £9.00
Non-vintage
Montlouis Mousseux Brut Berger (YAP)
Montlouis Mousseux Demi-sec Berger
  (YAP)
Vouvray Brut Jarry (YAP)
Vouvray Foreau (GE)
1993
Crémant de Loire Brut Gratien & Meyer
  (WS)
Saphir Bouvet-Ladubay (NI)

£9.00 → £9.99
Non-vintage
Crémant de Loire Château Langlois (CRO,
  ELL, DI, BEN)
Vouvray Foreau (AD, GAU)

£10.00 → £10.99
Non-vintage
Vouvray Brut Brédif (ROB)
Vouvray Méthode Champenoise, Huet
  (RAE)

SWEET WHITE

Under £7.00
1994
Coteaux d'Ancenis Malvoisie, Guindon
  (YAP)
1992
Coteaux du Layon Rablay, Caves de la
  Pierre Blanche (YAP)

£7.00 → £8.99
1986
Coteaux du Layon Leblanc (RAE)
1985
Montlouis Moelleux Deletang (RAE)

£9.00 → £12.99
1994
Coteaux du Layon Clos de Ste-Catherine,
  Baumard (EL, SOM)
Vouvray Clos du Bourg, Huet (RAE)
1992
Coteaux du Layon Clos de Ste-Catherine,
  Baumard (HOG)
1989
Coteaux du Layon Leblanc (RAE)
1985
Montlouis Moelleux Domaine des Liards,
  Jean & Michel Berger (VIG)
Quarts-de-Chaume Château de Bellerive
  (CRO)

£13.00 → £15.99
1993
Quarts-de-Chaume Baumard (SOM, EL)
1990
Vouvray le Haut Lieu Moelleux, Huet (NI)
1989
Coteaux du Layon Domaine de la Petit
  Croix (VIG)
Quarts-de-Chaume Château de Bellerive
  (WS)
Vouvray Domaine Peu de la Moriette (TAN)
Vouvray Moelleux Bourillon Dorléans (VIG)
1988
Quarts-de-Chaume Baumard (NO, GAU)
Vouvray Moelleux Huet (RAE)
1986
Vouvray Clos du Bourg, Huet (WS)
1985
Coteaux du Layon Chaume, Château de
  la Guimonière (VIG)
Vouvray Clos Naudin, Foreau (NO, HOG)
Vouvray le Haut Lieu Moelleux, Huet (NO)
1983
Anjou Moulin, Touchais (EL)

£16.00 → £19.99
1993
Coteaux du Layon Clos de Ste-Catherine,
  Baumard (UB)
1990
Bonnezeaux Château de Fesles (TAN)
Quarts-de-Chaume Baumard (HOG)
Vouvray Moelleux Bourillon Dorléans (ELL)

1989
Montlouis Moelleux Deletang (WS)
Quarts-de-Chaume Château de
  l'Echarderie (YAP)
1976
Anjou Moulin, Touchais (WRI)
1973
Vouvray Clos Naudin, Foreau (CRO)
1971
Coteaux du Layon Ravouin-Gesbron (AD)
1969
Anjou Moulin, Touchais (FOR)

£20.00 → £29.99
1993
Vouvray Cuvée Constance, Huet (RAE, GAU)
1990
Bonnezeaux la Chapelle, Château de
  Fesles (WS)
Quarts-de-Chaume Château de Bellerive
  (NO)
Vouvray Clos du Bourg, Huet (GAU)
1989
Bonnezeaux la Chapelle, Château de
  Fesles (GAU)
Coteaux du Layon Clos de Ste-Catherine,
  Baumard (CRO)
Quarts-de-Chaume Baumard (GAU)
Vouvray Clos du Bourg, Huet (WS, AD)
1979
Anjou Moulin, Touchais (WRI)
1976
Vouvray le Haut Lieu Moelleux, Huet
  (CRO)
1975
Anjou Moulin, Touchais (EL)
1971
Vouvray Clos Naudin, Foreau (CRO)

£30.00 → £49.99
1990
Vouvray le Mont, Huet (GAU)
1989
Vouvray Cuvée Constance, Huet (BUT)
1959
Anjou Moulin, Touchais (FOR)

> *Please remember that*
> ***Webster's*** *is a price*
> *GUIDE and not a price*
> *LIST. It is not meant to*
> *replace up-to-date*
> *merchants' lists.*

Bonnezeaux Château des Gauliers, Mme
  Fourlinnie (CRO)
Vouvray Brédif (CRO)
Vouvray le Haut Lieu Moelleux, Huet (CRO)
Vouvray Moelleux Bourillon Dorléans (YOU)

£50.00 → £79.99
1969
Vouvray Clos du Bourg, Huet (AD)
1962
Vouvray Clos du Bourg, Huet (RAE)
1959
Vouvray Clos du Bourg, Huet (NO)
1953
Vouvray le Mont, Huet (RAE)
1947
Vouvray Brédif (CRO)
Vouvray le Haut Lieu Moelleux, Huet (REI)
1935
Bonnezeaux Château des Gauliers, Mme
  Fourlinnie (NO)

c. £80.00
1955
Vouvray le Haut Lieu Moelleux, Huet (WS)

c. £194.00
1921
Vouvray Brédif (CRO)

ROSÉ

Under £5.00
1993
Anjou Rosé Cellier de la Loire (NI)

£5.00 → £7.99
1995
Reuilly Pinot Gris, Cordier (YAP)
Reuilly Pinot Noir, Beurdin (AD)
1994
Touraine Rosé Noble Jouée, Clos de la
  Dorée (AD)

c. £9.00
1994
Sancerre Rosé André Dezat (NI)

£10.00 → £10.99
1995
Sancerre Rosé André Dezat (PIP)
Sancerre Rosé Delaporte (LEA)
1994
Sancerre Rosé les Romains, Vacheron (BEN)

RED

Under £4.99

1992
Saumur Cave des Vignerons de Saumur (AD)
1989
Bourgueil la Hurolaie, Caslot-Galbrun (TES)

£5.00 → £6.99

1995
Saumur Cave des Vignerons de Saumur (YAP)
Vin de Thouarsais, Gigon (YAP)
1994
Anjou Rouge Logis de la Giraudière, Baumard (EL)
Chinon Château de Ligre (EL)
Gamay de Touraine Domaine de la Charmoise, Marionnet (BIB)
Gamay du Haut Poitou Cave Co-op. (FOR)
1993
Bourgueil Clos de la Henry, Morin (AV)
1992
Bourgueil la Hurolaie, Caslot-Galbrun (TES)

Saumur Domaine du Langlois-Château (DI)
1991
Anjou Rouge Tijou (HIG)
1989
Saumur-Champigny Château de Parnay (WAT)

£7.00 → £8.99

1995
Chinon l'Arpenty, Desbourdes (YAP)
Sancerre André Dezat (NI)
1993
Chinon Cuvée Prestige, Gouron (KA)
St-Nicolas-de-Bourgueil Vieilles Vignes, Taluau (WS)
Saumur-Champigny Château de Targé (SOM)
Saumur-Champigny Château des Chaintres (WS)

1992
Chinon Clos de Danzay, Druet (BY)
Menetou-Salon Domaine de Chatenoy, Clement (DI)
Menetou-Salon Rouge, Pellé (ENO)
1990
Bourgueil Domaine des Raguenières (UB)
Chinon Clos de l'Echo, Couly-Dutheil (WAT)
St-Nicolas-de-Bourgueil Mabileau (PLA, LAY)
1988
Chinon Clos de l'Echo, Couly-Dutheil (WAT)
1987
Bourgueil Cuvée Reserve, Druet (BY)
Bourgueil Beauvais, Druet (BY)
Bourgueil Grand Mont, Druet (BY)

£9.00 → £10.99

1994
Sancerre André Dezat (TAN)
1993
Bourgueil Domaine des Ouches (PIP)
Menetou-Salon Domaine de Chatenoy, Clement (VIG)
Saumur-Champigny Vieilles Vignes, Filliatreau (YAP)
1991
Sancerre la Bourgeoise, Henri Bourgeois (SOM)
1990
Sancerre Domaine de Montigny, Natter (RAE)

£11.00 → £12.99

1992
Chinon Clos de la Dioterie, Joguet (AD)
Sancerre Cotat (RAE)
1990
Anjou Rouge Château de la Roche, Nicolas Joly (GAU)
Bourgueil Beauvais, Druet (CRO)
1989
Chinon Clos de l'Echo, Couly-Dutheil (NO)

£13.00 → £19.00

1990
Bourgueil Grand Mont, Druet (YAP)
1976
Bourgueil Caslot-Galbrun (VIG)

c. £39.00

1978
Chinon Olga Raffault (CRO)

ALSACE

Are they wrong, or just misunderstood? Alsace wines seem to correspond with everything we want from wine, and yet we still decline to drink them

Wine consumption in Britain is heavily weighted in favour of white, and the production of Alsace is dominated by six white grape varieties. Many of us, although we claim to prefer steely, crisp whites, often find something rounded and fruity much more palatable, which corresponds to the flavour of Alsace. So why don't we drink more of it?

In addition Alsace, in a world with a growing number of fully paid-up members of the ABC – Anything But Chardonnay – club, offers flavours that have absolutely nothing to do with that ubiquitous variety. The only form of Chardonnay you might encounter in Alsace is in sparkling wine, blended with Pinot Blanc or Pinot Noir, for in theory it is forbidden in still wine.

Again, in a world in which new oak rules all too many regions and dominates all too many flavours, there is a refreshing absence of barriques in the average Alsace cellar. In the large village co-operatives you are most likely to see stainless steel vats, while smaller, more traditional producers tend to favour large old barrels, made of oak from the Vosges, and these may be as much as a hundred years old. New barriques are really only used for maturing Pinot Noir, and even then in very limited quantities.

The six principal white grapes range from steely dry Rieslings to ripe, even overblown, Gewürztraminers. While the British market tends to favour Pinot Blanc for easy drinking and Gewürztraminer for its more obvious and immediately recognisable flavours, in Alsace itself it is Riesling that is most keenly appreciated, while Tokay-Pinot Gris is growing in popularity. In some ways Pinot Gris is the unsung hero of Alsace. But it only represents seven or eight per cent of production and there is little opportunity to increase that, despite the demand. It takes time to change the composition of a vineyard, and there is an EU ban on new vineyard plantings.

Variety show

Surprisingly perhaps, some producers see a move away from varietal wines as a way of winning new consumers, not with Edelzwicker, which now has a decidedly tarnished reputation, but with more upmarket blends. Willm has always had its Gentil de Clos Gaensbronnel, made from Gewürztraminer and Sylvaner, planted together in the vineyard. Hugel too has taken up the idea with its Gentil, a blend of Riesling, Gewürztraminer, Pinot Gris and Muscat, as well as a substantial amount of Sylvaner. Kuentz-Bas sees a future in a similar blend.

Meanwhile many of us continue to be misled by the Germanic appearance of the traditional tall green bottles, with their teutonic-sounding vineyard and producer names. Not only are there the names of the 50 grands crus, but also those of countless other lieu-dits or individual vineyards. In addition, some key producers like Hugel and Trimbach prefer to stick with their cuvée names, like Jubilee and Cuvée Frédéric Émile, for they feel that the concept of the grands crus has been grossly devalued. There may be 50 in all, but only 15 or 20 are significantly better than the run of Alsace vineyards, and to make things worse, some of the better grands crus have been extended in area.

Flavours too can be confusing. With long hours of sunshine, the grapes here are usually rich in sugar, which in turn results in high alcohol levels. Sometimes they can be too high, and for the sake of balance a producer might leave some residual sweetness in his wine. In the hands of a skilled winemaker this can be subtle, but there are less scrupulous producers who are tempted to take the easy option and use sugar to mask the deficiencies of fruity and flavour that are caused by squeezing too high yields from the vines.

Another answer to the question of why Alsace wines don't sell here is price. The good-value wines we are so used to from the New World come from highly mechanised vineyards or countries with low labour costs. In contrast in Alsace there are slopes so steep that mechanisation of any kind is impossible, and French labour costs are some of the highest in Europe. That, combined with the strong franc, makes Alsace wines expensive. Prices in Alsace have been fairly static for the last three years, but now they are due to rise again with the small 1995 vintage.

Bertrand Denoune, the export manager of Willm, argues fluently that it is a question of attitude. The British wine trade is set in its idea that Alsace wines don't sell – but put them in the right place, for example as a house wine in a lively restaurant, and suddenly they do sell. But then, if we all started buying Alsace, would there be enough to go round? And what would happen to prices then? **ROSEMARY GEORGE MW**

GRAPES & FLAVOURS

In Alsace wines are generally labelled according to their grape variety. Blends of two or more varieties are allowed, but account for just four per cent of the total production, and are mostly sold as cheap Edelzwicker.

AUXERROIS This is officially only tolerated in Alsace and not encouraged. The name only appears on the label if it is unblended, and usually it is blended with Pinot Blanc to add acidity. It's fatter and more buttery than Pinot Blanc, with a touch of spice and musk. Best: *André Kientzler, Marc Kreydenweiss, Jos Meyer, Landmann-Ostholt, Rolly Gassmann, Bruno Sorg*.

CHASSELAS Rare now in Alsace, Chasselas has never been complex, but the few true examples can be vibrantly fruity and must be drunk young, while they retain their freshness. Best: *André Kientzler, Jos Meyer, Schoffit*.

CLASSIC BLENDS These can be superb, and their producers avoid the Edelzwicker designation like the plague. Best: *Hugel Gentil, Marc Kreydenweiss Clos du Val d'Eléon, Co-op de Ribeauvillé Clos du Zahnacker, Schlumberger Réserve, Jean Sipp Clos du Schlossberg, Louis Sipp Côtes de Ribeauvillé, Willm Gentil Clos*

Gaensbroennel. They will almost all be best in riper years.

EDELZWICKER These are mostly lacklustre blends. Occasionally an Edelzwicker with an extra dollop of Gewürztraminer or Tokay-Pinot Gris will be good. *Schlumberger Cristal-Maree* has been on good form lately.

GEWÜRZTRAMINER Gewürztraminer is the least dry of all Alsace. The high street ones are usually decent, and *Beyer Cuvée des Comtes d'Eguisheim* and *Trimbach Cuvée des Seigneurs de Ribeaupierre* are bone dry. Gewürztraminer is the most voluptuous, upfront and fat of all Alsace wines, overflowing with exotic aromas. Young Gewürz often smells of banana and the more it does so, the more finesse it will have when mature. Best: *Kuentz-Bas, Ostertag, Trimbach, Weinbach, Willm Clos Gaensbroennel, Zind-Humbrecht*.

MUSCAT Light, fragrant, wonderfully grapy. Imagine crushing a fistful of green grapes and gulping the juice. That's how fresh and grapy a good Muscat should be. Hotter years give heavy wines that are far from ideal. 1993 is the best current vintage. Look for *Becker, Ernest Burn, Joseph Cattin, Dirler, Charles Koehly, Marc*

Kreydenweiss, Kuentz-Bas, Rolly Gassmann, Pfaffenheim co-op, Schlumberger, Bruno Sorg, Weinbach, Zind-Humbrecht.

PINOT Most are Pinot Blanc, but the rules permit any variety of Pinot. Not very long ago, many Pinots were dull and neutral, but reduced yields and stricter selection are giving wines that are plump, rich and ripe, with apple or floral overtones and a long creamy finish. Best: J B Adam, Camille Braun, Théo Cattin, Co-opérative de Cléebourg, Marcel Deiss, Hugel, Charles Koehly, Albert Mann, Rolly Gassmann, Schlumberger, Martin Spielmann, Zind-Humbrecht. Can also be called Klevner.

PINOT NOIR The Burgundy grape makes light reds, although richer, oakier wines are becoming more common. Typically they are perfumed and strawberryish, but lack complexity. 1990 was an exceptional year. Best include J B Adam, Jean Becker, Marcel Deiss, René Fleith, Albert Hertz, Hugel, Jacques Iltis, Albert Mann, Co-opérative de Pfaffenheim, Turckheim co-op, Wolfberger.

RIESLING Powerful, structured, steely wines that grow 'petrolly' with age. It's with Riesling that the subtleties of grand cru soils are most evident. Can be long-lived. Best: Becker, Beyer, Paul Blanck, Deiss, Dirler, Pierre Freudenreich, Pierre Frick, Mader, Frederic Mallo, Frederic Mochel, Edgar Schaller, Schlumberger, Sick-Dreyer, Jean Sipp, Louis Sipp, Bruno Sorg, Trimbach, Weinbach, Wunsch & Mann, Zind-Humbrecht.

SYLVANER Light, tart, slightly earthy. With age it tastes of tomatoes, for some reason. Best: Christian Dolder, J Hauller, Ostertag, Rolly Gassmann, Martin Schaetzel, Schoffit, Albert Seltz, Zind-Humbrecht.

TOKAY-PINOT GRIS Rich, musky and honeyed, though can run to flab if badly made. Even the lighter ones are luscious behind their dry fruit. The best can age well. Best: Lucien Albrecht, Barmès-Buecher, Léon Beyer, Ernest Burn, Claude Dietrich, Robert Dietrich, Pierre Frick, Marc Kreydenweiss, Kuentz-Bas, Frédéric Mallo, Schlumberger, Schoffit, Bruno Sorg, Turckheim co-op, Weinbach, Zind-Humbrecht.

CLASSIFICATIONS

VIN D'ALSACE, AC This is the simple generic appellation that covers the whole Alsace region, and it is normally used in conjunction with a grape name. Thus a wine would be called 'Riesling – Appellation d'Origine Contrôlée Alsace'.

CRÉMANT, AC White, Champagne-method fizz, made mainly from Pinot Blanc. Some producers make the wine from Riesling or Pinot Gris, the former racy and flowery, the latter more musky and rich. But both are atypical. Chardonnay may also be used, and Pinot Noir for rosé. Look for wines from Paul Blanck, Robert Dietrich, Dopff & Irion, Dopff Au Moulin, Laugel, Co-opérative de Pfaffenheim, Co-opérative de Turckheim, Wolfberger.

GRAND CRU A decree of 1992 classified 50 historically excellent vineyards as grand cru.

They must meet stricter regulations than ordinary Alsace, and can only be planted with Riesling, Tokay-Pinot Gris, Gewürztraminer or Muscat. Notably lower (but still high) yields apply. They are recognized by the words Appellation Alsace Grand Cru Contrôlée on the label.

The 50 grands crus cover 1700 hectares, just over eight per cent of the 20,250ha classified as AC Alsace. But only 600ha are declared as grand cru, amounting to about four per cent of the total yield. The fascination of grands crus is that they reflect the great variety of soils to be found in Alsace – limestone, schist, granite, clay, sandstone – offering a superb palate of flavours and nuances. But great wine can only be made, even from grand cru sites, if yields are modest. Otherwise the wines do not reflect the terroirs that were the reason why the grand cru sites were selected.

SÉLECTION DE GRAINS NOBLES
The higher of the two 'super-ripe' legal descriptions. It only applies to wines from Riesling, Tokay-Pinot Gris, Muscat (very rare) and Gewürztraminer and is not disimilar to Sauternes in style, though not flavour. Acidity levels can be lower, especially from Pinot Gris or Gewürztraminer.

VENDANGE TARDIVE
The lesser of the 'super-ripe' categories, made from late-picked grapes, as opposed to the botrytized ones used for Sélection de Grains Nobles. Only applies to Riesling, Tokay-Pinot Gris, Muscat (rare) and Gewürztraminer. They are very full, fairly alcoholic and vary in sweetness from richly dry to dessert-sweet.

MERCHANTS SPECIALISING IN ALSACE
see Merchant Directory (page 424) for details

Adnams (AD), Bennetts (BEN), Bute Wines (BUT), Butlers Wine Cellar (BU), Anthony Byrne (BY), Croque-en-Bouche (CRO), Direct Wine (DI), Eldridge Pope (EL), J E

Hogg (HOG), Lay & Wheeler (LAY), Oddbins (OD), Thos Peatling (PE), Reid Wines (REI), T&W Wines (TW), Thresher (THR), The Ubiquitous Chip (UB), Wine Society (WS)

ALSACE VINTAGES

1995 Similar to 1994, but possibly with lower acidity. A wet September resulted in rot in the vineyards, and a sharp reduction in yields among the conscientious producers who eliminated the rotten grapes. Warm weather in October redeemed the quality.

1994 A wet September marred a promising vintage. Many growers panicked and picked too soon, making light wines. Those who waited were rewarded with a sunny October and phenomenally rich late-harvest wines.

1993 Good to average wines. Muscat and Gewürztraminer are fresh, and there is excellent Riesling, which resisted rot better than other varieties. Be selective.

1992 An easy vintage after a hot, dry summer. The best producers thinned the crop in the summer to reduce yields. The wines are healthy, and range from dilute to excellent.

1991 The main problem, after a splendid summer, was late September and October rains. Careful vinification will have produced fresh, clean wines, but it is not a late-harvest year.

1990 With healthy grapes and no noble rot, 1990 was a *vendange tardive* year. The early harvest was already too hot for Muscat. Rieslings are powerful and will age well.

1989 An abundant harvest of very good but not top quality. They have lively fruit, though some are low in acidity. Abundant and superb late-harvest wines.

1988 Rain at harvest time made for pleasant, but hardly inspiring wine. Tokay-Pinot Gris and Riesling are the most successful.

1987 Not great, but better than first thought. Good single-vineyard wines.

1986 The best are at their peak. Good *vendange tardive* and even some *SGN*.

1985 An absolute corker – wonderful wines to drink now but they will keep.

1983 A great year, but only at the top level. These are brilliant, and will still keep.

ALSACE

WHITE

Under £4.50
1994
Pinot Blanc Cave Co-op. Turckheim (SO)
1993
Pinot Blanc Cave Co-op. Turckheim (FUL)

£4.50 → £4.99
1995
Pinot Blanc Cave Co-op. Turckheim (SAF)
1994
Gewürztraminer Cave Co-op. Turckheim (SO)
Pinot Blanc Dopff & Irion (EL, HOG)
Pinot Blanc Tradition, Cave Co-op. Turckheim (AME)
Riesling Cave Co-op. de Ribeauvillé (LEA)
Sylvaner Dopff & Irion (EL)
Tokay-Pinot Gris Cave Co-op. Turckheim (OD)

£5.00 → £5.99
1994
Muscat Réserve, Cave Co-op. Turckheim (OD)
Tokay-Pinot Gris Cave Co-op. Turckheim (WR, THR, BOT)
Tokay-Pinot Gris Tradition, Cave Co-op. Turckheim (AME)
1993
Gewürztraminer Cave Co-op. Turckheim (FUL)
Tokay-Pinot Gris Cave Co-op. Turckheim (POR)
1991
Edelzwicker Rolly Gassmann (WR, BOT, THR)

£6.00 → £6.99
1994
Gewürztraminer Dopff & Irion (HOG)
Pinot Blanc Muré (NEZ)
Pinot Blanc Schlumberger (EY)
Pinot Blanc Trimbach (HOG)
Riesling Réserve, Cave Co-op. Turckheim (QUE)
Riesling Seigneur d'Alsace, Dopff & Irion (EL)
Sylvaner Schleret (YAP)
Tokay-Pinot Gris Dopff & Irion (EL, HOG)
Tokay-Pinot Gris Tradition, Cave Co-op. Turckheim (QUE)

1993
Gewürztraminer Caves de Bennwihr (PE)
Gewürztraminer Réserve Prestige, Cave Co-op. Turckheim (NI)
Muscat Muré (NEZ)
Muscat Réserve, Cave Co-op. Turckheim (QUE)
★ Pinot Blanc Fuchs (PIP)
Pinot Blanc Muré (DI)
Pinot Blanc Schlumberger (HOG)
Riesling Cave Co-op. de Ribeauvillé (PLA)
Riesling Caves de Bennwihr (PE)
1992
Gewürztraminer Seigneur d'Alsace, Dopff & Irion (UB)
Pinot Blanc Louis Gisselbrecht (HIC)
Sylvaner Zind-Humbrecht (CRO, BY)
1990
Riesling les Faitières (CHA)
Sylvaner Vieilles Vignes, Ostertag (GAU)
1989
Riesling Hugel (REI)
Sylvaner Faller (BUT)
1988
Pinot Blanc les Amours, Hugel (BUT)
Pinot Blanc Trimbach (BUT)

£7.00 → £7.99
1995
Pinot Blanc Cave de Kientzheim (LAYT)
1994
Gewürztraminer Dopff au Moulin (CRO)
Pinot Blanc Schlumberger (NI, WRI, PLA)
Pinot Blanc Trimbach (GAU)
Riesling Muré (NEZ)
Riesling Schleret (YAP)
Sylvaner Vieilles Vignes, Ostertag (MV)
1993
Edelzwicker Rolly Gassmann (SEC, WS)
Gewürztraminer Muré (DI)
Gewürztraminer Réserve, Cave Co-op. Turckheim (QUE)
Gewürztraminer Schléret (YAP)
Muscat Wiederhirn (HIG)
Pinot Blanc Cattin (CB)
Pinot Blanc Hugel (DI)
Pinot Blanc Schlumberger (BEN)
Pinot Blanc Zind-Humbrecht (BY)
Riesling Tradition, Kuentz-Bas (WS)
Riesling Zind-Humbrecht (BY)
Sylvaner Schlumberger (PLA)

1992
Gewürztraminer Herrenweg, Zind-
  Humbrecht (WR)
Muscat Réserve, Trimbach (REI)
Pinot Blanc Tradition, Kuentz-Bas (BER)
Pinot Blanc Trimbach (UB)
Riesling Beyer (AME)
Tokay-Pinot Gris Louis Gisselbrecht (WHI)
Tokay-Pinot Gris Wiederhirn (HIG)
1991
Pinot Blanc Rolly Gassmann (BIB)
Pinot Blanc Willy Gisselbrecht (ROB)
Riesling les Murailles, Dopff & Irion (HOG)

Riesling Rolly Gassmann (BIB)
Sylvaner Zind-Humbrecht (GAU)
1990
Riesling Louis Gisselbrecht (HIC)

£8.00 → £8.99

1995
Riesling Cave de Kientzheim (LAYT)
1994
Muscat Koehly (HAH)
Muscat les Amandiers, Dopff & Irion (EL)
Pinot Blanc Schleret (YAP)
Sylvaner Vieilles Vignes, Ostertag (BEN)
Tokay-Pinot Gris Tradition, Kuentz-Bas
  (HOG)
1993
Gewürztraminer Beyer (BER)
Gewürztraminer Louis Gisselbrecht (HIC)
★ Gewürztraminer Reserve Personelle,
  Fuchs (PIP)
Gewürztraminer Sipp (WHI)
Gewürztraminer Zind-Humbrecht (BY)
Muscat Réserve, Trimbach (REI, BOT, THR)
★ Muscat Riquewihr, Bott-Geyl (SUM)
Pinot Blanc Tradition, Kuentz-Bas (AV)
Riesling des Princes Abbés, Schlumberger
  (BEN)
Riesling Louis Gisselbrecht (TAN)
Tokay-Pinot Gris les Maquisards, Dopff &
  Irion (EL)
Tokay-Pinot Gris Tradition, Kuentz-Bas (AV)

1992
Gewürztraminer Hugel (OD, AD, WR, BOT)
Gewürztraminer les Sorcières, Dopff &
  Irion (EL)
Muscat Hugel (DI)
Riesling des Princes Abbés, Schlumberger
  (HOG)
Riesling les Murailles, Dopff & Irion (EL)
Riesling Trimbach (BER)
Tokay-Pinot Gris Barriques, Ostertag (SOM)
1991
Gewürztraminer les Sorcières, Dopff &
  Irion (HOG)
Gewürztraminer Trimbach (REI, HOG)
Pinot Blanc Zind-Humbrecht (REI)
Tokay-Pinot Gris les Maquisards, Dopff &
  Irion (HOG)
1990
Tokay-Pinot Gris Ostertag (CRO)
1989
Muscat les Amandiers, Dopff & Irion (HOG)
Muscat Réserve, Trimbach (GAU)
Muscat Schlumberger (NO)
Riesling Dopff & Irion (UB)
Riesling Hugel (DI)
1988
Gewürztraminer Trimbach (BUT)

£9.00 → £10.49

1995
Gewürztraminer Kientzheim, Blanck (LAYT)
1994
Muscat Schleret (YAP)
Pinot Blanc Zind-Humbrecht (BY)
Tokay-Pinot Gris Koehly (HAH)
Tokay-Pinot Gris Schlumberger (NI)
1993
Auxerrois Rolly Gassmann (RAE, GAU, BIB)
Gewürztraminer Hugel (PE, DAV, DI)
Gewürztraminer Tradition, Hugel (OD)
Muscat Schlumberger (PLA)
Muscat Trimbach (CRO)
Riesling Herrenweg, Zind-Humbrecht (BY)
Riesling Rolly Gassmann (RAE)
Riesling Turckheim, Zind-Humbrecht (BY)
Tokay-Pinot Gris Schlumberger (EY)
1992
Gewürztraminer Beyer (AME)
Gewürztraminer des Princes Abbés,
  Schlumberger (PLA, TAN)
Gewürztraminer Herrenweg, Zind-
  Humbrecht (BY)
Gewürztraminer Willy Gisselbrecht (ROB)
Muscat Réserve, Trimbach (VIG)
Muscat Zind-Humbrecht (BY)

Pinot Blanc Rolly Gassmann (TAN)
Riesling Réserve, Cave Co-op. Turckheim
   (POR)
Tokay-Pinot Gris Schlumberger (HIC, BEN)
1991
Gewürztraminer Rolly Gassmann (SEC, RAE)
Muscat Réserve, Trimbach (PLA)
Tokay-Pinot Gris Réserve, Trimbach (PLA)
Tokay-Pinot Gris Tradition, Kuentz-Bas
   (BER)
1990
Gewürztraminer des Princes Abbés,
   Schlumberger (BEN)
Riesling Dopff & Irion (CRO)
1989
Gewürztraminer Réserve, Trimbach (GAU)
Riesling Réserve Particulière, Faller (BUT)
Tokay-Pinot Gris Tradition, Hugel (DI)
1987
Muscat Moench Reben, Rolly Gassmann
   (RAE)
Tokay-Pinot Gris Réserve, Rolly
   Gassmann (CRO)
1985
Gewürztraminer Osterberg, Sipp (WHI)
Gewürztraminer Trimbach (BUT)
Tokay-Pinot Gris Réserve, Trimbach (CRO)

£10.50 → £12.99
1994
Gewürztraminer Bollenberg, Cattin (CB)
Gewürztraminer Herrenweg, Zind-
   Humbrecht (BY)
Muscat Goldert, Zind-Humbrecht (BY)
Riesling Clos Haüserer, Zind-Humbrecht
   (BY)
Riesling Herrenweg, Zind-Humbrecht (BY)
Tokay-Pinot Gris Barriques, Ostertag (MV)
Tokay-Pinot Gris Deiss (LEA)
Tokay-Pinot Gris Hatschbourg, Cattin (CB)
Tokay-Pinot Gris Schleret (YAP)

1993
Auxerrois Rolly Gassmann (UB)
Riesling Herrenweg, Zind-Humbrecht (WR)
Riesling Schoenenberg, Dopff au Moulin
   (HOG)
Riesling Schoenenberg, Wiederhirn (HIG)
1992
Gewürztraminer Hugel (UB, AV)
Riesling Zind-Humbrecht (LAY)
Tokay-Pinot Gris Rolly Gassmann (TAN)
Tokay-Pinot Gris Schlumberger (PLA)
Tokay-Pinot Gris Trimbach (ROB)
1991
Gewürztraminer Dopff au Moulin (POR)
Riesling Saering, Schlumberger (HOG, NI)
1990
Gewürztraminer Jubilee, Hugel (WS)
Riesling Tradition, Hugel (AD)
1989
Gewürztraminer Réserve Particulière,
   Faller (BUT)
Riesling Rolly Gassmann (TAN)
Riesling Schlossberg, Domaine Weinbach
   (BUT)
1988
Gewürztraminer Jubilee, Hugel (HOG)
Gewürztraminer Réserve, Trimbach (BUT,
   UN)
Muscat Zind-Humbrecht (CRO)
Riesling Réserve, Trimbach (TW)
1987
Riesling Brand, Zind-Humbrecht (BY)
1985
Riesling Réserve Personnelle, Hugel (REI)

£13.00 → £14.99
1993
Gewürztraminer Clos Windsbuhl, Zind-
   Humbrecht (BY)
Gewürztraminer Goldert, Zind-
   Humbrecht (BY)
Gewürztraminer Sonnenglanz Vieilles
   Vignes, Bott-Geyl (SUM), Zind-
   Humbrecht (CRO)
Muscat Moench Reben, Rolly Gassmann
   (BIB)
1992
Gewürztraminer Herrenweg, Zind-
   Humbrecht (CRO)
Riesling Muenchberg, Ostertag (ELL, ENO)
Riesling Trimbach (AV)
Tokay-Pinot Gris Millesime, Rolly
   Gassmann (UB)
1991
Muscat Goldert, Zind-Humbrecht (BY)

1990
Riesling Jubilee, Hugel (ws)
Riesling Tradition, Hugel (AV)
1989
Gewürztraminer Kessler, Schlumberger
(POR)
Riesling Frédéric Émile, Trimbach (HOG)
Riesling Kitterlé, Schlumberger (HOG)
1988
Gewürztraminer Seigneurs de
Ribeaupierre, Trimbach (HOG)
1986
Riesling Frédéric Émile, Trimbach (CRO,
TW)
1983
Gewürztraminer Réserve Personnelle,
Hugel (BUT, DI)
Riesling Réserve Personnelle, Hugel (DI,
BUT)
1981
Riesling Frédéric Émile, Trimbach (GAU)

£15.00 ➜ £19.99
1994
Riesling Brand, Zind-Humbrecht (BY)
Riesling Dopff & Irion (CRO)
1993
Riesling Ste-Cathérine, Domaine
Weinbach (OD)
1992
Gewürztraminer Rangen, Zind-
Humbrecht (BY)
Gewürztraminer Seigneurs de
Ribeaupierre, Trimbach (UN)
Gewürztraminer Tradition, Hugel (AV)
Riesling Clos Haüserer, Zind-Humbrecht
(CRO)
Riesling Frédéric Émile, Trimbach (UN)
1991
Gewürztraminer Clos Windsbuhl, Zind-
Humbrecht (BY, GAU)
Gewürztraminer Herrenweg, Zind-
Humbrecht (GAU)
Gewürztraminer Kessler, Schlumberger
(NI)
Gewürztraminer les Sorcières, Dopff &
Irion (UB)
1990
Muscat Goldert, Zind-Humbrecht (BY, GAU)
Riesling Frédéric Émile, Trimbach (LAY,
VIG)
Tokay-Pinot Gris Kitterlé, Schlumberger
(REI, VIG, BEN)
Tokay-Pinot Gris Réserve Personnelle,
Trimbach (WS)

1989
Gewürztraminer Fronholz Vendange
Tardive, Ostertag (MV)
Gewürztraminer Kessler, Schlumberger
(BEN, TAN, PLA)
Riesling Altenberg de Bergheim, Koehly
(BUT)
Riesling Frédéric Émile, Trimbach (REI, NO,
WR, THR, BOT, EY, GAU, CRO, PLA)
Tokay-Pinot Gris Kitterlé, Schlumberger
(LAY)
Tokay-Pinot Gris Réserve, Rolly
Gassmann (BIB)
1988
Gewürztraminer Jubilee, Hugel (WS, TAN)
Gewürztraminer Seigneurs de
Ribeaupierre, Trimbach (PLA)
Riesling Frédéric Émile, Trimbach (WS)
Riesling Jubilee, Hugel (TAN)
1987
Riesling Clos Ste-Hune, Trimbach (FA)
1986
Gewürztraminer Herrenweg Vendange
Tardive, Zind-Humbrecht (BY)
Riesling Kitterlé, Schlumberger (BEN)
1985
Gewürztraminer Seigneurs de
Ribeaupierre, Trimbach (WS, GAU)
Riesling Jubilee, Hugel (DI)
Riesling Kitterlé, Schlumberger (CRO)
Riesling Vendange Tardive, Faller (REI)
Tokay-Pinot Gris Réserve, Rolly
Gassmann (CRO)
1983
Gewürztraminer Seigneurs de
Ribeaupierre, Trimbach (REI)
Gewürztraminer Vendange Tardive,
Wiederhirn (HIG)
Riesling Réserve Personnelle, Hugel (TW)

£20.00 ➜ £24.99
1992
Tokay-Pinot Gris Clos St-Urbain, Zind-
Humbrecht (CRO)
1990
Gewürztraminer Herrenweg, Zind-
Humbrecht (CRO)
1989
Gewürztraminer Kitterlé, Schlumberger
(HOG, BEN)
Riesling Herrenweg, Zind-Humbrecht (CRO)
Tokay-Pinot Gris Kitterlé, Schlumberger
(VIG)
1986
Riesling Clos Ste-Hune, Trimbach (FA)

1985
Gewürztraminer Schlumberger (BO)
Gewürztraminer Vendange Tardive,
    Dopff & Irion (EL)
Gewürztraminer Vendange Tardive,
    Hugel (DI)
Pinot Blanc Tradition, Kuentz-Bas (BO)
Riesling Frédéric Émile, Trimbach (CRO)
1983
Gewürztraminer Vendange Tardive,
    Ostertag (YOU)
Riesling Frédéric Émile, Trimbach (TW, CRO)
Riesling Vendange Tardive, Dopff & Irion
    (EL, HOG)
Tokay-Pinot Gris Vendange Tardive,
    Dopff & Irion (HOG)
1982
Riesling Clos Ste-Hune, Trimbach (CRO)
1981
Riesling Schoenenberg Vendange Tardive,
    Dopff au Moulin (CRO)
1976
Muscat les Amandiers, Dopff & Irion (CRO)
1969
Muscat Trimbach (FA)

£25.00 → £29.99
1989
Gewürztraminer Herrenweg Vendange
    Tardive, Zind-Humbrecht (FA)
1986
Gewürztraminer Herrenweg Vendange
    Tardive, Zind-Humbrecht (BU)
1985
Riesling Frédéric Émile, Trimbach (TW)
1983
Gewürztraminer Cuvée Christine,
    Schlumberger (BUT)
Gewürztraminer Vendange Tardive,
    Dopff & Irion (HOG)
Gewürztraminer Vendange Tardive,
    Hugel (REI)
Gewürztraminer Vendange Tardive
    Sélection Personnelle, Hugel (DAV)
Riesling Réserve Personnelle, Hugel (CRO)
1976
Riesling Vendange Tardive, Hugel (BU)
1971
Gewürztraminer Réserve Exceptionelle,
    Hugel (REI)

£30.00 → £39.99
1990
Gewürztraminer Cuvée Christine,
    Schlumberger (HOG, TAN)

1989
Gewürztraminer Herrenweg Vendange
    Tardive, Zind-Humbrecht (BU)
Gewürztraminer Herrenweg, Zind-
    Humbrecht (BUT)
Gewürztraminer Vendange Tardive,
    Hugel (DI)
1988
Riesling Clos Ste-Hune, Trimbach (BER)
Tokay-Pinot Gris Sélection de Grains
    Nobles, Dopff au Moulin(BU)
Tokay-Pinot Gris Vendange Tardive,
    Hugel (WS)
1986
Riesling Clos Ste-Hune, Trimbach (AD, PLA)
1985
Gewürztraminer Cuvée Anne Vendange
    Tardive, Rolly Gassmann (RAE)
Gewürztraminer Vendange Tardive,
    Domaine Weinbach (BUT)
Gewürztraminer Vendange Tardive,
    Hugel (AV)
Riesling Clos Ste-Hune, Trimbach (CRO)
1983
Gewürztraminer Seigneurs de
    Ribeaupierre, Trimbach (CRO)
Gewürztraminer Sélection de Grains
    Nobles, Dopff & Irion (HOG)
Gewürztraminer Vendange Tardive,
    Hugel (BUT)
Gewürztraminer Vendange Tardive,
    Trimbach (BUT)
Riesling Clos Ste-Hune, Trimbach (BUT)
Riesling Schoenenberg Vendange Tardive,
    Dopff au Moulin (CRO)
Riesling Sélection de Grains Nobles,
    Dopff & Irion (EL, HOG)
Riesling Vendange Tardive, Hugel (BEN)
Riesling Vendange Tardive, Wiederhirn
    (CRO)
Tokay-Pinot Gris Vendange Tardive,
    Hugel (BEN)
1976
Riesling Vendange Tardive, Dopff & Irion
    (CRO)
1969
Muscat Réserve, Trimbach (VIG)

£40.00 → £49.99
1989
Gewürztraminer Cuvée Anne,
    Schlumberger (TAN, YOU, NO)
1986
Gewürztraminer Sélection de Grains
    Nobles, Hugel (EY)

1985
Gewürztraminer Cuvée Anne Vendange
   Tardive, Rolly Gassmann (UB)
Gewürztraminer Cuvée Christine,
   Schlumberger (CRO)
1983
Riesling Clos Ste-Hune, Trimbach (GAU)
Riesling Frédéric Émile Vendange Tardive,
   Trimbach (TW)
Tokay-Pinot Gris Sélection de Grains
   Nobles, Beyer (REI)
Tokay-Pinot Gris Vendange Tardive,
   Faller (CRO)
1976
Gewürztraminer Seigneurs de
   Ribeaupierre, Trimbach (CRO)
Riesling Frédéric Émile, Trimbach (CRO)
Riesling Réserve Personnelle, Hugel (CRO)
Riesling Vendange Tardive, Hugel (REI)
Tokay-Pinot Gris Vendange Tardive,
   Hugel (VIG)
1971
Gewürztraminer Eichberg Vendange
   Tardive, Dopff au Moulin (REI)
Tokay-Pinot Gris Réserve, Trimbach (VIG)
1966
Riesling Réserve, Trimbach (VIG)

£50.00 → £59.99
1989
Gewürztraminer Cuvée Anne,
   Schlumberger (BEN)
1986
Gewürztraminer Sélection de Grains
   Nobles, Hugel (DI)
1983
Gewürztraminer Sélection de Grains
   Nobles, Hugel (REI)
Riesling Clos Ste-Hune, Trimbach (CRO)
1976
Riesling Vendange Tardive, Hugel (TW)
Riesling Vendange Tardive Sélection de
   Grains Nobles, Hugel (NO)
Tokay-Pinot Gris Vendange Tardive,
   Hugel (TW)

£60.00 → £74.99
1988
Gewürztraminer Sélection de Grains
   Nobles, Hugel (VIN)
Tokay-Pinot Gris Sélection de Grains
   Nobles, Dopff au Moulin (BER)
1983
Gewürztraminer Sélection de Grains
   Nobles, Hugel (BEN)

1976
Gewürztraminer Cuvée Anne,
   Schlumberger (CRO)
Gewürztraminer Sélection de Grains
   Nobles, Hugel (CRO)
Riesling Clos Ste-Hune, Trimbach (CRO,
   TW)
Riesling Sélection de Grains Nobles,
   Hugel (REI)
Riesling Vendange Tardive, Hugel (CRO)

£90.00 → £94.99
1976
Gewürztraminer Cuvée Christine,
   Schlumberger (CRO)
Tokay-Pinot Gris Sélection de Grains
   Nobles, Hugel (CRO)

RED

Under £10.00
1993
Pinot Noir Hugel (WS)
1991
Pinot Noir Rolly Gassmann (BIB)
1989
Pinot Noir Hugel (BUT)

£10.00 → £17.99
1995
Pinot Noir Schleret (YAP)
1992
Pinot Noir Herrenweg, Zind-Humbrecht
   (BY)
Pinot Noir Rolly Gassmann (UB)
1985
Pinot Noir Réserve Personnelle, Hugel
   (REI, TW)

c. £25.00
1971
Pinot Noir Beyer (CRO)

SPARKLING

Under £9.00
Non-vintage
Crémant d'Alsace Cuvée Julien, Dopff au
   Moulin (HOG)
Crémant d'Alsace Dopff & Irion (EL)

£9.00 → £11.99
Non-vintage
Crémant d'Alsace Cuvée Julien, Dopff au
   Moulin (BEN, ROB)

SOUTHERN FRANCE

The biggest improvement has been in Languedoc-Roussillon, with Chardonnay and Cabernet making the running. Viognier is increasingly fashionable – but Petit Manseng could be a rival

The trade association that represents the vins de pays producers of France launched a new promotional campaign this year under the slogan, 'There's a new world of French wines to choose from.' Geddit? New World? If anybody doubted that the French wine industry had abandoned its traditional aloofness towards competition from elsewhere, here is the evidence.

Although that campaign took in country wines from all over France, it is undoubtedly in the South, particularly the Midi, that most of the innovation has been taking place. Here is where the flying winemakers have had the most dramatic impact, so that small vineyard owners who may have been churning out undemanding mediocrity for years are suddenly finding themselves doing things the Barossa way. So far Chardonnay and Cabernet – those failsafe cash crops – have made most of the running.

D'Oc lands development
Gradually, though, that picture is changing. Varietal wines bottled under the Vin de Pays d'Oc designation are increasingly reaching out to embrace other, less familiar varieties. Grenache, when it isn't smothered in oak and pumped up to headbanging alcohol levels, is beginning to demonstrate fine potential, while Viognier has been the great white hope of the South lately, turning out some deliciously apricot-scented numbers without the galumphing weight (or the galumphing price) of Condrieu.

The Languedoc and Roussillon reds are shaking off their image as cheap and cheerful Rhône substitutes, with Minervois, St-Chinian and Costières de Nîmes outshining most basic Côtes du Rhône. White wines will never make the same kind of splash because most of the varieties used are fairly neutral. (So is most négociant Chablis, of course, but that tends to cost at least £3 more.) There are exceptions, such as grapefruity Picpoul de Pinet, which enjoys its own subdivision of the Coteaux de Languedoc AC, and those still wines of Limoux that use the tartly appley Mauzac.

Provence has some extraordinary whites, unexpectedly delicate in structure but highly aromatic. Foremost are Cassis and white Bandol, but they are still too seldom encountered outside their native region. Much is made of the assertive flavours of Mourvèdre in Provence's reds, and plantings have grown at the expense of the less distinguished Carignan. Cabernet, too, is spreading, but is being used to flesh out the lighter reds rather than being made a virtue in itself. Veterans of the Mediterranean beaches will know that some of France's most fresh and fruit-filled rosés are made in Côtes de Provence, particularly from Cinsaut, with the local Tibouren grape often adding power without brutality.

The best wines of the South-West are already familiar. Cahors, Gaillac and Côtes du Frontonnais lead the red challenge to Bordeaux, while the dry and sweet whites of Jurançon show that the Petit Manseng grape is as worthy as the trendier Viognier.

Corsica continues on its mission of modernisation at its own unspectacular pace. Most of the wine is still made by co-operatives, but EU funds have seen temperature-controlled fermentation breaking out all over. The northern tip of the island, the Cap Corse, now has an AC for its vin doux naturel Muscats.

And yes – as elsewhere, 1995 was a great vintage across the South; better even than the fine 1994, and there's more of it to go round. **STUART WALTON**

WINES AND WINE REGIONS

BANDOL, AC (Provence; red, white) The magnificent, pine-protected, terraced vineyards of Bandol reign over the sea beneath. The reds can be world class. Here Mourvèdre is king, but is assisted by the classic southern grapes: Grenache, Cinsaut and Syrah make herby, tobaccoey, classically long-lived wines. The serious spicy rosés can also be excellent. Best estates: *Ch. Pradeaux, Ste-Anne, Dom. Bastide Blanche, Dom. du Cageloup, Dom. le Galantin, Dom. de Pibarnon, Dom. Ray-Jane, Dom. Tempier, Dom. Terrebrune.* The whites are made from the southern Rhône grapes, together with an enlivening dash of Sauvignon, and can be delicious, with a lovely aniseed-and-apple bite to them. *Dom. de Pibarnon* and *Dom. Lafran Veyrolles* are among the most interesting: both of these vineyards have a soil constituent, blue marl, which is very rare around here and seems to give an extra dash of elegance to their wines.

BANYULS, AC (Languedoc-Roussillon; Vin doux naturel, red) This Grenache-based (50 per cent minimum) wine comes from old, low-yielding vines on terraces above the sea. It can be red or tawny, sweet or dryish, and can come, too, in a maderized *rancio* style with burnt caramel flavours. *Dom. de la Rectorie, Mas Blanc* and *Mas Casa Blanca* are good. Wines aged for two and a half years in wood may be labelled *grand cru*.

LES BAUX-DE-PROVENCE, AC

(Provence, red, rosé) A mountainous enclave at the western end of the larger Coteaux d'Aix-en-Provence AC, Les Baux was awarded its own appellation for red and rosé wines in 1994. More intense and complex than their big brothers, these wines are often produced in vineyards blasted from the rock. There are splendid rosés and several startlingly good reds, like the organic *Domaine de Trévallon*, a complex Cabernet-Syrah blend which makes most analogous Aussie wines look positively simple. Other organic wines are made at *Mas de la Dame* and *Mas de Gourgonnier. Mas Ste-Berthe* also produces a good red.

BÉARN, AC (South-West; red, rosé) Wines from the far South-West. The reds are predominantly from the Tannat grape, but with other local varieties and both Cabernets thrown in. In spite of this they are basically undistinguished but you could try the wines of the *Vignerons de Bellocq* co-op, or the co-op at *Crouseilles.*

BELLET, AC (Provence; red, white) An unusual nutty Rolle and Chardonnay white with a good local reputation. *Ch. de Crémat* and *Ch. de Bellet* are worth seeking out, though like everything else near Nice, they're expensive. There are also a few good, dark reds made in *Ch. de Bellet* and *Ch. de Crémat.*

BERGERAC, AC (South-West; red, rosé) An eastward extension of the St-Émilion vineyards, Bergerac is a kind of Bordeaux understudy, but with more mixed results. The rosés are often extremely good, deep in colour, dry and full of fruit, but the reds are more exciting, with the fruit and bite of a good, simple Bordeaux without the rough edges. Like St-Émilion, it relies on the Merlot grape, with help from both Cabernets and Malbec, but the Bergerac reds are less substantial than St-Émilions. Sadly, most British merchants cut the prices too much for the potential of the area to be seen, so that what we get here is frequently tough, meaty, medicinal and charmless. Bergerac Rouge is usually at its best at between one and four years old, depending on vintage and style. *Château la Jaubertie* is very good and has also produced a wood-aged *Reserve. Château le Barradis* and *Château Belingard* are also good, and *Château Court-les-Mûts* makes a delicious rosé and a good red. Many wines over here come from the central co-op, and quality depends on paying a few extra centimes for a better vat.

BERGERAC SEC, AC (South-West; white) A Bordeaux lookalike from east of Bordeaux, planted largely with Sémillon and Sauvignon. *Château Belingard, Château Court-les-Mûts* and *Château de Panisseau* are good but the star is *Château la Jaubertie* where tremendous flavour and panache are extracted from a Sauvignon, Sémillon and Muscadelle blend; this last grape is now also being made into a 100 per cent varietal.

BUZET, AC (South-West; white) Used to be labelled Côtes de Buzet. The most exciting of the claret lookalikes from a region that was historically considered part of Bordeaux. Made from Bordeaux grapes with Cabernet predominant, they can combine a rich blackcurrant sweetness with an arresting grassy greenness. They are for drinking at between one and five years old, depending on vintage and style. Look out for the wines of the co-op, which dominates the area: its *Château de Gueyze, Château Padère* and *Baron d'Ardeuil* are all pretty special. It also has a real rarity – its own cooper. Almost all the wine spends at least a couple of months in wood, and this contributes massively to Buzet's serious-but-soft appeal.

CABARDÈS, VDQS (Languedoc-Roussillon; red) The aromatic originality and liveliness of these wines, from a region just north of Carcassonne, derive from the influence of two different climates, one from the Atlantic and one from the Mediterranean, and from the marriage of southern and south-western grape varieties, such as Merlot, Cabernet, Fer Servadou and Cot (Malbec). Bordeaux varieties are planted in the heavier, deeper clay soil, whereas the Mediterranean varieties are grown in chalky soil. Best producers include *Château de la Bastide, Château de Rayssac, Domaine Jouclary, de Brau, Ventenac.*

The price guides for this section begin on page 215.

CAHORS, AC (South-West; red) Of all the south-western country wines, Cahors is the most exciting. It's grown on both banks of the River Lot in the region of Quercy, practically due east of Bordeaux (though hotter, because it's well away from the influence of the sea). It's at least 70 per cent Auxerrois (Bordeaux's Malbec), the rest being made up of varying proportions of Merlot and Tannat.

Two hundred years ago, it was one of France's most famous wines, and the 'Black Wine of Cahors' is still held up as an example of how it used to be done. The wine was made black by the simple trick of giving the grapes a quick crushing and then, literally, boiling the must. Just as boiling gets the stain out of a shirt, so it gets the tannin and colour out of a grape skin. Fruit? Er, no, but strength (it was sometimes even fortified) and stability and massive aging potential – yes. Though without fruit, it's difficult to know what age was expected to do.

Adopting modern wine-making methods has added some lovely sweet fruit to the still dark, but now less aggressively tannic wines. There's a clear whiff of fine wine about some of the big, firm products of private growers. With age, they are often almost honeyed and raisiny, with plummy fruit that gets deeper, spicier and darker, often resembling tobacco and prunes. But another sort of Cahors has sprung up, too, lighter and easier, for drinking young. It can sometimes be very good. The raw materials for these are quite different: the best, traditional land of Cahors is up in the hills, but most grapes are now grown in easier vineyards on the valley slopes. One third of the wine comes from the co-op, *Côtes d'Olt,* which, after a pusillanimous, fruitless start, is beginning to produce wine with real style. Its *Château des Bouysses* is the sort of thing, and it's responsible for ten other châteaux. Its basic wine is on the light side. Good names: *Château de Cayrou, Château de Chambert, Château de Haute-Serre, Clos de Gamot, Château St-Didier, Château de Treilles, Domaine du Cèdre, Clos la Coutale, Clos Triguedina, Domaine Eugénie, Domaine de Gaudou, Domaine de Paillas, Château de Poujol* and *Domaine de Quattre.*

CASSIS, AC (Provence; red, white, rosé)
Some flavoursome reds and rosés can be
unearthed here, notably *Dom. du Bagnol* and
Dom. de la Ferme Blanche. The white is fine but
expensive. The addition of Sauvignon Blanc to
the classic southern varieties gives a welcome
zingy lift to the wines. Look out for *Domaine
du Paternel* and *Clos Ste-Magdelaine*.

CLAIRETTE DU LANGUEDOC, AC
(Languedoc-Roussillon; white) The Clairette
can be a difficult grape to vinify, but the quality
of wines like *Dom. de la Condamine Bertrand,*
the co-op at *Cabrières* and *Domaine St-André*
show just what can be done.

COLLIOURE, AC (Languedoc-Roussillon;
red) Startling, intense reds from very low
yields, dominated by Grenache, with increasing
contributions from Mourvèdre. This ancient
vineyard, tucked in between the Pyrenees and
the Med, boasts several fine estates, such as
*Dom. de la Rectorie, Dom. du Mas Blanc, Clos
des Paulilles* and *Mas Casa Blanca*.

CORBIÈRES, AC (Languedoc-Roussillon;
red, white, rosé) This region stretches from
the beaches near Narbonne to the dramatic
peaks of the Hautes-Corbières. Its red wines
can be dramatic too, ranging from juicy
upfront carbonic maceration wines to
powerful, serious, traditionally made bottles
like those of the marvellous *la Voulte-
Gasparets*. Others: *Château Cabriac, Étang des
Colombes, Château Hélène, Château les Ollieux,
les Palais, Caraguilhes, Fontsainte, Villemajou,
St-Auriol, Dom. du Révérend*. There is less white,
but it's increasingly good.

**COTEAUX D'AIX-EN-PROVENCE,
AC** (Provence; red, white, rosé) An increasing
use of Cabernet and Syrah, more rigorous
selection and subtle use of new oak are
combining to make several interesting
individual reds and rosés in a semi-Bordelais
style – such as *Château Vignelaure*. Also good:
Château Crémade, Château de Calissanne and
Château du Seuil. There is little white, and
frankly it's not that thrilling.

COTEAUX DU LANGUEDOC, AC
(Languedoc-Roussillon; red, white) This
sprawling appellation, running from Narbonne
to Nîmes, incorporates 12 demarcated *terroirs*
that may state their names on the labels to
distinguish themselves from wines of the basic
AC. Among the better ones for reds are St-
Saturnin, Pic St-Loup and La Clape.

Since 1985 it has all been happening here.
The classic southern grapes are used, and the
growing presence of Syrah and Mourvèdre can
be discerned in the complexity and breed of
many recent wines. Some of the myriad
outstanding producers: *Château Moujan,
Calage, Capion, Flaugergues, Pech-Céleyran,
Pech-Redon, Lascaux, Domaine de la Coste,
de la Roque, d'Aupilhac, Domaine de Payre-Rose,
Domaine de Cazeneuve, Domaine de Brunet,
Domaine de la Roque, de Terre-Mégère* and
Domaine de l'Hortus, where the rosé is
particularly notable. The co-ops at *Cabrières,
Montpeyrous, Neffiès, St-Saturnin* and *Gabian*
(*la Carignano*) are setting very high standards.
But perhaps the greatest genius of all in the
appellation is the young, gangling Olivier Jullien,
who's always trying something new, and
always succeeding, whether it's red, white,
rosé, or a Sauternes-style *moelleux*. White
wine-making is being also taken more and
more seriously, and among the best are those
from La Clape, based on Bourboulenc
(*Chamayrac* and *Boscary* are the stars).
Another rediscovery is the Picpoul de Pinet
grape which has been grown around the Étang
de Thau since the Middle Ages. It is dry,
medium-bodied with tingling grapefruit
flavours and a touch of pepper on the finish.
Delicious with seafood, it would knock many a
good Muscadet off its perch. Best producers:
Claude Gaujal, Mas Jullien, Terre Mégère and the
co-ops at *Pine, Pomérols* and *St-Saturnin* (for its
Chenin-based *le Lucian*).

COTEAUX VAROIS, AC (Provence; red,
rosé) This large region, promoted from VDQS
in 1995, can produce some very good, cheap
reds and rosés, such as *Château St-Jean de
Villecroze, Château St-Estève, Dom. de Triennes*
and *Dom. du Loou*.

CÔTES DE BERGERAC, AC (South-West; red, rosé)

This is to Bergerac what Bordeaux Supérieur is to Bordeaux: from the same region, but with slightly higher minimum alcohol. It should be better, and often is. Many are still basic Bergerac, although the excellent *Château Court-les-Mûts* now uses the AC.

CÔTES DE DURAS, AC (South-West; red, white)

Light, grassy claret lookalikes. *Château de Pilar* and *le Seigneuret* from the co-op are quite good and cheap. Also fairly good Sauvignon-based white that can be as fresh as good Bordeaux Blanc, but just a little chubbier. *Château de Conti* is good, as is *le Seigneuret* from the co-op.

CÔTES DU FRONTONNAIS, AC (South-West; red, rosé)

This largely uses the local Négrette grape, plus both Cabernets, Malbec and Fer Servadou. At their best they are silky and plummy, sometimes with a touch of raspberry and liquorice, but always with the savoury tang of fresh black pepper. The distinctive Négrette grape is wonderfully tasty and there are now some 100 per cent Négrettes from *Bellevue-la-Forêt* and *Flotis*. Great value, but drink young, as the Négrette needs the Cabernets for staying power. There is some new oak too, but it deforms the flavour of Négrette, unless it is very sensitively used. Best are *Dom. de Baudare, Ch. Bellevue-la-Forêt, Ch. Flotis, Ch. Montauriol, Ch. la Palme*.

CÔTES DE LA MALEPÈRE, VDQS (Languedoc-Roussillon; red)

Lying west-south-west of Carcassonne, this is another fascinating *terroir*, with a huge variety of soil composition. Using grape varieties similar to those of Cabardès, it is also entitled to draw on Cabernet Franc, which thrives in this milieu, where the Atlantic influence is even more pronounced. The Malepère co-op produces *Ch. de Festes* which shone in *Webster's* southern French tasting a couple of years back. The *Cave du Razès*, harnessing passion to high tech, produces an array of splendid wines. *Dom. de Matibat* makes a really fine Bordeaux-style wine.

CÔTES DU MARMANDAIS, AC (South-West; red)

Simple, soft, fruity wines for drinking young, made from Cabernet Sauvignon, Cabernet Franc, Merlot, Fer and Abouriou. A few are designed for more serious aging, but it doesn't suit them.

CÔTES DE PROVENCE, AC (Provence; red, white, rosé)

A sprawling area which far too often spews out millions of trivial *petits rosés d'été* for the fried beach potatoes of the Provençal coast. There are, however, many growers who do take their calling seriously and proffer top-grade red and pink wines – such as the *Commanderie de Peyrassol, Domaines de la Bernarde, St-Baillon, Rimauresque, Richeaume, Jas d'Esclans, Aumerade, Château de Selle* (too expensive), *Mas de Cadenet* and the very distinguished *Domaine de Courtade*. The co-op of the *Presqu'île de St-Tropez* produces wines of surprisingly good quality. The brilliant whites of *Dom. Arnaude, Clos Bernarde, Ch. Ferry-Lacombe, de Rasque, Dom. Richeaume, Castel Roubine, St-André de la Figuière* and *Réal Martin* are in the lead here – the last made with 100 per cent Ugni Blanc. Who said Ugni was only ever a dull workhorse variety?

COTES DE ST-MONT, VDQS (South-West, red, white)

Just north of Madiran, the predominantly red wines of Côtes de St-Mont are increasingly being made in a fresh, blackcurranty, modern style – quite an achievement when the ferocious Tannat has to make up no less than 70 per cent of the blend. By far the best wines come from the *Plaimont* co-op.

FAUGÈRES, AC (Languedoc-Roussillon; red)

The grapes for these reds are Grenache, Mouvèdre, Syrah and (though declining in use) Carignan. The vines grow in schist soil and give wines of real depth, class and character in which cassis, black cherries and liquorice predominate. In mature Faugères wines, complex game and leather aromas can often emerge. *Alquier, Louison, Lubac, Ollier-Taillefer, Vidal* and the co-op at *Laurens* must be in anyone's top ten.

FITOU, AC (Languedoc-Roussillon; red) A highly variable, old-style red in which Carignan has traditionally been dominant, but Grenache and, increasingly, Syrah and Mourvèdre are being used to add interest. *Paul Colomer* and *Robert Daurat-Fort* are the leading lights, along with co-ops at *Villeneuve* and at *Tuchan*, where the *Caves de Mont Tauch* is producing some of the most serious Fitou of all.

GAILLAC, AC (South-West; red, white) North-east of Toulouse and south of Cahors, Gaillac makes more white wine than red, based on the bracing Mauzac grape. It can be *moelleux* (medium-sweet), *perlé* (very faintly bubbly) or dry; the dry is usually a little neutral, though a few have a quite big apple-and-liquorice fruit. The sparkling wines can be superb: peppery, honeyed, apricotty and appley all at the same time. From producers like *Boissel-Rhodes*, *Canto Perlic* (a newcomer), *Cros* or *Robert Plageoles*, they are very good value. Other still wine producers to look out for are *Château Larroze*, *Domaine du Bosc Long* and *Domaine de Labarthe*. The co-op at *Labastide de Lévis* is the main, and improving, force in the area, but still has a fair way to go.

There are two styles of red, Duras plus Fer Servadou and Syrah, or Duras plus Merlot and Cabernet. Mostly, this is co-op land, but the growers who care make remarkable red. *Domaine Jean Cros* is delicious. Others: *Lastours*, *Mas Pignou*, *Labarthe*, *Larroze*.

IROULÉGUY, AC (South-West; red) A small AC in the Basque country. The co-op dominates, and the wine is mostly quite rough, Tannat-based red, supplemented by both Cabernet Sauvignon and Cabernet Franc. Try *Domaine Brana* and *Domaine Ilarria*.

JURANÇON, AC (South-West; white) Sweet, medium or dry wine from the Pyrenean foothills. Based on the Petit Manseng, Gros Manseng and Courbu, the dry wines are light and can be ravishingly perfumed, while the sweet wines are honeyed, raisiny and peachy, yet with a lick of acidity. New oak is appearing in some cellars. Most wine is from the local co-op, but I'd plump for a grower's wine. The pace-setter is *Henri Ramonteu*, who is experimenting avidly with different blends, picking times, and the aging of both sweet and dry whites in oak. His latest innovation is a dry white Petit Manseng, the grape more commonly reserved for the sweet wines. Others are *Clos de la Vierge* (dry), *Cancaillaü* (sweet), sweet *Cru Lamouroux*, *Clos Uroulat* (sweet), *Dom. de Cauhapé*, *Dom. de Souch*, *Dom. Bru-Baché* (dry), *Clos Thou* (dry), *Dom. Larredya*, *Clos Lapeyre*, *Dom. Castera*.

LIMOUX, AC (South-West; white) Brilliant AC Chardonnays are finally seeping into the consciousness of the *cognoscenti* and causing Burgundians to reach for their worry-beads. The sophisticated *Caves du Sieur d'Arques* is at the bottom of this dastardly plot and and there is no limit to its audacity: Mauzac, Chenin, Cabernet – you name it, it can do it, and very well, too. It also makes a fine range of sparkling Blanquette de Limoux and Crémant de Limoux (the latter must contain 30 per cent Chardonnay and/or Chenin Blanc, while the former is mainly Mauzac). Other excellent Crémants are made by *Antech*, *Delmas*, *Robert*, *Philippe Collin* and *Sev Dervin*, a spy who came in from the cold of Champagne.

MADIRAN, AC (South-West; red) Grown near Armagnac, Madiran is often likened to claret, but only rarely approaches its finesse. Generally about half Tannat, along with the Cabernets and occasionally Fer, it spends 20 months minimum in wood. It can be astringent and too tannic, though a new generation of growers is mellowing its sturdy flavours. Some are even producing a pure Tannat with some success, while others soften it with Cabernets Sauvignon and Franc. New oak barriques are popping up, too. Good ones include *Ch. d'Arricau-Bordes*, *Ch. d'Aydie* (alias *Dom. Laplace*), *Ch. Montus*, *Ch. Boucassé*, *Ch. Peyros*, *Dom. du Crampilh*, *Dom. Meinjarre*, *Laffitte-Teston*, *Dom. Berthoumieu* and *Dom. Moureou*.

MAURY, AC (Languedoc-Roussillon; Vin doux naturel; red) Grenache again, without

WINES FROM AROUND THE WORLD

THAT DON'T COST THE EARTH

the finesse of Banyuls, but more explosive in its nutty, toffee, prunes-in-brandy intensity. It, too, can be *rancio*. Try *Mas Amiel* and the co-op at *Maury*.

MINERVOIS, AC (Languedoc-Roussillon; red, white, rosé) This AC is producing more and more interesting reds with good peppery berry fruit – such as those made by the co-op at *la Livinière*. *J-P Ormières*, with a magic formula of Grenache, Syrah, Mourvèdre, new oak and baroque music in the cellars makes subtle, distinguished, wine at *Château Fabas*. Other serious producers: *Château de Gourgazaud, Villerambert-Julien, la Combe Blanche, Château du Donjon, Domaine Maris, Ste-Eulalie, la Tour Boisée* and the co-ops at *Peyriac* and *Azillanet*. White Minervois is increasingly good and aromatic, and there are experiments with oak aging.

MONBAZILLAC, AC (South-West; white) This is one of the most famous names in the sweet wine world. The occasional true Monbazillac is fine, rich and honeyed, yet never as good as a top Sauternes – more like a good Loupiac or Ste-Croix-du-Mont. There are few quality-conscious single properties making the real thing, and with the banning of machine harvesting matters are improving. Ones worth seeking out include *Château les Hébras, Château du Treuil de Nailhac, Château Haut-Bernasse* and *Clos Fontindoule*. Grab any 1990s you can still find: coming from one of the hottest, most botrytized vintages for years, the best are a bargain.

MONTRAVEL, AC (South-West; white) Dry white from the Dordogne. Côtes de Montravel is *moelleux* from the same area; Haut-Montravel is a separate area and sweeter. All are mostly sold as Bergerac or Côtes de Bergerac.

MUSCAT (Vin doux naturel; white) These can range from the syrupy *Tradition* made by the *Frontignan* co-op to the elegant *Château de la Peyrade* (Frontignan), *Domaine de la Capelle* (Mireval), *Grés St-Paul* (Lunel), *Domaine de*

Barroubie and the co-op in *St-Jean-de-Minervois*. The co-op at Frontignan also makes an elegant, floral Muscat – with the help of Bordeaux white-wine whizz Denis Dubourdieu. All of these are made from the Muscat à Petits Grains which gives more finesse than the Muscat d'Alexandrie, used in Muscat de Rivesaltes (*Cazes* and *Brial* are the masters here).

PACHERENC DU VIC-BILH, AC (South-West; white) From the Madiran area near Armagnac, this is one of France's most esoteric whites, a blend of Gros and Petit Manseng and Arrufiac – a grape peculiar to the AC. At its best when dry and pear-skin-perfumed – and sometimes when rich and sweet. Best are: *Château d'Aydie, Château Boucassé* and *Domaine du Crampilh*.

PALETTE, AC (Provence; red, white, rosé) A tiny AC dominated by *Château Simone*. The rosé beats the others.

PÉCHARMANT, AC (South-West; red) The best red wine of Bergerac from the best slope of the region, east of Bordeaux, this must be aged for a minimum of a year before sale to distinguish it from Bergerac, which can be sold after only six months. It is deliciously blackcurranty when young. *Château de Tiregand* is very good indeed, but *Domaine du Haut-Pécharmant* is even better, resembling a top-line Médoc.

ROUSSILLON, AC (Languedoc-Roussillon; red, white, rosé) While many good, fruity, dusty reds are made here, there isn't quite the same sense of pioneering adventurousness as there is in the Languedoc. The Côtes du Roussillon-Villages AC accounts for most of the best reds in the northern part of the Côtes du Roussillon AC *Vignerons Catalans* uses carbonic maceration very skilfully: its *Mas Camo* and *Château Cap de Fouste* are excellent. Other serious winemakers here include the delightful, innovative *Cazes* brothers, plus *Château Corneilla* and *Domaine Sarda-Malet*.

ST-CHINIAN, AC (Languedoc-Roussillon; red, rosé) Improving wines from between Minervois and Faugères. Tthe soil can be either schist or clay-chalk, the latter giving wines with greater aging potential. Among the top must be *Dom. des Jougla, Dom. Madalle, Ch. Cazal-Vieil, Ch. Coujan, la Dournie* and *Ch. Milhau-Lacugue* (especially for its brilliant rosé). The co-ops at *Roquebrun, Roueire* and *Berlou* are outstanding.

VIN DE CORSE, AC (Corsica; red, white, rosé) Corsican growers use the southern French grapes plus the indigenous Nielluccio and Sciacarello. *Dom. de Torraccia* makes a tasty red redolent of spices and rosemary. Also good: *Clos Landry, Capitoro, d'Alzeto, Dom. Filippi* and *Dom. Peraldi*. There are interesting whites and rosés, too. Most wines of better than vin de table status take the all-island designation Vin de Pays de l'Île de Beauté.

VIN DE PAYS (red, white, rosé) This is where it's all happening. With no aging AC rules to tie them in knots, the most innovative winemakers love the vin de pays classification for the freedom it gives them. There's plenty of Cabernet Sauvignon being used here, but some of the most exciting flavours come from Syrah and the other good grapes of the South, like Grenache or Mourvèdre. There are some excellent varietals, particularly Syrah, Cabernet Sauvignon and Chardonnay, coming from the Vin de Pays d'Oc region. Look for *Fortant de France, la Grange des Quatre Sous, Dom. de Condamine-l'Evêque, de l'Aigle, Quatre Sous, Peyrat, Cousserges, Raissac, Dom. de la*

Colombette, du Bosc, and *Dom. de l'Arjolle,* not to mention the mouth-watering, inky black *Dom. de Limbardié,* and the Australian-inspired *Chais Baumière* and *Dom. Virginie.*

In the Gard, knee-deep in salt marshes and corralled by Camargue horses, *Listel* is living proof that a thriving empire can be built on sand. In the same region, *Dom. de Gournier* and *Mas Montel* are the ones to watch; and, in the Roussillon, *Chichet, Laporte* and *Vaquer.*

The ultimate accolade here must go, however, to the ebullient, combative Aimé Guiber in the Hérault, whose *Mas de Daumas Gassac* reds are explosively concentrated and who makes marvellous, Viognier-based white.

On the western side of France the Charente produces some good, grassy-fresh whites with fairly sharp acidity – which sometimes gets the better of the fruit. The region here is Vin de Pays Charentais. The equivalent from Armagnac country is Vin de Pays des Cotes de Gascogne. The Ugni Blanc is the major grape, in more abundant supply since the drop in Armagnac sales, and the Colombard adds a touch of class. They're trying out the Gros and Petit Manseng, Chardonnay and Sauvignon, too, and oak aging and *vendanges tardives*. The co-op of *Plaimont* supplies many of those on sale in Britain at reasonable prices but variable quality. However, the mood of change sweeping the south-western co-ops is evident here too. There are several labels available from the *Grassa* family estates – notably *Dom. de Plantérieu* and *de Tariquet,* which are very good, full, dry and acid. Also good are *Dom. St-Lannes, Dom. le Puts* and *San Guilhem.*

MERCHANTS SPECIALISING IN SOUTHERN FRANCE
see Merchant Directory (page 424) for details

Most good merchants have some. For particularly good lists try: Adnams (AD), Averys of Bristol (AV), Bibendum (BIB), Anthony Byrne (BY) always enterprising, Davisons (DAV), Direct Wine (DI), Eldridge Pope (EL), Ben Ellis (ELL), Enotria Winecellars (ENO), Forth Wines (FOR), Fullers (FUL), Gauntleys (GAU), Gelston

Castle (GE), J E Hogg (HOG), Lay & Wheeler (LAY), Majestic (MAJ), Oddbins (OD), The Nobody Inn (NO), James Nicholson (NI), Thos. Peatling (PE), Terry Platt (PLA), Raeburn Fine Wines (RAE), Reid Wines (REI), Sainsbury (SAI), Somerfield/Gateway (SO), Tanners (TAN), Thresher (THR), Ubiquitous Chip (UB), The Wine Society (WS)

LANGUEDOC/ROUSSILLON

RED

Under £3.50

1994

VdP de l'Aude Cabernet Sauvignon, Foncalieu (WAI)

VdP d'Oc Cépage Merlot, Domaine des Fontaines (WAI)

£3.50 → £3.99

Non-vintage

Fitou Mme Claude Parmentier (VIC, WR)

1993

Corbières Château les Ollieux (THR, WR)

Costières de Nîmes Château de Campuget (POR)

Fitou Caves du Mont Tauch (MAR)

★ Minervois Domaine des Murettes (MAJ)

VdP de l'Hérault, Domaine de Chapître (YOU)

VdP des Coteaux de Murviel, Domaine de Limbardie (SOM)

1992

Corbières Château St-Auriol (BOT)

1991

Fitou Resplandy (BO)

£4.00 → £4.99

Non-vintage

Côtes du Roussillon-Villages Vignerons Catalans (MAR)

1995

VdP d'Oc Domaine Virginie sur lie (MV)

1994

Corbières Château de Cabriac (FUL, DAV)

Corbières Château les Palais (DI)

Coteaux du Languedoc La Clape Château de Pech-Celeyran (AD)

Fitou Cave Pilote (EL)

VdP de l'Hérault, Domaine de Chapître (MV)

VdP des Coteaux de Murviel, Domaine de Limbardie (MV, DAV)

VdP des Côtes de Thongue Cépage Syrah, la Condamine l'Évêque (TAN, LEA)

1993

Corbières Château de Cabriac (EY, EL)

Corbières Château de Montrabech (AV)

Corbières Château la Baronne (SEC)

Corbières Château St-Auriol (WAI)

Corbières Chatellerie de Lastours (POR)

★ Costières de Nîmes Lamargue (EL)

Coteaux du Languedoc La Clape Château de Pech-Celeyran (EY, WS)

Côtes de la Malepère Château Malvies (KA)

St-Chinian Coujan (VIG)

VdP des Coteaux de Murviel, Domaine de Limbardie (AD, TAN, YOU)

1992

Fitou Caves du Mont Tauch (HOG)

Minervois Château de Gourgazaud (REI)

Minervois Domaine de Ste-Eulalie (WR, THR, BOT)

1991

Minervois Domaine la Tour Boisée (WAT)

VdP des Côtes de Thongue Domaine Comte de Margon (ARM)

VdP du Gard Domaine Mas de Montel (NEZ)

£5.00 → £6.99

1994

Coteaux du Languedoc Château Flaugergues (MAJ)

Coteaux du Languedoc La Clape Château de Pech-Celeyran (TAN)

Minervois Domaine de Ste-Eulalie (TAN)

1993

Collioure les Clos de Paulilles (OD)

Costières de Nîmes Château de la Tuilerie (AV)

Coteaux du Languedoc Domaine de l'Abbaye de Valmagne (EL, DI)

★ Fitou Château de Segure (UN)

VdP des Côtes de Thongue Cuvée de l'Arjolle, Teisserenc (CRO)

VdP d'Oc La Cuvée Mythique, DuBernet/Vign. de Val d'Orbieu (SAF)

1992

Faugères Château de Grézan (POR)

VdP du Mont Baudile, Domaine d'Aupilhac (AD)

1991

Corbières Château de Cabriac (NO)

Corbières Château de Lastours (WR)

VdP d'Oc La Cuvée Mythique, DuBernet/Vign. de Val d'Orbieu (NI)

1990

Corbières Château de Lastours (POR)

Minervois Domaine de la Combe Blanche (AME)

Minervois Domaine la Tour Boisée (WAT)

£7.00 → £9.99

1994
VdP du Mont Baudile, Domaine
   d'Aupilhac (LEA)
1993
Côtes du Roussillon-Villages Domaine
   Cazes (ENO)
1992
Collioure Domaine de la Rectorie (REI)
VdP de l'Hérault, Mas de Daumas Gassac
   (BOT, WR, THR, OD, POR)
1990
Faugères Cuvée Spéciale, Gilbert Alquier
   (SUM)

£10.00 → £14.99

1993
VdP de l'Hérault, Mas de Daumas Gassac
   (AD, VIG)
1991
Coteaux du Languedoc Prieuré de St-Jean
   de Bébian (GAU)
1988
VdP de l'Hérault, Mas de Daumas Gassac
   (BUT, GAU, SOM)

£15.00 → £24.99

1985
VdP de l'Hérault, Mas de Daumas Gassac
   (CRO)
1983
VdP de l'Hérault, Mas de Daumas Gassac
   (CRO, NO)

WHITE

Under £4.50

1995
VdP d'Oc Sauvignon, Domaine St Marc
   (SAI)
1994
Picpoul de Pinet Cave Bonlouis (THR, WR)
VdP de l'Aude Enclos de Lilas (SAI)
VdP d'Oc Cépage Chardonnay, Ryman
   (SAF)
VdP d'Oc Chardonnay, Cave de la
   Cessanne (SAI)
VdP d'Oc Chardonnay, Domaine
   d'Aubian (SAI)
VdP d'Oc Chardonnay, Fortant de France
   (VIC)
VdP d'Oc Chardonnay, Philippe de Baudin
   (alias Chais Baumière) (SAI)
VdP d'Oc Sauvignon Blanc, Philippe de
   Baudin (SAI, SAF)

£4.50 → £6.99

1995
VdP des Côtes de Thongue la Croix Belle
   (LEA)
1994
VdP d'Oc Viognier, Père Anselme (SAI)
VdP de l'Hérault Cépage Muscat Sec, du
   Bosc (WS)
1993
VdP d'Oc Chardonnay, Four Terroirs (SAI)

£14.00 → £17.99

1994
VdP de l'Hérault, Mas de Daumas Gassac (AD)
1993
VdP de l'Hérault, Mas de Daumas Gassac
   (BOT, WR)

1992
VdP de l'Hérault, Mas de Daumas Gassac
   (NI, NO, BEN, ARM)

ROSÉ

Under £7.00

1993
Costières de Nîmes Château de la
   Tuilerie (AV)

£7.00 → £9.99

1991
VdP de l'Hérault, Mas de Daumas Gassac
   (BUT)
1987
VdP de l'Hérault, Mas de Daumas Gassac
   (BUT)

SPARKLING

Under £7.00

Non-vintage
Blanquette de Limoux Brut, Cave de
   Blanquette de Limoux (FUL)

c. £9.00

1993
Blanquette de Limoux Brut, Cave de
   Blanquette de Limoux (LAYT)

PROVENCE

RED

Under £5.00
1994
VdP des Maures, Domaine d'Astros (BIB)
1993
Coteaux d'Aix-en-Provence Château de Fonscolombe (LAY)

£5.00 → £6.99
1993
Coteaux d'Aix-en-Provence Château Calissanne (BOD, SUN)
Coteaux d'Aix-en-Provence Domaine de la Vallonge (SOM)
1992
Côtes de Provence les Maîtres Vignerons de St-Tropez (NEZ)
1991
Côtes de Provence Domaine de Rimauresq (HOG)

£7.00 → £10.99
1994
Côtes du Lubéron Château de Canorgue (YAP)
1992
Bandol Domaine Tempier (WS)
1991
Bandol Mas de la Rouvière, Bunan (YAP, ROB)
Les Baux-de-Provence Mas de Gourgonnier (BEN)
1990
Coteaux d'Aix-en-Provence Domaine de la Vallonge (ROB)
Côtes du Lubéron Château Val Joanis (CRO)

£11.00 → £14.99
1993
Bandol Cuvée Migoua (VIG)
Bandol Cuvée Tourtine (VIG)

Côtes de Provence Domaine de Trevallon (YAP)
Les Baux-de-Provence Domaine de Trévallon (VIG)
1992
Bandol Cuvée Migoua (VIG)
Bandol Domaine Tempier (DI)
Coteaux d'Aix-en-Provence Domaine de Trévallon (DI)
Côtes de Provence Domaine de Trevallon (YAP)
1991
Bandol Cuvée Tourtine (VIG, DI)
Bandol Domaine Tempier (DI)
Coteaux d'Aix-en-Provence Domaine de Trévallon (DI)
Côtes de Provence Domaine de Trévallon (YAP)
1990
Bandol Château de la Rouvière, Bunan (YAP)
Bandol Cuvée Tourtine (WS)
1989
Bandol Domaine Tempier (DI)
1986
Bellet Château de Crémat, Jean Bagnis (CRO)

£15.00 → £16.99
1992
Côtes de Provence Domaine de Trevallon (GAU)
1990
Palette Château Simone (YAP)

c. £26.00
1991
Les Baux-de-Provence Domaine de Trévallon (UB)

WHITE

Under £7.00
1994
Coteaux d'Aix-en-Provence Château de Fonscolombe (LAY)
Côtes du Lubéron la Vieille Ferme (ROB)

£7.00 → £9.99
1994
Bandol Mas de la Rouvière, Bunan (YAP)
Cassis Clos Ste-Magdeleine, Sack (YAP)

£10.00 → £17.99

1993
Bandol Château de la Rouvière, Bunan (YAP)
Palette Château Simone (VIG)
1992
Palette Château Simone (YAP)

ROSÉ

Under £4.00

Non-vintage
VdP des Sables du Golfe du Lion Gris de Gris, Listel (FUL)

£5.00 → £9.99

1995
Bandol Mas de la Rouvière (YAP)
1993
Bandol Mas de la Rouvière (UB)
Côtes du Lubéron Château Val Joanis (CRO)

£14.00 → £15.99

1993
Palette Château Simone (YAP)
1992
Palette Château Simone (VIG)

VINS DOUX NATURELS

Under £10.00

Non-vintage
Muscat de Frontignan, Château de la Peyrade (ELL)
Muscat de St-Jean-de-Minervois, Cave de St-Jean-de-Minervois (REI)
Rasteau Domaine la Soumade (PIP)
1993
Banyuls Domaine de la Rectorie (UB)

£10.00 → £14.99

Non-vintage
Rasteau Domaine la Soumade (CRO)
1994
Maury Mas Amiel (LEA)
1993
Muscat de Rivesaltes Domaine Cazes (ROB)
1986
Maury Mas Amiel (VIG)
1982
Maury Mas Amiel (VIG)

c. £16.00

1980
Vieux Rivesaltes Domaine Cazes (ROB)

SOUTH-WEST FRANCE

RED

Under £3.50

1994
Côtes du Marmandais Cave de Cocumont
(SO)
1993
Côtes de St-Mont, Producteurs Plaimont
(SOM)

£3.50 → £3.99

1993
Côtes de St-Mont, les Hauts de Bergelle
(FUL)
Côtes du Frontonnais Château Baudare
(DI)
1992
Côtes de St-Mont, les Hauts de Bergelle
(SOM)

£4.00 → £4.99

1994
Côtes de St-Mont, Producteurs Plaimont
(AD, TAN)
Côtes du Frontonnais Château Bellevue-
la-Forêt (NI)
Gaillac Domaine de Labarthe (SOM)
★ VdP des Côtes de Gascogne Domaine
Loubadère (EL)
VdP d'Orange, Cuvée des Templiers
(LAYT)
1993
Cahors Château de Gaudou (SOM)
Côtes de St-Mont, les Hauts de Bergelle
(TAN)
1992
Gaillac Château Clement Termes (HOG)

£5.00 → £5.99

1994
Marcillac Domaine du Cros, Teulier
(AD)
1993
Cahors Château de Gaudou (ENO)
Cahors Clos la Coutale (WS)

> In each price band wines
> are listed in vintage order.
> Within each vintage they
> are listed in A–Z order.

1992
Pécharmant Château de Tiregand (SAI)
1990
Bergerac Château la Jaubertie (NI)
Cahors Château d'Eugénie (HIC)
Cahors Château St-Didier-Parnac, Rigal
(OD)

£6.00 → £7.99

1994
Madiran Domaine de Moureau (LEA)
1993
Cahors Château de Gaudou (EY)
Madiran Domaine de Moureau (TAN)
1992
Madiran Domaine Damiens (BIB)
Pécharmant Château de Tiregand (TAN)
1990
Cahors Domaine de la Pineraie (HOG)
Côtes de St-Mont, Château de Sabazan
(WS)
1989
Buzet Château de Gueyze (YOU)

Madiran Cave de Crouseilles (SAI)
1988
Cahors Domaine de Paillas (BIB)

£8.00 → £9.99

1993
Cahors Château Lagrezette (NEZ)
1992
Madiran Château Montus (REI)
1990
Cahors Château de Chambert (DI)
1988
Cahors Prince Probus, Clos Triguedina
(YOU)
1987
Côtes du Frontonnais Château Flotis (CRO)
1982
Madiran Château de Peyros (CRO)

£10.00 → £12.99

1991
Madiran Château Montus (YOU, VIG)
1990
Cahors Domaine de Paillas (UB)
1989
Madiran Château d'Aydie (VIG)
Madiran Château Montus (YOU)
1985
Pécharmant Château de Tiregand (CRO)

WHITE

Under £3.50

1995
VdP des Côtes de Gascogne Producteurs
Plaimont (MAR)
1994
VdP des Côtes de Gascogne Domaine le
Puts (MAJ)

£3.50 → £3.99

1995
VdP des Côtes de Gascogne Domaine de
Planterieu (WAI)
VdP des Côtes de Gascogne Domaine de
Tariquet (WR, BOT, THR)
1994
Côtes de Duras, Moulin des Groyes
(SAI)
Côtes de St-Mont, les Hauts de Bergelle
(FUL)
VdP des Côtes de Gascogne Domaine
Bordes (SAI)
VdP des Côtes de Gascogne Domaine San
de Guilhem (HOG)
VdP des Côtes de Gascogne Domaine de
Rieux (EY)
VdP du Comte Tolosan Colombard
Chardonnay, le Lizet (SAI)
1993
Côtes de St-Mont, les Hauts de Bergelle
(SOM)

£4.00 → £4.99

1995
Bergerac Château la Jaubertie (CO)
Côtes de St-Mont, Producteurs Plaimont
(LAY)
VdP des Côtes de Gascogne Domaine San
de Guilhem (MV)
VdP des Côtes de Gascogne Domaine de
Rieux (AD, TAN)
VdP des Côtes de Gascogne Producteurs
Plaimont (AD)

1994
Côtes de St-Mont, Producteurs Plaimont
(AD, TAN)
1993
Côtes de St-Mont, les Hauts de Bergelle
(TAN)
VdP des Côtes de Gascogne Domaine de
Rieux (PE)
1992
Pacherenc du Vic-Bilh Domaine du
Crampilh (WAT)

£5.00 → £5.99

1995
Bergerac Sec Château de Tiregand (TAN)
1994
Bergerac Domaine de Grandchamp (SAI)
1992
Bergerac Château le Fagé (BER)

£6.00 → £6.99

1995
VdP des Côtes de Gascogne Domaine des
Cassagnoles (BOD, SUN)
1994
Pacherenc du Vic-Bilh Domaine Boucassé
(REI)
Pacherenc du Vic-Bilh Domaine Damiens
(BIB)

£7.00 → £9.99

1994
Bergerac Château la Jaubertie (NO)
Jurançon Sec Domaine Cauhapé (MV, ELL,
TAN)
1993
Pacherenc du Vic-Bilh Domaine Boucassé
(YOU)

SWEET WHITE

Under £10.00

1994
Monbazillac Château Theulet (ROB)

c. £18.00

1990
Jurançon Moelleux, Domaine Cauhapé
(NO)

ROSÉ

c. £6.00

1995
Bergerac Château la Jaubertie (VIC)

JURA & SAVOIE

These are wines for the adventurous drinker, prepared to venture off the beaten track of familiar grape varieties

If you should happen to want a wine that comes from a region so far untouched by the influence of international wine styles, you have a surprisingly small choice. If you want it to be French as well your choice is even more limited. Flying winemakers have not so far turned their attention to the Jura, with its Mondeuse and Savagnin grapes, although there is a sprinkling of Chardonnay for anyone suffering withdrawal symptoms.

It's probably the distinctive flavours that hold them back over here. That and the fact that they're not cheap and are not made in vast quantities anyway. The generally oxidized style doesn't help, either, although after a few days in the region you may find that you are beginning to understand and even like the taste. It reaches its apogee in *vin jaune*, the sherry-style wine that is yet totally different from sherry, seldom as good, and at least three times the price. But nobody who likes to try new flavours should be put off.

In Savoie and the Bugey, too, the wines are hardly sold outside the region, although Varichon & Clerc's traditional method Seyssel Mousseux, made from Molette and Roussette grapes, is sold abroad under the name of Royal Seyssel.

Otherwise the principal appellation is simply Vin de Savoie, with its 16 *cru* villages, a handful of which are worth seeking out. There are Abymes and Apremont, for steely whites made from the Jacquère grape, and Chignin, which has the curiosity Chignin Bergeron – a tiny enclave of the Roussanne grape of the northern Rhône. Mondeuse, grown in Arbin and featuring in the *cru* of Chautagne, sometimes has some earthy, berry fruit and may benefit from some barrel aging; Chasselas, otherwise known as Fendant, grows in the vineyards closer to Lake Geneva and Switzerland. A simple Vin de Savoie, with a grape variety and no *cru*, can also be worth trying, as can an equally simple Vin du Bugey. Savoie is popular with tourists, who go there in the winter for the snow and in the summer for the mountain air, and who are happy to drink the local product in the cafés.

WINES & WINE REGIONS

ARBOIS, AC (red, white, rosé) The general appellation for wines of all types from the northern part of the Jura around the town of Arbois. Reds are mostly Trousseau and thuddingly full of flavour. Savagnin weaves its demonic spells on the whites, though Chardonnay is sometimes used to soften it. Interestingly there are some attractive light reds and rosés from Pinot Noir or Poulsard which seem positively out of place, they are so delicate. *Henri Maire* is the biggest producer, but the best wines come from the village of Pupillin, where the co-op produces delicious Chardonnay and a fizz.

BUGEY, VDQS (red, white) This little VDQS half-way between Savoie and Beaujolais, is a rising star in France for its deliciously crisp Chardonnays, although it also uses the other Savoyard grapes for whites and reds. It is one of the most refreshing, zippy Chardonnays in France, and has become a fad wine with some of the local Michelin-starred restaurants – which at least means the growers will keep producing it.

CÔTES DU JURA, AC (red, white, rosé) These are the wines, of all colours, from the centre and south of the Jura region. They are virtually indistinguishable in style and flavour (and grape varieties) from Arbois wines, though they are sometimes a little less disturbing in their weirdness.

CRÉPY, AC (white) The least interesting Savoie region, situated south of Lake Geneva, where the Chasselas grape produces an even flimsier version of the already delicate Swiss Fendant, if that's possible. Drink young and fast, or not at all.

L'ÉTOILE, AC (white) This is a small area in the south of the Jura region, producing whites from Savagnin and Chardonnay and, occasionally, from the red Poulsard, vinified without the colour-giving skins. Also Savagnin *vins jaunes*.

ROUSSETTE DE SAVOIE, AC (white) This wine can be the fullest and softest of the Savoie whites. It is usually a blend of as much as 50 per cent Chardonnay with Altesse (also known as Roussette, hence the name of the wine), unless it is produced in one of the four villages or *crus*, of which Frangy is the best known, in which case it is pure Altesse. Even at its most basic level, it's good, crisp, strong-tasting white.

SEYSSEL, AC and SEYSSEL MOUSSEUX, AC (white) The Roussette (blended with a little Molette) makes quite full, flower-scented but sharp-edged whites in this zone of the Haute-Savoie and the Ain. Sparkling Seyssel, with its Molette base, is also good, light but pepper-pungent and available in the UK from *Varichon et Clerc*.

VIN JAUNE (white) The kind of wine of which more than a small glass makes you grateful it is as rare as it is. It grows the same

yeasty *flor* as dry sherry, and its startlingly, painfully intense flavours just get more and more evident as it matures. In fact it seems virtually indestructible, as long as the cork remains healthy.

Château-Chalon AC – the 'Montrachet' of *vin jaune*. Well, that's what they think, anyway. This is the most prized – and most pricy – of the *vins jaunes*, and is difficult to find even in the region. *Vins jaunes* are sold in small 62cl *clavelin* bottles, which of course the EU at one point tried to ban. That threat left me in two minds. I felt that 75cl of *vin jaune* would be just too much for anyone to handle, and indeed 37.5cl might be more like it. But I was blowed if the EU was going to destroy yet another great vinous original in the stultifying name of conformity. The EU, however, backed down and the 62cl *clavelin* lives. Actually there is a reason for the 62cl size, in that 100 litres of wine, kept in barrels for six years without being topped up, slowly evaporates to 62 litres, or 100 bottles. So it can be ordered in nice round numbers.

VIN DE SAVOIE, AC (red, white) Vin de Savoie covers the whole Savoie area, but produces the most interesting results in the South. These alpine vineyards are some of the most beautiful in France and produce fresh, snappy wines. The white, from the Jacquère, Chardonnay or Chasselas, can be excellent, dry, biting, but with lots of tasty fruit. Avoid aging them for too long. The reds from Pinot Noir or Gamay are subtly delicious, while the Mondeuse produces some real beefy beauties when the vintage is hot enough. A *cru* name is often found tacked on to the best wines. Ones worth looking out for are the *crus* of Abymes, Apremont, Chignin, Cruet and Montmélian, with Chautagne and Arbin also quite important for reds.

MERCHANTS SPECIALISING IN JURA AND SAVOIE
see Merchant Directory (page 424) for details

Nobody exactly specialises in these areas, but the following have some: Anthony Byrne (BY), Enotria Winecellars (ENO),

Terry Platt (PLA), Seckford Wines (SEC), Summerlee Wines (SUM), Tanners (TAN), Wine Society (WS)

JURA & SAVOIE

JURA: RED

Under £5.00

Non-vintage
Bonchalaz Maire (ROB)

£7.00 → £7.99

1992
Côtes du Jura Rouge Bourdy (WS)
1988
Côtes du Jura Rouge Bourdy (AD)

JURA: WHITE

Under £10.50

Non-vintage
Vin de Paille La Vignière, Maire ½ bottle
  (CRO)
1992
Côtes du Jura Blanc Bourdy (WS)
1990
Côtes du Jura Cépage Savagnin, Boilley (ROB)

£19.00 → £29.99

1992
Vin Jaune de Gard, d'Arlay (REI)
1988
Vin Jaune Château-Chalon, Bourdy (WS)
1986

Vin Jaune Côtes du Jura Château d'Arlay,
  Laguiche (SUM)
1983
Vin Jaune d'Arbois, Tissot (PLA)
1982
Vin Jaune Château-Chalon, Maire (ROB)
1981
Vin Jaune d'Arbois, Tissot (CRO)

c. £41.00

1979
Vin Jaune Château-Chalon, Bourdy (WS)
1973
Vin Jaune Château-Chalon, Bourdy (UB)

JURA: ROSÉ

Under £4.00

Non-vintage
Vin Gris Cendré de Novembre Maire (HOG)

SAVOIE: WHITE

Under £5.50

1995
Vin de Savoie Abymes, Cave Co-op (EL)

c. £7.00

1995
Apremont les Rocailles, Pierre Boniface
  (TAN)

SAVOIE: SPARKLING

c. £6.50

Non-vintage
Seyssel Blanc de Blancs Mousseux
  Varichon & Clerc (EY, REI)

VINS DE PAYS

Improve or go under is the word here – and, accordingly, some of France's most innovative wines are vins de pays

Vin de pays can provide some of the best and some of the worst drinking in France. Contrast superstar Mas de Daumas Gassac with a Vin de Pays de l'Hérault from a regional co-op, made from whatever grapes its conservative-minded members have delivered, be it Carignan and Cinsaut or even Aramon and Alicante Bouschet.

The good news is that the Midi is full of experimentation, for good producers are untrammelled by appellation regulations. If they wish to plant Roussanne or Gamay, they may; if they wish to try Viognier or Pinot Noir, why not? The new heroes in particular are Sauvignon, Viognier, Roussanne and Marsanne for whites, while Syrah and Mourvèdre are increasingly making excellent reds, full of rich, spicy fruit.

So far Sauvignon Blanc seems the least successful of the whites – it's probably just a bit too hot – while the more traditional varieties like Terret Blanc and Grenache Blanc are benefiting from the improved control of fermentation temperatures – but then they tend not to taste of all that much anyway. Similarly the taste of Carignan has improved enormously with vinification by carbonic maceration.

Foreign investment is important in the Midi, and those who can't compete on quality terms will go under. This will not mean the end of wines with a taste of the region – indeed, there is increasing emphasis on wines with a genuinely regional taste.

Vins de pays come in three categories:

VINS DE PAYS RÉGIONAUX

There are four of these. Vin de Pays du Jardin de la France covers the whole Loire basin across almost to Chablis and down to the Charente. Vin de Pays du Comté Tolosan is for the South-West, starting just below Bordeaux, and covering Bergerac, Cahors, the Tarn and down to the Pyrenees, but not including the Aude and Pyrénées Orientales. Vin de Pays des Comtés Rhodaniens includes the northern Rhône and Savoie; Vin de Pays d'Oc covers Provence and the Midi right down to the Spanish border.

VINS DE PAYS DÉPARTEMENTAUX

These are also large groupings, and each one is defined by the boundaries of the *département*. So, for instance, any wine of vin de pays quality grown in the *département* of Vaucluse will qualify for the title 'Vin de Pays du Vaucluse'.

VINS DE PAYS DE ZONE

These are the tightest-controlled of the categories, and can apply to actual communes or carefully defined localities. The allowed yield is lower and there may be more control on grape varieties. So, for example, we could have a Vin de Pays de la Vallée du Paradis which is in the Aude, and could also be sold as Vin de Pays de l'Aude, or as Vin de Pays d'Oc.

MERCHANTS SPECIALISING IN VINS DE PAYS
see Merchant Directory (page 424) for details

Most merchants have some, but for particularly good ranges try: Adnams (AD), Avery's of Bristol (AV), Bibendum (BIB), Anthony Byrne (BY), Davisons (DAV), Eldridge Pope (EL), Enotria Winecellars (ENO), Forth Wines (FOR), Lay & Wheeler (LAY), Majestic (MAJ), James Nicholson (NI), Oddbins (OD), Thos. Peatling (PE), Thresher (THR), The Ubiquitous Chip (UB), Wine Society (WS)

GERMANY

The new stars of German wine are in the Mosel and the Pfalz, although not in the Rheingau. But just try finding their most exciting wines in your local British wine merchant

During the last few years the German wine industry has been turned upside down. Germany's top dozen producers are currently making some of the world's greatest white wines, although the names of contemporary stars such as Dönnhoff, Gunderloch, Reinhold Haart, Franz Künstler, Dr Loosen and Müller-Catoir were virtually unknown ten years ago. Yet the German wines on supermarket shelves and in off-licences across Britain are nearly all mass-produced plonk selling for £3.50 or less per bottle. Thanks to modern wine-making technology these are generally clean and palatable, but they bear only the faintest resemblance to the nation's noble Rieslings. Unfortunately, the same can be said of the wines from many of the large estates which formed Germany's wine élite a decade and more ago. Today the number of them who continue to play in the nation's first division of wine producers can be counted on one hand. Five years ago Erwin Count Matuschka of Schloss Vollrads presented himself as the prophet of Germany's dry wine revolution. Today the only reason people talk about him is his court battle with Germany's wine writers.

Cheap – if you can find it

The radical transformation in Germany has both pluses and minuses for British wine drinkers. The up side is that when you find good German wines the prices are modest. From which other countries can you find world-class white wines for £8 to £12 per bottle? Even in the intensely competitive £5 to £7 range Germany offers a wealth of excellent quality. The down side of the often lukewarm interest in good German wines here is that most British wine merchants and supermarkets feel disinclined to give Germany much list or shelf space. The worst consequence of this is that the marvellous Weissburgunder and Grauburgunder (Pinot Blanc and Pinot Gris respectively) dry whites, and the magificent Pinot Noirs that have been made since 1990 by a group of red wine pioneers do not make it to Britain at all. The top estates of Baden, the region producing the majority of these wines, are therefore almost invisible in Britain.

Thankfully, with Riesling things look much better. We have not missed out on the abundant fruits of the tremendous quality renaissance in the Mosel-Saar-Ruwer during the last decade. The richly aromatic, elegant wines made from the precipitously steep vineyards of its beautiful river valleys by its top producers are unique. Nowhere in Germany are there more old vineyards, nowhere is the harvesting later and more selective, and nowhere are the wines more hand-crafted than here. The strong personalities of its leading winemakers are reflected in wines as individual as any in the world. During the last years Rheinhold Haart, von Hövel, Karthäuserhof, von Kesselstatt, Dr Loosen, Willi Schaefer, Selbach-Oster, Dr Wagner and Zilliken have matched the achievements of the established élite of Fritz Haag, Egon Müller, J J Prüm and von Schubert (Maximin Grünhaus) and earned the region pole position in Germany.

Taste the wines of the last five harvests from these estates and you would think that Germany has been blessed with a string of excellent vintages. However, each of these years presented winemakers with a considerable challenge, and those winemakers who worked most uncompromisingly for quality, made wines far superior to the norm. The situation is comparable to that in Burgundy, where a handful of top domaines turn out sensational wines almost every year, while the general quality shoots up and down.

Mines in the Rhine

Nowhere are the contrasts between greatness and ghastliness more pronounced than in the Rheingau. Until the late 1970s it was the nation's flagship wine region, but now it is a minefield. A handful of brilliant small estates such as Johannishof, Franz Künstler and Josef Leitz are overshadowed by underperforming dinosaurs such as Schloss Groenesteyn and the Staatsweingüter Kloster Eberbach. Thankfully, it has two large-scale producers, in the form of dry wine specialist Georg

Breuer and dessert wine superstar Robert Weil to keep the flag flying. However, for a region whose wines were the most expensive in the world a century ago, this is a pitiful showing.

During the last decade the rich dry wines of the Pfalz have comprehensively outclassed those of the Rheingau on the latter's own territory. The warm, sunny climate here gives wines which combine the body of those from neighbouring Alsace with the vibrant fruit and crispness typical of Germany. The wines from Müller-Catoir are spectacular examples of this style, the aromas pouring from the glass and almost overwhelming the palate with their intensity. Reclusive wine-making genius Hans-Günther Schwarz achieves this with a wide range of grapes (look for Rieslaner

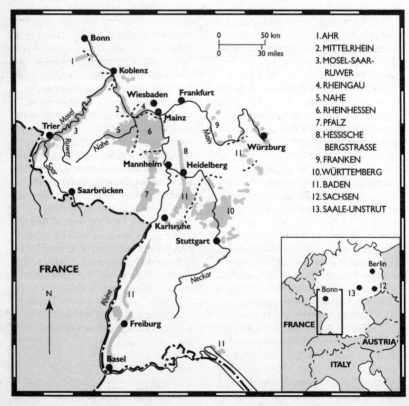

0 — 50 km	1. AHR
0 — 30 miles	2. MITTELRHEIN
	3. MOSEL-SAAR-RUWER
	4. RHEINGAU
	5. NAHE
	6. RHEINHESSEN
	7. PFALZ
	8. HESSISCHE BERGSTRASSE
	9. FRANKEN
	10. WÜRTTEMBERG
	11. BADEN
	12. SACHSEN
	13. SAALE-UNSTRUT

Bonn
Koblenz
Wiesbaden Frankfurt
Trier Mainz
Mosel Nahe Würzburg
Ruwer Main
Saar Mannheim Heidelberg
Saarbrücken
Karlsruhe
Stuttgart
FRANCE
Neckar
N
Rhine
Freiburg
Basel

Berlin
Bonn 13
FRANCE
AUSTRIA
ITALY

and Scheurebe as well as Riesling); an example followed by other top Pfalz estates such as Bergdolt, Fuhrmann-Eymael, Koehler-Ruprecht (Germany's most concentrated dry Rieslings, and amazing Pinot Noir), Lingenfelder, Georg Mosbacher, Messmer, Rebholz and Dr Wehrheim. But few leading producers here concentrate on just one grape variety as Riesling specialists Josef Biffar and Bürklin-Wolf do.

Rheinhessen and the Nahe are regions that lack the image of their neighbours, but each has a handful of first-class producers. The classic-style Riesling Kabinett and Spätlese wines from Gunderloch in Rheinhessen, and Dönnhoff in the Nahe put the entire Rheingau in the shade. In Rheinhessen St Antony and Heyl zu Herrnsheim and in the Nahe Schlossgut Diel, Emrich Schönleber and Crusius are almost in the same league. The effusively fruity, racy Rieslings from Mittelrhein producers such as Tony Jost and Ratzenberger are also worth tracking down. The contrast between the dynamism of these regions and the slumber in which the winemakers of Franken and Württemberg are apparently sunk is striking. If these latter regions do not rapidly wake up, they will get left behind even on the domestic market, where regional patriotism has long enabled them to get away with selling mediocre wines for high prices. **STUART PIGOTT**

CLASSIFICATIONS

The German classification system is based on the sugar levels, and therefore the ripeness and the potential alcohol, of the grapes when they are picked. The main categories are as follows:

DEUTSCHER TAFELWEIN Basic German table wine of supposedly tolerable quality; low natural alcoholic strength, sugared at fermentation to increase alcohol, no specific vineyard origin stated. Deutscher Tafelwein must be 100 per cent German. From a good source, like the major supermarkets, it can be better than many QbAs. The most commonly available are labelled Rhine (or Hock) or Mosel and bear some resemblance to QbAs from the Rhine or Mosel areas. Cheaper wines labelled EU Tafelwein are not worth looking at – they are usually bottled in Germany from very cheap imported wine, sweetened to a more or less Germanic style. However, at the other end of the price spectrum are expensive 'designer table wines', red and white wines from adventurous producers who may age them in oak barriques.

LANDWEIN German *vin de pays*, slightly up-market and drier table wine from one of 20 designated areas. It can be *Trocken* (dry) or *Halbtrocken* (half-dry).

QbA (Qualitätswein bestimmter Anbaugebiete) Literally 'quality wine from designated regions' – the specific areas being Ahr, Hessische Bergstrasse, Mittelrhein, Nahe, Rheingau, Rheinhessen, Pfalz, Franken, Württemberg, Baden, Mosel-Saar-Ruwer, plus two regions in what was East Germany: Saale-Unstrut and Sachsen. QbAs can be mediocre, but are not necessarily so. In modest vintages such as 1987 and 1991 they can be very good indeed, as QbAs may be chaptalized, giving wines of better body and balance than minor Kabinetts. They may also include the products of prestigious single vineyards, where growers set standards far above those required by the law. These wines can offer outstanding value for money when produced by top estates.

QmP (Qualitätswein mit Prädikat) Quality wine with special attributes, classified in

The price guides for this section begin on page 236.

ascending order according to the ripeness of the grapes: Kabinett, Spätlese, Auslese, Beerenauslese, Eiswein, Trockenbeeren-auslese. Chaptalization is not allowed, and in each category up to and including Auslese, the sugar content may range from almost non-existent to positively luscious. Drier wines may be either Trocken (dry) or Halbtrocken (half-dry). Depending on the vintage conditions, some or all of the following QmP categories will be made.

KABINETT Made from ripe grapes from a normal harvest. Usually lighter in alcohol than ordinary QbA, and often delicious.

SPÄTLESE From late-picked (therefore riper) grapes. Often moderately sweet, though there are now dry versions.

AUSLESE From selected bunches of very ripe grapes. Usually sweet and sometimes touched by noble rot. In many southern regions, such as Baden, they are fermented dry, giving rich and powerful wines.

BEERENAUSLESE (BA) From selected single grapes almost always affected by 'noble rot', a fungus that concentrates the sugar and acidity in the grapes. BA from new, non-Riesling grapes can be dull: Huxelrebe takes to noble rot so easily that you can make a BA before you've even picked Riesling. But Riesling BA, and many a Scheurebe or Silvaner, will be astonishing.

EISWEIN Just that – 'ice wine' – often picked before a winter dawn when the grapes are frozen. They are dashed to the winery by the frost-bitten pickers; once there, quick and careful pressing removes just the slimy-sweet concentrate; the water, in its icy state, stays separate. Eiswein always has a high acidity that needs to be tamed by bottle-age, though you do lose the lovely frosty, green apple flavours of youth.

TROCKENBEERENAUSLESE (TBA) 'Shrivelled berries gathered late.' That's a pedestrian translation of one of the world's great tastes. To be TBA, juice has to reach about 22 degrees potential alcohol, and can reach 30 or more. But that stifles the yeasts – so much so that fermentation may hardly get going, and a year later the liquid may have five to six degrees alcohol but 15 to 20 degrees of unfermented sugar. A top Sauternes might be picked with 20 degrees potential alcohol, but end up with 14 degrees or more, so that TBAs are usually among the sweetest wines in the world. But the tendency is to produce a slightly drier, more alcoholic style. Few growers try to make TBAs because of the risk and the cost. Remember that the vines are making a glass of wine each instead of a bottle, and the weather can easily ruin it all anyway. That's why TBAs are expensive – usually starting at £20 a half-bottle ex-cellars. But, even then, a grower won't make money; it's his pride that makes him do it. And the wines can age for as long as most of us.

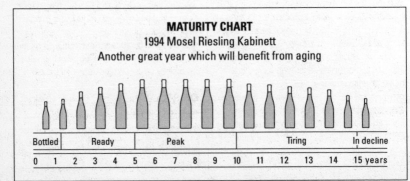

MATURITY CHART
1994 Mosel Riesling Kabinett
Another great year which will benefit from aging

Bottled	Ready	Peak	Tiring	In decline

0   1   2   3   4   5   6   7   8   9   10   11   12   13   14   15 years

GRAPES & FLAVOURS

DORNFELDER (red) A red variety grown mainly in the Rheinhessen and Pfalz which at its best produces deep-coloured reds with great fruit concentration combined with firm structure. Made in two styles, either reminiscent of Beaujolais and for early drinking (try *Lingenfelder's*) or aged in barriques for longer keeping. *Siegrist* produces one of the best. Best producers: *Knipser, Lergenmüller, Lingenfelder, Messmer, Siegrist, Heinrich Vollmer* (Pfalz).

MÜLLER-THURGAU (white) The most widely planted German grape, this cross was propagated in 1883 to get Riesling style plus big yields and early ripening. Just like saying, 'Hey, I've just found a way to turn this plastic bowl into a gold chalice.' You can't do it. It produces soft, grapy wines when ripe – and grassy, sharp ones when not. When aged in oak as a dry wine, Müller-Thurgau can be known as Rivaner, though this name can also be used for non-oaked versions, too. The oaked style is particularly successful in Baden, but only when yields are severely reduced. Stars of the oaked style are *Dr Loosen, Gunderloch, Karl Johner.*

RIESLANER (white) A sensational crossing of Riesling and Silvaner, but not widely planted because of its sensitivity to soil and site. Like Riesling it attains astonishing ripeness but has even higher acidity. When it's ripe it tastes of apricots; when it's unripe it tastes, less appealingly, of gooseberries and grass. Best as dessert wine from the Pfalz (especially *Müller-Catoir*) and Franken. Best producers: *Juliuspital, Rudolf Fürst, Robert Schmitt, Schmitt's Kinder* (Franken).

RIESLING (white) Most of Germany's best wines (except in Baden-Württemberg, where the soils are usually unsuitable) are made from this grape. A slow-ripening variety, it mostly grows on the best sites in each village, and when yields are controlled, it produces wonderful flavours: from steely, slaty and dry as sun-bleached bones, through apples, peaches, apricots – more or less sweet according to the ripeness of the grapes and the intentions of the winemaker – and finally arriving at the great sweet wines. These can be blinding in their rich, honeyed concentration of peaches, pineapples, mangoes and even raisins, with acidity like a streak of fresh lime that makes them the most appetizing of sweet wines.

RULÄNDER (white) The French Pinot Gris. As Ruländer the style is strong, sweetish, rather broad-shouldered, with a whiff of kasbah spice and a splash of honey. When sold as Grauburgunder it is firm, dry, often aged in small oak barriques and can make exciting drinking. Best producers: *Schlossgut Diel* (Nahe); *Koehler-Ruprecht, Müller-Catoir, Münzberg* (Pfalz); *Bercher, Dr Heger, Karl H Johner, Salwey, Stigler* (Baden); *Johann Ruck* (Franken)

SCHEUREBE (white) A tricky grape. When it's unripe, it can pucker your mouth with a combination of raw grapefruit and cat's pee. But properly ripe, it is transformed. The grapefruit is still there, but now it's a fresh-cut pink one from Florida sprinkled with caster sugar. There's honey too, lashings of it, and a crackling, peppery fire which, in the Pfalz, Baden and Franken, produces dry wines as well as sweeter, sometimes outstanding Auslese and Beerenauslese. Best producers: *Darting, Lingenfelder, Messmer, Müller-Catoir* (Pfalz); *Andreas Laible, Wolff-Metternich* (Baden); *Rudolf Fürst, Wirsching* (Franken).

SILVANER (white) This was the workhorse before Müller-Thurgau. At its worst it's a broad, earthy wine – dull, fat and vegetal. It is at its best in Franken, where it is impressive and powerful and develops honeyed weight with age. It suits the local porky cookery; good with asparagus, too.

SPÄTBURGUNDER (red) Throughout the southerly regions of Germany a red wine revolution has taken place during the last decade. Though most German wines from the Spätburgunder (the Pinot Noir of Burgundy) remain pale and thin, the pioneers of the new, deeply coloured, rich and powerful style and now making some stunning wines. Top producers: *Meyer-Nakel* (Ahr); *August Kelleler* (Rheingau); *Knipser, Koehler-Ruprecht* (Pfalz); *Bercher, Dr Heger, Bernhard Huber, Karl H Johner* (Baden); *Rudolf Fürst* (Franken); *Dautel* (Württemberg).

WEISSBURGUNDER or **WEISSER BURGUNDER** (white) The Pinot Blanc is increasingly grown in Nahe, Rheinhessen, Pfalz and Baden to make full dry whites, often as a Chardonnay substitute. It ripens more easily than Chardonnay, though, and in the right hands can produce soft, creamy wines with a peach, melted butter, caramel and nuts. The top producers are *Dönnhoff* (Nahe); *Heyl zu Hermsheim, Schales* (Rheinhessen); *Bergdolt, Müller-Catoir, Rebholz, Wehrheim* (Pfalz); *Bercher, Dr Heger, Karl H Johner, Franz Keller, Salwey* (Baden).

WINES & WINE REGIONS

AHR This small area contrives to be famous for red wines, though the flavour and the colour are pretty light, and its Rieslings are in fact more interesting. Top producers: *Deutzerhof, Meyer-Näkel.*

BADEN In the distant, balmy south of the country, Baden makes some red and rosé in the hills near Freiburg. Dry Ruländer and Weisser Burgunder can be really special – more reliable than those of Alsace, only ten minutes' drive away. In southern Baden, everyone drinks the pleasant, nondescript Gutedel, but Silvaner from the Kaiserstuhl area can be more interesting. There's only a little Riesling, but it's good, although Spätburgunder is definitely on top. In the Ortenau area there is a clutch of fine producers of dry Riesling.The area is dominated by the vast *Badische Winzerkeller* co-operative. Top producers: *Bercher, Dr Heger, Bernhard Huber, Karl H Johner, Franz Keller, Andreas Laible, Schloss Neuweier, Salwey, Seeger, Wolff-Metternich.*

DEUTSCHER SEKT Often a sure route to intestinal distress and sulphur-led hangover, although Deinhard makes a decent Riesling; version called *Lila*; *Dr Richter's* and *Georg Breuer's* are outstanding, but expensive. Interesting smaller brands are Graeger, Menger-Krug, Schloss Vaux, but at the time of writing they are not shipped to Britain. Avoid

at all costs the stuff made from imported wines, labelled Sekt (not Deutscher Sekt), or worse, Schaumwein.

FRANKEN (Franconia) This is dry wine country. The slightly earthy, slightly vegetal, big and beefy Franken wines in their flagon-shaped 'Bocksbeutel' bottles are usually based on Silvaner or Müller-Thurgau. The quality is very mixed, with only a handful of estates making wines worth the relatively high prices. Top producers: *Rudolf Fürst, Juliusspital, Johann Ruck, Egon Schäffer, Schmitt's Kinder, Robert Schmitt, Wirsching.*

HALBTROCKEN Half-dry. The general run of German wines used to go from slightly sweet to very sweet, and this classification was created mostly to satisfy the Germans' own desire for dry wines to drink with food. First efforts were mean and unbalanced but three ripe vintages have shown that producers are learning how to preserve the fruit without oversweetening. In the Mosel and Rheingau this is a sensible style, but in the Pfalz, Franken and Baden it's better to go for dry wines. Riesling Halbtrockens need at least three years to soften.

HESSISCHE BERGSTRASSE A tiny side valley of the Rhine running down to Heidelberg, where, presumably, most of its wine is drunk – because it never gets much further. The central town of Bensheim has one of the highest average temperatures of any wine region in Germany, so the wine is worth seeking out. In general the Rieslings are of good quality. The *Staatsweingut Bergstrasse* is the best producer.

LIEBFRAUMILCH Liebfraumilch was a brilliant invention, an innocuous, grapy liquid, usually from the Rheinhessen or Pfalz, that dramatically fulfilled a need in both the UK and US: as the perfect 'beginner's wine', it broke through the class barriers and mystique of wine. Unfortunately our passion for ever-cheaper wine has meant that most Liebfraumilch these days is dire and best avoided. There are drinkable generic wines, and *Blue Nun* isn't bad, but then it's not one of the cheapest.

MITTELRHEIN The Rhine at its most beautiful, providing all the label ideas for castles clinging to cliffs high above the boats and river-front cafés. It really is like that, and tourists sensibly flock there and just as sensibly drink most of its wine. One grower whose wines have got away is *Toni Jost* – his racy Rieslings are worth trying. *Fritz Bastian, Dr Randolf Kauer, Helmut Mades* and *Ratzenberger* also make good Rieslings.

MOSEL-SAAR-RUWER When they are based on Riesling and come from one of the many steep, slaty, south-facing sites in the folds of the river, or strung out, mile upon mile, along the soaring, broad-shouldered valley sides, these northerly wines are unlike any others. They can achieve a thrilling spring flowers flavour, allied to an alcohol level so low that it leaves your head clear. Most Mosel comes from the river valley itself, but the Saar and Ruwer tributaries are also part of the region. Their top wines are the lightest yet most intense Rieslings in the world, and the best Mosel-Saar-Ruwer Rieslings have an intensely minerally character from the slate soil. Some of the best come from *Joh. Jos. Christoffel, Fritz Haag, Reinhold Haart, von Hövel, Karthäuserhof, von Kesselstatt, Dr Loosen, Joh. Jos. Prüm, Max Ferd. Richter, Schloss Saarstein, Willi Schaefer, von Schubert, Selbach-Oster, Dr Wagner, Dr Weins-Prüm, Zilliken.*

NAHE Important side-valley off the Rhine, snaking south from Bingen. Many of the best Kabinetts and Spätlesen come from its middle slopes of this geologically complex area, wines with a grapy taste, quite high acidity and something slightly mineral too. Away from this hub of quality, the wines are less reliable. The best wines now come from *Dönnhoff*, but *Crusius, Schlossgut Diel, Emrich-Schönleber, Kruger-Rumpf and Mathern* also make good wines. The *Staatliche Weinbaudomäne* is still struggling to regain top form.

PFALZ This used to be called the Rheinpfalz, and is still sometimes known in English as the Palatinate. The northern half clusters round some extremely good villages like Forst, Wachenheim, Deidesheim and Ruppertsberg. There's lots of fiery Riesling, and Scheurebe is also excellent. The South is Germany's great success story of recent years, with fewer big names to fly its flag but an astonishing overall improvement in quality. The Pfalz is now arguably the most dynamic wine region in Germany. Look for *Bergdolt, Josef Biffar, Dr Bürklin-Wolf, Fuhrmann-Eymael, Knipser, Koehler-Ruprecht, Messmer, Georg Mosbacher, Müller-Catoir, Rebholz, Karl Schaefer, Werheim, Werlé.*

RHEINGAU This wine area spreads north and east of Bingen. It posseses some of Germany's most famous vineyards and renowned aristocratic wine estates, and its supremely elegant Rieslings once defined top-quality German wines. However, many of the big estates here have been resting on their laurels for years. High yields, poor vineyard management and sloppy wine-making have pushed several to the edge of bankruptcy. The region's drive to promote its dry wines through the Charta association during the 1980s did not convince many outside Germany. Thankfully a small group of family-owned or -directed estates regularly prove that the region can produce great dry and dessert Rieslings. Look for: *Georg Breuer, Domdechant Werner, August Eser, Johannishof, August Kesseler, Frank Künstler, Josef Leitz, Schloss Reinharshausen, J Wegeler (Deinhard), Robert Weil.*

RHEINHESSEN The contrasts between Rheinhessen's regular products and its top wines could not be more extreme. This large expanse of vine-covered hills is one of the main sources of Liebfraumilch and generic wines such as Bereich Nierstein and Niersteiner Gutes Domtal. In the hands of talented winemakers, though, Nierstein's top vineyards can give dry and naturally sweet Rieslings that can match anything from the Rheingau. Unfortunately, the German wine law allows inferior wines from nearby villages to carry the Nierstein name. This has robbed the region's new star winemakers such as the Hasselbachs of the Gunderloch estate, and the Michalskys of St Antony, of much well-deserved limelight. The new Rheinhessen Selection programme is designed to focus attention upon the region's traditional dry white wines from the Silvaner, Weissburgunder, Grauburgunder and Riesling grapes. Top producers: *Gunderloch, Heyl zu Hermsheim, Keller, St Antony, Schales, Georg Albrecht Schneider.*

REGIONAL DEFINITIONS

German wine is classified according to provenance and ripeness of grapes. The country is divided into wine regions (alphabetically listed on these pages – Rheingau, Rheinhessen etc, and two in the former East); inside these there are three groupings. There is widespread agreement that the law needs reform, but the conflicting interests of small growers and large co-operatives is delaying the process.

Bereich This is a collection of villages and vineyard sites, supposedly of similar style, and grouped under a single name – generally that of the most famous village. So 'Bereich Nierstein' means 'a wine from the general region of Nierstein'. It could come from any one of 50 or more villages, regardless of quality.

Grosslage A group of vineyards supposedly all of similar type, based on one or more villages. The plan was to make sense of thousands of obscure vineyard names. But it doesn't work. Among the 152 designated names, there are a few good Grosslagen – like Honigberg, which groups the vineyards of Winkel in the Rheingau, or Badstube, which covers the best sites in Bernkastel. In these Grosslagen, a blend of several different vineyard sites produces wine of good quality and local character. But most Grosslagen debase the whole idea of a 'vineyard' identity. Take Germany's most famous Grosslage, Niersteiner Gutes Domtal. Gutes Domtal was originally a not terribly special vineyard of 34 hectares in Nierstein. The Niersteiner Gutes Domtal Grosslage covers 1300 hectares, almost all of which share no quality traits with Nierstein whatsoever. From 1997 the VDP association of top growers will forbid their members to market wines under Grosslage names. It is expected that other estates will follow suit, leaving the field open to wholesalers and co-ops, who will supply supermarkets and airlines who demand wines in the quantities that only Grosslagen can produce.

Einzellage This is a real single vineyard wine, corresponding to a *cru* in Burgundy or Alsace. There are about 2600 of these, ranging from a mere half a hectare to 250 hectares. All the best wines in Germany are from Einzellagen, though only a distressingly small proportion actually have real individuality. Some growers are using Einzellage names less, and emphasizing their estate and grape names more, or naming QbA and QmP wines simply with the village name, such as Nierstein or Deidesheim. There are moves, especially in the Rheingau, to institute a classification system that will single out the very best sites.

SAALE-UNSTRUT Three large producers dominate the largest of the wine regions in what we used to call East Germany. The climate is similar to Franken, the grapes are mainly Müller-Thurgau and Silvaner. *Lutzkendorf* has good Riesling and Traminer.

SACHSEN Germany's smallest wine-growing region, in the Elbe Valley close to Dresden and Meissen, is rapidly overcoming the legacy of its GDR past. Müller-Thurgau dominates the vineyards, but the best dry wines come from Weissburgunder, Grauburgunder, Kerner, Traminer and Riesling. *Klaus Zimmerling* is the best producer, but *Schloss Proschwitz* and *Jan Ulrich* are also good.

SEKT bA (Sekt bestimmter Anbaugebiete). Deutscher Sekt increasingly comes from private estates, and is sometimes made by the traditional Champagne method. If the wine comes from one specific quality region it can be labelled accordingly – Rheinhessen Sekt for instance – and is generally a step above Deutscher Sekt. Riesling Sekt bA is especially worth looking out for. Try *Schloss Wachenheim* or *Winzersekt*, or *Dr Richter's*.

TROCKEN Dry. These are the driest German wines, austere and acidic in unripe vintages, but especially harsh in the Mosel. The richer, more alcoholic wines of the Pfalz, Baden and Franken respond well to being fully fermented into a *trocken* style, but be wary of dry Rheingau and Mosel except in the very ripest vintages such as 1992.

WÜRTTEMBERG We haven't seen much Württemberg wine here because most has been drunk on the spot. Württemberg's claim to fame – if fame is the right word – is for red, which accounts for half of the production. The best grape is Lemberger, which makes dark, spicy wines suited to oak aging. Good ranges of wines from *Graf Adelmann, Dautel, Graf von Neipperg, Haidle* and *Hohenlohe-Ohringen*.

WINERY PROFILES

GEORG BREUER ★★★★ (Rheingau) Bernhard Breuer has long been the most active and convincing promoter of dry Rheingau Riesling. Since the 1992 vintage his wines have been amongst the region's very best, particularly those from the Rüdesheimer Berg Schlossberg and Rauenthaler Nonnenberg vineyards.

H DÖNNHOFF ★★★★★ (Nahe) Classic-style Rieslings of great aromatic subtlety and racy intensity have made wine-making genius Helmut Dönnhoff the very top producer in the Nahe. There is magnificent Kabinett and Spätlese from the Niederhäuser Hermannshöhle vineyard, and sensational Auslese and Eiswein.

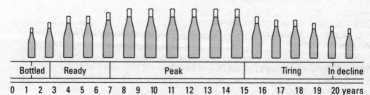

MATURITY CHART
1994 Rheingau Riesling Spätlese
Riesling Spätlese develops a more refined character after three years in bottle

Bottled	Ready	Peak	Tiring	In decline

0 1 2 3 4 5 6 7 8 9 10 11 12 13 14 15 16 17 18 19 20 years

GUNDERLOCH ★★★★★ (Rheinhessen)
Fritz and Agnes Hasselbach's explosively fruity,
rich, seductive Rieslings from the great
Nackenheimer Rothenberg are among the
finest wines being made on the Rhine today.
The Jean Baptiste Kabinett is very good value
for money; there is also Beerenauslese and
Trockenbeerenauslese of other-worldly
concentration and density.

FRITZ HAAG ★★★★ (Mosel-Saar-Ruwer)
Mosel wines of crystalline clarity and racy
refinement from the great Brauneberger Juffer-
Sonnenuhr vineyard made by Wilhelm Haag,

untiring president of the region's Grosser Ring
association of (genuinely) top estates.

VON HÖVEL ★★★★ (Mosel-Saar-Ruwer)
Always a very good producer of Saar Rieslings,
since the 1992 vintage, Eberhard von Kunow's
wines have taken a dramatic jump up in
quality. Best are the succulent, beautifully
balanced wines from the Oberemmeler
Hütte site.

KOEHLER-RUPRECHT ★★★★★ (Pfalz)
Bon vivant Bernd Philippi not only makes the
powerful dry Rieslings that could be mistaken

VINTAGES

1995   For Germany's top Riesling producers, at least, this looks to be the best vintage
since 1990. The marvellous summer was followed by another rainy harvest, but those who
waited for the October sun harvested very ripe grapes with excellent acidity. Few BAs and
TBAs, but lots of excellent Spätlese and Auslese.

1994   Rain in September thwarted the chance of a great vintage, but the Rieslings
harvested during the Indian summer of late October are very good. Strongest in the
Mosel-Saar-Ruwer, but the standard quality wines are lighter and more acidic than the
1993s. Only at BA and TBA level is the vintage really outstanding..

1993   Like 1994, this is a vintage which would have been great had it not rained in
September. Rich, occasionally opulent wines that have developed quite quickly. It was best
in the Rheingau, Pfalz and Middle Mosel. Very good for dry Riesling. Drink during the next
few years.

1992   Very good. Like 1989 its problem may be acidity, making for opulent wines which
may be short on bite. In the Mosel rain put paid to hopes of making much Auslese, but
Spätlesen should be excellent. Rigorous selection in Sachsen and Saale-Unstrut shows that
they may be catching on.

1991   Drought stress during the very hot summer robbed the wines of some depth, but
the best Rieslings from the Mosel-Saar-Ruwer and the Pfalz are like smaller versions of the
1990s. They will show much better with a year or two more aging.

1990   Clearly the best vintage for every region in Germany since at least 1971. Very
concentrated, racy wines with great aging potential. Currently most are closed up, but the
best Riesling Spätlese and Auslese will be magnificent from the end of the decade. The rare
BA and TBA wines are breathtaking.

1989   A mixed vintage: many Kabinett and Spätlese wines are tiring fast and/or turning
bitter. Best in the Mosel-Saar-Ruwer, Nahe and Pfalz. Some wonderful Auslese, BA and
TBA that are beginning to show well, but even these categories are a mixed bag.

1988   A wonderful vintage for the Middle Mosel, giving rich wines with marvellous
balance. Elsewhere very good, but relatively few highlights. The best Riesling Spätlese and
Auslese will still improve.

for top Alsace wines like Clos Ste Hune, he also produces a range of excellent oak-aged varietal whites and Germany's best Pinot Noir reds, which are sold under the Philippi label.

FRANZ KÜNSTLER ★★★★★
(Rheingau) Young Gunter Künstler is the Rheingau's number one winemaker, demonstrating that Hochheim's vineyards can give the most powerful and long-lived Rieslings in the region. Best are the majestic dry and dessert wines from the Hochheimer Hölle.

DR LOOSEN ★★★★★ (Mosel-Saar-
Ruwer) Impish, cosmopolitian Ernst Loosen makes the most concentrated and complex Rieslings in the Middle Mosel from old, ungrafted vines. His Spätlese and Auslese from the Urziger Würzgarten, Erdener Prälat and Treppchen are among Germany's greatest wines. The regular quality wines are sold without vineyard names and offer excellent value for money.

EGON MÜLLER ★★★★★ (Mosel-Saar-
Ruwer) The Riesling Auslese, Beerenauslese, Trockenbeerenauslese and Eisweins which Egon Müller Jr makes at this estate and its Le Gallais sister property are the ultimate German dessert wines. No honey tastes this good. However, be perpared to pay world-class prices for world-class quality.

MÜLLER-CATOIR ★★★★★ (Pfalz)
Leading estate of the Pfalz producing a wide range of highly expressive, rich dry and naturally sweet wines. Look for the superb Scheurebe and Rieslaner as well as for the Rieslings. Müller-Catoir's winemaker Hans Günther Schwarz is the father figure for the region's talented new generation of wine producers.

JOH. JOS. PRÜM ★★★★★ (Mosel-Saar-
Ruwer) No German estate has been at the top longer than this, the established star of the Middle Mosel. Dr Manfred Prüm's wines need time to show their best, but after a few years of aging they are supremely elegant. Look for the wines from the Wehlener Sonnenuhr, which can age for decades without losing their vigour.

VON SCHUBERT ★★★★★ (Mosel-Saar-
Ruwer) Dr Carl von Schubert's Maximin Grünhaus estate makes exquisitely delicate, fragrant Rieslings that gain enormously with long aging. The state is composed of three monopoly vineyards, but the art nouveau label is gloriously impossible to read, so their names hardly matter. There are excellent quality wines from QbA right up to TBA, and prices to match.

WEINGUT ROBERT WEIL ★★★★
(Rheingau) Large Rheingau estate recently dramatically revitalised under the ownership of Japanese drinks giant Suntory, and the direction of young Wilhelm Weil. Makes class-style Rieslings which manage to combine opulent fruit with clarity and crisp acidity. Best are the wines from the Kiedricher Gräfenberg, all the other wines being sold without vineyard names.

MERCHANTS SPECIALISING IN GERMANY
see Merchant Directory (page 424) for details

So unfashionable, and so hard to sell, that the majority of merchants only list basic wines. Brave merchants prepared to stick their necks out include: Adnams (AD), Averys of Bristol (AV), Bennetts (BEN), Bibendum (BIB), Butlers Wine Cellar (BU) particularly old vintages, Direct Wine (DI), Eldridge Pope (EL), Philip Eyres (EY),

Gelston Castle Fine Wines (GE), Douglas Henn-Macrae (HE), J E Hogg (HOG), Lay & Wheeler (LAY), Oddbins (ODD), Majestic (MAJ), James Nicholson (NI), The Nobody Inn (NO), Thos. Peatling (PE), Reid Wines (1992) Ltd (REI), Summerlee Wines (SUM), Tanners (TAN), The Ubiquitous Chip (UB), Waterloo Wine (WAT), Wine Society (WS)

GERMANY

Kab.	=	Kabinett
Spät.	=	Spätlese
Aus.	=	Auslese
BA	=	Beerenauslese
TBA	=	Trockenbeerenauslese

RHINE WHITE

Under £4.00

1995
Liebfraumilch Black Tower (CO, SO)
Liebfraumilch Blue Nun (CO, SO, THR, BOT, WR)
1994
Liebfraumilch Black Tower (SAF)
Niersteiner Gutes Domtal, Deinhard (HOG)
Niersteiner Gutes Domtal, Rudolf Müller (HAH)
Rüdesheimer Rosengarten, Rudolf Müller (TAN)
1993
Liebfraumilch Blue Nun (UN)
Niersteiner Gutes Domtal, Rudolf Müller (PEN)
1992
Johannisberger Erntebringer Riesling Kab., Müller (FUL)
Liebfraumilch Black Tower (BOT, THR, WR)

£4.00 → £4.49

1995
Liebfraumilch Black Tower (WHI)
1993
Niersteiner Gutes Domtal, Rudolf Müller (CB)
Oppenheimer Krötenbrunnen, Rudolf Müller (CB)

£4.50 → £5.49

1995
Liebfraumilch Black Tower (FOR)
Liebfraumilch Blue Nun (WHI, FOR)
1994
Deidesheimer Hofstück Kab., Rudolf Müller (FOR)
Niersteiner Spiegelberg Riesling Kab., Rudolf Müller (TAN)

1993
Johannisberger Erntebringer Riesling Kab., Müller (FOR)
Oestricher Doosberg Riesling Aus., Deinhard (FUL)

£5.50 → £6.49

1995
Hochheimer Hölle Riesling Kab., Aschrott (ASD)
1994
Niederhäuser Pfingstweide Riesling, Paul Anheuser (SUM)
1993
Binger Scharlachberg Riesling Kab., Villa Sachsen (TES)
Mainzer Domherr Bacchus Kab., Guntrum (PIP)
Oppenheimer Schloss Müller-Thurgau Trocken, Guntrum (WRI)
1992
Niersteiner Spiegelberg Kab., Guntrum (WRI, DAV)
1989
Eltviller Sonnenberg Riesling Kab., von Simmern (WAT)
1988
Kiedricher Sandgrub Riesling Kab., Schloss Groenesteyn (VIC)
Schloss Vollrads Blau-Gold, Matuschka-Greiffenclau (EL)

1983
Oestricher Doosberg Riesling Kab., Schönborn (SO)

£6.50 → £7.49

1990
Ruppertsberger Gaisböhl Riesling Kab., Bürklin-Wolf (TAN)
Wachenheimer Luginsland Riesling Kab., Bürklin-Wolf (DI)

£7.50 → £8.49

1994
Schlossböckelheimer Kupfergrube
  Riesling Kab., Staatliche
  Weinbaudomäne (TAN)
1992
Forster Ungeheuer Riesling Kab.,
  Bassermann-Jordan (GAU)
Rauenthaler Gehrn Riesling Kab.,
  Staatsweingüter Eltville (HE)
1990
Kiedricher Sandgrub Riesling Kab.,
  Schloss Groenesteyn (HOG)
Niersteiner Oelberg Spät., Gessert (SUM)
Schloss Vollrads Blau-Silber, Matuschka-
  Greiffenclau (HOG)
1989
Niederhäuser Hermannsberg Riesling
  Spät., Staatliche Weinbaudomäne (EY)
Riesling Spät. Trocken, Lingenfelder (NI)
1988
Niersteiner Pettenthal Riesling Spät.,
  Balbach (VIC)
1987
Rüdesheimer Berg Roseneck Riesling
  Kab., Deinhard (PEN)
1986
Niederhäuser Hermannsberg Riesling
  Kab., Staatliche Weinbaudomäne (REI)
Ruppertsberger Gaisböhl Riesling Kab.,
  Bürklin-Wolf (DI)

£8.50 → £9.99

1995
Scheurebe Spät. Trocken, Lingenfelder (AD)
1993
Schlossböckelheimer Kupfergrube
  Riesling Kab., Staatliche
  Weinbaudomäne (LAY)
Steinberger Riesling Kab., Staatsweingüter
  Eltville (HE)
★ Ungsteiner Herrenberg Scheurebe Spät.,
  Pfeffingen (SUM)
1990
Kreuznacher Kahlenberg Riesling Spät.,
  Paul Anheuser (ROB)
Niederhäuser Hermannsberg Riesling
  Spät., Staatliche Weinbaudomäne (EY)
Oppenheimer Kreuz Riesling Spät.
  Trocken, Guntrum (GE)
1989
Erbacher Marcobrunnen Riesling Kab.,
  Staatsweingüter Eltville (AV)
Steinberger Riesling Kab., Staatsweingüter
  Eltville (HOG)

1988
Deidesheimer Hohenmorgen Riesling
  Spät., Bassermann-Jordan (EY, RAE)
Forster Ungeheuer Riesling Spät.,
  Deinhard (PEN)
1986
Wachenheimer Goldbachel Riesling Spät.,
  Bürklin-Wolf (DI)

1983
Johannisberger Hölle Riesling Kab., Eser
  (REI)

£10.00 → £11.99

1993
Schloss Reichartshausen Riesling Kab.,
  Ress (SUM)
1992
Riesling Spät. Trocken, Lingenfelder (AD)
Schloss Johannisberg Riesling Kab.,
  Metternich (BEN)
1989
Schlossböckelheimer Kupfergrube
  Riesling Spät., Staatliche
  Weinbaudomäne (HOG)
1986
Niersteiner Oelberg Riesling Aus., Senfter
  (HOG)
1979
Grünstadter Höllenpfad Scheurebe Aus.,
  Winzerkeller Leiningerland (HE)

£12.00 → £14.99

1994
Erbacher Marcobrunnen Riesling Spät.,
  von Simmern (TAN)
1991
Forster Kirchenstück Riesling Kab.,
  Bassermann-Jordan (BIB)
1989
Wachenheimer Gerümpel Riesling Spät.,
  Bürklin-Wolf (PIP)
1983
Wachenheimer Königswingert Aus.,
  Bürklin-Wolf (REI)

£15.00 → £19.99

1989
Schlossböckelheimer Kupfergrube
   Riesling Aus., Staatsdomäne (HOG)
1988
Schlossböckelheimer Kupfergrube
   Riesling Aus., Staatsdomäne (AD)
1983
Hochheimer Herrenberg Riesling Aus.,
   Nagler (UB)
Wachenheimer Mandelgarten Scheurebe
   Aus., Bürklin-Wolf (UB)
1976
Schlossböckelheimer Burgweg Riesling
   Aus., Pleitz (HE)

£20.00 → £29.99

1985
Wachenheimer Rechbächel Riesling Aus.,
   Bürklin-Wolf (AD)
1976
Niersteiner Kranzberg Riesling BA,
   Senfter (CRO)
Oppenheimer Krötenbrunnen, Deinhard
   (PEN)

c. £43.00

1976
Binger Scharlachberg Riesling BA,
   Staatliche Weinbaudomänen (UB)

RHINE RED

Under £6.00

1990
Traisener Nonnengarten Portugieser
   Halbtrocken, Pleitz (HE)

MOSEL WHITE

Under £3.50

1990
Wiltinger Scharzberg Riesling Kab.,
   Zentralkellerei (TES)

£3.50 → £3.99

Non-vintage
Bereich Bernkastel, Rudolf Müller (FUL)
1995
Bereich Bernkastel Riesling, Schneider
   (PLA, EL)
Piesporter Michelsberg Reh (MAR)
Piesporter Michelsberg Schneider (PLA)
1994
Piesporter Michelsberg Schneider (EL)

1993
Bereich Bernkastel Riesling, Schneider
   (WHI)
Piesporter Michelsberg Schneider (WHI)

£4.00 → £5.99

1995
Graacher Himmelreich Riesling Kab.,
   Kesselstatt (ASD)
1994
Bereich Bernkastel, Rudolf Müller (CB)
Ockfener Bockstein Riesling Kab., Rudolf
   Müller (FOR)
Piesporter Michelsberg Rudolf Müller
   (PEN, CB)
1993
Deinhard Green Label (HOG, WHI)
Scharzhofberger Riesling Kab., Rudolf
   Müller (SO)
1985
Bernkasteler Badstube Riesling Kab.,
   Thanisch (FUL)

£6.00 → £7.99

1994
Ockfener Scharzberg Riesling, F-W-
   Gymnasium (TAN)
1993
Erdener Treppchen Riesling Spät.,
   Monchhof (WAI)
1992
Brauneberger Juffer Riesling Kab., Richter
   (BER)
Graacher Himmelreich Riesling Kab., F-
   W-Gymnasium (EY)
Trittenheimer Apotheke Riesling Spät.,
   Weingut Hubertushof (HE)
Wehlener Sonnenuhr Riesling Kab.,
   Richter (BER)
1991
Graacher Himmelreich Riesling Kab., F-
   W-Gymnasium (EL)
Trittenheimer Apotheke Riesling Spät.,
   Weingut Hubertushof (HE)
Wehlener Sonnenuhr Riesling Kab.,
   Richter (AV, SUM)

> *Please remember that*
> ***Webster's** is a price*
> *GUIDE and not a price*
> *LIST. It is not meant to*
> *replace up-to-date*
> *merchants' lists.*

1990

Graacher Himmelreich Riesling Spät., F-
W-Gymnasium (EY)
Oberemmeler Hutte Riesling Spät., von
Hövel (EY)
Reiler Mullay Hofberg Riesling Spät.,
Rudolf Müller (CB)

1989

Brauneberger Juffer Riesling Kab.,
Kesselstatt (BY)
Serriger Schloss Saarsteiner Riesling Kab.,
Schloss Saarstein (SUM)

£8.00 → £9.99

1994

Scharzhofberger Riesling Kab., Kesselstatt
(EL)
Wehlener Sonnenuhr Riesling Kab.,
Loosen (AD, NO, WRI)

1993

Brauneberger Juffer Riesling Kab., Richter
(AV)
Ockfener Bockstein Riesling Spät., Dr
Fischer (AV)

1992

Graacher Himmelreich Riesling Spät., F-
W-Gymnasium (EY)
Serriger Schloss Saarsteiner Riesling Kab.,
Schloss Saarstein (SUM)
Wehlener Sonnenuhr Riesling Kab.,
Loosen (ELL, NI)
Wehlener Sonnenuhr Riesling Kab., J.J.
Prüm (PIP)

1990

Bernkasteler Lay Riesling Kab., Loosen (GE)
Graacher Himmelreich Riesling Spät., F-
W-Gymnasium (YOU)
Scharzhofberger Riesling Kab., Kesselstatt
(BY)
Scharzhofberger Riesling Spät., Kesselstatt
(NI)
Wehlener Sonnenuhr Riesling Kab.,
Richter (GE)

1989

Eitelsbacher Marienholz Riesling Spät.,
Bischöfliches Konvikt (PE)
Enkircher Steffenberg Riesling Spät.,
Immich (GE)
Graacher Himmelreich Riesling Spät., Max
Ferd Richter (SUM)
Josephshofer Riesling Spät., Kesselstatt (BY)
Ockfener Bockstein Riesling Spät.,
Staatlichen Weinbaudomänen (HOG)
Wehlener Sonnenuhr Riesling Kab., J.J.
Prüm (NI)

£10.00 → £11.99

1994

Wehlener Sonnenuhr Riesling Kab.,
Loosen (LEA)

1993

Erdener Treppchen Riesling Kab., Dr
Loosen (AV)

1992

Erdener Treppchen Riesling Spät., Dr
Loosen (ELL)
Wehlener Sonnenuhr Riesling Kab., J.J.
Prüm (WS)

1990

Erdener Treppchen Riesling Kab., Dr
Loosen (NO)
Graacher Himmelreich Riesling Spät., F-
W-Gymnasium (ROB)

1989

Bernkasteler Lay Riesling Kab., Loosen
(BER)
Ockfener Bockstein Riesling Spät.,
Staatlichen Weinbaudomänen (UB)
Scharzhofberger Riesling Spät., Hohe
Domkirche (HOG)

1988

Josephshofer Riesling Aus., Kesselstatt (NI)
Trittenheimer Apotheke Riesling Aus., F-
W-Gymnasium (VIC)

1983

Eitelsbacher Marienholz Riesling Spät.,
Bischöfliches Konvikt (UB)

1975

Graacher Himmelreich Riesling Spät.,
Deinhard (REI)

£12.00 → £14.99

1994

Maximin-Grünhäuser Abtsberg Riesling
Kab., Schubert (AD, LAY)
Serriger Schloss Saarsteiner Riesling Spät.,
Schloss Saarstein (SUM)

1993
Scharzhofberger Riesling Kab., Egon
    Müller (LAY)
Wehlener Sonnenuhr Riesling Spät.,
    Prüm-Erben (CB)
1990
Eitelsbacher Karthäuserhofberger Sang
    Spät., Werner Tyrell (WS)
Maximin-Grünhäuser Herrenberg Riesling
    Spät., Schubert (EY)
Wehlener Sonnenuhr Riesling Spät.,
    Deinhard (BEN)
1989
Scharzhofberger Riesling Aus., Kesselstatt
    (WS)
Wehlener Sonnenuhr Riesling Kab.,
    Weins Prüm (UB)
Wehlener Sonnenuhr Riesling Spät.,
    Prüm-Erben (DI)
1983
Bernkasteler Bratenhöfchen Riesling Aus.,
    Deinhard (PEN)
Graacher Himmelreich Riesling Aus., F-
    W-Gymnasium (REI)
Piesporter Goldtröpfchen Riesling Aus.,
    Tobias (ROB)
Wehlener Sonnenuhr Riesling Aus., F.W.
    Prüm (PE)
1971
Ockfener Herrenberg Riesling Spät.,
    Deinhard (REI)

£15.00 → £19.99
1994
Brauneberger Juffer Sonnenuhr Riesling
    Aus., Fritz Haag (LAY)
Maximin-Grünhäuser Abtsberg Riesling
    Spät., Schubert (WS)
1993
Ayler Kupp Riesling Aus., Bischöfliches
    Priesterseminar (TAN)
1989
Wehlener Sonnenuhr Riesling Aus., S.A.
    Prüm-Erben (DI)
1988
Maximin-Grünhäuser Herrenberg Riesling
    Aus., Schubert (EY)

£20.00 → £29.99
1991
Scharzhofberger Riesling Spät., Egon
    Müller (UB)
1989
Brauneberger Juffer Sonnenuhr Riesling
    Aus., Fritz Haag (VIG)

Josephshofer Riesling Aus., Kesselstatt (BY)
Maximin-Grünhäuser Abtsberg Riesling
    Aus., Schubert (LAY)
1987
Mulheimer Helenkloster Riesling Eiswein,
    Richter ½ bottle (SUM)
1985
Bernkasteler Doctor Riesling Spät.,
    Deinhard (PEN)

£30.00 → £49.99
1993
Mulheimer Helenkloster Riesling Eiswein,
    Richter ½ bottle (SUM)
1992
Mulheimer Helenkloster Riesling Eiswein,
    Richter ½ bottle (SUM)
1990
Mulheimer Helenkloster Riesling Eiswein,
    Richter ½ bottle (SUM, BER)
1989
Mulheimer Helenkloster Riesling Eiswein,
    Richter ½ bottle (SUM)
1985
Bernkasteler Doctor Riesling Aus.,
    Bergweiler (UB)
1976
Graacher Himmelreich Riesling Aus., J.J.
    Prüm (WS)

c. £53.00
1983
Bernkasteler Graben Riesling Eiswein,
    Deinhard ½ bottle (AD)

FRANKEN WHITE

Under £8.00
1994
Schloss Castell Silvaner Trocken, Fürstlich
    Castell'sches Domänenamt (TAN)

£10.00 → £14.99
1992
Escherndorfer Lump Riesling Kab.,
    Gebietswinzergenossenschaft (UB)
1989
Iphofener Julius Echterberg Riesling Kab.,
    Juliusspital (SUM)

SPARKLING

£6.00 → £6.99
Non-vintage
Henkell Trocken (UN)

ITALY

Be prepared for an influx of new DOC wines from Italy as the new wine law brings great swathes of vineyard under the DOC umbrella. And we're talking about traditional wines, not international grape varieties

The world's largest wine industry has begun to pursue new goals that by previous standards seem to be remarkably ambitious. Italy's first order of business is rapidly to increase the volume of officially classified wines in the national total. Until recently, less than 15 per cent of production qualified as DOC or DOCG, while the rest, ranging in quality from the lowest levels of plonk right up to Italy's highest levels of oenological skill, fell into the odds and ends bin as vino da tavola.

The avowed aim of Ezio Rivella, chairman of the National Wine Committe, is to raise the quota of classified wines to 50 per cent of the total by the year 2000, a mandate that seems rather optimistic in a country renowned for its casual approach to official denominations. Yet Rivella's grand design of regionwide DOCs, bolstered by the recently activated category of wines of indicazioni geografiche tipiche (IGT), seems to have the makings of eventual success.

The regional model is his native Piedmont, where the established catalogue of 41 DOC/DOCG zones has been extended with the broad new appellations of Langhe, Colline Novaresi and the comprehensive Piemonte DOC. Similar systems are already in effect in Trentino-Alto Adige, Sardinia, Valle d'Aosta and Abruzzi, while Tuscany has been moving towards a Toscana DOC that would create special niches for most of the premium vini da tavola often referred to as Super-Tuscans.

At one point Rivella had suggested that DOCs for each of Italy's 20 regions could be developed to cover virtually all wines of quality, so that IGT might not be needed. But the DOC reforms haven't come quickly enough to cover everything, so as an alternative the government has finally introduced IGT to cover wines typical of certain regions, provinces or large areas equivalent to France's Vins de Pays.

Vini tipici had been approved by the Common Market as early as the 1970s, though Italy managed to stall a system generally opposed by producers who tended to view 'typical' as synonymous with 'common'. But now, under mounting pressure from their European partners, Italians have begun to fall into line, with scores of IGTs for wines that range in class from super premium to strictly mediocre. Many IGTs, introduced from the 1995 vintage on, are identified by regions or provinces or places with recognizable names, but others are certain to create confusion with obscure appellations like Terra del Placentiano, Alta Valle della Greve and Fortana del Taro.

How the other half lives

Well, at least the official status should help to bring Italian wine some of the credibility that's been lacking up to now among foreign consumers. In a sense, Italy's goal of classifying 50 per cent of its wine might seem modest, considering that France sanctions 55 per cent of its total, and Germany manages to rank a massive 98 per cent. But the fact is that Italy continues to rely on profits from bulk wines, mainly from southern regions, that are shipped for blending to France, Germany and Spain.

Italy has so rapidly reduced its volume of production over the last few vintages that the country has suddenly found itself with a shortage of wine. The reduction is due primarily to the uprooting of vineyards under a long-term EU policy of ridding the continent of once chronic wine surpluses. But recently, following a series of scarce

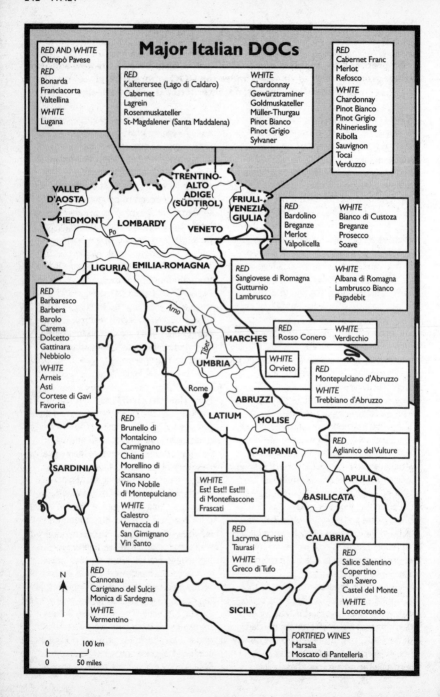

Major Italian DOCs

RED AND WHITE
Oltrepò Pavese

RED
Bonarda
Franciacorta
Valtellina

WHITE
Lugana

RED
Kalterersee (Lago di Caldaro)
Cabernet
Lagrein
Rosenmuskateller
St-Magdalener (Santa Maddalena)

WHITE
Chardonnay
Gewürztraminer
Goldmuskateller
Müller-Thurgau
Pinot Bianco
Pinot Grigio
Sylvaner

RED
Cabernet Franc
Merlot
Refosco

WHITE
Chardonnay
Pinot Bianco
Pinot Grigio
Rhineriesling
Ribolla
Sauvignon
Tocai
Verduzzo

VALLE
D'AOSTA

TRENTINO-
ALTO
ADIGE
(SÜDTIROL)

FRIULI-
VENEZIA
GIULIA

PIEDMONT

LOMBARDY

VENETO

Po

RED
Bardolino
Breganze
Merlot
Valpolicella

WHITE
Bianco di Custoza
Breganze
Prosecco
Soave

LIGURIA

EMILIA-ROMAGNA

RED
Sangiovese di Romagna
Gutturnio
Lambrusco

WHITE
Albana di Romagna
Lambrusco Bianco
Pagadebit

RED
Barbaresco
Barbera
Barolo
Carema
Dolcetto
Gattinara
Nebbiolo

WHITE
Arneis
Asti
Cortese di Gavi
Favorita

Arno

TUSCANY

MARCHES

RED Rosso Conero

WHITE Verdicchio

Tiber

UMBRIA

WHITE
Orvieto

RED
Montepulciano d'Abruzzo

WHITE
Trebbiano d'Abruzzo

Rome

ABRUZZI

LATIUM

MOLISE

RED
Brunello di
Montalcino
Carmignano
Chianti
Morellino di
Scansano
Vino Nobile
di Montepulciano

WHITE
Galestro
Vernaccia di
San Gimignano
Vin Santo

CAMPANIA

RED
Aglianico del Vulture

SARDINIA

APULIA

BASILICATA

WHITE
Est! Est!! Est!!!
di Montefiascone
Frascati

RED
Lacryma Christi
Taurasi

WHITE
Greco di Tufo

CALABRIA

RED
Salice Salentino
Copertino
San Savero
Castel del Monte

WHITE
Locorotondo

N

RED
Cannonau
Carignano del Sulcis
Monica di Sardegna

WHITE
Vermentino

SICILY

FORTIFIED WINES
Marsala
Moscato di Pantelleria

0   100 km

0   50 miles

harvests caused in part by adverse weather, the demand for Italian wine has far surpassed supply, and prices are rising.

Italy's 1995 vintage turned out to be the smallest since 1961, with just 53 million hectolitres produced, 17 per cent less than the average of recent years, and nearly 40 per cent less than the record 86.5 million hectolitres of 1980. Bulk wine prices continued to rise during 1996, in some cases to more than double those of the previous year.

Italian producers of premium wines have been showing more self-discipline than usual in holding the line on prices to remain competitive on international markets. Yet increases of 15 per cent to 20 per cent have been normal for the prestigious wines of Tuscany, Piedmont, the Veneto, Friuli-Venezia Giulia and Trentino-Alto Adige. In Chianti Classico, where excess had been the rule for decades, stocks of wines from earlier vintages are now exhausted.

Pulling too hard

The market crunch has given new purpose to the Italian movement to stop the EU vine-pull programme before it's too late. Leading the opposition is Mario Fregoni, professor of viticulture and former chairman of the National Wine Committee, who had been warning for years that the reduction rate is too drastic. If the current pace is maintained, he predicts that by the turn of the century Europe – which produces about two-thirds of the world's wine – will no longer have enough to meet domestic demands, and will need to rely on imports to make up the difference. With Italy's exports steadily on the rise, Fregoni insists that policies should be aimed at strengthening the country's position as the world's prime producer of wine.

Italy also remains the world's leading consumer of wine – closely rivalled by France – though the per capita consumption rate has levelled off at about 55 litres a year, about half the figure of three decades ago. Those statistics don't reflect a rejection of wine by Italians, 90 per cent of whom drink wine on occasion, and nearly 50 per cent of whom drink it daily.

After an era in which white wines and light reds and rosés gained ground steadily on the Italian market, the trend over the last few years has been a return to favour of aged reds. The turnaround is due in part to published reports of the benefits of moderate consumption of red wine to health. But credit also seems due to a change in dining habits, as the vogue for creative cuisine has given way to a return to tradition, with the emphasis on regional dishes that call for robust red wines.

The great 1989 and 1990 vintages in Piedmont heralded a return to favour of Barolo and Barbaresco among Italians, after years in which exports to northern Europe rose, while domestic sales declined. In Tuscany, production of Brunello di Montalcino continues to mount at impressive rates, as does Vino Nobile di Montepulciano. Chianti has now become so popular that estates can no longer meet demand.

The renaissance of noble red wines is reflected in the planting of new vines. Sangiovese, the source of Chianti, Brunello and Vino Nobile, is not only Italy's most diffused variety but also the most in demand at vine nurseries. Next comes Barbera, the once workaday Piedmontese vine that has gained new status in recent years, followed by Merlot, Apulia's Negro Amaro and Montepulciano, widely planted along the Adriatic, notably in Abruzzi.

It's interesting to note that all but one of the leading varieties are native. Merlot's stronghold is the north-eastern regions of the Veneto and Friuli, where it has been established for well over a century. New plantings of Merlot, Cabernet Sauvignon, Pinot Noir and Syrah continue in many regions, but the pace has slowed after the vogue of the 1980s. The allegation that Italians are forsaking their native vines in favour of trendy international varieties doesn't hold water.

GRAPES & FLAVOURS

AGLIANICO (red) A very late-ripening grape of Greek origin, grown in the South. At its most impressive in Aglianico del Vulture (Basilicata) and Taurasi (Campania).

BARBERA (red) The most prolific grape of Piedmont and the North-West. The wines traditionally have high acidity, a slightly resiny edge and yet a sweet-sour, raisiny taste or even a brown-sugar sweetness. But they don't always have to be like this: witness some of the lighter but intensely fruity Barberas from the Asti and Monferrato hills. The grape reaches its peak in the Langhe hills around Alba where growers like *Altare, Conterno-Fantino* and *Gaja* have used low yields to great effect. Experiments with barrique aging are also encouraging, and wines like *Aldo Conterno*'s are outstandingly rich.

BONARDA (red) Low acid, rich, plummy reds, often with a liquoricy, chocolaty streak and sometimes a slight spritz. The grape is most common in the Colli Piacentini of Emilia-Romagna where it is blended with Barbera as Gutturnio; it is also found in the Oltrepò Pavese.

CABERNET SAUVIGNON (red) The debate over the way in which Cabernet's powerful character swamped the local character of the native grapes has subsided. Fevered brows have been soothed as traditionalists have realized that the French interloper will not replace their beloved native vines, while the flag-waving revolutionaries have reduced the prominence that Cabernet once had. Cabernet has come of age in Italy – it is now part of the intelligent new DOC for Bolgheri Superiore – but so have the producers. It is still important in the North-East and Tuscany, but it is no longer regarded as a panacea for all ills.

CABERNET FRANC (red) Fairly widely grown in the north-east of Italy, especially in Alto Adige, Trentino, Veneto and Friuli. It can make gorgeous grassy, yet juicy-fruited reds – wines that are easy to drink young but also capable of aging.

CHARDONNAY (white) The new law alters Chardonnay's DOC status. The typical Italian style is unoaked: lean, floral and sharply balanced from the Alto Adige and usually more neutral, Mâconnais-style from elsewhere. There is exciting, creamy, spicy, barrique-aged wine being made by the likes of *Gaja, Marchesi di Gresy* and *Pio Cesare* in Piedmont, *Zanella* in Lombardy, *Maculan* in the Veneto and both *Caparzo (Le Grance)* and *Avignonesi (Il Marzocco)* in Tuscany. However the best of the oak-free lobby are making some ravishing stuff by focusing on low yields and picking at the optimum moment. *Zeni* (Trentino) and *Gradnik* (Friuli) are prime examples.

DOLCETTO (red) Piedmont's answer to Gamay but, as you might expect from the region that gave us Barolo, slightly more robust. From the hills of Asti, it is light and refreshing, while from some producers in Alba, notably *Mascarello,* it is Dolcetto with attitude. The 1993s are delicious.

GARGANEGA (white) The principal grape of Soave. Well, it's *supposed* to make up the majority of the blend, and when well made it is refreshing, soft, yet green-apple fresh. However, it has to compete with Trebbiano Toscano in cheaper blends, and often loses. Good producers use Trebbiano di Soave, which is much better, or Chardonnay.

GEWÜRZTRAMINER (white) Although this is supposed to have originated in the Alto Adige (Südtirol) village of Tramin, most of the plantings there now are of the red Traminer, rather than the spicier, more memorable Gewürztraminer of Alsace. Gewürztraminer can be lovely, needing some time in bottle to develop perfume.

GRECO/GRECHETTO (white) An ancient vine introduced to southern Italy by the Greeks, it makes crisp, pale and refreshing wines with lightly spicy overtones in Calabria and Campania and, as Grecanico, in Sicily. Grechetto is part of the same family and its delicious, nutty, aniseed character adds dramatically to Trebbiano-dominated blends in central Italy, as well as sometimes surfacing under its own colours in Umbria, where *Adanti* makes a splendid version.

LAGREIN (red) Local grape of the Alto Adige (Südtirol) and Trentino, making delicious, dark reds, strongly plum-sweet when they're young, aging slowly to a smoky, creamy softness. It also makes one of Italy's best rosés, called Lagrein Kretzer.

MALVASIA (white) This name and the related Malvoisie seems to apply to a range of grape varieties, some not related. Malvasia is found mostly in Tuscany, Umbria and Latium, where it gives a full, creamy nuttiness to dry whites like Frascati. It also produces brilliant, rich dessert wines with the density of thick brown-sugar syrup and the sweetness of raisins, in Sardinia and the islands of Lipari north of Sicily.

MERLOT (red) Widely planted in the North-East. Often good in Friuli; provides lots of jug wine in the Veneto but when blended with Cabernet Sauvignon by *Loredan Gasparini* (Venegazzù) or *Fausto Maculan* (Trentino) achieves greater stature. Other Cabernet-Merlot blends are produced by *Mecvini* in the Marche and Trentino's *Bossi Fedrigotti* (Foianeghe). *Avignonesi* and *Castello di Ama* in Tuscany are getting promising results, while *Ornellaia's Masseto* (also Tuscany) is outstanding.

MONTEPULCIANO (red) A much underrated grape. Yes, it is tough, and yes it is tannic, but it also has lots of plummy, herby fruit behind that toughness. *Banfi* in Montalcino has high hopes for it. It grows mostly on the Adriatic Coast.

MOSCATO (white) The Alto Adige (Südtirol) has various sorts of Muscat, including the delicious Rosenmuskateller and Goldmuskateller, making dry wines to equal the Muscats of Alsace and sweet wines of unrivalled fragrance. But it is at its best in Piedmont, where Asti is a delicious, grapy, sweetish fizz and Moscato Naturale is a heartily perfumed sweet wine, full of the fragrance of grapes, honey, apples and cigars. Moscato is best young, but *Ivaldi's* Passito from Strevi can age beautifully. It also makes fine dessert wines on the island of Pantelleria, south of Sicily.

MÜLLER-THURGAU (white) This is a soft, perfumy workhorse grape in Germany, but on the high, steep Alpine vineyards of the Alto Adige (Südtirol), it produces glacier-fresh flavours; not bad in Trentino and Friuli either.

NEBBIOLO (red) The big, tough grape of the North-West, making – unblended – the famous Barolos and Barbarescos as well as Gattinara, Ghemme, Carema, Spanna and plain Nebbiolo. This is a surly, fierce grape, producing wines that can be dark, chewy, unyielding and harsh behind a shield of cold-tea-tannin and acidity for the first few years; but which then blossom out into a remarkable richness full of chocolate, raisins, prunes, and an austere perfume of tobacco, pine and herbs. In the past, sloppy wine-making has been all too evident in the wines on sale here but shops are now more willing to fork out for the best.

The latter half of the 1980s saw a transformation. Whereas once the wines were unapproachable until about five years after the vintage, now the 1990s, which are bursting with fruit, seem ready to be drunk almost immediately. True, there is still a fairly hefty whack of tannin in most, but clever wine-making seems to have sheathed this in sleek and velvety fruit. A few growers (*Altare, Clerico, Conterno-Fantino* and *Voerzio*) are producing some superb *vini da tavola* by aging their wines in barrique, or blending it with Barbera, or both, as in *Sebaste's* Briccoviole.

PINOT BIANCO (white) Produces some of its purest, honeyed flavours in the Alto Adige (Südtirol), and can do very well in Friuli where the best are buttery and full.

RHEINRIESLING/RIESLING RENANO (white) The true German Riesling is grown in the Alto Adige (Südtirol), making sharp, green, refreshing, steely dry wines – as good as most Mosel or Rhine Kabinett in Germany. It can be OK, and slightly fatter, in Friuli and Lombardy. Riesling Italico, nothing to do with real Riesling, is the dreaded Olasz/ Laski/Welsch Rizling, which so despoils Riesling's name across Eastern Europe.

SANGIOVESE (red) This grape, the mainstay of Chianti and all the other major Tuscan DOCGs, is the Scarlet Pimpernel of Italian viticulture. Numerous experiments are being carried out into its nature, but they seem to produce as many questions as answers. The problem is that it is very sensitive to its environment, and changes it character completely when planted in the cool hills of Chianti, the warm clay soil of the coastal strip or the arid slopes of Montalcino. This sensitivity, which once led people to assume that the problem lay in clones, also accounts for the fact that many of the vineyards in Chianti Classico, for instance, don't produce the quality they should. Hardly surprising: the soil is too rich, the slopes too gentle and the density of planting too high. The sensitive Sangiovese might respond better if it were moved up the hill a bit, where the soil is stonier. This is the lesson people are now learning, and early results show wines of great colour, depth and vibrancy. The austere edge remains, but is balanced by the flesh, which augurs well for the future.

SAUVIGNON BLANC (white) Quite common in the North, and gives some acid bite to far-southern blends like Sicily's *Regaleali*. It can be spicy, grassy and refreshing from the Alto Adige (Südtirol) and Friuli, though the style is usually more subtle than New World Sauvignon. *Volpaia* and *Castellare*

have started making it in Chianti land as have *Banfi* in Montalcino and *Avignonesi* in Montepulciano.

SCHIAVA (red) Light reds with a unique taste that veers between smoked ham and strawberries. An Alto Adige (Südtirol) grape, Schiava is at its best in Kalterersee (Lago di Caldaro) and Santa Maddalena. The locals, who mostly speak German, call it Vernatsch.

SYLVANER (white) Grown very high in the northern valleys of the Alto Adige, at its best this can be chillingly dry, lemon-crisp and quite delicious. But there are still quite a few fat, muddy examples around.

TREBBIANO (white) The widely planted Trebbiano Toscano is a wretched thing, easy to grow, producing vast quantities of grapes with frightening efficiency. It is responsible for an awful lot of fruitless, oxidized, sulphured blaagh-ness. However, attempts to pick it early and vinify it sharp and fresh are having some effect, and at least its use in red, yes *red* Chianti is now severely restricted. Trebbiano di Soave, the Veneto clone, is much better. Lugana is a Trebbiano DOC of character (*Zenato's* is widely available and good). Abruzzi has a strain which *can* be tasty from producers like *Tenuta del Priore, Pepe* and *Valentini*.

VERNACCIA (white) There are several types of Vernaccia – including some red – but we mostly just see two. Vernaccia di Oristano in Sardinia is a sort of Italian version of sherry, best dry – when it has a marvellous mix of floral scents, nutty weight and taunting sourness – but also medium and sweet. Vernaccia di San Gimignano *can* be Tuscany's best traditional white – full, golden, peppery but with a softness of hazelnuts and angelica. *Fagiuoli, Teruzzi e Puthod,* and *Sainsbury's* own-label show what can be done. Some have tried barriques, but so far *Teruzzi e Puthod* is the only producer to understand that you need lots of fruit in the wine in order to balance the oak.

WINES & WINE REGIONS

AGLIANICO DEL VULTURE, DOC

(Basilicata; red) High up gaunt Monte Vulture, in the wilds of Italy's 'instep', the Aglianico grape makes a superb, thick-flavoured red wine. The colour isn't particularly deep, but the tremendous almond paste and chocolate fruit is matched by a tough, dusty feel and quite high acidity. What's more, it's *not* very expensive. Two good producers are *Paternoster, Fratelli d'Angelo*. D'Angelo's barriqued *Canneto d'Angelo* is good.

ALBANA DI ROMAGNA, DOCG

(Emilia-Romagna; white) I resent putting DOCG against this uninspiring white, which some not particularly cynical people say was made DOCG *(a)* because it was the first to apply, *(b)* because they *had* to have a white DOCG and all the others were too frightful to contemplate and *(c)* because the politicos in Bologna have a lot of clout. What's the wine like? Well, it's dry or sweet, still or slightly fizzy, or very fizzy; you see what I mean. At least these days it's less likely to be oxidized and, at its best, the dry version can be delicately scented with an almondy finish. The only really decent producers are *Fattoria Paradiso* and *Zerbina*.

ALTO ADIGE various DOCs (red, white,

rosé) The locals up here by the Austrian border answer more warmly to *grüss Gott* than to *buon giorno* so this area is often referred to as Südtirol. Wines from these dizzily steep slopes are much more Germanic than Italian. Most are red – attractive light wines made from the Vernatsch/Schiava grape, especially Kalterersee and St Magdalener. Cabernet, Pinot Nero, Lagrein and the tea-rose-scented Rosenmuskateller all make reds – and rosés – with more stuffing and personality. This is also one of Italy's most successful white regions. The wines are light, dry and intensely fresh, with spice and plenty of fruit. The best are from *Tiefenbrunner*, in his uplifting, aromatic style and *Lageder* who

makes fuller, rounder wines. Both are experimenting with barrel maturation to good effect. Also *Haas*, a young producer of promise, *Hofstätter, Schloss Schwanburg, Walch* and *Terlan, Schreckbichl*, and *St Michael-Eppan* co-ops.

ARNEIS (Piedmont; white) Potentially

stunning, apples-pears-and-liquorice-flavoured wines from an ancient white grape of the same name, with high prices to match – but since there's a feel of ripe white Burgundy about the best of them, that's not such a turn-off. Unfortunately it is trendy so some may bear the name and not much more. *Arneis di Montebertotto* by *Castello di Neive* is intense yet subtle. *Bruno Giacosa*'s softer, sweeter one has a taste of hops. *Deltetto, Malvirà, Negro, Vietti, Voerzio* are good.

ASTI, DOCG (Piedmont; white) Elevation

to DOCG status means that the tacky 'Spumante' has been dropped from the name of the wine. Other more serious attempts are being made to improve quality, and the fact that prices have risen rapidly since DOCG came into effect on 1 February 1994 cannot be a million miles removed from the fact that there were rumoured to be about 12 million bottles of fraudulent Asti on the market. If

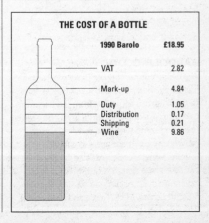

THE COST OF A BOTTLE

	1990 Barolo	£18.95
VAT		2.82
Mark-up		4.84
Duty		1.05
Distribution		0.17
Shipping		0.21
Wine		9.86

promotion to DOCG status does nothing more than eliminate these fraudsters and take us back to the wonderfully frothy, fruit-bursting young wine that is Asti at its best, then I'll gladly open a bottle or two to toast its success.

BARBARESCO, DOCG (Piedmont; red) Toughness and tannin are the hallmarks of the Nebbiolo, Barbaresco's only grape, and they can often overshadow its finer points: a delicious soft, strawberryish maturity, edged with smoke, herbs and pine. The Riserva category (four years' aging) still exists, but most producers these days stick to the minimum two years' aging (one in wood) the law requires. When it works, the Nebbiolo can show more nuances and glints of brilliance than any other Italian grape. Best: *Luigi Bianco, Castello di Neive, Cigliuti, Glicine, Giuseppe Cortese, Gaja, Bruno Giacosa, Marchesi di Gresy, Moresco, Pasquero, Pelissero, Pertinace, Pio Cesare, Produttori del Barbaresco, Roagna, Scarpa, La Spinona* and *Vietti*.

BARBERA, DOC (Piedmont and others; red) Barbera is Italy's second most widely planted red vine after Sangiovese, and makes a good, gutsy wine, usually with a resiny, herby bite, insistent acidity and fairly forthright, dry raisin sort of fruit. It is best in Piedmont, where it has four DOCs, Barbera d'Alba, d'Asti, del Monferrato and Rubino di Cantavenna, and in Lombardy under the Oltrepò Pavese DOC; also found in Puglia, Campania, Emilia-Romagna, Liguria, Sicily, Sardinia.

BARDOLINO, DOC (Veneto; red, rosé) A growing number of pale pinky reds with a frail wispy cherry fruit and a slight bitter snap to the finish are appearing from the banks of Lake Garda, along with some lovely Chiaretto rosés and some excellent, *very* fresh-fruited Novello wines. There are also a few fuller, rounder wines like *Boscaini*'s *Le Canne* which can take some aging. As quality has risen, so have the prices. Also *Arvedi d'Emilei, Guerrieri-Rizzardi, Lenotti, Masi (Fresco* and *La Vegrona), Portalupi* and *Le Vigne di San Pietro*.

BAROLO, DOCG (Piedmont; red) Praise be – I'm a Barolo fan! Who'd have thought it: some years ago I couldn't find *any* I liked. The raw material is still the Nebbiolo grape, a monstrously difficult character that has had to be dragged squealing and roaring into the latter half of the twentieth century. But many growers are trying to stress fruit rather than raw, rough tannins and not only will these wines be enjoyable younger – in five years rather than 20 – they will (according to the basic tenet of the modern school) actually *age better* because you can't age a wine without balance, and balance, too, makes a wine enjoyable young.

It would be easy to say only expensive Barolo is any good, just as it is easy to say that only expensive Burgundy is any good. The efforts of some of our High Street buyers show that bargains can be found, though the very nature of the zone, with only a relatively small area of low-yielding Nebbiolo planted, makes it impossible to get anything respectable for under £7. But to glimpse the real majesty of Barolo, you need, as in the Côte d'Or, to step up to the great names, where the remarkable flavours of the Nebbiolo – plums and cherries, tobacco and chocolate, liquorice and violets – whirl like a maelstrom in the glass. The modernization that has taken place in the past decade – better control during fermentation, a closer eye on aging and earlier bottling – has accentuated these flavours. This is nowhere more evident than in the glorious 1989s and '90s, though the lighter '91s, due out in 1995, should be more accessible.

The area of production is small, around 1200 hectares in total, and is divided into five main communes, all with individual styles. La Morra is the largest and makes the most forward and perfumed wines, ripe and velvety from around five years. Barolo itself tends to make wines of more richness and weight, but without the concentration and structure of the wines from Castiglione Falletto, and which need aging. Monforte, the southernmost commune, is known for rich and powerful wines often needing ten years in bottle. To the east, Serralunga is famous for the tough, jaw-locking style which ages more slowly than the others.

Over the last 20 years, producers have been fighting for official classification of the top sites: the new law should do this. Many are already citing vineyards on the label; for now, the ones to look for are: Arborina, Monfalletto, Marcenasco Conca, Rocche, Rocchette, Brunate, La Serra and Cerequio (La Morra); Cannubi, Sarmassa, and Brunate and Cerequio which straddle the two communes (Barolo); Bricco Boschis, Rocche, Villero, Bric del Fiasc (Castiglione Falletto); Bussia Soprana, Santo Stefano and Ginestra (Monforte); Marenca-Rivette, Lazzarito, La Delizia, Vigna Rionda, Prapo, Baudana and Francia (Serralunga). Best producers: *Altare, Azelia, Borgogno, Bovio, Brovia, Cavallotto, Ceretto, Clerico, Aldo* and *Giacomo Conterno, Conterno-Fantino, Cordero di Montezemolo, Fontanafredda* (only its *cru* wines), *Bruno Giacosa, Marcarini, Bartolo* and *Giuseppe Mascarello, Pio Cesare, Pira, Prunotto, Ratti, Rocche dei Manzoni, Sandrone, Scarpa, Scavino, Sebaste, Vajra, Vietti* and *Voerzio*.

BIANCO DI CUSTOZA, DOC (Veneto; white) Thought of as a Soave lookalike, though I wonder if Soave isn't a Bianco di Custoza lookalike. It contains Tocai, Cortese and Garganega, as well as Trebbiano, which helps. But the lack of pressure to make any old liquid as cheaply as possible must be as important. *Gorgo, Portalupi, Santa Sofia, Tedeschi, Le Tende, Le Vigne di San Pietro* and *Zenato* are good.

BOLGHERI, DOC (Tuscany; red, white, rosé) This zone near the coast has extended its DOC from white and rosé to cover red wines based on Cabernet, Merlot or Sangiovese in various combinations, while creating a special category for Sassicaia. This wine, previously *vino da tavola*, has intense Cabernet character but higher acidity and slightly leaner profile than most New World Cabernets. It needs about eight to ten years to begin to show at its best; 1968 was the first vintage, and remains, with '72 and '82, one of the best, but '85, '88 and '90 are also excellent. Pre-1994 vintages are labelled *vino da tavola*.

BONARDA (Lombardy; red) Delicious, young, plummy red with a dark bitter chocolate twist from Lombardy and Emilia. *Castello di Luzzano* is particularly good, with great tannic length, the right fruit impact and gently peppery push.

BREGANZE, DOC (Veneto; red) Little-known but excellent claret-like red from near Vicenza. There's Pinot Nero, Merlot and Cabernet (Sauvignon and Franc), and these Bordeaux grapes produce a most attractive grassy, blackcurranty red, with a touch of cedar. Very good stuff. *Maculan* ages it in new wood, which makes it more exciting.

BRUNELLO DI MONTALCINO, DOCG (Tuscany; red) A big, strong neighbour of Chianti traditionally better known for its ridiculous prices than for exciting flavours, but slowly coming to terms with a world in which people will pay high prices, but demand excellence to go with them. The reason why the wine can be disappointing is that it can lose its fruit during the three and a half years' wood-aging required by law. But in the right hands, in a good, clean cellar, the fruit can hold out, and then the wine can achieve an amazing combination of flavours: blackberries, raisins, pepper, acidity, tannin and a haunting sandalwood perfume, all bound together by an austere richness resembling liquorice and fierce black chocolate. Such wines are a growing minority, especially with the excellent 1988 vintage, though scary prices are still the norm. The best wines come from producers like *Altesino, Argiano, Campogiovanni, Caparzo, Casanova, Case Basse, Il Casello, Castelgiocondo, Col d'Orcia, Costanti, Pertimali, Il Poggione, Talenti* and *Val di Suga. Biondi Santi* is the most famous and the most expensive producer of all but I've never had a bottle that justified the enormous cost.

CAREMA, DOC (Piedmont; red) The most refined of the Nebbiolo wines, from a tiny mountainous zone close to Valle d'Aosta. *Luigi Ferrando* is the best producer, especially his 'black label', but almost all are good – and need five to six years to be at their best.

CARMIGNANO, DOCG (Tuscany; red)
Although the advent of Cabernet Sauvignon in Tuscany is often talked of as being an entirely recent development, Carmignano – a small

enclave inside the Chianti zone just to the west of the city of Florence – has been adding in ten to 15 per cent of Cabernet Sauvignon to its wine ever since the eighteenth century. The soft, clear blackcurranty fruit of the Cabernet makes a delicious blend with the somewhat stark flavours of the Sangiovese, which is the majority grape. There is also some good toasty, creamy rosé and some *vin santo*.

NORTH-WEST ITALY VINTAGES

North-West vintages are difficult to generalize about because it isn't always easy to catch them at their best, and a good year for Nebbiolo may not have been a good one for Dolcetto. And vice versa. Also, styles of wine-making may vary from one producer to the next. In general, Dolcetto needs drinking in its youth, Barbera can last but is often at its best young, when the fruit is most vibrant, and although there are Barolo and Barbaresco wines which you can drink after five years or so, the best last for 20 years or more. Whites should be drunk as young as possible.

1995   Rain in September hampered the early maturing white varieties, including Cortese and Moscato. Dolcetto was also below par. But a sunny, warm October produced some excellent Barolo and Barbaresco.

1994   Dolcetto, Moscato and Arneis were picked in mid-September in perfect conditions, but Barbera and Nebbiolo were badly hit by rain.

1993   High hopes were dashed by October rains, but the colour is deeper and the fruit richer than in '92, and some excellent wines were made. Particularly good for Dolcetto.

1992   September rains meant grey hairs for the producers and light, early drinking wines.

1991   A very fragmented year. Those wines picked before the rains in Piedmont, Gattinara and Gavi were good. It was difficult in Lombardy but there was good Valtellina and some exceptional whites. Fair to good overall.

1990   A fabulous vintage: wines of tremendous colour, richness and perfume, Barolo and Barbaresco for long aging and delicious Barbera. Wonderful Dolcetto again.

1989   Unlike the rest of Italy, Piedmont basked in glorious sunshine in 1989. Dolcetto looks even better than in the last five (excellent) vintages, and the Barbera is very good.

1988   Dolcetto and Barbera have concentration and fruit. Nebbiolo got caught by the rain, but the good growers waited.

1987   Very good for Dolcetto and the whites, but patchy Barolo and Barbaresco.

1986   Barbaresco and Barolo are overshadowed by the great '85s but quality is good.

1985   An exciting vintage when more growers decided to emphasize fruit and perfume.

1983   All but the best are fading.

1982   Excellent, big ripe reds which have the fruit to age.

The zone rose to DOCG status in 1990. *Capezzana* is the original estate and the only one which is regularly seen over here. Its 1985 and 1988 Riservas are special.

CHIANTI, DOCG (Tuscany; red) The first few times I had real Chianti, fizzy-fresh, purple-proud, with an invigorating, rasping fruit, I thought it was the most perfect jug wine I'd ever had. It still can be. But following the introduction of DOC in 1963, vineyards expanded all over the place to meet a buoyant demand. Chianti and especially Chianti Classico suffered more than their fair share of investors who cared only about profit and knew nothing about wine.

But Chianti might have stood more chance if the chief grape, the Sangiovese, had not been debased, first by planting the sensitive vine in poor, easily workable sites, and second by the traditional admixture of too much white juice from Trebbiano and Malvasia grapes with the red. Growers could at one time legally mix in almost one-third white grapes – yes, white grapes in red wine – and the inevitable result was wines that faded before they even made it into bottle.

Thankfully, DOCG regulations now limit the proportion of white grapes to between two and five per cent. This measure seems to have stemmed the flow of thin, colourless Chianti, and own-label examples from companies like *Asda* can be very good indeed.

Another development in the Chianti region has been the emergence of Cabernet Sauvignon as a component of the red wines. Although not really permissible for more than ten per cent of the total, a number of growers use it to delicious effect, though as clonal selection of better Sangiovese develops, there may come a day when this is no longer necessary. The Chianti Classico Consorzio has set in train an operation called 'Chianti Classico 2000' which is intended to ensure that as replanting takes place only top clones of Sangiovese and Canaiolo are used. By 2000 we may well be classing Chianti Classico, at least, as one of the world's great red wines once again.

The Chianti territory is divided into seven sub-zones as follows: Classico, Colli Aretini, Colli Fiorentini, Colli Senesi, Colline Pisane, Montalbano and Rufina. Classico and Rufina are almost always marked on the label, where appropriate, but most wines from the other zones are simply labelled 'Chianti'.

CHIANTI STYLES There are two basic styles of Chianti. The first is the sharp young red that used to come in wicker flasks and just occasionally still does. This starts out quite purple-red, but quickly takes on a slightly orange tinge and is sometimes slightly prickly, with a rather attractive taste: almost a tiny bit sour, but backed up by good, raisiny-sweet fruit, a rather stark, peppery bite and tobacco-like spice. This style is traditionally made by the *governo* method, which involves adding – immediately after fermentation – either a small quantity of grapes dried on racks, or concentrated must, together with a dried yeast culture, so that the wine re-ferments. Apart from the prickle, this process leaves the wine softer, rounder and more instantly appealing, but it also makes it age more quickly.

The second type has usually been matured for several years and, in the bad old days before the advent of DOCG, had all the acidity and tannin it needed. Unfortunately the only fruit on show was a fistful of old raisins and a curious, unwelcome whiff of tomatoes. Nowadays there are enough exceptions around to reckon that the good wines are becoming the rule. The Chiantis of top estates, especially in fine vintages such as 1985, '86, '88 and '90 are gaining a range of slightly raw strawberry, raspberry and blackcurrant flavours backed up by a herby, tobaccoey spice and a grapeskins roughness that makes the wine demanding but exciting. Top estates making wines to look for include *Badia a Coltibuono, Castellare, Castello di Ama, Castello dei Rampolla, Castello di San Polo in Rosso, Castello di Volpaia, Felsina Berardenga, Fontodi,*

The price guides for this section begin on page 265.

Montesodi and Nipozzano (Frescobaldi), Isole e Olena, Pagliarese, Peppoli (Antinori), Riecine, San Felice, Selvapiana, Vecchie Terre di Montefili and Villa di Vetrice.

COLLI EUGANEI, DOC (Veneto; red, white) These hills near Padua produce an array of wines, including white and sparkling, that generally may be taken lightly, though the Vignalta estate produces a Cabernet Riserva and Merlot-based Gemola that get high ratings.

COPERTINO, DOC (Apulia; red) The blend of Negroamaro and Malvasia Nera produces robust red wines that can be both elegant and outstanding bargains. Best producer: the Copertino co-op.

DOLCETTO, some **DOC** (Piedmont; red) At its best, delicious. It's a full but soft, fresh, and dramatically fruity red, usually for gulping down fast and young, though some will age a few years. Wonderful ones come from Altare, Castello di Neive, Clerico, Aldo Conterno, Giacomo Conterno, Marcarini, Mascarello, Oddero, Pasquero, Prunotto, Ratti, Sandrone, Scavino, Vajra, Vietti and Voerzio.

ERBALUCE DI CALUSO, DOC (Piedmont; white) Half the price of Gavi, with a soft, creamy flavour, this is clean-living, plumped-out, affordable white. Boratto, Ferrando and Marbelli are good; Boratto also makes a rich but refreshing Caluso Passito.

FIANO DI AVELLINO, DOC (Campania; white) After numerous attempts to stomach this inexplicably famous wine from near Naples I got hold of a bottle of Mastroberardino's single-vineyard Fiano di Avellino Vignadora and found a brilliant spring flowers scent and honey, peaches and pear skins taste. But it may just have been a flash in the pan.

FRANCIACORTA, DOCG (Lombardy; red, white) Sparkling Franciacorta, made by the Champagne method from Pinots Bianco

and Nero and Chardonnay grapes, has become Italy's latest DOCG. Ca' del Bosco and Bellavista lead the field, though Cavalleri, Monte Rosa, Ricci Curbastro and Uberti are also recommended. The DOC of Terre di Franciacorta makes fine white from Pinot and Chardonnay, and tasty red from Cabernet, Barbera, Nebbiolo and Merlot.

FRASCATI, DOC (Latium; white) True Frascati, unfortunately, remains a mirage: most relies on bland Trebbiano or is spoilt by mass production. But with enough Malvasia to swamp the Trebbiano and careful wine-making, it has a lovely, fresh, nutty feel with an unusual, attractive tang of slightly sour cream. Antonio Pulcini is way ahead with Colli di Catone, Villa Catone and Villa Romana; his cru Colle Gaio is very special. Fontana Candida's limited releases are also worth a try.

FRIULI, some **DOC** (red, white) Six different zones (of which Friuli Grave DOC is by far the most important quantitatively) stretching from the flat lands just north of Venice right to the Slovenian border. The red wines are marked by vibrant fruit. In particular, 'international' grape varieties like Cabernet Franc and Merlot have an absolutely delicious, juicy stab of flavour; and Refosco has a memorable flavour in the tar-and-plums mould – sharpened up with a fresh grassy acidity. There is some good Cabernet from Ca' Ronesca and Russiz Superiore. La Fattoria and Collavini make excellent Cabernet and Merlot too and Pintar in the Collio area makes good Cabernet Franc. Borgo Conventi's reds are very good and worth looking out for. There are also some very good fruity and fresh whites, particularly above-average Pinot Bianco, good Pinot Grigio, Chardonnay, better Gewürz, Müller-Thurgau, Riesling Renano, Ribolla and Sauvignon, and the brilliantly nutty and aromatic white Tocai, all capturing the fresh fruit of the varietal for quick, happy-faced drinking. Prices are generally in the mid- to upper range, but they are good value, especially from names like Abbazia di Rosazzo, Attems, Borgo Conventi, Villa Russiz, Collavini, Dri,

Eno Friulia, Volpe Pasini, Gravner, Jermann, Livio Felluga, Puiatti, Ronchi di Cialla, Schiopetto. Of the big names *Collavini* is best, but getting pricy. The almost mythical Picolit sweet wine is beautifully made by *Al Rusignul* – who is the *only* producer I've found who takes this difficult grape variety seriously.

GALESTRO (Tuscany; white) A collective brand name created to mop up the Trebbiano and Malvasia no longer used in red Chianti. Low alcohol, simple, lemony, greengage taste, high-tech style, best on its home territory.

GATTINARA, DOCG (Piedmont; red) This Nebbiolo-based red from the Vercelli hills in Piedmont can be good but often has an unappealingly volatile character. *Antoniolo, Brugo, Dessilani* and *Travaglini* are reliable.

GAVI, DOC (Piedmont; white) Cortese is the grape here, Gavi the area. The wine is dry and sharp, like Sauvignon minus the tang, and fairly full, like Chardonnay without the class. So it should be a refreshing, straight-up gulper at a pocket-easy price. But restaurant chic in Italy coos over it. *Deltetto* and *Arione* are fresh, though not cheap, and the atypical oaked *Gavi Fior di Rovere* from *Chiarlo* and *Ca' Bianca* are also good.

KALTERERSEE/LAGO DI CALDARO, DOC (Alto Adige; red) Good, light, soft red with an unbelievable flavour of home-made strawberry jam and woodsmoke, made from the Schiava (alias Vernatsch) grape in the Alto Adige (alias Südtirol). It is best as a young gulper. Best producers: *Gries* co-op, *Lageder, Muri-Gries, Hans Rottensteiner, St Michael-Eppan* co-op, *Tiefenbrunner* and *Walch*.

LACRYMA CHRISTI DEL VESUVIO, DOC (Campania; red, white) The most famous wine of Campania and Naples. It can be red, white, dry or sweet: *Mastroberardino*'s is the best one to look for.

CLASSIFICATIONS

Only about 13 per cent of the massive Italian wine harvest comes under the heading of DOC or DOCG, and the regulations are treated in a fairly cavalier manner by many growers. At the same time producers, rebelling against the constraints imposed on their originality and initiative, have often chosen to operate outside the regulations and classify their – frequently exceptional – wine simply as *vino da tavola*, the lowest grade. This situation is changing, with up to 50 per cent of Italy's wines becoming subject to the law, and the so-called Super-Tuscans and other premium *vini da tavola* coming under the umbrella of regional DOCs like Toscana DOC, or more specific ones like Bolgheri.

Vino da Tavola This is currently applied to absolutely basic stuff but also to maverick wines of the highest class such as Gaja's Piedmontese Chardonnay.

Indicazione Geografiche Tipici (or IGT for short) This will apply to wines which are typical of their regions, but which do not qualify for DOC. It is equivalent to vin de pays.

Denominazione di Origine Controllata (DOC) This applies to wines from specified grape varieties, grown in delimited zones and aged by prescribed methods. Nearly all of Italy's traditionally well-known wines are DOC, but more get added every year. In future, the wines will also undergo a tasting test (as DOCG wines do now).

Denominazione di Origine Controllata e Garantita (DOCG) The top tier – a tighter form of DOC with more stringent restrictions on grape types, yields and a tasting panel. First efforts were feeble, but a run of good vintages in 1983, '85, '86, '88 and '90 gave the producers lots of fine material to work with. The revised DOCG should give due recognition to particularly good vineyard sites in future.

LAGREIN DUNKEL, some **DOC** (Alto Adige; red) Dark, chewy red from the Alto Adige (Südtirol) with a remarkable depth of flavour for the product of a high mountain valley. These intense wines have a tarry roughness jostling with chocolate-smooth ripe fruit, the flavour being a very successful mix between the strong, chunky style of many Italian reds and the fresher, brighter tastes of France. The *Gries* co-op, *Lageder, Muri-Gries, Niedermayr* and *Tiefenbrunner* are all good names to seek out. *Tiefenbrunner* also makes very good pink Lagrein Kretzer.

LAMBRUSCO, some **DOC** (Emilia-Romagna; red, white) Good Lambrusco – lightly fizzy, low in alcohol, red or white, dry to vaguely sweet – should *always* have a sharp, almost rasping acid bite to it. Real Lambrusco with a DOC, from Sorbara, Santa Croce or Castelvetro (and it will say so on the label), is anything but feeble and is an exciting accompaniment to rough-and-ready Italian food. But most Lambrusco is not DOC and is softened for the British market for fear of offending us. *Cavicchioli* is one of the few 'proper' ones to brave British shelves.

LANGHE, DOC (Piedmont, red, white) This recent DOC in the Langhe hills around Alba in southern Piedmont covers wines previously sold as *vino da tavola*. Producers of Barolo, Barbaresco and Nebbiolo d'Alba may now sell tasty young Langhe Nebbiolo at attractive prices. The DOC also applies to red Dolcetto and Freisa and white Arneis, Chardonnay and Favorita.

LUGANA, DOC (Lombardy; white) The Trebbiano di Lugana grape grown along the southern shores of Lake Garda makes whites of solid structure and appealingly fruity flavours from producers such as *Ca' dei Frati, Premiovini, Provenza, Visconti* and *Zenato.*

CENTRAL ITALY VINTAGES

1995   October sun favoured an unexpected recovery after a dismal summer; producers of Chianti, Brunello and other Tuscan reds refer to it as a miracle vintage. Also good in Umbria, the Marches and the Abruzzo, though generally better for reds than for whites.

1994   September rain stopped by the time the vintage was due, and the spring and summer had been good. All in all, probably the best year overall since 1990.

1993   Another year that did wonders for sales of the ulcer drug Zantac. Those grapes that ripened early, like the whites, or those zones, like Montalcino, where they harvest earlier, dodged the rain. Others were less lucky, though quality seems better than in 1992.

1992   Those who reduced yields have produced decent, light- to medium-bodied reds for early drinking. Carmignano was nearly as good as 1990. The Marches were also fortunate.

1991   Outstanding in Tuscany. Red and white Torgiano is very good, as are the Marches.

1990   Excellent in Tuscany: deeply coloured wines of tremendous perfume, built to last.

1989   The spring was good, the summer and early autumn wet. Buy good producers only.

1988   Anyone who couldn't make good wines this year ought to give up. Exciting reds.

1987   Reasonable reds such as Carmignano and nice young Chiantis.

1986   Some people are now rating 1986 Chianti Riserva more highly than the 1985s.

1985   Hardly a drop of rain from the Lords Test until September; some big, rich wines.

MARSALA (Sicily; fortified) This has, at its best, a delicious, deep brown-sugar sweetness allied to a cutting, lip-tingling acidity that makes it surprisingly refreshing for a fortified dessert wine. The rare Marsala Vergine is also good – very dry, lacking the tremendous concentration and deep brown texture that makes an old *oloroso seco* sherry or a Sercial Madeira so exciting, but definitely going along the same track. But a once-great name is now in decline. A few good producers keep the flag flying; *De Bartoli* outclasses all the rest, and even makes an intense, beautifully aged, but *unfortified* non-DOC range called *Vecchio Samperi*. His *Josephine Dore* is in the style of *fino* sherry.

MONTEFALCO, DOC and **SAGRANTINO DI MONTEFALCO, DOCG** (Umbria; red) Montefalco Rosso, a blend of Sangiovese, Merlot, Barbera and Sagrantino, is a tasty red that can show style. DOCG has been granted to Sagrantino, a red of great size and strength, that comes in both a dry version and a sweet Passito, made from semi-dried grapes. Both can age impressively from top producers like *Adanti*, *Antonelli* and *Caprai*.

MONTEPULCIANO D'ABRUZZO, DOC (Abruzzi; red) Made on the east coast of Italy from the gutsy Montepulciano grape, a good one manages to be citrus-fresh and plummily rich, juicy yet tannic, ripe yet with a tantalizing sour bite. Fine wines are made by producers such as *Mezzanotte* and *Pepe*, while the standard of co-ops such as *Casal Thaulero* and *Tollo* is high. Other good names to look for include *Colle Secco* (from Tollo), *Illuminati* and *Valentini*.

MORELLINO DI SCANSANO, DOC (Tuscany, red) A backwater DOC that occasionally comes up with something interesting, like *Le Sentinelle Riserva* from *Mantellassi*. With a similar grape-mix to that of Chianti, its wines have a fine, dry austerity with earthy tannins, deep, ripe fruit, and remarkable tarry spice.

MOSCATO D'ASTI, DOCG (Piedmont; white) Celestial mouthwash! Sweet, slightly fizzy wine that captures all the crunchy green freshness of a fistful of ripe table grapes. Heavenly ones come from *Ascheri*, *Dogliotti*, *Gatti*, *Bruno Giacosa*, *I Vignaioli di Santo Stefano*, *Michele Chiarlo*, *Rivetti* and *Vietti*. *Gallo d'Oro* is the most widely available.

MOSCATO PASSITO DI PANTELLERIA (Pantelleria; white) From an island closer to Tunisia than Sicily, a big, heavy wine with a great wodge of rich Muscat fruit and a good slap of alcoholic strength.

OLTREPÒ PAVESE, some **DOC** (Lombardy; red, white, rosé) This covers reds, rosés, dry whites, sweet whites, fizz – just about anything. Almost the only wine we see is non-DOC fizz, usually Champagne-method, and based on Pinot Grigio/Nero/Bianco. Most Oltrepò Pavese is drunk in nearby Milan, where regularity of supply is more prized than DOC on the label. We see some red – ideally based on Barbera and Bonarda, which is good, substantial stuff, soft and fruity – though if you happen to drink it in Milan, don't be surprised to find it's fizzy.

ORVIETO, DOC (Umbria; white) Umbria's most famous wine has shaken off its old, semi-sweet, yellow-gold image and emerged less dowdy and rather slick and anonymous. It used to be slightly sweet, rich, smoky and honeyed from the Grechetto and Malvasia grapes. Its modern, pale, dry style owes more to the feckless and uninteresting Trebbiano. I must say I'm looking forward to Orvieto getting back to its golden days and there are signs that good producers are starting to make this happen. *Scambia* is lovely, peach-perfumed wine; *Barberani* and *Palazzone* are even better. *Decugnano dei Barbi* is good, while exciting wines, fragrant, soft and honeyed, come from *Bigi*, whose *Cru Torricella Secco* and *Cru Orzalume Amabile* (medium-sweet) are exceptional and not expensive. *Antinori*'s is a typical over-modern, under-flavoured dry, though its medium version is delicious, and the

Chardonnay, Grechetto, Malvasia and Trebbiano *vino da tavola* called *Cervaro della Sala*, also from *Antinori*, is outstanding. Sweet, unctuous, noble-rot affected wines (*Antinori's Muffato della Sala* and *Barberani's Calcaia*) are rarely seen but delicious.

PIEMONTE, DOC (Piedmont, red, white) This recently introduced regional appellation applies to quality wines not covered by the established DOCs of Piedmont. The reds include Barbera, Bonarda, Brachetto and Grignolino. White wines, which may also be sparkling, come from Chardonnay, Cortese, Moscato, Pinot Bianco, Pinto Grigio and Pinot Nero.

POMINO, DOC (Tuscany; red, white) A DOC for red, white and the dessert wine *vin santo* in the Rufina area of Chianti. The red, based on Sangiovese with Canaiolo, Cabernet and Merlot, becomes rich, soft, velvety and spicy with age. The only producers are *Frescobaldi* and *Giuntini*.

PROSECCO, some **DOC** (Veneto; white) This can be either still or sparkling. It's a lovely fresh, bouncy, light white, often off-dry, at its best in the neighbourhoods of Conegliano and Valdobbiadene. *Sainsbury's* does a typical easy-going crowd-pleaser. Other names to look for include *Canevel, Le Case Bianche, Carpenè Malvolti, Collavini*.

ROSSO CONERO, DOC (Marches; red) A very good, sturdy red from the east coast of Italy opposite Florence and Siena. Combining the tasty Montepulciano grape and up to 15 per cent Sangiovese, Rosso Conero blends herb and fruit flavours; sometimes with some oak for richness. Producers to look for: *Bianchi, Garofoli, Marchetti, Mecvini* and *San Lorenzo (Umani Ronchi)*.

ROSSO DI MONTALCINO, DOC (Tuscany; red) DOC introduced in 1984 as an alternative for producers of Brunello who didn't want to age wine for Brunello's statutory four years, or who, like the top châteaux of Bordeaux, wanted to make a 'second wine'. Softer, more approachable and cheaper than Brunello di Montalcino.

ROSSO DI MONTEPULCIANO, DOC (Tuscany; red) This is to Vino Nobile de Montepulciano what Rosso di Montalcino is to Brunello di Montalcino: for 'lesser' Montepulciano, aged for less time in the cellar. Pretty much the same style as its big brother, but lighter and more approachable and therefore drinkable younger.

SALICE SALENTINO, DOC (Apulia; red) Impressive wines from Negroamaro and Malvasia Nera grown in the Salento peninsula: deep in colour, ripe and chocolaty, acquiring hints of roast chestnuts and prunes with age. Producers to look for are *Candido, Taurino, Leone De Castris* and *Vallone*.

SOAVE, DOC (Veneto; white) At last turning from the tasteless, fruitless, profitless mass-market bargain basement to show as an attractive, soft, fair-priced white. The turn-around in the last few years has been quite amazing. More often than not now an own-label Soave from a good producer will be pleasant, soft, slightly nutty, even creamy. Drink it as young as possible, though; it doesn't improve. *Pasqua, Bertani* and *Zenato* are supplying a lot of the decent basic stuff.

On a higher level *Anselmi* is outstanding, if expensive (try *Capitel Foscarino*) and *Pieropan*, especially single-vineyard wines *La Rocca* and *Calvarino*, is very good. Other good ones are *Boscaini, Zenato, Costalunga, Bolla's Castellaro, Santi's Monte Carbonare, Lenotti, Tedeschi's Monte Tenda* and the local co-operative's *Costalta. Anselmi* also makes a *Recioto di Soave dei Capitelli* which is shockingly good in its pungent sweet-sour way, and *Pieropan's* unoaked *Recioto di Soave* is gorgeously redolent of apricots.

SPANNA (Piedmont; red) A Nebbiolo-based wine with a lovely raisin and chocolate flavour in the old style. Even cheap Spannas are usually a pretty good bet.

TAURASI, DOCG (Campania; red)
Remarkable, plummy yet bitingly austere red
grown inland from Naples. To be honest, I'm
not totally convinced. Recent releases haven't
had the fruit or, as with the 1983, are
impossibly tannic. *Mastroberardino* is the most
important producer here.

TOCAI, DOC (Friuli; white) Full, aromatic,
with a colour that is sometimes copper-tinged,
sometimes clear as water, this grape makes
lovely, mildly floral and softly nutty, honeyed
wines in Friuli, as well as increasingly good
wines in the Veneto. Best producers include:
*Abbazia di Rosazzo, Borgo Conventi, Cà Bolani,
Livio Felluga, Caccese, Collavini, Lazzarini,
Maculan, Schiopetto, Villa Russiz, Volpe Pasini.*

TORGIANO, DOC and **DOCG** (Umbria;
red) A region south-east of Perugia whose
fame has been entirely created by *Lungarotti*.
The reds are strong, plummy, sometimes
overbearing, usually carrying the trade name
Rubesco. Single-vineyard *Monticchio* and *San
Giorgio* Cabernet Sauvignon are exciting. In

1990 Torgiano Rosso Riserva became DOCG.
White wines here are also clean and good.
Lungarotti also makes a good flor-affected
sherry-type wine called *Solleone.*

TRENTINO, DOC (red, white)This
northern region, below Alto Adige (Südtirol),
can make some of Italy's best Pinot Bianco and
Chardonnay, as well as some interesting
whites from Riesling, Müller-Thurgau and
excellent dry Muscat. But until they stop
grossly overproducing we're never going to
see the full potential. The tastiest come from
the mountainous bit north of the town of
Trento. Trento Classico DOC applies to
Champagne-method sparkling wines. Look
especially for *Conti Martini, Gaierhof, Istituto di
San Michele, Mandelli, Pojer e Sandri, Spagnolli*
and *Zeni.* Trentino also makes sparkling wine
from Chardonnay and Pinot Bianco (*Ferrari*
and *Equipe 5*), and fair *vin santo* (equivalent to
Tuscan dessert wines) comes from *Pisoni* and
Simoncelli. Reds are either from local varieties
such as Lagrein, Teroldego and Marzemino or
from international grapes like Cabernet,

NORTH-EAST ITALY VINTAGES

1995 A damp, cool late summer meant a small crop of fair to middling whites in Friuli-
Venezia Giulia and Trentino-Alto Adige. Valpolicella was outstanding, as was Amarone and
Recioto.

1994 Drought was followed by rain in September. There will be some good wines, but
quantities are well down.

1993 Whites from Verona, the Alto Adige and Friuli have more richness, perfume, length
– well, more of everything than the 1992s, while the reds are excellent.

1992 Whites are mostly ripe and perfumed if lacking the body of 1991, and the reds
medium-bodied and forward. Only where yields were low is the quality good.

1991 Veneto blessed its good fortune. It was more difficult in Trentino-Alto Adige, and
some excellent reds and elegant whites were made in Friuli.

1990 Very good. The best wines show impressive balance and concentration.

1989 Good, aromatic whites; the reds, though, were less concentrated.

1988 The quantity was reduced, but the quality was tremendous, in particular for reds.

1986 Good, balanced wines, but not exciting save for Amarone and Ripasso Valpolicella.

Merlot and Pinot Noir. Too often their attractive fruit is hopelessly diluted by overcropping; a pity, because some lovely Cabernet and Teroldego in particular has come from the good producers of the region, such as *Conti Martini, Foradori, Istituto di San Michele, Guerrieri-Gonzaga, Pojer e Sandri, de Tarczal* and *Zeni*.

VALPOLICELLA, DOC (Veneto; red) Uses a variety of local grapes, especially Corvina, Rondinella and Molinara. Valpolicella *should* have delicious, light, cherry-fruit and a bitter almond twist to the finish – a bit fuller and deeper than nearby Bardolino with a hint more sourness. But it's a pretty forlorn quest unless you can find *Tedeschi's Capitel Lucchine*. It's worth going for a Classico or a single-vineyard wine every time, if you can find one. The Superiore has higher alcohol, but these are wines you must drink young. Producers with good flavours are *Allegrini, Boscaini, Guerrieri-Rizzardi, Quintarelli, Le Ragose, Santi, Tedeschi, Masi* and *Zenato*.

There are a few single-vineyard wines, like *Masi's Serègo Alighieri*, which are way ahead of the 'generic' stuff. They cost more, but *Allegrini's La Grola* or *Tedeschi's Ca' Nicalo* show what Valpolicella should be about. You might also look for wine made by the traditional *ripasso* method. In this system, new wine is pumped over the skins and lees of Recioto or Amarone, starting a small re-fermentation and adding an exciting sweet-sour dimension to the taste. *Masi, Quintarelli* and *Tedeschi* all do this really well.

But the wine which can be really great is the weird and wonderful Recioto Amarone della Valpolicella. This is a wine that is imitated nowhere else. *Amaro* means bitter, and this huge wine, made from half-shrivelled Valpolicella grapes, *is* bitter, but it also has a brilliant array of flavours – sweet grape skins, chocolate, plums and wood smoke – which all sound sweet and exotic and, up to a point, they are. Yet the genius comes with that shocking, penetrating bruised sourness which pervades the wine. The good stuff is usually about three times the price of simple

Valpolicella, but it's still good value for what is a remarkable wine. If the label simply says 'Recioto della Valpolicella', the wine will be sweeter and may still be excellent but will be, to my mind, a little less strangely special. Fine examples come from producers like *Allegrini, Bertani, Masi, Quintarelli, Le Ragose* and *Tedeschi*.

VALTELLINA, DOC (Lombardy; red) Nebbiolo wine from along the Swiss border, north-east of Milan. I find it generally a little stringy, but someone must be drinking it because it has the largest output of Nebbiolo of any DOC, including all the numerous ones in Piedmont.

VERDICCHIO, DOC (Marches; white) Of Italy's numerous whites, only Soave is made in greater quantities than Verdicchio. It comes from the grape of the same name (with a little Trebbiano and Malvasia added) on the east coast opposite Florence and Siena. The wines are reliable rather than exciting – usually extremely dry, lean, clean, nutty with a streak of dry honey, sharpened by slightly green acidity. Occasionally you find fatter styles, and *Fazi-Battaglia's* single-vineyard *vino da tavola Le Moie* shows the the area's potential. There is also a Verdicchio fizz. The two leading areas are Verdicchio dei Castelli di Jesi and Verdicchio di Matelica. The rarer Matelica wines often have more flavour. Good producers: *Brunori, Bucci, Fabrini, Fazi-Battaglia, Garofoli, Mecvini, Monte Schiavo, Umani Ronchi, Zaccagnini*.

VERDUZZO, DOC (Friuli and Veneto) This is usually a soft, nutty, low acid yet refreshing light white. The DOC also includes a lovely, gentle fizz, and in Friuli Colli Orientali there are some of Italy's best sweet wines, in particular *Dri's Verduzzo di Ramandolo* and *Abbazia di Rosazzo's Amabile*.

VERNACCIA DI SAN GIMIGNANO, DOCG (Tuscany) The DOCG applies from the 1993 vintage, and officially sanctions a long-standing practice of adding up to ten per cent of Chardonnay to the blend. Can be attractively nutty, but is too often a model of bland neutrality. Exceptions are produced by the following: *Frigeni, Fagiuoli, Falchini, San Quirico, Teruzzi & Puthod* and *La Torre*.

VINO NOBILE DI MONTEPULCIANO, DOCG (Tuscany)

A neighbour of Chianti, with the same characteristics, but more so. Usually, this means more pepper, acid and tannin at a higher price; but increasingly fine Vino Nobile is surfacing, deep wines with a marvellously dry fragrance reminiscent almost of sandalwood, backed up by good Sangiovese spice, and a strong plumskins-and-cherries fruit. Time was when you wouldn't go out of your way to find it, but that's not the case any more. There's also more of it about. Best producers: *Avignonesi, Bindella, Boscarelli, Fattoria di Casale, La Casalte, Fassati, Fattoria del Cerro, Fognano, Poliziano* and *Trerose*.

VIN SANTO Holy Wine? Well, I wouldn't be too pleased with these if I were the Almighty because too much *vin santo* is vaguely raisiny and very dull. It *should* have all kinds of splendid, rich fruit flavours – apricots, apples, the richness of ripe grape skins, the chewiness of toffee, smoke and liquorice. But it's sadly rare and only *Isole* e *Olena* has provided me with this thrill so far. If you can't get a bottle of that try *La Calonica* or *Avignonesi* in Tuscany or *Adanti* in Umbria.

VINI DA TAVOLA

The category of *vini da tavola* isn't dead, but it does seem condemned to wither away as the conveniently anonymous cover for some of Italy's finest wines. The term for table wine represents a catch-all category with virtually no rules of quality control, though it had applied to more than 80 per cent of Italian production, ranging from the lowest in class to the highest.

The premium *vino da tavola* phenomenon emerged in the early 1970s with Sassicaia, the Cabernet from Tuscany that fostered a generation of renegade red wines that came to be called Super-Tuscan. The fashion spread through other regions of Italy, as winemakers adopted trendy grape varieties (mainly Cabernet, Merlot, the Pinots and Chardonnay) and avant-garde methods (including aging in small French oak barrels) that weren't permitted under the tradition-oriented rules of DOC. Since these unclassified wines represented the utmost in enterprise and creativity, they were often sold at prices that surpassed the cream of classified bottlings.

But lately the Italians, under pressure from their European partners, have begun to bring premium table wines under meaningful official appellations. Technically speaking, *vini da tavola* may be sold only with the wine's colour on the label – rosso, bianco or rosato – with no reference to vintage, grape variety or place of origin.

Nevertheless, for the next couple of years, such table wines may continue to carry geographical indications, thanks to the inevitable extension granted to producers reluctant to comply with the rules. But, after the grace period, they must either qualify under the new category of indicazioni geografiche tipiche (IGT), the Italian equivalent of the French vins de pays, or they must be brought under the DOC system. Sassicaia recently acquired a DOC of its own under the Bolgheri appellation, a precedent that other illustrious table wines seem destined to follow.

ALTE D'ALTESI A 30 per cent Cabernet, 70 per cent Sangiovese blend from *Altesino*, aged for about a year in new barriques. 1986, '88 and '90 are the years to look for.

BALIFICO *Volpaia's* 'special', two-thirds Sangiovese, one-third Cabernet Sauvignon aged for 16 months in French oak. Exciting, exotic, oaky-rich wine, rather French in its youth, more Tuscan as it ages.

CABREO IL BORGO From *Ruffino* in Tuscany, vervy wine: blackcurrants one moment to raspberries and brambles the next.

CABREO LA PIETRA This is *Ruffino's* white counterpart to Cabreo il Borgo: a succulent, oak-aged Chardonnay.

CA' DEL PAZZO Brunello and Cabernet from *Caparzo* in Montalcino. Powerful wine behind juicy blackcurrant fruit and vanilla oak.

CAMARTINA From *Querciabella,* an estate high in the hills of Chianti Classico. A blend of about 80% Sangiovese and 20% Cabernet, this is one of the best of the breed.

CARANTAN Merlot with both Cabernets, this, from *Marco Felluga* in Friuli, is big, savoury and tannic. The 1988 still needs more time.

CEPPARELLO Very fruity, rich wine from *Isole e Olena,* with the oak beautifully blended: one of the leaders of the super-Sangioveses.

CERVARO DELLA SALA (white) Chardonnay and Grechetto grapes from Umbria, made by *Antinori* and aged in French oak. Complex, nutty stuff, delicious and long-lived.

COLTASSALA *Castello di Volpaia's* Sangiovese-Mammolo blend, leaner and less rich than most. It's lovely, austere wine, needing plenty of time to soften and blossom.

FLACCIANELLO DELLA PIEVE *Fontodi's* Sangiovese, aged in barrique and with a little *governo* used. Cedary, tightly grained fruit, oak and elegance.

FONTALLORO 100 per cent Sangiovese from *Felsina Berardenga,* fatter and richer than the *Flaccianello,* with a spicy rather than a cedary oak character, which takes a long time to come out of its tannic shell.

GHIAIE DELLA FURBA Made at *Villa di Capezzana* from roughly equal parts of both Cabernets and Merlot, and better each vintage. The 1990 is outstanding, '89 less than impressive.

GRIFI *Avignonesi's* Sangiovese-Cabernet Franc blend. It's cedary and spicily rich but lacks the class of his Vino Nobile di Montepulciano. The '85 is the best yet; '88 and '90 are also good.

MAURIZIO ZANELLA Both Cabernets and Merlot, from Ca' del Bosco in Lombardy. It's expensive but it is impressive, with roasted, smoky fruit. The '88 is potentially the best, with '89 and '87 not far behind.

ORNELLAIA The creation of Ludovico *Antinori,* brother of Piero, so presumably first cousin to Sassicaia. It's mostly Cabernet Sauvignon plus some Merlot and Cabernet Franc, made in a winery built for the purpose, and prices are sky-high. Quality is pretty terrific, too, particularly in 1990.

PALAZZO ALTESI 100 per cent Brunello, barrique-aged at *Altesino* in Montalcino, packed with delicious fruit and oakiness, and though it needs five years to develop and display its full splendour, its brilliant blackberry fruit makes it drinkable much younger.

LE PERGOLE TORTE From Montevertine, the first of the 100 per cent Sangiovese, barrique-aged wines. It is intensely tannic and oaky when young, and needs at least five years to open up.

SAMMARCO *Castello dei Rampolla's* blend of 75 per cent Cabernet Sauvignon, 25 per cent Sangiovese. Magnificently blackcurranty, Sammarco is built to last.

SANGIOVETO Made from carefully selected old vines (about 40 years old) at *Badia a Coltibuono* in Chianti Classico. Yields are minute (15–20 hectolitres per hectare) giving tremendous concentration.

SASSICAIA Cabernet (Sauvignon and Franc) from *Bolgheri*, south-east of Livorno. The first vintage was 1968, and this is still one of the best years. Since the 1994 vintage this has had the DOC of Bolgheri: see page 249.

I SISTRI This barrique-aged Chardonnay from *Felsina Berardenga* in Tuscany is fresh, zingy and grapy, with a rich ice-cream core.

IL SODACCIO 85 per cent Sangiovese, 15 per cent Canaiolo from Montevertine. It could have been a Chianti, but was too oaky when young. Elegant; drink young.

I SODI DI SAN NICCOLÒ One of the most distinctive of the new wave wines., made by *Castellare*. A little rare Malvasia Nera adds sweet and floral perfume to the Sangiovese.

SOLAIA Piero *Antinori*'s attempt to match Sassicaia. A blend of 80 per cent Cabernet Sauvignon and 20 per cent Sangiovese. Sassicaia beats it for sheer beauty of flavour but Solaia does have tremendous rich fruit and a truly Tuscan bitterness to balance.

TAVERNELLE *Villa Banfi*'s 100 per cent Cabernet made from young vines at Montalcino. It has good style and varietal character.

TIGNANELLO First made in 1971 by *Antinori,* when it was Canaiolo, Sangiovese and Malvasia, it is now about 80 per cent Sangiovese and 20 per cent Cabernet. It was superb in the late 1970s, and '88 and '90 are excellent, rich, plummy and fleshy, putting this groundbreaking wine right back at the top of the Super-Tuscan league table.

TUSCAN WINERY PROFILES

ALTESINO This was one of the first of the new style producers in Montalcino, now making an excellent Brunello – the 1988 shows a return to form after an indifferent patch in the middle of the decade – and some good *vini da tavola*, notably under the name of Palazzo Altesi.

ANTINORI Indisputably one of the great names of Chianti, boasting 600 years of wine-making history. Excellent Chianti Classico from its estates Pèppoli and Badia a Passignano; it also initiated the moves towards modern wine-making in Tuscany, with the development of wines like Tignanello, the archetypal barrique-aged Sangiovese-Cabernet blend. Its Orvieto estate, Castello della Sala, is the source of exciting experiments with white grapes. The wines show terrific style, but don't expect them to be cheap.

AVIGNONESI An old Montepulciano family, but a relative newcomer to the ranks of serious producers of Vino Nobile. They also make two excellent Chardonnays: Terre di Cortona, without oak, and Il Marzocco,

oak-fermented and aged wine of considerable depth. I Grifi is barrel-aged Prugnolo and Cabernet Franc.

BANFI Oenologist Ezio Rivella's space-age winery in the hills of Montalcino, created with the money of the Mariani brothers, who took Lambrusco to the USA. Wines include Brunello di Montalcino, Pinot Grigio, Fontanelle Chardonnay, Sauvignon, Tavernelle Cabernet, Castello Banfi, a blend of Pinot Noir, Cabernet Sauvignon and Sangiovese, and Moscadello Liquoroso. New versions of Pinot Noir and Syrah will be released soon. The Banfi Spumante is one of Italy's best.

BIONDI SANTI A legendary family making a fabulously priced, but not necessarily legendary wine; however there are indications that quality is improving again, with some modernization in the cellars of its Il Greppo estate. 1988 saw its celebration of the centenary of Brunello di Montalcino.

CAPARZO One of the new wave of Montalcino estates; investment from Milan has turned it into a serious wine producer of not only Brunello di Montalcino and Rosso di Montalcino, but also an oak-fermented Chardonnay called Le Grance, and Ca' del Pazzo, a barrique-aged blend of Cabernet Sauvignon and Sangiovese.

CASTELLO DI AMA Excellent single-vineyard Chianti Classico: San Lorenzo, La Casuccia, Bellavista; also a Merlot that had critics raving in 1990. Promising Chardonnay and Pinot Grigio.

FATTORIA DEI BARBI is owned by one of the old Montalcinese families, the Colombinis. Traditional methods produce serious Brunello and Rosso di Montalcino, as well as Brusco dei Barbi, and a single-vineyard wine, Vigna Fiore.

FATTORIA DEL CERRO Traditional producer of Vino Nobile, now experimenting with barriques. Its best wine remains the DOCG Vino Nobile: both 1985 and '86 were excellent and '88 will be even better.

FELSINA BERARDENGA Winery very much on the up. Vigneto Rancia is a single-vineyard Chianti, I Sistri a barrique-aged Chardonnay. Fontalloro is a Sangiovese, aged in barrique for 12 months.

FONTODI Sleek Sangiovese, in the form of single-estate Chianto Classico or *vino da tavola* Flaccianello, marks this out as one of Tuscany's

top names. From 1991 it has also been the source of one of Tuscany's best Pinot Noirs (best of a rather small category, that is).

FRESCOBALDI The best Frescobaldi estate is Castello di Nipozzano, with a special selection Montesodi, from Chianti Rufina. It is also the producer of some excellent Pomino, including an oak-aged white, Il Benefizio. It now owns the Castelgiocondo estate further south near Montalcino, and produces an excellent Brunello. It also makes a good white wine under the new Capitolato label. Mormoreto is a fine, Cabernet-style red.

ISOLE E OLENA Rapidly gaining a reputation for fine Chianti Classico. Also Cepparello, a rich pure Sangiovese wine, made from the oldest vines of the estate; outstanding *vin santo* and a superb varietal Syrah.

RICASOLI As well as sound Chianti, Brolio makes a host of other Tuscan wines. The Chianti is currently looking quite good.

RUFFINO One of the largest producers of Chianti. Riserva Ducale is its best wine.

TERUZZI & PUTHOD Commonly acknowledged to be the best producer of Vernaccia di San Gimignano. Its most expensive wine is the oak-aged Terre di Tufo. It also produces Chianti Colli Senesi and fresh, modern Galestro.

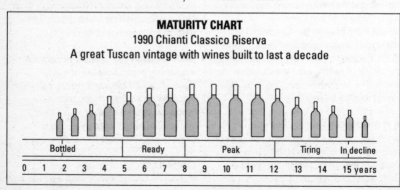

MATURITY CHART
1990 Chianti Classico Riserva
A great Tuscan vintage with wines built to last a decade

Bottled	Ready	Peak	Tiring	In decline

| 0 | 1 | 2 | 3 | 4 | 5 | 6 | 7 | 8 | 9 | 10 | 11 | 12 | 13 | 14 | 15 years |

PIEDMONT WINERY PROFILES

ABBAZIA DELL'ANNUNZIATA
(Barolo, La Morra) One of the greats. All the wines are full of excitement, strongly perfumed and develop wonderfully.

ELIO ALTARE
(Barolo, La Morra) New wave producer – wines of firm structure and tannin behind perfumed fruit. Highly successful Barolo. Very good Barbera and Dolcetto and barrique-aged Barbera Vigna Larigi and Nebbiolo Vigna Arborina.

BRAIDA-GIACOMO BOLOGNA
(Rochetta Tanaro) Saw early the potential of Barbera in barrique: cru Bricco dell' Uccellone continues to impress with depth, balance and richness. An equally good Bricco della Bigotta. Unoaked, youthful Barbera, La Monella. Good Moscato d'Asti and Brachetto d'Acqui.

CASTELLO DI NEIVE
(Barbaresco, Neive) Impeccable, finely crafted, austerely elegant Barbaresco from Santo Stefano. Barrique-aged Barbera from single cru Mattarello and firm, classic Dolcetto from three sites, the best of which is Basarin. Revelatory Arneis.

CERETTO
Known for both Barolo and Barbaresco. Barolo Bricco Rocche Bricco Rocche (yes) and Barbaresco Bricco Asili are legendary with prices to match. Also Barolos Brunate, Prapo, Zonchera, and Faset in Barbaresco. Light Barbera and Dolcetto. Arneis is disappointing.

CLERICO
(Barolo, Monforte) Top-notch producer using barriques to fine effect in Nebbiolo-Barbera blend Arte. Barolo from two crus (Bricotto Bussia, Ciabot Mentin Ginestra) are among the best moderns.

ALDO CONTERNO
(Barolo, Monforte) Great Barolo, traditionally made, slow to mature but worth the wait. Bussia Soprana is very special, Cicala and Colonello remarkable. Gran Bussia is made in the best years only. Il Favot (barrique-aged Nebbiolo), powerful Barbera, Dolcetto and Freisa also good.

CONTERNO FANTINO
(Barolo, Monforte) Guido Fantino and Diego Conterno have earned a reputation for fine Barolo from the Ginestra hillside. Rich but forward, perfumed wines; should age well.

CARLO DELTETTO
(Roero, Canale) Good understated, intriguing whites from Arneis and Favorita. Reliable Roero and Gavi.

ANGELO GAJA
(Barbaresco, Barbaresco) Uses barriques for most wines, including all Barbarescos: Costa Russi, Sorì San Lorenzo, Sorì Tildìn. In vanguard of Piedmontese

MATURITY CHART
1990 Barolo
A superb year in Piedmont, but patience is needed for the tannins to soften

| Bottled | Ready | Peak | Tiring | In decline |

0 1 2 3 4 5 6 7 8 9 10 11 12 13 14 15 16 17 18 19 20 21 22 23 24 25 years

Cabernet (Darmagi) and Chardonnay (Gaia and Rey) production. Two Barberas (straight and *cru* Vignarey), two Dolcettos (straight and *cru* Vignabajla), Freisa and top Barolo from the Marenca Rivette vineyard.

BRUNO GIACOSA (Barbaresco, Neive) Traditional wines of, at their best, mind-blowing quality, especially Barbaresco *cru* Santo Stefano and, best of all, Vigna Rionda Barolo. Rich, concentrated not overbearing, elegant. Also white Arneis and good fizz. .

MARCHESI DI GRESY (Barbaresco, Barbaresco) The leading site, Martinenga, produces Barbaresco, two *crus* – Camp Gros and Gaiun, and a non-wood-aged Nebbiolo called Martinenga; elegant wines.

GIUSEPPE MASCARELLO (Barolo, Castiglione Falletto) Superb *cru* Monprivato at Castiglione Falletto. Also Villero and other *crus* from bought-in grapes. Barbera d'Alba Ginestra is notable. Excellent inky Dolcetto comes from a different vineyard each year.

PAOLO CORDERO DI MONTEZEMOLO (Barolo, La Morra) Wines with the accent on fruit. Standard-bearer is *cru* Monfalletto from La Morra. *Cru* Enrico VI is from Castiglione Falletto, refined, elegant, scented. Also Barbera and Dolcetto.

FRATELLI ODDERO (Barolo, La Morra) Barolo, Barbera and Dolcetto from own vineyards in prime sites in the area and Barbaresco from bought-in grapes. Wines of good roundness, balance, style and value.

PIO CESARE (Barolo, Alba) Full spread of Barolo, Barbaresco, Nebbiolo d'Alba, Dolcetto, Barbera, Grignolino and Gavi. Wines are gaining elegance, losing a bit of punch but gaining harmony and balance. Experiments with barriques; also Nebbio (young-drinking Nebbiolo), Piodilei (barriqued Chardonnay).

GIUSEPPE RIVETTI (Asti, Castagnole Lanze) Smallish quantities of magical Moscato d'Asti which sell out in a flash.

LUCIANO SANDRONE (Barolo, Barolo) A small producer making tiny quantities of perfumed Barolo with lovely raspberry and black cherry flavours from the Cannubi-Boschis vineyard. Also excellent Dolcetto.

PAOLO SCAVINO (Barolo, Castiglione Falletto) Hailed locally as one of the emerging masters of Barolo, Scavino makes superb wines which combine purity of fruit with depth and structure. Barolo Bric' del Fiasc' is his top wine; Cannubi and straight Barolo are not far behind. Delicious Dolcetto and Barbera.

VIETTI (Barolo, Castiglione Falletto) Classically perfect wines of their type, with a punch of acidity and tannin, plus elegance and class. Barolo (straight plus *crus* Rocche, Villero and Brunate) and Barbaresco (*normale* plus *crus* Masseria, Rabajà) are intensely complex. Dolcetto and Barbera very good. Also one of the top Moscato d'Astis. Very good Arneis.

ROBERTO VOERZIO (Barolo, La Morra) Ultra-modern approach. Fine wines full of fruit and perfume, made with great skill, giving Roberto (not to be confused with brother Gianni) a reputation as a rising star. Produces Barolo, Dolcetto d'Alba, Barbera d'Alba, Freisa, and delicious barrique-aged Barbera-Nebbiolo blend Vignaserra, as well as fine Arneis.

MERCHANTS SPECIALISING IN ITALY
see Merchant Directory (page 424) for details

Adnams (AD), Bennetts (BEN), Bibendum (BIB), Butlers Wine Cellar (BU), Anthony Byrne (BY), Direct Wine (DI), Enotria Winecellars (ENO), J E Hogg (HOG), Lay & Wheeler (LAY), James Nicholson (NI), Reid Wines (REI), Roberson (ROB), T&W Wines (TW), The Ubiquitous Chip (UB), Valvona & Crolla (VA)

ITALY

NORTH-WEST RED

Under £5.00
1988
Barbera d'Asti Viticoltori dell'Acquese (BUT)

£6.00 → £6.99
1994
Dolcetto d'Alba Ascheri (EL)
1993
Dolcetto d'Alba Ascheri (VA)
1992
Inferno Nino Negri (HOG)
1991
Barolo Terre del Barolo (POR)
1990
Barolo Giacosa Fratelli (TES)
1986
Gattinara Berteletti (HOG)

£7.00 → £7.99
1994
Dolcetto d'Alba Prunotto (EY)
1993
Barbera d'Asti Guasti Clemente (HOG)
1992
Barolo Terre del Barolo (SAF, VIC, CO)
1990
Inferno Nino Negri (VA)
1989
Dolcetto d'Alba Giacomo Conterno (CRO)
1985
Barbaresco Fontanafredda (PEN)

£8.00 → £9.99
1994
Dolcetto d'Alba Aldo Conterno (NI)
Dolcetto d'Alba Prunotto (DI)
1991
Barolo Ascheri (OD, AME)
Barolo Fontanafredda (QUE)
1990
Barbera d'Alba Pio Cesare (DI)
Barolo Fontanafredda (HOG, BOT, WR, THR)
Barolo Gemma (SAT)
Gattinara Travaglini (EL)
1987
Barolo Borgogno (DI)
1985
Ronco de Mompiano Pasolini (CRO)

£10.00 → £12.49
1993
Barbera d'Alba Conca Tre Pile, Aldo Conterno (ENO)
1992
Barbera d'Alba Conca Tre Pile, Aldo Conterno (BEN)
Barolo Ascheri (ENO, VA)
Barolo Terre del Barolo (HAH)
1991
Barolo Oddero (ROB)
1990
Barbaresco Santo Stefano, Castello di Neive (VA)
1989
Bricco Manzoni, Rocche dei Manzoni (ELL)
1982
Barolo Riserva Fontanafredda (HOG)

£12.50 → £14.99
1993
Barbera d'Alba Aldo Conterno (NI, VA)
Vignaserra Voerzio (ENO)
1991
Barolo Ascheri (EL)
Barolo Zonchera Ceretto (DI)
Nebbiolo d'Alba Vignaveja, Gaja (REI)
1988
Barolo Pio Cesare (HOG)
Bricco Manzoni, Rocche dei Manzoni (ROB)
1986
Barbaresco Riserva Bricco Faset, la Spinona (LAYT)
Barolo Pio Cesare (DI)
1979
Barolo Montanello, Monchiero (ENO)
1976
Barolo Vigneto Villero, Ceretto (REI)

£15.00 → £19.99
1994
Nebbiolo Il Favot, Aldo Conterno (PIP)
1991
Barolo Monprivato, Mascarello (WS, ENO)
Barolo Sandrone (TAN)
1990
Barolo Bussia, Prunotto (YOU)
Sfursat Nino Negri (VIG)
1987
Nebbiolo Il Favot, Aldo Conterno (BU)
1978
Barbera d'Alba Vietti (CRO)

Barolo Gattinera, Fontanafredda (HOG)
Barolo Prunotto (CRO)
1970
Barolo Montanello, Monchiero (BU)
1967
Barolo Borgogno (ENO)

£20.00 → £29.99

1991
Barbaresco Gaja (REI)
Barolo Bussia Soprana, Aldo Conterno
   (REI, NI)
Barolo la Serra di la Morra, Voerzio (ENO)
1990
Barbaresco Bricco Asili, Ceretto (YOU)
Barbera d'Alba Vignarey, Gaja (VA)
Barbera Vignarey, Gaja (FA)
Barolo Bricco Rocche Brunate, Ceretto
   (YOU)
Barolo Bussia Soprana, Aldo Conterno
   (ELL)
1989
Barolo Bussia, Prunotto (VIG)
Barolo Bussia Soprana, Aldo Conterno
   (GAU)
1988
Maurizio Zanella, Ca' del Bosco (VA)
1985
Barbaresco Camp Gros, Tenute Cisa
   Asinari dei Marchesi di Gresy (WHI)
Barolo Monprivato, Mascarello (GAU)
Darmagi Gaja (VA)
1969
Barolo Mascarello (ENO)
1967
Barolo Ceretto (ENO)

£30.00 → £39.99

1990
Barolo Monprivato, Mascarello (BEN)
1989
Barbaresco Gaja (FA)
1986
Barbaresco Gaja (DI, CRO)
1983
Darmagi Gaja (VA)

1978
Barolo Borgogno (VA)
1974
Barolo Pio Cesare (BU)
1969
Barolo Zonchetta, Ceretto (ENO)

£40.00 → £59.99

1991
Barbaresco Gaja (TW)
1990
Barolo Ciabot Mentin Ginestra, Clerico
   (SEC)
1986
Barbaresco Sori San Lorenzo, Gaja (DI)
Darmagi Gaja (CRO)
1978
Barolo Bussia, Prunotto (RES)
1974
Barolo Monfortino, Giacomo Conterno
   (FA)
1968
Barolo Giacomo Conterno (ENO)
1964
Barolo Bussia, Prunotto (REI)
1961
Barolo Pio Cesare (ENO)

£60.00 → £79.99

1989
Barbaresco Costa Russi, Gaja (FA)
Barbaresco Gaja (LAY)
Barbaresco Sori San Lorenzo, Gaja (FA)
1986
Barbaresco Sori San Lorenzo, Gaja (TW, NO)
1982
Barbaresco Gaja (UB)
1964
Barbaresco Gaja (ENO)

£90.00 → £95.99

1979
Barbaresco Sorì Tildìn, Gaja (REI)
1978
Barbaresco Costa Russi, Gaja (REI, BEN)

c. £118.00

1978
Barbaresco Sori San Lorenzo, Gaja (TW)

NORTH-WEST WHITE

Under £6.00

1995
Gavi Fontanafredda (ENO)

1993
Arneis del Piemonte, Castello di Neive
(BOT)

£6.00 → £7.99
1995
Moscato d'Asti Bricco Quaglia, la
  Spinetta-Rivetti (AD)
1994
Arneis del Piemonte, Castello di Neive
  (VA)
Arneis del Piemonte San Michel, Deltetto
  (REI)
Arneis del Roero, Malvirà (BIB)
Favorita Malvira (AD)
Gavi Fontanafredda (ROB)
Gavi La Raja (BIB)

£9.00 → £10.99
1994
Arneis Blange Ceretto (YOU)
Arneis del Piemonte Renesio, Damonte
  (AD)

£12.00 → £17.99
1994
Arneis del Roero, Vietti (PEN)
1993
Chardonnay Rossj Bass, Gaja (REI, YOU)

c. £22.00
1993
Gavi dei Gavi, la Scolca (ROB)

NORTH-WEST SPARKLING

Under £6.00
Non-vintage
Asti Baldovino (PLA)
Asti Cinzano (HOG)
Asti Gancia (QUE)
Asti Martini (SAF, TES, CO)
Asti Sandro (WAT)
Gancia Pinot di Pinot (VA)
Gancia Spumante (VA)

£6.00 → £6.99
Non-vintage
Asti Martini (SO, WAI, VIC, TAN, FUL, UN,
  FOR, WRI, SAT, DAV, OD)

£7.00 → £7.99
Non-vintage
Asti Fontanafredda (VA)
Asti Martini (PLA, VIN, WR, THR, BOT, EL)

NORTH-EAST RED

Under £4.50
1994
Valpolicella Classico Negarine (SAI)
1992
Valpolicella Classico Tedeschi (MAJ)

£4.50 → £4.99
1995
Bardolino Portalupi (VA)
1994
Bardolino Classico Ca' Bordenis (HOG)
Cabernet Sauvignon Morago (SAI)
Valpolicella Classico Bolla (ELL)
Valpolicella Classico Castello d'Illasi, Santi
  (HOG)
1993
Bardolino Classico Superiore Masi (DI)
Valpolicella Classico Masi (OD)
Valpolicella Classico Superiore Masi (YOU)
Valpolicella Classico Superiore Rizzardi
  (HOG)
1992
Valpolicella Classico Allegrini (SOM)

£5.00 → £5.99
1994
Bardolino Classico Superiore Masi (PIP)
Valpolicella Classico Allegrini (POR)
1993
Valpolicella Classico Castello d'Illasi, Santi
  (TAN)
1992
Valpolicella Classico Superiore Valverde,
  Tedeschi (AD)
Valpolicella Classico Superiore Zenato
  (DAV)
Valpolicella Classico Tedeschi (BEN)

£6.00 → £7.99
1995
Marzemino del Trentino Letrari (WS)
Molinara Quintarelli (VA)
Valpolicella Classico Allegrini (ENO)
Valpolicella Classico Superiore La Grola,
  Allegrini (WS)
1994
Bardolino Classico Ca' Bordenis (TAN)
1993
Cabernet Grave del Friuli, Collavini (VA)
Campo Fiorin Masi (PIP)
Maso Lodron Letrari (WS)
1991
Recioto Amarone Sartori (SAI)

£8.00 → £9.99

1995
Molinara Quintarelli (AD)
1994
Marzemino di Isera de Tarczal (ROB)
1992
Valpolicella Classico la Grola, Allegrini
(SOM, HOG, ENO)
Valpolicella Classico Palazzo della Torre,
Allegrini (ENO)
Venegazzù della Casa Loredan-Gasparini
(SOM)
1991
Campo Fiorin Masi (NO, DI)
Palazzo della Torre, Allegrini (VA)
Recioto Amarone Masi (OD)
★ Recioto Amarone della Valpolicella
Classico, Rocca Sveva (UN)
Valpolicella Classico Superiore La Grola,
Allegrini (POR)
1990
Recioto Amarone Negrar (EL)
Recioto Amarone Tedeschi (MAJ, FUL)
1988
Valpolicella Classico Palazzo della Torre,
Allegrini (GAU)

£10.00 → £12.99

1991
Recioto Amarone Santi (BU)
Valpolicella Classico Palazzo della Torre,
Allegrini (LAY)
1990
Recioto Amarone Montresor (HOG)
Recioto Classico Capitel Monte Fontana,
Tedeschi (SOM)
Venegazzù della Casa Loredan-Gasparini
(ROB)
1988
Recioto Amarone della Valpolicella
Allegrini (AME, WS)
1987
Valpolicella Valpantena Bertani (AD)

£13.00 → £14.99

1991
Recioto Amarone Masi (DI)
Venegazzù della Casa Black Label,
Loredan-Gasparini (VA)
1990
Recioto Amarone della Valpolicella
Allegrini (VA)
Recioto Amarone Montresor (VA)
Valpolicella Classico Superiore Quintarelli
(AD)

1989
Valpolicella Classico Superiore Quintarelli
(BIB)
1988
Recioto Amarone Bolla (VA)
Recioto Amarone della Valpolicella
Allegrini (YOU)

£15.00 → £19.99

1992
Valpolicella Classico Superiore La Grola,
Allegrini (PIP)
1991
Recioto Classico della Valpolicella
Allegrini (ENO)
1990
Recioto Amarone Vaio Armaron,
Alighieri (PIP)
1988
Recioto Amarone Classico Superiore
Allegrini (DI)
Recioto Amarone della Valpolicella
Allegrini (TAN)
Recioto Classico Capitel Monte Fontana,
Tedeschi (DI)
1986
La Poja, Allegrini (POR)
Recioto Amarone Le Ragose (ROB)
1985
Recioto Amarone Le Ragose (VIG)
1981
Recioto Amarone Fieramonte, Allegrini
(ELL)

£20.00 → £29.99

1991
La Poja, Allegrini (ENO)
1988
La Poja, Allegrini (VA)
1986
La Poja, Allegrini (AD, BEN)
1985
Recioto Amarone Le Ragose (UB)
1980
Recioto della Valpolicella Classico
Quintarelli (AD)

£30.00 → £35.00

1986
Recioto Amarone Quintarelli (VA)
1983
Recioto della Valpolicella Quintarelli (ENO)
1979
Recioto della Valpolicella Riserva
Quintarelli (RAE)

NORTH-EAST WHITE

Under £4.00

1995
Bianco di Custoza Geoff Merrill (SAI)
Pinot Grigio Ca' Donini (VIC)
1994
Soave Classico Tedeschi (MAJ)
Soave Zonin (DAV)

£4.00 → £4.99

1995
Lugana Riserva Villa Flora, Zenato (WAI)
Pinot Grigio Ca'vit (NEW)
Soave Classico Zenato (WAI)
1994
Pinot Grigio Ca'vit (POR)
Soave Boscaini (CO)
Soave Classico Superiore Masi (YOU)
1993
Lugana di San Benedetto, Zenato (SAI)
Soave Classico Superiore Masi (YOU, DI)

£5.00 → £5.99

1995
Soave Classico Superiore Masi (PIP)
1994
Chardonnay Atesino Geoff Merrill (SAI)
Lugana di San Benedetto, Zenato (DAV)
Pinot Grigio Grave de Friuli, Collavini (UB)
Soave Classico Monte Tenda, Tedeschi (AD)
Soave Classico Zenato (DAV)
1993
Soave Classico Pieropan (UB)
Soave Classico Superiore Gini (YOU)
1992
Chardonnay Tiefenbrunner (WHI)

£6.00 → £7.99

1995
Lugana Cà dei Frati, Dal Cero (ENO)
Soave Classico Anselmi (ENO)
Soave Classico Pieropan (ENO)
Soave Classico Superiore Anselmi (VA)
1994
Lugana Cà dei Frati (SOM, POR)
Pinot Grigio Collio, Puiatti (SOM)
Pinot Grigio Grave de Friuli, Collavini (ROB)
Soave Classico di Monteforte Santi (TAN)
Soave Classico Pieropan (NI)
Soave Classico Superiore Pieropan (SOM, POR, TAN, VA)
Soave Classico Vigneto la Rocca, Pieropan (WS)
Tocai EnoFriulia (ENO)

1993
Chardonnay Lageder (NI)
Soave Classico Monte Carbonare, Tessari (AD)
Soave Classico Pieropan (BEN)
1990
Soave Classico Vigneto Calvarino, Pieropan (GAU)

£8.00 → £9.99

1995
Chardonnay EnoFriulia (PIP, ENO)
Pinot Bianco Jermann (NI)
Pinot Grigio EnoFriulia (ENO)
Soave Classico Col Baraca, Masi (PIP)
1994
Lugana Cà dei Frati (ROB)
Lugana Cà dei Frati, Dal Cero (TAN, VA, BEN)
Pinot Grigio Collio, Puiatti (VA)
Pinot Grigio Jermann (REI)
Soave Classico Monte Carbonare, Suavia (BIB)
Soave Classico Superiore Anselmi (UB)
Soave Classico Vigneto Calvarino, Pieropan (ENO, EY)
Soave Classico Vigneto la Rocca, Pieropan (ENO)
1993
Pinot Bianco Collio, Puiatti (ELL)
1990
Soave Classico Vigneto la Rocca, Pieropan (GAU)
1989
Chardonnay Maculan (REI)

£10.00 → £11.99

1995
Chardonnay Collio, Puiatti (ENO)
Pinot Bianco Collio, Puiatti (ENO)
Pinot Grigio Collio, Puiatti (ENO)
Sauvignon Collio, Puiatti (ENO)
Soave Classico Capitel Foscarino, Anselmi (ENO, VA)
1994
Pinot Grigio Collio, Puiatti (BEN)
Pinot Grigio Jermann (UB, LEA)
1993
Chardonnay Jermann (REI)
Pinot Bianco Jermann (VA, UB, ROB)
Recioto di Soave le Colombare, Pieropan (WS)
Soave Classico Vigneto la Rocca, Pieropan (AD, CRO)
1992
Recioto di Soave Capitelli, Anselmi (ROB)

£15.00 → £19.99

1994
Recioto di Soave Capitelli, Anselmi (ENO)
1993
Vintage Tunina, Jermann (ENO)
1992
Vintage Tunina, Jermann (REI)
1991
Recioto di Soave le Colombare, Pieropan
(ENO)
Vintage Tunina, Jermann (VA)

c. £26.00

1991
Torcolato Vino Liquoroso Maculan (AD)

NORTH-EAST ROSÉ

c. £5.00

1995
Bardolino Chiaretto, Portalupi (VA)

NORTH-EAST SPARKLING

Under £4.50

Non-vintage
Alionza Frizzante di Castelfranco (SUN,
BOD)

£7.50 → £8.50

Non-vintage
Prosecco di Conegliano Carpenè Malvolti
(LEA, VA)

c. £15.00

Non-vintage
Berlucchi Brut (VA)

c. £19.00

Non-vintage
Ferrari Brut (VA)

CENTRAL RED

Under £4.50

1994
Carmignano Barco Reale, Capezzana (WR)
Rosso Conero San Lorenzo, Umani
Ronchi (MAJ, CO)
1993
Chianti Rufina Villa di Vetrice (POR)
Rosso Conero San Lorenzo, Umani
Ronchi (ENO)
1992
Chianti Rufina Villa di Vetrice (SOM, EY)

1991
Chianti Colli Senesi Cecchi (VIC)
Chianti Rufina Villa di Vetrice (SAT)

£4.50 → £4.99

1994
Chianti Classico Briante (SAI)
Chianti Rufina Villa di Vetrice (VA, ENO)

1993
Chianti Classico Rocca delle Macie (MAJ)
1992
Chianti Rufina Villa di Vetrice (TAN, HAH)
1991
Chianti Rufina Villa di Vetrice (YOU, AME)
Parrina Rosso La Parrina (THR, BOT, WR)
1990
Chianti Rufina Riserva Villa di Vetrice (WR,
BOT, THR)
Parrina Rosso La Parrina (GAU)

£5.00 → £5.99

1994
Chianti Classico Aziano, Ruffino (HOG)
Chianti Classico Rocca delle Macie (NI,
DAV)
Chianti Classico Ruffino (VA)
Chianti Fattoria di Gracciano (BIB)
Chianti Rufina Riserva Tenuta di Remole,
Frescobaldi (VA)
Montefalco Rosso d'Arquata Adanti (OD)
Rosso di Montalcino Campo ai Sassi,
Frescobaldi (WAI)
Rosso di Montalcino Villa Banfi (MAJ)
Santa Cristina, Antinori (LAY, DI)
1993
Chianti Classico Castello di Fonterutoli
(WAI)
Chianti Rufina Selvapiana (WS)
Parrina Rosso La Parrina (ENO)
Rosso Conero San Lorenzo, Umani
Ronchi (BOT, WR, THR)
1992
Chianti Classico Castello Vicchiomaggio
(NEW)

Parrina Rosso La Parrina (YOU, LAY, BEN, VA)
Rosso Conero San Lorenzo, Umani
  Ronchi (VA)
Santa Cristina, Antinori (BUT)
1991
Santa Cristina, Antinori (VIC)
1990
Chianti Rufina Riserva Villa di Vetrice (EY,
  SOM, YOU, GAL, PIP, AME, ENO)
Vino Nobile di Montepulciano Cerro
  (HOG)
1989
Morellino di Scansano Poggio Valente (GAU)
1985
Chianti Rufina Riserva la Piève (SAI)

£6.00 → £6.99

1994
Chianti Classico Castello di Volpaia (EY)
Chianti Classico la Lellera, Matta (WHI)
Chianti Classico San Felice (HOG)
1993
Carmignano Barco Reale, Capezzana (ROB)
Chianti Classico la Lellera, Matta (EL)
Chianti Classico Riserva Villa Antinori
  (FUL)
Chianti Classico San Jacopo,
  Vicchiomaggio (ROB)
Chianti Classico Villa Antinori (MAJ)
1992
Chianti Classico Castello di Volpaia (REI)
Chianti Classico San Jacopo,
  Vicchiomaggio (DI)
Chianti Rufina Villa di Vetrice (HIC)
Rosso di Montalcino Col d'Orcia (POR)
1991
Chianti Classico Riserva Castello di
  Nipozzano, Frescobaldi (HOG)
Chianti Classico Villa Antinori (HOG)
Chianti Rufina Castello di Nipozzano (VA)
Chianti Rufina Riserva Castello di
  Nipozzano (OD)
Vino Nobile di Montepulciano Cecchi (SAI)
1990
Chianti Classico Riserva Antinori (NEW)
Chianti Classico Riserva Villa Antinori
  (SAI)
Chianti Classico Villa Antinori (SAI)
Chianti Classico Villa Cafaggio (GE)
1989
Chianti Classico Riserva Villa Antinori
  (BOT, THR, WR)
1985
Chianti Rufina Riserva Villa di Vetrice (AD,
  ENO, SAT)

£7.00 → £7.99

1995
Carmignano Barco Reale, Capezzana (ENO)
1994
Carmignano Barco Reale, Capezzana (AD,
  DI)
1993
Chianti Classico Brolio (ENO)
Chianti Classico Castello di Volpaia (AD,
  HAH)
Chianti Classico Fontodi (WS)
Chianti Classico Riserva Pèppoli, Antinori
  (TAN)
Chianti Classico Rocca delle Macie (AV)
Chianti Classico Villa Banfi (PEN)
Chianti Rufina Selvapiana (ENO, LAY)
Rosso di Montalcino il Poggione (AD)
Rosso di Montalcino Villa Banfi (PEN)
1992
Chianti Classico Castello di Fonterutoli
  (LEA)
Chianti Classico Isole e Olena (SOM)
Ornellaia Le Volte, Tenuta dell'Ornellaia
  (AME)
Vino Nobile di Montepulciano Avignonesi
  (WAI)
1991
Chianti Classico Riserva Villa Antinori (VA)
Parrina Reserva, La Parrina (SOM, EY, VA)
Rubesco Rosso di Torgiano Lungarotti
  (ROB, TAN)
1990
Chianti Classico Riserva Ducale, Ruffino
  (FOR, HOG)
Chianti Classico Riserva Rocca delle
  Macie (QUE)
Chianti Classico Vignamaggio (ELL)
Parrina Reserva, La Parrina (YOU, AME,
  BEN)
1989
Chianti Rufina Riserva Castello di
  Nipozzano (WHI)
1988
Chianti Classico Villa Antinori (BUT)
Parrina Reserva, La Parrina (GAU)
1986
Vino Nobile di Montepulciano Bigi (PEN)

£8.00 → £8.99

1994
Ornellaia Le Volte, Tenuta dell'Ornellaia
  (PIP, ENO)
Rosso di Montalcino Talenti (BIB)
1993
Chianti Classico Felsina Berardenga (PIP)

Chianti Classico Isole e Olena (GAL)
Chianti Classico Villa Cafaggio (WRI)
Ornellaia Le Volte, Tenuta dell'Ornellaia
(CO, VA)
1992
Chianti Classico Castello dei Rampolla (CB)
Chianti Classico Castello di Ama (VA)
Chianti Classico Fontodi (ENO)

Chianti Rufina Selvapiana (AD)
Vino Nobile di Montepulciano Bindella
(BIB)
1991
Chianti Classico Castell'in Villa (CB)
Chianti Classico Felsina Berardenga (AME)
Chianti Rufina Riserva Castello di
Nipozzano (UN)
Rubesco Rosso di Torgiano Lungarotti
(HAH)
1990
Chianti Classico Riserva Felsina
Berardenga (SOM)
Chianti Classico Riserva Santa Cristina,
Antinori (CRO)
Chianti Rufina Selvapiana (BER)
Fontalloro, Felsina Berardenga (SOM)
1989
Grifi Avignonesi (REI)
1985
Chianti Classico Riserva Montagliari (WS)

£9.00 → £9.99
1993
Chianti Classico Felsina Berardenga (ENO)
Chianti Classico Isole e Olena (ENO)
1992
Chianti Classico Felsina Berardenga (DI)
Chianti Classico Isole e Olena (NI, BEN)
1991
Chianti Classico Isole e Olena (HIC)
Chianti Classico Pèppoli, Antinori (VA)
Chianti Classico Riserva Villa Banfi (PEN)
1990
Chianti Classico Riserva Brolio (ENO)
Chianti Classico Riserva Castello di
Volpaia (AD)
Chianti Classico Riserva di Fizzano, Rocca
delle Macie (VA)
Chianti Classico Riserva Villa Cafaggio (GE)
Ser Gioveto, Rocca delle Macie (VA)
1989
Sagrantino di Montefalco, Adanti (LAY)
1986
Chianti Classico Riserva Monsanto (RAE)
1977
Chianti Rufina Riserva Villa di Vetrice (GAU)

£10.00 → £11.99
1993
Chianti Classico Pèppoli, Antinori (DI)
1992
Vino Nobile di Montepulciano le Casalte
(TAN)
Vino Nobile di Montepulciano Trerose
(DI)
1991
Vino Nobile di Montepulciano le Casalte
(BEN, UB, AD)
Vino Nobile di Montepulciano Trerose
(AV)
1990
Brunello di Montalcino Castelgiocondo
(HOG)
Chianti Classico Isole e Olena (CRO)
Chianti Classico Riserva Felsina
Berardenga (ENO)
Palazzo Altesi, Altesino (POR)
Vino Nobile di Montepulciano Avignonesi
(VA)
Vino Nobile di Montepulciano Baiocchi (VA)
Vino Nobile di Montepulciano le Casalte
(AME, ROB)
Vino Nobile di Montepulciano Riserva,
Avignonesi (REI)
1985
Tavernelle Villa Banfi (NO)

£12.00 → £14.99

1993
Grosso Senese, Il Palazzino (BIB)
1991
Brunello di Montalcino Argiano (WS, SOM)
Brunello di Montalcino il Poggione (AD)
Coltassala Castello di Volpaia (AD)
1990
Balifico Castello di Volpaia (REI)
Brunello di Montalcino Altesino (POR)
Brunello di Montalcino Val di Suga (DI)
Brunello di Montalcino Villa Banfi (PEN)
Chianti Classico Felsina Berardenga (CRO)
Chianti Classico Riserva Badia a
    Coltibuono (ELL)
Chianti Classico Riserva Fontodi (BEN)
Chianti Classico Riserva Marchese
    Antinori (AV)
Chianti Classico Riserva Vigneto Rancia,
    Felsina Berardenga (WS, YOU, ENO, BEN)
Chianti Rufina Riserva Bucerchiale,
    Selvapiana (WS)
Chianti Rufina Selvapiana (CRO)
Coltassala Castello di Volpaia (REI)
Ghiaie della Furba, Capezzana (YOU)
Vino Nobile di Montepulciano le Casalte
    (BER)
1989
Tavernelle Villa Banfi (PEN)
1988
Palazzo Altesi, Altesino (GAU)
1986
Cepparello, Isole e Olena (GAU)
1985
Bongoverno Farneta (NO)
Sangioveto Badia a Coltibuono (NO)
1983
Chianti Classico Riserva Castell'in Villa
    (UB)
Chianti Classico Riserva Rocca delle
    Macie (BUT)

£15.00 → £19.99

1993
Cepparello, Isole e Olena (ENO)
Tignanello Antinori (NI)
1992
Ghiaie della Furba, Capezzana (TAN)
1991
Brunello di Montalcino Argiano (ENO, PIP)
Brunello di Montalcino Barbi (NI)
Brunello di Montalcino Fattoria dei Barbi
    (ENO, BY)
Brunello di Montalcino Talenti (BIB)
Cabernet Sauvignon Isole e Olena (ENO)

Cepparello, Isole e Olena (REI, NI)
Flaccianello della Pieve, Fontodi (ENO)
Quercia Grande, Capaccia (VA)
Syrah Isole e Olena (ENO)
Tignanello Antinori (NI, FUL)
1990
Brunello di Montalcino Argiano (YOU, BEN)
Carmignano Riserva, Villa Capezzana
    (TAN, ENO)
Cepparello, Isole e Olena (ELL, VA, BEN)
Chianti Rufina Montesodi, Frescobaldi
    (VA)
Fontalloro, Felsina Berardenga (YOU, ENO,
    CRO, LEA)
Grifi Avignonesi (LEA)
Mormoreto Predicato di Biturica,
    Frescobaldi (RES)
Solatio Basilica Villa Cafaggio (GE)
Syrah Isole e Olena (REI)
1989
Brunello di Montalcino Barbi (EY, QUE, VIG)
Ornellaia Tenuta dell'Ornellaia (GOE)
1988
Brunello di Montalcino Altesino (CRO)
Cepparello, Isole e Olena (GAU)
Grifi Avignonesi (LEA)
I Sodi di San Niccolò, Castellare (DI, AD)
Solatio Basilica Villa Cafaggio (GE)
1986
Chianti Classico Riserva Felsina
    Berardenga (BER)
Fontalloro, Felsina Berardenga (BER)
Il Sodaccio, Monte Vertine (ROB)
Tignanello Antinori (GAU)
Vino Nobile di Montepulciano Bindella
    (CRO)
1983
Chianti Classico Riserva Santa Cristina,
    Antinori (CRO)
1979
Rubesco Torgiano Riserva Vigna
    Monticchio Lungarotti (CRO)

£20.00 → £24.99

1993
Tignanello Antinori (LEA)
1992
Ornellaia Tenuta dell'Ornellaia (PIP)
1991
Ornellaia Tenuta dell'Ornellaia (DI, TAN,
    LAY, VA)
Tignanello Antinori (VA, HAH, WR, BOT,
    TAN, LAY, GOE, DI, LEA)
1990
Chianti Classico Riserva San Felice (UB)

Flaccianello della Pieve, Fontodi (LEA)
Tignanello Antinori (HOG)
1989
Cepparello, Isole e Olena (YOU)
1988
Alte Altesi, Altesino (CRO)
Brunello di Montalcino Castelgiocondo (VA)
Tignanello Antinori, (BUT)
1983
Brunello di Montalcino Altesino (CRO)
1982
Coltassala Castello di Volpaia (CRO)
Tignanello Antinori (BUT)
1981
San Giorgio Lungarotti (CRO)
1980
Brunello di Montalcino Riserva,
   Castelgiocondo (CRO)
1978
Chianti Classico Riserva Badia a
   Coltibuono (CRO)

£25.00 → £29.99
1992
Ornellaia Tenuta dell'Ornellaia (ENO)
1991
Sammarco Castello dei Rampolla (CB)
Tignanello Antinori (AV)
1990
Chianti Rufina Riserva Bucerchiale,
   Selvapiana (CRO)
1988
Chianti Classico Riserva Felsina
   Berardenga (CRO)
Tignanello Antinori (NO, CRO)
1984
Sassicaia Incisa della Rocchetta (CRO)
1983
Tignanello Antinori (CRO)
1978
San Giorgio Lungarotti (CRO)
1975
Brunello di Montalcino Poggio alle Mura
   (PEN)
1974
Chianti Classico Riserva Badia a
   Coltibuono (CRO)
1972
Chianti Classico Riserva Badia a
   Coltibuono (REI)

£30.00 → £39.99
1992
Sassicaia Incisa della Rocchetta (FA, REI,
   LEA, LAY)

1991
Sassicaia Incisa della Rocchetta (TAN, WR,
   THR, BO, BOT, LEA, VA)
1987
Sassicaia Incisa della Rocchetta (BUT)
1986
Sassicaia Incisa della Rocchetta (GAU)
1985
Tignanello Antinori (BUT)
1982
Tignanello Antinori (CRO)
1977
Brunello di Montalcino Barbi (BU)
1975
Brunello di Montalcino Poggio alle Mura
   (BU)
1970
Vino Nobile di Montepulciano Fassati
   (CRO)
1968
Brunello di Montalcino Fattoria dei Barbi
   (REI)

£40.00 → £49.99
1993
Sassicaia Incisa della Rocchetta (LEA)
1992
Masseto Tenuta dell'Ornellaia (BU)
Sassicaia Incisa della Rocchetta (DI)
1990
Sassicaia Incisa della Rocchetta (NO)
1989
Solaia Antinori (FA)
1988
Solaia Antinori (NI)
1987
Sassicaia Incisa della Rocchetta (GOE)
1986
Sassicaia Incisa della Rocchetta (BUT)
1985
Solaia Antinori (BUT)
1980
Brunello di Montalcino Biondi-Santi (BU)
Sassicaia Incisa della Rocchetta (CRO)
1978
Tignanello Antinori (CRO)
1977
Tignanello Antinori (REI)
1971
Brunello di Montalcino Barbi (BU)
1968
Chianti Classico Riserva Badia a
   Coltibuono (CRO)
1967
Brunello di Montalcino Barbi (BU)

£50.00 → £79.99

1991
Solaia Antinori (DI)
1990
Ornellaia Tenuta dell'Ornellaia (FA)
Sassicaia Incisa della Rocchetta (BUT)
1988
Sassicaia Incisa della Rocchetta (REI, BUT, CRO)
Solaia Antinori (NO)
1986
Sassicaia Incisa della Rocchetta (GOE, BEN)
1982
Sassicaia Incisa della Rocchetta (CRO)
Solaia Antinori (CRO)
1977
Brunello di Montalcino Biondi-Santi (VA)
1976
Brunello di Montalcino Riserva, Biondi-Santi (REI)
1970
Brunello di Montalcino Riserva, Biondi-Santi (CRO)

£100.00 → £149.99

1988
Sassicaia Incisa della Rocchetta (VA)
1985
Sassicaia Incisa della Rocchetta (CRO)
1982
Sassicaia Incisa della Rocchetta (BUT)
Solaia Antinori (BUT)
1975
Brunello di Montalcino Biondi-Santi (VA)

CENTRAL WHITE

Under £4.00

1995
Frascati Colli di Catone (ASD)
1993
Orvieto Secco Conte Vaselli (TES)

£4.00 → £4.49

1994
Est! Est!! Est!!! di Montefiascone, Bigi (SAI)
Frascati Superiore Colli di Catone (OD)
Frascati Superiore Gotto d'Oro (NEW)
Orvieto Classico Secco Antinori (HOG)
1993
Frascati Superiore Monteporzio (FOR)

£4.50 → £4.99

1995
Frascati Superiore Fontana Candida (MAJ)

Orvieto Classico Antinori (DAV)
Orvieto Classico Secco Antinori (FUL, MAJ)
Orvieto Secco Bigi (VA)
Verdicchio dei Castelli di Jesi Classico, Umani Ronchi (VA)
1994
Frascati Superiore Cantine San Marco (SAI)
Frascati Superiore Fontana Candida (NI)
Frascati Superiore Monteporzio (HOG)
Orvieto Classico Abboccato Antinori (HOG)
Orvieto Secco Antinori (NEW)
1993
Galestro Antinori (HOG)
Orvieto Classico Secco Antinori (WR, BOT, THR)

£5.00 → £5.99

Non-vintage
Frascati Superiore Fontana Candida (QUE)
1995
Bianco Vergine Valdichiana, Avignonesi (BOD, SUN)
Frascati Superiore Monteporzio (VA)
Galestro Antinori (VA)
Orvieto Classico Abboccato Antinori (LAY)
Orvieto Classico Amabile Bigi (VA)
Orvieto Secco Antinori (PIP, DI)
Verdicchio dei Castelli di Jesi Classico, Casal di Serra (VA)
1994
Bianco Villa Antinori (LAY, LEA, DI)
Frascati Superiore Gotto d'Oro (LAY)
Galestro Antinori (LEA)
Orvieto Classico Secco Antinori (LAY, ROB)
Orvieto Classico Vigneto Torricella, Bigi (SOM)
Verdicchio dei Castelli di Jesi, Brunori (BIB)
Verdicchio dei Castelli di Jesi Classico, Casal di Serra (REI)
Vernaccia di San Gimignano Falchini (SEC, RAE)
1992
Orvieto Classico Abboccato Antinori (BOT, WR, THR)

£6.00 → £6.99

1995
Bianco Villa Antinori (TAN)
Orvieto Classico Abboccato Antinori (TAN)
Orvieto Classico Vigneto Torricella, Bigi (ENO, VA)
Verdicchio dei Castelli di Jesi Classico, Casal di Serra (NI)

1994
Frascati Superiore Satinata, Colle di
   Catone (DI, BEN)
Pomino Frescobaldi (HOG)
Verdicchio dei Castelli di Jesi Classico,
   Fazi-Battaglia (TAN)
Vernaccia di San Gimignano Teruzzi e
   Puthod (SOM, REI)
1993
Verdicchio dei Castelli di Jesi Classico,
   Casal di Serra (VIC)
Vernaccia di San Gimignano Falchini (BER)

£7.00 → £9.99

Non-vintage
Vin Santo Antinori (HOG, VA)
1995
Vernaccia di San Gimignano Montenidoli
   (BIB)
Vernaccia di San Gimignano Teruzzi e
   Puthod (PIP)
1994
Borro della Sala, Antinori (DI)
Vernaccia di San Gimignano Teruzzi e
   Puthod (EY, ENO, HIC, ROB, DI)
1993
Pomino Frescobaldi (UN, ROB)
1979
Vin Santo Villa di Vetrice (YOU)

£10.00 → £12.99

1993
Chardonnay I Sistri, Felsina Berardenga
   (ENO, HIC, YOU)
Chardonnay Isole e Olena (ENO)
Pomino il Benefizio, Frescobaldi (VA)
1992
Chardonnay I Sistri, Felsina Berardenga
   (AME)
Pomino il Benefizio, Frescobaldi (PIP, AD)
1989
Vin Santo Antinori (DI)

£13.00 → £16.00

Non-vintage
Vin Santo Isole e Olena (SOM)
1995
Vernaccia di San Gimignano Teruzzi e
   Puthod (VA)
1994
Vernaccia di San Gimignano Terre di Tufi,
   Teruzzi e Puthod (ENO, BEN, LEA)
1993
Chardonnay I Sistri, Felsina Berardenga
   (LAY, BEN)

1990
Vin Santo Antinori (LEA)
1987
Cabreo La Pietra Ruffino (HOG)
1968
Vin Santo Capelli (CRO)

£19.00 → £19.99

1993
Cervaro della Sala, Antinori (LAY)
1992
Cervaro della Sala, Antinori (VA)
1991
Cervaro della Sala, Antinori (DI)

CENTRAL ROSÉ

Under £7.00

1995
Carmignano Vinruspo Rosato, Capezzana
   (ENO)

CENTRAL SPARKLING

Under £4.00

Non-vintage
Lambrusco Amabile Luigi Gavioli (HOG)
Lambrusco Bianco Ca' de Medici (WAI, WAT)
Lambrusco Ca' de Medici (WAI)
Lambrusco Grasparossa di Castelvetro
   (WAI)

c. £4.50

Non-vintage
Lambrusco di Sorbara Cavicchioli (ELL)

SOUTHERN RED

Under £4.00

1995
Montepulciano d'Abruzzo Tollo (ASD)
1994
Montepulciano d'Abruzzo Umani Ronchi
   (VIC, WAI)
1993
Montepulciano d'Abruzzo Tollo (VA)
Settesoli Rosso (HOG)

£4.00 → £5.99

1994
Montepulciano d'Abruzzo Cornacchia (VA)
1993
Cirò Classico Librandi (POR)
Copertina Riserva, Cantina Copertina
   (ENO, VA)

Corvo Rosso Duca di Salaparuta (HOG, UN)
Montepulciano d'Abruzzo Cornacchia (MAJ)
Montepulciano d'Abruzzo Illuminati (HOG)
Salice Salentino Riserva Candido (MAJ)
1992
Cirò Classico Librandi (YOU)
Montepulciano d'Abruzzo Umani Ronchi (NI)
Salice Salentino Candido (VA)
Salice Salentino Riserva Candido (POR, SOM, PIP, NI, ENO)
1991
Corvo Rosso Duca di Salaparuta (FOR)

1990
Copertina Riserva, Cantina Copertina (DI)
Salice Salentino Riserva Candido (WS, REI, AME, YOU, WR, BOT, THR, BEN)

£6.00 ➜ £8.99
1994
Montepulciano d'Abruzzo Cornacchia (LAYT)
1993
Regaleali Rosso (PIP)
1992
Regaleali Rosso (DI)
1991
Aglianico del Vulture, Fratelli d'Angelo (VA, ROB, TAN)
1990
Salice Salentino Riserva Candido (KA)

c. £15.00
1987
Taurasi Mastroberardino (DI)

c. £22.00
1981
Taurasi Riserva Mastroberardino (CRO)

SOUTHERN WHITE

Under £4.00
1995
Settesoli Bianco (VA)
Vermentino di Sardegna C.S. di Dolianova (OD)
1994
Settesoli Bianco (HOG)

£4.00 ➜ £5.99
1994
Corvo Bianco Duca di Salaparuta (HOG)
Locorotondo (ENO)
Vermentino di Sardegna C.S. di Dolianova (UB)
1993
Corvo Bianco Duca di Salaparuta (UN)
Terre di Ginestra vdt (ROB)

£6.00 ➜ £7.99
1995
Corvo Bianco Duca di Salaparuta (VA)
1994
Regaleali Bianco (LEA)
Regaleali Conte Tasca d'Almerita (VA)
Terre di Ginestra vdt (AD)
1993
Regaleali Bianco (DI, ROB)

c. £11.00
1995
Lacryma Christi del Vesuvio, Mastroberardino (VA)

SOUTHERN FORTIFIED

Under £8.50
Non-vintage
Josephine Dore de Bartoli (BEN)

£10.00 ➜ £14.99
Non-vintage
Josephine Dore de Bartoli (ENO)
Marsala Vigna la Miccia, de Bartoli (ENO)
Moscato Passito di Pantelleria Tanit (CRO)
Vecchio Samperi 10-year-old, de Bartoli (ENO, BEN)

£20.00 ➜ £21.99
Non-vintage
Il Marsala 20-year-old de Bartoli (VA, ENO)
1989
Moscato Passito di Pantelleria Bukkuram, de Bartoli (CRO, BEN)

SPAIN

The new classic wines of Spain are emerging from regions we'd scarcely heard of a few years ago, and the secrets are very simple: good grapes, good soils and good wine-making

Why is Rioja famous? What was its first step on the road to stardom? You can argue about this, but I'd like to offer an answer which is also a metaphor for what has been happening in Spanish wine-making over the past three or four years.

Rioja wine as we know it today dates back to the day in 1856 when Don Camillo Hurtado de Améxaga, the Marqués de Riscal, arrived back from France at his estates in Elciego with Bordeaux barrels, a French winemaker and Cabernet Sauvignon vines. But this was not, I respectfully submit, the breakthrough.

French grapes, techniques and oak were the catalyst, but the precious metal of Rioja wine was something else: the Tempranillo grape, native to the region since time immemorial and scarcely considered as anything more than a simple country red – under which name, Tinto del País, it's still grown in Ribera del Duero. The breakthrough came when winemakers realised that, given the same care in cultivation, handling and elaboration, the Tempranillo could perform at least as well as the Cabernet in average years, and much better in drier years, of which Spain has something of a surplus. Even in the 1860s the message was there, although few outside Rioja and Navarra took notice.

One hundred and thirty years later, they were singing the same song in Galicia: the Albariño, with its putative German origins, was producing top-class wines, particularly in Rías Baixas – albeit at silly prices. But the breakthrough has come in the last 18 months as winemakers have discovered that, once again, the humble Treixadura and Torrontés in Ribeiro, the excellent Godello in Valdeorras and even the over-cropping Palomino can produce delicious, crisp,

lipsmacking white wines at relatively modest prices when harvested early, pressed immediately, fermented cool – but not too cold – and marketed in the spring following the vintage. Indeed, Galicia is proving to be a rich source of excellent quality, fruity, dry white wines: look out, too, for the new DOs of Ribeira Sacra and Val de Monterrei. I predict that Galicia – though not necessarily Rías Baixas – will win the battle to provide the 'classic' white wines of Spain.

Unless, that is, Rueda follows the lead of its new-wave winemakers. Sauvignon has made great inroads here and is available everywhere at good prices, but it is work with the Verdejo which has been the real eye-opener since the 1994 vintage. This particular grape, its juice and its wine oxidize faster than a politician distancing himself from culpability. However, satellite pressing-plants, must-chillers and rigorous attention to grape quality and speed of delivery is gradually excising the dull-and-dusty style and producing wines with more gooseberries than a chaperoned tea-dance.

DO your worst

Elsewhere, encouraging developments have been sighted in all parts, and I'd like to offer two examples to show that the new thinking is now beginning to run deep. The first is Méntrida, the most despised of all the DO wines of Spain, in the province of Toledo. Every reference book you pick up will tell you how appalling the wines are, how ill-advised it was that an area such as this should be awarded a Europe-wide quality classication, how dreadfully souply/overheated/oxidized and generally thoroughly nasty the flavours are. This is nonsense: it's true they don't have the money to build new wineries but they do prove that it's the workman rather than his tools which makes the difference between poor, adequate and half-way decent wine. I saw a winery still using concrete tinajas for fermentation, where temperature control was effected by the cellarman turning up or down the cold-water tap on his metal plates, inserted into the tank to chill the must. And his wine was honest stuff – with some acidity, plenty of fruit... and quite a lot of alcohol. Robert Parker wouldn't rate it, but the fact that they're prepared to go to extra trouble for an obscure wine for the local market shows how things are changing. Oh, and they'd never seen a British journalist before. So where did all those denigratory articles come from?

Clos call

At the other end of the scale, on a visit to the province of Tarragone in early 1996 I saw the vinous equivalent of the Holy Grail in the obscure and scarcely known town of Gratallops in DO Priorato. There was an experiment here, engendered by one René Barbier (son of the father but no relation, now, to the Cava/Penedés company, which belongs to Freixenet) which saw the establishment of a number of small bodegas growing a mixture of French, Catalan and Spanish grapes and all calling their wine 'Clos' something-or-other. Several survive, most notably Clos l'Obac, Clos Martinet, Clos Erasmus, Clos Dofi and Clos l'Ermita, and they all win prizes at international tastings far out of proportion to the size of their vineyard holdings. The last two are managed by a young winemaker from Rioja called Alvaro Palacios.

The highland vineyards of Gratallops are all based on a crumbly, limey schist, and this, according to Palacios, is the secret of its wines. This schist (say geologists) is the same stratum which stretches all the way across north-central Spain, through Ribera del Duero, Rueda, Toro and into Portugal,

Demarcated wine regions (DOs)

where it provides the subsoil for the finest port vineyards. If you wanted an argument in favour of *terreño* (what the French call *terroir*), then this is it; if you wanted a French parallel then Gratallops is, perhaps, the Haut-Médoc of Spain. They grow Garnacha, Cabernet, Tempranillo, Cariñena and Syrah mixed, matched and blended according to the individual winemaker's whim, and then give it up to a year's aging in French oak. The results range from outstanding to unbelievable. The best of all is Clos l'Ermita.

Clos l'Ermita is a vineyard at 45° to the horizontal in a natural amphitheatre high in the hills above Gratallops. Many of the vines are over 100 years old, and production per vine is pitifully small. The finished wine is likely to be 85 per cent Garnacha with five per cent each of Garnacha Blanca, Cariñena and Cabernet to make up the difference. The wine made by Alvaro Palacios has a

concentration, fruit, structure and class which leads me to compare it to Mouton-Rothschild. It's different, of course – being mainly Garnacha. And it's different in price, too. Palacios claims to have made 4000 bottles of the 1995 Clos l'Ermita and sold the lot before bottling at an opening price of 16,000 Pts (£80) per bottle. Mouton-Rothschild has seldom commanded such a price en primeur. Indeed, one wonders if the good Baronne has ever even noticed the humble Grenache grape.

What's the secret? Well, yields in Pauillac from the Cabernets, Merlot, Malbec et al average out at about 30 hectolitres per hectare. Clos l'Ermita is happy with about 16 hl/ha from its ancient Garnacha vines. So this year's formula for great wine – from Spain or anywhere else is a trinity – low yields, old vines, inspired wine-making. What do you mean, what's new? **JOHN RADFORD**

GRAPES & FLAVOURS

AIRÉN (white) This plain and simple grape hardly deserves its prominence, but it covers far, far more land than any other grape on earth. It holds sway over Spain's central plateau, where the summers are baking hot, irrigation is banned, and the vines are widely spaced to survive. As a result, the Airén must be a front-runner for another record: the *smallest* producer per hectare. Traditionally, these grapes have yielded tired, alcoholic, yellow plonk to service the bars of Madrid. But new, cool wine-making methods can transform it into some of the most refreshing basic white yet produced in Spain, with a delicious light apple, lemon and liquorice flavour.

ALBARIÑO (white) The great white hope of the DO Rías Baixas, producing lovely, peachy, fresh and delicious wines with tremendous fruit and elegant acid balance. Some authorities believe that the grape is actually the Riesling of Germany taken to Galicia on the Camino de Santiago in the 17th

century by German monks. It's also grown over the border in Portugal for Vinho Verde, but it's called Alvarinho there. The wine has had the disadvantage of being very expensive, but as vineyards mature it's possible to buy decent Albariño at reasonable prices. A good example is *Condes de Albarei* from Victoria Wine.

BOBAL (red) This is proving quite good for deep-coloured, fruity red and stylish rosado wines in Utiel-Requena and Valencia. It has reasonable acidity and relatively low alcohol, which keep the wines comparatively fresh and appetizing.

CARIÑENA (red) A high-yielding grape (the Carignan of southern France) producing dark and prodigiously tannic wine. It is believed to have originated in the region of the same name, south of Zaragoza, but plays only a small part in the DO wine which carries its name, and the region is now dominated by Garnacha and Bobal. Most Cariñena is grown in Catalonia, usually as a beefy blender. It is also a minority grape in Rioja under the name Mazuelo. With its high tannin and acidity, and its aroma of ripe plums and cherries, it complements the Tempranillo so well – adding to its aging potential – that, each vintage, the Rioja bodegas fight over the little available. Try the varietal Mazuelo from *Campo Viejo* to see what it can do.

GARNACHA (red) This is Spain's – and the world's – most planted red grape variety. It grows everywhere except Andalusia, and makes big, broad, alcoholic, sometimes peppery or spicy wines. The French, who know it as Grenache, moan about its lack of colour; but here in Spain, where burning heat and drought naturally restrict its yield, there's more dark skin in proportion to pale juice, and the wines turn out darker. They don't last well, but they can be delicious drunk young, whether as red, or fresh, spicy *rosado*. In Navarra Garnacha is giving way to Tempranillo and Cabernet. In the Rioja Baja, one or two bodegas are producing a varietal Rioja Garnacha, which offers the triple benefits of early drinking, pleasant fruit and a modest price. Garnacha's greatest wines, however, are to be found in the highland vineyards of Priorato.

GARNACHA BLANCA (white) A relation of the red Garnacha, and like the red, it makes wines high in alcohol, low in acidity and with a tendency to oxidize, so they are usually blended in with wines of higher acidity, like Viura. Good growers are grubbing it up, but its high yields keep it popular, especially among winemakers in Navarra.

GRACIANO (red) On the verge of extinction, the excellent Graciano grape has been rescued by the DOC upgrade in Rioja, where conscientious winemakers are seeking it out once again for the extra quality it gives to the wine.

MALVASÍA (white) This interesting, aromatic, flavourful grape tends, in Spain, to produce wines of low acidity that turn yellow and oxidize rapidly unless extreme care is taken. It is also low-yielding and prone to rot, so many growers in its traditional homelands of Rioja and Navarra have been ousting it in favour of the less interesting Viura. Only five per cent of the Rioja vineyard is now planted with Malvasía, although there are hints of new interest appearing from bodegas like *Marqués de Cáceres*. When well made, Malvasía wine is full-bodied, fairly strongly scented, spicy or musky, often with a hint of apricots, and sometimes slightly nutty as well. It blends well with Viura, which raises its acidity, but more and more wooded white Riojas are now based solely on Viura, which can't meld in oaky softness as successfully as Malvasía. Ten years ago, good white Rioja *reservas* really *did* taste like white Burgundy – because of the high proportion of Malvasía used in the blend. Still flying the flag for this late-lamented style are the excellent *Marqués de Murrieta* and *CVNE*, with its *Monopole* and its *Reserva*. But Malvasia is also still widely grown in the new DOs of the Canary Islands where, for generations, it's made the sweet, fortified 'Canary Sack' of Shakespeare. Today it also makes light, fresh whites, sometimes mixed with Viura/Macabeo.

MENCÍA (red) A grape native to Ribeiro and Bierzo. Believed to share a common ancestor with the Cabernet Franc, it is mainly used in light, fruity young wines, but older examples made in Bierzo before the DO was awarded indicate that it may have a future as a grape for oak aging.

MERSEGUERA (white) Valencia's mainstay white grape, also grown in Alicante and Tarragona, produces light, delicately aromatic and characterful wines.

MONASTRELL (red) Spain's second most planted red variety, used to add body and guts to many Catalonian Tempranillo blends. Produces good crops of dark, tasty, alcoholic reds and rosados right down the eastern seaboard in Alicante, Jumilla, Almansa, Yecla and Valencia – usually dry and stolid but sometimes made sweet. Jumilla's *Altos de Pio* is traditional in style, while Yecla's *Pozuelo* is more elegant.

MOSCATEL (white) Almost all Spanish Moscatel is the second-line Muscat of Alexandria rather than the top-quality Muscat à Petits Grains. Even so, it makes a lot of good wine – mostly rich and brown in Málaga, or fresh and grapy in Valencia. *Torres* makes a good, off-dry, aromatic version mixed with Gewürztraminer in Penedés, as does *de Muller* in Tarragona. The Muscat de Chipiona from *Burdon* is wonderfully rich and peachy. Moscatel is also used for sweetening cream sherries. One or two sherry bodegas are experimenting with a pure Moscatel fortified during fermentation (like port) and aged in oak. Early examples are encouraging, but it may not get the DO.

PALOMINO (white) This is the dominant grape of the sherry region, making up all of the dry sherries, and an increasing proportion of the others. Although it produces great fortified wine it is not in itself a great grape. It plays a minor role in Montilla-Moriles. As a table wine grape, it produces dull, fat stuff, even with modern winemaking techniques, but in the sherry bodegas it reacts brilliantly to the flor yeast which imparts to *fino* that characteristic bone-dry, stark-sour nose.

PARELLADA (white) Touted as the provider of all the perfume and finesse in Catalonia's whites and in Cava fizz, but Parellada doesn't honestly have a great deal to say for itself, except in the hands of the best producers. *Torres Viña Sol* is refreshing and lemony; other good examples include *Ferret i Mateu* and *Miret*.

PEDRO XIMÉNEZ (white) In decline in Jerez, where it used to be the chief component of sweet sherries. It is sometimes made into dessert wine, deeply coloured and thick. It constitutes 95 per cent of the nearby Montilla-Moriles vineyards, as well as providing richness in Málaga; otherwise used extensively for rather dull dry white wines in the south of the country.

TEMPRANILLO (red) The fine red grape of Rioja and Navarra crops up all over Spain even (for Vino de la Tierra) as far south as the province of Cádiz, but with a different name in almost every region (some may be a slightly different strain). It's Cencibel on the plains of La Mancha and Valdepeñas, Tinto Fino in Ribera del Duero; elsewhere it may be Tinto de Madrid, Tinto de Toro, Tinto del País... It is being introduced into new areas (Cariñena, Somontano, the Rioja Baja...) and extended elsewhere. The wines have a spicy, herby, tobacco-like character, with plenty of sweet strawberry or sour cherry fruit, firm acidity and some tannin. Tempranillo makes vibrantly fruity wines for gulping down young, as well as more robust wines for longer aging – and its flavours mix brilliantly with oak. It's often blended, especially with Garnacha.

VERDEJO (white) This native of Rueda on the River Duero is one of Spain's more interesting white grapes. Nowadays it's used more for table wines than for Rueda's traditional fortifieds, and makes a soft, creamy and slightly nutty white, sometimes a touch honeyed, with good, green acidity and less alcohol than Viura. The oxidation problems of the past few years seem to have been sorted out by the influence of flying winemakers with New World ideas, such as picking in the dark of the early morning, pressing in the vineyard, or transporting in pressurised isothermic containers. The 1994 and 1995 vintages from the best houses show tremendous improvement.

VIURA (white) The main white grape of Rioja, made nowadays apple-fresh and clean and, at best, rather neutral-flavoured; at worst it is sharp and grapefruity. It achieves similarly mixed results, under the name Macabeo, in Catalonia (where it also forms part of the Cava fizz blend). Made in this light, modern style, it's a wine for gulping down young, in its first year. But if you take the trouble to blend it with Malvasía, top it up with a slug of acidity and leave it to age for a while in oak barrels, the Viura can make some wonderful, rich, almost Burgundy-like white Riojas. What white Rioja used to be like, in fact.

XAREL-LO (white) One of the three main white grapes of Catalonia, this is heavier, more alcoholic and even less aromatic than the barely aromatic Parellada and Macabeo, with which it is generally blended. Some producers of Cava and still wines like to use it for the extra body and alcohol it gives to the wine, while others scorn it for its coarseness. Scorn or not, it accounts for a third of all white plantings in Penedés. In Alella, it's called Pansá Blanca.

CLASSIFICATIONS

Spain has the largest area under vine in the EU, but only 51 demarcated quality wine areas. The country is divided into 17 'Autonomías' and 50 provinces, as well as two offshore territories on the Moroccan coast. Some of these Autonomías consist of only one province (e.g. La Rioja, Navarra) and some consist of rather more – Castilla-León has nine provinces and Andalusia has eight. Fourteen of the Autonomías produce at least one quality wine, although some of the DO zones may overlap more than one province, or more than one Autonomía.

As with every country in the EU, Spain's wines divide into two grades: Table Wine (Vino de Mesa) and Quality Wine (Vino de Calidad Producido en Región Demarcada, or VCPRD). Each of these further subdivides as follows:

TABLE WINE

Vino de Mesa may not carry any kind of regional name, nor a vintage date, but may be blended from any region or regions of the bottler's choice. If the producer wants to put a vintage date on it – as with maverick winemakers such as the Marqués de Griñón in Toledo and the Yllera family in Rueda, then a legal nicety allows them to use a general regional name with no real meaning at all. In Griñón's case it's 'Vino de Mesa Toledo' (the name of a province); Yllera uses 'Vino de Mesa de Castilla-León' (the name of the whole Autonomía). **Country Wines** fall into two groups. The first comprises 27 fairly large areas known colloquially as **Vinos Comarcales**: perhaps 'County Wines' is the nearest translation into English. These have some local significance but few pretensions to promotion. The second and more important group comprises 22 **Vinos de la Tierra**, which translates as 'Country Wines' and is cognate with Vin de Pays in France, Vini Tipici in Italy, and so on. These are smaller areas, more tightly controlled and, in many cases, with ambitions to apply for DO status at some time in the future: three of them have achieved this since the last issue of this Guide.

QUALITY WINE

Denominación de Origen (DO) is roughly equivalent to the French AOC, except that it tends to be administered locally (rather in the manner of the Italian DOC) with a Consejo Regulador (Regulating Council) consisting of vineyard owners, winemakers, representatives from local and national government, oenologists and viticulturalists. Most decisions are made by the Consejo in the regions, and then subsequently sent for approval to INDO (the Instituto Nacional de Denominaciones de Origen) in Madrid.
Denominación de Origen Calificada (DOC) is a new super-category (equivalent to the Italian DOCG) for wines which have a long tradition of high quality and are prepared to submit themselves to more rigorous quality scrutiny. There is considerable argument over what this scrutiny is, or should be, and there are myriad theories about what Rioja ought to have done or could have done instead, but although the transition to DOC has attracted some criticism in and out of Spain, most bodegas are making a genuine effort to show that they're worthy of the new accolade. Sherry, Penedés and Ribera del Duero have been mooted as the next DOCs, but in best politician style, they're all hotly denying it. So it's probably true.

WINES & WINE REGIONS

ALELLA, DO (white) Catalan region gradually disappearing under suburban sprawl, whose best-known wine is the off-dry, very fruity *Marqués de Alella*. Also look for the light, pineapple-fresh Chardonnay and appley *Marqués de Alella Seco*, as well as the sparkling *Parxet*, which beats most famous Cavas hands down with its greengagey flavour.

ALICANTE, DO (red) Heavy, earthy reds made in south-east Spain from Monastrell and mostly useful as blending wines.

ALMANSA, DO (red) Falling between the high La Mancha plain and the near coastal plains of Alicante and Valencia, up-and-coming Almansa produces strong spicy reds from Monastrell and Garnacha, and even better reds from Tempranillo. The producer *Bodegas Piqueras* makes very good wines under the *Castillo de Almansa* and *Marius* labels.

AMPURDÁN-COSTA BRAVA, DO (red, white, rosado) This part of Catalonia is a major supplier to the Costa Brava beaches. Seventy per cent is rosado, catering to the sun-freaks, but it also produces some so-called 'Vi Novell', supposedly modelled on the fresh, fruity style of Beaujolais Nouveau.

BIERZO, DO (red) Emergent zone growing the possibly promising Mencía grape. Older wines are pre-DO blends, so the aging potential is pretty unknown.

BINISSALEM, DO (red, white, rosado) Young and *crianza* reds from Mallorca, made from Manto Negro and Callet grapes; there are young rosados, too. Whites are lightweight, mainly from Moll, Xarel-lo and Parellada. However, the main producer, *Bodegas Franja Roja*, has invested massively in new plant and equipment, and has some experimental (and good) *crianzas* on the market. One to watch.

BULLAS, DO (red) In the province of Murcia, great big heady Monastrell reds, mostly from co-operatives, but watch out for *Las Reñas* should it appear over here – co-operative yes, everyday no.

CALATAYUD, DO (red) Mainly Garnacha reds, plus some Tempranillo, usually for drinking young. The area supplements neighbouring Cariñena and Campo de Borja, though it (generally) has slightly lower quality.

CAMPO DE BORJA, DO (red) Situated in the heart of Aragón between Navarra and Cariñena. Hefty alcoholic reds made from Cariñena and Garnacha, now making way for lighter reds and very good rosados. *Bodegas Bordejé*, the *Borja* co-op and the *Santo Cristo* co-op look promising.

MATURITY CHART
1990 Rioja Reserva
In general, Reservas are ready to drink when they are released, though they may stay at their peak for some years

Bottled		Ready		Peak		Tiring		In decline	

| 0 | 1 | 2 | 3 | 4 | 5 | 6 | 7 | 8 | 9 | 10 | 11 | 12 | 13 years |

CANARY ISLANDS By the time this book is published there will be eight DOs in the islands: Abona, El Hierro, Lanzarote, La Palma, Tacoronte-Acentejo, Valle de Güimar, Valle de la Orotava and Ycoden-Daute-Isora. Most of the wines are white (Tacoronte-Acentejo is the only serious producer of red) and mainly pleasant enough for beach consumption. There is still some sweet, fortified and vin doux naturel Malvasia ('Canary Sack'), but it seems unlikely that much of it will be seen outside the islands.

CARIÑENA, DO (red) A lot of basic red from Cariñena, south-east of Rioja, finds its way as common *tinto* into Spain's bars, but the best co-ops (they make most of it) produce pleasant, full, soft reds. The main grape is the fat, jammy Garnacha, though a certain amount of Tempranillo firms up the better reds. Whites and rosados can be pleasant, but are mostly dull. The reds of the *Bodegas San Valero* co-operative are well made, sold here as *Don Mendo* and *Monte Ducay*.

CAVA, DO (white, rosado) The Spanish name for Champagne-method fizz. Around 95 per cent of it comes from Catalonia, and the authorities in Barcelona have been given the task of supervising the Denominación de Origen for the whole of Spain. Various other small vineyard enclaves have been granted the DO, odd patches of Rioja and Aragon for instance. When Cava was promoted to DO status, several regions lost the right to use the name, and their wines (some, admittedly excellent) must now be called *Método Tradicional*. However, the two biggest outsiders, *Bodegas Inviosa* in Extremadura and *Torre Oria* in Valencia have (supposedly temporary) permission to continue using the name, even though the grapes do not come from classified Cava vineyards. Their wines are good, and their financial and political clout is probably even better.

However, most Cava comes from the top right-hand corner of Spain, and it gets criticized in Britain for its earthy, old-fashioned style. There are those who criticize the grape varieties – Xarel-lo, Parellada and Macabeo – and a number of producers add Chardonnay to help the blend, but careful wine-making seems to be a bigger factor, as evidenced by the new generation of Cavas.

RIOJA CLASSIFICATIONS

Rioja is divided into three geographical sub-regions: Rioja Alta, Rioja Alavesa and Rioja Baja: most wines will be a blend from all three. The wine's age, indicated on the label, falls into one of four categories.

Sin crianza Without aging, or with less than a year in wood; wine sold in its first or second year. (The words 'sin crianza' are not seen on the label.)

Crianza With a minimum of 12 months in wood and some further months in bottle; cannot be sold before its third year. Whites will have had a minimum of six months in cask before bottling.

Reserva Selected wine from a good harvest with a minimum of 36 months' aging, in cask and bottle, of which 12 months minimum in cask. It cannot leave the bodega until the fifth year after the vintage. Whites have at least six months in cask, and 24 months' aging in total.

Gran Reserva Wine from an excellent vintage (supposedly) that will stand up to aging: 24 months minimum in cask and 36 months in bottle, or vice-versa. It cannot leave the bodega until the sixth year after the vintage. White wines have six months in cask and 48 months' aging in total.

Some companies are starting to turn out fresher, less earthy Cavas by better wine-making and less excessive aging, and by including some Chardonnay; *Cavas Hill, Codorníu, Juvé y Camps, Mont Marçal* and *Rovellats* look hopeful, though there's a distressing trend to raise prices with the use of Chardonnay. But most are stuck with their grape varieties, none of which will ever be renowned for its perfume or fruit. Most appetizing are *Cavas Hill Reserva Oro Brut Natur, Codorníu Première Cuvée Brut, Mont Marçal Cava Nature* (and *Chardonnay*), *Parxet, Raïmat, Segura Viudas* and *Rovellats, Freixenet* and its subsidiary company *Condé de Caralt*.

CEBREROS, (DEp, 1986) Vino de la Tierra (red) In Castilla-León, a source of good, honest local wines, mostly red and cheap. DEp means Provisional Denominación Específica. But it's still VdlT as far as the law's concerned.

CIGALES, DO (red, rosado) Near Ribera del Duero, famed for rosados but with some serious reds as well, made from Tempranillo/Garnacha mixes.

CHACOLÍ, DO (red, white) There are two of these, made in the neighbouring north-coast Basque provinces of Guipúzcoa (or Gipuzkoa) and Vizcaya (Bizkaia): Chacolí de Getaria (the local spelling is Getariako Txakolina) and Chacolí de Bizcaia (Bizkaiko Txakolina) respectively. They're sharp, fresh and uncomplicated with the local seafood and are made from the (unpronounceable) Hondarribi Zuri grape. They're seldom seen outside the area, however.

CONCA DE BARBERÁ, DO (red, white) In the highlands inland from Penedés, this region has the potential for some excellent red wines. First seen in Britain is a Merlot from *Concavins SA*, which shows very well indeed what might be accomplished here. A pioneer of 'double vintaging', this bodega now has Hugh Ryman making the Santara brand weeks before the main crop is picked.

CONDADO DE HUELVA, DO (white, fortified) Faces Jerez across the Guadalquivir river, with broadly similar climate and soils. Wines not unlike Montilla are made and mostly drunk locally, though some reaches here. Tesco's *Tio Cani* is the sort of thing.

COSTERS DEL SEGRE, DO (red, white) Formerly a virtual one-producer DO (*Raïmat*) in the Catalan province of Lérida. It's desert, but has been irrigated to grow cereals, fruit and vines, despite the fact that irrigation is banned both in Spain and in the EU for DO wines. But there are two let-out clauses: if your vineyard is 'experimental', or if you can claim unusual local conditions, you can turn on the tap. *Raïmat Abadía*, based on Cabernet Sauvignon, Tempranillo and Garnacha and aged in oak, is normally good, as is the Pinot Noir. The Cabernet Sauvignon is also very good – ripe but light, blackcurranty-oaky wine. The Tempranillo isn't so very different; Merlot is plummy and rich. Whites include the light, lemony, gently oaked Chardonnay, as well as a good sparkler, Chardonnay Blanc de Blancs. *Castell del Remei*, producing Cabernet, Merlot, Chardonnay, Macabeo and Tempranillo, is now also in Britain.

JUMILLA, DO (red) Usually a palate-buster of a red from super-ripe Monastrell grapes grown in the dust bowls of Murcia. Much of it is sold in bulk for beefing up blends elsewhere. However, French investment is now creating a new fresh-flavoured red style. The *Condestable* brands, *Castillo de Jumilla* and *Con Sello*, are quite good and gentle as is the ripe, plummy *Taja* from French merchants *Mahler-Besse*. The *San Isidro* co-operative is the biggest in Spain.

LANZAROTE, DO See Canary Islands.

MÁLAGA, DO (fortified) We don't see much Málaga here – in fact no-one sees much anywhere because Malaga's wine industry is beset by encroaching tourism. Málaga is usually full, brown and sweet in a raisiny, but not a gooey way and is slightly smoky too. There is some dry Málaga, but you'll have to take a long

weekend on the Costa del Sol to see much. *Scholtz Hermanos* has closed, leaving only one producer, *Bodega López Hermanos,* of any size. It has substantial soleras of old wines. Enjoy it.

LA MANCHA, DO (red, white) Spain's enormous central plateau – making 40 per cent of all its wine – is bringing in cool fermentation and drawing out unexpectedly fresh flavours – and at rock-bottom prices. Some are bland, but fresh and fruity, or else surprisingly young and bright-eyed. Only ten per cent is red, most of which is pale semi-red plonk for the bars of Madrid. The reds *can* be enjoyable, yet so far only *Vinicola de Castilla, Cueva del Granero* and *Bodegas Rodriguez & Berger* are proving this with any regularity. *Arboles de Castillejo* from *Bodegas Torres Filoso* is a Tempranillo worth a try. But you have to catch them *very* young. In 1993 a government commission was set up with a three-year brief to split La Mancha into (probably) three DOs, each with its own Consejo Regulador, to speed up the quality process throughout the region. It should have reported by the summer of 1996. Best: *Casa la Teja, Castillo de Alhambra, Lazarillo, Señorío de Guadianeja, Viña Santa Elena, Yuntero, Zagarrón.*

MANCHUELA, (DOp, 1982) Vino de la Tierra (red) Mainly traditional-style robust red wines made from the Bobal between Madrid and Valencia. Look out for *Viñaclar* and *Montefiel* from the giant *Bodegas y Bebidas* group – it's a ripe, plummy, good-value red which points the way for this region.

MÉNTRIDA, DO (red) Strong, sturdy reds produced bang in the middle of Spain.

MONTILLA-MORILES, DO (fortified) Montilla wines are usually thought of as lower-priced – and lower-strength – sherry lookalikes but there is a great deal of quite good wine here. The problem is getting any UK retailer to ship it. In general the dry wines, from Pedro Ximénez grapes, do not have the bite of really good sherry, but some of the mediums and sweets can be all right.

NAVARRA, DO (red, white, rosado) This large region just north of Rioja grows the same grapes, but with more Garnacha. The officially funded experimental winery here, EVENA, is one of the most impressive in Europe, and its influence is already showing, with Garnacha giving way to Tempranillo and Cabernet.

The best red is the single-estate *Magaña,* which has Cabernet and Merlot, not really DO-permitted varieties. Other potentially good names are *Chivite* and *Bodegas Príncipe de Viana,* which also uses the label *Agramont. Monte Ory* and *Bodegas Ochoa* are now much fresher. *Vinicola Navarra* makes old-fashioned, oaky reds – look for *Castillo de Tiebas* – and the modernized *Bodegas Irache* is producing both fruity and oak-aged styles. The whites used to be mostly very ordinary, cool-fermented, neutral Viura which died in the bottle waiting for someone to buy it. However, young and fresh white Navarra is pleasant and slurpable, and serious work at EVENA and by certain bodegas is producing more exciting wines. New yeast strains, some maceration on the skins and a return to tradition is making its mark: look for *Agramont* from *Bodegas Príncipe de Viana,* which is fermented in new Alliers oak. This could be the future.

LA PALMA, DO See Canary Islands.

PENEDÈS, DO (red, white, rosado) Catalonia's leading wine region. The example set by Torres and other innovative winemakers is finally starting to filter down to the general run of bodegas, although there is still some way to go. And there are high spots. *Jean León's* Cabernet Sauvignon is one such – a weighty, impressively long-lasting red, though sadly lighter since 1980. *Torres* is another, from the rich, rather sweetly oaky basic reds, right up to the exciting Cabernet Sauvignon-based *Mas La Plana* and the 100% Pinot Noir *Mas Borras.* Torres also extracts a lean, lemony, sharply refreshing flavour from his Parellada. *Jean León* makes a delicious oaky, pineappley Chardonnay. Other names to look out for are *Cavas Hill, Ferret i Mateu, Masia Bach, Mont Marçal, Vallformosa, René Barbier, Jaume Serra.*

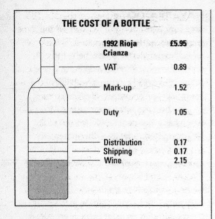

THE COST OF A BOTTLE

	1992 Rioja Crianza	£5.95
VAT		0.89
Mark-up		1.52
Duty		1.05
Distribution		0.17
Shipping		0.17
Wine		2.15

PRIORATO, DO (red) You need 13.5 degrees of alcohol here to get your DO. Cool, mountainous region, abutting the west of Tarragona. The reds from Garnacha and Cariñena are renowned – rich and full-bodied in style, and *Masia Barril, Scala Dei* and *de Muller* are worth trying. Experimental vineyards around Gratallops in the highest part of the DO are producing stunning wines from Garnacha, Cabernet Sauvignon, Merlot, Syrah et al. Look out for *Masia Duch, Clos Dofi, Clos Martinet, Clos l'Obac, Clos Mogador* and – if you've won the lottery – *Clos l'Ermita*.

RÍAS BAIXAS, DO (red, white) Three separate areas make up this DO on the Galician coast, north of Portugal. Val de Salnes, around Cambados makes whites from almost pure Albariño – fresh and fragrant when well made. *Martín Codax* is good. Further south, Condado de Tea and O Rosal make Albariño-dominated wines, sometimes with a dash of Loureiro and Treixadura. As the wines become more fashionable in Spain, the prices are rising. *Bodegas Morgadío, Santiago Ruiz, Granja Fillaboa* and *Lagar de Cervera* are all good and worth a try.

RIBEIRA SACRA, DO (white) One of Galicia's new DOs which are taking advantage of the boom in Galician white wines. Excellent and good value whites from Godello, Albariño, Trexadura, and so on.

RIBEIRO, DO (red, white) Since this Galician area was granted DO status, a zone once known for flabby dry whites has been benefitting from investment. Fresh white wine made from Treixadura and Torrontés is a distinct improvement on the old regime, though as in nearby Rías Baixas, demand is causing prices to rise. A pleasant example at a reasonable price is *Casal da Barca*, from *Bodega Alanis* (Thresher £3.49).

RIBERA DEL DUERO, DO (red) This region follows the river Duero westwards towards Portugal, with vineyards ranging from nearly 900 metres to just under 800 metres in altitude. Its three main qualities are its soil (up to 18 per cent chalk), its climate (almost Alpine in its temperature range) and the Tinto Fino (Tempranillo) grape, which ripens here two weeks earlier than in Rioja and so avoids autumn frosts. The big name is *Vega Sicilia*, a seminal bodega established in 1864 with vines and technology from Bordeaux. Its wines are arguably the best in Spain, and unquestionably the most expensive. However, new names and faces are coming to the fore: *Pesquera* from Alejandro Fernández fetches high prices (usually too high). Others include *Félix Callejo, Señorío de Nava, Viña Pedrosa, Balbás, Vega Izan, Ribeño, La Cepa Alta* and (potentially excellent) *Pago de Carraovejas*. There seems to have been genuine progress after some recent hiccups in direction, and stability provided by good leadership from the Consejo Regulador has been crowned with two excellent vintages in 1994 and 1995. The auguries are good that, when released (the first *crianzas* will be seen in early 1997) this could prove to be the organised, sustainable rebirth for which the region has been waiting since 1989.

RIOJA, DOC (red, white) Classic reds that taste of oak and vanilla sweetness. Oak – and especially American oak, the type liked in Rioja – is full of vanilla, and wine leaches it out, taking up its buttery-vanilla-toffee aromas and flavours. The actual fruit in Rioja is usually rather light, sometimes peppery, with a strawberry jam sweetness.

Practically all the Rioja on sale here comes from firms who blend and age wines from different grapes and parts of the region to a house style. Some use more of the more elegant Tempranillo, some more of the fatter, riper Garnacha, perhaps adding a little of the two minority grapes, Graciano and Mazuelo. The Rioja Alavesa region makes more delicate, scented wines; Rioja Alta is firmer, leaner, slower to show its character but slower to lose it too, and the lower, hotter Rioja Baja grows mostly Garnacha, which gets super-ripe and rather lumpish. There is now pressure from the authorities (as well as from the market) to use both new and old wood, both French and American, for aging, and to age for much shorter periods than in the past. The light has finally dawned on some bodegas that their wine actually ages very well in bottle. Best are *Bodegas Riojanas, Campo Viejo, El Coto, CVNE, Faustino, López de Heredia, Marqués de Cáceres, Marqués de Murrieta, Martínez Bujanda, Montecillo, Muga, Olarra, La Rioja Alta, Palacio, Campillo, Amézola de la Mora,* and an improving *Marqués de Riscal.*

White Rioja *can* be buttery and rich, slightly Burgundian in style. It used to be made from a blend of Viura and the richer, more interesting Malvasía, aged for several years in oak. Some were awful, tired and flat; some were wonderful. The style is now starting to make a comeback. *Marqués de Murrieta* still makes a very good example, and so, with rather less oak, does *CVNE* with its *Monopole* and *Reserva,* and *Bodegas Riojanas* with its *Monte Reál. López de Heredia* makes an old-fashioned style, while *Navajas, Viña Soledad* from *Franco Españolas* and *Siglo Gold* from *AGE* are all in the oak-aged mould. The best new white Riojas are full of fresh, breath-catching raw fruit, with the acid attack of unsugared grapefruit.

There is little credence given, as yet, to the 'estate' mentality, but it will come, as expectations rise and the over-achievers of the area determine to set an individual stamp on their wines. It's already worth trying to search out the wines from Barón de Ley, Contino and Remelluri.

RUEDA, DO (white) Rueda used to be famous, or notorious, for its heavy, oxidized, sherry-type wines made from the Palomino grape of Jerez – high on alcohol, low on fruit and freshness. But production of these *vinos generosos* is now really limited to a couple of bodegas, and the rest of the region has switched over to light table wines, picked early and fresh and fermented cool. They have a natural advantage in their local grape, the Verdejo, which makes soft, full, nutty wines, sometimes padded out with the dull Palomino, or sharpened up with the more acid Viura. Most are best young, but there are oaked ones. The most interesting Ruedas are *Marqués de Griñon,* made at *Bodegas Castilla La Vieja.* Others include *Marqués de Riscal,* which is also growing Sauvignon Blanc and re-discovering the use of oak, and *Alvarez y Diez,* which makes stylish Sauvignon and Verdejo. Rueda has also recently introduced a new Champagne-method *espumoso,* made from 85 per cent Verdejo.

SHERRY (JEREZ-XÉRÈS-SHERRY, DO) (fortified) There are two basic sherry styles, *fino* and *oloroso,* each with sub-divisions. *Fino,* from Jerez or Puerto de Santa Maria, should be pale and dry, with an unnerving dry austerity. The tang comes from a layer of natural yeast, called *flor,* that forms on the surface of the wine in the barrels. The lightest wines are selected for *fino,* and they are less fortified than the heavier *oloroso* wines. *Fino* is drunk cool and fresh, often as an apéritif.

Manzanilla is a form of *fino* matured by the sea at Sanlúcar de Barrameda. It can be almost savoury-dry, and you might imagine a whiff of sea salt – if you catch it young enough. Best: *Barbadillo, Caballero, Diez-Merito, Don Zoilo, Garvey, La Gitana, Hidalgo, La Ina, Inocente, Lustau, La Riva, Sanchez Romate, Tío Pepe.* Good Puerto *fino* comes from *Burdon* and *Osborne.*

In Britain there can be a problem with freshness, as *fino* and *manzanilla* needs to be

The price guides for this section
begin on page 294.

turned round within a year if it has 17 per cent alcohol, and six months if it has less. Own-brands tend to suffer most, but since 1992 producers must put a lot number on every bottle. Systems vary, but a common way is to print four figures to signify the year ('3' for 1993, '4' for 1994) and the day (001 for 1 January and 365 for 31 December), so 14 February 1995 would be expressed as 5044 or 0445). So one should be able to make a rough stab at the age of a bottle.

Real *amontillado* begins life as *fino*, aged in cask until the flor dies and the wine deepens and darkens to a tantalizing, nutty dryness. In the natural state, as drunk in Spain, it is *completely* dry, and a proper *amontillado* will usually say *seco* ('dry'), on the label. But we've adulterated the word in English to mean a bland, downmarket drink of no interest. Look out for *almacenista* sherries, wines from small stockholders, which can be wonderful.

Look out also for *Príncipe* and *Solear* (a *manzanilla pasada*) from *Barbadillo*, *La Goya Manzanilla Pasada* and *Amontillado Fino Zuleta* (*Delgado Zuleta*), *Amontillado del Duque* (*Gonzalez Byass*), *Hidalgo Manzanilla Pasada*, *Sandeman Bone Dry Old Amontillado*, *Valdespino's Amontillado Coliseo* and *Don Tomás*. (*Manzanilla pasada* is an old *manzanilla* beginning to take on *amontillado* characteristics.)

Real *olorosos*, made from richer, fatter wines without any flor, are deep and dark, packed with violent burnt flavours – and usually dry, though you may find *oloroso dulce* (sweet). In Britain most are sweetened with Pedro Ximénez or Moscatel. They usually come as 'Milk', 'Cream' or 'Brown'. Pale Creams are sweetened (inferior) *fino*, and are some of the dullest drinks around. For the real, dry thing, once again, look for *almacenista olorosos* from Lustau. There are a few good, concentrated sweetened *olorosos* around, like *Apostoles* and the fairly sweet *Matúsalem*, both from *Gonzalez Byass*, *Solera 1842 (Valdespino)*. Dry: *Barbadillo*, *Don Zoilo*, *Sandeman*, *Valdespino Don Gonzalo*, *Williams & Humbert Dos Cortados*. These intense old wines are one of today's great bargains.

SOMONTANO, DO (red, white, rosado) The most exciting of Spain's newly demarcated regions in the cool foothills of the Pyrenees. Attractive, lightly scented table wines, and I've tasted some decent fizz. The *Cooperativa de Sobrarbe* under the *Camporocal* label is encouraging. *Covisa* has been doing well with both Spanish and foreign grapes. Other bodegas include *Enate*, with splendid, almost Burgundian barrel-fermented Chardonnay and excellent red *crianzas* and *reservas*, and *Bodegas Pirineos*, with very good *joven* and *crianza* reds.

TACORONTE-ACENTEJO, DO See Canary Islands.

TARRAGONA, DO (red, white, rosado) After years in the wilderness some progress is discernible here, following the collapse of some old co-ops and new investment in 'village' wineries. One of the best is at the tiny village of Capçanes in the region of Falset with some superb *crianzas* made from Cabernet Sauvignon, Garnacha and Tempranillo.

TERRA ALTA, DO (red) A region which is rapidly reinventing itself. Even the sleepy village co-ops are starting to harvest decent Tempranillo, and a new breed of boutique winery is springing up beside the old classics. The best of the old is the *Gandesa* co-op, and a good example of the new is *Ferrer Escod* – inspired by a woman (Barbarà Forés – the bodega's main brand), run by a woman and with a female winemaker. There's still work to be done, but lo! The bird is on the wing.

TIERRA DE BARROS, (DOp, 1979) Vino de la Tierra (red) The great hope of Extremadura, one major bodega (*Inviosa*) has blazed a trail in export markets with its excellent *Lar de Barros* made from Cencibel and Cabernet Sauvignon. Other bodegas, most notably *Viniberia*, are following, and promotion to DO is a real prospect here.

TORO, DO (red) This can make excellent, cheap, beefy, tannic but richly fruity reds from the Tinto de Toro – yet another alias for the Tempranillo. The best wines still probably come from *Bodegas Fariña,* whose *Gran Colegiata,* is aged French-style in small oak barrels. *Bodegas Frutos Villar* and the co-op at *Morales* are also on the British market, and offering good value at more modest prices.

UTIEL-REQUENA, DO (red, rosado) The reds, from the Bobal grape, are robust and rather hot and southern in style. The rosados *can* be better – delicate and fragrant.

VALDEORRAS, DO (red, white) Galician region with young reds only, though good results are promised from the Mencía. The ordinary whites, fresh and fruity at their best, are made from Palomino and Doña Blanca, but there is work being done with Godello.

VALDEPEÑAS, DO (red) Until recently the home of soft, unmemorable reds, this DO has improved recently. The wines for drinking young are often lightened with the white Airén grape. *Crianza* and others for aging in oak must, however, be made from 100% Cencibel (Tempranillo) and turn out deep and herby with good strawberry fruit – and excellent value at very low prices, even for *gran reservas*

with a decade's aging. Look for the soft reds, aged in new oak, of *Señorio de Los Llanos, Viña Albali* from *Bodegas Felix Solís* and the fruity *Marqués de Gastañaga* and *Casa de la Viña.*

VALENCIA, DO (red, white, rosado) Large quantities of wines that are fine for the beach. Some low-priced reds from *Schenk* and *Gandia Pla* can be good and the sweet Moscatels can be tasty and good value. *Castillo de Liria,* from *Gandía,* is an attractive red.

VALLE DE MONTERREI, DO (white) Another of Galicia's new 'superwhite' DOs. Good value whites from Godello, Doña Blanca and even Palomino.

VINOS DE MADRID, DO (red) Large area split into three parts around the capital: mainly young wines, plus some *crianza* from Tempranillo and Garnacha.

YECLA, DO (red, white) Sandwiched between Jumilla and Alicante, this dry region makes fairly full-bodied reds and more dubious whites. Some decent wines come from *Bodegas Castaño,* from the cheap and cheerful *Dominio de Espinal* (Thresher) to the better *Pozuelo Reserva.*

WINERY PROFILES

ANTONIO BARBADILLO (Sanlúcar de Barrameda) ★★★★(★) Best *manzanilla* bodega. Príncipe is tangy, nutty, well-aged.

CAMPO VIEJO ★★★ Decent Riojas, soft, traditional *reservas,* and a varietal range .

VINÍCOLA DE CASTILLA (La Mancha) ★★★ Up-to-date producer turning out 14 million litres a year, including white and oaky red Señorio de Guadianeja. Soft red Castillo de Alhambra is good value.

CODORNÍU (Penedés) ★★★ Giant Cava company, owned by the Raventós family, making some of the most likeably reliable

fizzes. Good soft and honeyed Anna de Codorníu fizz, and a very good, creamy Chardonnay Cava.

CONTINO (SOCIEDAD VINÍCOLA LASERNA) (Rioja) ★★★★(★) Excellent, single-vineyard wines, mainly Tempranillo, from a 45-hectare vineyard in prime Rioja Alavesa land. Big, plummy and spicily complex, Contino is made only as *reserva* and *gran reserva.* If you see any '82, snap it up.

CVNE (Rioja) ★★★(★) This bodega is back on form with a new £12m winery. Excellent *crianza* and *reserva* whites (Monopole and CVNE Reserva), but its fame rests on its two ranges of reds: Imperial and Viña Real, from *crianza* to *gran reserva* level.

DOMECQ (Jerez)★★★★(★) One of the oldest and most respected sherry houses, with top *fino* La Ina, Botaina *amontillado* and Rio Viejo *oloroso*. Also makes Rioja.

FAUSTINO MARTÍNEZ (Rioja) ★★★ A huge, family-owned bodega which makes good reds. Look out also for the new Campillo bodega.

FREIXENET (Penedés)★★ High-tech Cava firm best known for Cordon Negro, but also making good value Carta Nevada, Vintage Brut Nature which includes some Chardonnay, and upmarket Brut Barroco.

GONZÁLEZ BYASS (Jerez)★★★★★ Huge, family-owned company, producers of the best-selling fino Tío Pepe. GB also makes an impressive top range of wines, and a Rioja, Bodegas Beronia.

CAVAS HILL (Penedés) ★★(★) Table wines as well as fresh, clean Cava Reserva Oro Brut Natur. Look out for Blanc Cru and Oro Penedés Blanco Suave whites, and Rioja-style reds, Gran Civet and Gran Toc.

JEAN LEÓN (Penedés) ★★★★ Jean León makes some of Spain's most 'Californian' wines: super-oaky, pineapple-and-honey Chardonnay, and soft, blackcurranty Cabernet Sauvignon.

JULIÁN CHIVITE (Navarra)★★★ Export-minded and state-of-the-art bodega making a clean white from Viura, attractive *rosado* from Garnacha, and a good Tempranillo-based red, all under the Gran Feudo label.

LOS LLANOS (Valdepeñas) ★★★ The brightest spot here: wonderfully soft, oaky reds. 1978 *gran reserva* is especially good.

LÓPEZ DE HEREDIA (Rioja) ★★★★ Rich, complex whites, Viña Tondonia and Viña

Gravonia, and delicate, ethereal reds, Viña Cubillo and Viña Tondonia.

LUSTAU (Jerez) ★★★★ 'Reviving Traditional Sherry Values', to use its own phrase, with its range of *almacenista* wines.

MARQUÉS DE CÁCERES (Rioja) ★★★(★) Whites are cool-fermented and fresh, and reds have less wood-aging than usual, but still keep an attractive style.

MARQUÉS DE GRIÑÓN (Toledo) ★★★★ Carlos Falcó, Marqués de Griñón, makes very good Cabernet in his irrigated vineyard, aided by advice from Professor Émile Peynaud from Bordeaux. Since 1994 Falcó has had a joint venture with Berberana in Rioja, and Griñón Rioja is looking good.

MARQUÉS DE MURRIETA (Rioja) ★★★★ A remarkable, ultra-traditional winery built into a hill outside Logroño. Red, rosados and whites are oak-aged far longer than in any other Rioja bodega; the Etiqueta Blanca wines, the youngest sold, spend at least two years in barrel, and are richly oaky, pungent and lemony. The red is soft and fruity-oaky, while the *reservas* are deep and complex. The best wines of the very top years are sold as Castillo Ygay, and may sit in barrel for 40 years.

MARTÍNEZ BUJANDA (Rioja) ★★★ Wine is produced only from the family's own vineyards, and is very well made, from the super-fresh and lively Valdemar white to the strongly oaky *reserva* and *gran reserva* Condé de Valdemar.

MONTECILLO (Rioja) ★★★(★) Since 1973, this has belonged to Osborne, the sherry company, who built a new winery to turn out an aromatic white Viña Cumbrero, a raspberry and oak red, Viña Cumbrero *crianza*, and a *reserva*, Viña Monty.

MUGA (Rioja) ★★★(★) This has a sternly traditional image. For reds, it does nothing but good, and the *crianza* is fragrant and delicate, while the Prado Enea *reserva* or *gran reserva* is more complex, but still subtle and elegant. It's not cheap, though.

VIÑA PESQUERA (Ribera del Duero) ★★★(★) Prices have shot up since American wine writer Robert Parker likened this to Château Pétrus. Made from Tinto Fino and Garnacha, it's good but not *that* good, oaky and aromatic, with rich savoury fruit.

PRÍNCIPE DE VIANA (Navarra) ★★★(★) Innovative bodega which used to be a co-op, and became known as Bodegas Cenalsa. Agramont is its best-known UK brand, and look out for new Bodegas Guelbenzu, a Cabernet/Tempranillo estate in Cascante.

RAÏMAT (Costers del Segre) ★★★ The Raïmat Chardonnay Cava is honeyed, with grassy acidity. Abadía is an oak-enhanced blend of Cabernet, Tempranillo and Garnacha. Also Cabernet Sauvignon, Pinot Noir and Merlot.

REMELLURI (Rioja) ★★★★(★) Single-estate wine; the Rodriguez family have completely rebuilt the winery, installing stainless steel tanks, but the old wooden vats are still used for primary fermentation. The bodega now makes a fine, meaty *reserva*, barrel-aged for two to three years.

LA RIOJA ALTA (Rioja) ★★★★ A traditional bodega, firm believer in long barrel-aging: over half the wines qualify as *reserva* or *gran reserva*. Even the Viña Alberdi *crianza* has a delightfully oaky flavour. They make two styles of *reserva*, the elegant Viña Arana and the rich Viña Ardanza. In the best years, they make exceptional *gran reservas*.

RIOJANAS (Rioja) ★★★(★) Best reds are the *reservas*: the light, elegant, plummy Viña Albina and the richer, more concentrated Monte Reál. White Monte Reál *crianza* is soft and peachy, with just enough oak.

MIGUEL TORRES (Penedés) ★★★★ Viña Sol is a super-fresh modern white. Gran Viña Sol is Parellada and Chardonnay, fresh and pineappley, enriched with hints of vanilla oak. Gran Viña Sol Green Label pairs Parellada with Sauvignon Blanc, like oakier Sancerre. The superstar white is Milmanda Chardonnay. Viña Esmeralda is Gewürztraminer and Muscat d'Alsace. Mas la Plana is Torres' top red, a Cabernet Sauvignon. Viña Magdala is Pinot Noir and Tempranillo, Gran Sangredetoro is mainly Garnacha, Mas Borras is Pinot Noir, Las Torres is Merlot and Coronas – Tempranillo – is the least exciting.

VALDESPINO (Jerez) ★★★★★ Another family-owned bodega making a range of top-class, dry sherries. Inocente is one of the last traditional *finos* at 17.5 degrees. The Pedro Ximénez Solera Superior is one of the few examples of sherry's great sweetening wine bottled by itself. *Amontillados* and *olorosos* from here are about as good as you can get.

BODEGAS VEGA SICILIA (Ribera del Duero) ★★★★(★) Makers of Spain's most famous and expensive red wine. Vega Sicilia Unico, the top wine, is sometimes kept in barrel for ten years. Younger Valbuena, offers a cheaper glimpse of Vega Sicilia's glories.

VICENTE GANDIA (Valencia) ★★(★) Perhaps this DO's most go-ahead producer. Fresh white Castillo de Liria and juicy red and rosado from Bobal.

MERCHANTS SPECIALISING IN SPAIN
see Merchant Directory (page 424) for details

Adnams (AD), Bibendum (BIB), Direct Wine (DI), Eldridge Pope (EL), J E Hogg (HOG) particularly sherry, Lay & Wheeler (LAY), Lea & Sandeman (LEA), Moreno Wines (MOR) an entirely Spanish list, Thos. Peatling (PE), Reid Wines (1992) Ltd (REI) good sherries, Roberson (ROB), Tanners (TAN), Wine Society (WS)

SPAIN

RED

Under £3.50

Non-vintage
Vitorianas Don Darias, Vino de Mesa (TES, SAF, VIC)
Vitorianas Don Hugo, Alto Ebro, Vino de Mesa (WAI)
1995
Felix Solis Viña Albali, Valdepeñas (SAF)

£3.50 → £3.99

Non-vintage
Rivarey, Rioja (VIC)
Torres Sangredetoro, Penedés (BO)
1992
Fariña Gran Colegiata, Toro (MOR)
Señorio de los Llanos Reserva, Valdepeñas (POR)
Señorio de los Llanos, Valdepeñas (SOM)
1991
Condé de Caralt, Penedés (MOR)
1987
Señorio de los Llanos Reserva, Valdepeñas (TES)

£4.00 → £4.49

1993
Torres Sangredetoro, Penedés (DI, CO)
1992
Señorio de los Llanos Reserva, Valdepeñas (HOG, EY)
1991
Torres Sangredetoro, Penedés (TES)
1989
Felix Solis Viña Albali Reserva, Valdepeñas (FUL)

£4.50 → £4.99

1994
El Coto Crianza, Rioja (ROB)
Ochoa, Navarra (PLA, PEN, EL)
1993
Cellers Scala Dei, Priorato (WS)
El Coto Crianza, Rioja (DAV)
1992
Campo Viejo, Rioja (MOR)
Julián Chivite Gran Feudo, Navarra (DI)
CVNE, Rioja (PEN)
Torres Coronas, Penedés (DI)
Torres Sangredetoro, Penedés (SAT)

1991
Julián Chivite Gran Feudo, Navarra (HOG)
Fariña Colegiata, Toro (EL)
Felix Callejo Tinto F Callejo, Ribera del Duero (FUL)
Raïmat Abadia, Costers del Segre (UN)
Torres Coronas, Penedés (REI, HOG, UN, FUL)
Torres Sangredetoro, Penedés (THR, WR)
1990
Bodegas Principe de Viana Agramont Tinto, Navarra (BOT)
Julián Chivite Gran Fuedo Reserva, Navarra (THR, WR, BOT)
Torres Coronas, Penedés (WHI)
1989
Piqueras Castillo de Almansa, Almansa (DI)
Piqueras Marius Tinto Reserva, Almansa (LAY)
Raïmat Abadia, Costers del Segre (BO, TES)

Torres Coronas, Penedés (TES)
1984
Señorio de los Llanos Reserva, Valdepeñas (SOM)

£5.00 → £5.49

Non-vintage
Raïmat Merlot, Costers del Segre (BO)
1994
Señorio de Nava Crianza, Ribera del Duero (LAY)
1992
CVNE, Rioja (MOR, PLA, POR, BO)
Señorio de los Llanos Reserva, Valdepeñas (LAY)
1991
Berberana Carta de Oro, Rioja (YOU, UN)
Marqués de Cáceres, Rioja (HOG)
Raïmat Cabernet Sauvignon, Costers del Segre (CO)
Señorio de los Llanos, Valdepeñas (HIC)
Torres Gran Sangredetoro, Penedés (DI)

1990
CVNE, Rioja (WAT)
Marqués de Cáceres, Rioja (MOR)
René Barbier Reserva, Penedés (PLA)
1989
Piqueras Marius Tinto Reserva, Almansa
(TAN)
Torres Gran Sangredetoro, Penedés (CO)
1987
Piqueras Marius Tinto Reserva, Almansa
(AV)
1984
Señorio de los Llanos Gran Reserva,
Valdepeñas (MAJ)
1980
Felix Solis Viña Albali Gran Reserva,
Valdepeñas (SO)

£5.50 → £5.99
1994
Torres Las Torres, Penedés (HOG)
1993
Marqués de Cáceres, Rioja (WHI)
Torres Las Torres, Penedés (DI)
1992
Marqués de Cáceres, Rioja (LAY)
Ochoa Tempranillo, Navarra (REI, MAJ)
Olarra Añares, Rioja (AS)
Siglo Saco, Rioja (QUE)
Torres Coronas, Penedés (DAV, BY, PE)
Torres Las Torres Merlot, Penedés (FUL)
1991
Julián Chivite Gran Fuedo Reserva,
Navarra (DI)
Condé de Caralt Reserva, Penedés (TAN)
CVNE Viña Real, Rioja (BIB)
Felix Callejo Tinto F Callejo, Ribera del
Duero (RES)
La Rioja Alta Viña Alberdi, Rioja (SOM)
Marqués de Cáceres, Rioja (CRO, DI, DAV,
TAN, HAH, NEW)
Raïmat Tempranillo, Costers del Segre (UN)
Señorio de los Llanos Reserva,
Valdepeñas (ROB)
1990
Condé de Caralt Reserva, Penedés (MOR)
CVNE Viña Real, Rioja (WHI)
Señorio de los Llanos Gran Reserva,
Valdepeñas (EY)
Señorio de los Llanos Reserva,
Valdepeñas (BEN)
Señorio de Nava Crianza, Ribera del
Duero (FUL, ASD)
Siglo Saco, Rioja (MOR)
Torres Coronas, Penedés (MOR)

1989
Campo Viejo Reserva, Rioja (QUE, VIC)
Fariña Gran Colegiata Reserva, Toro (TAN)
Fariña Gran Colegiata, Toro (EL)
Gran Condal Reserva, Rioja (CO)
Señorio de los Llanos Gran Reserva,
Valdepeñas (MOR)
1987
Felix Solis Viña Albali Gran Reserva,
Valdepeñas (FUL)
Señorio de Nava Crianza, Ribera del
Duero (CO)

£6.00 → £6.49
1993
Ochoa Tempranillo, Navarra (PIP)
Viña Berceo, Rioja (AUR)
1992
CVNE, Rioja (LAY)
Ochoa Tempranillo, Navarra (HOG, WAT, EY)
★ Viña Valoria, Rioja (PE)
1991
Coto de Imaz Reserva, Rioja (DAV)
Ochoa Tempranillo, Navarra (YOU, BO)
Raïmat Abadia Reserva, Costers del Segre
(HIC)
Torres Gran Sangredetoro, Penedés (QUE)
1990
Raïmat Cabernet Sauvignon, Costers del
Segre (BOT, THR, WR)
Raïmat Tempranillo, Costers del Segre
(THR, WR, BOT)
1989
La Rioja Alta Viña Alberdi, Rioja (POR)
Torres Gran Sangredetoro, Penedés (UB,
SAT)
1988
Berberana Reserva, Rioja (YOU, FUL)
Campo Viejo Reserva, Rioja (MOR)
1985
La Rioja Alta Viña Ardanza Reserva, Rioja
(SO)

£6.50 → £6.99
1993
Torres Las Torres Merlot, Penedés (SAT)
1991
Barón de Ley, Rioja (ASD)
Compania Vitivinicola Aragonesa Viñas
del Vero Pinot Noir, Somontano (PLA)
CVNE Viña Real, Rioja (LEA)
Faustino V Reserva, Rioja (SAF, BOT, WR)
Marqués de Cáceres, Rioja (BER)
Torres Gran Coronas, Penedés (DI)
Torres Gran Sangredetoro, Penedés (WRI)

1990
Berberana Carta de Oro, Rioja (SAT)
Faustino V Reserva, Rioja (POR)
Marqués de Cáceres, Rioja (AV)
Marqués de Riscal Reserva, Rioja (MAJ)
Raïmat Abadia, Costers del Segre (MOR)
Raïmat Cabernet Sauvignon, Costers del
   Segre (MOR)
Torres Sangredetoro, Penedés (MOR)
1989
La Rioja Alta Viña Alberdi, Rioja (ELL)
Marqués de Riscal Reserva, Rioja (VIC)
Torres Las Torres, Penedés (PEN)
1988
Faustino V Reserva, Rioja (TES)
1987
Barón de Ley, Rioja (BOT, WR, THR)
Señorio de Sarria Cabernet Sauvignon,
   Navarra (BOT)
1984
Señorio de los Llanos Gran Reserva,
   Valdepeñas (CRO, PE, BEN)

£7.00 → £7.49
1991
La Rioja Alta Viña Alberdi, Rioja (AME, KA)
Torres Gran Coronas, Penedés (CO)
1990
Amézola de la Mora Viña Amézola, Rioja
   (BER)
Faustino V Reserva, Rioja (MOR)
Marqués de Murrieta, Rioja (HOG)
1989
Marqués de Riscal, Rioja (UN)
Piqueras Marius Tinto Reserva, Almansa
   (UB)
1986
CVNE Reserva, Rioja (WAT)
Montecillo Gran Reserva, Rioja (OD)
1981
Campo Viejo Gran Reserva, Rioja (SO)

£7.50 → £7.99
1993
★ Marqués de Griñon Dominio de
   Valdepusa Syrah, Rueda (TES)
1991
Compania Vitivinicola Aragonesa Viñas
   del Vero Pinot Noir, Somontano (BIB)
Marqués de Murrieta Reserva, Rioja (NI)
1990
Compania Vitivinicola Aragonesa Viñas
   del Vero Pinot Noir, Somontano (YOU)
Marqués de Murrieta Reserva, Rioja (AME)
Torres Gran Coronas, Penedés (QUE)

1989
Compania Vitivinicola Aragonesa Viñas
   del Vero Pinot Noir, Somontano (VIG)
La Rioja Alta Viña Alberdi, Rioja (DI)
1988
CVNE Reserva, Rioja (MOR, BO, PEN)
Muga Reserva, Rioja (DI)
1985
Ochoa Reserva, Navarra (WAT)
Siglo Saco Gran Reserva, Rioja (QUE)

£8.00 → £8.49
1991
Marqués de Riscal Reserva, Rioja (NEW)
Torres Gran Coronas, Penedés (EY, POR)
Viña Berceo Reserva, Rioja (NEW)
1990
Marqués de Cáceres Reserva, Rioja (POR)
Marqués de Murrieta Reserva, Rioja (AD,
   HAH)
Marqués de Murrieta, Rioja (ENO, BEN)
Muga Reserva, Rioja (EL)
Ochoa Reserva, Navarra (PIP)
Torres Gran Coronas, Penedés (MOR)
1989
CVNE Reserva, Rioja (PLA)
1988
Muga Reserva, Rioja (MOR)
1987
La Rioja Alta Viña Ardanza Reserva, Rioja
   (SOM)
Ochoa Reserva, Navarra (PEN)

£8.50 → £8.99
1992
Marqués de Griñon Cabernet Sauvignon,
   Rueda (FUL)
1991
Compania Vitivinicola Aragonesa Viñas
   del Vero Pinot Noir, Somontano (DI)
La Rioja Alta Viña Alberdi, Rioja (ROB)
Marqués de Murrieta Reserva, Rioja (WRI)
Marqués de Murrieta, Rioja (QUE, DAV)
Torres Gran Coronas, Penedés (PIP)
1990
Marqués de Murrieta Reserva, Rioja (PLA,
   MOR)
Marqués de Riscal, Rioja (PE)
Remelluri Reserva, Rioja (NO, ELL)
1989
Marqués de Murrieta Reserva, Rioja (RAE)
1988
Jean León Cabernet Sauvignon, Penedés
   (PE)
Olarra Cerro Anon Reserva, Rioja (AS)

1987
Ochoa Reserva, Navarra (KA)
1985
Campo Viejo Gran Reserva, Rioja (VIC)

£9.00 → £9.99
1991
Marqués de Murrieta Reserva, Rioja (ROB)
Pesquera, Alejandro Fernandez, Ribera del Duero (NI)
Viña Berceo Reserva, Rioja (AUR)
1990
Marqués de Murrieta Reserva, Rioja (LAY, PEN, NI)
1989
Contino Reserva, Rioja (WAT, VIC)
Marqués de Cáceres Reserva, Rioja (HAH)
1988
Contino Reserva, Rioja (PEN)
CVNE Imperial Reserva, Rioja (POR)
Jean León Cabernet Sauvignon, Penedés (AV)
1987
CVNE Imperial Reserva, Rioja (NO)
CVNE Reserva, Rioja (AV)
CVNE Viña Real Reserva, Rioja (SAT)
Faustino I Gran Reserva, Rioja (HOG)
La Rioja Alta Viña Ardanza Reserva, Rioja (POR, CRO, HOG)
Marqués de Cáceres Reserva, Rioja (DI)
Marqués de Griñon Crianza, Rueda (MOR)
1986
La Rioja Alta Viña Arana, Rioja (HOG)
Ochoa Reserva, Navarra (PLA)
1985
Campo Viejo Gran Reserva, Rioja (POR, MOR)
Fariña Colegiata, Toro (CRO)

£10.00 → £11.99
1994
Pesquera, Alejandro Fernandez, Ribera del Duero (OD)
1993
Pesquera, Alejandro Fernandez, Ribera del Duero (TAN)

> *Please remember that*
> ***Webster's** is a price*
> *GUIDE and not a price*
> *LIST. It is not meant to*
> *replace up-to-date*
> *merchants' lists.*

1990
Contino Reserva, Rioja (PIP)
1989
Contino Reserva, Rioja (YOU, MOR, LEA)
CVNE Imperial Reserva, Rioja (PIP)
CVNE Viña Real Reserva, Rioja (PIP)
La Rioja Alta Viña Ardanza Reserva, Rioja (EY, AD, KA)
Torres Mas Borras Pinot Noir, Penedés (DI)
1988
CVNE Imperial Reserva, Rioja (GAL, PLA, SAT, VIG, ROB)
CVNE Viña Real Reserva, Rioja (GAL, KA, VIG)
Torres Mas Borras Pinot Noir, Penedés (PEN)
1987
Conde de la Salceda Gran Reserva, Rioja (DI, TAN)
Contino Reserva, Rioja (LEA)
Faustino I Gran Reserva, Rioja (WHI, QUE, MOR, UB)
La Rioja Alta Viña Arana Reserva, Rioja (LAY)
1986
CVNE Imperial Reserva, Rioja (MOR)
CVNE Viña Real Gran Reserva, Rioja (ROB)
Marqués de Cáceres Gran Reserva, Rioja (DI)
1985
Conde de la Salceda Gran Reserva, Rioja (ELL)
Jean León Cabernet Sauvignon, Penedés (MOR)
Marqués de Cáceres Reserva, Rioja (VIN)
Marqués de Murrieta Reserva, Rioja (TW)
1983
Berberana Gran Reserva, Rioja (MOR)
1982
Marqués de Cáceres Gran Reserva, Rioja (MOR)

£12.00 → £13.99
1990
Contino Reserva, Rioja (EL, LAY)
1988
CVNE Viña Real Gran Reserva, Rioja (PIP)
La Rioja Alta Viña Ardanza Reserva, Rioja (AV)
1986
CVNE Imperial Gran Reserva, Rioja (MOR, SAT)
CVNE Viña Real Gran Reserva, Rioja (PEN, PLA)

1985
CVNE Viña Real Gran Reserva, Rioja (MOR)
Fariña Gran Colegiata, Toro (CRO)
La Rioja Alta Reserva 904 Gran Reserva, Rioja (SOM)
La Rioja Alta Viña Ardanza Reserva, Rioja (CRO)
Marqués de Cáceres Gran Reserva, Rioja (UB)
1984
Marqués de Murrieta Reserva, Rioja (CRO)
1982
Faustino I Gran Reserva, Rioja (MOR)
Jean León Cabernet Sauvignon, Penedés (DI)
Marqués de Cáceres Gran Reserva, Rioja (CRO)
Montecillo Gran Reserva, Rioja (MOR)
1980
Bilbainas Viña Pomal Gran Reserva, Rioja (SUM)

£14.00 → £15.99

1991
Pesquera Cosecha Especial, Alejandro Fernandez, Ribera del Duero (MOR)
1988
CVNE Imperial Gran Reserva, Rioja (PIP, BIB, PEN, TAN, VIG)
1987
Marqués de Murrieta Castillo Ygay Gran Reserva, Rioja (HOG, MOR, LAY)
1985
CVNE Imperial Reserva, Rioja (REI)
La Rioja Alta Reserva 904 Gran Reserva, Rioja (POR, REI)
La Rioja Alta Reserva 904, Rioja (NO, CRO)
Marqués de Murrieta Gran Reserva, Rioja (MAJ)
1983
La Rioja Alta Reserva 904 Gran Reserva, Rioja (HOG)
1982
Jean León Cabernet Sauvignon, Penedés (POR)
Marqués de Cáceres Gran Reserva, Rioja (VIN)

£16.00 → £19.99

1989
Torres Gran Coronas Black Label (Mas La Plana), Penedés (QUE)
1988
Torres Gran Coronas Black Label (Mas La Plana), Penedés (POR)

1987
Marqués de Murrieta Castillo Ygay Gran Reserva, Rioja (PLA)
Torres Gran Coronas Black Label (Mas La Plana), Penedés (DI, HOG)
1986
Vega Sicilia Valbuena 3rd year, Ribera del Duero (DI)
1985
La Rioja Alta Reserva 904 Gran Reserva, Rioja (LAY, DI, BEN)
Marqués de Murrieta Gran Reserva, Rioja (HAH, MOR)
Pesquera, Alejandro Fernandez, Ribera del Duero (CRO)
Torres Gran Coronas Black Label (Mas La Plana), Penedés (PEN)
Vega Sicilia Valbuena 3rd year, Ribera del Duero (PEN)
1982
Torres Gran Coronas Black Label (Mas La Plana), Penedés (NO)
Torres Gran Coronas, Penedés (PEN)
1981
Marqués de Riscal Gran Reserva, Rioja (MOR)
1978
Muga Gran Reserva, Rioja (MOR)
Viña Berceo Gran Reserva, Rioja (BU, AUR)
1970
CVNE Viña Real, Rioja (REI)

£20.00 → £29.99

1989
Torres Gran Coronas Black Label (Mas La Plana), Penedés (TAN)
1988
Torres Gran Coronas Black Label (Mas La Plana), Penedés (UB, ROB)
Vega Sicilia Valbuena 5th year, Ribera del Duero (DI)
1987
Vega Sicilia, Ribera del Duero (AV)
1985
Marqués de Murrieta Castillo Ygay Gran Reserva, Rioja (MOR)
Marqués de Murrieta Reserva, Rioja (CRO)
Torres Gran Coronas Black Label (Mas La Plana), Penedés (MOR, DI)
1983
La Rioja Alta Reserva 904 Gran Reserva, Rioja (UB)
La Rioja Alta Reserva 904, Rioja (CRO)
Marqués de Murrieta Gran Reserva, Rioja (CRO)

1982
Muga Gran Reserva, Rioja (MOR)
1977
Torres Gran Coronas Black Label (Mas La Plana), Penedés (REI)
1975
CVNE Viña Real Gran Reserva, Rioja (VIG, CRO)
Torres Gran Coronas Black Label (Mas La Plana), Penedés (NO, DI)
1973
CVNE Imperial Gran Reserva, Rioja (VIG)
1970
Berberana Gran Reserva, Rioja (CRO)
Marqués de Murrieta Gran Reserva, Rioja (NO, MOR)
1942
Marqués de Murrieta Castillo Ygay Gran Reserva, Rioja (BUT)

£30.00 → £49.99

1990
Vega Sicilia Valbuena 5th year, Ribera del Duero (TAN, VIG, CRO)
Vega Sicilia Valbuena, Ribera del Duero (ELL, PLA, BEN)
1985
Vega Sicilia Valbuena 5th year, Ribera del Duero (PEN)
1983
Vega Sicilia Valbuena 3rd year, Ribera del Duero (CRO)
1981
La Rioja Alta Reserva 890 Gran Reserva, Rioja (REI)
1980
Vega Sicilia Unico, Ribera del Duero (PEN)
1979
Vega Sicilia Unico, Ribera del Duero (DI)
1978
Torres Gran Coronas Black Label (Mas La Plana), Penedés (CRO)
1976
Ribera Duero Protos Gran Reserva, Ribera del Duero (MOR)
Torres Gran Coronas Black Label (Mas La Plana), Penedés (CRO)

In each price band wines are listed in vintage order. Within each vintage they are listed in A–Z order.

1975
Marqués de Murrieta Castillo Ygay Gran Reserva, Rioja (MOR)
Marqués de Murrieta Gran Reserva, Rioja (CRO)
1970
CVNE Imperial Gran Reserva, Rioja (CRO)
Faustino I Gran Reserva, Rioja (MOR)
1965
Marqués de Murrieta Gran Reserva, Rioja (MOR)
1964
Berberana Gran Reserva, Rioja (CRO)
1961
López de Heredia Viña Bosconia Gran Reserva, Rioja (MOR)
1952
Berberana Gran Reserva, Rioja (REI)

£50.00 → £69.99

1983
Vega Sicilia Unico, Ribera del Duero (BEN)
1975
Vega Sicilia Unico, Ribera del Duero (DI)
Vega Sicilia Valbuena, Ribera del Duero (VIG)
1974
Vega Sicilia Unico, Ribera del Duero (DI)
1970
Ribera Duero Protos Gran Reserva, Ribera del Duero (MOR)
1968
Marqués de Murrieta Castillo Ygay Gran Reserva, Rioja (NO, CRO, AD, MOR, ROB)
1964
Marqués de Murrieta Castillo Ygay Gran Reserva, Rioja (MOR)
Marqués de Murrieta Gran Reserva, Rioja (MOR)
1960
Marqués de Murrieta Gran Reserva, Rioja (MOR)

£70.00 → £99.99

1970
Vega Sicilia Unico, Ribera del Duero (CRO, ELL, VIG, BEN, FA)
1965
Vega Sicilia Unico, Ribera del Duero (VIG)
1964
Ribera Duero Protos Gran Reserva, Ribera del Duero (MOR)
1942
Marqués de Murrieta Castillo Ygay Gran Reserva, Rioja (CRO)

£100.00 → £121.00

1970
Torres Gran Coronas Black Label (Mas La Plana), Penedés (MOR)
1962
Vega Sicilia Unico, Ribera del Duero (BEN)
1952
Marqués de Murrieta Castillo Ygay Gran Reserva, Rioja (AD)
1942
Marqués de Murrieta Castillo Ygay Gran Reserva, Rioja (MOR)

WHITE

Under £3.50

Non-vintage
Castillo de Liria, Vicente Gandia, Valencia (WAI, VIC)
Moscatel de Valencia Castillo de Liria, Vicente Gandia, Valencia (WR, THR, BOT)
1994
Torres Viña Esmeralda, Penedés (CRO)

£3.50 → £3.99

Non-vintage
Moscatel de Valencia Castillo de Liria, Vicente Gandia, Valencia (WAI, FUL)
Rivarey Blanco, Rioja (VIC)
1994
Condé de Caralt, Penedés (MOR)
Marqués de Cáceres, Rioja (HOG)
1993
Hermanos Lurton Sauvignon Blanc, Rueda (CO)
Torres Gran Viña Sol, Penedés (CRO)
1992
Marqués de Cáceres, Rioja (EY, BO)
Torres Viña Sol, Penedés (TES)

£4.00 → £4.99

Non-vintage
Torres Viña Sol, Penedés (BO)
1995
El Coto, Rioja (DAV)
Marqués de Cáceres, Rioja (DI)
Torres Viña Sol, Penedés (CO, WAI, DAV)
1994
Barbadillo Castillo de San Diego, Vino de Mesa (HOG)
Cellers Scala Dei, Priorato (DI)
CVNE Viura, Rioja (PLA)
El Coto, Rioja (ROB)
Marqués de Cáceres, Rioja (NEW, HAH, LAY)
Marqués de Riscal, Rueda (MAJ)

Torres San Valentin, Penedés (DI)
Torres Viña Esmeralda, Penedés (HOG, FUL, DI)
Torres Viña Sol, Penedés (HOG, DI, FUL, TAN)
1993
Marqués de Cáceres, Rioja (AD, EL)
Torres Viña Sol, Penedés (WR, BOT, THR, MOR)

£5.00 → £5.99

Non-vintage
Faustino V, Rioja (TES)
1995
Faustino V, Rioja (QUE)
Torres Viña Esmeralda, Penedés (PIP)
1994
Faustino V, Rioja (MOR)
Marqués de Alella, Alella (WS)
Marqués de Cáceres, Rioja (UB)
Palacio de Bornos, Rueda (BER)
Raïmat Chardonnay, Costers del Segre (UN)
Torres Gran Viña Sol, Penedés (DI, BOT)
Torres Viña Esmeralda, Penedés (UB, WHI, TAN, PEN, WRI)
1993
CVNE Monopole, Rioja (SAF)
Marqués de Cáceres, Rioja (AV, BER, VIN)
Torres Viña Esmeralda, Penedés (WR, BOT, THR, AME, MOR)
1992
CVNE Monopole, Rioja (MOR)
Torres Viña Esmeralda, Penedés (EY)
1991
Compania Vitivinicola Aragonesa Viñas del Vero Chardonnay, Somontano (UB)
Torres Gran Viña Sol, Penedés (TES)
1988
Marqués de Murrieta Reserva, Rioja (AV)

£6.00 → £7.99

Non-vintage
Torres Moscatel Malvasia de Oro, Penedés (NO)
1995
Julián Chivite Gran Feudo Blanco, Navarra (HA)

> *Please remember that*
> **Webster's** *is a price*
> *GUIDE and not a price*
> *LIST. It is not meant to*
> *replace up-to-date*
> *merchants' lists.*

1994
CVNE Monopole, Rioja (PIP)
Marqués de Murrieta, Rioja (WHI)
Marqués de Riscal, Rueda (PLA)
Torres Gran Viña Sol, Penedés (WRI, HAH)
Torres Viña Esmeralda, Penedés (PE, ROB)
1993
Compania Vitivinicola Aragonesa Viñas
  del Vero Chardonnay, Somontano (PLA)
Torres Fransola, Penedés (REI, DI)
1992
Compania Vitivinicola Aragonesa Viñas
  del Vero Chardonnay, Somontano (VIG)
CVNE Monopole, Rioja (PEN, TAN)
1991
CVNE Monopole, Rioja (PE)
Faustino V, Rioja (UB)
Marqués de Murrieta Ygay Gran Reserva,
  Rioja (QUE)
Muga, Rioja (EL)
1990
Marqués de Griñon, Rueda (MOR)
1989
Marqués de Murrieta Reserva, Rioja (MAJ,
  WS, BOT, WR, WRI, PLA)
Marqués de Murrieta, Rioja (HOG, ENO)
Navajas, Rioja (UB)
Raïmat Chardonnay, Costers del Segre
  (MOR)
1987
CVNE Reserva, Rioja (VIG)

£8.00 → £10.99
1994
Cellers Puig & Roca, Augustus
  Chardonnay, Penedés (FUL)
Lagar de Cervera Hermanos, Galicia (TAN,
  LAY)
1993
Lagar de Cervera Hermanos, Galicia (ROB)
1990
Marqués de Murrieta, Rioja (CRO)
1989
La Rioja Alta Viña Ardanza Reserva, Rioja
  (ROB)
1986
Marqués de Murrieta Reserva, Rioja (RAE)

£11.00 → £19.99
1994
Torres Milmanda Chardonnay, Penedés
  (REI)
1992
Jean León Chardonnay, Penedés (DI, PEN)
Marqués de Alella, Alella (MOR)

1990
Torres Milmanda Chardonnay, Penedés
  (DI)
1988
Marqués de Murrieta Reserva, Rioja (UB)
1985
Marqués de Murrieta Ygay Gran Reserva,
  Rioja (VIG)
1984
Marqués de Murrieta, Rioja (CRO)
1983
Marqués de Murrieta Reserva, Rioja (NO)

£20.00 → £29.99
1991
Torres Milmanda Chardonnay, Penedés
  (NO)
1989
Torres Milmanda Chardonnay, Penedés
  (UB)
1988
Torres Milmanda Chardonnay, Penedés
  (NO)
1985
Marqués de Murrieta Ygay Gran Reserva,
  Rioja (MOR)
1978
Marqués de Murrieta Ygay Gran Reserva,
  Rioja (MOR)
1974
Bodegas Riojanas Monte Real, Rioja (VIG)
1970
Marqués de Murrieta Ygay Gran Reserva,
  Rioja (NO)

£30.00 → £40.00
1975
Marqués de Murrieta Ygay Gran Reserva,
  Rioja (AD, MOR)
1970
Marqués de Murrieta Ygay Gran Reserva,
  Rioja (MOR)
1966
Bodegas Riojanas Monte Real, Rioja (VIG)
1962
Marqués de Murrieta Ygay Gran Reserva,
  Rioja (CRO)

£50.00 → £59.99
1962
Marqués de Murrieta Ygay Gran Reserva,
  Rioja (MOR)
1948
Marqués de Murrieta Ygay Gran Reserva,
  Rioja (VIG)

c. £76.00
1940
Marqués de Murrieta Ygay Gran Reserva, Rioja (VIG)

c. £120.00
1946
Marqués de Murrieta Reserva Especial, Rioja (VIG)

ROSÉ

Under £4.00
1994
Marqués de Cáceres Rosado, Rioja (HOG)

£4.00 → £4.99
1994
Marqués de Cáceres Rosado, Rioja (NEW)
Torres de Casta, Penedés (EY)
1993
Marqués de Cáceres Rosado, Rioja (DI)
1992
Marqués de Cáceres Rosado, Rioja (MOR)
1991
Torres de Casta, Penedés (DI)

£5.00 → £5.99
1995
Faustino V Rosado, Rioja (QUE)
1993
Marqués de Cáceres Rosado, Rioja (UB)
Torres de Casta, Penedés (UB)
1992
Torres de Casta, Penedés (MOR)

SPARKLING

Under £5.50
Non-vintage
Segura Viudas Brut, Cava (HOG)

£5.50 → £5.99
Non-vintage
Codorníu Brut Première Cuvée, Cava (VIC)
Condé de Caralt Brut, Cava (MOR)
Condé de Caralt Rosado, Cava (MOR)
Condé de Caralt Semi-seco, Cava (MOR)
Freixenet Brut Nature, Cava (BO)
Freixenet Brut Rosé, Cava (VIC)
Freixenet Carta Nevada, Cava (BO, PIP)
Freixenet Cordon Negro Brut, Cava (PEN, HOG, MAR)
Mont Marçal Brut, Cava (BO)
Segura Viudas Brut, Cava (OD, DI)

£6.00 → £6.99
Non-vintage
Codorníu Brut, Cava (FUL)
Condé de Caralt Blanc de Blancs, Cava (SOM, MOR)
Freixenet Brut Rosé, Cava (PLA, WHI, MOR)
Freixenet Carta Nevada, Cava (WHI)
Freixenet Cordon Negro Brut, Cava (WHI, YOU, MAJ, FUL, VIC, POR, WAT, CO)
Segura Viudas Brut, Cava (LAY)
1993
Freixenet Cordon Negro Brut, Cava (THR, WR, BOT)
1992
Freixenet Cordon Negro Brut, Cava (PIP, PLA, ROB, WAI, UB)
Mont Marçal Brut, Cava (SAI)
1991
Freixenet Cordon Negro Brut, Cava (SAI, SAF)
1989
Freixenet Cordon Negro Brut, Cava (MOR)

£7.00 → £7.99
Non-vintage
Freixenet Cordon Negro Brut, Cava (DAV, SAT, EL, QUE, PE)
Raïmat Chardonnay Brut, Cava (MOR)
1992
Codorníu Chardonnay Brut, Cava (WAI)
1991
Freixenet Cordon Negro Brut, Cava (AUR)
1990
Codorníu Brut Première Cuvée, Cava (MOR)
Freixenet Brut Nature, Cava (MAJ)
1988
Segura Viudas Brut, Cava (DI)

c. £8.50
Non-vintage
Marqués de Monistrol Rosé Brut, Cava (VIC)

OTHER FORTIFIED

Under £4.50
Non-vintage
Bodegas Alvear Medium Dry, Montilla (TAN)
Bodegas Alvear Pale Dry, Montilla (TAN)

£9.00 → £10.50
Non-vintage
Scholtz Lagrima 10 años, Málaga (TAN)
Scholtz Solera 1885, Málaga (PE, ROB)

SHERRY

DRY

Under £4.50

Fino Hidalgo (PLA, HAH)
la Gitana Manzanilla, Hidalgo ½ bottle (REI, TAN, HAL, OD)
Valdespino Fino (WAT)

£4.50 → £4.99

Elegante, González Byass (HOG, WHI)
Fino de Sanlúcar, Barbadillo (AME, PIP)
la Gitana Manzanilla, Hidalgo (HAH)
Harvey's Luncheon Dry (HA)
Lustau Fino (DI, MAJ)
Manzanilla de Sanlúcar, Barbadillo (SUM, OD, PIP, AME)
Oloroso Seco Barbadillo (PIP)
Valdespino Fino (AS)

£5.00 → £6.99

Amontillado Napoleon, Hidalgo (NI, EY, WS)
Elegante, González Byass (BO, TES, FUL, WR, BOT, THR, SAF, WAI, DAV, UN, SAT)
Fino de Sanlúcar, Barbadillo (LAYT)
Fino Hidalgo (BIB, NI)
la Gitana Manzanilla, Hidalgo (HOG, REI, EL, PLA, EY, WAI, MAJ, BIB, WS, TW)
la Guita Manzanilla, Hidalgo (DI)
Harvey's Luncheon Dry (HOG, SAF, WHI, HAH, BO, SAT)
la Ina, Domecq (HA, HOG, WRI, WAT, HAH, BOT, WR, UN, THR)
Inocente Fino, Valdespino (HOG, WAT, WRI)
Lustau Dry Oloroso (DI)
Manzanilla de Sanlúcar, Barbadillo (PEN, HIC, CB, LAYT)
Manzanilla Pasada Solear, Barbadillo (HOG, PIP)
Oloroso Seco Barbadillo (NO)
Ostra Manzanilla (LAY)
San Patricio Fino, Garvey (HOG, MAJ, WS)
Tio Pepe, González Byass (HOG, WHI, THR, WR, BOT, TES, SAF, OD, WRI, BO, WAI, FUL)
Valdespino Fino (ROB)

£7.00 → £8.99

Amontillado Napoleon, Hidalgo (AD, TW)
Don Zoilo Finest Fino (HOG)
Don Zoilo Old Dry Oloroso (THR, BOT, WR)

Don Zoilo Pale Dry Manzanilla (WR, THR)
Don Zoilo Very Old Fino (AME)
Dos Cortados Old Dry Oloroso, Williams & Humbert (HOG)
la Guita Manzanilla, Hidalgo (HOG)
Harvey's Palo Cortado (HA)
la Ina, Domecq (EL, ROB)
Inocente Fino, Valdespino (ENO, OD, WS, AS, AD)
Manzanilla Pasada Almacenista, Lustau (DI)
Manzanilla Pasada de Sanlúcar, Hidalgo (TAN)
Manzanilla Pasada Solear, Barbadillo (HIC)
Oloroso Dry, Hidalgo (TAN, AD)
Oloroso Especial, Hidalgo (EL, LAY)
Oloroso Seco Barbadillo (AME)
Palo Cortado del Carrascal, Valdespino (WAT)
Palo Cortado, Valdespino (ENO)
Tio Diego Amontillado, Valdespino (ENO)
Tio Pepe, González Byass (HAH, UN, EL, ROB, SAT, QUE)

£9.00 → £9.99

Fino Especial, Hidalgo (LAY)
Jerez Cortado, Hidalgo (TAN, AD)
Oloroso Especial, Hidalgo (TW)
Oloroso Seco Barbadillo (HIC)
Tio Diego Amontillado, Valdespino (WS)

£10.00 → £12.99

Don Zoilo Palo Cortado (HOG)
Dos Cortados Dona Rosario Farfante (YOU)
Fino Especial, Hidalgo (TW)
Harvey's Palo Cortado (PLA)
Jerez Cortado, Hidalgo (LAY)
Manzanilla Pasada Almacenista, Lustau (REI, PEN, SAT)
Manzanilla Pasada de Sanlúcar, Hidalgo (TW)
Oloroso Seco Barbadillo (HOG)
Palo Cortado, Valdespino (WS)

> *Please remember that* **Webster's** *is a price GUIDE and not a price LIST. It is not meant to replace up-to-date merchants' lists.*

MEDIUM

Under £4.50
Amontillado Valdespino (WAT, OD)

£4.50 → £4.99
Amontillado de Sanlúcar, Barbadillo (NO, PIP, BIB)
Amontillado Lustau (DI, MAJ)
Amontillado Martial, Valdespino (HAH)
Amontillado Valdespino (AS)
Concha Amontillado, González Byass (HOG, WHI)
Dry Sack, Williams & Humbert (TES)
Harvey's Club Amontillado (HA, WR, BOT, THR)

£5.00 → £6.99
Amontillado de Sanlúcar, Barbadillo (SUM, HIC)
Caballero Amontillado, González Byass (TES, SAT)
Concha Amontillado, González Byass (WR, THR, BOT, WAI, SAT)
Dry Fly Amontillado, Findlater (WAI)
Dry Sack, Williams & Humbert (HOG, WRI, AME, QUE)
Harvey's Club Amontillado (HOG, WHI, WAI, TES, WRI, BO, HAH, DAV, ROB, SAT)
Tanners Medium Sherry (TAN)

£7.00 → £10.99
Amontillado Almacenista, Lustau (DI)
Amontillado Valdespino (ROB)
Don Zoilo Amontillado (BOT, WR, THR, HOG, BEN)
Harvey's Fine Old Amontillado (HA, PLA)
Oloroso de Jerez, Almacenista Viuda de Antonio Borrego (DI)
Solera 1842 Oloroso, Valdespino (TAN)

£11.00 → £12.99
Amontillado Almacenista, Lustau (PEN)
Oloroso Muy Viejo Almacenista, Lustau (PEN, ROB)
Sandeman Royal Corregidor Oloroso (HOG, ROB)
Sandeman Royal Esmeralda (HOG)

£18.00 → £24.99
Amontillado del Duque, González Byass (HOG, OD, PE, VIN)

Apostoles Oloroso, González Byass (HOG, PE, VIN)
Coliseo Amontillado, Valdespino (ENO)

SWEET

Under £5.50
Bertola Cream (HOG)
Double Century Oloroso (WR, THR, BOT)
Oloroso Lustau (MAJ)
Sanlúcar Cream, Barbadillo (PIP)

£5.50 → £6.99
Croft Original Pale Cream (HOG, BO, THR, WR, TES, BOT, WHI, UN, WAI, DAV, OD, WRI, EL, QUE)
Harvey's Bristol Cream (OD, BO, DAV, TES, BOT, THR, WR, HOG, HA, WHI, WAI, UN, WRI)
Harvey's Bristol Milk (HA)
Harvey's Copper Beech (HA)
Sanlúcar Cream, Barbadillo (HIC)

£7.00 → £9.99
Croft Original Pale Cream (ROB)
Don Zoilo Rich Old Cream (HOG)
Harvey's Bristol Cream (HAH, EL, SAT, ROB, QUE)
Lustau's Old East India (MAJ, HOG)
Pedro Ximenez, Barbadillo (PIP)

£18.00 → £23.99
Matusalem Oloroso, González Byass (HOG, NO, PE, ROB, VIN)

PORTUGAL

Portuguese wine has improved beyond recognition – but is that enough? Now we want more individuality, more character – and yes, more clever use of tradition

Not so long ago Portuguese wine meant Mateus Rosé, Vinho Verde, some run-of-the-mill reds from Dão, and Barca Velha – a mysterious cult wine of legendary quality, but of such rarity that it was known only to a lucky few. Although it was possible to find the occasional old bottle which demonstrated that Portugal was capable of reaching the heights, most table wine was branded, and much came from co-operatives using primitive, hit-or-miss techniques where concrete tanks and hot fermentation were the rule. The result? Reds which were coarse, unbalanced and over-tannic, and whites which were heavy, tired and oxidized. And although this was what appealed to the native palate, these styles found few friends in export markets.

Today things are very different. Portugal can now boast some of the most up-to-date vinification equipment, and even in the co-ops stainless steel and temperature control are becoming the norm. After the 1974 revolution many estates which had previously sold their grapes to the co-ops, began to appear on the market under their own labels. Now they have become so numerous that they confuse the consumer. Other areas, always wine producers, have come into increasing prominence – first Bairrada, then the Douro and the Alentejo.

Two Australians, Peter Bright and David Baverstock, were at the forefront of improvements in wine-making techniques, and their current influence is still profound. However, a new generation of talented native winemakers has sprung up within the last decade, and although many of them still go to Bordeaux, California and Australia to gain experience, university departments at Vila Real, Coimbra, Carcavelos and Évora provide courses on (or including) oenology, and there are countless current research projects into every aspect of wine production. But perhaps the greatest impetus came when Portugal joined the EU, bringing an infusion of cash from which the co-ops largely benefited, with grants of up to 60 per cent towards improvement. The wines that have resulted, with their strong emphasis on fruit character, are dramatically different from the wines of old, and they continue to improve.

Old, tired, unwanted
There still remain things to be done. Although there has been striking progress in wine-making, viticulture still lags behind. Without good grapes to start with, you are unlikely to end up with good wine. Again, although a legally controlled denomination system is now in place for all wine areas, some of the controls actually hamper progress – for example, in Dão and Bucelas, where compulsory aging is geared to producing the older, tired wines which no-one wants any more. The explosion of quinta wines has been a mixed blessing. Sadly, many quintas produce indifferent wine or worse, and one should beware of thinking that being a quinta wine is some sort of guarantee of quality. Here more control might be a blessing.

What of the current situation and the future? The good news is that, after the vintages of 1993, which was quite disastrous both in terms of quality and quantity, and 1994, which was average in quality (except for the favoured Douro) and only slightly better in quantity, 1995 provided very high quality even if the quantity was still 20 per below average yields. Although these shortfalls have depleted stocks of older wines and this has pushed up prices by about 15 per cent, this seems modest compared with increases of double that in Spain and Italy.

For a while there was a trend towards producing wines from non-native grape varieties in a bid to cash in on consumer fashion. The results with the ubiquitous Cabernet Sauvignon, with a few striking exceptions like Quinta de Pancas, have been only average, and the grape is now mostly blended. As for the whites, Chardonnay has given a few Australian lookalikes, but other exotica like Gewürztraminer are decidedly unexciting. Happily this movement appears to be going into reverse and the tendency is now towards more native varieties.

The Alentejo goes from strength to strength, and was recently granted full DOC status in recognition of its increasing quality. It is currently the region which is best organized in terms of consistent quality and a strong promotional image, and it has perhaps the best qualified winemakers. José Saramago is an old-fashioned winemaker who has been experimenting with good results, and some of the red wines from the Co-operativa Agricola de Granja are excellent. David Baverstock has been improving the wines at Herdado do Esporão.

God's own country

A friend from the Douro recently remarked to me that in the North, when the wines are good, the credit is due to God rather than to the winemaker. Although this may be unduly severe, it is certainly true that this region, as well as providing some of the most impressive of Portugal's wines, still

provides too many of its disappointments. The whites are uniformly rather dull. It succeeds, however, with some young, fruity reds, and at its best produces serious wines

PORTUGUESE CLASSIFICATIONS

Portugal's wines are divided into four tiers of quality. At the top there are **Denominaçoes de Origem Controlada** or DOCs. **Indicações de Proveniência Regulamentada** or IPRs, are similar to the French VDQS. VQPRD (**Vinho de Qualidade Produzido em Região Determinada/Demarcada**) is similar, and can also apply to the DOC regions. **Vinhos Regionais** are Regional Wines, and **Vinhos de Mesa** are table wines.

to rival Barca Velha, such as Quinta do Côtto Grande Escolha, Quinta da Gaivosa (made from 60-year-old vines), and Redoma. This last is a new to the market, made by Dirk van der Niepoort (of the port firm), who is clearly a winemaker to watch. A white Redoma is due for release in 1997, as is a red from Quinta de Passadouro, which has had such a success with its single-quinta port.

There is nothing much to report about Vinho Verde, where prices remain relatively high in relation to quality, which is extremely variable. In Dão there have been no really exceptional recent developments apart from Vergilio Loureiro's Quinta das Maias and Quinta dos Roques. The best news in Bairrada has been the emergence of Rui Alves as a winemaker of great talent, responsible for stunning reds from Casa de Saima and from the estates of Gonçalves Faria and Sidonio de Souza. Alves is a traditionalist: he believes in old vines, uses 90 per cent Baga grapes (usually without destemming) and he ages in old wooden barrels. No stainless steel here: Casa de Saima is made by treading the grapes. The

results amply demonstrate that it is still possible to make world-class wines by the careful use of old-fashioned methods.

And the future? Portugal continues to be a wine producer of great promise but only modest progress. True, what has been achieved is considerable when compared with how things used to be. But it is no good getting too carried away by wines which, in general, are remarkable only by contrast with those of the past but which, in world terms, remain pretty average. Most of the new-style wines go too far towards the opposite extreme from the traditional style and lack complexity, staying power and personality. They offer easy drinking – which, admittedly, is what most of the market is looking for – but they will not build Portugal a reputation for great wines. While we may expect continued steady progress along the lines of the past decade, the most interesting developments in the future may well come from makers like Alves, and small independent growers, who pursue the ideal of individual character and excellence, and who will adapt rather than jettison traditional methods. **ALEX LIDDELL**

WINES & WINE REGIONS

ALENTEJO, DOC (red, white) Unfettered by Portugal's legendary bureaucracy, the Alentejo comes on in leaps and bounds. With EU help the co-ops are showing more initiative here than anywhere else in the country. Stainless steel and temperature control are now the norm. Borba led the way but Redondo is now producing some round, fruity reds and some good peachy whites. Roseworthy-trained David Baverstock deserves another mention, having left his job in the port trade to revitalize the vast Esporão estate at Reguengos de Monsaraz. The whites from here, from the Roupeiro grape, make the most of its tropical, guava-like flavours. The large José Maria da Fonseca company, a leading innovator, has invested a lot of time and energy in the region. Apart from Fonseca's

blends, and the Tinto Velho from the J S Rosado Fernandes estate, which Fonseca now owns, the best wines are from various co-ops. The reds from the Redondo co-op, with their big, brash grapy fruit show the potential waiting to be tapped. The upfront rich damson-and-raspberry fruit of the Paço dos Infantes from Almodovar shows the same marvellously untamed excitement. The Borba co-op, Cartuxa, Esporão and Reguengos de Monsaraz are producing reds with terrific fruit. Look for Pera Manca and also for local red blend Quinta da Anfora. The Rothschilds have bought a share of Quinta do Carmo, near Estremoz, and other foreign investors are looking.

ALGARVE (red, white) The south coastal strip of the country, making undistinguished wines – mostly alcoholic reds. Once a Região Demarcada, it has now been split into four Denominaçoes de Origem Controlada, Lagos, Portimão, Lagoa and Tavira. All deserve demotion from DOC status. Among producers, the *Lagoa* co-op is the best bet.

BAIRRADA, DOC (red, white) In the flat land down towards the sea from the hilly Dão region, vineyards mingle with wheatfields, olive trees and meadows, and the reds frequently overshadow the more famous Dão wines. The reds are apt to be tannic, often the result of fermenting them with the grape stalks, but the Baga grape, the chief one in the blend, gives a sturdy, pepper, plum-and-blackcurrant fruit to the wine which can often survive the over-aging, and at ten years old, although the resiny bite and peppery edge are apparent, a delicious, dry fruit is more in command. The best Bairrada wines age remarkably well. Luis Pato, who sells under his own name, blends in a dollop of softening Cabernet Sauvignon and is consciously aiming at a New World style, though some of his wines lack elegance. Is it a mark of his success that he's already had some of his wine turned down by the Bairrada Região as untypical because he'd used new oak instead of old?

Some Portuguese merchants will tell you that their own *garrafeira* wines are based on Bairrada, though the label won't say so. That's probably true, because of the traditional Portuguese approach to high quality reds – buy where the grapes are best, blend and age at your company's cellars, and sell the result under your own name. Since 1979, however, the Bairrada region has been demarcated and bulk sales have been banned, and the challenging, rather angular, black fruit flavours of the wines now sport a Bairrada label. *São João* produces wine of world class, though increasingly hard to find. *Aliança* and *Sogrape* (look for its *Nobilis*) are good. The best co-op is *Vilharino do Bairro*, and *Cantanhede* and *Mealhada* aren't bad. Leading the increasing number of single-estate wines are *Casa de Saima* (especially the *garrafeira* and *reserva* versions), *Gonçalves Faria* and *Sidonia de Souza*.

There are also some increasingly good dry whites from the Maria Gomes grape. *Sogrape*, maker of *Mateus Rosé*, has done the most to freshen up flavours. Try the crisp, floral *Quinta de Pedralvites*. Also very good: peachy *Sogrape Bairrada Reserva* and *Caves Aliança*'s inexpensive dry white.

BEIRAS (red, white) Much of this area, in the centre of the country close to the Spanish border, is mountainous, but it has fertile plains to the north and south. Traditionally a source for sparkling wines, but a few interesting reds are starting to appear. Look for *Quinta da Foz de Arouce.*

BUCELAS, DOC (white) Popular in Wellington's day, this dry white was almost extinct, with *Caves Velhas* left as the sole producer. However, two new ones have appeared. Look out for *Quinta da Romeira* under the *Prova Regia* label.

CARCAVELOS, RD (fortified) Just when Carcavelos looked as if it was about to disappear for ever, along comes a new vineyard. *Quinta dos Pesos* is making a good, nutty, fortified rather like an aged Tawny port.

COLARES, DOC (red) Grown in the sand dunes on the coast near Lisbon from the doughty but scented Ramisco grape. Almost all the wine is vinified at the local Adega Regional, stalks and all, aged in concrete tanks for two to three years, then sold to merchants for further maturation and sale. The young wine has fabulous cherry perfume but is *numbingly* tannic. As it ages it gets an exciting rich pepper-and-bruised-plums flavour, but the 1974s are only just ready. The Adega no longer has a monopoly on Colares, but only *Carvalho, Ribeiro & Ferreira* shows interest in exploiting the new freedom, and it may be too late to save the region from extinction.

DÃO, DOC (red, white) This upland eyrie, ringed by mountains, reached by steep, exotic, forest-choked river gorges, makes Portugal's most famous, if not always her most appetizing reds. They are reputed to become velvet-smooth with age. My experience is that they rarely achieve this and could do with less aging in wood and more in bottle. They are made from a mixture of six grapes, of which the Touriga Nacional is the best, and they develop a strong, dry, herby taste, almost with a pine resin bite.

The protectionist rules that allowed companies to buy only finished wine, not grapes, from growers, and that forbade firms from outside the region to set up wineries there, have been abolished and Sogrape, with its own winery in the region, is now making the most of it. Among the others, Caves São João deserves an honourable mention along with Caves Aliança and José Maria da Fonseca for its brand, Terras Altas. Other firms are persuading their co-op suppliers to leave the grape stalks out of the fermentation vats and make cleaner, more modern wines. However, two very promising single-estate wines, Quinta das Maias and Quinta dos Roques, which combine a modern style with interesting wood treatment, indicate that change is beginning, though there's still a long way to go.

White Dão was traditionally (and mostly still is) yellow, tired and heavy. But a few companies are now making a lighter, fresher, fruitier style, and now that the co-ops are losing the upper hand with production, others look set to follow suit. White Grão Vasco, now made in Sogrape's shiny new winery at Quinta dos Carvalhais is a significant departure from tradition with its crisp lemon-zest appeal. Sadly, local regulations insist that the wine should be at least six months old before bottling, so it pays to catch the wine young. Look out for oak-aged reservas in future.

DOURO, DOC (red, white) The Douro Valley is famous for the production of port. But only a proportion of the crop – usually about 40 per cent – is made into port, the rest being sold as table wine. Sogrape, which owns Ferreira, produces a number of these from the rare and expensive Barca Velha, through Reserva Espécial, to the young and fruity Esteva. Other port shippers are beginning to

follow suit, with Redoma from Niepoort a notable newcomer, and single-quinta port producers, such as Quinta de la Rosa, are doing the same. The flavour can be delicious – soft and glyceriny, with a rich raspberry-and-peach fruit, and a perfume somewhere between liquorice, smoky bacon and cigar tobacco. Look out for Quinta da Cismeira, Calços do Tanho, Seara d'Ordem among the easy drinkers, and Quinta do Côtto Grande Escolha and Quinta da Gaivosa among the heavyweights.

Nearly all the best table wines are red, though the Planalto white from Sogrape, the Mateus-makers, is full and honeyed and good, as is its oaked Douro Reserva, and Esteva from Ferreira is clean and crisp. Quinta do Valprado Chardonnay, made by Raposeira, is big and honeyed.

MADEIRA, RD (fortified) Each Madeira style is supposedly based on one of four grapes, Malmsey (Malvasia), Bual, Verdelho and Sercial, though at the moment only the more expensive Madeiras really live up to their labels – the cheaper ones, up to 5 years old, are almost all made from the inferior Tinta Negra Mole. The Madeira Wine Company is voluntarily enforcing the EU table wine rule that 85 per cent of a wine labelled with a grape variety should be made from it, so the cheaper Madeiras are now calling themselves, more honestly, 'Pale Dry', 'Dark Rich', and so on.

The Malmsey grape makes the sweetest Madeira, reeking sometimes of Muscovado sugar, dark, rich and brown, but with a smoky bite and surprisingly high acidity that makes it positively refreshing after a long meal. The Bual grape is also rich and strong, less concentrated, sometimes with a faintly rubbery whiff and higher acidity. Verdelho makes pungent, smoky, medium-sweet wine with more obvious, gentle fruit, and the Sercial makes dramatic dry wine, savoury, spirity, tangy, with a steely, piercing acidity. To taste what Madeira is all about you need a 10-year-old, and, frankly, really good Madeira should be two or three times that age.

Recent large scale investments by the Madeira Wine Company (controlled by the

Symingtons, the port family), and by *Henriques and Henriques*, indicate a much-needed determination to reverse the declining fortunes of Madeira.

OESTE (red, white) North of Lisbon, Portugal's largest wine region (in terms of both area and volume of wine produced) is dominated by huge co-ops, some of which are just beginning to do something about quality. The region sub-divides into seven principal IPR regions: Arruda, Alenquer, Óbidos, Torres Vedras, Alcobaça, Estremadura and Encostas d'Aire. Arruda makes strong, gutsy reds, while Alenquer makes softer, glyceriny wine. Look out for Quinta da Boa Vista's *Espiga, Quinta das Setencostas* and *Palha Canas* made by José Neiva. The *Obidos* reds are drier, more acidic, but good in a cedary way. *Torres Vedras'* reds are lighter than Arruda, with a climate more influenced by cool Atlantic air. Single-estate *Quinta de Abrigada* makes light, creamy whites and stylish damson-and-cherry reds. *Casa de Pancas* in Estremadura has a Cabernet (blended with 15 per cent Periquita) and a Chardonnay. These two are the only private estates doing much so far, though *Paulo da Silva's Beira Mar* and *Casal de Azenha* are both good Oeste blends.

PORT (DOURO, DOC) (fortified) The simplest and cheapest port available in Britain is labelled simply 'Ruby' and 'Tawny'. Ruby is usually blended from the unexceptional grapes of unexceptional vineyards to create a tangy, tough, but warmingly sweet wine to knock back uncritically. It should have a spirity rasp along with the sweetness. Cheap Tawny at around the same price as Ruby is simply a mixture of light Ruby and White ports, and is almost never as good as the Ruby would have been, left to itself.

Calling these inferior concoctions 'Tawnies' is very misleading because there's a genuine 'Tawny', too. Proper Tawnies are kept in wooden barrels for at least five, but preferably ten or more years, to let the colour leach out and a gentle fragrance and delicate flavour of nuts, brown sugar and raisins develop. Most of

these more expensive Tawnies carry an age on the label, which must be a multiple of ten: 10, 20, 30 or even 40 years old, but the figure indicates a style rather than a true date: a 10-year-old Tawny might contain some 6-year-old and some 14-year-old wine. Lack of age on a Tawny label – however often it says 'Fine', 'Old', and so on – is a bad sign and usually implies a cheap Ruby-based blend, though there are some good brands like *Harvey's Director's Bin Very Superior Old Tawny* or *Delaforce's His Eminence's Choice*. Most Tawnies reach their peak at somewhere between ten and 15 years, and few ports improve after 20 years in barrel, so don't pay inflated prices for 30- and 40-year-old wine. Try *Cockburn 10-year-old, Ferreira 10-* and *20-year-old, Fonseca 10-* and *20-year-old, Harvey's Director's Bin, Sainsbury's 10-year-old. Colheitas* – single-vintage Tawnies – are increasingly available, usually from Portuguese houses, and can be really delicious. *Cálem* and *Niepoort* are also good.

VINTAGE PORTS are the opposite of the Tawnies, since the object here is to make a big, concentrated rather than a delicate mouthful. Vintage years are 'declared' by port shippers when the quality seems particularly good – usually about three times a decade. The wines are matured in wooden casks for two years or so, then bottled and left to age for a decade or two.

The final effect should have more weight and richness than a Tawny of similar age, since the maturation has taken place in the almost airless confines of the bottle, which ages the wines more slowly. There should also be a more exciting, complex tangle of flavours; blackcurrant, plums, minty liquorice, pepper and herbs, cough mixture and a lot more besides. Vintage port you get animated and opinionated about, while Tawny is more a wine for quiet reflection.

If you want a peek at what a declared Vintage port can be like, buy single-quinta wine. Single-quintas (or farms) are usually from the best vineyards in the slightly less brilliant years when a declaration is not made, but

MATURITY CHART
Vintage Ports
1977 has always been destined for the long term
1983 will be easier to enjoy earlier

1977

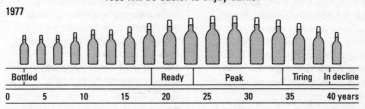

Bottled				Ready	Peak		Tiring	In decline

| 0 | 5 | 10 | 15 | 20 | 25 | 30 | 35 | 40 years |

1983

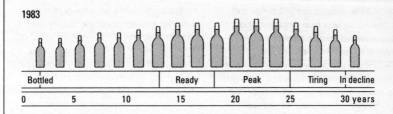

Bottled			Ready	Peak		Tiring	In decline

| 0 | 5 | 10 | 15 | 20 | 25 | 30 years |

1985 and 1991 are both excellent vintages to cellar,
the 1991 vintage may develop slightly earlier.

1985

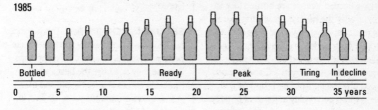

Bottled			Ready	Peak		Tiring	In decline

| 0 | 5 | 10 | 15 | 20 | 25 | 30 | 35 years |

1991

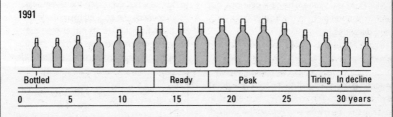

Bottled			Ready	Peak		Tiring	In decline

| 0 | 5 | 10 | 15 | 20 | 25 | 30 years |

instead of being bottled and shipped after only two years or so, they are bottled after two years, stored for up to ten years, and shipped ready to drink. Growers' single-quintas are also available in generally declared years. Single-quinta wines can be extremely good. Look particularly for Taylor's *Quinta da Vargellas*, Dow's *Quinta do Bonfim*, Warre's *Quinta da Cavadinha*, Fonseca's *Quinta do Panascal*, Niepoort's *Quinta do Passadouro*, Cockburn's *Quinta da Eira Velha*, and *Quinta do Vesuvio*. Among growers' quintas look out for *Quinta de la Rosa*.

Another good-value Vintage lookalike is Crusted port. This is a blend of wines from two or three vintages, shipped in cask and bottled slightly later than Vintage, at about three years old, so they retain the peppery attack of the top wines and also keep a good deal of the exotic perfumed sweetness of real 'Vintage'. They are called Crusted because of the sediment that forms after three or four years in bottle. More and more houses are producing Crusted ports, and they can be very good, although single-quinta wines can offer more excitement and good aged Tawnies more complexity.

Two other types of port like to think of themselves as vintage-style. Vintage Character and Late Bottled Vintage are bottled four to six years after the harvest. Ideally, this extra time maturing in wood should bring about an effect similar to a dozen years of bottle-aging. Bottled at four years, and not too heavily filtered, it still can, but most VC and LB ports are too browbeaten into early decline and have as much personality as a pan of potatoes. The best, labelled with the year of bottling, are from *Fonseca, Niepoort, Smith Woodhouse, Ramos Pinto* and *Warre*. They are delicious, but can throw a sediment in the bottle, and may need decanting.

There are two styles of White port, dry and sweet. In general, the flavour is a bit thick and alcoholic, the sweet ones even tasting slightly of rough grape skins. But there are a few good dry ones, though I've never felt any great urge to drink them anywhere except in the blinding mid-summer heat of the Douro Valley when they're refreshing with a few ice-cubes and a big splash of lemonade or tonic.

RIBATEJO (red, white) Portugal's second-largest region, in the flat lands alongside the River Tagus, provides the base wine for some important brands and some of Portugal's best *garrafeira* wines – in particular the *Romeira* of Caves Velhas. Carvalho Ribeiro and Ferreira, owned by Costa Pina, a subsidiary of Allied Domecq, also bottles some good *garrafeiras*, and with multi-national backing its wines are likely to improve. The co-op at *Almeirim* markets good wine under its own name, including the price-busting red and white *Lezíria*, a good white for Safeway called *Falcoaria* and classier white under the *Quinta das Varandas* label. The *Torre Velha* brand isn't bad. Australian Peter Bright is also making white under his new *Bright Bros.* label at *Quinta da Granja*. The *Margaride* estate is the Ribatejo's leading estate. The wines are sold as *Dom Hermano, Margarides* and under the names of their properties, *Casal do Monteiro* and *Convento da Serra*. The wines are patchy, but can be very good. The region is being split up into six IPRs (*Indicação de Proveniência Regulamentada*), the six being Almeirim, Cartaxo, Chamusca, Santarém, Tomar and Coruche.

SETÚBAL, DOC (fortified) This is good, but it's always a little spirity and never quite as perfume-sweet as one would like, perhaps because they don't use the best sort of Muscat. It comes in a 6-year-old and a 25-year-old version, and the wines do gain in concentration with age – the 25-year-old does have a lot more character and less overbearing spiritiness – but even then the sweetness veers towards the cooked marmalade of southern French Muscats rather than the honeyed, raisined richness of the Australian versions. You can still occasionally find older

The price guides for this section begin on page 317.

wines like *José Maria da Fonseca's 1934*, or its intense, pre-phylloxera *Torna Viagem*, with a powerful treacle toffee character balanced by a sharp acidic tang.

TERRAS DO SADO (red, white) This Vinho Regional is centred on Setúbal, and there is plenty of technical expertise. The best wines are produced on the limestone of the Arrábida hills from where comes an oak-aged Chardonnay, *Cova da Ursa*. J P Vinhos is one of the leading lights for reds and whites; the Muscat is especially good. *José Maria da Fonseca* likes local grapes for reds and whites, though Chardonnay gives a lemony lift to the white *Pasmados*, and *Quinta da Camarate* boasts Riesling, Gewürztraminer and Muscat. Cabernet Sauvignon and Merlot are made as varietals and used in blends with local grapes like Periquita.

TRÁS-OS-MONTES (red, white) This is the large and remote region in the north-east of the country adjacent to Vinho Verde and the Douro. It is not uncommon to see vines growing as bushes here, and export production is only just beginning. Look out for *Casal de Valle Pradinhos*.

VINHO VERDE, DOC (red, white) Sixty per cent of all Vinho Verde produced is red, made from four different grapes, of which the Vinhão is best. The wine is wonderfully sharp, harsh even, is hardly ever seen outside the country and goes a treat with traditional Portuguese dishes like *bacalhau*, or salt cod. Adnams have the red from the *Ponte da Lima* co-op, for anybody feeling brave.

But the wine we see is white, and Verde means green-youthful, un-aged, not the colour of a croquet lawn. Ideally, the whites are bone dry, positively tart, often aromatic, and brilliantly suited to heavy, oily northern Portuguese food. But we almost always get the wines slightly sweetened and softened, which is a pity, although it is in its peculiar way a classic wine style.

Most wines come from co-ops or are sold under brand names, but some larger private producers bottle their own. There is also some characterful single-quinta Vinho Verde. *Palacio da Brejoeira*, from the Alvarinho grape, is more alcoholic and full-bodied, and expensive, for that matter, than the general run. Vinho Verde can be made from a variety of grapes, but there's often more Loureiro in the estate wines. Indeed, there's quite rightly a lot of interest in Loureiro, with its dry, apricotty, Muscatty aroma and taste. It is more attractive than the much-praised Alvarinho, and it gives the wines a much more tangy but fruity character. *Solar das Bouças* and *Quinta de Tamariz* are almost entirely Loureiro. *Quinta da Franqueira*, *Casa de Sezim* and *Terras de Corga* are also good. From the large firms *Gazela* is just off-dry and reliable. *Aveleda* also makes some good ones, including one made entirely from the Trajadura grape. Its best is called *Grinalda*, a perfumed blend of Loureiro and Trajadura grapes.

PORT SHIPPER PROFILES

CÁLEM ★★★★ Important Portuguese shipper founded in the last century and still family owned. Cálem produce excellent 10-, 20-, 30- and 40-year-old Tawnies, good Colheitas, and good Vintage port from the reliable Quinta da Foz at Pinhão.

CHURCHILL GRAHAM ★★★(★) Established in 1981, this was the first independent port shipper to be founded in more than 50 years. John Graham is establishing a reputation for intense and concentrated wines which are designed to last well.

COCKBURN ★★★★ Shippers of the best-selling 'Fine Old Ruby' and 'Special Reserve'. At the forefront of research into viticulture in the Upper Douro. Recent Vintage ports have been stunning.

CROFT ★★(★) Quinta da Roeda near Pinhão forms the backbone of Croft's Vintage wines, but many wines are over-delicate.

DELAFORCE ★★(★) The Tawny, His Eminence's Choice, is its best-known wine.

DOW ★★★★★ Quinta do Bomfim at Pinhão produces the backbone of Dow's firm-flavoured, long-living Vintage and has also been launched as a single-quinta wine.

FERREIRA ★★★★ One of the best Portuguese-owned shippers, making elegant, early-maturing Vintages and two superb Tawnies: 10-year-old Quinta do Porto and 20-year-old Duque de Bragança. Bought by Sogrape in 1988.

FONSECA GUIMARAENS ★★★★★ Family-run shippers belonging to the Yeatman side of Taylor, Fladgate and Yeatman. Fonseca's wines are sweeter and less austere than Taylor's. The Vintage ports are often outstanding, and the quality of its commercial releases is reassuring.

GOULD CAMPBELL ★★★★ The Gould Campbell name is used mainly for Vintage ports which tend to be ripe and mature relatively early.

GRAHAM ★★★★★ Usually rich and sweet. Apart from Vintage there is Malvedos, produced in off-vintage years, and fine Tawnies.

NIEPOORT ★★★★★ Tiny firm run by a Dutch family with total commitment to quality. Look for aged Tawnies, traditional LBVs, Colheitas and long-lasting Vintage. It launched a new single-quinta, Quinta do Passadouro, in 1994.

OFFLEY FORRESTER ★★★(★) Famous for 'Boa Vista' Vintage and LBV ports. Vintage is mostly based on its own Quinta da Boa Vista and can be insubstantial. Excellent Baron de Forrester Tawnies.

QUINTA DO NOVAL ★★★ Bought out recently by the French insurance group AXA. Noval's Nacional wines, made from ungrafted vines, are legendary and fetch a stratospheric price at auction. Other Noval wines don't attempt such heights, but are usually good, if light. Noval LB is widely sold, but isn't actually that special; the Tawnies and Colheitas are much better.

RAMOS PINTO ★★★★ There are delicious Tawnies from two single-quintas – Ervamoira and Bom Retiro – both of which are elegant, nutty and delicate. The firm is now owned by the house of Louis Roederer of Champagne.

REAL VINICOLA ★★ Sells ports under seven different names including that of Royal Oporto. They can sometimes be good. Vintage is generally early maturing.

SANDEMAN ★★★ Currently being shaken up, and heading towards quality rather than quantity. It launched its first single-quinta, Quinta do Vau, in 1993; and a new ruby port, Partners, in 1994.

SMITH WOODHOUSE ★★★★ Some delicious Vintage and LBVs. Concentrated Vintage wines which tend to mature early. Full-flavoured Crusted.

TAYLOR, FLADGATE AND YEATMAN ★★★★(★) Taylor's has a very high quality range, but some recent commercial releases have seen standards slip a bit, and its Vintage port is no longer ahead of the field. However, the excellent Quinta de Vargellas is still one of the best single-quinta wines about.

WARRE ★★★★★ This was the first port company in which the entrepreneurial Symington dynasty became involved. Warre produces serious wines: good LBVs and Vintage and fine 'Nimrod' Tawny. Quinta da Cavadinha has recently been launched as a single-quinta wine.

PORT CLASSIFICATION

If you think that Burgundy and Bordeaux make a meal out of classifying their vineyards, just look at how rigidly port is controlled. Nothing is left to chance. The age of the vines is classified on a scale from 0 to 60 points. The level of upkeep of the vines is ruthlessly marked from -500 to +100 points. The objective is to score as many points as possible. The highest possible score would be +1660 points, while the bottom score possible would be a massively embarrassing -2880. The classification, based on points scored, is from A to F, and controls how many litres of juice per 1000 vines can be turned into port. The rest has to be made into table wine, which gives a smaller (although often quicker) return.

The Vineyard Calculation
Productivity (Ranging from about 500 litres per 1000 vines to about 2000 litres; the lower the yield the higher the points scored.)
Worst: 0 points   Best: +80 points
Altitude (Ranging from a highest allowable altitude of 650 metres to a lowest of 150 metres.)
Worst: -900 points   Best: +150 points
Soil (Scored according to type. Schist scores best, granite worst.)
Worst: -350 points   Best: +100 points
Geographical position (Predetermined locations score different marks.)
Worst: -50 points   Best: +600 points

Upkeep of vineyard (Good housekeeping awards for various factors.)
Worst: -500 points   Best: +100 points
Variety and quality of grapes
Worst: -300 points   Best: +150 points
Gradient (From 1-in-6 to 1-in-30 – the steeper the better.)
Worst: -100 points   Best: +100 points
Shelter
Worst: 0   Best: +70 points
Age of vines (With 5-year-olds scoring 30; up to 25-year-olds scoring 60.)
Worst: 0   Best: +60 points
Distance root to root (The distance from the end of one vine's root to the start of the next root – too close is frowned upon.)
Worst: -50 points   Best: +50 points
Nature of land
Worst: -600 points   Best: +100 points
Aspect
Worst: -30 points   Best: +100 points

THE TOTAL
The experts then add up all these points and classify the vineyards according to score, allowing each group to make a certain number of litres of wine per 1000 vines, as follows:

A (1201 points or more)	600 litres
B (1001–1200 points)	600 litres
C (801–1000 points)	590 litres
D (601–800 points)	580 litres
E (401–600 points)	580 litres
F (400 points or less)	260 litres

MERCHANTS SPECIALISING IN PORTUGAL
see Merchant Directory (page 424) for details

Nearly all merchants sell some port, but only a few have interesting table wines. Adnams (AD), Bibendum (BIB) especially port, on fine wine list, Davisons (DAV) especially port, Direct Wine (DI) for port and Madeira, Eldridge Pope (EL) ditto, Farr Vintners (FA) for Vintage port, J E Hogg (HOG) especially port, Lay & Wheeler (LAY),

Thos. Peatling (PE), Raeburn Fine Wines (RAE) old colheitas from *Niepoort*, Reid Wines (1992) Ltd (REI) particularly for port, T&W Wines (TW) including ports back to 1937, Tanners (TAN) particularly port, Thresher (THR), Wine Society (WS), Peter Wylie Fine Wines (WY) old ports and Madeiras

PORT VINTAGES

Not every year produces a crop of fine enough quality for vintage-dated wine to be made, and a few houses may not make Vintage port even in a generally good year. Announcing the intention to bottle Vintage port is known as 'declaring'. It all depends on the quality the individual house has produced, although it is extremely rare for a house to declare two consecutive years.

1995   A vintage with a lot of colour and tannin, but slightly unbalanced because of the strong summer heat. Above average, but missed being top grade.

1994   After severe winter weather everything came right to produce a fine vintage which is now certain to be widely declared.

1992   Declared by four shippers: *Fonseca, Taylor, Niepoort* and *Burmester*. Rich, fruity wines, lusher and fleshier than the 1991s. Cynics note that 1992 was Taylor's tercentenary.

1991   Generally declared, but quantities were small.

1987   *Ferreira, Martinez, Niepoort* and *Offley* declared this small but good vintage. Most shippers opted instead for single-quinta wines for medium-term drinking.

1985   Declared by every important shipper. The quality is exceptionally good. The wines don't quite have the solidity of the 1983s but they make up for this with a juicy ripeness of fruit. Although *Taylor* isn't as outstanding as usual, several perennial under-achievers like *Croft* and *Offley* are very good, *Cockburn* is very attractive, and *Fonseca* is rich and lush. However, my favourites are *Graham, Warre, Dow, Gould Campbell* and *Churchill Graham*.

1983   Marvellous wine, strong and aggressive, but with a deep, brooding sweetness which is all ripe, clean fruit. Not one of the most fragrant vintages, but it will be a sturdy classic.

1982   Not as good as it was at first thought. *Croft* and *Delaforce* are already drying out, and most need to be drunk already.

1980   A good vintage, though excessively expensive when first offered. Although they were consequently unpopular, the wines are developing a delicious, drier than usual style. Try from 1995 onwards.

1977   Brilliant wine, now beginning to mature. The flavour is a marvellous mixture of great fruit sweetness and intense spice and herb fragrance.

1975   These in general don't have the stuffing that a true vintage style demands, but some have surprisingly gained weight and richness and are excellent for drinking now. *Noval, Taylor, Dow, Warre* and *Graham* need no apologies. Most of the others do.

1970   Exceptional, balanced port, already good to drink, sweet and ripe with a fascinating citrus freshness – and it'll last. All the top houses are special, led by *Fonseca, Taylor, Warre, Graham* and *Dow*, but lesser houses like *Cálem* and *Santos Junior* are also excellent.

1966   This has gained body and oomph and is now approaching its best. Doesn't *quite* have the super-ripe balance of the '70 or the startling, memorable character of the '63, but a very good year. *Fonseca* is the star at the moment.

1963   The classic year. It's big, deep, and spicy, with remarkable concentration of flavours. One or two have lost colour, but *Fonseca, Taylor, Graham, Dow* or *Cockburn* are excellent.

PORTUGAL

RED

Under £3.50

Non-vintage
Tinto da Anfora J P Vinhos (THR, BOT, WR, FUL)
1995
Dão Novo (SAI)

£3.50 → £3.99

1991
Dão Grão Vasco (VIC)
1990
Periquita J.M. da Fonseca (TES)
1989
Bairrada Reserva Dom Ferraz (BOT, THR)
Dão Reserva Dom Ferraz (THR, WR, BOT)
1987
Periquita J.M. da Fonseca (CRO)

£4.00 → £4.99

1993
Alentejo Borba Adega Co-operativa (UN)
Dão Grão Vasco (DAV)
Douro Quinta de la Rosa (POR)
1992
Dão Reserva, Caves Aliança (DI, PEN)
Periquita J.M. da Fonseca (WAI, MAJ)
1991
Bairrada Reserva Caves Aliança (POR, DI)
Periquita J.M. da Fonseca (YOU)
1990
Bairrada Frei João (WS)
Bairrada Terra Franca (SAT)
Dão Dom Ferraz (UN)
1989
Dão Porto dos Cavaleiros (WS)
1987
Dão Terras Altas J.M. da Fonseca (SAT)
1985
Bairrada J.M. da Fonseca (SAT)
1984
Garrafeira J.M. da Fonseca (TES)

£5.00 → £5.99

1994
★ Douro Quinta de la Rosa (GE, PLA, MV)
1993
Alentejo Vinha do Monte Sogrape (VIC)
1992
Dão Duque de Viseu (CO)
Dão Terras Altas J.M. da Fonseca (PIP)

1991
Douro Quinta de la Rosa (CRO)
Quinta da Bacalhôa (SAI)
1990
Dão Garrafeira Grão Vasco (PE)
Douro Vila Regia (SAT)
Pasmados J.M. da Fonseca (PIP, WRI)
1989
Garrafeira Particular Caves Aliança (DI)
1988
Pasmados J.M. da Fonseca (YOU)
1985
Beira Mar Reserva, da Silva (ROB)
Garrafeira Particular Caves Aliança (BO)

£6.00 → £8.00

1990
Quinta da Camarate, J.M. da Fonseca (PIP)
Tinto da Anfora J P Vinhos (DI)
1989
Quinta da Camarate, J.M. da Fonseca (PE)
1988
Tinto Velho J.M. da Fonseca (UB)
1986
Tinto Velho Reguengos (WRI)

£10.00 → £13.99

1990
Quinta do Côtto Grande Escolha,
  Champalimaud (AD)
1971
Periquita J.M. da Fonseca (CRO)

c. £27.00

1985
Barca Velha, Ferreira (ELL)

WHITE

Under £3.50

Non-vintage
João Pires Branco (FUL)
Vinho Verde Aveleda (HOG)
1992
Bairrada Caves Aliança (SO)

£3.50 → £3.99

1995
João Pires Branco (CO)
1993
Santa Sara (SAI)
Vinho Verde Chello Dry (VIC)

£4.00 → £4.99

Non-vintage
Vinho Verde Casal Mendes Caves Aliança (DI)
Vinho Verde Gazela (OD, DAV, TAN)
1995
Vinho Verde Quinta de Aveleda (PIP)
1994
Bairrada Caves Aliança (DI)
Dão Grão Vasco (PE)
Dry Palmela Moscato, João Pires (MAJ)
João Pires Branco (WHI)
1993
Bairrada Reserva Sogrape (SAF)
Dry Palmela Moscato, João Pires (FUL)
1992
Bairrada Reserva Sogrape (VIC)
Vinho Verde Aveleda (SAT)
Vinho Verde Quinta de Aveleda (SAT)

£5.00 → £5.99

Non-vintage
Vinho Verde Casal Garcia (PE)
1994
Dão Terras Altas J.M. da Fonseca (PIP)
1993
Dry Palmela Moscato, João Pires (UB)

£6.00 → £7.99

1993
Bucelas Quinta de Romeira (VIN)
Cova da Ursa Chardonnay, J.P. Vinhos (DI)
1992
Cova da Ursa Chardonnay, J.P. Vinhos (THR, BOT, WR)
1991
Cova da Ursa Chardonnay, J.P. Vinhos (YOU)

ROSÉ

Under £4.00

Non-vintage
Mateus Rosé (CO, SAF, WAI, SO, BOT, WR, THR, SAI, VIC, TES, UN)

£4.00 → £4.99

Non-vintage
Mateus Rosé (HOG, BO, WHI)

FORTIFIED

£20.00 → £22.99

Non-vintage
Moscatel de Setúbal 20-year-old J.M. da Fonseca (NO, TAN)

PORT

Under £6.50

Non-vintage
Cockburn's Fine Tawny (HA, HOG)
Quinta do Noval Old Coronation Ruby (HOG)
Smith Woodhouse Fine Tawny (UN)
Van Zellers Ruby (WHI)
1985
Dow (BOT, WR, THR)

£6.50 → £6.99

Non-vintage
Cockburn (WR, THR, BOT)
Cockburn's Fine Ruby (WHI, BOT, THR, WR, BO, VIC)
Graham Ruby (NI)
Quinta do Noval Old Coronation Ruby (AUR)
Sandeman Tawny (BOT, THR, WR, OD)
Taylor Chip Dry White Port (FOR)
Warre's Tawny (VIC)

£7.00 → £8.99

Non-vintage
Churchill Dry White (LEA, BO)
Churchill's Finest Vintage Character (PIP)
Cockburn's Fine White (UN)
Cockburn's Special Reserve (HA, FUL, HOG, BO, SAF, WAI, VIC, WHI, UN, OD)
Delaforce Special White Port (THR, WR)
Dow's Fine Tawny (PEN, ROB)
Dow's No. 1 White (PEN)
Fonseca Bin 27 (HOG, VIC, ENO, NEW, FUL)
Graham Tawny (BO)
Quinta do Noval Extra Dry White (DI)
Quinta do Noval Late Bottled (HOG, WHI, AUR, FUL, WRI, ROB, UN)
Ramos-Pinto Ruby (BEN)
Ramos-Pinto Tawny (PEN, QUE)
Sandeman Fine Old White (BO, EL)
Sandeman Founder's Reserve (FUL)
Taylor Special Tawny (BEN)
Warre's Warrior (TES, AME, WR, BOT, VIC, FUL, MAJ, SAF, UN, THR, DI)
1989
Graham Late Bottled (NI)
Sandeman Late Bottled (OD)
1988
Dow's Late Bottled (OD, WAI)
1987
Dow's Late Bottled (FUL)
Ramos-Pinto Late Bottled (HOG, HAH)

£9.00 → £10.99

Non-vintage
Churchill's Crusted Port (PIP)
Churchill's Finest Vintage Character (GAL)
Cockburn's Special Reserve (EL)
Croft Late Bottled (WR, THR, BOT)
Delaforce His Eminence's Choice (HOG)
Delaforce Special White Port (AV)
Dow's Crusted Port (VIC, TES)
Dow's Fine Ruby (LAYT)
Dow's Vintage Character (PEN, WRI)
Fonseca Bin 27 (FOR, WRI, QUE, BEN, ROB)
Graham 10-year-old Tawny (NI)
Graham Late Bottled (QUE)
Quinta do Noval Late Bottled (TAN)
Taylor Chip Dry White Port (HOG, PLA, DAV)
Taylor Late Bottled (THR, BOT, WR, QUE)
Warre's Warrior (LAYT, PEN)
1990
Dow's Late Bottled (AME)
Taylor Late Bottled (AUR)
1989
Dow's Late Bottled (VIC)
Graham Late Bottled (VIC, HOG, HAH)
Ramos-Pinto Late Bottled (BEN)
Sandeman Late Bottled (NEW)
Taylor Late Bottled (HOG, MAJ, VIC, FOR, UN)
1988
Cockburn's Late Bottled (HA, UN)
Dow's Late Bottled (SUM, SAT, AV)
Graham Late Bottled (REI, WAI, SAF, BO, UN)
Taylor Late Bottled (SAF, WAI, BO, FUL)
1987
Churchill's Crusted Port (PLA)
Graham Late Bottled (WAT, TES, WR, BOT, THR, MAJ, HIC)
1985
Feuerheerd (THR, WR, BOT, OD)
Royal Oporto (FUL)
1984
Delaforce Quinta da Corte (OD)
1983
Royal Oporto (ELL)

£11.00 → £12.99

Non-vintage
Churchill's Crusted Port (WRI)
Cockburn's 10-year-old Tawny (HA)
Quinta da Ervamoira 10-year-old Tawny (NEZ)
Quinta do Noval 10-year-old Tawny (WAI)
Tanners Crusted (TAN)

1991
Dow's Crusted Port (AUR)
1990
Graham Malvedos (NI)
Quinta de la Rosa (MV)
1989
Dow's Late Bottled (LAYT)
Graham Late Bottled (TAN)
1988
Dow's Crusted Port (AV)
Quinta de la Rosa (PLA, YOU, ELL)
1987
Cálem Colheita (HOG)
Churchill's Crusted Port (SOM, WR, BOT)
1985
Cockburn (BIB)
Delaforce (OD)
1984
Delaforce Quinta da Corte (POR)
1982
Graham Malvedos (NI)
Royal Oporto (TES)
1980
Warre (WY)
1970
Martinez (BUT)

£13.00 → £14.99

Non-vintage
Dow's 10-year-old Tawny (THR, BOT, WR)
Fonseca 10-year-old Tawny (ENO, FUL, ELL)
Graham 10-year-old Tawny (OD)
Martinez 10-year-old Tawny (HIC, PIP, AME)
Quinta da Ervamoira 10-year-old Tawny
  (QUE)
Quinta do Noval 10-year-old Tawny (UN)
Taylor 10-year-old Tawny (WHI, PLA, FOR,
  PEN, EY, BO, DAV)
Warre's Nimrod Old Tawny (DI)
1988
Quinta de la Rosa (MV, CB)
1985
Churchill (GOE)
Croft (FA, THR, BOT, WR)
Dow (BIB, FA, BUT)
1983
Feuerheerd (BU)
Gould Campbell (ELL)
Royal Oporto (DI, WRI)
Smith Woodhouse (PIP)
Warre (BUT)
1982
Croft (GOE)
Fonseca Guimaraens (HOG)
Quinta do Noval (DI)

Sandeman (WAT, WR, BOT, THR)
Taylor Quinta de Vargellas (HOG)
Warre's Late Bottled (NO, PIP, HAH, WAI)
1981
Smith Woodhouse Late Bottled (ROB)
Warre's Late Bottled (HIC)
1980
Delaforce Quinta da Corte (POR)
Graham (BIB)
Quinta de la Rosa (GAU)
Taylor ½ bottle (HAL)
1979
Warre's Quinta da Cavadinha (SUM)
1975
Croft (BIB)
Delaforce (MAJ)
1967
Taylor Quinta de Vargellas (FA)

£15.00 → £16.99

Non-vintage
Cockburn's 20-year-old Tawny (HA)
Dow's Vintage Character (BUT)
Taylor 10-year-old Tawny (TAN, WRI, BOT,
  MAJ, THR, WR, BEN, VIN)
Warre's 10-year-old Tawny (AV)
1992
Quinta de la Rosa (YOU)
1991
Fonseca Guimaraens (REI)
Gould Campbell (PIP)
Graham (NI)
Smith Woodhouse (BO)
Warre (DI)
1987
Quinta da Eira Velha (NO, AME)
1985
Delaforce (POR)
Gould Campbell (DI)
Quarles Harris (PIP)
Quinta do Noval (TAN)
Smith Woodhouse (DI)
1984
Delaforce Quinta da Corte (AV)
Taylor Quinta de Vargellas (FOR, PLA, HAH)
Warre's Quinta da Cavadinha (WHI, MAJ, DI)
1983
Croft Quinta da Roeda (POR)
Dow (BUT, FA, NO)
Graham (REI)
Warre (BIB, BOT, THR, WR, YOU)
1982
Churchill (BER)
Quinta do Noval (HOG, YOU)
Taylor Quinta de Vargellas (UN)

1980
Dow's Crusted Port (BUT)
Fonseca (FOR, HOG)
Sandeman (BU)
Taylor (WY)
Warre (DAV, FOR)
1978
Croft Quinta da Roeda (REI)
1977
Offley Boa Vista (FA)
1967
Martinez (BEN)

£17.00 → £18.99

Non-vintage
Cockburn's Special Reserve (BUT)
Dow Quinta do Bomfim (SAT)
Graham 20-year-old Tawny (REI)
Quinta do Bom Retiro 20-year-old Tawny
  (NEZ)
1991
Cálem (TAN)
Cockburn (HA)
Dow (FUL)
Gould Campbell (CB)
Smith Woodhouse (DAV)
Taylor Quinta de Vargellas (ELL)
Warre (BO)
1987
Quinta da Eira Velha (DI)
1985
Graham (EL, NI)
Sandeman (WAT)
1984
Dow Quinta do Bomfim (THR)
Taylor Quinta de Vargellas (TAN, WRI)
Warre's Quinta da Cavadinha (WAI, AME)
1983
Cockburn (BUT, HOG)
Dow (GOE, TAN)
Fonseca (GAL, BUT)
Gould Campbell (NO)
Graham (BIB)
Royal Oporto (UN)
Taylor (FUL)
1982
Croft (ROB, VIC)
Martinez (AD)
Quinta do Noval (VIC)
Taylor Quinta de Vargellas (TES, VIC)
Warre's Quinta da Cavadinha (ROB)
1980
Fonseca (WY, RES, WR, BOT, THR)
Gould Campbell (BER)
Graham (REI, DAV)

Quarles Harris (AME)
Sandeman (NEW)
Taylor (WHI)
1978
Fonseca Guimaraens (PEN, BEN, RES, ENO)
Quinta do Noval (PEN, EY)
Taylor Quinta de Vargellas (BOT, WR, THR)
1977
Offley Boa Vista (CB)
Quarles Harris (REI, BUT, LAYT, BO)
1976
Fonseca Guimaraens (THR, WR, BOT, QUE)
1975
Cockburn (BER)
Dow (REI)
Smith Woodhouse (PEN)
1970
Royal Oporto (REI)
1960
Delaforce (REI)

£19.00 → £20.99

Non-vintage
Fonseca Guimaraens (SAF)
Graham 20-year-old Tawny (NI)
1986
Churchill's Crusted Port (BUT)
1985
Cockburn (PLA, HA, VIC)
Dow (BO, ELL, LAY, VIC)
Graham (BO, BUT, VIC)
Quinta do Noval (PIP, AUR)
Taylor (BO)
Warre (HOG, HAH, PLA, YOU)
1984
Graham Malvedos (NO)
Warre's Quinta da Cavadinha (PIP, AV, TAN)
1983
Churchill's Quinta do Agua Alta (AD)
Dow (HOG, POR, LAY, YOU, ROB)
Fonseca (HOG, FUL)
Taylor (HOG)
1982
Graham Malvedos (BOT, WR, THR)
Quinta do Noval (VIG)
1980
Dow (DAV)
Sandeman (ROB)
Warre (EL, DI)
1979
Dow Quinta do Bomfim (ROB)
Graham Malvedos (AV, HAH)
1978
Quinta do Noval (VIC, RES)
Taylor Quinta de Vargellas (EL, BU)

1977
Delaforce (GOE, POR, DI, OD)
Quarles Harris (BER, WR, BOT, THR)
Warre (BUT, REI)
1976
Fonseca Guimaraens (ELL, PEN)
1975
Croft (POR, BER)
Dow (BER, FUL)
Graham (NI)
Quinta do Noval (PEN)
1970
Martinez (REI)
Sandeman (BIB)

£21.00 → £22.99

Non-vintage
Dow's 20-year-old Tawny (WAI)
Sandeman 20-year-old Tawny (OD)
1991
Cockburn (CB)
Quinta do Vesuvio (BO)
1987
Churchill's Quinta do Agua Alta (BO, TAN)
1985
Churchill (BUT)
Fonseca (GAL)
Taylor (EL, VIC)
1984
Dow Quinta do Bomfim (VIN)
1983
Fonseca (NO, DAV, BIB)
Gould Campbell (WS)
Graham (PEN, UN, DAV, HAH)
Taylor (ROB, DAV, FOR)
Warre (UN, DAV, GAU, VIC)
1980
Fonseca (LEA)
Taylor (ROB, HOG, QUE)
Warre (BER, YOU)
1977
Croft (FA)
Sandeman (SEC)
1972
Taylor Quinta de Vargellas (BU)
1970
Cockburn (FA)
Delaforce (WHI)
Taylor ½ bottle (CRO)
1960
Rebello Valente (REI)

£23.00 → £24.99

Non-vintage
Dow's 20-year-old Tawny (QUE)

Ferreira Duque de Braganca 20-year-old
   Tawny (NO)
Taylor 20-year-old Tawny (EL)
1992
Quinta do Vesuvio (AD)
1991
Fonseca Guimaraens (ROB)
Taylor Quinta de Vargellas (ROB)
1985
Cockburn (DAV)
Graham (DAV)
Warre (ROB, DAV, RES)
1984
Graham Malvedos (LAY)
1983
Cockburn (HA, NO)
Taylor (VIC)
1980
Fonseca (BER, VIC, EL)
Graham (BER)
Taylor (FOR)
Warre (VIC)
1977
Gould Campbell (WHI)
Offley Boa Vista (VIC)
Quarles Harris (AD)
Royal Oporto (DAV)
Warre (BIB, FA)
1975
Graham (BER, WHI)
1967
Cockburn (YOU)

£25.00 → £29.99

Non-vintage
Ferreira Duque de Braganca 20-year-old
   Tawny (ENO)
Fonseca 20-year-old (PLA, BEN)
Taylor 20-year-old Tawny (UN, FOR, LAY)
1992
Quinta do Vesuvio (LAY)
1990
Quinta do Vesuvio (NO)
1989
Quinta do Vesuvio (DI)
1985
Fonseca (ROB, HOG)
Taylor (FOR, PLA, HOG, WHI, LAY)
1980
Taylor (EL)
1977
Croft (REI, BER)
Dow (WAT, GOE, DI, FA, BUT, FUL)
Graham (REI)
Sandeman (BER, ROB, LEA)

Smith Woodhouse (WHI)
Warre (WAT, GOE, TAN, GE, NI, POR)
1975
Taylor (BER)
1970
Cockburn (WY, WS, GAU)
Croft (WY, WHI, BEN, TAN)
Delaforce (BER)
Quinta do Noval (BIB, MV, BO)
Rebello Valente (VIC)
1967
Fonseca Guimaraens (VIC)
1966
Quinta do Noval (FA)
1960
Sandeman (BUT)

£30.00 → £39.99

Non-vintage
Taylor 20-year-old Tawny (ROB, TAN, BEN)
1992
Fonseca (FA)
1980
Dow (VIN)
1977
Dow (LAY, WS, PEN, BER, DAV, EL, VIG, YOU)
Graham (BO, GOE, FA, BIB, SOM, DAV, YOU)
Offley Boa Vista (VIN)
Taylor (HOG, REI, FA)
Warre (LAY, EL, BO, HA, DAV)
1970
Cockburn (HA, DAV)
Graham (DAV, BUT, WS)
Quinta do Noval (TAN, PLA, LEA, BER, ROB)
Warre (ELL, DAV, DI, BUT, BER, HAH)
1966
Gould Campbell (BER)
Quinta do Noval (BU, REI, PEN)
Rebello Valente (BUT)
1964
Taylor Quinta de Vargellas (VIG)
1963
Croft (FA)
Dow (DI)
Feuerheerd (BU)
1960
Cockburn (BUT)
Croft (YOU)

> **Webster's** is an annual
> publication. We welcome
> your suggestions for next
> year's edition.

Dow (BU, DI)
Fonseca (REI, SEC)
Graham (BUT, SUM)
Sandeman (ROB)
1958
Mackenzie (BU)
Warre (POR)

£40.00 → £49.99

1986
Quinta do Noval Nacional (FA)
1977
Graham (EL, ROB)
Taylor (WY, BIB, DAV, BO, BEN)
1970
Dow (RES)
Graham (FA, GOE, BIB, NI)
Taylor (WY, EY, CRO, BIB, FA, GOE)
Warre (ROB, EL, RES)
1969
Dow's 30-year-old Tawny (SOM)
1967
Cockburn (PEN)
1966
Ferreira (VIG)
Graham (BU, REI, FA)
Taylor (DAV, BUT, BEN, REI)
Warre (DI)
1964
Taylor Quinta de Vargellas (VIG)
1963
Croft (BIB, MV, WY, WS)
Quinta do Noval (REI, BEN, MV)
Sandeman (BU)
Warre (BIB, FA)
1960
Fonseca (RES)
Warre (TAN, ROB, YOU)
1950
Dow (CRO)

£50.00 → £74.99

Non-vintage
Taylor 40-year-old Tawny (PEN, FOR, UN)
1980
Quinta do Noval Nacional (FA)
1977
Taylor (NO, ROB)
1970
Fonseca (WY, BER, EL)
Graham (EL, ROB, LEA)
1966
Dow (RES)
Quinta do Noval (VIG)
Sandeman (VIG)

1963
Dow (FA)
Fonseca (BUT)
Quinta do Noval (EL, LEA, ROB)
Warre (GOE, GAU, WS, DI, LAY, BEN, BUT)
1960
Gonzalez (SOM)
Taylor (YOU, RES)
1955
Cockburn (SEC)
Quinta do Noval (POR)
Rebello Valente (FOR)
1950
Sandeman (BEN)
1944
Royal Oporto (TW)
1934
Martinez (WY)
1924
Rebello Valente (WY)

£75.00 → £99.99

1963
Fonseca (GOE, BIB)
Graham (FA, GOE)
Taylor (CRO, SOM, FA, SEC, RES, BIB, VIG)
Warre (RES)
1955
Croft (WY, ROB)
Dow (BEN, CRO)
Fonseca (FA)
1947
Quinta do Noval (CRO)
1942
Sandeman (SOM)

£100.00 → £149.99

1985
Quinta do Noval Nacional (NO)
1980
Quinta do Noval Nacional (TW)

1955
Graham (SOM)
Taylor (BU, REI, BIB)
1948
Graham (CRO)
1945
Quinta do Noval (BUT)
1934
Martinez (RES)
1927
Gould Campbell (BEN)
1924
Dow (WY, BEN)
1920
Gould Campbell (SEC)

£150.00 → £199.99

1958
Quinta do Noval Nacional (FA)
1955
Taylor (ROB)
1945
Croft (RES)
Quinta do Noval (RES)
1935
Graham (CRO)
Sandeman (REI)
1930
Taylor (REI)
1927
Cockburn (RES)
1920
Warre (WY)
1908
Cockburn (REI)
Sandeman (BEN)

£200.00 → £299.99

1948
Taylor (BEN)
1945
Croft (WY)
Graham (ROB)
Sandeman (WY, RES)
1935
Taylor (RES)
1927
Cockburn (WY)
Taylor (ROB)
1912
Croft (RES)

£590.00 → £600.00

1963
Quinta do Noval Nacional (NO, TW)

MADEIRA

Under £8.00

Non-vintage
Bual Old Trinity House Rutherford &
Miles (FUL)
Full Rich Henriques & Henriques (FOR)
Medium Rich Henriques & Henriques (FOR)
Sercial Henriques & Henriques (FOR)
Sercial Old Custom House Rutherford &
Miles (FUL)
Viva Dry Cossart Gordon (HAH)

£8.00 → £9.99

Non-vintage
Bual Old Trinity House Rutherford &
Miles (HAH, ROB)
Full Rich Blandy (NI)
Full Rich Good Company Cossart
Gordon (DI)
Full Rich Henriques & Henriques (ELL, LEA)
Medium Dry Blandy (QUE)
Medium Dry Henriques & Henriques (PEN)
Medium Rich Blandy (WAT, NI)
Medium Rich Cossart Gordon (PEN)
Medium Rich Henriques & Henriques (ELL)
Rainwater Good Company Cossart
Gordon (DI)

Sercial Henriques & Henriques (PEN)
Sercial Old Custom House Rutherford &
Miles (AME, ROB)
Special Dry Blandy (NI, QUE)

£10.00 → £14.99

Non-vintage
10-year-old Bual Rutherford & Miles (NO)
10-year-old Malmsey Blandy (WAT, NI, NO,
WR, THR, BOT)

5-year-old Bual Cossart Gordon (DI, WR,
BOT, THR, HIC)
5-year-old Malmsey Cossart Gordon
(BOT, WR, THR, AD)
5-year-old Sercial Cossart Gordon (DI,
WR, THR, BOT, HAH)
Bual Reserve Rutherford & Miles (QUE)
Finest Old Bual Cossart Gordon (PIP)
Finest Old Malmsey Cossart Gordon (PIP)
Finest Old Sercial Cossart Gordon (PIP)
Full Rich Blandy (VIN)
Medium Dry Blandy (VIN)
Medium Rich Blandy (VIN)
Special Dry Blandy (VIN)

£15.00 → £19.99

Non-vintage
10-year-old Bual Rutherford & Miles (VIG)
10-year-old Malmsey Blandy (HOG, WAI,
HAH, QUE, ROB)
10-year-old Malmsey Cossart Gordon (DI,
HIC)
10-year-old Verdelho Cossart Gordon
(THR, WR, BOT, AD)
5-year-old Malmsey Cossart Gordon (DI)
Very Old Sercial Duo Centenary
Celebration Cossart Gordon (HAH)

£20.00 → £49.99

Non-vintage
Bual Solera 1845 Cossart Gordon (FUL)

c. £79.00

1952
Malmsey Jubilee Selection Leacock (CRO)

£110.00 → £124.00

Non-vintage
Verdelho Solera 1880 Blandy (VIG)
1944
Sercial Henriques & Henriques (CRO)
1940
Sercial Rutherford & Miles (VIG)

> *Please remember that*
> ***Webster's*** *is a price*
> *GUIDE and not a price*
> *LIST. It is not meant to*
> *replace up-to-date*
> *merchants' lists.*

UNITED KINGDOM

It's our fault – we knock it, just because it's English. But supposing England started producing good sparkling wine: would we pay the price then? So far, the omens are good

The main problem with English wine is the English. 'Once we've persuaded people to like English wine, then we're home and dry': this is the view of the enthusiastic couple who own Hidden Springs Vineyard in East Sussex. They are not alone. Other owners and winemakers lament the Anglo-Saxon tendency to decry the local product. New Zealanders were just the same until a few years ago, and even now there are many New Zealanders who prefer to buy Australian wine.

There are other parallels to be drawn with New Zealand. Both countries have had false starts, following the trail of German grape varieties. Now there has been a definite shift away from Germanic wine-making styles here, to the extent that England is almost becoming the next New World country. At Denbies a Roseworthy graduate from Australia has replaced a German winemaker, and the difference can be tasted in a comparison of the 1995 and 1992 vintages of Riesling. The older wine has a mouthwatering streak of acidity, while the 1995 is fragrant and harmonious. Others following New World techniques include John Worontschak from the Harvest Group, and David Cowdroie, who is the man behind Chapel Down. David Sax, who now produces Saxon Valley, trained in New Zealand and has worked three vintages there. He sees similarities between the two countries. Both risk heavy rain at vintage time and may be saved by wonderful Indian summers, as was the case in England in 1995. Like New Zealand, England needs to do more work on matching grape varieties to climate.

There is an increasing amount of Chardonnay planted, much of which is destined for sparkling wine. Nyetimer,

outside Pulborough, has nearly 50 acres, with a little Pinot Noir and Pinot Meunier, all intended for sparkling wine, of which the first release, the 1992 vintage, appeared in the summer of 1996. Sparkling wine has long been one of the objectives of the Harvest Group, with Heritage Brut and others. The new winemaker at Denbies is working to improve the sparkling wine, by giving it longer on the lees and by including some barrel-fermented Chardonnay in the blend. One of the longest established vineyards, Breaky Bottom, is also producing its first fizz. There is no doubt that the potential for bubbles from the chalky North and South Downs is tremendous, and this may prove England's real strength.

Anglo-Saxon attitudes

The other attitude problem that the English wine producer has to confront is the assumption that if it is local it should be cheap. It is possible to buy English wine at £2.99 a bottle, but this is usually a clearance price. When £1.05 a bottle goes in excise duty and VAT, a bottle of English wine needs to be at least £5 a bottle if there is to be any profit in it for the grower.

Nor is cross-Channel shopping helping. Some growers and wineries have gone out of business in the last few years. They need considerable marketing acumen to survive: banding together in associations like the Harvest Group or the English Wine Producers is one way; being based in a tourist area is another.

While it is true that the quality range of English wine is broad – there are professional winemakers and there are distinctly amateur ones – overall quality is improving. So try it. You may be pleasantly surprised. **ROSEMARY GEORGE MW**

GRAPES AND FLAVOURS

BACCHUS (white) In Germany, this new crossing usually produces fat, blowsy, marmalade-Muscatty flavours. In England it is more likely to produce sharp, strong flavours of gooseberry, elderflower and orange rind. Best: *Barkham, Partridge Vineyard, Three Choirs, Coddington and Shawsgate.*

CABERNET SAUVIGNON (red) *Beenleigh* in Devon has been growing this in plastic tunnels, along with Merlot, and the 1991 version, blended with Merlot, is clean and fresh, if light.

FABER (white) A crossing of Pinot Blanc and Müller-Thurgau, making fragrant wines with good acidity. One of the few varieties in which you can actually taste Riesling characteristics.

HUXELREBE (white) A cross (of Gutedel, alias Chasselas, with Courtillier Musqué) that in Germany beetles to overripeness in no time at all. The wine there is usually rich, flat and grapy. In England it's generally the exact opposite, renowned for a grapefruit-pith taste and a greenish bite. For this reason it is often softened up by blending. *Lamberhurst* and *Biddenden* are full; *Staple St James* more grapefruity and smoky. *Nutbourne Manor*'s is concentrated, while *Three Choirs* picks it late and tries to make a sweetie.

KERNER (white) A bright, new German crossing of Riesling and Trollinger that has been producing good results.

MADELEINE ANGEVINE (white) Basically a table grape, but performs quite well in England, where its somewhat fruit-juicy character is matched by good acidity, either in a green but refreshingly elderflower-perfumed style, or a more honeyed but appley style. *Sharpham*'s is good, sometimes barrel fermented.

MÜLLER-THURGAU (white) This used to be the English workhorse. However, it has

fallen from over one-third of the acreage to 15 per cent. *Wootton, Bruisyard St Peter, Breaky Bottom, St Nicholas of Ash, Staple St James* and *St George*'s are good. And it can make very attractive, slightly sweet wine (through the addition of *Süssreserve,* or unfermented grape juice, just before bottling), as at *Rowney.*

ORTEGA (white) German cross making fat, rich, grapy wine mostly in the Mosel, of all places, but better suited to England. *Hidden Spring* is concentrated, and *Biddenden,* in particular, makes a delicious, slightly sweet but tremendously fruity elderflower and apricot-tasting example. It is usually blended and rarely seen on its own.

PINOT NOIR (red) There are now 46 hectares and rising of the great Burgundy grape planted. and full reds seem to be an increasingly viable proposition. *Thames Valley*'s Pinot Noir is the best so far. Kent has several patches making very good rosé; *Denbies* also makes a nice light, scented rosé; *Chiddingstone* blends it with Pinot Meunier to make a delicious wine redolent of eucalyptus; *Bodiam Castle* makes a tasty rosé blended with Blauburger, as well as a dry, honeyed Blanc de Pinot Noir white; *Biddenden* mixes it with Dornfelder and Gamay for a light, cherryish red; and *Tenterden*'s blend with Dunkelfelder makes a gently honeyed, smoky, mango-flavoured pink. *Three Choirs* rosé from Pinot Noir has earthy raspberry-and-Morello-cherry fruit; *Conghurst*'s grapy, herbaceous rosé is also good. Some estates, particularly *Denbies Estate* and *Nyetimber*, have planted it for fizz.

REICHENSTEINER (white) A real EU grape, since it is a crossing of French Madeleine Angevine, German Müller-Thurgau

The price guides for this section begin on page 330.

and Italian Calabrese. Does this multi-coloured background make it an exciting, tempestuous grape? Sadly, it's more of a Brussels bureaucrat clone, taking up 12 per cent of the total acreage. Usually pretty dull when dry, but made slightly sweet, it can develop a pleasant, smoky, quince-and-peaches taste which ages well. *Carr Taylor* and *Rock Lodge* use it for Champagne-method fizz, *Northbrook Springs* is barrel fermented. *Nutbourne Manor*'s is also good.

SCHEUREBE (white) Silvaner crossed with Riesling, capable of producing good grapefruity, curranty wines in good years. It needs a hot site. It goes into *Thames Valley*'s *Clocktower Selection Botrytis*, when it's made, along with Reichensteiner.

SCHÖNBURGER (pink) A good grape, that makes a fat wine by English standards, with a pears-and-lychees flavour and good acidity. Dry versions like *Saxon Valley*'s need ripe fruit to balance the acidity, and it needs expert wine-making or it can end up tasting like bathroom detergent. The best are made by *Wootton*, *Carr Taylor*, *Coxley* and *Three Choirs*.

SEYVAL BLANC (white) A French hybrid with 12 per cent of the UK acreage, and falling slightly. *Breaky Bottom* is the most successful – dry and Sauvignon-like when young, honeyed like Burgundy after four to five years – but it is generally best blended with something more exotic like Schönburger or Huxelrebe, or made sweetish. *Three Choirs* blends it with Reichensteiner and *Adgestone* with Reichensteiner and Müller, while *Tenterden* makes a very good oaked Reserve. *Thames*

Valley is oaked. *Hidden Spring* blends it successfully with Ortega and gives it some oak, as in 1992.

TRIOMPHE (red) There are only about 11 hectares planted to this hybrid, which used to be called Triomphe d'Alsace until the EU decreed otherwise, but the best examples have a fresh, raspberry-and-spice character like *Meon Valley*'s *Meonwara* or *Thames Valley*'s *Ruscombe*. The trick, as with all reds in England, is to settle for a light, graceful wine and not to over-extract flavour.

OTHER REDS There is also some potential in Dunkelfelder and Dornfelder, plus plantings of Léon Millet and Maréchal Foch, both more commonly seen in Canada. Gamay is being used by *Thames Valley* for a sparkler. *Dunkery*'s *Prometheus* (from Somerset) is delicious.

OTHER WHITES Numerous other varieties are being tried. The most interesting are Gewürztraminer at *Barton Manor* on the Isle of Wight where it was planted in plastic tunnels in 1984, and Ehrenfelser, aged in a 4000-litre oak barrel, at *Penshurst*; *Wootton*'s Auxerrois is a pungent, salty-sappy wine. *Carr Taylor* has achieved good results with Pinot Blanc for its concentrated *Kemsley Dry*. There are also some efforts with Chardonnay, at, for example, the 250-acre *Denbies Estate* at Dorking in Surrey, England's biggest vineyard project yet. Chardonnay now has all of 36 hectares planted in England (Kerner has 23) and most of them are at *Denbies* and *Nyetimber*, with *Thames Valley*'s *Clocktower* label also in the running. Denbies' Riesling is also showing potential.

MERCHANTS SPECIALISING IN ENGLAND
see Merchant Directory (page 424) for details

Nobody has very long lists of English wines, but the following have a fair selection: Averys of Bristol (AV), The Nobody Inn (NO), Thos. Peatling (PE), Terry Platt (PLA) well, wines from Wales actually,

Safeway (SAF), Tanners (TAN), Thresher (THR) an exceptionally long list, Unwins (UN), Wine Society (WS). Otherwise the best thing is to buy direct from the vineyard itself.

UNITED KINGDOM

WHITE

Under £4.50

Non-vintage
Lamberhurst Sovereign (SAI, DAV)
Wootton Trinity (SAI)
1995
Carr Taylor Hastings Medium Dry
(SAI)
1993
Saxon Valley (BOT, WR, THR)
Three Choirs Medium Dry (SAI)
1992
Denbies (SAI)
1990
Three Choirs Seyval Blanc/Reichensteiner
Dry (SAF)

£4.50 → £4.99

1993
Three Choirs Medium Dry (TAN)
1990
Bruisyard St Peter Müller-Thurgau
(BER)

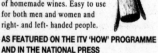
1989
Staple St-James Müller-Thurgau (BER)

£5.00 → £5.99

1994
Astley Severn Vale (TAN)
Wake Court (EL)
1993
Elmham Park Madeleine Angevine (SAT)
Elmham Park Medium Dry (SAT)
Three Choirs Medium Dry (WS)
1992
Moorlynch (WR, THR, BOT)
Wootton Auxerrois (WS)
1991
Wootton Schönburger (HIC)
1989
Staple St-James Huxelrebe (BER)

£6.00 → £7.99

1992
Breaky Bottom Seyval Blanc (WS)
1990
Elmham Park Müller-Thurgau (HA)
Pulham Vineyards Magdalen Rivaner
(TW)
1989
Lamberhurst Schönburger (BER)

£8.00 → £8.99

1993
Sharpham Barrel-Fermented Dry (THR,
BOT, WR)
1992
Thames Valley Fumé Blanc (WR, THR, BOT,
NO)

c. £12.50

1992
Sharpham Barrel-Fermented Dry (NO)

RED

c. £6.00

1992
Denbies Red (SAI)

SPARKLING

c. £10.50

Non-vintage
Carr Taylor (CRO)

EASTERN EUROPE

We're going to have to pay more for the best wines from eastern Europe, but there's nothing unfair about that. If we're not prepared to pay, we can't expect decent wines

Evolution not revolution: that's what's happening in eastern Europe. We are seeing growth in both sales and quality but we don't expect the wines to be in the mid-price bracket. We still want nicely aged Cabernets and Pinot Noirs or barrique-fermented Chardonnays for less than £4 and we walk away if we don't. In the medium term this will be bad news for both producers and consumers. All the ex-Iron Curtain countries have had serious inflation; all of them badly need to make big capital investments, and all feel that they need and deserve to see some return if they invest in quality production. Privatisation and disillusion are forcing good vineyard land out of production. Other countries, notably the USA, CIS and Germany, are beginning to compete for the available volume. Investment only comes when all parties involved feel confident that sales will make the necessary return on capital; it would be a tragedy to lose many of these vineyards.

In other words: don't expect to see too much more Bulgarian Cabernet Sauvignon at £1.99; you'll be lucky to find the best ones at under £3.50 in future. If one comes highly recommended at a price you don't associate with eastern Europe, give it a whirl; it will still be value for money in international terms and you'll be helping to save a vineyard's life.

The good news is that white wine production is getting more and more reliable. Applying the careful hygiene and controlled temperature disciplines of flying wine-making to any good white grapes is a bit like bathing and dressing up Calamity Jane. They 'clean up real pretty'. Pinot Gris from Murfatlar or Tărnave in Romania or via the Nesmelye winery in Hungary are fine examples. So are Chardonnays from various Hungarian vineyards (make sure it's young), Khan Krum/Preslav in Bulgaria, South-Eastern Romania (Murfatlar/Medgedia/Cernavodă) and Moldova, where Hugh Ryman is finally well-established, having toughed out the first few appallingly difficult years. These are all great countries for Sauvignon Blanc, which is widely planted and suffers only from the lack of necessary investment in the winery.

Just desserts

Ever since the gold rush to buy up premium bits of Tokaji in Hungary started, we have been waiting to see the real results. This year should see the first wide ranging offer of the dessert wines which are setting out to prove what non-oxidative handling can do for Furmint and Hárslevelü grapes.

Red wines, on the other hand, are not really advancing so fast. Hungarian reds remain, with a very few honourable exceptions (and none from the 1994 vintage) the thinnest, lightest, least attractive and durable in the country. Their nicest surprises are the best of the pure Cabernet Francs, which can have a very good colour and perfumy, black plum taste. Macedonia is the newest entrant, with some cheap but earthy reds of good colour and chunky tannin. Bulgaria didn't have a good harvest in 1995 and is scraping around for decent fruit. Whenever this happens, the least expensive wines show leaner and duller than usual, and are probably best avoided. The best news is probably that of the young Romanian reds. There are a lot of good vineyards here, and 'young vatted' Cabernet, Pinot Noir and above all Merlot (if the Californians don't grab it all first) are the wines that are showing some real, rich, balanced fruit. **ANGELA MUIR MW**

BULGARIA

We are still drinking more and more Bulgarian wine. This is worrying, as we now account for not far off 20 per cent of what's officially made. Privatisation here, as elsewhere, includes the return of small vineyard plots to families of former owners. To do this often involves breaking up larger, more professionally farmed vineyards. Here, and throughout most former Iron Curtain countries, this is resulting in the disappearance of around 20 to 30 per cent of grapes from the 'professional' wine-making market. Furthermore, many of the major wineries were sited on the outskirts of towns and cities, so that workers could easily get there. These, of course, are now prime development sites and often half empty following the Gorbachev purges of the mid-80s, which removed half the Bulgarian vineyard. Although they had fixed contracts with their growers, they don't any more. The scrabble for grapes in a scarce year is a major fight for survival. The winners may stay in the game; the losers are likely to be 'privatised' to property developers. Since

Bulgaria needs to lose about half its production capacity, this isn't total disaster, but it is a brake on capital development despite our national faith in Bulgaria as a reliable source of red wine.

Potential survivors include the prosperous and reliable Lovico-Suhindol where the farmers own the winery and have about 60 per cent of the land planted with Cabernet Sauvignon; Iambol, too far out of town and heading well in to private hands, and Khan Krum, which has taken kindly to flying wine-making. With a following wind, Russe, one of the biggest and the best red wine wineries, should continue to do well with its 'young vatted' styles. (Young vatted simply means it was made to show strong, youthful fruit and it didn't go into oak.) Slaviantzi and Svishtov both produce good buying samples, the former particularly for white.

There is quiet, solid, joint venture work going on between local winemakers and Antipodeans. Results are increasingly fresh whites and good young reds.

HUNGARY

There is Tokaji and there is everything else. This is unfair, since Tokaji is just one fairly small quality region out of 20 – but it is the area which is piloting central and eastern Europe into a new era. It alone in all eastern Europe has professionally run, premium 'boutique' wineries. Six very rich western investors own good sized holdings in the region. They came in determined to restore fame and fortune to the area, and they started to apply similar methods to those used in Sauternes and Graves. The results look exciting. But they weren't achieved without a lot of damage to local pride, and a questioning of whether Tokaji should not legitimately remain an oxidative wine like tawny port.

'Everything else' is capable of producing between 30 and 40 million cases of wine a

year, twice as much as Bulgaria these days. Privatisation and inward investment are gathering momentum. Flying winemakers are less of a feature than they were, but their legacy includes some very good native Hungarian winemakers. This means that more of the wine finding its way here is at least reliable. Bottlings from the Nesmelye winery, which may well show another region like Sopron, Mór, Tök or Szedszárd on the label, get better every year, especially the whites. One of the two wineries where Kym Milne operates, Balatonboglár, is now German owned, although this has had no effect so far. More worrying is the German purchase of Gyöngyös, home of Hugh Ryman and Adrian Wing's revolutionary Chardonnay and Sauvignon.

MACEDONIA

One of the most unlikely looking Aussie trained winemakers ever, Steve Clarke, has been helping to reform wine handling and bottling here for the past two years. It's paying off for at least one winery, Povardarié, which sent several hundred thousand cases, mainly of country red, here last year. Vranac is the main red grape, and can be used to make rich, crude but solid and balanced wines for drinking or keeping. The whites need cooler handling than the winery can yet afford to give them, but they show some leafy, lively and positive fruit flavours that may please those who like a white to have some real structure.

MOLDOVA AND POINTS EAST

A vast vineyard strip runs across Moldova, Ukraine, Belorusse, Georgia and on into Azerbaijan. Beyond Moldova, it is all too clear that this is not Europe. It's an enormously rich wine-producing area, but little of its production comes west. The exception is the Hugh Ryman operation based on Hincesti winery in Moldova, selling under the Kirkwood brand. The flavours are archetypal flying winemaker, right down to the slight oakiness.

ROMANIA

The biggest producer of all, Romania has a lot of good traditional vineyard land. Some of the finest reds come from Dealu Mare: names like Tohani, Urlati, Săhăteni and Ceptura are now beginning to appear on bottles of Merlot and Cabernet Sauvignon. Sometimes the wood is clean and the wines astonishing. The young vatted styles are safer, although these themselves were the origins of much of the aged Pinot Noir that was so popular a while back.

Tămave or Tirnave makes less ripe, more delicately aromatic whites like Sauvignon, Pinot Gris and Gewürztraminer.

There are also a very few potentially outstanding natural sweet wine producers: the research station of Pietroasele, Cotnari and parts of Murfatlar. Tămîioasă Românească and Grasă are Romania's own noble rot varieties. Murfatlar uses overripe classic white grape types. Recent vintages have been badly bottled, but occasionally come out delicious.

SLOVAKIA AND CZECH REPUBLIC

For protectionist and currency reasons the wines of both countries are poor value. This is a pity. They have some good grapes, and privatisation is just beginning to exert a positive influence after having been a dead hand on development for some years now.

SLOVENIA AND CROATIA

Prices are high for the better fresh, dry whites. Lutomer Laski Rizling is not quite dead yet, but is certainly no longer typical of the best. Pinot Blanc, Chardonnay, Sauvignon Blanc, Gewürztraminer and Sipon (a local grape) are grown in the hills; many of the north-eastern Italian red grapes are found on the Dalmatian coast.

GRAPES & WINES

ALIGOTÉ (white; Romania, Bulgaria, Moldova) Used for sparkling wine and some passable neutral dry white. Often blended with Chardonnay.

BURGUND MARE (red; Romania) Probably Blauburgunder. Produces a light shadow of Pinot Noir style.

CABERNET FRANC (red; Hungary, Moldova, Bulgaria) Lovely velvety, fruity young reds in Hungary.

CABERNET SAUVIGNON (red; Macedonia, Bulgaria, Romania, Moldova, SW Hungary) Can produce ripe, long-lived wines in Romania, Moldova and Bulgaria.

CHARDONNAY (white; Bulgaria, Hungary, Moldova, Romania) Good dry whites. Yields are a bit too high in Hungary.

DIMIAT (white; Bulgaria) Bulk producer, blended with Muscat and Rhine Riesling.

FETEASCĂ ALBĂ/LEANYKA/ MÄDCHENTRAUBE (white; Romania, Hungary) Rich, floral, short-lived, flabby wines.

FETEASCĂ NEAGRĂ (red; Romania) At best dark, slightly vegetal with sooty tannins. Can easily become too vegetal.

FURMINT (white; Hungary) The top Tokaji grape; good acidity, concentration, long life.

GAMZA (red; Bulgaria) Soft, light, and early maturing.

GEWÜRZTRAMINER (white; everywhere) Usually known as Traminer, and has typical spicy style. Amazing dessert wines in Moldova.

GRÜNER VELTLINER (white; CZ, Slovakia) Intense greengage fruit at best; hard acidity if not ripened properly.

HÁRSLEVELÜ (white; Hungary) Earthy, big, peachy, long-lived.

EASTERN EUROPEAN CLASSIFICATIONS

BULGARIA   In order of quality there are Katchestveno vino (equivalent to Vin de Pays); Vina ot declariran geografski rayon (equivalent to DOC or AOC); Vinas controlirano naimenovanie za proizhod (equivalent to DOCG); Kolektziono/Rezera (Reserve: implies aging controls).

HUNGARY   Tájbor (Vin de Pays equivalent); Minöségi bor (quality wine; normally higher alcohol level); Különleges minöségu bor (top quality wine, often comes with an extra qualification. For example, all the Tokaji descriptions such as 'aszu 4 puttonyos').

ROMANIA   Vinuri de calitate superioară (Vin de Pays equivalent); Vinuri de calitate superioară cu denumire de origine controlată (AOC equivalent); Vinuri de calitate superioară cu denumire de origine controlată si trepte de calitate (this is usually followed by a further term normally to do with the sweetness level; may carry aging implications as well); Vin de vinotecă (wine aged in bottle in its own cellar for a minimum time before release); Rezervă (carries minimum bulk aging requirements).

SLOVENIA   All six Yugoslav republics shared a system. Premium (Kvalitetno) Wine is from a specific region. Select Wine (Cuveno or Vrhunsko Vino) can be from a single vineyard.

THE CZECH STATE, SLOVAKIA, CIS STATES   No system of classifications.

IRSAY OLIVER (white; CZ, Slovakia, Hungary) A Muscat cross, very perfumed and intense.

KADARKA (red; Hungary) Seldom allowed to produce the weight and tannin which made its reputation. Usually small, tough, green wines.

KÉKFRANKOS/FRANKOVKA/ BLAUFRANKISCH (red; Hungary, CZ, Slovakia) Vegetal young reds. Yields have to be small for good quality.

KÉKOPORTO/BLAUER PORTUGUEISER (red; Hungary) Light, ordinary, short-lived reds.

MAVRUD (red; Bulgaria) Hefty dark reds.

MERLOT (red; everywhere except CZ and Slovakia) Very successful in Romania, good in southern Bulgaria.

MISKET (white; Bulgaria) Claims not to be a Muscat, but has a lightly perfumed style, and a tendency to blow over quickly.

MÜLLER-THURGAU (white; CZ, Slovakia, Hungary) Floral, early-drinking Germanic type. Widely cultivated.

MUSCAT OTTONEL (white; everywhere) Good but short-lived, vulgar Muscat styles.

PAMID (red; Romania, Bulgaria) Short-lived, empty, high yielder; occasionally blends well with Merlot.

PINOT BLANC (white; Hungary, CZ, Slovakia) Very similar to dry Alsace when properly handled.

PINOT GRIS (white; Hungary, CZ, Slovakia, Romania, Moldova) Can make outstanding dry and off-dry wines with wonderful spicy aroma.

PINOT NOIR (red; Romania, Hungary, Moldova, Slovakia) Can be true to type and elegant, but often too poorly handled.

RHINE RIESLING (white; everywhere) Can be lemony and true to type; rarely as intense as good German versions.

ST LAURENT/BLAUER LIMBERGER/ SVATOVAVRINECKE (red; CZ, Slovakia) Delicious soft reds with real black cherry flavours when allowed to ripen.

SAUVIGNON (white; everywhere) Needs good technology; grassy and vegetal otherwise.

SMEDEREVKA (white; Macedonia and elsewhere in former Yugoslavia) Can make good, fresh wine; often poorly handled.

TAMIÎOASĂ ROMANEASCĂ/ TAMIANKA (white; Romania, Bulgaria) Classic noble rot grape, probably related to the Muscat family. Very sweet, raisiny flavours, long-lived.

VRANAC (red; Macedonia) Good solid performer. Takes well to oak.

WELSCHRIESLING/LASKI RIZLING/ VLASSKY RIZLING/OLASZ RIZLING/ RIZLING ITALICO (white; everywhere) Usually and confusingly referred to as Riesling, though nothing to do with Rhine Riesling. Earthy, lowish-acid wines, but reliable yielder and ripener. **ANGELA MUIR MW**

MERCHANTS SPECIALISING IN EASTERN EUROPE
see Merchant Directory (page 424) for details

Butlers Wine Cellar (BU) good for curiosities, Enotria Winecellars (ENO) particularly Hungary, Morris & Verdin (MV) a good range from Bodegas Oremus in

Hungary, Thos. Peatling (PE), Sainsbury (SAI), Safeway (SAF), T&W Wines (TW) old Tokaji, Thresher (THR), Wines of Westhorpe (WIW)

EASTERN EUROPE

BULGARIA RED

Under £2.50

Non-vintage
Russe Cabernet Sauvignon/Cinsaut (WIW)
Suhindol Cabernet Sauvignon/Merlot
(WIW)
Suhindol Merlot/Gamza (WIW)

£2.50 → £2.99

Non-vintage
Bulgarian Cabernet Sauvignon/Merlot (UN,
OD)
Pavlikeni Cabernet Sauvignon/Merlot (VIC)
Petrich Cabernet Sauvignon/Melnik (MAJ)
Russe Cabernet Sauvignon/Cinsaut (CO,
THR, WR, BOT)
Suhindol Cabernet Sauvignon (FUL)
Suhindol Cabernet Sauvignon/Merlot
(THR, BOT, WR)
1995
Bulgarian Merlot/Gamza (WAI)
1994
Bulgarian Merlot (WHI)
1993
Suhindol Cabernet Sauvignon (WIW)
Suhindol Gamza (WIW)
1992
Assenovgrad Mavrud (ASD)
Oriahovitza Cabernet Sauvignon Reserve
(WIW)
Sakar Mountain Cabernet Sauvignon (WIW)
Suhindol Cabernet Sauvignon (WIW)
Suhindol Cabernet Sauvignon Reserve
(WIW)
Suhindol Gamza (WIW)
1991
Assenovgrad Mavrud (WIW)
Oriahovitza Cabernet Sauvignon Reserve
(WIW, ASD)
Suhindol Cabernet Sauvignon (ASD)
Svischtov Cabernet Sauvignon (MAR)
1990
Bulgarian Gamza Reserve (SAI)
Sakar Mountain Cabernet Sauvignon (WIW)
Suhindol Cabernet Sauvignon Reserve
(WIW)

£3.00 → £3.99

Non-vintage
Bulgarian Cabernet Sauvignon (SAI)
Bulgarian Cabernet Sauvignon/Merlot (DI)

Bulgarian Merlot (SAI)
Haskovo Merlot (VIC, LAY)
Oriahovitza Cabernet Sauvignon Reserve
(FUL)
Russe Cabernet Sauvignon Reserve (VIC)
Svischtov Cabernet Sauvignon (LAY)
1993
Suhindol Cabernet Sauvignon (OD)
1992
Suhindol Merlot/Gamza (SAF)
1991
Bulgarian Cabernet Sauvignon (WHI, UN)
Oriahovitza Cabernet Sauvignon (TAN)
Suhindol Reserve Merlot (SAI)
Svischtov Cabernet Sauvignon (TAN)
1990
Bulgarian Merlot (UN)
Oriahovitza Cabernet Sauvignon/Merlot
(SAI)
Plovdiv Cabernet Sauvignon (WR, BOT, THR)
Russe Cabernet Sauvignon Reserve (CO)
Stambolovo Merlot Reserve (SO)
Stambolovo Merlot Special Reserve (CO)
Svischtov Reserve Cabernet Sauvignon
(WHI)
Yantra Valley Cabernet Sauvignon (SAI)
1989
Haskovo Merlot (SAT)
Oriahovitza Cabernet Sauvignon Reserve
(SAI)
Russe Cabernet Sauvignon Reserve (MAJ)
Stambolovo Merlot Reserve (WR, BOT,
THR, UN)
Suhindol Cabernet Sauvignon Reserve
(SAI)
Svischtov Cabernet Sauvignon (WIW)
1988
Svischtov Reserve Cabernet Sauvignon
(SAI)
1987
Sakar Merlot (WIW)
Svischtov Cabernet Sauvignon (WIW)

£4.00 → £4.99

Non-vintage
Russe Cabernet Sauvignon Reserve (LAY)
1989
Haskovo Merlot (TAN)
Svischtov Cabernet Sauvignon (WHI)
1987
Oriahovitza Cabernet Sauvignon Reserve
(SAT)

Svischtov Cabernet Sauvignon (BOT, WR)
1985
Sakar Mountain Cabernet Sauvignon (SAT)

c. £6.00
1986
Stambolovo Merlot Special Reserve (UB)

BULGARIA WHITE

Under £2.50
Non-vintage
Burgas Muscat/Ugni Blanc (WIW)

£2.50 → £2.99
Non-vintage
Burgas Muscat/Ugni Blanc (FUL, WAI, UN, MAJ)
Preslav Chardonnay (WIW, FUL)
1993
Khan Krum Chardonnay (WIW)

£3.00 → £3.99
Non-vintage
Khan Krum Special Reserve Chardonnay (FUL)
1995
Novi Pazar Chardonnay (WIW)
1994
Preslav Chardonnay (OD)

ESTATE BOTTLED · 75cl
Bulgarian
Chardonnay
PRESLAV REGION
A fine white wine · 12% vol

1993
Khan Krum Special Reserve Chardonnay (OD)
Novi Pazar Chardonnay (WIW)
1992
Khan Krum Chardonnay (TAN)

HUNGARY WHITE

Under £3.00
Non-vintage
Chapel Hill Irsai Oliver (CO)
1995
Nagyréde Pinot Blanc (SAF)

1994
Chapel Hill Irsai Oliver (SAI)

£3.00 → £3.99
1995
Gyöngyös Estate Chardonnay (CO, BOT, THR, BO, WR)
Gyöngyös Estate Sauvignon Blanc (THR, BO, WR, BOT)
Safeway Nagyréde Chardonnay (SAF)
1994
Chapel Hill Chardonnay (SAI)
Gyöngyös Estate Chardonnay (SAI, FUL, UN)
Gyöngyös Estate Sauvignon Blanc (FUL, HAH, UN)
1993
Gyöngyös Estate Chardonnay (SO)
Gyöngyös Estate Sauvignon Blanc (SO)
1988
Tokay Szamorodni Dry ½ litre (WIW)
Tokay Szamorodni Sweet ½ litre (WIW)

£4.00 → £5.99
1994
Tokay Furmint (TAN)
1988
Tokay Aszú 3 Putts ½ litre, Tokay Kereskedöhóz (WIW)
Tokay Aszú 5 Putts ½ litre, Tokay Kereskedöhóz (WIW)

£6.00 → £7.99
Non-vintage
Tokay Aszú 3 Putts ½ litre, Tokay Kereskedöhóz (SAT, PE)
1988
Tokay Aszú 5 Putts ½ litre, Tokay Kereskedöhóz (AUR)
Tokay Szamorodni Dry ½ litre (AD, ROB)
Tokay Szamorodni Sweet ½ litre (UN)
1986
Tokay Szamorodni Sweet ½ litre (DI)
1981
Tokay Aszú 3 Putts ½ litre, Tokay Kereskedöhóz (BO)
Tokay Aszú 4 Putts ½ litre, Tokay Kereskedöhóz (CRO)

£8.00 → £12.99
Non-vintage
Tokay Aszú 4 Putts ½ litre, Tokay Kereskedöhóz (SAT)
Tokay Aszú 5 Putts ½ litre, Tokay Kereskedöhóz (SAT)

1988
Tokay Aszú 4 Putts ½ litre, Tokay
  Kereskedöhóz (DI)
Tokay Aszú 5 Putts ½ litre, Château
  Megyer (SOM)
1983
Tokay Aszú 3 Putts ½ litre, Tokay
  Kereskedöhóz (ROB)
Tokay Aszú 5 Putts ½ litre, Tokay
  Kereskedöhóz (CRO, UN, AD)
1981
Tokay Aszú 5 Putts ½ litre, Tokay
  Kereskedöhóz (CRO)
1979
Tokay Aszú 5 Putts ½ litre, Tokay
  Kereskedöhóz (CRO)

£14.00 → £16.99
1991
Tokay Aszú 5 Putts ½ litre, The Royal
  Tokay Wine Company (REI, TAN)
Tokay Aszú 5 Putts ½ litre, Tokay
  Kereskedöhóz (ROB)
1981
Tokay Aszú 5 Putts ½ litre, Tokay
  Kereskedöhóz (ROB)

c. £50.00
1956
Tokay Aszú 5 Putts ½ litre, Tokay
  Kereskedöhóz (AD)

£60.00 → £75.00
1964
Tokay Aszú Essencia ½ litre (SOM)
1963
Tokay Aszú Muskotalyos ½ litre (AD)
1957
Tokay Aszú Essencia ½ litre (CRO)
1956
Tokay Aszú 4 Putts ½ litre, Tokay
  Kereskedöhóz (AD)

c. £87.00
1964
Tokay Aszú Essencia ½ litre (REI)

> *Please remember that*
> ***Webster's*** *is a price*
> *GUIDE and not a price*
> *LIST. It is not meant to*
> *replace up-to-date*
> *merchants' lists.*

HUNGARY RED

Under £3.00
Non-vintage
Eger Bull's Blood (SO)
1995
Eger Bull's Blood (WIW)
1994
Eger Bull's Blood (CO)

£3.00 → £4.99
1993
Villany Cabernet Sauvignon (BOT, WR,
  THR)

MOLDOVA

c. £15.00
1978
Negru de Purkar (CRO)

c. £21.00
1975
Negru de Purkar (CRO)

ROMANIA

Under £3.00
1990
Pinot Noir Dealul Mare (UB)

£3.00 → £3.99
1995
Tamaioasa (CO)
1990
Classic Pinot Noir (DAV)
Pinot Noir Dealul Mare (WHI)
1989
Tamaioasa (UB)

c. £5.50
Non-vintage
Tamaioasa (SAT)

£9.00 → £9.99
1979
Muscat Ottonel White (CRO)
1960
Tamaioasa (BU)

SLOVENIA WHITE

Under £4.00
Non-vintage
Lutomer Laski Rizling (BO, UN, FUL)

UNITED STATES

'Wine is made in the vineyard' is the new US mantra. Unfortunately it's priced on the balance sheet, and soaring demand has sent prices sky high

The wine boom shows no signs of letting up in the United States – to the point that a market glutted with wines only a few years ago now faces a severe shortage. Increased sales – five per cent growth in table wine sales in 1995 for the second consecutive year – are part of the problem, but there have also been two short crops of premium wine grapes in a row. Add to this the vine pest phylloxera, which is devastating some North Coast vineyards, and there isn't enough wine to go around.

Supply is so short that some California wineries that have done a brisk business in bottlings at under $5 are buying bulk wine from Chile, France and elsewhere, shipping it back to California and putting California lookalike bottles on the market – all quite legal if the right forms are followed.

The increased demand for wine was, once again, spurred by the US obsession with health. News of the Copenhagen City Heart Study, which recommended three to five glasses of wine daily as the way to stay heart-healthy, received major play on network television. Late in the year, the federal government in its US Dietary Guidelines acknowledged, for the first time, that moderate consumption of wine could be beneficial as part of a regular diet.

So, with demand up and supply down, it shouldn't be any surprise to learn that prices are climbing. Modest Chardonnays that were selling for $8 a bottle only a year ago are now closing in on $15. Run-of-the-press Zinfandel that was lucky to move off the shelf at $6 is now being blown away at $12. Napa Cabernet? If you have to ask the price, maybe you should stick to a glass of Central European plonk. Top niche producers like Caymus are routinely breaking the $100 barrier and just-below-

the-top brands like Groth are easily getting $70 or $75 for reserve bottlings. New wineries with hardly any track record are offering first or second releases of Cabernet at over $30.

But don't despair. Relief is at hand. If you are hunting for a bargain in California wines, look for the simple California appellation on the label, rather than Napa or Sonoma. With prices for grapes soaring, more and more wineries are turning to the Central Valley and the Central Coast as a source for grapes. One area of the Central Valley, the Lodi-Woodbridge appellation, is now the largest supplier of premium wine grapes in California, outdistancing the famed North Coast counties.

Central balance

Lodi-Woodbridge is seldom seen on a wine label, with the major exception of the Robert Mondavi Woodbridge budget wines, but it is a credible area. Vineyards are planted on the delta of the Sacramento River, about 50 miles upstream from San Francisco Bay. Unlike much of California's Central Valley, the grapes do receive some cooling night air and occasional morning fog, which helps balance the grapes and the wine. Wineries like Kendall-Jackson, Benziger and Sebastiani are able to offer under-$10 bottlings of decent, quaffable wine, thanks in large part to Lodi-Woodbridge.

Another alternative is to break out of the California syndrome and look for wines from the Pacific Northwest, New York State – even Texas. Too often, when one mentions American wines, the California bias pops up. Some of the best red wines I've tasted recently have come from Washington, like the marvellous vineyard-designated Cabernets from Columbia Winery, the delicious, fruity Merlots from Chateau Ste Michelle or Staton Hills, or the richly concentrated wines from L'Ecole No. 41 or Leonetti Cellar.

New York New York

More and more wines from New York State's Long Island and Finger Lakes appellations are coming to market. Look for elegant, balanced Riesling and Chardonnay from Finger Lakes producers like Lamoreaux Landing Wine Cellars or Heron Hill. Some of the best Merlot and Pinot Noir in America is being produced on Long Island, an hour's nerve-wracking drive from downtown Manhattan. Look for Peconic Bay, Lenz, Palmer Vineyards or Pindar.

In the 1980s, the winemakers were the superstars of the American wine world. Vintners trotted them out like prize exhibits at special winemaker's dinners where adoring consumers paid high prices to learn what magic they applied to the grapes. In the 1990s, as Americans explore wines from different parts of the country and from around the world as imports grow, both consumers and winemakers are learning to pay more attention to exactly where the grapes are planted. They are beginning to understand the lesson that Europeans realized centuries ago: the *terroir*, that combination of soil, climate and exposure to the sun that makes a vineyard unique, has a direct influence on the taste of the wine.

Now, rather than winemakers waving a magic wand and gaining media glory, the grubby guys in blue jeans out in the vineyards are suddenly at the centre of the action. The new mantra from California to Long Island is, 'Wine is made in the vineyards'. And, by and large, even the winemakers are beginning to believe it.

With this emphasis on the vineyard that began in the late 1980s, American wines are getting better. Everyday wines are more balanced, with accessible fruit that makes them ready for short-range drinking – the PQ, pleasure quotient, has soared. The emphasis on the vineyard will, in the long run, also benefit wines for cellaring, leading to elegant, richer wines a few years down the road.   **LARRY WALKER**

GRAPES & FLAVOURS

BARBERA (red) The Italian variety most grown in California. *Louis M Martini, Sebastiani* and *Bonny Doon* are good, as is *Monteviña* with an intense, blackberry-and-black-cherry wine; *Preston Vineyards* (Sonoma County) is also worth a try.

CABERNET SAUVIGNON (red) The string of outstanding vintages for Cabernet Sauvignon was probably broken in 1995, with an erratic growing season leading to patchy results, especially in Napa and Sonoma. However, with the outstanding 1992s and the almost as good '93s now coming on to the market, there's no need to worry yet. From the 1980s, the '85s and '86s are drinking well, having delightful upfront fruit quality. Don't wait too long for the '84s and '87s, which are peaking now. Washington State Cabernet continues to improve as the vines age, yielding intense fruit and concentration. For serious cellaring, good names are: *Beringer Reserve, Buena Vista, Burgess, Cain, Carmenet Reserve, Caymus Special Selection, Clos du Val, Conn Creek, Cuvaison, Diamond Creek, Dunn, Franciscan, Grgich Hills, Groth, Heitz Bella Oaks, Kenwood Artist Series, La Jota, Laurel Glen, Louis M Martini, Robert Mondavi Reserve* and *Opus One, Chateau Montelena, Newton, Raymond Reserve, Ridge Monte Bello, Sequoia Grove, Shafer Hillside Select, Spotteswoode, Stag's Leap Cask 23, Sterling Vineyards Diamond Mountain Ranch* (California); *Ste Chapelle* (Idaho); *Fall Creek Vineyards, Llano Estacado, Messina Hof, Oberhellmann, Pheasant Ridge* (Texas); *Arbor Crest, Hogue Cellars, Chateau Ste Michelle,*

Columbia, *Staton Hills* (Washington). For a lighter Cabernet, the list is practically endless, but here are a few worthies: *Beringer* (Napa Valley), *Caymus Liberty School, Chateau Souverain, Clos du Bois, Cosentino, Fetzer, Estancia, Foppiano, Kendall-Jackson, Wente* (California); *Columbia Crest* (Washington).

CHARDONNAY (white) Chardonnay continues to be the white wine of choice in the US. Because of a short supply of grapes, winemakers are turning to grapes from different areas of California – such as the Central Coast and the Lodi-Woodbridge appellation in the northern Central Valley – to supply the thirst for Chardonnay. Many of the more popular brands – such as *Kendall-Jackson* and *Sebastiani* – have a slightly sweet finish to make them more commercial.

American Chardonnay will age, but look for the controlled balanced fruit of *Acacia, Arrowood, Beringer, Buena Vista, Chalone, Chateau St Jean, Cuvaison, Dehlinger, Flora Springs, Franciscan, Kistler, Mondavi Reserve, Newton, Raymond Reserve, Signorello, Simi* and *Sonoma-Cutrer* (California); *Bridgehampton* (New York); *Prince Michel* (Virginia). For more instant fun, try *Callaway, Clos du Bois, Estancia, Matanzas Creek, Kendall-Jackson, Morgan, Mirassou, Phelps, Monterey Vineyards, Wente Bros* (California); *Fall Creek* (Texas); *Chateau Ste Michelle, Columbia Crest, Hogue Cellars* (Washington).

GEWÜRZTRAMINER (white) This is looking up in quality, but California still falls far short of Alsace. The problem is that the grape ripens too fast, too soon in California's hotter climate. A few people are beginning to get it right, making wines with that spiciness that keeps you reaching for another glass. Look for *Adler Fels* (sometimes), *Lazy Creek, Handley Cellars, Rutherford Hill, Obester* (California); *Llano Estacado* (Texas); *Columbia, Chateau Ste Michelle* (Washington).

MERLOT (red) There is a virtual consumer frenzy centring on Merlot. Especially in California, vintners are rushing young-vine

Merlot to the market and charging prices that are a bit out of line. Many new bottlings have a bubble-gum, tutti-frutti quality that leaves more than a little to be desired. At its best, American Merlot shows lovely black cherry with a pleasing brambly edge. Best are *Arrowood, Bellerose, Cuvaison, Duckhorn, Gundlach-Bundschu, Murphy-Goode, Newton, St Francis, Pine Ridge, Silverado, Sinskey, St Clement, Sterling, Vichon,* (California); *Bedell Cellars, Bridgehampton, Peconic Bay* (New York); *Chateau Ste Michelle, Columbia, Columbia Crest, Hogue Cellars, Leonetti, Staton Hills, Paul Thomas* (Washington).

PETITE SIRAH (red) This is emphatically not the same as the great red Syrah grape of the Rhône Valley or the Shiraz of Australia. It produces big, stark, dry, almost tarry wines – impressive in their way, but usually lacking real style. *Ridge* is the exception, and in good years capable of making real Rhône Syrah blush. Also look for *Christopher Creek, Stag's Leap* and *Foppiano.*

PINOT NOIR (red) It may be time to stop asking if California or Oregon can make great Pinot Noir, and start asking how many can be made. Oregon, after several bad years, seems to be getting back on track, while in California good to very good Pinot Noir is turning up all over the place: the Carneros region in Napa/Sonoma, the lower Russian River Valley in Sonoma, north-eastern Monterey County and parts of Santa Barbara County. And there's also Long Island, where an occasional flash of excellent Pinot can be seen. Try *Au Bon Climat, Acacia, Bonny Doon, Bouchaine, Byron, Calera, Carneros Creek, Chalone, Dehlinger, De Loach, Gary Farrel, Iron Horse, Lazy Creek, Robert Mondavi, Saintsbury, Sinskey, Whitcraft, Wild Horse, Zaca Mesa* (California); *Bridgehampton* (New York); *Adelsheim, Amity, Drouhin, Elk Cove, Eyrie, King Estate, Knudsen Erath, Rex Hill, Scott Henry, Sokol Blosser* (Oregon).

SYRAH/RHÔNE VARIETIES (red) There has been an explosion of interest in the vines of the Rhône in California; they seem in many ways more suited to the climate than the Bordeaux or Burgundian grapes, and they add to the US range of flavours. Most eyes are on Syrah, but there is also Mourvèdre, Cinsaut, Grenache and Carignan, the last two of which used to be used in Central Valley jug wines. The best so far are from *Bonny Doon, Duxoup, Kendall-Jackson, La Jota, McDowell Valley, Joseph Phelps Mistral* series, *Preston Vineyards, Qupé, Santino* (all California).

RIESLING (white) Like Gewürz, most Riesling in California has been planted in the wrong (warm) place. Riesling (in the US called Johannisberg or White) makes a dull wine then; it is the cooler areas of California, Oregon, New York and Washington that are beginning to show what it can do. Best are *Alexander Valley Vineyards, Konocti, Navarro* (California); *Lamoureux Landing, Wagner Vineyards* (New York); *Amity* (Oregon); *Chateau Morrisette, Prince Michel* (Virginia); *Hogue Cellars, Columbia Cellars, Chateau Ste Michelle, Kiona* (Washington).

SAUVIGNON BLANC/FUMÉ BLANC (white) Now being tamed; its tendency to extreme herbal/grassy tastes is now often moulded into complex spicy/appley fruit. If you are a fan of the big, grassy wines, those that smell like a field of new-mown hay, you'll like *Dry Creek Vineyards Reserve,* which carries that as far as it can go. For more restraint try *Chateau St Jean, Ferrari-Carano, Hanna, Markham, Robert Mondavi, Murphy-Goode, Simi,* *Sterling, William Wheeler* (California); *Hargrave* (New York); *Arbor Crest, Columbia* (Washington).

SEMILLON (white) Usually added to Sauvignon Blanc for complexity (*Clos du Val, Carmenet, Vichon,* California). For stand-alone Semillon try *Alderbrook, R H Phillips, Ahlgren* (California); *Chateau Ste Michelle* (Washington).

ZINFANDEL (white) Zinfandel has joined the swing to red wines in the US. Encouraged by media reports that emphasize wine, especially red wine, as good for your heart, sales of red Zinfandel have soared. A particular favourite is 'old vine' Zinfandel – wine made from vines ranging from 50 to 100 years old (there is no exact legal definition of the term) which have become increasingly popular, harder to find, and more expensive. White or rosé Zinfandel, usually made in a sweet style, continues to sell well. Zins are popular in both the big rustic styles and the lighter, elegant styles. Best of the white Zins are *Sutter Home, Buehler* and *Amador Foothills.* For the big Zins, look for *Cline Cellars, Deer Park, Kendall-Jackson Ciapusci Vineyard, Murrieta's Well, Preston Vineyards, La Jota, A Rafanelli, Ravenswood, Rosenblum, Shenandoah, Joseph Swan.* For a more elegant approach, try *Buehler, Buena Vista, Burgess, Clos du Val, Fetzer, Haywood, Kendall-Jackson Mariah Vineyard, Kenwood, Louis M Martini, Nalle, Quivira, Ridge.* Best for blush wines are *Amador Foothill, Beringer, Buehler, Ivan Tamas.*

MATURITY CHART
1994 Carneros Chardonnay
The best Carneros Chardonnays have the elegance and balance to age well

Bottled	Ready	Peak	Tiring	In decline

| 0 | 1 | 2 | 3 | 4 | 5 | 6 | 7 | 8 | 9 | 10 years |

WINE REGIONS

CARNEROS (California; red, white) At the southern end of the Napa and Sonoma valleys, snuggled against San Francisco Bay. Breezes from the Bay hold the temperature down and create an ideal climate for Pinot Noir and Chardonnay. Many of California's best Pinot Noirs come from here.

CENTRAL VALLEY (California; red, white) Once a vast inland sea, the Central Valley runs from the San Joaquin/Sacramento river delta in the north to the unappealing flatlands of Bakersfield in the south, from the foothills of the Sierra Range in the east to the Coastal Ranges in the west. It can be 110°F during the day, and hardly cooler at night. It's a brutal life, but with modern techniques there are some decent quaffs. Chardonnay, especially, is much improved.

LAKE COUNTY (California; red, white) Grapes were grown in Lake County (north of Napa County and east of Mendocino County) in the last century; recently there has been a revival of interest with major plantings by *Louis M Martini, Konocti* and *Guenoc*. It's good Cabernet Sauvignon and Sauvignon Blanc territory, with warm days and cool nights, and a very long growing season.

LIVERMORE VALLEY (California; red, white) One of California's oldest vine-growing regions, this largely suburban valley has been enjoying a bit of a comeback. It was the first in California to put a varietal label on Sauvignon Blanc and the century-plus old *Wente Bros* winery in Livermore is increasingly good for that. The region is also proving good for Cabernet Sauvignon. Several small wineries have recently sprung up or been revived; early bottlings are promising.

MENDOCINO COUNTY (California; red, white) A rugged, coastal county with one major inland valley, and several cool east–west valleys running from the interior to the rocky

coastline. These pocket climates make it possible to grow a range of grapes, with Cabernet Sauvignon at its best in Round Valley in the interior but excellent Riesling, Gewürztraminer, Pinot Noir and Chardonnay doing well in the cool Anderson Valley, where Pacific fog and winds follow the Anderson River inland. This valley is also becoming a leading sparkling wine district, with *Roederer Estate,* the US off-shoot of Champagne Roederer, making some outstanding bubbly. The tiny *Handley Cellars Brut is* one of the best sparkling wines in California.

MISSOURI (red, white) At the turn of the century this midwestern state was the third largest wine producer in the US. Now it's making a comeback, growing both standard vinifera grapes and a range of French hybrids like Vidal, as well as native American grapes like Cynthiana/Norton. *Stone Hill Winery*'s Norton red wine has been compared favourably to a Rhône. There are also some very pleasing Rieslings made in the state (*Mount Pleasant Vineyard*) as well.

MONTEREY COUNTY (California; red, white) This came late to wine: only in the early 1970s did pioneering plantings by *Mirassou* and *Wente Bros* begin to bear fruit. Early Cabernets had a distinct taste of green peppers and other less appealing vegetal smells, which indicated that the climate was a touch too cool. Now growers have found more suitable grapes, like Riesling, Chenin Blanc and Pinot Noir. Even Cabernet Sauvignon has made a comeback, and is to be found on hillsides in the cool Carmel Valley and the Arroyo Seco region.

NAPA COUNTY (California; red, white) There are several important sub-regions within Napa: Calistoga, Carneros, Chiles Valley, Howell Mountain, Mount Veeder, Oakville, Pope Valley, Rutherford, Spring Mountain and Stags Leap. Some of these are formally designated viticultural regions. This is California's classic wine country. Napa's strong suit is red – Cabernet Sauvignon and Merlot – with Pinot Noir in Carneros.

NEW MEXICO (red, white) Northern New Mexico grows mostly hybrid grape varieties but some interesting wines are coming from irrigated vineyards in the South. Good producers are *Anderson Valley*, especially for Chardonnay, and a fizz from *Devalmont Vineyards* under the Gruet label.

NEW YORK STATE (red, white) The big news in New York continues to be Long Island, with outstanding Chardonnay and Pinot Noir. The Chardonnays here are very different from those of California, with more austere flavours, a bit like ripe Chablis. There's also decent Chardonnay and outstanding Riesling coming from the Finger Lakes and the Hudson River Valley areas. The Lake Erie-Niagara region is lagging behind the other three, and still has more native grapes planted. Try the wines of *Bedell Cellars, Bridgehampton, Brotherhood, Hargrave, Lenz, Pindar* and *Wagner*.

OREGON (red, white) Oregon has suffered from too much attention over the years. Hyped by press notices of the 1983 vintage for Pinot Noir, perhaps too much was expected of Oregon, too soon. Now that the dust has settled a bit and Oregon winegrowers have begun to sort out their *terroir*, the early promise for Pinot Noir is showing signs of paying off. A new generation of winemakers, with the technical skills and cash capital that were sometimes lacking in the Oregon pioneers, are showing what can be done on a consistent basis with Oregon Pinot Noir. Oregon's second-best grape is Pinot Gris, which can often be charming. Riesling can also be quite good, although it is a little short on that floral intensity one looks for in a great Riesling. For Pinot Gris, try *Adelsheim, Amity, Eyrie, King Estate* or *Knudsen Erath*. Oak Knoll has the best Riesling. For Pinot Noir recommendations see page 341.

SAN LUIS OBISPO COUNTY (California; red, white) A Central Coast growing area with the best wines coming from cool regions in canyons opening in from the coast. There are some good sites here for Pinot Noir, Chardonnay and there are a few surprising old Zinfandel vineyards. Edna Valley is the chief sub-region with a deserved reputation for Chardonnay.

SANTA BARBARA COUNTY (California; red, white) This growing region north of Los Angeles is divided into two major sub-regions, the Santa Maria and Santa Ynez valleys. Both are coastal valleys with openings to the Pacific which means that both days and nights are fairly cool. There are some outstanding Pinot Noirs from both regions with some good Sauvignon and Merlot from the Santa Ynez Valley.

SANTA CRUZ MOUNTAINS (California; red, white) Just south of San Francisco, this has lured several people who believe it to be Pinot Noir heaven. Despite some occasional successes, the track record is patchy, but progress is being made. *David Bruce* and *Santa Cruz Mountain Winery* have made Pinot with various degrees of success. Surprisingly, for a cool-climate region, some very good Cabernet has been made – notably from *Mount Eden* and *Ridge Vineyards*. Ridge has even made a notable Chardonnay here.

SIERRA FOOTHILLS (California; red, white) California's gold country was one of the busiest wine zones in the state in the last century but only a few Zinfandel vineyards survived Prohibition. These are the basis of the area's reputation today, plus good Sauvignon Blanc and Barbera. Sub-regions include Amador County, El Dorado County and Calaveras County. Best are *Amador Foothill Winery, Boeger Winery, Monteviña, Santino* and *Shenandoah Vineyards*.

The price guides for this section begin on page 351.

SONOMA COUNTY (California; red, white) On the West Coast, people are beginning to realize that Sonoma's Chardonnay, long in the shade of Napa, need take a back seat to no-one. Sonoma Valley is the main sub-region, but there are many others, in particular Alexander Valley, Chalk Hill, Dry Creek, Knight's Valley, and the Russian River Valley itself (including its sub-region Green Valley). Cabernet Sauvignon and Chardonnay yield the best wines, and they're usually a little fruitier and softer than they are in Napa. There's also some first rate Pinot Noir emerging from the lower Russian River Valley.

TEXAS (red, white) Texas wines continue to surprise. Major regions are the Austin Hills and the Staked Plains region of west Texas, centred around Lubbock. Cabernet Sauvignons from Texas have a drink-me-now rich fruitiness and the Chardonnays and Sauvignon Blancs are looking better every year. In short, it's goodbye Chateau Redneck. Best producers currently are *Fall Creek, Llano Estacado, Messina Hof, Oberhellmann* and *Pheasant Ridge.*

VIRGINIA (red, white) Growing good wine grapes in Virginia's hot, humid climate is certainly a man-over-nature drama. Besides the heat and the humidity, there is the occasional hurricane to contend with. Nevertheless, there are some good Rieslings and Chardonnays being made. Top producers are *Chateau Morrisette, Ingleside Plantation* and *Prince Michel.*

WASHINGTON STATE (red, white) There are those – and they're increasing in number – who believe that in the long run, the finest wines from North America may come from Washington State. There is an incredible intensity of fruit to be found right across the board in all varietals that is simply astonishing. When the first serious wines started appearing only about 15 years ago, the best were Riesling and Chardonnay; but now the Cabernets and Merlots can be outstanding, as can the Sauvignon Blanc and Semillon, varieties which are taken very seriously in Washington State. Good wineries include the following names: *Arbor Crest, Chateau Ste Michelle, Columbia Cellars, Columbia Crest, Hogue Cellars, Staton Hills.*

WINERY PROFILES

ACACIA ★★★(★) (Carneros/Napa) Acacia continues to produce attractive Pinot Noir and delightfully understated Chardonnay.

ADLER FELS ★★(★) (Sonoma) A quirky winery, taking chances that sometimes miss. Outstanding Gewürztraminer and an unusual Riesling sparkler that is a treat.

ARROWOOD ★★★★ (Sonoma) Richard Arrowood was the founding winemaker at Chateau St Jean, and now makes a superb Cabernet Sauvignon and Merlot.

AU BON CLIMAT ★★★★ (Santa Barbara) Fine Pinot Noir. The best is soft and approachable, with intense black cherry fruit. Chardonnay can also be impressive.

BEAULIEU VINEYARDS ★★★ (Napa) The top-of-the-line George de Latour Private Reserve Cabernet Sauvignon is still marvellous and capable of extended aging. The big surprise here is a lean, supple Carneros district Chardonnay. There is also an inexpensive Beautour Cabernet, which is good value.

BERINGER ★★★★(★) (Napa) This out-standing performer just gets better and better. A string of great Reserve Cabernets, beginning in 1986, are top of the line. A Sbragia Chardonnay (he's the winemaker) is a rich, almost over-the-top wine, loaded with buttery oak. Also several vineyard select bottlings of Cabernet, depending on the vintage. You can't go far wrong with any of them, or with the good-value second label, Napa Ridge.

BETHEL HEIGHTS ★★★(★) (Oregon) Impressive, intense Pinot Noirs. The Reserves can be among Oregon's finest and most concentrated.

BONNY DOON ★★★★ (Santa Cruz) One of California's most innovative winemakers, Randall Grahm makes some of the most delicious wines in California from his mountain-top winery a few miles from the Pacific Ocean. His work with Grenache (Le Cigare Volant) and Mourvèdre (Old Telegram, a pun on Châteauneuf's Vieux Télégraphe, if you hadn't guessed) have opened new vistas for California winemakers. A new line of Italian-style wines under the Ca' Del Solo label is winning him more friends.

BRIDGEHAMPTON ★★★(★) (New York) A first-class Chardonnay from Long Island vineyards as well as a fresh, light quaffable Pinot Noir and a fruity, forward Merlot.

BUENA VISTA ★★★(★) (Sonoma/Carneros) The Buena Vista winery has made a big comeback in recent years, with balanced, understated varietal Merlot, Pinot Noir and Cabernet Sauvignon to its credit. A new line of Reserve wines adds intensity and depth. One of California's better Sauvignon Blancs is made by Buena Vista from Lake County grapes.

CAKEBREAD CELLARS ★★★ (Napa) Wines from here are always sound, and are sometimes outstanding: it makes one of California's very best Sauvignon Blancs.

CALERA ★★★★(★) (San Benito) Possibly the best Pinot Noir in California comes from this winery. Rich, intense wine. The Jensen Vineyard is the best of the lot. Also fine Viognier and Chardonnay.

CAYMUS ★★★★ (Napa) Benchmark California Cabernet which shows no sign of faltering. There is also a good Zin and good value wines under the Liberty School label.

CHALONE ★★★★(★) (Monterey) A reputation for individualistic Pinot Noir and big, buttery Chardonny. Also some nice Pinot Blanc and Chenin Blanc.

CHATEAU POTELLE ★★★(★) (Napa) Run by two transplanted French wine buffs. Results fo far include distinctly promising Sauvignon Blanc and Cabernet and an outstanding Zinfandel.

CHATEAU ST JEAN ★★★(★) (Sonoma) This winery was born in the 1970s as a Chardonnay specialist, and it also made wonderful late-harvest dessert wines. Chardonnay is still important, but recent bottlings of Cabernet and Merlot, especially a reserve Merlot, have been outstanding.

CHATEAU STE MICHELLE ★★★(★) (Washington) Consistently good to outstanding white and red with Cabernet Sauvignon and Merlot being the real strengths; a pretty good bubbly as well. Columbia Crest, which began as a good-value label, is now a stand-alone winery with terrific Cabernet Sauvignon.

CHIMNEY ROCK ★★★(★) (Napa) After a faltering beginning, winemaker Doug Fletcher stepped in to put this Stags Leap district winery on the right track, with powerful yet elegant Cabernet Sauvignon and a reserve-style Bordeaux blend called Elevage. The wines are superb, with deep, rich, and complex fruit.

CLOS DU BOIS ★★★(★) (Sonoma) Now owned by Hiram Walker-Allied Vintners, Clos du Bois makes consistently good Merlots, Chardonnays and a claret-style blend called Marlstone.

CLOS DU VAL ★★★(★) (Napa) Bordeaux-trained owner and winemaker Bernard Portet makes elegant, well-balanced reds, with an emphasis on austere fruit. Best wines from this underrated winery are Cabernet Sauvignon and Zinfandel.

COLUMBIA ★★★★ (Washington) David Lake's pioneering winery, founded in 1962 by a group of university professors, makes a basketful of varietals including Semillon, Gewürztraminer, Chardonnay and Riesling (especially Wyckoff vineyard); plus Syrah, soft, peppery Pinot Noir, seductive Merlot (Red Willow vineyard), and surprisingly ripe Cabernet Sauvignon (Otis vineyard).

CUVAISON ★★★ (Napa) Winemaker John Thacher turns out delicious but unpredictable Merlot, Pinot Noir and Cabernet, at best elegant and understated with unexpected layers of complexity.

DEHLINGER ★★★★ (Sonoma) Makes one of the best Pinots in North America from cool vineyards along the Russian River Valley, just a few miles from the Pacific. Also good Cabernets including a good value Young Vine Cabernet.

DOMAINE CARNEROS ★★★(★) (Napa) This Taittinger-owned sparkling wine house has moved near the top in California fizz with a remarkable vintage Brut and a silky, powerful Blanc de Blancs.

DOMAINE CHANDON ★★★ (Napa) Owned by Champagne house Moët & Chandon, Domaine Chandon has shown good consistency and quality over the years, with a series of reasonably priced non-vintage bubblies. The rich and creamy Reserve bottlings are especially worth seeking out, as is a new Blanc de Blancs made entirely from Carneros grapes.

DOMAINE MUMM ★★★★ (Napa) Winemaker Greg Fowler, who helped establish Schramsberg as the top gun in American fizz, is now at Domaine Mumm and well on form. Early releases have been simply outstanding, especially the Brut and an impressive Blanc de Noirs.

DROUHIN ★★★★ (Oregon) With the 1991 Pinot Noir, this Oregon winery owned by the Burgundy wine firm, earned a fourth star, and has kept it with subsequent vintages. Only the winery's estate grapes are used. This is the Pinot Noir we have all been waiting for Oregon to make.

DRY CREEK VINEYARDS ★★(★) (Sonoma) This winery made its reputation with Sauvignon Blanc in a big, grassy style. Recently that wine has grown more subtle. Zinfandel and Cabernet Sauvignon are reliable if unremarkable.

DUCKHORN ★★★ (Napa) Intensely flavoured, deep, rich Merlot and weighty Cabernet.

ELK COVE VINEYARDS ★★★(★) (Oregon) Producer of one of Oregon's best Pinot Noirs, particularly in the estate version. It also makes a very good Pinot Gris.

EYRIE ★★★ (Oregon) David Lett is Oregon's Pinot pioneer. He has spawned a whole industry, and his wines can still be some of the best: generally supple, light but flavoursome. Pinot Gris, though, forms the bulk of production.

FALL CREEK VINEYARDS ★★★ (Texas) These wines can hold their heads up anywhere: a delicious Proprietor's Red (Cabernet, Ruby Cabernet, Merlot and Carnelian), a charming Semillon and a first-rate Cabernet Sauvignon.

FETZER ★★★ (Mendocino County) This large producer, now owned by Brown-Forman, a spirits corporation, makes reliable, middle of the road Cabernets and Chardonnay, with an occasional better-than-usual Zinfandel, especially the Ricetti Vineyard bottling. A new line of wines made from organically-grown grapes, Bonterra, is attracting favourable attention.

FLORA SPRINGS ★★★(★) (Napa) Excellent Chardonnay and a fair blend of both Cabernets and Merlot called Trilogy. Soliloquy is a creamy, rich, floral white that belies its Sauvignon Blanc base.

FOPPIANO★★(★) (Sonoma) This historic family winery has had a few more downs than ups recently. A Reserve bottling of Zinfandel and Petite Sirah are a cut or two above average.

FRANCISCAN ★★★★ (Napa) This Napa estate was down and out 15 years ago, but has recovered to a startling degree. The estate-bottled Chardonnays, especially the Cuvée Sauvage, so called because it's fermented with wild yeast, are outstanding. Straight Cabernets and Bordeaux blends are usually superb. Estancia is a better than usual second label, made from grapes from several parts of California.

HANDLEY CELLARS ★★★★ (Mendocino) The big story here is the limited production sparkling wines, especially the Brut and a delightful rosé. There are two bottlings of Chardonnay, equally good. One is from family-owned vineyards in the Dry Creek Valley of Sonoma County, the other from the cool estate vineyards in the Anderson Valley of Mendocino County.

HEITZ ★★★ (Napa) The Martha's Vineyard Cabernet Sauvignon has a devoted following and fetches high prices, but it seems a bit of a dinosaur compared with the elegant, sleek Cabernets of today.

IRON HORSE ★★★★ (Sonoma) Terrific racy, incisive fizz; this producer is now engaged in a joint venture with Laurent-Perrier of Champagne. Very good Pinot Noir and Chardonnay. Its second label, Tin Pony, is good value.

JORDAN ★★★★(★) (Sonoma) A rich, ripe Cabernet Sauvignon that ages well and a plausible 'wannabe Meursault' Chardonnay from this French lookalike winery in northern Sonoma. An outstanding sparkling wine called J was released in the spring of 1991.

KENDALL-JACKSON ★★★ (Lake) Owns what is probably the biggest Chardonnay vineyard in the world (1200 acres) in Santa Barbara, making smooth, rich, sometimes spicy Chardonnay which is invariably seamless with a spoonful of sugar; Proprietor's Grand Reserve is intense and buttery. Juicy Sauvignon Blanc and rather dense Pinot Noir.

KENWOOD ★★★(★) (Sonoma) A consistent producer of well-above-average quality. The Jack London and Artist Series Cabernets are outstanding, as is the Zinfandel and Sauvignon Blanc.

KUNDE ESTATE WINERY ★★★ (Sonoma) The Kunde family have been wine-grape growers for at least a century, and in 1990 they decided to start producing wines – the early results have been spectacular, with a powerful, buttery Reserve Chardonnay getting raves, and a richly satisfying old vine Zinfandel.

LAMOREAUX LANDING ★★★ (New York) The Finger Lakes region of New York is vying with Long Island as that state's most important wine area. Lamoreaux Landing, established in 1990, has quickly become one of the most important Finger Lakes wineries. Its Chardonnay is a consistent medal winner, and the Pinot Noir improves with each vintage.

LAUREL GLEN ★★★★ (Sonoma) Winemaker Patrick Campbell makes only Cabernet Sauvignon at his Sonoma Mountain winery and it is very, very good Cabernet Sauvignon. With intense black cherry fruit, it's a treat for short-term drinking but there is every reason to believe it will age very well. He releases three wines, a regular bottling called Counterpoint, which is wine not quite good enough for the A-list cut and a wine called Terra Rosa which he blends from bulk wine purchases.

LENZ VINEYARDS ★★★ (New York) Lenz is one of the strongest voices in Long

Island wine-making, with wines going from strength to strength. Merlot is an elegant, powerful wine with soft, balanced tannins, and dry Gewürztraminer is spicy and tasty – a good aperitif. In good vintages, the Pinot Noir has deep, ripe fruit.

LOUIS MARTINI ★★★ (Napa) This once top-rated family winery has been slowing down and giving ground lately. Money problems have forced the sale of some vineyards, and the latest bottlings don't quite seem up to the standards of bottlings from the 1960s and '70s. One exception is the Zinfandel, made from old vines in the Monte Rosso Vineyards.

MAYACAMAS ★★★ (Napa) A reputation in the past for big, hard Cabernets that would take decades to come around. There are signs that the reputation is justified, but a lot of people are still waiting.

ROBERT MONDAVI ★★★★(★) (Napa) Mondavi's major strength is in reds: both the straight and Reserve Cabernets are among the best in the world, though Opus One reds seem to lack the Reserve's intensity. Recent bottlings of Pinot Noir from Carneros are terrific.

NEWTON ★★★★ (Napa) Excellent, reasonably priced Chardonnay; cedary, cinnamon-spiced Cabernet and increasingly succulent Merlot.

PECONIC BAY VINEYARDS ★★★ (New York) This Long Island winery has a well deserved reputation for Chardonnay, which it makes in a light, unoaked style called Petite Chardonnay, and a barrel-fermented Reserve Chardonnay which is complex and filled with buttery, ripe flavours.

PHEASANT RIDGE ★★(★) (Texas) There has been quite good Chardonnay and Semillon, and promising Cabernet Sauvignon, coming from this producer in recent vintages. One to watch.

PHELPS ★★★(★) (Napa) Best here is the Insignia Vineyard Cabernet Sauvignon but exciting things are happening with Rhône grape varieties, particularly the Syrah, released under the Mistral label. There's also a nice light touch with that most civilized of wines, the Riesling.

RAVENSWOOD ★★★★ (Sonoma) Joel Peterson, one of California's leading Zin masters, established Ravenswood in 1976, with the sole purpose of making Zinfandel. Peterson makes several versions, varying the menu from year to year. The Dickerson Vineyard, Old Hill and Old Vines bottlings are super, with ripe, concentrated fruit, at once bold and stylish.

RIDGE ★★★★(★) (Santa Clara) Benchmark Zinfandel. The Monte Bello Cabernets are also remarkable, with great balance and long-lasting, perfumed fruit. Petite Sirah from York Creek is brilliant, under-valued and under-appreciated.

ROEDERER ESTATE ★★★★ (Mendocino County) Located in the cool Anderson Valley, Roederer's first two releases of bubbly had wine lovers doing hand-springs. The style is unlike that of most California sparkling wine, austere with understated fruit; the parent company in fact set out to make a Champagne-style sparkler. The brut and the rosé are also terrific.

SAINTSBURY ★★★★ (Napa) A young Carneros winery with a growing reputation for Pinot Noir and Chardonnay. Garnet, from young Pinot Noir vines, is delicious.

SANFORD WINERY ★★★(★) (Santa Barbara) At its best, Sanford Pinot Noir can be a real treat, with spicy, lush, intense fruit. Good Sauvignon and Chardonnay.

SCHRAMSBERG ★★★★ (Napa) The best sparkling wine in California can still come from this winery, but the challengers are rapidly gaining ground. The vintage sparklers from

Schramsberg age beautifully into lush, rich wines.

SHAFER ★★★★ (Napa) There's very good, very long-lived Cabernet Sauvignon and Merlot here, grown up on hillside vineyards rather than on the valley floor.

SIMI ★★★(★) (Sonoma) Rich, sometimes voluptuous, always reliable Chardonnay from winemaker Zelma Long. The concentrated Cabernets can be drunk young, but really need time. Reserves are excellent, as is Sauvignon Blanc.

SONOMA-CUTRER ★★★★ (Sonoma) Uses Chardonnay from three different Russian River Valley vineyards. Les Pierres is a restrained classic, made to age. Russian River Ranches is more forward and fruity, while the Cutrer is rich, full and more in the California tradition.

STAG'S LEAP WINE CELLARS ★★★★ (Napa) After a few years unaccountably adrift, the estate-bottled Cabernet Sauvignon is focussed and back on track, especially the Cask 23 and the SLV Vineyard bottlings. These wines will age beautifully over the next eight to ten years. Also an elegant Chardonnay with lean, appley fruit.

STATON HILLS VINEYARD ★★★(★) (Washington) Watch out for this Yakima Valley winery, which is set to become one of the superstars of Washington State wines.

The Merlot and Cabernet Sauvignon, both of which are made in a silky Bordeaux style, are lovely wines with rich, vivid fruit and good staying power.

STEELE WINES ★★★(★) (Lake County) Owner and winemaker Jed Steele is a master blender. He has the uncanny skills of sourcing grapes from vineyards all over California, and shaping them into exciting wines, usually featuring vivid, supple fruit. But he also offers single-vineyard wines and has, in current release, no fewer than four Chardonnays. His Zinfandels are often superb, with full-blown, spicy fruit. Shooting Star is a second, budget label.

ROD STRONG VINEYARDS ★★★(★) (Sonoma) At this much underrated winery on the Russian River, former dancer Rod Strong makes some very fine Cabernet Sauvignon, Pinot Noir and Zinfandel from river-terrace vineyards.

TREFETHEN ★★★ (Napa) Recent hillside Cabernet Sauvignon has raised the quality level of Trefethen, although other bottlings of Cabernet and Chardonnay are still stuck in a middle-of-the-road rut. There's a delightful just off-dry Riesling as well as a good value red and white under the Eschol label.

ZD WINES ★★★ (Napa) A source of excellent Cabernet Sauvignon, Pinot Noir and Chardonnay, all of which have lovely intensity and depth. The Pinot Noir, in particular, seems to get better with each vintage.

MERCHANTS SPECIALISING IN USA
see Merchant Directory (page 424) for details

Nearly all merchants have some, though few have very long lists of North American wines, often because of the high prices. And that can be as much the fault of the dollar (or the pound) as the producers. For longer-than-average lists, with unusually imaginative selections, try the following merchants: Adnams (AD), Averys of Bristol (AV) a New World pioneer, Bennetts (BEN), Bibendum (BIB), Croque-en-Bouche (CRO), Enotria Winecellars (ENO), Lay & Wheeler (LAY), Oddbins (ODD), Majestic (MAJ), Morris & Verdin (MV) very good for Rhône rangers, James Nicholson (NI), The Nobody Inn (NO), Reid Wines (REI), T&W Wines (TW), The Ubiquitous Chip (UB)

UNITED STATES

CALIFORNIA RED

Under £4.00

Non-vintage
E&J Gallo Dry Reserve (CO, SAF, SO, BOT,
WR, THR, BO, SAI, VIC)

£4.00 ➜ £4.99

Non-vintage
E&J Gallo Cabernet Sauvignon (SAF, SAI,
CO, VIC, BO)
E&J Gallo Dry Reserve (DAV)
E&J Gallo Zinfandel (CO)
South Bay Vineyards Pinot Noir (SAI)
South Bay Zinfandel (SAI)
Thornhill Pinot Noir (FUL)
1993
Fetzer Zinfandel (SOM)
1992
Glen Ellen Cabernet Sauvignon (HOG)
1991
E&J Gallo Zinfandel (UN)
1988
Glen Ellen Cabernet Sauvignon (SO)

£5.00 ➜ £5.99

1994
★ Quady Elysium Black Muscat ½ bottle (UN)
1993
Fetzer Zinfandel (SAF, OD)
Robert Mondavi Woodbridge Cabernet
Sauvignon (NI)
Quady Elysium Black Muscat ½ bottle
(PEN)
1992
Robert Mondavi Woodbridge Cabernet
Sauvignon (CRO, FOR)
1991
Robert Mondavi Woodbridge Cabernet
Sauvignon (WR, THR, BOT)
1989
Inglenook Cabernet Sauvignon (HOG)
1988
Inglenook Petite Sirah (WRI)

£6.00 ➜ £7.99

Non-vintage
Quady Elysium Black Muscat (NI)
1995
★ Bonny Doon Clos de Gilroy Grenache (MV)
1994
Ca' del Solo Big House Red (MV, BO)

Quady Elysium Black Muscat ½ bottle
(ROB, NO)
Washington Hills Merlot (SAI)
1993
Beringer Zinfandel (NEZ, PIP)
Ca' del Solo Big House Red (SOM, REI, YOU)
Carneros Creek Fleur de Carneros Pinot
Noir (MAJ)
Fetzer Zinfandel (DI)
★ Laurel Glen Terra Rosa (NI)
Quady Elysium Black Muscat ½ bottle (UN)
Sterling Diamond Mountain Ranch
Cabernet Sauvignon (OD)
1992
Beringer Zinfandel (MAJ, CO)
Kenwood Zinfandel (VIC)
1989
Robert Mondavi Woodbridge Cabernet
Sauvignon (BER)
Mountain View Cabernet Sauvignon (KA)

£8.00 ➜ £9.99

1994
Ca' del Solo Big House Red (TAN, ROB)
Quady Elysium Black Muscat (AD)
★ Qupé Syrah (MV)
Ravenswood North Coast Vintners Blend
Zinfandel (ARM)
1993
Lytton Springs Zinfandel (VIG)
Robert Mondavi Pinot Noir (MAJ)
Saintsbury Garnet Pinot Noir (HAH, FUL)
1992
Dry Creek Zinfandel (DI)
Firestone Cabernet Sauvignon (HA)
Firestone Merlot (BOT)
Ravenswood North Coast Vintners Blend
Zinfandel (UB)
Saintsbury Garnet Pinot Noir (GE)
1991
Beringer Cabernet Sauvignon (MAJ, VIC)
Pedroncelli Cabernet Sauvignon (LAY)
1990
Firestone Cabernet Sauvignon (LEA)
1989
Firestone Cabernet Sauvignon (HOG)
1988
Rutherford Hill Cabernet Sauvignon (HOG)
1987
Clos du Bois Cabernet Sauvignon (BU)
Dry Creek Cabernet Sauvignon (HOG)
Franciscan Cabernet Sauvignon (PEN)

£10.00 → £11.99

1993
Clos du Bois Merlot (DI)
Fetzer Barrel Select Cabernet Sauvignon (DAV)
Robert Mondavi Pinot Noir (WAT)
Quivira Zinfandel (HIC)
Qupé Syrah Bien Nacido (PLA)
Saintsbury Pinot Noir (SOM, NI, HAH)
1992
Bonny Doon Le Cigare Volant (NI)
Il Podere dell'Olivos Nebbiolo (MV)
Qupé Syrah Bien Nacido (BEN)
1991
Beringer Cabernet Sauvignon (PIP)
Fetzer Barrel Select Cabernet Sauvignon (DI, LEA)
Firestone Cabernet Sauvignon (PIP)
Ridge Paso Robles Zinfandel (HOG)
Rutherford Hill Merlot (AV)
Saintsbury Pinot Noir (GE)
1990
Grgich Hills Zinfandel (EL)
Jade Mountain Mourvèdre (CRO, YOU)
1989
Fetzer Barrel Select Cabernet Sauvignon (CRO)
1988
Conn Creek Cabernet Sauvignon (NO)
Rutherford Hill Cabernet Sauvignon (PEN)
Simi Cabernet Sauvignon (CB)
1987
Beringer Cabernet Sauvignon (SO)
1986
Renaissance Cabernet Sauvignon (PEN)
1984
Dry Creek Cabernet Sauvignon (CRO)
Ridge York Creek Cabernet Sauvignon (GAU)

£12.00 → £14.99

1994
Au Bon Climat Pinot Noir (REI, MV, ELL)
Jade Mountain La Provençale (MV)
Saintsbury Pinot Noir (AD)
1993
Acacia Iund Pinot Noir (BIB)
Au Bon Climat Pinot Noir (POR, YOU, BEN)
Bonny Doon Le Cigare Volant (AD, PLA)
Calera Jensen Pinot Noir (PIP)
Duxoup Syrah (BIB)
Robert Mondavi Pinot Noir (TAN)
Ridge Geyserville Zinfandel (MAJ)
Saintsbury Pinot Noir (BEN)
Sanford Pinot Noir (SOM)

1992
Bonny Doon Le Cigare Volant (RAE)
Calera Central Coast Pinot Noir (VIG)
Joseph Swan Frati Ranch Zinfandel (UB)
Lytton Springs Zinfandel (NI)
Mount Eden Cabernet Sauvignon (RAE)
Ojai Syrah (BEN)
Qupé Syrah Bien Nacido (MV)
Ridge Mataro (OD)
Saintsbury Pinot Noir (DI)
Sanford Pinot Noir (DI)
Shafer Merlot (ELL, AD)
1991
Bonny Doon Le Cigare Volant (ELL, YOU)
Joseph Phelps Le Mistral (BEN)
Ridge Geyserville Zinfandel (GE)
Saintsbury Pinot Noir (CRO)
Shafer Merlot (ROB)
1990
Au Bon Climat Pinot Noir (CRO)
Bonny Doon Le Cigare Volant (BEN)
Cuvaison Merlot (HOG)
Fetzer Barrel Select Cabernet Sauvignon (UB)
Simi Cabernet Sauvignon (ROB)
Stag's Leap Cabernet Sauvignon (ELL)
1989
Au Bon Climat Pinot Noir (ROB)
Joseph Phelps Cabernet Sauvignon (REI)
Newton Cabernet Sauvignon (DI)
1988
Grgich Hills Zinfandel (CRO)
Trefethen Cabernet Sauvignon (BER)
1987
Ojai Syrah (CRO)
1986
Renaissance Cabernet Sauvignon (CRO)
1985
Ridge Paso Robles Zinfandel (CRO)
1984
Beringer Private Reserve Cabernet Sauvignon (YOU)
1983
Clos du Val Merlot (CRO)

£15.00 → £19.99

1994
Au Bon Climat Pinot Noir (VIG)
1993
Duckhorn Merlot (LAY)
Lytton Springs Zinfandel (PIP)
Marimar Torres Estate Don Miguel Pinot Noir (DI)
Nalle Zinfandel (YOU)
Sanford Pinot Noir (BEN)

1992
Groth Cabernet Sauvignon (ARM)
Lytton Springs Zinfandel (VIG)
Newton Merlot (BEN)
Qupé Syrah Bien Nacido (YOU, VIG)
Ridge Geyserville Zinfandel (DI, BEN)
Saintsbury Pinot Noir Reserve (NI)
Sanford Pinot Noir (NO, UB)
Stag's Leap Cabernet Sauvignon (ROB)
1991
Au Bon Climat Pinot Noir (PLA)
Bonny Doon Le Cigare Volant (NO, UB)
De Loach Pinot Noir (ELL)
Grgich Hills Cabernet Sauvignon (EL)
Joseph Phelps Cabernet Sauvignon (LEA)
Lytton Springs Zinfandel (VIG)
Matanzas Creek Merlot (OD)
Robert Mondavi Pinot Noir Reserve (FOR)
Newton Merlot (POR)
Philip Togni Cabernet Sauvignon (REI)
Ridge Geyserville Zinfandel (NO)
Saintsbury Pinot Noir Reserve (GE, SOM)
1990
Joseph Phelps Syrah (BEN)
La Jota Cabernet Sauvignon (YOU)
Shafer Cabernet Sauvignon (BER)
Stag's Leap Cabernet Sauvignon (DI)

1989
Bonny Doon Le Cigare Volant (CRO)
Newton Cabernet Sauvignon (NI)
1988
Robert Mondavi Pinot Noir Reserve (REI)
Qupé Syrah Bien Nacido (GAU)
Stag's Leap Cabernet Sauvignon (BER)
1987
Bonny Doon Le Cigare Volant (BUT)
1985
Simi Cabernet Sauvignon (CRO)
1984
Carmenet Cabernet Sauvignon (NO)
Cuvaison Cabernet Sauvignon (CRO)
Mayacamas Cabernet Sauvignon (GAU)
Renaissance Cabernet Sauvignon (PEN, NO)
1982
Acacia St Clair Pinot Noir (BUT)

1978
Robert Mondavi Cabernet Sauvignon (CRO)
1976
Firestone Pinot Noir (BUT)
1975
Firestone Cabernet Sauvignon (CRO)

£20.00 ➜ £29.99
1993
Matanzas Creek Merlot (LEA)
1992
Calera Jensen Pinot Noir (REI)
Robert Mondavi Pinot Noir Reserve (BEN)
Saintsbury Pinot Noir Reserve (BEN)
1991
Beringer Private Reserve Cabernet
  Sauvignon (NEZ)
Calera Jensen Pinot Noir (BEN)
Saintsbury Pinot Noir Reserve (CRO)
1990
Bonny Doon Le Cigare Volant (MV)
1989
Dominus Christian Moueix (YOU)
1988
Robert Mondavi Cabernet Sauvignon
  Reserve (FOR)
1986
Dominus Christian Moueix (HAH)
Grgich Hills Cabernet Sauvignon (CRO)
1985
Heitz Bella Oaks Cabernet Sauvignon (BUT)
1984
Shafer Cabernet Sauvignon Hillside Select
  (CRO)
1982
Jekel Cabernet Sauvignon Private Reserve
  (BUT)
Mayacamas Cabernet Sauvignon (CRO)
1980
Robert Mondavi Cabernet Sauvignon
  Reserve (REI)
1979
Clos du Val Cabernet Sauvignon (CRO)
1977
Robert Mondavi Cabernet Sauvignon
  Reserve (GAU)
1973
Heitz Cabernet Sauvignon (CRO)

£30.00 ➜ £39.99
1993
Diamond Creek Volcanic Hill Cabernet
  Sauvignon (LAY)
1992
Philip Togni Cabernet Sauvignon (REI)

1991
Dominus Christian Moueix (CB)
1990
Robert Mondavi Cabernet Sauvignon
  Reserve (FOR)
1989
Ridge Monte Bello Cabernet Sauvignon
  (BEN)
1987
Robert Mondavi Cabernet Sauvignon
  Reserve (GAU)
Mondavi/Rothschild Opus One (BUT, BO)
1986
Dominus Christian Moueix (CRO)
1985
Robert Mondavi Cabernet Sauvignon
  Reserve (NO)
1984
Dominus Christian Moueix (REI)
1982
Heitz Martha's Vineyard Cabernet
  Sauvignon (NO)
1980
Ridge Monte Bello Cabernet Sauvignon
  (BUT)
1978
Jekel Cabernet Sauvignon (BUT)
1976
Heitz Fay Vineyard Cabernet Sauvignon
  (CRO)
1975
Chalone Pinot Noir (BUT)
Robert Mondavi Cabernet Sauvignon (BUT)

£40.00 → £49.99
1992
Mondavi/Rothschild Opus One (NI)
1991
Mondavi/Rothschild Opus One (POR, UN)
1990
Mondavi/Rothschild Opus One (UN)

1988
Mondavi/Rothschild Opus One (NO, BEN)
1987
Mondavi/Rothschild Opus One (NO)
1986
Dominus Christian Moueix (UB)
Mondavi/Rothschild Opus One (NO, BUT)
1984
Heitz Martha's Vineyard Cabernet
  Sauvignon (BUT)
Mondavi/Rothschild Opus One (NO)
1981
Ridge Monte Bello Cabernet Sauvignon
  (CRO)
1978
Robert Mondavi Cabernet Sauvignon
  Reserve (CRO, REI)
1975
Heitz Fay Vineyard Cabernet Sauvignon
  (CRO)

£50.00 → £59.99
1992
Mondavi/Rothschild Opus One (ROB)
1991
Mondavi/Rothschild Opus One (TAN)
1987
Mondavi/Rothschild Opus One (CRO)
1982
Heitz Martha's Vineyard Cabernet
  Sauvignon (CRO)
1978
Ridge Monte Bello Cabernet Sauvignon (AD)

£60.00 → £69.99
1985
Dominus Christian Moueix (BUT)
Heitz Martha's Vineyard Cabernet
  Sauvignon (BUT)
1976
Heitz Martha's Vineyard Cabernet
  Sauvignon (YOU)

CALIFORNIA WHITE

Under £4.00
Non-vintage
E&J Gallo Chenin Blanc (THR, SAI, WR, BOT,
  UN)
E&J Gallo French Colombard (WR, BOT,
  SAF, THR, VIC, SO, CO, BO, UN)
E&J Gallo Sauvignon Blanc (VIC, CO, WR,
  BO, THR, BOT)
1992
E&J Gallo Sauvignon Blanc (SAF)

1991
E&J Gallo Chenin Blanc (DAV)
E&J Gallo French Colombard (DAV)
E&J Gallo Sauvignon Blanc (SAI)

£4.00 → £5.99

Non-vintage
E&J Gallo Chardonnay (CO, THR, WR, SAF)
E&J Gallo Reserve Chardonnay (BO)
Glen Ellen Chardonnay (BO)
South Bay Chardonnay (SAI)
1994
Beringer Fumé Blanc (MAJ)
Glen Ellen Chardonnay (CO, ELL)
Washington Hills Chardonnay (SAI)
1993
Quady Essensia Orange Muscat ½ bottle
(PEN)
Robert Mondavi Woodbridge Sauvignon
Blanc (NI)
Robert Mondavi Woodbridge Zinfandel
(FOR)
1992
Robert Mondavi Woodbridge Sauvignon
Blanc (FOR, EY)

£6.00 → £7.99

Non-vintage
Quady Essensia Orange Muscat (NI)
1995
★ Ca' del Solo Malvasia Bianca (MV)
1994
Beringer Fumé Blanc (NEZ, PIP)
Ca' del Solo Malvasia Bianca (REI, ELL, WRI)
Dry Creek Chenin Blanc (BEN)
Firestone Riesling (WR, BOT)
★ Geyser Peak Chardonnay (VIC)

Quady Essensia Orange Muscat ½ bottle
(WRI, ROB)
Round Hill Chardonnay (LAY)
Sterling Chardonnay (OD)

1993
Beaulieu Vineyard Chardonnay (POR)
Quady Essensia Orange Muscat ½ bottle
(BEN)
Robert Mondavi Fumé Blanc (MAJ)
1992
Ca' del Solo Malvasia Bianca (REI, RAE)
Renaissance Riesling (AD)
Villa Mt Eden Cellar Select Chardonnay
(POR)
1991
Ca' del Solo Malvasia Bianca (SOM)
1990
Quady Essensia Orange Muscat ½ bottle
(WHI, NO)
1989
Wente Bros Chardonnay (SO)
1988
Renaissance Riesling (PEN)
1986
Jekel Johannisberg Riesling (CRO)

£8.00 → £9.99

1995
Murphy Goode Fumé Blanc (AD)
1994
Ca' del Solo Malvasia Bianca (TAN, ROB)
Clos du Bois Chardonnay (HA)
Dry Creek Fumé Blanc (DI)
Firestone Chardonnay (SAI)
1993
Ca' del Solo Il Pescatore (MV)
Edna Valley Chardonnay (HOG, BIB)
Firestone Chardonnay (WR, BOT, HOG)
Quady Essensia Orange Muscat ½ bottle
(UB)
Saintsbury Chardonnay (SOM)
1992
Beringer Chardonnay (MAJ)
Clos du Val Chardonnay (REI)
Pedroncelli Chardonnay (LAY)
Simi Sauvignon Blanc (PLA)
1991
Dry Creek Chardonnay (EY)
Firestone Riesling (BER)
Il Podere dell'Olivos Arioso (MV)
Murphy Goode Fumé Blanc (HAH)
Rutherford Hill Jaeger Chardonnay (PEN)

> *Stars (★) indicate wines
> selected by Oz Clarke in the
> 100 Best Buys section which
> begins on page 8.*

1990
Grgich Hills Fumé Blanc (CRO)
Philip Togni Sauvignon Blanc (CRO)
1989
Robert Mondavi Fumé Blanc (REI)
1988
Renaissance Sauvignon Blanc (PEN)
Saintsbury Chardonnay (GE)
Swanson Chardonnay (PEN)
1985
Quady Essensia Orange Muscat ½ bottle
  (CRO)
Renaissance Riesling Select Late Harvest
  ½ bottle (GAU)
1983
Mark West Johannisberg Riesling Late
  Harvest ½ bottle (CRO)

£10.00 → £11.99
1994
Estancia Chardonnay (OD)
Fetzer Barrel Select Chardonnay (DAV)
Saintsbury Chardonnay (WS)
1993
Acacia Chardonnay (LEA)
Beringer Chardonnay (PIP)
Ca' del Solo Il Pescatore (YOU)
Ca' del Solo Malvasia Bianca (CRO)
Carmenet Meritage White (WS)
Clos du Val Chardonnay (PIP)
Edna Valley Chardonnay (BEN, LEA)
Frog's Leap Chardonnay (MV)
Saintsbury Chardonnay (NI)
Shafer Chardonnay (ELL)
1992
Fetzer Barrel Select Chardonnay (DI)
Robert Mondavi Fumé Blanc (TAN)
Saintsbury Chardonnay (HAH)
1991
Cuvaison Chardonnay (HOG)
Grgich Hills Fumé Blanc (EL)
Newton Chardonnay (DI)
Rutherford Hill Jaeger Chardonnay (AV)
Simi Chardonnay (PLA)
Marimar Torres Estate Don Miguel
  Vineyard Chardonnay (POR, DI)

> *Please remember that*
> ***Webster's** is a price*
> *GUIDE and not a price*
> *LIST. It is not meant to*
> *replace up-to-date*
> *merchants' lists.*

1988
Newton Chardonnay (NO)
1983
Renaissance Botrytis Sauvignon ½ bottle
  (NO)
1979
Robert Mondavi Fumé Blanc (BUT)

£12.00 → £14.99
1994
Au Bon Climat Chardonnay (MV, ELL, BEN,
  ROB)
Frog's Leap Chardonnay (MV)
Newton Chardonnay (NI, OD, AME)
Qupé Chardonnay (MV, BER)
1993
Au Bon Climat Chardonnay (YOU)
Chalone Pinot Blanc (BIB)
Frog's Leap Chardonnay (ROB)
Matanzas Creek Chardonnay (BOT)
Matanzas Creek Sauvignon Blanc (LEA)
Morgan Chardonnay (BOT)
Robert Mondavi Chardonnay (TAN)
Saintsbury Chardonnay (AD, BEN)
Shafer Chardonnay (BER)
Sonoma-Cutrer Chardonnay (LEA)
1992
Au Bon Climat Chardonnay (MV, PLA)
Swanson Chardonnay (HOG)
Marimar Torres Estate Don Miguel
  Vineyard Chardonnay (CRO)
1991
Au Bon Climat Chardonnay (POR)
Flora Springs Chardonnay (REI)
Newton Chardonnay (POR)
Robert Mondavi Chardonnay Reserve
  (FOR)
Simi Chardonnay (ROB, CB)
Marimar Torres Estate Don Miguel
  Vineyard Chardonnay (PEN)
1990
Qupé Chardonnay (PLA)
Sanford Chardonnay (NI)
Sonoma-Cutrer Chardonnay (PEN)
1989
Iron Horse Chardonnay (NO)
Marimar Torres Estate Don Miguel
  Vineyard Chardonnay (NO)
1988
Edna Valley Chardonnay (NO)
1986
Joseph Phelps Johannisberg Riesling
  Selected Late Harvest ½ bottle (CRO)
Robert Mondavi Chardonnay Reserve
  (GAU)

£15.00 → £19.99

1993
Bonny Doon Le Sophiste (REI, MV, OD, YOU)
Chalone Chardonnay (BIB)
Clos du Bois Calcaire Chardonnay (BEN)
Saintsbury Reserve Chardonnay (AD, BEN)
Stag's Leap Chardonnay (ROB)
Swanson Chardonnay (AV)
1992
Bonny Doon Le Sophiste (AD, RAE)
Iron Horse Chardonnay (BER)
Matanzas Creek Chardonnay (LEA)
Saintsbury Reserve Chardonnay (NI)
Sanford Chardonnay (UB)
Swanson Chardonnay (CRO, LEA)
1991
Clos du Bois Calcaire Chardonnay (DI)
Grgich Hills Chardonnay (EL)
Matanzas Creek Chardonnay (YOU)
Robert Mondavi Chardonnay (BEN)
Saintsbury Reserve Chardonnay (DI)
Sonoma-Cutrer les Pierres Chardonnay (CRO, AD)
1990
Robert Mondavi Chardonnay Reserve (PLA)
Sonoma-Cutrer les Pierres Chardonnay (HOG, UB, AV, PEN)
1988
Au Bon Climat Chardonnay (BUT)
Chalone Chardonnay (LEA)
Far Niente Chardonnay (NO)
Robert Mondavi Chardonnay Reserve (CRO)
1985
Joseph Phelps Johannisberg Riesling Selected Late Harvest ½ bottle (NO)
1984
Acacia Chardonnay (BUT)
1983
Joseph Phelps Johannisberg Riesling Selected Late Harvest ½ bottle (HAL)

£20.00 → £24.99

1992
Bonny Doon Le Sophiste (PLA)
Kistler Chardonnay Dutton Ranch (AD)
1991
Far Niente Chardonnay (AV)
Saintsbury Reserve Chardonnay (CRO)
Sonoma-Cutrer les Pierres Chardonnay (LEA)
1990
Kistler Chardonnay Dutton Ranch (CRO)

1989
Grgich Hills Chardonnay (CRO)
1985
Robert Mondavi Chardonnay Reserve (NO)
1983
Stag's Leap Chardonnay (CRO)

c. £31.00

1988
Kistler Chardonnay Dutton Ranch (CRO)
1983
Robert Mondavi Sauvignon Blanc Botrytis (CRO, REI)

CALIFORNIA ROSÉ

Under £4.00

Non-vintage
E&J Gallo White Grenache (VIC, CO)
1994
E&J Gallo White Grenache (SAF)
1993
E&J Gallo White Grenache (BO)

£4.00 → £4.99

1994
E&J Gallo White Grenache (UN)
Robert Mondavi White Zinfandel (NI)

£6.00 → £6.99

1993
Robert Mondavi White Zinfandel (WHI, ROB)

CALIFORNIA SPARKLING

Under £9.00

Non-vintage
Mumm Cuvée Napa Brut (BO, UB, FUL, BOT, WR, THR, CO, OD, SAI, POR)
1991
Mumm Cuvée Napa Brut (SAF)

£9.00 → £9.99

Non-vintage
Mumm Cuvée Napa Brut (SEC)
1989
Mumm Cuvée Napa Brut (OD)

£10.00 → £14.99

Non-vintage
Mumm Cuvée Napa Brut (CRO)
Schramsberg Blanc de Blancs (LEA)
Schramsberg Blanc de Noirs (LEA)

1988
Schramsberg Blanc de Blancs (YOU)
1987
Schramsberg Blanc de Noirs (AD, LAY, YOU)

£15.00 → £21.00
1989
Schramsberg J Schram (LAY)
1988
Schramsberg Blanc de Blancs (ROB)
1986
Iron Horse Brut (CRO)

OTHER USA: RED

Under £7.00
1988
Covey Run Lemberger (HE)
1986
Covey Run Cabernet Sauvignon (HE)
1984
Texas Vineyards Ivanhoe Red (HE)

£7.00 → £9.99
1994
Firesteed Pinot Noir (ENO, VIG)
1993
Columbia Pinot Noir (FOR)
Covey Run Merlot (PLA)
Elk Cove Estate Pinot Noir (PIP, PLA)
Firesteed Pinot Noir (HOG, BU, YOU, UB)
Knudsen Erath Pinot Noir (POR)
1991
Knudsen Erath Pinot Noir (CRO)

1990
Columbia Crest Merlot (YOU, CRO)
Staton Hills Cabernet Sauvignon (CB)
1988
Columbia Crest Cabernet Sauvignon (YOU)
1987
Columbia Crest Cabernet Sauvignon (CRO)
Llano Estacado Cabernet Sauvignon (HE)
1986
Elk Cove Estate Pinot Noir (HE)

£10.00 → £19.99
1991
Domaine Drouhin Pinot Noir (REI, SOM)
Ponzi Pinot Noir (DI)
1990
Domaine Drouhin Pinot Noir (OD, REI)
Eyrie Vineyard Pinot Noir (DI)
1989
Domaine Drouhin Pinot Noir (CRO)
1988
Chateau Ste Michelle Cabernet Sauvignon
  (CRO, WRI)

£20.00 → £24.99
1993
Domaine Drouhin Pinot Noir (BEN)
1991
Domaine Drouhin Pinot Noir (PLA, BEN)
1990
Domaine Drouhin Pinot Noir (MAJ)
1988
Eyrie Vineyard Pinot Meunier (CRO)

OTHER USA: WHITE

Under £6.00
1994
Columbia Gewurztraminer (FOR)
1993
Columbia Crest Sauvignon Blanc (NEW,
  YOU)
1988
Fall Creek Emerald Riesling (HE)
1987
Covey Run Aligoté (HE)
1986
Texas Vineyards Johannisberg Riesling (HE)
1984
Texas Vineyards Ivanhoe Blanc (HE)

£6.00 → £7.99
1993
Columbia Chardonnay (FOR)
1988
Columbia Chardonnay (PEN)

£8.00 → £9.99
1993
Elk Cove Estate Chardonnay (PIP)
1990
Salishan Chardonnay (DI)
1988
Llano Estacado Chardonnay (HE)
1987
Elk Cove Estate Chardonnay (HE)

AUSTRALIA

Oak trees can start to breathe again: Australian winemakers will be needing fewer of them in future. But as well as a move away from over-oaking, there's greater emphasis on individuality

It wasn't looking good at the beginning of 1995, but Australia has not only weathered the storm caused by a severely short vintage but has reinforced its position as the source of the best value-for-money wines in the mid-price bracket. It was a close run thing. Australia was suckered into believing it could be all things to all prices when it was obvious that there were never going to be enough grapes about to satisfy demand at the bottom end of the market. But now it is doing what it should have been doing all along, concentrating on the middle market and leaving the others to scrap over low margins.

It won't be all plain sailing. Reds will still be thin on the ground (if not on the palate) for a year or so, prices are at the mercy of an exchange rate that continues to dip, while South Africa, Chile and the south of France are producing increasingly convincing wines. It isn't in the Australian psyche to give up without a fight, though, and with vast new plantings about to bear fruit, success in exports is going to be vital. It all adds up to good news for us.

Australian wine is also finding a new sense of identity. This has meant searching out the most appropriate techniques, pioneering new regions and also reappraising wine-making techniques. The result is that the terms 'Old World' and 'New World' are becoming increasingly blurred. Australian producers are using techniques from Burgundy, Bordeaux and Italy, while European producers are adapting techniques that have been tried and tested in Australia. The downside is that there are tankerloads of bland international beverages swilling about in the world, but on the positive side it shows a willingness by quality-conscious producers to look, find and adapt appropriate methods to make their wines speak of their origins. It's not uncommon these days to find Australian winemakers saying that they are fed up with too much flavour, too much alcohol. Some may say they are becoming European in outlook, which is a touch simplistic; rather it is the result of the speed at which the industry is maturing.

All this doesn't mean that flavour has been shown the back door, but it does indicate that the industry is responding to a market which is wanting increasingly elegant wines. In any case, if quality is the underlying principle, it should be inevitable that there will be an evolution in style. So winemakers are scaling down the oak, switching from American oak barrels to French, giving the whites more barrel fermentation, filtering the reds less, using a wider range of yeasts, and generally making the wine-making more natural. In the past one often had the feeling that there were still a lot of university manuals being used in the winery; not any more. Duplication of a standard style is not the way forward; instead individuality is in, and that means a concentration on vineyard, variety and region, and the discovery of new sites to give new flavours.

Orange's is not the only fruit

Australia is not what you would call small. There are millions of hectares, still unplanted, that would be suitable for quality wines. Almost every winery is drooling over some new region with an unfamiliar name, like Orange, Koppamurra or Burra. Watch out for these, and those of longer established areas like Margaret River, Eden Valley or Mount Barker; they are at the forefront of Australia's vinous development for the simple reason that they have been chosen specifically to produce a certain style of fruit. At the same time the established areas like McLaren Vale and the Barossa are seeing a renaissance as winemakers re-examine their strengths.

This trend is all part of a recognition that you need more than a price ticket and a varietal label to guarantee a sale. The right vines are, by and large, now going into the right vineyards, which means that there is a wider choice of style. Not only can one see the differences between Shiraz from the Barossa and from the Hunter, but there is increasingly good Grenache, pockets of Viognier, Zinfandel and, especially in Victoria, mutterings of the potential of Italian varieties.

Glad to be single

A further demonstration of individuality is the embracing of the idea by the major firms: more boutique-style releases, more single-vineyard wines, more emphasis on regions. Brands like BRL Hardy's Reynella and Leasingham, Yalumba's Heggies and Hill-Smith releases and Rosemount's single vineyard series are not new, but they have taken on an added importance. It's a backhanded compliment to the smaller players, justifying what they have been preaching for years; and there are plenty casting anxious glances over their shoulders as the big boys try to nick their clothes.

The question is what Britain will make of all this change. Producers may be accentuating differences, but retailers aren't – yet. To do so will mean looking at the balance of a range, and marketing the wines differently. It's what they have always done with European wines, so why should Australia be any different? The support given to the first wave of wines got many consumers into drinking wine in the first place, but that doesn't mean the job is finished. There are still whole states that are badly underrepresented, in particular Western Australia and Victoria. It's time to catch the next wave. **Dave Broom**

GRAPES & FLAVOURS

CABERNET SAUVIGNON (red) This can be rich and chocolaty in the Barossa, austere and minty in Victoria's Pyrenees, full of moss, tobacco and cedar flavours in the Eden Valley, and dense, phenolic and black in the Hunter. Sometimes it can be all of these, sometimes it can taste of nothing more than simple blackcurrant jelly. Winemakers tend to give it their best, which often means too much new wood. But when it's good, it's breathtaking. It's also often blended with other grapes, particularly Shiraz or the Bordeaux varieties Cabernet Franc and/or Merlot. Best: *Clancy's Shiraz-Cabernet, Greenock Creek, Peter Lehmann, Rockford, Seppelt's Dorrien* (Barossa); *Grosset, Tim Knappstein, Leasingham Cabernet-Malbec* and *Classic, Wendouree* (Clare); *Bowen Estate, Hollick's Ravenswood, Katnook, Lindemans' Pyrus, Lindemans' Limestone Ridge* and *Lindemans' St George, Leconfield, Orlando, Parker, Penley Estate, Petaluma, Wynns'* *Coonawarra* and *John Riddoch, Yalumba* (Coonawarra); *Heggies, Henschke, Hill-Smith Estate, Mountadam The Red, Seppelt's Partalunga* (Eden Valley); *Chateau Tahbilk* (Goulburn Valley); *Mt Langi Ghiran* (Great Western); *Frankland Estate, Goundrey, Howard Park, Plantagenet* (Great Southern); *Brokenwood, Lake's Folly, Rothbury Shiraz-Cabernet* (Hunter); *Chapel Hill The Vicar, Chateau Reynella, Coriole Shiraz-Cabernet, Mount Hurtle, Reynella Basket Press, Shottesbrooke, Wirra Wirra* (McLaren Vale); *Cape Mentelle, Capel Vale, Chateau Zanadu, Cullen, Devil's Lair, Leeuwin Estate, Lenton Brae, Moss Wood, Sandstone, Vasse Felix* (Margaret River); *Dromana Estate* (Mornington); *Taltarni* (Pyrenees); *Freycinet, Domaine A* (Tasmania); *Seppelt's Drumborg, Tisdall Mt Helen* (Victoria); *Coldstream Hills, Mount Mary, Seville Estate, St Hubert's, Yarra Yering* (Yarra); *Geoff Merrill, Penfolds* (various).

CHARDONNAY (white) Australia has done more than most to give this grape mass appeal, and is now embarking on a search for a new, more restrained identity. While this means that the old in-yer-face styles of the past are no more, although the richness of fruit is still there. What's happened is that the best wines have been scaled down a couple of notches, and have gained complexity, while not losing appeal. Best: *Shaw & Smith Reserve, Ashton Hills, Petaluma* (Adelaide Hills); *Andrew Garrett, St Hallett, Greenock Creek, Peter Lehmann* (Barossa); *Giaconda* (Beechworth); *Grosset* (Clare); *Katnook* (Coonawarra); *Richmond Grove* (Cowra); *Henschke, Hill-Smith Estate, Mountadam, Seppelt's Partalunga* (Eden Valley); *Bannockburn* (Geelong); *Michelton Preece* (Goulburn); *Frankland Estate, Howard Park, Plantagenet, Wignalls* (Great Southern); *Allandale, Allanmere, Brokenwood, McWilliams' Mount Pleasant, Rosemount, Scarborough* (Hunter); *Tim Knappstein, Stafford Ridge* (Lenswood); *Chateau Reynella, Geoff Merrill, Wirra Wirra* (McLaren Vale); *Cape Mentelle, Chateau Xanadu, Cullen, Evans & Tate, Leeuwin Estate, Lenton Brae, Moss Wood, Pierro* (Margaret River); *Dromana Estate* (Mornington); *Goundry* (Mount Barker); *Eileen Hardy, Lindemans* (Padthaway); *Pipers Brook* (Tasmania); *Coldstream Hills* (Yarra Valley); *Koonunga Hill* (various).

CHENIN BLANC (white) The Australian incarnation of this grape ripens to a much fuller, fruitier and blander style than its steelier Loire counterpart. *Moondah Brook* (Swan Valley) does a good example.

GEWÜRZTRAMINER (white) Gewürz should never be confused with Sydney's predilection for the oily, sweet and dim 'Traminer Riesling', often made of Muscat and Semillon. Fine, faintly spicy cool-climate Gewürztraminers smelling of lychees and honeydew melon are made by *Brown Brothers, Delatite* and *Lillydale* (Victoria), and *Tim Knappstein* (Clare). *Orlando Wyndham's Flaxman's* (Eden Valley) is always good, as is *Tolleys* (Barossa).

GRENACHE (red) Here's proof that there's more to Aussie reds than Cabernet and Shiraz. The Southern Vales around Adelaide are the heartland of this southern French variety, and the rediscovery of old vines sitting there squeezing out more and more concentrated grapes has resulted in a range of wonderful wines. Be prepared for some more examples: Grenache's star is in the ascendant. Best: *Rockford, Turkey Flat, St Hallett's Gamekeeper's Reserve, Yalumba Bush Vine Grenache* and *The Reserve, Charles Melton* and *RBJ* (Barossa); James Halliday Shiraz-Grenache, Michelton III (Goulburn); *D'Arenberg Ironstone Pressings* (McLaren Vale). *Yaldara Reserve*. The *Turkey Flat* vines have been in constant production since 1847.

MARSANNE (white) In Central Victoria, both *Chateau Tahbilk* and *Mitchelton* have made big, broad, ripe Marsanne.

MUSCAT (white) There are two types of Muscat in Australia: first, the bag-in-box *Fruity Gordo* or Muscat of Alexandria – fruity, sweetish, swigging wine, from a heavy-cropping lowish-quality grape grown in irrigated vineyards along the Murray River; second, Liqueur Muscat, made from the Brown Muscat, a strain of the top quality Muscat à Petits Grains, grown in Victoria. It is a sensation: dark, treacly even, with a perfume of strawberry and honeyed raisins. Best producers include *All Saints, Baileys, Bullers, Campbells, Yalumba, Chambers, Morris* and *Stanton & Killeen*.

PINOT NOIR (red) Winemakers are an obsessive lot, and there is no grape that is as likely to get them wound up as this one. Why? Because, first, Burgundy makes some of the best reds in the world and few have even come close to emulating them, and second, because it's a bastard to grow. But things are changing with Pinot, and as winemakers come to terms with this trickiest of all grapes the Burgundy copies are going and a true Australian Pinot style is beginning to appear. Best: *Ashton Hills, Hillstowe, Pibbin* (Adelaide

Hills); *Giaconda* (Beechworth); *Mountadam* (Eden Valley); *Bannockburn* (Geelong); *Lenswood, Ashton Hills* (Lenswood); *Wignall's* (Great Southern); *Tyrrell Vat 6* (Hunter); *Henschke, Tim Knappstein* (Lenswood); *Moss Wood* (Margaret River); *Freycinet, Spring Vale, Piper's Brook, Tasmania Wine Co* (Tasmania); *Coldstream Hills, Mt Mary, St Hubert's, Tarrawarra, Yarra Yering* (Yarra).

RIESLING (white) What has the world got against this variety? It has properties which elevate it far above Chardonnay, be it searingly dry or lusciously sweet. But who buys it? No-one, unless you take the name off the label. It's a shame, because Australia has highly individual, lime-scented examples, clean and crisp (*Ashton Hills, Pewsey Vale, Leeuwin Estate*), softer and more rounded (*Heritage, Skillogalee*), others that beg to be aged (*Orlando Steingarten, Mount Langhi Ghiran*); all sharing a lime aroma. It's a wonderful apéritif and the perfect partner for Thai and Pacific Rim cooking: not many white wines could stand up to those flavours, but Australian Riesling sails through them. Other good ones: *Rockford* (Barossa); *Tim Adams, Jim Barry, Grosset, Tim Knappstein, Mitchell, Petaluma, Pike* (Clare); *Heggies, Hill-Smith Estate, Lindemans' Leo Buring, Orlando St Helga, Seppelt's Partalunga* (Eden Valley); *Frankland Estate, Howard Park* (Great Southern); *Henschke* (Lenswood or Eden Valley); *Pipers Brook* (Tasmania); *Delatite* (Victoria). Best botrytis-afffected wines: *Petaluma, Mt Horrocks* and *St Huberts.*

SAUVIGNON BLANC (white) Aussie winemakers are fed up to the back teeth with people praising New Zealand Sauvignon Blancs to the skies. 'Who wants to drink wine made from unripe fruit?' they ask time and time again. Sour grapes? Perhaps, but there is an increasingly assured bunch of Aussie Sauvignon Blancs on the market, proof that the newer cool-climate regions are coming up with the goods. Adelaide Hills is proving its worth, with *Shaw & Smith, Stafford Ridge* and *Lenswood*, while Margaret River's richer styles

are like southern hemisphere Graves (*Cullen, Evans & Tate*). Best: *Jim Barry, Pike* (Clare); *Katnook* (Connawarra); *Hill-Smith Estate* (Eden Valley); *Bannockburn* (Geelong); *Frankland Estate, Wignalls* (Great Southern); *Ribbon Vale, Amberley Estate* (Margaret River); *Mount Hurtle, Wirra Wirra* (McLaren Vale); *Hardy, Lindemans* (Padthaway); *Bridgewater Mill* (various).

SEMILLON (white) This is slowly gaining the respect of the public, and about time too, as Australia's home-grown style. The Lower Hunter leads the way with wines which are lean and grassy when young, and that take on aromas of toast and honey with age (even though they see no wood). In Western Australia it can be powerful and exotically perfumed. Best: *Heritage, Peter Lehmann, Rockford* (Barossa); *Grosset, Mitchell, Mount Horrocks* (Clare); *Hill-Smith Estate* (Eden Valley); *Cassegrain* (Hastings Valley); *Brokenwood, Lindemans, McWilliams, Petersen, Rothbury* (Hunter); *Knappstein* (Lenswood); *Evans & Tate, Moss Wood, Sandstone* (Margaret River); *Simon Hackett* (McLaren Vales); *Brown Bros.* Best blends with Sauvignon: *St Hallett* (Barossa); *Brokenwood* (Hunter); *Cape Mentelle, Pierro, Xanadu Secession* (Margaret River); *Wirra Wirra* (McLaren Vale). *Geoff Merrill* blends with Chardonnay. Best stickies: *Peter Lehmann, Tim Adams, de Bortoli.*

SHIRAZ (red) The most widely planted red vine in Oz, and the one which squeezes out the most distinctive flavours in wines of the greatest opulence and longevity. Old gnarled Shiraz vines seem to slurp up sunlight, in return offering grapes with the dense, black iron intensity of Clare, the chocolate, earth and moss of the Barossa, the black pepper of the cooler bits of Victoria and WA, or the simple red berry sweetness of the over-irrigated, hot Murray Valley. Try: *Grant Burge Meshach, Greenock Creek, Peter Lehmann, Charles Melton, Rockford, St Hallett, Yalumba Octavius* (Barossa); *McWilliams* (Barwang); *Jasper Hill, Passing Clouds* (Bendigo); *Cape Mentelle* (Margaret River); *Tim Adams, Jim*

Barry, Mitchell, Pike's, Wendouree (Clare); *Bowen, Majella, Wynns, Zema* (Coonawarra); *Craneford, Henschke, David Wynn Patriarch* (Eden); *Bannockburn* (Geelong); *Ch. Tahbilk* (Goulburn); *Mt Langi Ghiran* (Great Western); *Plantagenet* (Great Southern); *Allandale Matthew, Brokenwood, McWilliams Old Paddock and Old Hill, Tulloch Hector, Rothbury* (Hunter); *Craiglee* (Macedon); *Chapel Hill, Chateau Reynella, D'Arenberg Old Vine, Hardy* (McLaren Vale); *Goundrey* (Mount Barker); *Dalwhinnie, Taltarni* (Pyrenees); *Baileys* (Rutherglen); *Yarra Yering* (Yarra); *Hardy, Penfolds, Yaldara Reserve*.

OTHER WHITES A sure sign that a new wine-producing country is growing more sophisticated is a widening range of grape varieties, and that's increasingly what we're seeing. *Heggies* is increasing its plantings of Viognier, *Michelton* is going the whole hog in its attempt to turn the Goulburn Valley into the Rhône with its *Michelton III* blend; *St Hallett's Poacher's Blend* is a wonderfully easy-drinking wine, while Verdelho – best known as a Madeira grape – makes fleshy, refreshing wines in the heat of Cowra (*Richmond Grove*) and the Swan Valley (*Moondah Brook*).

WINES & WINE REGIONS

The new Australian Geographical Indication system, the finer details of which are still being thrashed out in smoke-filled rooms all over the continent but which do not yet appear on labels, has to encompass certain Australian peculiarities. The main one is the system of inter-regional blending: that is, trucking grapes from several different regions, possibly in different states, to a central winery for blending together. So the Australian system has more layers than most, starting with the most general designation, which is Produce of Australia. Anything sold solely under this appellation will not be able to have a grape variety or a vintage on its label.

The next most general is South-Eastern Australia, an appellation which already exists and is much seen; it covers, in fact, most of the wine-producing areas of the country. Then there is the more specific State of Origin, and then there are zones. A zone is smaller than a state but larger than an individual region: Central South Australia incorporates both McLaren Vale and the Barossa, for example. Then come regions, like Barossa itself (not Barossa Valley, note: by dropping the Valley they can incorporate the Clare Valley with it). Finally there are sub-regions. In all there will be about 400 Geographical Indications but, as always, there are arguments over boundaries.

ADELAIDE HILLS (South Australia) This area, which lies 400m above sea level to the north of Adelaide, was pioneered by Petaluma's search for cooler climate sites for its still whites and sparkling wine. It has now been joined by firms such as *Shaw & Smith, Stafford Ridge, Henschke* and *Lenswood*, who are establishing the area with classically pure Sauvignon Blanc, Chardonnays with great length and some classy Pinot Noir.

BAROSSA VALLEY (South Australia) The heart of the wine industry, and a wonderful mix of huge wineries and small family vineyards planted originally by immigrants from Silesia. Most of Australia's wine passes through the Barossa, if only for bottling or aging. Big: *Penfolds, Orlando-Wyndham*. Medium: *Peter Lehmann, Mildara-Blass*. Tiny: *Rockford, Greenock Creek, Charles Melton, Grant Burge*.

BENDIGO (Victoria) This 19th-century region, destroyed by phylloxera, has been replanted with excellent Cabernet, good Shiraz and some Pinot Noir. *Balgownie* is the leader, with *Chateau Le Amon, Craiglee, Harcourt Valley, Heathcote, Mount Ida, Passing Clouds* and *Yellowglen* important.

CANBERRA DISTRICT (ACT) In the Australian Capital Territory, with some modest wineries producing wines to match.

CENTRAL VICTORIA Goulburn Valley is the most important area, with *Chateau Tahbilk* producing big, old-style Shiraz and Cabernet, and some interesting Marsanne. *Tisdall* makes superbly fruity Cabernet, Chardonnay and Sauvignon; *Mitchelton* is also good. *Delatite* makes delicate whites and intense reds in cool-climate conditions.

CLARE (South Australia) An upland complex of four valleys (Skillogallee, Clare, Watervale and Polish River), Clare is cool and dry and produces steely, limy Riesling (*Leo Buring, Tim Knappstein, Jim Barry, Pike* and *Grossett*), soft, light Chardonnay (*Penfolds*), rounded Semillon (*Mitchell*) and long-living reds (*Wendouree, Knappstein, Skillogallee, Leasingham* and *Watervale*).

COONAWARRA (South Australia) A big, flat, wide open landscape dotted with 300-year-old red gums with the famous cigar-shaped strip of *terra rossa* soil which is the heart of Coonawarra. This is Australia's most profitable red wine vineyard, and its incredibly expensive land is jam-packed with great names. In recent years, more white grapes have been planted, but these are best for sparkling wines. Coonawarra is best at Cabernet and unirrigated Shiraz. Try: *Bowen, Brand's, Hardy/Reynella, Hollick, Lindemans, Majella, Mildara, Orlando, Penfolds, Penley, Petaluma, Rouge Homme, Rosemount, Wynns* and *Zema*.

EDEN VALLEY (South Australia) A network of upland valleys, home to some of Australia's oldest vineyards, like *Henschke's* 120-year-old Hill of Grace, and some of the newest and most high-tech (*Mountadam* and *Seppelt's Partalunga*). Most of the major Barossa companies take fruit from these rolling uplands. The *Yalumba* winery is here too, with its *Heggies* and *Hill-Smith Estate* vineyards.

GEELONG (Victoria) Best are intense Cabernets from vineyards like *Idyll* and *Bannockburn*, Pinot Noir from *Prince Albert* and *Bannockburn*, whites from *Idyll*.

GLENROWAN-MILAWA (Victoria) Famous for *Baileys* torrid, palate-blasting reds from Cabernet and Shiraz and (more importantly) Liqueur Muscats. These are intensely sweet, the very essence of the overripe brown Muscat grape, full of an exotic tangle of orange and honey. *Brown Brothers* makes a wide range, but its best are from the Koombahla vineyard, and the high-altitude Whitlands site.

GOULBOURN VALLEY (Victoria) One of Victoria's biggest premium regions, this houses *Mitchelton*, a medium-sized modern winery, and *Tahbilk*, one of the nation's oldest, still making traditional intense reds and long-lived Marsanne. Tiny, highland, high-tech *Delatite* is nearby.

GRANITE BELT (Queensland) This sits on a 1000m-high plateau: altitude and southern latitude allow grapes to be grown in a banana and mango belt. Most wines serve the captive local markets and some (*Ballandean, Koninos Wines, Rumbalara, Robinsons Family* and *Stone Ridge*) are good. *Ironbark Ridge* is one to watch.

GREAT SOUTHERN (Western Australia) This huge, wild, remote region is host to just a handful of widely scattered vineyards, and even fewer wineries, but it is one of Australia's most promising. It has Rieslings as good as those of the Clare and Eden valleys, and delightful limy Chardonnays. Its Shiraz is lithe and peppery, its Pinot lush and fleshy, and its Cabernet magnificent, full of cedar, spice, moss, fern and earth. Soon Cabernet from here will give those from Margaret River a very hard run for their money. The wineries are *Goundrey, Alkoomi, Plantagenet* and the new *Frankland Estate*. Also new is the stunning *Howard Park*, home of the *Madfish Bay* blends.

GREAT WESTERN (Victoria) Historic area best known as the source of base wine for *Seppelt's Great Western* fizz, but more exciting for its reds. Shiraz is superb, full of chocolate, coconut and cream as at *Cathcart*

Ridge, or dry, liquoricy and with impressive pepper as at *Mount Langi Ghiran*. *Best's*, *Montara* and *Seppelt* are other top names. There is also excellent Chardonnay from *Best's* and *Seppelt*, good Cabernet Sauvignon from *Mount Langi Ghiran* and 'vintage port' from *Montara*.

HUNTER VALLEY (New South Wales) Only a madman would plant in the Lower Hunter, with its dry winters and wet summers, but the quality produced by *McWilliams Mount Pleasant*, *Tyrrells*, *Rothbury* and *Allandale* go some way to justifying the gnawed fingernails. This old-established region is home to wonderfully individual Semillons that will last for decades, and great leathery Shiraz. The Upper Hunter is hard, drought-prone land, home to *Rosemount* and its *Roxburgh* vineyard, while *Reynolds* is producing assured, elegant wines.

LOWER GREAT SOUTHERN (Western Australia) A vast, rambling area of great promise, especially round Mount Barker. *Alkoomi*, *Forest Hill*, *Goundrey*, *Howard Park* and *Plantagenet* are good. The whites are fragrant and appetizing, with zesty Riesling and Sauvignon, but the reds are best, with spicy, tobaccoey Cabernets.

MARGARET RIVER (Western Australia) Increasingly poised wines are coming from this high-quality strip of land whose wines reek of a sense of place, combining richness of fruit with elegance of structure. *Moss Wood, Cape Mentelle, Cullen, Pierro, Vasse Felix* and *Leeuwin Estate* are the names to watch, and while Semillon and Sauvignon (as varietals and blends), Cabernet and Chardonnay are the most common wines, experimentation is continuing. *Cape Mentelle* is making great Zinfandel and there are experiments with Malbec, Sangiovese and Nebbiolo.

MCLAREN VALE (South Australia) This area has been under threat from the spread of the Adelaide suburbs, and sadly some wonderful old Shiraz vineyards are now under the tarmac of Ramsay Street-type neighbourhoods. Thankfully the building has been slowed by a revival of interest in the singular quality of the area's fruit, in particular the boldness of the black pepper Shiraz and the sweet concentration of Grenache. Recommended are *Chateau Reynella Basket Press Shiraz, Coriole Redstone Shiraz-Cabernet, D'Arenberg Shiraz-Grenache, Geoff Merrill Chardonnay* and *Cabernet, Mount Hurtle Cabernet, Old Vine Shiraz, Ironstone Pressings.*

MORNINGTON PENINSULA (Victoria) One of the coolest Aussie wine zones, this is a weekend playground for the Melbourne rich. It has 80 vineyards and wineries, among the best of which are *Dromana, Stonier's Merricks* and *Moorooduc Estate*.

MUDGEE (New South Wales) Able to make good table wines owing to a late spring

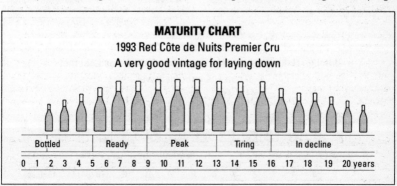

MATURITY CHART
1993 Red Côte de Nuits Premier Cru
A very good vintage for laying down

| Bottled | Ready | Peak | Tiring | In decline |

0 1 2 3 4 5 6 7 8 9 10 11 12 13 14 15 16 17 18 19 20 years

and cold nights. Though established on Shiraz (*Montrose* is outstanding), the best reds have been tarry, plummy Cabernets. But Chardonnay is even better, usually rich, soft and full of fruit-salad flavours. Best: *Montrose, Craigmoor, Huntington, Miramar.*

MURRUMBIDGEE IRRIGATION AREA/GRIFFITH (New South Wales) The

vast irrigated MIA provides ten to 15 per cent of the total Australian crop. Most of it is bulk wine, but *McWilliams* makes some attractive wines, as does de Bortoli, including a Sauternes-style Semillon.

ORANGE (New South Wales) This cool-

climate fruit-growing region was first planted with vines in 1986 and already there are 36 estates spread over 1000ha. It is high up (the vineyards are between 700m and 1000m), and so the fruit quality is distinctive. It's also near Sydney, which is handy. Already some intense Loire-style Sauvignon Blanc (*Highland Heritage*) and cashew nut Chardonnay *(Rosemount)* have appeared, while the reds, notably Cabernet, Merlot and Shiraz (from *Bloodwood, Reynolds* and *Rosemount)* are outstanding.

PADTHAWAY (South Australia) High

quality and increasingly important for whites, notably Chardonnay, Riesling and Sauvignon Blanc. Established in the 1960s when pressure on land in Coonawarra made wineries look elsewhere. Padthaway has some of the *terra rossa* soil which makes Coonawarra so special.

Grapes are grown here for sparkling wine, and there is some excellent sweet Riesling. Best: *Hardy, Lindemans, Seppelt;* major names like *Orlando* and *Penfolds* also use the grapes.

'PORT' Shiraz and other Rhône-type grapes are often used to make high-quality 'port'. Vintage is wonderful. One day they'll stop calling it port. Best: *Chateau Reynella, Lindemans, Montara, Penfolds, Saltram, Seppelt, Stanton & Killeen, Yalumba.*

PYRENEES (Victoria) Very dry Shiraz and

Cabernet reds, and mostly Sauvignon whites. Tops: *Dalwhinnie, Mount Avoca, Redbank, Taltarni, Warrenmang,* and for fizz, *Chateau Remy* and *Taltarni. Chateau Remy* also makes some stylish Cabernet and Chardonnay.

RIVERLAND (South Australia) The grape

basket of Australia – a vast irrigation project on the Murray river providing a large chunk of the national crop. Dominated by the huge *Angoves* winery, and the even bigger *Berri-Renmano-Loxton* group (now part of BRL Hardy), it makes enormous amounts of bag-in-box wines of consistently good quality. But it also yields fresh, fruity Rhine Riesling, Chardonnay, Sauvignon, Colombard, Chenin, Cabernet and Shiraz.

RUTHERGLEN (Victoria) The centre of

the fortified wine tradition. The white table wines are generally dull, except for the reliably fine *St Leonards.* The reds are rich and robust.

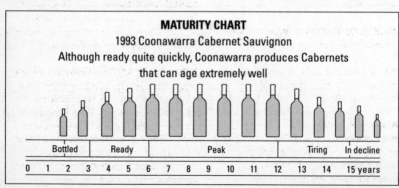

MATURITY CHART
1993 Coonawarra Cabernet Sauvignon
Although ready quite quickly, Coonawarra produces Cabernets that can age extremely well

Bottled	Ready	Peak	Tiring	In decline

0 1 2 3 4 5 6 7 8 9 10 11 12 13 14 15 years

The fortifieds, either as solera-method 'sherries', as 'vintage ports', or as intense, brown sugar-sweet Tokays, are all memorable. The true heights are achieved by Liqueur Muscats, unbearably rich but irresistible with it. Best: *Bullers, Campbells, Chambers, Morris, Stanton & Killeen*.

SPARKLING WINES Along with Pinot Noir, quality fizz is a Holy Grail here. In the lead are *Croser, Green Point* (otherwise known as *Domaine Chandon), Yalumba D, Salinger* and *Jansz*. Cheaper ones include: *Seaview, Angas Brut, Orlando Carrington*. Upmarket: *Seppelt's Blanc de Blancs* and *Pinot Noir-Chardonnay*. And try *Yalumba's Cabernet* and *Seppelt's Shiraz* (sparkling reds).

SWAN VALLEY (Western Australia) One of the hottest wine regions anywhere, this made its reputation on big, rich reds and whites, but even the famous *Houghton Supreme* is now much lighter and fresher. Good names: *Bassendean, Evans & Tate, Houghton, Moondah Brook, Sandalford*.

TASMANIA Only tiny amounts, but there is some remarkable Chardonnay from *Pipers Brook* and *Tasmanian Wine Co.*, and Cabernet from *Freycinet* and *Domaine A*. Pinot Noir can be terrific.

YARRA VALLEY (Victoria) This pretty valley is Victoria's superstar. It is cold, and suits the Champagne grapes, Pinot Noir and Chardonnay, for fizz, plus Riesling and Gewürztraminer, and even Cabernet and Pinot for superb reds. The scale is quite small, the quality very high. Best: *Coldstream Hills, de Bortoli, Diamond Valley, Lillydale, Mount Mary, St Huberts, Seville, Tarrawarra, Yarra Burn, Yarra Ridge, Yarra Yering* and *Yeringberg*.

WINERY PROFILES

TIM ADAMS ★★★★(★) (South Australia) Spectacular early results: spellbinding Semillon and a dense, full-flavoured Shiraz. Tiny amounts but building a cult following.

ALLANDALE ★★★(★) (Lower Hunter) Small winery showing that consistent quality is possible in a tricky climate. One of the best Hunter Semillons; also complex, slightly honeyed Chardonnay and the excellent Matthew Shiraz.

BAILEYS OF GLENROWAN ★★★★ (Victoria) Greatest of Australia's fortified winemakers, its 'Founder' Liqueur Muscat is an unbearably delicious concentration of sweet, dark flavours. Also reassuringly traditional Cabernet and Shiraz.

BANNOCKBURN ★★★★ (Victoria) Gary Farr, winemaker at Domaine Dujac in Burgundy, produces some of cool-climate Geelong's best wines: a rich Pinot Noir, full-bodied Chardonnay and Shiraz.

BAROSSA VALLEY ESTATES ★★(★) (South Australia) Berri Renmano Hardy-owned, this specializes in high-quality cheap wine.

JIM BARRY ★★★★ (South Australia) Clare Valley winery producing outstanding Chardonnay, Rhine Riesling, Sauvignon Blanc and a splendid Shiraz, The Armagh.

BASEDOWS ★★★★ (South Australia) Old Barossa winery now surging ahead with big, oaky Chardonnay, fine Watervale Riesling, hearty, chocolaty Shiraz and Cabernet.

BERRI RENMANO and HARDY ★★★★ (South Australia) This public company, which crushes 25 per cent of all Australian wine, is the result of the merger of Berri Renmano and the family company of Hardy. It's a powerful combination, with Berri's high standard, cheap own-labels and Hardy's impressive quality across the range from Nottage Hill to Chateau Reynella and Eileen Hardy.

WOLF BLASS ★★★(★) (South Australia) Though now owned by Mildara, Wolf Blass still has a knack of producing what people like: wines of tremendous fruit and well-judged oak. There's good Riesling, voluptuous Chardonnay and five styles of red which are, in rising price order, red, yellow, grey, brown and black labels.

DE BORTOLI ★★★(★) (New South Wales) Shot to fame with an astonishing sweet 1982 botrytis Semillon, and has since put together a string of well-priced basics. De Bortoli's new Yarra Valley property makes some of the region's best Chardonnay, Cabernet and Shiraz.

BOWEN ESTATE ★★★★ (South Australia) The best value in Coonawarra: elegant Cabernet-Merlot and razor-fine Shiraz renowned for consistency and quality. Very good Riesling, Chardonnay.

BROKENWOOD ★★★★(★) (New South Wales) Small, high-class Hunter Valley winery noted for eclectic blends such as Hunter/Coonawarra Cabernet and latterly Hunter/McLaren Vale Semillon/Sauvignon Blanc. Low-yielding Graveyard vineyard produces one of Australia's best Shiraz: concentrated, profound and long-living.

BROWN BROTHERS ★★★ (Victoria) Family firm, and a huge range of good wine. The best vineyards are the cool Koombahla and even cooler Whitlands; look for Muscat, Semillon, Chardonnay, Koombahla Cabernet, Whitlands Gewürz and Riesling.

CAPE MENTELLE ★★★★(★) (Western Australia) Important Margaret River winery now part-owned by Veuve Clicquot with founder David Hohnen; also owns New Zealand's buzz winery Cloudy Bay. Excellent Cabernet and variations on the Semillon/Sauvignon theme as well as Shiraz – and Zinfandel, of all things to find in Australia.

CHAPEL HILL ★★★★ (McLaren Vale) Former Wynn's winemaker Pam Dunsford is now in charge of this medium-sized high tech winery that can be run by two people. The early results are highly impressive: wines with restraint and style.

CHATEAU TAHBILK ★★★★ (Victoria) Historic Goulburn Valley winery with great traditional reds.

COLDSTREAM HILLS ★★★★ (Victoria) Aussie wine writer James Halliday opted for practising what he preached, producing world-class Pinot Noir, exciting Chardonnay and Cabernet.

CULLEN ★★★★(★) (Margaret River) A pioneer of the region, Cullen has made consistently intense wines from the word go, and is getting better with each vintgage. Releases include a benchmark Sauvignon Blanc

---

MATURITY CHART
1995 Clare Riesling
The best age as well as German Rieslings but go into a shell between three and six years old

Bottled	Ready	Peak		Tiring	In decline

0 1 2 3 4 5 6 7 8 9 10 11 12 13 14 15 16 17 18 19 20 years

and a richly elegant Cabernet. Wines with personality and style that go a long way to explain why people get excited about the Margaret River.

D'ARENBERG ★★★★ (McLaren Vale) This old-established producer is now undergoing a renaissance. Though in the hands of a new generation the wine-making remains firmly traditional (open fermenters are still used for the reds) to produce powerfully rich Shiraz capable of almost infinite aging, sweetly fruity Grenache and the densely structured Ironstone Pressings.

DELATITE ★★★★ (Victoria) 'A magic piece of dirt, it could grow anything' is how the owners describe the Delatite vineyard. The wines have an individuality of fruit plus superb wine-making which puts them in the top class. Dry Riesling is delicious, the sweet version superb, while Pinot Noir, Gewürz, Cabernet and Shiraz are brilliant.

DOMAINE CHANDON ★★★★ (South Australia) Moët & Chandon's Aussie offshoot Green Point Estate in the Yarra Valley makes outstanding Champagne-method sparkling wines.

DROMANA ★★★(★) (Victoria) Excellent Chardonnay, promising Pinot Noir and Cabernet-Merlot in the Mornington Peninsula, as well as the good-value Schinus-Molle label.

EVANS & TATE ★★★(★) (Western Australia) With vineyards in both Margaret River and Swan Valley, Evans & Tate is getting the best of WA's characteristically rich fruit and is producing a range of beautifully crafted, stylish wines; in particular weighty Semillon (straight and blended with Sauvignon), Merlot and Shiraz.

GOUNDREY ★★★(★) (Western Australia) Drawing fruit from the massive Great Southern region of WA, Goundrey is showing the potential of this (almost) virgin

territory with a range of wines which have real concentration, including the Windy Hill pairing of Chardonnay and Cabernet, and the soft, coffee bean aromas of Shiraz from Mount Barker.

GREEN POINT ★★★★ (Yarra Valley) Moët & Chandon's Australian outpost is now running with a full head of steam. The vineyards, spread across the Yarra Valley, are more mature than they were, the fruit is richer and the style increasingly elegant. Australia's best sparkler?

HENSCHKE ★★★★★ (South Australia) Old red vines, some of them 100 years old, that yield deep, dark, curranty wines of top class. Whites equally stunning – Riesling, Semillon and Chardonnay.

HERITAGE ★★★(★) (Barossa) In a region filled with boisterous winemakers, Heritage is a hidden gem, quietly producing classic wines from a wide range of varieties – limy Riesling, softly honeyed Semillon and an elegant Cabernet Franc.

HILL-SMITH/YALUMBA ★★★★ (South Australia) A large Barossa company producing good wines under the Yalumba and Hill-Smith labels, and exceptional ones under the Signature, Heggies and Pewsey Vale Vineyard labels, where dry and sweet Rieslings are some of the finest in Australia. Yalumba D is very good fizz.

HOLLICK ★★★ (South Australia) With vineyards on the best soils of Coonawarra, Ian Hollick and winemaker Pat Tocaciu harvest some of the region's suavest reds; a soft and tobaccoey Cabernet-Merlot and an outstanding Cabernet cuvée, Ravenswood. They make fine Pinot and Chardonnay fizz and the district's most successful Riesling.

The price guides for this section begin on page 373.

HOWARD PARK ★★★(★) (Western Australia) Expensive but superb, long-living wines. The Riesling is intense, perfumed and austere, the Cabernet deep and structured. Both need cellaring.

LAKE'S FOLLY ★★★★ (New South Wales) Tiny Hunter Valley winery making highly idiosyncratic Chardonnay and Cabernet, very exciting with age.

LEEUWIN ESTATE ★★★★ (Western Australia) Ultra-high profile, ultra-high prices for exciting Chardonnay and Pinot Noir, blackcurrant-and-leather Cabernet Sauvignon, good Riesling and Sauvignon.

LINDEMANS ★★★★ (Victoria) Remarkable firm, now part of Penfolds. Has land in the Hunter, Padthaway, Barossa and Coonawarra. Exceptionally good basic varietals, while Coonawarras, Padthaways and old-style Hunters are among Australia's finest. Coonawarra reds Limestone Ridge and St George are tip-top, as is the Bordeaux blend, Pyrus.

MCWILLIAMS ★★(★) (New South Wales) Old-fashioned giant now rapidly improving its quality. Though traditionally a Hunter Valley company, much McWilliams wine now comes from Griffith in the MIA. Blends like the Hillside Colombard-Chardonnay show what can be done with fairly basic fruit.

CHARLES MELTON ★★★★ (South Australia) A 1000-case Barossa winery with Grenache-based Nine Popes and a Shiraz of exceptional concentration and character.

GEOFF MERRILL ★★★(★) (South Australia) Walrus-moustached, charismatic and irreverent Geoff Merrill combines an instinct for wine with tremendous marketing ability. He makes worthy Cabernet, full Chardonnay, crisp Sauvignon-Semillon and thirst-quenching Grenache rosé at Mount Hurtle.

MILDARA-BLASS★★(★) (South Australia) Large group comprising 13 wineries and whose labels include Jamieson's Run and Robertson's Well. Quality tends to be erratic, though prices are fair. Owns Yellowglen and Balgownie in Victoria and Krondorf in South Australia. See also Wolf Blass and Tisdall.

MITCHELTON ★★★(★) (Victoria) Wide range of styles in the Goulburn Valley, notably fine, full-flavoured Rieslings, good Chardonnay under the Preece label and the speciality of the house, Marsanne.

MOORILLA ESTATE ★★(★) (Tasmania) The first of the new wave Tasmanian wineries, producing a polished range of crisp, cool-climate wines. Pinot Noir is a speciality; aromatic Riesling, Chardonnay and Gewürztraminer are also good.

MORRIS ★★★★(★) (Rutherglen) Now owned by Orlando, Morris has maintained its reputation as the leading producer of sweet liqueur Muscat and Tokay which give a new meaning to the words 'intense' and 'concentrated'.

MOSS WOOD ★★★★ (Western Australia) Superbly original wines from one of Margaret River's best. Semillon, with and without wood-aging, is some of the best in Australia. Pinot Noir is daring and delicious, Chardonnay less daring but just as delicious, Cabernet rich and structured.

MOUNTADAM ★★★★(★) (South Australia) David Wynn established this Adelaide Hills vineyard after selling his original company, Wynns in Coonawarra, and searching high and low for the ideal site. His son Adam makes complex, Burgundian Chardonnay, substantial Pinot Noir, idiosyncratic Riesling and lean Cabernet.

MOUNT LANGI-GHIRAN ★★★★ (Victoria) Great Western winery making richly flavoured, dry, intense Shiraz and long-lived Cabernet.

MOUNT MARY ★★★★ (Victoria) Finely structured Cabernet-based Bordeaux blend and a Pinot Noir improving with age. Tiny production, much sought-after.

ORLANDO ★★★ (South Australia) Barossa winery with fine quality at every level. Its boxed wine is outstanding, its RF Cabernet, Riesling and Chardonnay are usually the best in the price bracket, and St Helga Riesling, St Hilary Chardonnay and St Hugo Cabernet are among the best.

PENFOLDS ★★★★★ (South Australia) The greatest red winemakers in Australia, and now good in whites too. Its basics are clean and tasty, its varietals packed with flavour, and its special selection reds, culminating in the deservedly legendary Grange Hermitage, are superlative, hugely structured wines of world class. If you can't afford Grange, try Bin 28, Bin 128, Bin 389 or the new Bin 407 Cabernet Sauvignon.

PENLEY ESTATE ★★★★ (South Australia) Kym Tolley is a scion of the Penfolds and Tolley families, hence the name Penley. He planted his Coonawarra estate in 1988, but so far his award-winning Shiraz, Cabernet-Shiraz and Chardonnay come from bought-in grapes.

PETALUMA ★★★★(★) (South Australia) The baby of Brian Croser is on excellent form. Some of his Rieslings, sweet and dry, (Chardonnays, too) have been tip-top, and his Cabernet-based reds are now top quality. Also 'Croser' fizz.

PIPERS BROOK ★★★★ (Tasmania) Keenly sought wines which combine classy design, clever marketing and skilful wine-making by Andrew Pirie. Steely aromatic Riesling, classically reserved Chardonnay, serious Pinot Noir and tasty, barrel-fermented Sauvignon Blanc are the best.

PLANTAGENET ★★★(★) (Western Australia) In an unglamorous apple-packing shed in chilly Mount Barker, John Wade and Tony Smith make a fine range of wines. Noted for peppery Shiraz, melony/nutty Chardonnay, fine limy Riesling and elegant Cabernet Sauvignon.

REYNOLDS ★★★★ (Upper Hunter Valley) This recently established estate has already built a reputation with excellent chocolaty Cabernet, powerful Shiraz and well-structured Semillon. One of the backers of Orange, a region just coming to the fore, Reynolds is due to release its first 100 per cent Orange wine this year.

ROCKFORD ★★★★(★) (South Australia) The individuality of Rocky O'Callaghan's wines, especially his Basket Press Shiraz, has made him a Barossa cult.

ROSEMOUNT ★★★(★) (New South Wales) The company which did more than any to help Australia take Britain by storm with Chardonnay, Fumé Blanc and Cabernet. The last two are no longer so good, though Chardonnay is on the way back and the single-vineyard Roxburgh and Show Reserve Chardonnays are impressive. Worldwide, the Chardonnays have set new standards for affordable, tasty quality. We are seeing surprising Pinot Noir and excellent Semillon and Shiraz.

ROTHBURY ★★★★ (New South Wales) One of the leading Hunter companies founded by the indomitable Len Evans. Its wines went through a bad patch a few years ago, but are now back on form and showing classic flavours. The Chardonnay and Semillon are now some of the Hunter Valley's best and the Pinot Noir and the Shiraz are increasingly good.

ST HALLETT ★★★★ (South Australia) Big Bob McLean (a small winemaker in only one sense), with Stuart Blackwell and the Lindner family in the Barossa, makes full, oaky Semillon and Chardonnay and a rich Shiraz, Old Block, from old vines.

ST HUBERTS ★★★★ (Victoria) Now owned by Rothbury and right back at the top, making brilliant whites and reds; Look out for the Chardonnay and Cabernet Sauvignon, which are exceptional.

SEPPELT ★★★ (Victoria) Leading makers of quality fizz from Champagne grapes, peaking with Salinger. Also fruity, easy-drinking styles. Now part of Penfolds.

SHAW & SMITH ★★★★ (South Australia) Itinerant winemaker Martin Shaw and his cousin, Michael Hill-Smith MW, make fine Sauvignon Blanc and Chardonnay in the Southern Vales. A duo to watch.

STAFFORD RIDGE ★★★★ (★) (Adelaide Hills) Former Hardy winemaker Geoff Weaver headed for the hills behind the city to establish his own cool climate vineyard, producing crisply intense and pure Sauvignon Blanc and delicate but long Chardonnay.

STONIER'S MERRICKS ★★★ (Victoria) Good cool climate Chardonnay and Cabernet from this Mornington Peninsula winery.

TALTARNI ★★★ (Victoria) Remarkable bone-dry, grassy-sharp Fumé Blanc; fine Cabernet and Shiraz which soften (after about a decade) into classy, if austere reds.

TISDALL ★★★ (Victoria) Owned by Mildara, this Goulburn winery makes fresh, easy-to-drink reds and whites and cool-climate, quality classics from its Mount Helen grapes.

TYRRELL'S ★★★(★) (New South Wales) Eccentrically brilliant Hunter winery which sells 'port' and 'blackberry nip' to tourists through the front door while making some classic wines out the back. There has never been a more exciting Aussie Chardonnay than the Vat 47 of the early 1980s, and for years Tyrrell's was the only maker of good Pinot Noir in the whole country. Vat 1 Semillon is also excellent, as is his 'plonk' – Long Flat Red and White, named after the vineyard.

VASSE FELIX ★★★★ (Western Australia) This is one of the original Margaret River wineries, and produces a classic regional style of rich, leafy, curranty Cabernet and spicy, fleshy Shiraz.

WIRRA WIRRA★★★★ (South Australia) Fine, concentrated reds, whites and sparkling wine, and exceptional Angelus Cabernet Sauvignon.

WYNNS ★★★★ (South Australia) Big, oaky Chardonnay, refined Cabernet and Shiraz from this Coonawarra company. Top-line John Riddoch Cabernet is expensive but worth every penny.

YARRA YERING ★★★★★ (Victoria) Wonderful Yarra Valley winery, where Bailey Carrodus labels his Cabernet-based wine Dry Red No.1 and his Shiraz-based wine Dry Red No.2: exceptional, powerful and concentrated yet fragrant reds. He makes fine Pinot Noir and Chardonnay as well, but the style is very personal.

MERCHANTS SPECIALISING IN AUSTRALIA
see Merchant Directory (page 424) for details

Everybody wants to buy Australian wines, and virtually every merchant will be able to sell you something. But if you want something other than the usual names, try: Adnams (AD), Australian Wine Centre (AUS), Averys of Bristol (AV), Bennetts (BEN), Bibendum (BIB), Anthony Byrne (BY), Direct Wine (DI), Eldridge Pope (EL), Enotria Winecellars (ENO), Lay & Wheeler (LAY), Oddbins (OD), James Nicholson (NI), The Nobody Inn (NO), Terry Platt (PLA), Raeburn Fine Wines (RAE), Roberson (ROB), Sainsbury (SAI), Safeway (SAF), Sommelier Wine Co (SOM), Tanners (TAN), Thresher (THR), The Ubiquitous Chip (UB), Wine Society (WS)

AUSTRALIA

RED

Under £4.00

1995
Hardys Stamp Shiraz/Cabernet Sauvignon
   (CO)
1994
Hardys Stamp Shiraz/Cabernet Sauvignon
   (SAF, SAI, VIC)
Orlando Jacob's Creek Red (CRO)
Tollana Cabernet Sauvignon/Shiraz (WR,
   THR, BOT)
1993
McWilliams Cabernet Sauvignon (SAI)
1992
Penfolds Shiraz/Mataro Bin 2 (SOM)

£4.00 → £4.49

1994
Orlando Jacob's Creek Red (HOG, SO,
   NEW, DAV, FUL)
1993
Orlando Jacob's Creek Red (SAI, UN)
1992
Lindemans Shiraz Bin 50 (FUL)
Orlando Jacob's Creek Red (FOR)

£4.50 → £4.99

1994
Lindemans Cabernet Sauvignon Bin 45
   (CO, VIC, NEW)
Lindemans Shiraz Bin 50 (NEW)
Penfolds Koonunga Hill Cabernet
   Sauvignon/Shiraz (SOM)
Penfolds Shiraz/Mataro Bin 2 (HOG, VIG,
   BOT, WR, THR)
Yalumba Oxford Landing Cabernet
   Sauvignon/Shiraz (WR, THR, BOT)
1993
Hardys Nottage Hill Cabernet
   Sauvignon/Shiraz (SAF, SAI)
Lindemans Cabernet Sauvignon Bin 45 (POR)
Lindemans Shiraz Bin 50 (MAJ, UN)
Penfolds Shiraz/Mataro Bin 2 (FUL)
Peter Lehmann Shiraz (ASD)
Tollana Cabernet Sauvignon/Shiraz (UN)
1992
Lindemans Cabernet Sauvignon Bin 45
   (SAI, FUL, MAJ)
Orlando RF Cabernet Sauvignon (FOR)
Yalumba Oxford Landing Cabernet
   Sauvignon/Shiraz (FUL, NI)

1991
Lindemans Shiraz Bin 50 (POR)
1990
Hardys Nottage Hill Cabernet
   Sauvignon/Shiraz (SO)

£5.00 → £5.49

1994
David Wynn Cabernet Sauvignon (SOM)
David Wynn Pinot Noir (SOM)
Lindemans Cabernet Sauvignon Bin 45
   (PEN)
Orlando RF Cabernet Sauvignon (VIC)
Penfolds Shiraz/Mataro Bin 2 (VIC)
Tyrrells Long Flat Red (PIP, AME)
Yalumba Oxford Landing Cabernet
   Sauvignon/Shiraz (EY)
1993
Berri Cabernet Sauvignon/Shiraz (NEW, YOU)
Lindemans Cabernet Sauvignon Bin 45
   (WHI)
Lindemans Shiraz Bin 50 (WHI)
Orlando Cabernet Sauvignon (DAV)
Penfolds Koonunga Hill Cabernet
   Sauvignon/Shiraz (HOG)
Penfolds Shiraz/Mataro Bin 2 (SAI)
1992
Berri Cabernet Sauvignon/Shiraz (FUL)
Orlando Cabernet Sauvignon (HOG, SAI)
Orlando RF Cabernet Sauvignon (UB, NEW)
Rouge Homme Shiraz/Cabernet
   Sauvignon (ELL, YOU, FUL)

£5.50 → £5.99

1995
★ Yaldara Whitmore Old Vineyard
   Grenache (WAI)
1994
★ Kingston Estate Murray Valley Mataro (TES)
Penfolds Koonunga Hill Cabernet
   Sauvignon/Shiraz (EY, BOT, DAV, WHI, WR)
Rothbury Shiraz (FUL)
★ Tatachilla Cabernet Sauvignon (WAI)
Tyrrells Long Flat Red (TAN)
Tyrrells Old Winery Cabernet Merlot
   (SAI)
1993
★ Ironstone Cabernet-Shiraz (MAJ)
Lindemans Shiraz Bin 50 (BY, BEN)
Penfolds Koonunga Hill Cabernet
   Sauvignon/Shiraz (POR, UN, VIC, OD, BO,
   SAI, SAF)

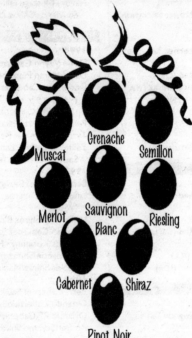

Peter Lehmann Shiraz (QUE)
Rosemount Shiraz (MAR)
Rothbury Shiraz (BO)
Tyrrells Long Flat Red (AV)
Wynns Shiraz (BOT, THR, WR)
1992
Berri Cabernet Sauvignon (NEW)
Krondorf Shiraz/Cabernet Sauvignon (HOG)
Penfolds Koonunga Hill Cabernet
   Sauvignon/Shiraz (FUL, TES)
Rouge Homme Shiraz/Cabernet
   Sauvignon (LEA, AME)
1991
Berri Cabernet Sauvignon (UN)
Mildara Cabernet Sauvignon/Merlot (PEN)
Rouge Homme Cabernet Sauvignon (AME)
1990
★ Wakefield Cabernet Sauvignon (UN)
1986
Rouge Homme Shiraz/Cabernet
   Sauvignon (GAU)

£6.00 → £6.49
1994
Basedows Cabernet Sauvignon (VIC)
Best's Victoria Shiraz (FUL, POR)
Rosemount Cabernet Sauvignon (UN, WR,
   BO, DAV, THR, BOT)
Rothbury Shiraz (OD)
Wolf Blass Yellow Label Cabernet
   Sauvignon (HOG)
1993
Brown Bros Shiraz (WHI)
Rosemount Cabernet Sauvignon (VIC,
   FUL)Rothbury Cabernet Sauvignon (SAI)
Rouge Homme Shiraz/Cabernet
   Sauvignon (WHI)
St Halletts Cabernet Merlot (REI)
Tyrrells Pinot Noir (PEN)
Wyndham's Shiraz Bin 555 (KA, DAV)
Wyndham's Cabernet Sauvignon Bin 444
   (DAV)
1992
Houghton Cabernet Sauvignon (WS)
Penfolds Kalimna Shiraz Bin 28 (SOM)
Penfolds Koonunga Hill Cabernet
   Sauvignon/Shiraz (AV)
Wyndham's Cabernet Sauvignon Bin 444
   (QUE, KA)
1991
Mildara Shiraz (PEN)
1989
Seppelt Dorrien Cabernet (FUL)
Seppelt Partalunga Cabernet Sauvignon
   (FUL)

£6.50 → £6.99
1994
Best's Victoria Shiraz (BU, SAT)
Brown Bros Cabernet Sauvignon (PIP)
Brown Bros Shiraz (DI, PIP, POR)
David Wynn Cabernet Sauvignon (AD)
Penfolds Koonunga Hill Cabernet
   Sauvignon/Shiraz (BEN)
Rosemount Cabernet Sauvignon (WHI)
Tyrrells Old Winery Cabernet Merlot (UN)
Wolf Blass Cabernet Sauvignon (WHI)
Wolf Blass Yellow Label Cabernet
   Sauvignon (VIC)
1993
Basedows Shiraz (HOG, VIC)
Brown Bros Cabernet Sauvignon (CO, DI)
Brown Bros Shiraz (UB)
Chateau Reynella Cabernet Merlot (CO)
David Wynn Cabernet Sauvignon (HIC)
Rothbury Shiraz (DI, POR)
Wolf Blass Yellow Label Cabernet
   Sauvignon (POR, NEW, SAF)
1992
Brown Bros Cabernet Sauvignon (POR)
Jamiesons Run Coonawarra Red (HOG)
Penfolds Coonawarra Shiraz Bin 128 (SOM)
Penfolds Kalimna Shiraz Bin 28 (THR, WR,
   BOT, SO, VIC)
Peter Lehmann Clancys Barossa (SAI)
St Halletts Cabernet Merlot (SAI)
1991
Berri Cabernet Sauvignon (CRO)
Jamiesons Run Coonawarra Red (BO)
Knappstein Cabernet Sauvignon/Merlot
   (SAI)
Penfolds Kalimna Shiraz Bin 28 (BO)
Rouge Homme Cabernet Sauvignon (WRI,
   ROB, LEA, YOU, DI)
Rouge Homme Shiraz/Cabernet
   Sauvignon (AV)
Taltarni Merlot (REI)
1990
Rosemount Cabernet Sauvignon (CRO)
Wynns Coonawarra Cabernet Sauvignon
   (VIC)
1989
Lindemans Cabernet Sauvignon Bin 45
   (BUT)
1988
Lindemans Shiraz Bin 50 (BUT)
Rosemount Hunter Valley Shiraz (BUT)
1987
Lindemans Shiraz Bin 50 (BUT)
1985
Lindemans Shiraz Bin 50 (BUT)

£7.00 → £7.49

1994
Brown Bros Shiraz (PEN, PE)
Jim Barry Cabernet Sauvignon (TAN)
Mitchell Peppertree Shiraz (EY)
Rosemount Cabernet Sauvignon (SAT)
Rosemount Pinot Noir (SAT)
Rosemount Shiraz (SAT)
1993
Brown Bros Cabernet Sauvignon (PE)
Wolf Blass Yellow Label Cabernet
  Sauvignon (QUE)
1992
Brown Bros Cabernet Sauvignon (PEN, AD)
Penfolds Coonawarra Shiraz Bin 128 (HOG)
Penfolds Kalimna Shiraz Bin 28 (HOG)
Pewsey Vale Cabernet Sauvignon (SAI)
Rockford Dry Country Grenache (REI)
Taltarni Shiraz (REI)
1991
Rouge Homme Shiraz/Cabernet
  Sauvignon (CRO)
1990
Jamiesons Run Coonawarra Red (PEN)
Knappstein Cabernet Sauvignon (OD)
Merricks Estate Cabernet Sauvignon (SAI)
Orlando St Hugo Cabernet Sauvignon
  (HOG)

£7.50 → £7.99

1994
Brown Bros Shiraz (TAN)
Cape Mentelle Zinfandel (NO)
★ Chapel Hill McLaren Vale Shiraz (AUS)
Mitchell Peppertree Shiraz (SOM, LAY)
Stonier's Pinot Noir (WAT)
Wolf Blass Yellow Label Cabernet
  Sauvignon (BY)
1993
Basedows Shiraz (BIB)
Brown Bros Cabernet Sauvignon (TAN)
Cape Mentelle Shiraz (NI)
Chateau Reynella Cabernet Merlot (ASD,
  SAI)
Penfolds Kalimna Shiraz Bin 28 (DAV, WHI,
  OD)
Rockford Dry Country Grenache (YOU)
★ Stonier's Cabernet (WAT)
1992
Cape Mentelle Shiraz (REI)
Charles Melton Shiraz (SOM)
★ Doonkuna Shiraz (AUS)
Penfolds Cabernet/Shiraz Bin 389 (SOM)
Penfolds Coonawarra Cabernet
  Sauvignon (SOM)

Penfolds Coonawarra Shiraz Bin 128 (VIG,
  THR, BOT, WR)
Rouge Homme Cabernet Sauvignon (YOU)
Tasmanian Wine Company Pinot Noir
  (POR)
1991
Mount Langi Ghiran Shiraz (AME)
Penfolds Coonawarra Cabernet
  Sauvignon (DAV)
Wynns Coonawarra Cabernet Sauvignon
  (VIG)
1990
Penfolds Coonawarra Shiraz Bin 128 (TES)
1989
Orlando St Hugo Cabernet Sauvignon (FOR)
1988
Wynns Coonawarra Cabernet Sauvignon
  (VIG, AME)
1986
Seppelt Cabernet Sauvignon Black Label
  (GAU)
1983
Brown Bros Shiraz/Cabernet Sauvignon
  (VIC)

£8.00 → £8.49

1994
Coriole Shiraz (TAN)
★ Dennis McLaren Vale Cabernet Sauvignon
  (PE)
Rosemount Shiraz (CRO)
Tasmanian Wine Company Pinot Noir
  (PEN)
1993
Coldstream Hills Pinot Noir (OD)
Coriole Sangiovese (BO)
★ Dennis McLaren Vale Shiraz (PE)
Penfolds Kalimna Shiraz Bin 28 (PIP, TAN)
Wirra Wirra Angelus (SOM)
Wolf Blass Yellow Label Cabernet
  Sauvignon (CRO)
1992
Cape Mentelle Zinfandel (POR)
Penfolds Kalimna Shiraz Bin 28 (PEN)
Penley Estate Coonawarra Cabernet
  Sauvignon/Shiraz (AUS)
St Halletts Old Block Shiraz (SOM)
Taltarni Shiraz (YOU)
1991
Taltarni Cabernet Sauvignon (WS)
Taltarni Shiraz (AME)
1990
Penfolds Koonunga Hill Cabernet
  Sauvignon/Shiraz (CRO)
Rouge Homme Cabernet Sauvignon (AV)

£8.50 → £8.99

1995
★ Stonier's Pinot Noir (WAT)
1994
Cape Mentelle Zinfandel (KA, RAE)
Charles Melton Shiraz (REI, AUS)
Rockford Dry Country Grenache (TAN)
★ Tim Adams The Fergus (AUS)
1993
Cape Mentelle Shiraz (OD)
Charles Melton Nine Popes (REI)
Coldstream Hills Pinot Noir (NEZ, NI)
Penfolds Coonawarra Cabernet
  Sauvignon (CO, VIC)
Penfolds Kalimna Shiraz Bin 28 (BY)
Taltarni Shiraz (PLA)
Tim Adams Shiraz (TES, AUS)
1992
Bowen Estate Shiraz (ENO)
Cape Mentelle Shiraz (PLA)
Mitchell Peppertree Shiraz (AV, VIG)
Mount Langi Ghiran Shiraz (SOM)
Penfolds Cabernet/Shiraz Bin 389 (THR,
  BOT, HOG, WR, FUL, WHI)
Penfolds Coonawarra Cabernet
  Sauvignon (POR, THR, WR, BOT)
Penfolds Coonawarra Shiraz Bin 128 (BY)
St Halletts Old Block Shiraz (REI)
1991
Hollick Coonawarra Cabernet
  Sauvignon/Merlot (YOU, ELL)
Mount Langi Ghiran Cabernet Sauvignon
  (YOU)
Penfolds Coonawarra Shiraz Bin 128
  (BEN)
Taltarni Merlot (YOU, AME)
Tasmanian Wine Company Pinot Noir
  (PLA)
Wynns Coonawarra Cabernet Sauvignon
  (MAJ)
1990
Bannockburn Pinot Noir (NI)
Rosemount Show Reserve Cabernet
  Sauvignon (TES)
Seville Estate Cabernet Sauvignon (RAE)
Wynns Coonawarra Cabernet Sauvignon
  (LEA)
1989
Cape Mentelle Shiraz (RAE)
Taltarni Cabernet Sauvignon (PLA)
1988
Chateau Tahbilk Cabernet Sauvignon
  (AUR)
Penfolds St-Henri Shiraz/Cabernet (SOM)
Taltarni Cabernet Sauvignon (AME)

£9.00 → £9.99

1994
Bowen Estate Shiraz (AUS)
Charles Melton Nine Popes (AUS, SOM)
David Wynn Patriarch Shiraz (AD)
Mitchell Peppertree Shiraz (PIP)
Mount Langi Ghiran Shiraz (ENO)
Stonier's Pinot Noir (DI)
Wirra Wirra Angelus (OD)
1993
Bowen Estate Cabernet Sauvignon (AUS)
Cape Mentelle Shiraz (AD)
Coriole Sangiovese (ROB)
David Wynn Patriarch Shiraz (NI)
Idyll Cabernet Sauvignon/Shiraz (DAV)
Mitchell Peppertree Shiraz (YOU)
Mount Langi Ghiran Shiraz (GAL)
Penfolds Cabernet/Shiraz Bin 389 (ASD)
Plantagenet Shiraz (ELL)
Taltarni Shiraz (LAYT)
Wirra Wirra Angelus (FUL)
1992
Best's Victoria Shiraz (PLA)
Cullen Pinot Noir (GAU)
Hollick Coonawarra Cabernet
  Sauvignon/Merlot (LAY)
Mount Langhi Ghiran Shiraz (YOU)
Penfolds Cabernet/Shiraz Bin 389 (TAN,
  BY, OD)
Penfolds Coonawarra Cabernet
  Sauvignon (BY)
Penfolds St-Henri Shiraz/Cabernet (CO)
Pipers Brook Pinot Noir (HOG)
St Halletts Old Block Shiraz (POR, AD, ENO)
St Huberts Cabernet Sauvignon (EY)
Taltarni Merlot (PLA)
1991
Blue Pyrenees Estate Cabernet
  Sauvignon/Merlot/Shiraz (WHI)
Cassegrain Cabernet Sauvignon (ROB)
Charles Melton Nine Popes (GAU)
Charles Melton Shiraz (GAU)
Hollick Coonawarra Cabernet
  Sauvignon/Merlot (BER)
Katnook Cabernet Sauvignon (VIC)
Lindemans Pyrus (POR, UN)
Mount Langi Ghiran Cabernet Sauvignon
  (DI)

> *Stars (★) indicate wines
> selected by Oz Clarke in the
> 100 Best Buys section which
> begins on page 8.*

Penfolds Coonawarra Cabernet
Sauvignon (MAJ)
Penley Estate Coonawarra Cabernet
Sauvignon/Shiraz (YOU)
Petaluma Coonawarra Cabernet
Sauvignon (NI)
Pipers Brook Pinot Noir (SOM)
Rockford Cabernet Sauvignon (YOU)
Taltarni Merlot (TAN)
Wolf Blass President's Selection Cabernet
Sauvignon (HOG)
1990
Orlando St Hugo Cabernet Sauvignon (UN)
Tyrrells Vat 9 Winemakers Selection
Shiraz (AV)
1989
Jamiesons Run Coonawarra Red (NO)
Lindemans St George Cabernet Sauvignon
(BO)
1988
Cape Mentelle Shiraz (BUT)
1987
Lindemans Cabernet Sauvignon Bin 45
(CRO)
1985
Brown Bros Koombahla Cabernet
Sauvignon (YOU, BO)
1983
Brown Bros Shiraz/Cabernet Sauvignon
(DI)
1982
Tyrrells Long Flat Red (CRO)

£10.00 → £10.99
1995
Cullen Pinot Noir (PIP, AD)
1994
Coldstream Hills Pinot Noir (PIP)
Cullen Pinot Noir (AME)
Parker Coonawarra Estate Terra Rossa
Cabernet Sauvignon (CB)
Wolf Blass President's Selection Cabernet
Sauvignon (WHI)
1993
Charles Melton Nine Popes (POR)
Mount Langi Ghiran Shiraz (DI)

> *Please remember that*
> ***Webster's*** *is a price*
> *GUIDE and not a price*
> *LIST. It is not meant to*
> *replace up-to-date*
> *merchants' lists.*

Penfolds Coonawarra Cabernet
Sauvignon (TAN)
Petaluma Coonawarra Cabernet
Sauvignon (OD)
St Halletts Old Block Shiraz (AUS)
1992
Cape Mentelle Zinfandel (CRO)
Coriole Shiraz (CRO)
Katnook Cabernet Sauvignon (BIB)
Penley Estate Coonawarra Cabernet
Sauvignon (AUS)
Penley Estate Coonawarra Cabernet
Sauvignon/Shiraz (LAY)
Rockford Basket Press Shiraz (REI)
St Halletts Old Block Shiraz (NO)
Wignalls Pinot Noir (ROB)
Wirra Wirra Angelus (AUR)
Wolf Blass President's Selection Cabernet
Sauvignon (VIC)
1991
Penfolds Kalimna Shiraz Bin 28 (CRO)
Rockford Cabernet Sauvignon (VIG)
1990
Cape Mentelle Cabernet Sauvignon (KA)
Penfolds St-Henri Shiraz/Cabernet (PIP)
Wolf Blass President's Selection Cabernet
Sauvignon (QUE)
1988
Eileen Hardy Shiraz (NO)
Lindemans St George Cabernet Sauvignon
(NO)
1987
Cape Mentelle Cabernet Sauvignon (RAE)
1986
Balgownie Shiraz (CRO)
1985
Wolf Blass Yellow Label Cabernet
Sauvignon (CRO)
1983
Hardy Keppoch Cabernet
Sauvignon/Shiraz (CRO)

£11.00 → £11.99
1994
Charles Melton Nine Popes (ENO)
Charles Melton Shiraz (ENO)
Rosemount Diamond Reserve Cabernet
Sauvignon/Shiraz (FOR)
1993
Bannockburn Pinot Noir (HA)
Cape Mentelle Cabernet Sauvignon (TAN)
Charles Melton Nine Popes (BEN)
Coldstream Hills Pinot Noir (CRO, ARM)
Cullen Cabernet Sauvignon/Merlot (DI)
Mount Langi Ghiran Shiraz (WS, BY)

Mountadam Pinot Noir (WR, THR, BOT)
Plantagenet Shiraz (BER)
Wirra Wirra Angelus (CRO)
1992
Cullen Cabernet Sauvignon/Merlot (ELL)
E&E Black Pepper Shiraz (CO)
Lake's Folly Cabernet Sauvignon (YOU)
Moss Wood Cabernet Sauvignon (NO)
Penfolds St-Henri Shiraz/Cabernet (HOG)
Rockford Basket Press Shiraz (FUL)
Wignalls Pinot Noir (AUS)
1991
Cape Mentelle Cabernet Sauvignon (BEN)
Charles Melton Nine Popes (CRO)
Cullen Cabernet Sauvignon/Merlot (GAU)
Lindemans Limestone Ridge
  Shiraz/Cabernet Sauvignon (OD)
Lindemans Pyrus (OD)
Lindemans St George Cabernet Sauvignon
  (OD)
Rockford Basket Press Shiraz (POR)
1990
Lindemans Pyrus (MAJ)
Lindemans St George Cabernet Sauvignon
  (POR)
Moss Wood Pinot Noir (ELL)
Penley Estate Coonawarra Cabernet
  Sauvignon/Shiraz (DI)
Tyrrells Vat 9 Winemakers Selection
  Shiraz (DI)
1988
Cape Mentelle Cabernet Sauvignon (BUT)
Penfolds Kalimna Shiraz Bin 28 (CRO)
Penfolds Magill Estate Shiraz (SOM)
1985
Seaview Cabernet Sauvignon (CRO)
1984
Balgownie Cabernet Sauvignon (CRO)

£12.00 → £13.99
1994
Charles Melton Nine Popes (VIG, WRI)
Lake's Folly Cabernet Sauvignon (LAY)
Pipers Brook Pinot Noir (MV)
1993
Bannockburn Shiraz (BEN, ROB)
Chateau Xanadu Cabernet Sauvignon
  (DAV)
Moss Wood Pinot Noir (CRO)
Mountadam Pinot Noir (WRI)
Rosemount Cabernet Sauvignon (FOR)
Yeringberg Pinot Noir (BIB)
1992
Bannockburn Pinot Noir (BEN)
Cape Mentelle Shiraz (NO)

E&E Black Pepper Shiraz (SAI)
Henschke Mount Edelstone Shiraz (YOU,
  SOM)
Moss Wood Cabernet Sauvignon (WS)
Penfolds Magill Estate Shiraz (HOG)
Petaluma Coonawarra Cabernet
  Sauvignon (ENO)
Pipers Brook Pinot Noir (PLA)
Rockford Basket Press Shiraz (YOU, VIG,
  BEN, ENO, TAN, GAU, PLA, WS, DI)
Rosemount Shiraz (FOR)
1991
Cape Mentelle Cabernet Sauvignon (PLA)
Charles Melton Shiraz (CRO)

Henschke Cyril Henschke Cabernet
  Sauvignon (YOU)
Lindemans Limestone Ridge
  Shiraz/Cabernet Sauvignon (VIG, PEN)
Lindemans St George Cabernet Sauvignon
  (NO)
Mountadam Pinot Noir (HIC, NO)
Penfolds Magill Estate Shiraz (NO)
Penley Estate Coonawarra Cabernet
  Sauvignon/Shiraz (UB)
Pipers Brook Pinot Noir (PEN, UB)
Tyrrells Pinot Noir (REI)
Vasse Felix Cabernet Sauvignon (ROB)
1990
Lindemans Limestone Ridge
  Shiraz/Cabernet Sauvignon (AV)
Lindemans Pyrus (NO, AV)
Lindemans St George Cabernet Sauvignon
  (AV)
Penfolds Magill Estate Shiraz (POR)
Petaluma Cabernet Sauvignon/Merlot
  (BEN)
Wolf Blass President's Selection Cabernet
  Sauvignon (CRO)
1989
Lindemans Limestone Ridge
  Shiraz/Cabernet Sauvignon (NO)
Lindemans St George Cabernet Sauvignon
  (BY)
Rouge Homme Cabernet Sauvignon (CRO)

1988
Cape Mentelle Cabernet Sauvignon
(CRO)
Cape Mentelle Shiraz (CRO)
Dalwhinnie Cabernet Sauvignon (NO)
Moss Wood Cabernet Sauvignon (CRO)
Rosemount Show Reserve Cabernet
Sauvignon (CRO)
Taltarni Shiraz (CRO)
1986
Cullen Cabernet Sauvignon/Merlot (CRO)
Rosemount Kirri Billi Merlot (BUT)
Rosemount Show Reserve Cabernet
Sauvignon (BUT)
1985
Chateau Reynella Cabernet Sauvignon
(CRO)
Chateau Tahbilk Cabernet Sauvignon
(CRO)
Petaluma Cabernet Sauvignon (REI)
1984
Katnook Cabernet Sauvignon (NO)
Leeuwin Estate Cabernet Sauvignon (CRO)
1983
Cullen Cabernet Sauvignon/Merlot (CRO)
Seppelt Cabernet Sauvignon Black Label
(CRO)
1981
Balgownie Cabernet Sauvignon (CRO)

£14.00 ➜ £15.99
1993
Mount Edelstone Shiraz (WS)
★ Tyrrells Vat 8 Shiraz-Cabernet (UN)
1992
Henschke Cyril Henschke Cabernet
Sauvignon (SOM)
Mountadam Pinot Noir (ARM)
Penfolds Cabernet Sauvignon Bin 707
(SOM, HOG)
Penfolds Magill Estate Shiraz (AD)
Penley Estate Coonawarra Cabernet
Sauvignon (LAY)
Wynns John Riddoch Cabernet Sauvignon
(TES)
Yarra Yering Dry Red No.1 (Cabernet)
(SOM)
Yarra Yering Dry Red No.2 (Shiraz) (SO⁻)

Webster's is an annual
publication. We welcome
your suggestions for next
year's edition.

1991
Bannockburn Pinot Noir (ROB)
Dalwhinnie Cabernet Sauvignon (GAU)
Hollick Ravenswood Cabernet Sauvignon
(YOU)
Penfolds Cabernet Sauvignon Bin 707
(PIP)
Penfolds Magill Estate Shiraz (PIP)
Penley Estate Coonawarra Cabernet
Sauvignon (YOU)
Petaluma Cabernet Sauvignon/Merlot
(ROB)
1990
Bannockburn Pinot Noir (UB)
Hollick Ravenswood Cabernet Sauvignon
(OD)
Tyrrells Vat 9 Winemakers Selection
Shiraz (CRO)
1989
Penley Estate Coonawarra Cabernet
Sauvignon (NO)
Tyrrells Pinot Noir (REI)
1988
Dromana Estate Cabernet/Merlot (BUT)
Wynns John Riddoch Cabernet Sauvignon
(SAI)
1987
Moss Wood Cabernet Sauvignon
(CRO)
Wynns John Riddoch Cabernet Sauvignon
(VIG)
1985
Lindemans St George Cabernet Sauvignon
(GAU)
1984
Chateau Reynella Cabernet Sauvignon
(CRO)
1983
Brown Bros Family Reserve Cabernet
Sauvignon (PIP)

£16.00 ➜ £19.99
1993
Mount Edelstone Shiraz (LAY)
1992
Cyril Henschke Cabernet Sauvignon (LAY,
DI)
Henschke Mount Edelstone Shiraz (DI)
Penfolds Cabernet Sauvignon Bin 707
(THR, UN, WR, BOT, BY, BEN, VIC)
Penfolds Magill Estate Shiraz (PEN)
Yarra Yering Dry Red No.1 (Cabernet)
(POR, BEN)
Yarra Yering Dry Red No.2 (Shiraz) (POR,
BY)

1991
Giaconda Pinot Noir (NO)
Henschke Mount Edelstone Shiraz (CRO)
Hollick Ravenswood Cabernet Sauvignon
   (ELL)
Penfolds Cabernet Sauvignon Bin 707
   (NO, POR, BO, AV)
Wolf Blass Black Label Cabernet
   Sauvignon (OD)
Wynns John Riddoch Cabernet Sauvignon
   (VIG, LEA)
Yarra Yering Dry Red No.2 (Shiraz) (BEN)
1990
Penfolds Cabernet Sauvignon Bin 707
   (TES)
Penley Estate Coonawarra Cabernet
   Sauvignon/Shiraz (NO)
Wynns John Riddoch Cabernet Sauvignon
   (VIG)
Yarra Yering Dry Red No.1 (Cabernet)
   (NO)
Yarra Yering Dry Red No.2 (Shiraz) (NO)
1988
Lindemans Limestone Ridge
   Shiraz/Cabernet Sauvignon (CRO)
Lindemans St George Cabernet Sauvignon
   (CRO)
Wynns John Riddoch Cabernet Sauvignon
   (VIG)
1985
Lindemans Limestone Ridge
   Shiraz/Cabernet Sauvignon (BUT)
Lindemans Pyrus (CRO)
Lindemans St George Cabernet Sauvignon
   (BUT)
Wolf Blass Black Label Cabernet
   Sauvignon (POR)
1984
Blue Pyrenees Estate Cabernet
   Sauvignon/Merlot/Shiraz (CRO)
1982
Balgownie Cabernet Sauvignon (CRO)
Chateau Tahbilk Cabernet Sauvignon (CRO)
1978
Penfolds Kalimna Shiraz Bin 28 (CRO)

£20.00 → £29.99

1993
Jim Barry The Armagh Shiraz (TAN, OD)
1991
Henschke Hill of Grace Shiraz (SOM)
Yarra Yering Dry Red No.1 (Cabernet)
   (BER)
1990
Yarra Yering Pinot Noir (BEN)

1989
Henschke Cyril Henschke Cabernet
   Sauvignon (CRO)
Penfolds Cabernet Sauvignon Bin 707
   (CRO)
Penfolds Coonawarra Cabernet
   Sauvignon (CRO)
Penley Estate Coonawarra Cabernet
   Sauvignon (CRO)
Yarra Yering Dry Red No.2 (Shiraz) (CRO)
1988
Henschke Cyril Henschke Cabernet
   Sauvignon (CRO)
1987
Henschke Cyril Henschke Cabernet
   Sauvignon (CRO)
Henschke Mount Edelstone Shiraz (CRO)
Lake's Folly Cabernet Sauvignon (CRO)
Yarra Yering Dry Red No.1 (Cabernet)
   (CRO)
1986
Rosemount Kirri Billi Cabernet Sauvignon
   (BUT)
1985
Lindemans St George Cabernet Sauvignon
   (CRO)
Rosemount Show Reserve Cabernet
   Sauvignon (CRO)
1984
Lindemans Limestone Ridge
   Shiraz/Cabernet Sauvignon (CRO)
1983
Lake's Folly Cabernet Sauvignon (CRO)
1982
Blue Pyrenees Estate Cabernet
   Sauvignon/Merlot/Shiraz (CRO)
Penfolds St-Henri Shiraz/Cabernet (CRO)
Rouge Homme Cabernet Sauvignon (CRO)
Taltarni Shiraz (CRO)
1980
Lindemans St George Cabernet Sauvignon
   (GAU)
Taltarni Cabernet Sauvignon (CRO)
1976
Rouge Homme Shiraz/Cabernet
   Sauvignon (CRO)

£30.00 → £39.99

1991
Henschke Hill of Grace Shiraz (YOU)
1988
Parker Coonawarra Estate Terra Rossa
   Cabernet Sauvignon (CRO)
1987
Henschke Hill of Grace Shiraz (CRO)

1986
Henschke Cyril Henschke Cabernet
Sauvignon (CRO)
Henschke Mount Edelstone Shiraz (CRO)
1985
Henschke Cyril Henschke Cabernet
Sauvignon (YOU)
1982
Yarra Yering Dry Red No.2 (Shiraz) (CRO)
1978
Lindemans Limestone Ridge
Shiraz/Cabernet Sauvignon (CRO)
Penfolds Grange (BUT)

£40.00 → £49.99
1990
Penfolds Grange (PEN, BO, HOG)
1988
Henschke Hill of Grace Shiraz (CRO)
Penfolds Grange (BUT)
1987
Penfolds Grange (NO)
1977
Henschke Mount Edelstone Shiraz (YOU)

£50.00 → £59.99
1991
Henschke Hill of Grace Shiraz (ROB)
Penfolds Grange (AD)
1990
Penfolds Grange (BY, UN)
1989
Penfolds Grange (AV)
1975
Henschke Hill of Grace Shiraz (YOU)

£60.00 → £69.99
1989
Penfolds Grange (FA, BEN)
1987
Penfolds Grange (FA)

1985
Penfolds Grange (FA)
1983
Penfolds Grange (CRO)
1981
Penfolds Grange (CRO)

£75.00 → £99.99
1990
Penfolds Grange (BEN, FA)
1989
Penfolds Grange (BER, ROB)
1988
Penfolds Grange (ROB)
1986
Penfolds Grange (FA, CRO)
1983
Penfolds Grange (FA)
1982
Penfolds Grange (CRO)
1981
Penfolds Grange (FA)
1980
Penfolds Grange (FA, CRO)
1978
Penfolds Grange (CRO)

£115.00 → £125.00
1989
Penfolds Grange (UB)
1976
Penfolds Grange (CRO)

WHITE

Under £4.00
1995
Hardys Stamp Sémillon/Chardonnay (VIC,
SAI)
1994
Hardys Stamp Sémillon/Chardonnay (SAF)
Nottage Hill Chardonnay (ASD)

£4.00 → £4.49
Non-vintage
Barramundi Sémillon/Chardonnay (CO, SAI)
1995
Lindemans Chardonnay Bin 65 (MAR)
Orlando Jacob's Creek Dry Riesling (VIC,
TES)
Orlando Jacob's Creek
Semillon/Chardonnay (SAF, NEW, VIC, SAI,
CO, BOT, WR, THR, DAV, FUL)
Penfolds Koonunga Hill Chardonnay
(SOM)

Penfolds Semillon/Chardonnay Bin 21
(HOG, CO)
Saltram Chardonnay (SAI)
Wynns Riesling (SAI)
1994
Lindemans Chardonnay Bin 65 (SOM)
Orlando Jacob's Creek Dry Riesling (SAI)
Orlando Jacob's Creek
   Semillon/Chardonnay (HOG, UN, TES, SAI)
Orlando Jacob's Creek White (SO)
1992
Orlando Jacob's Creek
   Semillon/Chardonnay (TES)

£4.50 → £4.99
1995
Lindemans Chardonnay Bin 65 (POR, CO,
   OD, NEW, MAJ, VIC)
Nottage Hill Chardonnay (VIC, DAV, FUL)
Orlando Jacob's Creek White (VIC)
Penfolds Koonunga Hill Chardonnay (POR,
   SAI, WR, BOT, VIC, THR)
Penfolds Koonunga Hill
   Semillon/Chardonnay (OD)
Penfolds Semillon/Chardonnay Bin 21 (BY)
Peter Lehmann Semillon (ASD)
Yalumba Oxford Landing Chardonnay
   (WAI, HOG, THR, BOT, WR)
1994
Brown Bros Dry Muscat (HOG)
Lindemans Chardonnay Bin 65 (THR, UN,
   WR, BOT, SAF, SAI, SO, FUL)
Lindemans Semillon/Chardonnay Bin 77
   (UN)
Nottage Hill Chardonnay (UN, SAF)
Penfolds Koonunga Hill Chardonnay (FUL,
   SO)
Penfolds Semillon/Chardonnay Bin 21 (BY)
Rothbury Chardonnay (FUL)
Seaview Chardonnay (POR)
Yalumba Oxford Landing Chardonnay (FUL)
1993
Nottage Hill Chardonnay (SO, CO)
Penfolds Semillon/Chardonnay Bin 21 (POR)
Peter Lehmann Semillon (BO)
Yalumba Oxford Landing Chardonnay (NI)

£5.00 → £5.49
1995
Lindemans Chardonnay Bin 65 (AUR)
Mitchelton Un-oaked Marsanne (OD)
Orlando RF Chardonnay (DAV)
Rosemount Semillon/Chardonnay (VIC, SAF)
Tyrrells Long Flat White (PIP)
Wynns Chardonnay (SOM)

1994
Brown Bros Dry Muscat (PIP, WHI, AUR)
Denman Hunter Valley Chardonnay (SAI)
Lindemans Chardonnay Bin 65 (WHI)
Orlando RF Chardonnay (HOG, SAF, VIC,
   NEW)
Penfolds Semillon/Chardonnay Bin 21 (UN)
Rosemount Sémillon/Sauvignon Blanc
   (FUL, SAI)
Tyrrells Long Flat White (AME)
Wyndham's Chardonnay Bin 222 (MAJ)
Yalumba Oxford Landing Chardonnay (EY)
1993
Brown Bros Dry Muscat (AME)
Penfolds Semillon/Chardonnay Bin 21
   (WAT)
Pewsey Vale Riesling (TES)
Rosemount Semillon/Chardonnay (BO)
1992
Penfolds Semillon/Chardonnay Bin 21
   (TES)

£5.50 → £5.99
1995
Chateau Tahbilk Marsanne (AUR)
Lindemans Chardonnay Bin 65 (BY)
Penfolds Koonunga Hill Chardonnay (BY)
Rothbury Chardonnay (CO)
★ Salisbury Estate Chardonnay (ENO)
1994
Basedows Semillon (VIC)
Brown Bros Dry Muscat (DI, EY, WRI)
Chateau Tahbilk Marsanne (VIG)
Lindemans Chardonnay Bin 65 (BEN)
Lindemans Semillon/Chardonnay Bin 77
   (BY)
Nottage Hill Chardonnay (SAT)
Peter Lehmann Semillon (EL)
Rosemount Hunter Valley Chardonnay
   (SAF)
Rothbury Chardonnay (EY, HOG, POR, UN,
   DI)
Tyrrells Long Flat White (TAN, AV)
1993
Brown Bros Dry Muscat (AD, PEN)
Leasingham Semillon (CO)
Orlando RF Chardonnay (UN)
Rosemount Semillon/Chardonnay (SAI)
1992
Chateau Tahbilk Marsanne (HOG)
Penfolds Padthaway Chardonnay (SO)
1988
Brown Bros Dry Muscat (UB)
1986
Petersons Semillon (NEZ)

£6.00 → £6.49
1995
Rosemount Chardonnay (CO, DAV)
Rosemount Diamond Chardonnay (SAI)
Rothbury Chardonnay (DAV)
1994
★ Basedows Oscars Traditional Semillon
(VIC, BIB)
Jim Barry Watervale Riesling (TAN)
Penfolds South Australia Chardonnay
(HOG)
Rosemount Chardonnay (UN, VIC, BO, FUL,
ASD)
Rosemount Hunter Valley Chardonnay
(BOT, THR, WR)
Rosemount Semillon/Chardonnay (SAT)
Rosemount Sémillon/Sauvignon Blanc (SAT)
Wyndham Estate Oak-Aged Chardonnay
(MAJ)
Wyndham's Chardonnay Bin 222 (DAV)
1993
Leasingham Semillon (WS)
Penfolds South Australia Chardonnay
(FUL, MAJ)
Tyrrells Old Winery Chardonnay (PEN)
1992
Rosemount Chardonnay (TES)
1990
Leasingham Semillon (NO)

£6.50 → £6.99
1996
Wolf Blass Chardonnay (WHI)
1995
David Wynn Chardonnay (AD)
Rosemount Chardonnay (WHI)
St Halletts Sémillon/Sauvignon Blanc (AUS)
Wolf Blass Chardonnay (WHI, VIC)
1994
Basedows Chardonnay (VIC)
Basedows Semillon (BIB)
Brown Bros Dry Muscat (BER)
Brown Bros Sauvignon Blanc (PIP, DI)
Chateau Reynella Chardonnay (ASD)
Katnook Sauvignon Blanc (WR, THR, BOT)
Pewsey Vale Riesling (BEN)
Rothbury Chardonnay (BEN)
★ Tyrrells Old Winery Semillon (UN)
Wolf Blass Chardonnay (POR, NEW)
Wyndham's Chardonnay Bin 222 (TAN)
Wynns Coonawarra Chardonnay (SAI)
1993
Orlando RF Chardonnay (QUE)
Penfolds South Australia Chardonnay (VIG)
Richard Hamilton Chardonnay (OD)

Rosemount Hunter Valley Chardonnay
(SAT)
★ Saltram Mamrebrook Chardonnay (WAI)
Tyrrells Old Winery Chardonnay (THR, BOT)
Wynns Coonawarra Chardonnay (FUL)
1992
Brown Bros Semillon (YOU, DI)
Mitchelton Wood-Matured Marsanne
(MAJ)
Penfolds Padthaway Chardonnay (UN)
Penfolds South Australia Chardonnay (SOM)
Wynns Chardonnay (VIC)
1991
Brown Bros Semillon (AME)
1990
Lindemans Chardonnay Bin 65 (BUT)
Rosemount Chardonnay (BUT)
1989
Rosemount Chardonnay (BUT)

£7.00 → £7.49
Non-vintage
Hill-Smith Chardonnay (SAI)
1995
Delatite Riesling (ELL, AUS)
Tim Adams Riesling (AUS)
1994
David Wynn Riesling (ARM)
Tim Knappstein Chardonnay (OD)
Mitchell Watervale Riesling (HAH)
Wirra Wirra Chardonnay (SOM)
1993
David Wynn Chardonnay (HIC)
Jamiesons Run Chardonnay (PEN)
Lindemans Padthaway Chardonnay (HOG)
Tyrrells Old Winery Chardonnay (AV)
1992
Brown Bros Semillon (WRI, AD)
Orlando St Hilary Chardonnay (HOG)
Peter Lehmann Chardonnay (QUE)

£7.50 → £7.99
1995
Cape Mentelle Semillon/Sauvignon Blanc
(NI, RAE, MAJ)
Katnook Sauvignon Blanc (WAI)
Mitchell Wood-aged Sémillon (LAY)
Rosemount Sauvignon Blanc (CRO)
Wirra Wirra Chardonnay (OD)
Wolf Blass Chardonnay (BY)
1994
Basedows Chardonnay (BIB)
Brown Bros Chardonnay (PIP)
Cape Mentelle Semillon/Sauvignon Blanc
(CRO, NO)

1993
Brown Bros Chardonnay (DI)
Hill-Smith Chardonnay (HA)
Jamiesons Run Chardonnay (BO, SO)
Pewsey Vale Riesling (ROB)
Tim Adams Semillon (THR, WR, BOT)
Wolf Blass Chardonnay (ROB)
1992
Brown Bros Semillon (PE)
Lindemans Padthaway Chardonnay (VIC)
Mitchelton Wood-Matured Marsanne (UB)
Rouge Homme Chardonnay (YOU, AME)
1991
Lindemans Padthaway Chardonnay (TES)

£8.00 → £8.99

1995
Cape Mentelle Semillon/Sauvignon Blanc
  (AUR, TAN, HAH)
★ Delatite Limited Release Chardonnay (ARM)
Grosset Polish Hill Riesling (WS)
Tim Adams Semillon (AUS)
1994
Cape Mentelle Chardonnay (CRO)
Cape Mentelle Semillon/Sauvignon Blanc
  (EY, MV, PLA, AD)
Hill-Smith Chardonnay (WS)
Katnook Sauvignon Blanc (BO)
Rosemount Show Reserve Chardonnay
  (MAJ, CO, WR, THR, BOT)
Stafford Ridge Sauvignon Blanc (RAE)
1993
Brown Bros Chardonnay (PEN, PE, TAN)
Cape Mentelle Chardonnay (REI)
Coldstream Hills Chardonnay (NI)
Henschke Riesling (DI)
Mitchelton Wood-Matured Marsanne (WRI)
Pikes Polish Hill River Chardonnay (WRI)
Rosemount Show Reserve Chardonnay
  (SAI, VIC, FUL)
Rouge Homme Chardonnay (DI)
1992
David Wynn Riesling (UB)
Henschke Semillon (DI, YOU, POR)
Katnook Chardonnay (WR, BOT)
Lindemans Padthaway Chardonnay (BY)
Rockford Semillon (ENO)
Rouge Homme Chardonnay (AV)
Wirra Wirra Chardonnay (FUL)
Wynns Chardonnay (LEA)
Wynns Coonawarra Chardonnay (BY)
1991
Henschke Riesling (YOU)
Jamiesons Run Chardonnay (BER)
1990

Chateau Tahbilk Marsanne (NO)
Henschke Semillon (NO)
Mitchelton Reserve Marsanne (NO)
Rockford Semillon (VIG)
1989
Rockford Semillon (BO)
1988
Rockford Semillon (GAU)
1986
Rosemount Show Reserve Semillon (BUT)

£9.00 → £9.99

1995
Cape Mentelle Chardonnay (NI)
Coldstream Hills Chardonnay (NEZ)
★ Hanging Rock Jim Jim Sauvignon Blanc (PE)
Moss Wood Semillon (RAE)
Shaw & Smith Un-oaked Chardonnay (ENO)
1994
Cape Mentelle Chardonnay (OD)
Cullen Sauvignon Blanc (SOM)
Petaluma Rhine Riesling (BEN)
Rosemount Show Reserve Chardonnay
  (DAV)
Shaw & Smith Sauvignon Blanc (BEN, AUR)
1993
Henschke Semillon (LAY, BEN)
Pipers Brook Chardonnay (SOM)
Rockford Semillon (PLA)
Wirra Wirra Chardonnay (WS)
1992
Henschke Semillon (ROB)
Lindemans Padthaway Chardonnay (AV)
Petaluma Chardonnay (NI)
Rockford Semillon (AD)
1991
Shaw & Smith Chardonnay (REI)
Stafford Ridge Chardonnay (RAE)

GEOFF WEAVER

Stafford Ridge
LENSWOOD
CHARDONNAY
1991
STAFFORD RIDGE LENSWOOD SOUTH AUSTRALIA 5240
13.0% VOL   PRODUCT OF AUSTRALIA   750ml

1990
Rockford Semillon (POR)
Tyrrells Vat 1 Semillon (AV)

1989
Cape Mentelle Chardonnay (RAE)
Chateau Tahbilk Marsanne (VIG)
Schinus Molle Sauvignon (BUT)
1988
Evans & Tate Sémillon (UB)
1987
Chateau Tahbilk Marsanne (VIG)
1985
Petaluma Chardonnay (REI)

£10.00 → £12.99

1995
Chateau Xanadu Chardonnay (DAV)
Coldstream Hills Chardonnay (PIP)
Cullen Sauvignon Blanc (AD)
Pipers Brook Chardonnay (MV)
1994
Cape Mentelle Chardonnay (HAH, AD)
Moss Wood Chardonnay (CRO)
Petaluma Chardonnay (OD)
Pipers Brook Riesling (LEA)
Plantagenet Chardonnay (BER)
Rosemount Show Reserve Chardonnay
    (CRO)
Tyrrells Vat 47 Chardonnay (UN)
Wignalls Chardonnay (AUS)
1993
Bannockburn Chardonnay (BEN)
Cape Mentelle Chardonnay (BEN, PLA)
Coldstream Hills Chardonnay (ARM)
Cullen Chardonnay (GAU)
De Bortoli Chardonnay (WRI)
Giaconda Chardonnay (NO)
Katnook Chardonnay (BIB)
Mountadam Chardonnay (SOM, BOT, WR,
    THR, NI, AME, AD, CRO, NO)
Petaluma Chardonnay (BOT, THR, WR)
Pipers Brook Chardonnay (ROB)
Wignalls Chardonnay (ROB)
1992
Bannockburn Chardonnay (LEA)
Henschke Semillon (CRO)
Petaluma Chardonnay (TAN, ENO)
Pipers Brook Chardonnay (LEA)
Rouge Homme Chardonnay (CRO)

> *Please remember that*
> **Webster's** *is a price*
> *GUIDE and not a price*
> *LIST. It is not meant to*
> *replace up-to-date*
> *merchants' lists.*

1991
Moss Wood Wooded Semillon (CRO)
Mountadam Chardonnay (HIC)
Petaluma Chardonnay (NO)
Shaw & Smith Chardonnay (TAN, BEN)
1990
Cape Mentelle Chardonnay (BUT)
Mountadam Chardonnay (POR)
Petaluma Chardonnay (NO)
Pipers Brook Chardonnay (PEN)
1989
Cape Mentelle Chardonnay (BUT)
Mountadam Chardonnay (GAU)
Pikes Polish Hill River Sauvignon Blanc
    (BUT)
1988
Petaluma Chardonnay (NO)
1987
Lindemans Padthaway Chardonnay (CRO,
    BUT)

£13.00 → £15.99

1993
Lakes Folly Chardonnay (LAY, ROB)
Mountadam Chardonnay (ARM)
Petaluma Chardonnay (BEN, ROB)
Pipers Brook Chardonnay (CRO)
Tarrawarra Chardonnay (WS)
Tyrrells Vat 47 Chardonnay (AV)
1992
Bannockburn Chardonnay (UB)
Dalwhinnie Chardonnay (DI)
Pipers Brook Chardonnay (AV, UB)
1991
Leeuwin Estate Chardonnay (OD)
1989
Yeringburg Marsanne (VIG)
1987
Moss Wood Wooded Semillon (CRO)
Rosemount Giants Creek Chardonnay
    (BUT)
1986
Petersons Semillon (CRO)
Rosemount Whites Creek Semillon (BUT)

£16.00 → £18.99

1995
Rosemount Chardonnay (CRO)
1993
Moss Wood Chardonnay (CRO)
1991
Lakes Folly Chardonnay (REI)
Petaluma Chardonnay (CRO)
Petersons Chardonnay (REI)
Rosemount Roxburgh Chardonnay (AME)

1990
Yarra Yering Chardonnay (NO)
1988
Yarra Yering Chardonnay (BEN)
1987
Rosemount Roxburgh Chardonnay (CRO)

£22.00 → £26.00
1993
Tyrrells Vat 47 Chardonnay (CRO)
1989
Lakes Folly Chardonnay (CRO)
1986
Lakes Folly Chardonnay (CRO)
1985
Petaluma Chardonnay (CRO)

SPARKLING

Under £5.50
Non-vintage
Angas Brut (SOM)
Seaview (NEW)

£5.50 → £5.99
Non-vintage
Angas Brut (NI, CO, OD, DAV, THR, FUL, WR,
   BOT, SAI)
Angas Brut Rosé (CRO, NI, WAI, WR, TES,
   THR, FUL, BOT, OD, DAV, CO)
Cockatoo Ridge Brut (SAI)
Seaview (CO, WAI, POR, FUL, DAV, BO)
Taltarni Brut Taché (SOM)

£6.00 → £7.99
Non-vintage
Angas Brut (QUE, AD, BEN)
Angas Brut Rosé (EY, QUE, BEN)
★ Seaview Pinot Noir Chardonnay (SAI, UN)
Taltarni Brut (REI, HOG)
Taltarni Brut Taché (REI, HOG, POR, MAJ)
Yalumba Pinot Noir/Chardonnay (NI, FUL)
1992
Seaview Pinot Noir Chardonnay (BOT, THR)
1991
Seppelt Sparkling Shiraz (OD)
1990
Seppelt Sparkling Shiraz (POR, TES, BO)

£8.00 → £9.99
Non-vintage
Taltarni Brut (PLA, YOU, AD, LAYT)
Taltarni Brut Taché (PLA, YOU, AME, BEN)
Yalumba Pinot Noir/Chardonnay (SAI,
   BOT, THR, DAV, MAJ, WR)

1992
Green Point Brut Domaine Chandon
   (HOG)
1991
Seppelt Salinger Brut (OD, FUL)
1990
Croser (SOM)
Seppelt Salinger Brut (TES)
1989
Seaview Pinot Noir Chardonnay (ELL)
1988
Seppelt Salinger Brut (POR)

£10.00 → £10.99
Non-vintage
Green Point Brut Domaine Chandon
   (CO)
1993
Croser (OD)
Green Point Brut Domaine Chandon (FUL,
   DAV)
1992
Croser (THR, WR, BOT)
Green Point Brut Domaine Chandon (OD,
   WAI, DI, ROB)
1991
Green Point Brut Domaine Chandon (EY,
   SAI)
1990
Green Point Brut Domaine Chandon
   (WHI, TES)
Seppelt Salinger Brut (AME, YOU)
Seppelt Sparkling Shiraz (ROB)
1989
Green Point Brut Domaine Chandon
   (PLA)

£11.00 → £13.99
Non-vintage
Green Point Brut Domaine Chandon (LAY,
   AD, CRO)
Schinus Molle Chardonnay/Pinot Noir
   (BUT)
1992
Green Point Brut Domaine Chandon
   (TAN)

> Please remember that
> **Webster's** is a price
> GUIDE and not a price
> LIST. It is not meant to
> replace up-to-date
> merchants' lists.

1991
Croser (BEN)
Yalumba D (SOM)
1988
Seppelt Salinger Brut (DI)
Yalumba D (AD)
1983
Seppelt Sparkling Shiraz (NO)

c. £19.00
1988
Croser (CRO)

SWEET & FORTIFIED

Under £4.99
Non-vintage
Morris Liqueur Muscat (TES)
1995
Brown Bros Orange Muscat & Flora ½
bottle (DI, CO)
1994
Brown Bros Orange Muscat & Flora ½
bottle (POR)

£5.00 → £5.99
Non-vintage
Brown Bros Muscat Late Picked (QUE)
Stanton & Killeen Liqueur Muscat (BOT,
WR, THR)
1995
Brown Bros Orange Muscat & Flora (DAV)
Brown Bros Orange Muscat & Flora ½
bottle (AME, QUE, PIP, AUR, WRI, PE)
1994
Brown Bros Muscat Late Picked (HOG, PIP,
AME, DI, POR, AUR)
Brown Bros Orange Muscat & Flora (ROB)
Brown Bros Orange Muscat & Flora ½
bottle (FUL, UN, THR, BO, BOT, WR, PEN,
BEN, WHI)
1993
Brown Bros Muscat Late Picked (TES, PEN)
1992
Brown Bros Muscat Late Picked (UB)
Brown Bros Orange Muscat & Flora (WAT)
1982
Brown Bros Noble Late Harvest Riesling
½ bottle (DI, PIP)

£6.00 → £7.99
1994
Brown Bros Muscat Late Picked (PE, WRI)
Brown Bros Orange Muscat & Flora (VIN)
Brown Bros Orange Muscat & Flora ½

bottle (TAN, HAL, AD, UB)
1993
Brown Bros Orange Muscat & Flora ½
bottle (NO)
1992
Brown Bros Orange Muscat & Flora ½
bottle (SAT)
1982
Brown Bros Noble Late Harvest Riesling
½ bottle (PEN, WRI, UB)

£8.00 → £9.99
Non-vintage
Baileys Founder Liqueur Muscat (YOU)
Morris Liqueur Muscat (KA, QUE)
1992
Brown Bros Orange Muscat & Flora ½
bottle (CRO)
1991
Yalumba Pewsey Vale Botrytis Late
Harvest Riesling ½ bottle (BEN)

£10.00 → £10.99
Non-vintage
All Saints Rutherglen Liqueur Muscat
(AUR)
Brown Bros Liqueur Muscat (DI)
Campbells Rutherglen Liqueur Muscat
(NO)
Chambers Rosewood Liqueur Muscat
(GAU, AD, RAE)
Morris Liqueur Muscat (NO)
Stanton & Killeen Liqueur Muscat (YOU,
NO, AME, RAE)

£11.00 → £12.99
Non-vintage
Baileys Founder Liqueur Muscat (NO)
Baileys Founder Liqueur Tokay (NO)
Brown Bros Liqueur Muscat (PIP, WRI)
Campbells Rutherglen Liqueur Muscat
(ROB)
Chambers Rosewood Liqueur Muscat
(TAN)

£13.00 → £14.99
Non-vintage
Brown Bros Liqueur Muscat (WAT, BEN, NO)
Campbells Rutherglen Liqueur Muscat (LEA)
Morris Liqueur Muscat (UB)

c. £17.00
1982
Brown Bros Noble Late Harvest Riesling
(CRO)

NEW ZEALAND

Every month there are two more new wineries in New Zealand. Every decade sees a new generation of wine styles. So what's new? Just about everything

New Zealand winemakers are hoping for a bumper harvest in 1996. They need to repolish an image that became tarnished when rain affected the quality of Marlborough's 1995 Sauvignon Blanc.

Unfortunately some critics condemned the entire New Zealand crop on the basis of a single variety in a single region. That's a bit like assuming that Champagne, Burgundy and the Rhône all produced sub-standard wine because Bordeaux had a bad vintage.

In fact New Zealand's wine regions span 1500 kilometres of latitude. In 1995 rain caused a few problems in Marlborough and Nelson, while the rest of the South Island enjoyed near-perfect vintage conditions.

Unlike in many European regions, the vintage can last for up to eight weeks in each region. Rain certainly diluted the quality of some Marlborough Sauvignon Blanc but the early-harvested Chardonnay and Pinot Noir for bottle-fermented sparkling wine was rated by most winemakers as outstanding.

Winemaker influence also has a significant affect on the outcome of a vintage. The 1995 Marlborough Sauvignon Blanc produced by Hunter's and Cloudy Bay was better than most because both companies rejected a significant amount of grapes in order to preserve quality. Montana performed well thanks to old vines and plenty of production capacity.

The astute buyer of New Zealand wines needs to consider variety, vintage, region as well as winemaker – all have a bearing on quality and style.

The Wine Institute of New Zealand recognises eight wine regions, many of which have a number of smaller districts, each of which produces its own distinct wine style. There are now 226 wineries with an average of two newcomers appearing every month. Twenty-four different commercial grape varieties are planted in a national vineyard that totals around 8,500 hectares.

Ten-year turnaround

A rapid evolution of wine styles provides a further challenge to everyone who enjoys New Zealand wine. A new generation of wine styles seems to emerge every decade. Take Cabernet Sauvignon, for example: during the seventies New Zealand Cabernet was thin, green and acidic. In the next decade canopy management reduced and occasionally eliminated herbaceousness while adding flesh and ripe berry flavours. Unfortunately these riper flavours were often masked by strong toasty oak. The latest generation of Cabernet Sauvignon typically forms a useful partnership with Merlot and often Cabernet Franc. A subliminal influence of oak flatters rather than competes with the fruit. If you've always thought that New Zealand red is thin and weedy, buy a bottle of 1994 Cabernet Sauvignon-Merlot from Hawkes Bay or Waiheke and discover a new generation of red wine.

Other developments include richer and more complex Pinot Noir styles to replace the simple cherry and plum wines that dominated a few years ago. Bottle-fermented sparkling wines are becoming full and fruitier as winemakers endeavour to make better wine rather than pursue the Champagne benchmark. More fruit, subtle oak and lees influence is a definite trend in Chardonnay. Dry, full-bodied Riesling is now emerging to challenge the fruitier and slightly sweet Germanic wines that have ruled until recently.

From tiny acorns… Botrytis-affected Chardonnay (Millton claims to have harvested one at a staggering 68° Brix) is a relatively new, though still insignificant, style.

Shiraz falls into the 'anything they can do, we can do better' category. A small number of New Zealand wineries now make this wine in a very non-Australian, cracked black pepper style. Most are labelled as Syrah to distinguish them from the Aussie versions.

And the new vintage? At the time of writing the 1996 picking season is just changing out of low gear, and there are signs that it will be good in quantity terms, yielding some ten per cent more than last year, and good in quality terms as well. If the sun continues to shine as it has done for much of this summer until the last grapes are picked the image of New Zealand wine will reflect that lustre. **BOB CAMPBELL MW**

GRAPES & FLAVOURS

CABERNET SAUVIGNON (red) In the hotter North Island, Waiheke, Matakana and Hawkes Bay can make good Cabernet in most years, but the cooler South Island is less consistent. Merlot is often added to soften the unripe fruit in cool years and to add complexity in good vintages. NZ's best Cabernet has deliciously ripe berry flavours, often with a touch of mint. *Te Mata Coleraine* is the leader in stylishness, *Stonyridge Larose* wins for concentration while *Vidal* and *Villa Maria Reserve* deserve an award for consistency. Other top wines include *Waimarama, Matua Ararimu, Esk Valley, Heron's Flight, Te Motu, Fenton Estate* and *Delegat's*.

CHARDONNAY (white) NZ grows wine in so many latitudes that styles range from the soft peaches-and-cream of Gisborne to the grapefruit of Hawkes Bay and the light, zesty wines of Marlborough. Auckland, Nelson, Wairarapa and Canterbury have less defined styles. Best: *Babich* (Irongate), *Cloudy Bay, Collards* (Rothesay, Hawkes Bay), *Corbans* (Marlborough Private Bin, Gisborne Cottage Block), *Church Road, Coopers Creek, Delegats, Hunter's, Kumeu River, Matua Valley* (Ararimu), *Montana* (Ormond Estates), *Morton Estate* (Black Label), *Neudorf, Nobilo* (Dixon, Marlborough), *Te Mata, Vidal, Villa Maria*.

CHENIN BLANC (white) Often overcropped but can produce full-bodied wine when grown on heavy clay soils, and more aromatic and elegant wines on lighter,

sandy soils. Best: *Millton Vineyards* is a serious heavyweight, *Collards* and *Esk Valley* are lighter, more supple wines.

GEWÜRZTRAMINER (white) Gewürz is well suited to NZ's cool climate. Gisborne makes pungent, fleshy wines with strong lychee and apricot aromas. Fine, spicy wines with pure, focussed fruit flavours are produced in Central Otago, NZ's most southerly wine region, from *Rippon*. *Matawhero* put the variety on the map although quality has been variable lately. *Villa Maria* and *Montana Patutahi Estates* are good from Gisborne.

MERLOT (red) Mostly blended with Cabernet although there is an emerging band of top varietals from *Delegats'* (delicately plummy/peppery), *Corbans'* (rich and gamy) and the concentrated *Vidal*.

MÜLLER-THURGAU (white) The mainstay of bag-in-the-box production. Good ones in bottle include the White Cloud blend from *Nobilos,* and delicately fruity wines from *Babich* and *Montana*. Also good are *Collards* and *Matua Valley*.

PINOT NOIR (red) NZ might not keep many Burgundy producers awake at night but the best can hold their own in the New World. *Martinborough Vineyard* is closest to the Burgundy benchmark. *Ata Rangi* and *Dry River*, also from the Wairarapa, make more obviously New World Pinot Noir that relies on strong plum and cherry fruit. Others: *Waipara Springs, Rippon, Neudorf, Mark Rattray, Palliser* and *St Helena.*

RIESLING (white) NZ Riesling (often called Rhine Riesling) used to be bland and sweetish. Now styles have polarized towards both dry and lusciously sweet wines, and quality has risen. The best dry Riesling is made by *Dry River, Neudorf, Redwood Valley, Giesen* and *Corbans* (Amberley). For off-dry wines try *Corbans Stoneleigh, Montana, Coopers Creek, Collards* and *Millton.* The best sweet botrytized ones are made by *Villa Maria, Corbans, Coopers Creek* and *Palliser.*

SAUVIGNON BLANC (white) This can be divided into the pungently aromatic,

herbaceous and zesty South Island (mainly Marlborough) styles, and the fleshier, riper and softer stone fruit wines made on the North Island. Best of the South include: *Cloudy Bay, Hunter's, Jackson Estate, Montana, Selaks, Stoneleigh, Vavasour* and *Wairau River.* Best North Island: *Matua Valley, Morton Estate, Palliser* and *Vidals.*

SEMILLON (white) NZ has until recently used a Swiss clone of Semillon that seldom ripens well enough to lose its aggressively grassy flavours. It makes good blending wine but can overpower when made as a varietal. New clones are starting to emerge, and show good potential. *Villa Maria* and *Collards* are the best. *Selaks'* Sauvignon-Semillon is clearly the best blend.

WINES & WINE REGIONS

GISBORNE (North Island) They call this carafe country, because it yields the second highest grape tonnage after Marlborough. Above all it is home to Müller-Thurgau, which can yield 20 to 25 tons a hectare on the Poverty Bay alluvial flats. Matawhero is a high-quality sub-area, as are Tolaga and Tikitiki further north. Local growers and winemakers have dubbed their region the Chardonnay Capital of NZ to mark the high number of award-winning wines they have produced in recent years. Gisborne is also a spiritual home of Gewürztraminer with a consistent string of winners. Reds are less exciting, although expanding vineyards of Pinot Noir are now being grown for good Champagne-method sparklers.

HAWKES BAY (North Island) Potentially NZ's greatest wine region. Plenty of sun plus complex soil patterns help to give top Chardonnay, Cabernets Sauvignon and Franc and Merlot. It has been established for over 100 years and yet we are only now beginning to see what it can do. *Te Mata* is the region's leading resident winemaker with *Brookfields, Church Road, Esk Valley, Ngatarawa, Vidal* and

Waimarama close behind. Top producers of Hawkes Bay wines outside the region include *Babich, Cooks, Matua Valley, Mills Reef, Morton Estate* and *Villa Maria.*

MARLBOROUGH (South Island) NZ's biggest region by far was established in 1973 despite criticism that vines would be killed by frost. In their haste many planted ungrafted vines, and now over half of the vineyards must be replanted. Sauvignon Blanc is the leader with Riesling and Chardonnay also doing well in the long, cool ripening conditions. Reds have fared less well although Pinot Noir is in great demand when it can be spared from the buoyant Champagne-method fizz industry. There's good botrytized wine here as well.

REST OF NORTH ISLAND Matakana, north of Auckland, has received overnight acclaim for its stylish reds. Waiheke, an island in Auckland harbour, has been hailed by some as NZ's top red region thanks to robust Bordeaux blends from *Stonyridge, Te Motu* and *Goldwater. Kumeu River, Collards* and *Matua Valley* have shown that mainland Auckland can also produce the right stuff. Wairarapa is a small but significant region in the south of the North Island, and is home to *Martinborough Vineyard, Ata Rangi, Dry River* and *Palliser*, with Pinot Noir as the star.

REST OF SOUTH ISLAND Nelson has good performers in *Neudorf* and *Seifried*.

Canterbury is dominated by the excellent *Giesen* and a growing number in Waipara north of Christchurch, like *Waipara Springs* and the new *Mark Rattray Vineyard* and *Pegasus Bay*. Central Otago is NZ's most southerly region; *Rippon, Gibbston* and *Chard Farm* are the leading producers.

WINERY PROFILES

ALLAN SCOTT ★★★(★) Lively Marlborough Sauvignon Blanc, pungent medium-dry Riesling, elegant Chardonnay.

ATA RANGI★★★★ Good Pinot Noir, intense Cabernet-Merlot-Shiraz called Célèbre, and nice Chardonnay.

BABICH ★★★(★) Fresh Fumé Vert (Chardonnay, Semillon, Sauvignon), zesty Marlborough Sauvignon, elegant Irongate Chardonnay and Cabernet-Merlot.

CELLIER LE BRUN ★★★★(★) Excellent, Champenois-run specialist fizz producer.

CLOUDY BAY ★★★★★ Excellent, complex Sauvignon, fattened with a little Semillon. There's top Champagne-method fizz under the Pelorus brand, and Chardonnay is also good.

COLLARDS ★★★★ A top Chardonnay maker. Buttery Chenin Blanc and luscious botrytized Riesling when the vintage allows.

COOPERS CREEK ★★★★ The best Hawkes Bay Riesling in both medium dry and sweet styles, top range of Chardonnay from Hawkes Bay and Gisborne, attractive Marlborough Sauvignon Blanc, good Bordeaux-style reds.

CORBANS ★★★(★) Stoneleigh Sauvignon, Blanc, Chardonnay and Riesling range from reliable to very good. Cooks Winemakers Reserve Cabernet and Chardonnay are concentrated.

DELEGATS ★★★★ A Marlborough range called Oyster Bay. Fine Chardonnay and Cabernet with a good botrytized Riesling.

DE REDCLIFFE ★★★ State-of-the-art winery producing good, consistent Chardonnay and Riesling with occasionally very good oak-aged Savuignon Blanc.

DRY RIVER ★★★★★ Micro winery making mega quality. NZ's best Pinot Noir, Gewürztraminer and Pinot Gris. Among the best Chardonnay and botrytized styles.

GIBBSTON VALLEY ★★★ Small Otago winery making good Pinot Noir and Chardonnay. Sauvignon Blanc is variable.

GIESEN ★★★(★) Elegant dry and luscious sweet Riesling; big, buttery Chardonnay.

GOLDWATER ★★★★ Big Waiheke reds and the island's only Chardonnay, plus good Marlborough Chardonnay.

GROVE MILL ★★★(★) Weighty Riesling, rich Chardonnay. Top reds in good years.

HUNTER'S ★★★★(★) Top Sauvignon and elegant Chardonnay. Fizz with potential.

JACKSON ESTATE ★★★★ Classic Marlborough Sauvignon, complex Chardonnay and stunning fizz.

KUMEU RIVER ★★★★(★) Top Chardonnay – but not mainstream. Good North Island Sauvignon and Merlot-Cabernet.

MARTINBOROUGH VINEYARDS
★★★★ NZ's best-known Pinot Noir, big and complex Chardonnay, lovely Riesling.

MATUA VALLEY ★★★★ Top Ararimu Chardonnay and Cabernet. Luscious Sauvignon and Gewürztraminer, and good Shingle Peak range from Marlborough.

MILLS REEF★★★ Big, ripe Hawkes Bay Chardonnay, stylish limy Riesling and rich, ripe, mouthfilling fizz.

MISSION ★★★(★) A quality drive has produced impressive Chardonnays, delicate Riesling and an occasional sweet botrytis style.

MONTANA ★★★(★) Grassy Sauvignon. Top Champagne-method fizz (Deutz); good Chardonnay and botrytized Riesling.

MORTON ESTATE ★★★★ Chardonnay, especially Black Label. Good Sauvignon and Gewürztraminer, impressive fizz. Reds good.

NAUTILUS ★★★★ Tight, quality-focussed range includes top Marlborough Chardonnay, Sauvignon Blanc and bottle-fermented fizz.

NEUDORF ★★★★ Remarkably Burgundian Chardonnay; nice Sauvignon, Pinot Noir.

NGATARAWA ★★★ Attractive Chardonnay, Cabernet-Merlot and botrytized Riesling.

NOBILO ★★★(★) Good Dixon vineyard Chardonnay. Stylish Sauvignon. Popular White Cloud (Müller-Thurgau and Sauvignon blend).

PALLISER ★★★★ Nice Sauvignon, Pinot Noir and concentrated Chardonnay.

C J PASK ★★★(★) Flavoursome reds and Chardonnay from excellent vineyard sites.

PEGASUS BAY ★★★(★) Great Riesling, unconventional full-bodied Sauvignon Blanc-Semillon and big, chewy Pinot Noir.

ST CLAIR ★★★(★) Classic Marlborough Sauvignon Blanc, well made, elegant Chardonnay and pungent medium dry Riesling.

ST HELENA ★★★(★) Good Chardonnay, Pinot Gris and Pinot Blanc.

SELAKS ★★★★ Great Sauvignon and Sauvignon-Semillon. Founder's Selection is the top label.

STONYRIDGE ★★★★★ NZ's top red producer. Intense, ripe Cabernet blend (Larose) with less intense version as second label.

TE MATA ★★★★★ Coleraine and Awatea are sought-after Cabernet-Merlot blends. Burgundian-style Elston Chardonnay, and one of NZ's first Syrahs.

THE MILLTON VINEYARD ★★★★ NZ's first organic maker. Lush medium Riesling, big, rich Chenin Blanc, Chardonnay.

VAVASOUR ★★★★ Top Chardonnay and reds and very good Sauvignons.

VILLA MARIA ★★★★ Outstanding Vidal, Esk Valley and Villa Maria Reserve wines.

MERCHANTS SPECIALISING IN NEW ZEALAND
see Merchant Directory (page 424) for details

Nobody has very long lists of these (except FIZ), but most good merchants have at least a small selection. For a slightly wider choice, try: Adnams (AD), Averys of Bristol (AV), Anthony Byrne (BY), Enotria Winecellars (ENO), Fine Wines of New Zealand (FIZ), J E Hogg (HOG), Lay & Wheeler (LAY), Tanners (TAN), Thresher (THR), The Ubiquitous Chip (UB), Wine Society (WS)

NEW ZEALAND

RED

Under £5.50

1994
Cooks Cabernet Sauvignon (VIC, DAV)
Montana Marlborough Cabernet
Sauvignon (QUE, WR, THR, BO, VIC, BOT, CO)
1993
Montana Marlborough Cabernet
Sauvignon (TES)
1991
Cooks Cabernet Sauvignon (TES)

£5.50 → £6.99

1995
Montana Marlborough Cabernet
Sauvignon (PIP)
1994
Babich Henderson Valley Pinot Noir (HOG)
Matua Valley Pinot Noir (SAI)
Stoneleigh Marlborough Cabernet
Sauvignon (MAJ)
1993
Cooks Cabernet Sauvignon (UN)
Cooks Hawke's Bay Cabernet Sauvignon
(AS)
1992
Stoneleigh Marlborough Cabernet
Sauvignon (UB, TES)
1991
Nobilo Pinotage (HOG, AV)
Stoneleigh Marlborough Cabernet
Sauvignon (VIC)
1990
Stoneleigh Marlborough Cabernet
Sauvignon (KA)

£7.00 → £8.99

1994
C J Pask Roy's Hill Red (LAY)
Redwood Valley Estate Cabernet
Sauvignon (FIZ)
1993
Matua Valley Cabernet Sauvignon (NI)
Redwood Valley Estate Cabernet
Sauvignon (HOG)
Stoneleigh Marlborough Cabernet
Sauvignon (AS)
1992
Corbans Marlborough Private Bin Pinot
Noir (KA)

1991
Nobilo Pinotage (WRI)
Redwood Valley Estate Cabernet
Sauvignon (WAT)

£9.00 → £10.99

1994
Martinborough Pinot Noir (BO, ELL, AD, NI, OD)
Palliser Estate Pinot Noir (BY, WR, THR, BOT)
1993
C J Pask Cabernet Sauvignon (HAH)
Hunter's Pinot Noir (DI, KA)
Martinborough Pinot Noir (SOM, CRO, UB, YOU, LAY, WR, BOT, AME)
1992
Martinborough Pinot Noir (POR, YOU)
Morton Estate Black Label Cabernet
Sauvignon/Merlot (NEZ)
Villa Maria Cabernet Sauvignon (ROB)
Waipara Springs Pinot Noir (DI)
1991
C J Pask Cabernet Sauvignon (AV)
Cloudy Bay Cabernet Sauvignon/Merlot
(BUT)
Delegat's Cabernet Sauvignon (BEN)
Redwood Valley Estate Cabernet
Sauvignon (UB)
1989
Villa Maria Reserve Cabernet Sauvignon
(CRO)

£11.00 → £14.99

1994
Martinborough Pinot Noir (WS, NO, ROB, ENO)
Neudorf Moutere Pinot Noir (WS)
1992
Martinborough Pinot Noir (DI)
1991
Kumeu River Merlot/Cabernet Sauvignon
(BEN)
1988
Martinborough Pinot Noir (BUT, GAU)

£15.00 → £19.99

1994
Rippon Vineyard Pinot Noir (FIZ)
1991
Stonyridge Larose Cabernet (AD)
Te Mata Coleraine Cabernet Sauvignon
(AME)

WHITE

Under £4.00

1995
Timara Dry White (SAI)
Villa Maria Sauvignon Blanc (TES)

£4.00 → £4.99

1995
Cooks Sauvignon Blanc (DAV)
Montana Marlborough Chardonnay (HOG, CO, SAF, THR, WR, FUL, OD, DAV, BOT, VIC, BO)
Montana Marlborough Sauvignon Blanc (HOG, SO, VIC, BOT, TES, OD, WR, FUL, DAV, THR, SAF, BO, CO)
Nobilo Sauvignon Blanc (DAV)
Nobilo White Cloud (CRO, HOG, SO, VIC, DAV)

1994
Cooks Hawke's Bay Chardonnay (WAI, TES)
Cooks Sauvignon Blanc (NEW, TES)
Montana Marlborough Chardonnay (SAI, TES, SAT, WHI)
Montana Marlborough Sauvignon Blanc (SAT, WHI, SAI)
Nobilo White Cloud (CO, SAI, QUE, AV)

1993
Stoneleigh Riesling (WR, BOT, THR, MAJ)

1991
Cooks Sauvignon Blanc (KA)

£5.00 → £5.99

1996
Montana Marlborough Chardonnay (PIP)

1995
Aotea Sauvignon Blanc (FIZ)
Babich Hawke's Bay Sauvignon Blanc (HOG)
Delegat's Chardonnay (HOG)
★ Mills Reef Sauvignon Blanc (FOR)
Montana Marlborough Sauvignon Blanc (EL)
Stoneleigh Marlborough Sauvignon Blanc (AME)
Stoneleigh Sauvignon Blanc (SAI, BOT, VIC, THR, WR)
Villa Maria Chardonnay (BO)
Villa Maria Sauvignon Blanc (SAI, ELL, OD, BO, WR, BOT, WAI, THR)
★ Waipara Springs Riesling (WAT)

1994
Aotea Sauvignon Blanc (EL)
Matua Valley Late Harvest Muscat ½ bottle (PLA)
Montana Marlborough Sauvignon Blanc (UN)

Stoneleigh Sauvignon Blanc (UB, NEW)
Villa Maria Chardonnay (ELL)

1992
Stoneleigh Marlborough Sauvignon Blanc (KA)

1991
Matua Valley Late Harvest Muscat ½ bottle (BEN)
Montana Late Harvest Rhine Riesling ½ bottle (WR, BOT, THR)

£6.00 → £6.99

1995
Esk Valley Sauvignon Blanc (BO)
Matua Valley Sauvignon Blanc (NI, PLA)
★ Mills Reef Hawkes Bay Reserve Riesling (FOR)
Morton Estate Sauvignon Blanc (NEZ, DAV)
★ Oyster Bay Marlborough Sauvignon Blanc (MAJ)
Selaks Sauvignon Blanc (REI)
Stoneleigh Marlborough Sauvignon Blanc (SO, AUR, TAN)
Vidal Sauvignon Blanc (FIZ, VIC)
Villa Maria Sauvignon Blanc (NI, CRO)

1994
Aotea Sauvignon Blanc (MV, LEA, ROB, BER)
Babich Hawke's Bay Chardonnay (HOG)
Matua Valley Chardonnay (SAI)
Mills Reef Sauvignon Blanc (POR)
Nobilo Sauvignon Blanc (QUE)
Stoneleigh Marlborough Sauvignon Blanc (AS)
Villa Maria Sauvignon Blanc (HA)
Wairau River Sauvignon Blanc (SOM)

1993
Aotea Sauvignon Blanc (SUM)
Nobilo Gewürztraminer (AV)
Stoneleigh Chardonnay (TES, THR, WR, BOT)
Vidal Sauvignon Blanc (HOG)

1992
Babich Hawke's Bay Sauvignon Blanc (PEN)

£7.00 → £7.99

1995
Babich Hawke's Bay Sauvignon Blanc (PE)
Esk Valley Sauvignon Blanc (ROB)
Grove Mill Sauvignon Blanc, Marlborough (SAI)
Jackson Estate Marlborough Sauvignon Blanc (PIP, AME, TES, POR, DAV)
Nautilus Hawke's Bay Sauvignon Blanc (NI)
Ngatarawa Sauvignon Blanc (YOU)
★ Palliser Estate Sauvignon Blanc (BY, CB)
★ Waipara West Sauvignon Blanc (WAT)

1994
Aotea Sauvignon Blanc (CB)
Coopers Creek Marlborough Sauvignon Blanc (POR)
Dashwood Sauvignon Blanc (FUL)
Delegats Oyster Bay Chardonnay (MAJ)
Jackson Estate Marlborough Chardonnay (POR)
Matua Valley Sauvignon Blanc (ELL)
Millton Gisborne Chardonnay (SAF)
★ Mills Reef Hawkes Bay Reserve Chardonnay (FOR)
Montana Church Road Chardonnay (WHI, SAI, BOT, WR, FUL)
Redwood Valley Sauvignon Blanc (REI, HOG)
★ Stoniers Chardonnay (WAT)
Vidal Sauvignon Blanc (YOU)
Wairau River Chardonnay (REI)
Wairau River Sauvignon Blanc (FA, BO, YOU)
1993
Coopers Creek Chardonnay (TES)
Delegats Oyster Bay Chardonnay (SAI, QUE)
Montana Church Road Chardonnay (VIC)
Selaks Sauvignon Blanc (RAE)
Stoneleigh Chardonnay (AUR)
1992
Mills Reef Chardonnay (HOG)
Ngatarawa Sauvignon Blanc (YOU)
Nobilo Gisborne Chardonnay (AV)
1991
Corbans Fumé Blanc (KA)

£8.00 → £8.99
1995
Cloudy Bay Sauvignon Blanc (UN)
Dashwood Sauvignon Blanc (OD, BO, CB)
Delegats Oyster Bay Chardonnay (HIC)
Jackson Estate Marlborough Sauvignon Blanc (TAN, AD, PLA, WRI, AS, ELL)
★ Matua Marlborough Sauvignon Blanc (UN)
Nautilus Hawke's Bay Sauvignon Blanc (DAV)
Ngatarawa Sauvignon Blanc (VIG)
Redwood Valley Sauvignon Blanc (FIZ)
Selaks Sauvignon Blanc (HIC)
Te Mata Castle Hill Sauvignon Blanc (WS)
Wairau River Sauvignon Blanc (LEA, BEN, ENO)
1994
Babich Hawke's Bay Chardonnay (TAN)
Cloudy Bay Sauvignon Blanc (KA)
Coopers Creek Marlborough Sauvignon Blanc (QUE)
Dashwood Sauvignon Blanc (YOU, KA)
Jackson Estate Marlborough Chardonnay (ELL, AS, PLA, BOT, THR, WR)

Lawsons Dry Hills Chardonnay (BIB)
Martinborough Vineyards Chardonnay (SOM)
Matua Valley Sauvignon Blanc (UN)
Millton Chenin Blanc (AD)
Morton Estate Chardonnay (PIP)
Redwood Valley Chardonnay (REI)
Redwood Valley Sauvignon Blanc (WAT, WRI)
Selaks Kumeu Estate Sauvignon Blanc (AD)
Te Mata Castle Hill Sauvignon Blanc (YOU, AME)
Wairau River Chardonnay (SOM)
Wairau River Sauvignon Blanc (BEN, SEC, WR, THR, BOT)
1993
Hunter's Sauvignon Blanc (HOG)
1992
Kumeu River Sauvignon Blanc (FA)
Palliser Estate Sauvignon Blanc (BUT)
1991
Nobilo Dixon Chardonnay (AV)
Palliser Estate Martinborough Vineyard Sauvignon Blanc (BUT)

£9.00 → £10.99
1995
Cloudy Bay Sauvignon Blanc (VIC, WRI, HAH)
Dashwood Sauvignon Blanc (CRO, HAH)
Dry River Sauvignon Blanc (RAE)
Hunter's Sauvignon Blanc (FUL, OD, PIP, BEN, DI)
Jackson Estate Marlborough Sauvignon Blanc (CRO)
★ Mark Rattray Waipara Chardonnay (WAT)
Palliser Estate Martinborough Vineyard Sauvignon Blanc (CB)
Palliser Estate Sauvignon Blanc (BOT, WR, THR)
Vavasour Oak-Aged Reserve Sauvignon Blanc (KA)
Wairau River Sauvignon Blanc (CRO)
1994
Babich Irongate Chardonnay (HOG)
C J Pask Chardonnay (TAN, HAH)
Cloudy Bay Chardonnay (NI, TAN)
Dashwood Chardonnay (HAH)

Stars (★) indicate wines selected by Oz Clarke in the 100 Best Buys section which begins on page 8.

Delegat's Proprietors Reserve
Chardonnay (DI)
Hunter's Sauvignon Blanc (YOU, QUE, PLA)
Jackson Estate Marlborough Chardonnay
(TAN, WRI, UB, CRO)
Martinborough Vineyards Chardonnay
(AD, NI, OD)
Morton Estate Chardonnay (ROB)
Morton Estate Chardonnay Reserve (NEZ)
Ngatarawa Chardonnay (WS, VIG)
Palliser Estate Chardonnay (BY, WR, BOT,
THR)
Redwood Valley Chardonnay (FIZ, EL, LEA)
Wairau River Chardonnay (ENO, LEA)
1993
C J Pask Chardonnay (AV)
Cloudy Bay Sauvignon Blanc (BUT)
Hunter's Chardonnay (BOT, WR, DI, QUE)
Hunter's Gewürztraminer (UB)
Martinborough Vineyards Chardonnay
(LAY, AME, THR, BOT, WR)
Palliser Estate Martinborough Vineyard
Sauvignon Blanc (BUT)
Redwood Valley Chardonnay (WAT)
Vidal Chardonnay (ROB)
Villa Maria Reserve Chardonnay (CRO)
1992
Hunter's Chardonnay (OD, YOU, BEN)
Hunter's Sauvignon Blanc (GAU, KA)
Kumeu River Sauvignon Blanc (BEN)
Martinborough Vineyards Chardonnay
(POR, ENO, YOU)
1989
Nobilo Dixon Chardonnay (NO)

£11.00 → £12.99
1995
Hunter's Sauvignon Blanc (CRO)
1994
Cloudy Bay Chardonnay (NO, WRI, REI,
HAH, SEC, LAY, MV, AD)
Hunter's Sauvignon Blanc (BER, UB)
Hunter's Wood-Aged Sauvignon Blanc
(BEN, TAN, DI)
Martinborough Vineyards Chardonnay
(ROB)
Te Mata Elston Chardonnay (BOT, WR, THR)
Vavasour Oak-Aged Reserve Sauvignon
Blanc (CB)
1993
Hunter's Chardonnay (PIP)
Hunter's Wood-Aged Sauvignon Blanc (NO)
1992
Babich Irongate Chardonnay (TAN)
Te Mata Elston Chardonnay (AME)

1991
Babich Irongate Chardonnay (PEN)
Cloudy Bay Chardonnay (BUT)
Hunter's Chardonnay (NO)
1990
Cloudy Bay Chardonnay (BUT)
Palliser Estate Chardonnay (BUT)
1988
Martinborough Vineyards Chardonnay
(GAU, BUT)

£13.00 → £15.99
1995
Cloudy Bay Sauvignon Blanc (CRO, NO)
1994
Cloudy Bay Chardonnay (CRO)
Kumeu River Chardonnay (WS, BEN)
Vavasour Oak-Aged Reserve Sauvignon
Blanc (BER)
1993
Elston Chardonnay (BEN)
Kumeu River Chardonnay (FUL, REI, BEN)
1992
Te Mata Elston Chardonnay (VIG)

£16.00 → £21.99
1995
Cloudy Bay Sauvignon Blanc (UB)
1994
Kumeu River Chardonnay (WRI, CRO)
1993
Cloudy Bay Chardonnay (UB)

SPARKLING

Under £7.00
Non-vintage
Deutz Marlborough Cuvee (CO)
Lindauer Brut (WHI, FUL, BOT, WR, THR, BO,
OD, SAF, SAI, VIC, TES, POR)

£7.00 → £9.99
Non-vintage
Deutz Marlborough Cuvee (TES, VIC, OD,
BOT, WR, THR)
Lindauer Brut (CRO, AUR, SAT, ROB)

£10.00 → £11.99
Non-vintage
Daniel Le Brun Brut (PLA)
Deutz Marlborough Cuvee (CRO)

£12.00 → £13.99
Non-vintage
Daniel Le Brun Brut (CRO, YOU, NO, LEA)

CHILE

Chilean winemakers are starting to take risks – and sometimes, if you're experimenting in the winery, it doesn't pay to let the boss know what you're doing

I recently heard a UK wine buyer claim that in the £3 to £5 range, no other country comes near to Chile in value for money – an assertion backed up by Chilean wine sales here last year crashing through the million case mark. Each vintage sees higher quality, more wineries, and more consumers moving from tentative toe-dippers to complete pisco and salsa converts.

The same buyer predicted that if a £20 wine was to come out of South America, it would probably have Argentina and not Chile on the label. Now, the Recabarrens and Espinozas may beg to differ with this, but they would undoubtedly agree that a jump from good value to premium is one they must make (and make soon) if interest and loyalty is to be maintained. Can Chile make a £20 wine? Thanks to some persistent wine buyers and a radical switch in attitudes, the answer, I think, is yes.

Until now, the definition of premium in Chile has been Cabernet Sauvignon and, narrowing it down even further, usually Maipo Cabernet with at least a year in oak. There is nothing wrong with these wines – the fruit is there – but the inspiration is often lacking. But now the message appears to have got through that yes, premium does mean low yields, but more importantly it means taking risks in the winery; and it definitely does not involve telling the MD what you're doing. Last year, Valdivieso's boss Jorge Cordech intercepted a memo from Luis Simian to UK importer Tony Lamont mentioning 'Project L'. It transpired that Simian (who has since departed to Australia, though not because of the discovery) had secretly been blending various wines from different vintages, with a Chilean version of Grange in mind. The result is a wine called Loco (which

translates as mad or madman), a red blend made in tiny quantities, which will be given a number not a vintage. Valdivieso is not alone. There's Errázuriz's new wild yeast barrel-fermented Chardonnay, Concha y Toro's stunning Trio red made with low yield Merlot from Cachapoal and Casablanca, and Casa Lapostolle's 30-day maceration stunner from the same grape. The fear of failure that has stifled so much Chilean creativity in the past is at last loosening its grip.

Uncovering plots

Every year there is better fruit to work with, as viticulturalists and ampelographers sort out some very mixed-up vineyards. A cyclical history of rip it up, replant, then tear it out again (because of both short-term vision and political upheavals) caused so much varietal muddling that when experts were brought in to identify Sauvignonasse from true Sauvignon Blanc, a few other discoveries were made too. Concha y Toro came across a plot of Syrah in the middle of a Cabernet vineyard, and it recently found some Alicante Bouschet, a grape that is obscure in France and still more so in Chile. Whether a premium wine can be squeezed out of it is another matter.

Chile's biggest discovery is a grape that has the ability to straddle the good-value and premium ends of the price scale, and which seems to carry an identifiable Chilean stamp better than any other. For too long, Merlot has been neglected both in the vineyard, where it has become mixed up with Carmenère and Cabernet Franc, and in the winery, where traditionally it has played second fiddle to Cabernet. But booming US demands for Merlot and a worldwide trend towards softer reds has forced Chileans to rethink. A brilliant deep beetroot colour, and a rich flavour of damsons and plums are the identity tags of Chilean Merlot. It can either be drunk young and vibrant six months after the harvest (like those from Terra Noble, Carta Vieja and La Rosa) or left for five years to allow the oak and fruit to marry (like those from Valdivieso, Errázuriz, Carmen and Casa Lapostolle). The country's reputation may have been forged on Cabernet, but Merlot could entice drinkers into an even stronger allegiance to South America.

The only thing the Chileans still need is a few more wineries. The feeling of being a small community (exporting wineries still number fewer than 50) has been highlighted by the resignation of four of its most exciting winemakers. In Australia or South Africa, four changes wouldn't warrant mention; in Chile, these four affect a large proportion of the country's wine. Gaetane Carron has left Concha y Toro to join Agustin Hunneus' Franciscan operation in Casablanca; Luis Simian's departure left a short-term vacuum at Valdivieso, and Ed Flaherty was set to move from Cono Sur to Errázuriz in the wake of Brian Bicknell's return to New Zealand. It's worth watching these labels closely.   **RICHARD NEILL**

GRAPES & FLAVOURS

CABERNET SAUVIGNON (red) Characterized by relatively soft, well-rounded tannins; Chilean Cabernet often doesn't need Merlot to fill it out, unlike Cabernet from many other places. Unoaked versions are best within two years of the vintage. Over-oaking was a problem in the past, especially with premium wines, but greater restraint is now being shown. Best unoaked Cabernets: *Monte La Finca, La Rosa, Andes Peak*. Best premium: *Concha y Toro Don Melchor, Canepa Magnificum*.

CHARDONNAY (white) There are massive improvements in the handling of this grape, both in the vineyard and in the winery. A good crop of unoaked wines has emerged (like those of *La Rosa, Luis Felipe Edwards, Casa Porta, Santa Monica*) and at the top end of the quality range there are experiments with fermenting wines in oak barrels using wild yeasts (*Viña Casablanca, Errázuriz, Montes*). As with Cabernet, subtler oaking is increasingly the norm. Cool-climate Casablanca tends to produce a crisper, more citrussy Chardonnay than its Central Valley counterparts.

GEWÜRZTRAMINER (white) Ignacio Recabarren's lychee and rose petal packed *Viña Casablanca* wine shows that potential and consumer demand (it sells out almost immediately) are both there, but few others are trying. *Concha y Toro*'s vineyards in southerly Mulchen are showing good results, but frost is a major problem.

MERLOT (red) The grape of the moment. Bursting with colour and vibrant, plummy fruit. Try *La Rosa, Santa Monica, Carta Vieja, La Fortuna, Canepa* (all for drinking young); *Errázuriz Reserve, Casa Lapostolle, Carmen, Viña Porta, Montes, Concha y Toro* (all with aging potential).

PINOT NOIR (red) Only two wineries, *Valdivieso* and *Cono Sur*, have managed to tame this grape. Ed Flaherty's departure from the Chimbarongo Estate will not, one hopes, mean the end of the latter's aromatic raspberry and spice wine. *Concha y Toro*'s new Casablanca Pinot shows some promise.

RIESLING (white) Only minimal amounts of the great German grape are grown in Chile, and it's not being pursued with any great zeal. *Miguel Torres* makes a good Gewürztraminer-Riesling blend in the Curicó Valley, however; *Santa Monica* makes a minerally varietal; and *Santa Rita*'s example has good varietal character.

SAUVIGNON BLANC (white) Almost all of the inferior Sauvignonasse has now gone, and new clones, better canopy management and handling in the winery are resulting in cleaner flavours. Casablanca still leads and is the only region with a distinct style (ripe gooseberry and asparagus fruit, and firm acidity). *Viña Casablanca's Santa Isabel Estate, Villard, Concha y Toro* and *Caliterra* are the labels to watch. Outside Casablanca, the Curicó Valley is producing some goodies (*Viña Casablanca White Label, Montes, San Pedro*).

SEMILLON (white) Widely planted but rarely used in blended whites for the domestic market. For exports, *Carmen's* Alvaro Espinoza uses it in a good Chardonnay blend and a rich, oily Late Harvest Semillon. The quality of the few other varietal wines suggests efforts should be concentrated on other grapes.

WINE REGIONS

Although grapes are grown as far north as the Picso-producing region of Elqui (480km north of Santiago) and as far south as Mulchen on the edge of the Lake District (550km south of the capital), only a 400km strip of the Central Valley is responsible for producing quality wine. Frost and rain limit development further south, searing heat and desert to the north.

Recent appellation legislation splits the main wine growing region into Aconcagua (incorporating the sub-region of Casablanca), the Central Valley (including Maipo, Rapel, Curicó and Maule) and the Southern Region (including the valleys of Itata and Bío-Bío).

ACONCAGUA VALLEY To the north-west of Santiago, and dominated by one producer (*Errázuriz*) in Panqueheu. Temperatures here are maginally warmer than in Maipo, but are tempered by regular cool breezes coming off the Pacific. Light is a key factor here, with between 240 and 300 clear days a year. Most vines are irrigated, with the main variety being Cabernet Sauvignon (*Errázuriz' Don Maximiano* is one of the top Cabernets in Chile) and new plantings of Sangiovese, Nebbiolo and Zinfandel adding to the red bias.

CASABLANCA VALLEY Chile's premier white wine region, and the only one with an identifiable style. Barely 50km from the coast, Casablanca has a cool maritime climate, with almost clockwork 11am–3pm breezes taking the sting out of the summer heat. 80 per cent of the 1400ha planted is Chardonnay, with Sauvignon Blanc and Gewürztraminer making up the white balance, and small amounts of Cabernet Sauvignon, Merlot and Pinot Noir yielding impressive results. Poor soils, drip irrigation low yields (8 tons per hectare is the average) and new clones are helping quality. Chardonnay tends to be green and citrussy, often with figgy aromas, and Sauvignons are grassy and crisp with firm acidity. Best: *Viña Casablanca, Caliterra, Concha y Toro, Villard.*

MAIPO VALLEY Birthplace of the Chilean wine industry and home to some of the biggest and most traditional players (*Santa Rita, Concha y Toro, Santa Carolina*). Those in Alto Maipo (*Aquitania, Cousiño Macul, William Fèvre*) have larger diurnal temperature variations. Cabernet Sauvignon made the valley's name and is still the main grape, although excellent Chardonnay is made here, too. The spread of Santiago's suburbs and smog is creating pressure on some producers. Most innovative: *Carmen, Canepa, Concha y Toro.*

RAPEL A seedbed of new winery activity, particularly in the Colchagua Valley where new

The price guides for this section begin on page 404.

arrivals *Mont Gras, Luis Felipe Edwards* and *Casa Lapostolle* are producing equally good Chardonnay and Cabernet. Top Pinot Noir comes from Chimbarongo (*Cono Sur*), and Merlot seems to be well suited to the clay soils of the upper slopes of Cachapoal Valley, where *La Rosa* and *Concha y Toro* have extensive plantings. *Viña Porta* and *Santa Monica* are further north near Rancagua, making top-class Cabernet and Merlot.

CURICÓ About 200km south of Santiago, and split between the Teno and Lontué rivers, Curicó is mainly known for its Chardonnay (*Valdivieso, Montes, San Pedro, Caliterra*). Valdivieso has emerged as the leading

producer, also making beautiful Pinot Noir, Merlot and Cabernet.

MAULE Southerly region, home to large quantities of País grapes. A handful of producers (*Terra Noble, Domaine Oriental, Carta Vieja, Segu Olle*) are achieving variable results, with reds (particularly Merlot) beating whites on quality. Results from government-funded vineyard project at Cauquenes have drawn interest from the likes of Kendall-Jackson.

SOUTHERN REGION covers the largely País-filled valleys of Itata and Bío-Bío, but *Concha y Toro* has produced a top-class Gewürztraminer from Mulchen.

WINERY PROFILES

AQUITANIA ★★★ Bruno Prats of Ch. Cos d'Estournel and Paul Pontallier of Ch. Margaux know their real estate, but there are less polluted areas to make great Cabernet. It's questionable whether the Domaine Paul Bruno is worth its hefty price tag.

CANEPA ★★★★ The company behind many of the best own-labels here, Canepa also makes the good Montenuevo and Rowan Brook. Merlot, Zinfandel and Magificum Cabernet are its top reds.

CARMEN ★★★★ State-of-the-art sister operation to Santa Rita with innovative young winemaker. Reds are best; beautiful Merlot Reserve and Grande Vidure Cabernet. Petite Sirah is on the way.

CARTA VIEJA ★★★ Old Maule Valley winery with new quality drive and ability to deliver good value, inexpensive wine. Reds are superior to whites. Very good Merlot.

CASA LAPOSTOLLE ★★★(★) Collaboration between Rabat family and Marnier group with M Rolland consulting. Grassy Sauvignon, rich, buttery Chardonnay and spectacular oak-aged Merlot.

CONCHA Y TORO ★★★★ Chile's biggest winery has resources to reach both good value and premium ends. New Trio red and white are superb, as is the Amelia Chardonnay, a new Syrah, and constantly improving Don Melchor Cabernet.

CONO SUR ★★★★ Superb Pinot Noir from Chimbarongo and Isla Negra red are excellent value. At the time of writing, seeking a new winemaker after Ed Flaherty's departure.

COUSIÑO MACUL ★★ Traditionalist making old-style reds under the Santiago smog. A new location and a new wine-making philosophy would help.

ECHEVERRIA ★★★ One of the leading boutique wineries with vineyards in Curico Valley. Good reserve Chardonnay and Cabernet Sauvignon.

ERRÁZURIZ ★★★★ The arrival of Kiwi Brian Bicknell had a big impact, with an improvement in the Chardonnay and Reserve Merlot. His exit shouldn't disrupt projects like the wild yeast Chardonnay. Second label Caliterra ★★★(★) is now in a joint venture with Mondavi.

LA ROSA ★★★★ Top unwooded Chardonnay and Merlot from Cachapoal Valley with Ignacio Recabarren consulting. Watch out for new Cabernet from Palmeria Estate.

LOS VASCOS ★★★ A recent change of ownership – with Santa Rita taking over the Chilean stake of this venture with Lafite-Rothschild – will one hopes bring new impetus and direction. So far, the Cabernet has not lived up to potential.

LUIS FELIPE EDWARDS ★★★(★) Large single estate in Colchagua Valley specialising in Chardonnay and Cabernet.

MONTES ★★★ Curicó-based boutique winery with erratic tendencies. At the moment it's back on form with intense new Malbec, good Merlot and juicy unoaked La Finca Cabernet.

SAN PEDRO ★★★ Against a backdrop of severe financial difficulties, the space-age new winery and the new consultant, Jacques Lurton, are producing big improvements in quality. Best of the Castillo de Milina range is the Chardonnay Reserve.

SANTA CAROLINA ★★★ Reliable producer of reds, particularly Merlot from San Fernando. Whites are a dull comparison with the vibrant wines of its sister company Viña Casablanca.

SANTA MONICA ★★★ Small family-run winery with excellent Riesling and Merlot.

SANTA RITA ★★★ Erratic quality in recent years. The 120 range is the most

reliable, and the latest release of premium Casa Real shows welcome restraint with the new oak.

TERRA NOBLE ★★★★ Talca winery with Touraine wizard Henri Marionnet's very good Sauvignon Blanc and Merlot.

TORRÉON DE PAREDES ★★★(★) Large winery based in Rapel. Good wines throughout, particularly an award-winning Merlot.

TORRES ★★★ Another piece of foreign investment that hasn't delivered the goods. Whites are above average but not spectacular.

UNDURRAGA ★★★ Another of the old camp that needs an injection of inspiration. Merlot and Cabernet are good.

VALDIVIESO ★★★★ Traditional sparkling wine producer, now top of premium still wine table. Excellent oaked Pinot Noir, Merlot, and new red blend Loco.

VILLARD ★★★★ Thierry Villard makes good Sauvignon and Chardonnay from Casablanca, and fruity Merlot from Cachapoal.

VIÑA PORTA ★★★★ Boutique winery with French winemaker Yves Pouzet delivering consistently good oak-aged Chardonnay and Cabernet. A good new Merlot, too.

VIÑA CASABLANCA ★★★★ Ignacio Recabarren's baby. White label wines come from outside the Casablanca area (good new El Bosque Cabernet is from Maipo). Santa Isabel Estate Sauvignon, Chardonnay and Gewürztraminer are all excellent.

MERCHANTS SPECIALISING IN CHILE
see Merchant Directory (page 424) for details

This is another country where few merchants stock a long list. The following, however, have a good choice: Lay & Wheeler (LAY), Oddbins (OD) few

independent merchants have as much variety as Oddbins, Thos. Peatling (PE), Safeway (SAF), Tanners (TAN), Thresher (THR), The Ubiquitous Chip (UB)

CHILE

RED

Under £4.00

1995
Caliterra Cabernet Sauvignon (CO)
Concha y Toro Merlot (FUL)
1994
Concha y Toro Cabernet
   Sauvignon/Merlot (AUR)
Torres Cabernet Sauvignon (POR)
1993
Carmen Cabernet Sauvignon (MAR)

£4.00 → £4.49

1995
Concha y Toro Merlot (EY)
Cono Sur Pinot Noir (VIC, SAF)
1994
Caliterra Cabernet Sauvignon (DAV, FUL,
   BO, VIC)
Concha y Toro Cabernet Sauvignon (EY)
Montes Cabernet Sauvignon (AME)
1993
Torres Curico Cabernet Sauvignon (AME)
Torres Santa Digna Cabernet Sauvignon
   (PEN)
1992
Concha y Toro Cabernet
   Sauvignon/Merlot (UB)
1990
Santa Helena Siglo d'Oro Cabernet
   Sauvignon (HOG)

£4.50 → £4.99

1995
★ Errázuriz Merlot (OD)
Montes Cabernet Sauvignon (PIP)
1994
Carmen Reserve Cabernet Sauvignon
   (MAR)
Concha y Toro Merlot (UN)
Errázuriz Cabernet Sauvignon (FUL)
San Pedro Merlot (ROB)
Santa Carolina Cabernet Sauvignon (SOM)
Santa Rita 120 Cabernet Sauvignon (DI)
Undurraga Cabernet Sauvignon (WRI)
Viña Casablanca Cabernet Sauvignon
   Miraflores Estate (OD)
1993
Los Vascos Cabernet Sauvignon (REI, HOG)
Montes Cabernet Sauvignon (YOU, WHI)
San Pedro Merlot (ROB)

Santa Carolina Cabernet Sauvignon (BY)
Santa Rita Cabernet Sauvignon Reserva
   (MAJ)
Torres Cabernet Sauvignon (HOG)
1992
Concha y Toro Cabernet
   Sauvignon/Merlot (HIC)
Santa Rita 120 Cabernet Sauvignon (BEN)
Torres Santa Digna Cabernet Sauvignon
   (WHI)
1991
Montes Cabernet Sauvignon (REI)
Undurraga Cabernet Sauvignon (AV)
Viña Casablanca Cabernet Sauvignon
   Miraflores Estate (MOR)
1990
Santa Carolina Cabernet Sauvignon (BOT)
Undurraga Pinot Noir (TES)
1989
Cousiño Macul Antiguas Reservas
   Cabernet Sauvignon (BO)
★ Torreon del Paredes Cabernet Sauvignon
   Reserve (FOR)

£5.00 → £5.99

1995
Cono Sur Selection Reserve Pinot Noir
   (ASD, VIC)
1994
★ Alamos Ridge Malbec (BIB)
Cousiño Macul Cabernet Sauvignon (NI)
Undurraga Pinot Noir (WRI)
1993
Caliterra Cabernet Sauvignon (BOT, THR,
   WR)
Concha y Toro Cabernet Sauvignon (WRI)
Los Vascos Cabernet Sauvignon (CRO, PLA)
Torres Santa Digna Cabernet Sauvignon
   (DI)
Undurraga Pinot Noir (AV)
1992
Cousiño Macul Cabernet Sauvignon (UB)
Los Vascos Cabernet Sauvignon (POR)
Marqués de Casa Concha Cabernet
   Sauvignon (VIC)
Santa Rita Cabernet Sauvignon Reserva (DI)
Torres Cabernet Sauvignon (SUM)
1991
Concha y Toro Cabernet Sauvignon (UB)
Cousiño Macul Antiguas Reservas
   Cabernet Sauvignon (SOM)
Montes Cabernet Sauvignon (QUE)

1990
Cousiño Macul Antiguas Reservas
Cabernet Sauvignon (VIC)
Montes Cabernet Sauvignon (WRI)
Undurraga Cabernet Sauvignon Reserve
Selection (EY)
Villa Montes Cabernet Sauvignon (BER)

£6.00 → £6.99
1995
Cono Sur Selection Reserve Pinot Noir
(OD, WS, FUL)
Errázuriz Don Maximiano Reserva
Cabernet Sauvignon (VIC)
1992
Cousiño Macul Antiguas Reservas
Cabernet Sauvignon (WRI, TAN)
Los Vascos Cabernet Sauvignon (NO, ARM)
Montes Cabernet Sauvignon (TAN)
Undurraga Cabernet Sauvignon Reserve
Selection (PEN)
1991
Santa Helena Seleccion del Directorio
Cabernet Sauvignon (WRI)
1990
Cousiño Macul Antiguas Reservas
Cabernet Sauvignon (NI)
1989
Undurraga Cabernet Sauvignon Reserve
Selection (AV)

£7.00 → £7.99
1993
Santa Rita Cabernet Sauvignon Medalla
Real (DI)
1991
Marqués de Casa Concha Cabernet
Sauvignon (TAN)
Montes Alpha Cabernet Sauvignon (MAJ)
1990
Montes Alpha Cabernet Sauvignon (OD)
1989
Cousiño Macul Antiguas Reservas
Cabernet Sauvignon (MV)

£8.00 → £9.99
1991
Montes Alpha Cabernet Sauvignon (WRI,
PLA, AME, LAY)
1990
Montes Alpha Cabernet Sauvignon (YOU,
AD)
1984
Santa Rita Cabernet Sauvignon Medalla
Real (MOR)

£10.00 → £13.99
1992
Concha y Toro Don Melchor Cabernet
Sauvignon (TAN)
1990
Santa Rita Casa Real Cabernet Sauvignon
(DI, BEN)
1989
Concha y Toro Don Melchor Cabernet
Sauvignon (UB)

WHITE

Under £4.00
1995
Caliterra Sauvignon Blanc (VIC)
Carmen Chardonnay (CO)
Villa Montes Sauvignon Blanc (SAF)
1994
Caliterra Sauvignon Blanc (TES)

£4.00 → £4.99
1995
Caliterra Chardonnay (SAF, FUL, BO)
Carmen Chardonnay (VIC)
Errázuriz Chardonnay (OD)
Santa Rita 120 Sauvignon Blanc (DI)
Santa Rita Sauvignon Blanc Reserva
(MAJ)
Torres Santa Digna Sauvignon Blanc (PEN,
WHI)

Undurraga Sauvignon Blanc (WRI)
Viña Casablanca Chardonnay Santa Isabel
Estate (NI)
Viña Casablanca Sauvignon Blanc Santa
Isabel Estate (NI)
1994
Caliterra Chardonnay (DAV)
Caliterra Sauvignon Blanc (DAV)
Concha y Toro Chardonnay (UN)
Errázuriz Chardonnay (TES)
Torres Sauvignon Blanc (HOG, SUM)
Villard Aconcagua Sauvignon Blanc (BOT,
WR, THR)

1993
Caliterra Sauvignon Blanc (SAT)
Undurraga Sauvignon Blanc (AV)
1992
Caliterra Chardonnay (SAT)
Santa Rita Sauvignon Blanc Medalla Real (MOR)

£5.00 → £5.99
1995
Carmen Sauvignon Blanc (PLA)
Cousiño Macul Chardonnay (HIC, TAN)
Errázuriz Chardonnay (HA)
Santa Rita Sauvignon Blanc Reserva (DI)
Torres Santa Digna Sauvignon Blanc (DI)
Undurraga Sauvignon Blanc (PEN)
Villa Montes Chardonnay (PLA)
Villard Aconcagua Sauvignon Blanc (BU)
Viña Casablanca Gewürztraminer (BO, OD)
1994
Marqués de Casa Concha Chardonnay (VIC)
Santa Rita Sauvignon Blanc Reserva (BO)
Viña Casablanca Gewürztraminer (MOR)
1993
Undurraga Chardonnay (PEN, AV, WRI)
Undurraga Sauvignon Blanc (HIC)
1992
Santa Rita Chardonnay Medalla Real (MOR)

£6.00 → £6.99
1995
Viña Casablanca Gewürztraminer (NI)
Viña Casablanca Sauvignon Blanc Santa Isabel Estate (OD)

£7.00 → £7.99
1995
Viña Casablanca Chardonnay Santa Isabel Estate (WS)
Viña Casablanca Sauvignon Blanc Santa Isabel Estate (WS)
1994
Santa Rita Chardonnay Medalla Real (DI)

ROSÉ

Under £5.00
1995
Torres Santa Digna Cabernet Sauvignon Rosado (WHI)
1994
Torres Santa Digna Cabernet Sauvignon Rosado (HOG)

SOUTH AFRICA

If 'fruit first' is the current catchphrase in South African wine, does that mean it's all going to taste the same? And where does one look for some regional character?

As South African winemakers have opened their eyes and ears to the outside world, so the outside world has bombarded them with one very clear message: give us riper fruit. But while riper wines would be an improvement, there is an obvious danger that by trying to squeeze into some sort of Australian mould, South Africa will lose its own identity.

Evidence from the 1996 vintage suggests the new generation of young winemakers (less tainted by the Germanic influence of old) are keen to get more colour and flavour into the bottle. They can do this, first, because they have access to far better grapes than their predecessors. The quiet but massive achievements of the KWV-funded 'Vine Improvement Association' has caused a widespread clean-up of virus-affected vineyards, and has brought in new clones with cleaner flavours. Second, proper site selection for individual varieties has taken the place of the old 'put whites here, reds there' attitudes that had been born out of a bulk- and brandy-led past. Third, winemakers are at last daring to pick later. The green stalky flavours of the past were caused by picking the grapes when they were ripe in terms of sugar content, but not in terms of flavour or tannins. And it is these latter that give depth to wines.

Lost and fined

All this hard work is of course redundant if these new wines are then over-fined and filtered to death; and because of a dire shortage of bottling lines in the Cape, this sucking out of character, colour (why else should South African whites be so pallid?) and life from the wines is a common problem. The ubiquitous sharing of bottling facilities means long queues and a lack of control, so fantastic tank samples turn up six months later on the shelves tasting like worn-out wrecks. Forget the shiny new visitors' centre; the money would be far better spent on a boring new bottling line.

But, assuming this 'fruit first' revolution continues to sweep across the country, will any sort of national, and indeed regional style start to emerge? In the past, the off-flavours born of heavily virus-infected vines made it relatively easy to spot South African wines in blind tastings. Post clean-up, the task is thankfully harder, but the challenge now is to maintain originality while also providing what the market wants. At the moment, the style of each producer is more important than the style of any region – this is hardly a shock, given the lack of attention to soils and mesoclimates in the past, and the fact that only one region, Walker Bay, was demarcated according to the potential of the land, and not (as was the case with Paarl, Stellenbosch and the rest) by civil service boundaries. Regionality will only emerge when *terroir* and mesoclimate determine the boundaries of wine regions.

The variations that do exist are caused by differences in attitudes, not differences in soil. Winemakers in areas like Robertson and Franschhoek appear to have a much stronger common purpose and far less complacency than their counterparts in the heartland of the industry. The emerging regions, often dismissed by Stellenbosch traditionalists as 'those places over the mountain' have greater openness to change. Bold, ripe Chardonnays from Robertson, pungent Pinotage from Worcester and Swartland, subtle and supple Pinot Noir from Walker Bay. These are the wines to watch for. Packed with fruit, but also packed with Cape personality. **RICHARD NEILL**

GRAPES & FLAVOURS

CABERNET SAUVIGNON, CABERNET FRANC AND BORDEAUX BLENDS (red)

The varieties and blends that best demonstrate the improvements in the clones in the vineyards. Out go the dusty, earthy tones of the past; in come clean, minty aromas and far fresher fruit. However, a tough greenness still remains in many, with unripe tannins and poor oak selection the culprits. The Bordeaux blends tend to be more successful than straight Cabernet of either variety. Best varietal Cabernets: *Avontuur Reserve, Backsberg, Bellingham, Blaauwklippen Reserve, Neil Ellis, Excelsior, Glen Carlou, Hartenberg, Landskroon Cabernet Franc, Le Bonheur, Liefland, Nederburg, Plaisir de Merle, Stellenryck, Swartland Co-operative, Thelema.* Best Bordeaux-style blends: *Avontuur Baccarat, Buitenverwachting Grand Vin, Clos Malverne Auret, Fairview Charles Gerard Red Reserve, Glen Carlou Les Trois, Groot Constantia Gouverneur's Reserve, Klein Constantia Marlbrook, La Motte Millennium, Lievland DVB, Meerlust, Nederburg Auction, Rustenberg Gold, Villiera Cru Monro, Zonnebloem Laureat.*

CHARDONNAY (white)

The tendency is still to pick too early and then over-oak, but a growing number of producers are allowing the grapes to ripen properly, then toning down the wood. As a result they get better length and balance in their wines. The best wines have lingering lemon-lime freshness with subtle oak. Best: *Alphen, Avontuur Le Blush* (fermented in ex-Merlot barrels), *Backsberg, Graham Beck Lonehill, Bellingham Reserve, Blaauwklippen, Bouchard Finlayson, Buitenverwachting, De Leuwen Jagt, De Wetshof Bateleur, Dieu Donne, Neil Ellis, Hamilton Russell, Klein Constantia, Glen Carlou Reserve, Groot Constantia, Louisvale, Van Loveren, Nederburg Auction, Simonsig, Stellenryck, Thelema, Vergelegen Les Enfants, Weltevrede, Zandvliet, Zevenrivieren, Zevenwacht, Zonnebloem.*

CHENIN BLANC (white)

One of the most neglected varieties (despite making up 30 per cent of the Cape's vines) and usually dominates the blend in off-dry commercial whties. However, a new drive to revive its fortunes is under way. Dry versions are best drunk young, when their crisp, honeyed guava flavours are freshest. Best include: *Boland, Boschendal, Glen Carlou, Van Zylshof, Villiera, Wildekrans.*

CINSAUT (red)

Recently overtaken by Cabernet as the most planted variety. Cinsaut's greatest claim to fame here is that, crossed with Pinot Noir, it produced the Pinotage. By itself it gives light, undistinguished red.

COLOMBARD (white)

Second only in quantity to Chenin Blanc (Steen) in South Africa, Colombard makes crisp, commercial whites. A flowery freshness is about all they can ever aspire to.

MERLOT (red)

Arrived in appreciable quantity only in 1985, but already making itself felt. By itself Merlot makes rich, ripe, easy reds – even better aged in new oak. Blended with Cabernet, it smooths over the austere edges to give most of the best reds. Good are *Avontuur Reserve, Bellingham, Boschendal, Fairview Reserve, Glen Carlou, Meerlust, Steenberg, Uiterwyk, Villiera, Warwick, Wildekrans, Zonnebloem.*

MUSCAT (white)

Two types of the Muscat grape are grown in South Africa, Muscadel (a version of the high-quality Muscat Blanc à Petits Grains) and Muscat of Alexandria (known as Hanepoot). Muscadel can be red or white, and is always sweet. The best sweet Muscadels include: *De Leuwen Jagt Muscadel, Klein Constantia Vin de Constance, KWV White Muscadel, Nederburg Eminence, Van Loveren Blanc de Noir, Van Loveren Red Muscadel, Vredendal Muscadel.*

PINOTAGE (red) This crossing of Pinot Noir with Cinsaut can be used to make either light and easy rosé or red, or reds that are a great deal more substantial. The abrasive, estery styles of old are being taken over by cleaner, more intense fruit. Good examples include those from the following producers: *KWV Cathedral Cellars, Simonsig, Swartland co-op, Wildekrans.*

PINOT NOIR (red) Most of South Africa's vineyards are too warm for great Pinot Noir. The cliff-top slopes above Hermanus are the furthest south and the coolest, and give Pinots of European elegance and subtlety. Why Walter Finlayson can do it at *Glen Carlou* on the (hotter) south-west outskirts of Paarl, or indeed Achim von Amim at *Cabrière Estate* in Franschhoek, is a mystery. Fortunately, the 'I have to make a Pinot' mentality doesn't seem to have struck the country. Best: *Bouchard Finlayson, Glen Carlou, Hamilton Russell, Haute Cabrière.*

RIESLING (white) Riesling ripens every year here, but it keeps its acidity, and gives the best sweet Rieslings to be found outside Germany. The dry and off-dry ones can be excellent, too. Best dry: *Buitenverwachting, Neethlingshof.* Best off-dry: *De Leuwen Jagt, Klein Constantia,*

Liefland, Sinnya. Best botrytized sweet Rieslings: *Danie De Wet Edeloes, KWV Noble Late Harvest, Nederburg Noble Late Harvest and Neetlingshof Noble Late Harvest.*

SAUVIGNON BLANC (white) Cape winemakers seem desperate to succeed, yet the pale, dilute and varietally challenged wines being offered as Sauvignon Blanc suggests that other grape varieties are better suited to the country's hot climate. Poor site selection and over-early picking (to compensate for the heat) are the chief problems. Elgin, Constantia and Durbanville seem to deliver the most intensity of flavour. Try examples from *Bellingham, Neil Ellis, Klein Constantia, Steenberg, Villiera.*

SHIRAZ (red) Shiraz used to be the grape South African winemakers forgot until they'd harvested their Cabernet. By that time it was often overripe and good only for 'port'. Now a few are trying harder. As with Cabernet, growers are hampered by the lack of really good clones, but Shiraz can make savoury, raspberry-fruited wines, perhaps lacking the fleshy sweetness of the best of the northern Rhône and Australia. Best examples: *Bertrams, Fairview, Groot Constantia, Hartenberg, La Motte, Lievland, Zonnebloem.*

CLASSIFICATIONS AND WINE LAWS

Every bottle of wine sold in South Africa must bear the Wine of Origin seal. This certifies, through vineyard inspection, cellar checking, analysis and an official tasting panel, the wine's area of origin, grape variety (or varieties) and vintage. Varietal wines must contain at least 75 per cent of the stated grape if sold on the domestic market, and 85 per cent if exported. Blends must state the grapes in descending order of proportion, and if any varieties are present under 20 per cent the percentage must be stated.

Chaptalization (addition of sugar to grape must to increase the alcohol level) is not allowed, but acidification (addition of acidity) is.

To qualify as an 'estate', producers must vinify their wines from grapes grown only on their property. Most then bottle and mature it on the estate, too, but this is not strictly essential.

'Methode Cap Classique' (MCC) is the new name for South African Champagne-method fizz. Best brands so far are *Graham Beck, Blaauwklippen Barouche, Boschendal, Charles de Fere Tradition, Pierre Jourdan* (from *Clos Cabrière*), *J C Le Roux Chardonnay* and *Pongracz.*

WINES & WINE REGIONS

CONSTANTIA SA's oldest existing wine region is one of its most dynamic, thanks to massive 1980s investment. *Steenberg's* 1996 Sauvignon shows the results. A strict green belt policy means there will never be more than the existing five estates. *Buitenverwachting* and *Klein Constantia* are the others to watch.

DURBANVILLE Cape Town is threatening the vineyards of Durbanville. A pity, since it's cool. Sauvignon Blanc is particularly good.

FRANSCHHOEK An enclosed valley with a sense of purpose, and showing a dramatic improvement in quality. White grapes rule, yet the new reds are promising. *Cabrière* makes excellent fizz and Pinot Noir, *Bellingham* has a fantastic new Cabernet Franc, *Dieu Donne* and *Haute Provence* good Cabernet Sauvignon.

OLIFANTS RIVER Irrigated semi-desert area, with yields that are rarely less than 20 tons per hectare. The *Vredendal co-op* is now run by an accountant and is likely to respond to rising brandy demand . Hugh Ryman's Impala wines from the *Citrasdal co-op* taste great in SA, less good after UK bottling. *Klawer* and *Spruitdrift* co-ops both make good Merlot.

PAARL The *KWV* is based in the town of Paarl, as is *Nederburg*. There is also *Backsberg, Villiera, Glen Carlou, Fairview, De Leuwen Jagt* and *Landskroon*, with good wines from almost every variety. *Villiera* even has a good Sauvignon, and *Glen Carlou* one of South Africa's best Pinot Noirs, despite the heat.

ROBERTSON Horse-breeding and brandy country, gaining a reputation for Chardonnay. *Danie de Wet* was the first to realise the potential, and *Van Loveren, Sandvliet, Weltevred* and *Astonvale* are following. *Van Zylshof* makes good Chenin Blanc. Look out for the new *Sinnya* red and white: blends of vintages and grapes from eight different growers.

STELLENBOSCH The heart of the wine industry. *Stellenbosch Farmers' Winery, Bergkelder* and *Gilbeys* are all here. Both reds and whites are successful, with Devon Valley (*Clos Malverne* and *Bertrams*) good for reds. Also: *Avontuur, Blaauwklippen, Hartenberg, Kanonkop, Lievland, Meerlust, Mulderbosch, Neetlingshof, Neil Ellis, Rust-en-Vrede, Simonsig, Stellenzicht, Thelema, Vriesenhof, Zevenwacht.*

SWARTLAND Called 'black land' because of the dark grey scrub that covers the hills, Hhot and dry, with cereals outnumbering vineyards. Yields are very low, and Chenin Blanc, Sauvignon Blanc, Colombard and Pinotage do best. The *Swartland* and *Riebeek* co-ops and *Allesverloren* estate are the best.

WALKER BAY Cool coastal region with three river valleys: Onrust, where *Hamilton-Russell* and *Bouchard Finlayson* are making Pinot Noir and Chardonnay in a style somewhere between that of the Old and New Worlds; Bot River, where *Wildekrans* is making good Chenin and Pinotage; and Klein River, home of *Southern Right* Pinotage. Further inland, high Elgin shows promise.

WINERY PROFILES

BACKSBERG ★★★★ Luscious Chardonnay and superb reds. Top Malbec and Pinotage.

BELLINGHAM ★★★★★ Super flinty Sauvignon, elegant, peachy Chardonnay. New Cabernet Franc is stunning.

BOSCHENDAL ★★★★(★) Stronger on reds than whites. Intense, peppery Shiraz, juicy, chocolaty Merlot, and superb Lanoy red blend.

BOUCHARD FINLAYSON ★★★★★ Burgundian-style Chardonnays and Pinot Noir.

CABRIÈRE ESTATE ★★★★ Assertively dry and steely Pierre Jourdan Brut, elegant Blanc de Blanc, and perfumed, raspberry-packed Pinot Noir.

CATHEDRAL CELLAR ★★★ KWV's top range. Good New World-style Cabernet Sauvignon, vibrant Pinotage and grassy Sauvignon Blanc.

DE WETSHOF ★★★(★) Top Chardonnays and spicy Rhine Riesling.

FAIRVIEW ★★★★(★) Great Cabernet, Shiraz, Merlot, and new Zinfandel-Cinsaut blend. Sauvignon-Semillon blend is top of the whites.

GLEN CARLOU ★★★★ Tropically rich, leesy Chardonnay and impressive red Bordeaux blends.

HAMILTON RUSSELL ★★★★★ Elegant Chardonnay and Pinot Noir that brilliantly straddle Old and New Worlds.

KANONKOP ★★★★★ Pinotage king of the Cape. There's also rich, mouthfilling Cabernet and complex Paul Sauer Bordeaux blend.

KLEIN CONSTANTIA ★★★★ Stunning Sauvignon Blanc, toasty Chardonnay and classic claret-style Marlbrook red.

LA MOTTE ★★★★ Excellent reds; big spicy Shiraz and ripe oak-splashed Cabernet.

LOUISVALE ★★★ Buttery, biscuity Chardonnay and a good Cabernet-Merlot blend.

MEERLUST ★★★★ Stunning new Chardonnay, complex Rubicon Cabernet blend and a soon-to-arrive range of grappa.

NEIL ELLIS WINES ★★★(★) Top negociant producing excellent Sauvignon from Elgin and Darling. Tropical Chardonnay, intense Cabernet.

PLAISIR DE MERLE ★★★(★) Rapidly improving Chardonnay and Cabernet.

RUSTENBERG ★★★ Cabernet blends that cellar well, but the new Kiwi winemaker should improve the whites.

SIMONSIG ★★★★ Concentrated, unwooded Pinotage and brilliant peppery Shiraz.

STEENBERG ★★★(★) Constantia's rising star. Crisp, nettley Sauvignon Blanc and powerful, inky Merlot.

THELEMA ★★★★ First-rate Sauvignon Blanc and Chardonnay, gutsy Cabernet Reserve and fruit-driven Cabernet-Merlot blend.

VILLIERA ★★★★ Consistently excellent Merlot and a new Chenin that nudges ahead of the tangy Sauvignon.

VRIESENHOF ★★★(★) Very intense Chardonnay and super Kallista Bordeaux blend.

WARWICK ★★★★(★) Fabulous bush-trained Pinotage, dense, mouthfilling Cabernet Franc and complex Bordeaux blend called Trilogy.

MERCHANTS SPECIALISING IN SOUTH AFRICA
see Merchant Directory (page 424) for details

Averys of Bristol (AV), Bibendum (BIB), Cape Province Wines (CAP) who do nothing else, Direct Wine (DI), J E Hogg (HOG), Lay & Wheeler (LAY), Oddbins (OD), Thos. Peatling (PE), Terry Platt (PLA), Roberson (ROB), Sainsbury (SAI), Tanners (TAN), Thresher (THR), The Ubiquitous Chip (UB)

SOUTH AFRICA

RED

Under £3.50

1994
Pinotage Culemborg Paarl (WAI)

£3.50 → £3.99

1995
Fairview Pinotage (ASD)
1993
KWV Roodeberg (HOG, UN)
1992
KWV Cabernet Sauvignon (UN, HOG)
KWV Pinotage (UN)
KWV Shiraz (UN)

£4.00 → £4.99

Non-vintage
★ Beyers Truter Pinotage (TES)
KWV Cabernet Sauvignon (BO)
KWV Pinotage (BO)
KWV Roodeberg (BO)
1995
★ Avontuur Pinotage (WAI)
★ Beyerskloof Pinotage (OD)
1994
KWV Cabernet Sauvignon (AUR)
KWV Roodeberg (AUR)
Nederburg Pinotage (NEW)
1993
Backsberg Cabernet Sauvignon (WHI)
KWV Roodeberg (FUL, WAI, VIC, DAV)
KWV Shiraz (FUL)
Nederburg Pinotage (HOG)
1992
Backsberg Pinotage (HOG)
Klein Constantia Shiraz (VIC)
KWV Cabernet Sauvignon (DAV, CAP, FUL)
KWV Pinotage (HOG, DAV, WR, THR, BOT, CAP)
KWV Roodeberg (CAP)
KWV Shiraz (CAP)
Nederburg Edelrood (HOG)
Nederburg Paarl Cabernet Sauvignon (HOG)
1991
KWV Cabernet Sauvignon (BOT, WR, THR)
KWV Pinotage (WHI)
KWV Roodeberg (THR, WR, BOT, WHI)
KWV Shiraz (HOG)
Nederburg Edelrood (QUE)
Nederburg Paarl Cabernet Sauvignon (POR)

£5.00 → £5.99

Non-vintage
Zonnebloem Shiraz (BO)
1994
★ Fairview Cabernet Sauvignon (VIC)
Fairview Shiraz (AD)
KWV Shiraz (AUR)
Nederburg Pinotage (CAP)
1993
Backsberg Cabernet Sauvignon (PLA, CAP)
Backsberg Pinotage (CAP)
KWV Roodeberg (BY)
Nederburg Baronne (CAP)
Nederburg Edelrood (CAP)
Nederburg Paarl Cabernet Sauvignon (NEW)
Nederburg Pinotage (WRI)
Zonnebloem Pinotage (DAV)
1992
Backsberg Klein Babylonstoren (QUE)
Backsberg Pinotage (KA)
Klein Constantia Shiraz (AV)
Nederburg Paarl Cabernet Sauvignon (TAN)
Rustenberg Dry Red (TAN)
1991
Backsberg Cabernet Sauvignon (HOG)
KWV Shiraz (BY)
Nederburg Paarl Cabernet Sauvignon (QUE)
Neil Ellis Cabernet Sauvignon (UB)
Rustenberg Dry Red (AV)
1990
De Leuwen Jagt Merlot (PEN)
1989
Diemersdal (CAP)
Fairview Pinotage (PEN)
1988
Klein Constantia Shiraz (PEN)
Zonnebloem Cabernet Sauvignon (BU)
1959
Nederburg Paarl Cabernet Sauvignon (UB)

£6.00 → £7.99

1995
Fairview Pinotage (ENO)
1994
Fairview Shiraz (AS, POR)
Kanonkop Pinotage (SOM)
★ Neil Ellis Pinotage (FOR)
1993
Hamilton Russell Pinot Noir (GAU, HOG)
Kanonkop Pinotage (TES)
Klein Constantia Shiraz (DI)
Zonnebloem Pinotage (CAP)

1992
Backsberg Pinotage (AD)
Groot Constantia Cabernet Sauvignon (CAP)
Groot Constantia Pinotage (CAP)
Groot Constantia Shiraz (CAP)
Hamilton Russell Pinot Noir (DI)
Klein Constantia Shiraz (UN)
Thelema Cabernet Sauvignon (CO)
Warwick Farm Cabernet Sauvignon (VIC)
Zonnebloem Pinotage (PLA)
Zonnebloem Shiraz (CAP)
1991
Allesverloren Tinta Barocca (CAP, DI)
Backsberg Shiraz (KA, PIP)
Groot Constantia Cabernet Sauvignon (HOG)
Klein Constantia Cabernet Sauvignon (CAP)
Meerendal Pinotage (CAP)
Zonnebloem Cabernet Sauvignon (CAP, DAV)
1990
Allesverloren Tinta Barocca (HOG, WRI)
Klein Constantia Cabernet Sauvignon (HOG, EY, TAN)
Klein Constantia Marlbrook (HOG, WRI)
Rustenberg Cabernet Sauvignon (HOG, POR)
Zandvliet Shiraz (CAP)
1989
Meerendal Pinotage (MAJ)
Zandvliet Shiraz (WRI)
1988
Backsberg Cabernet Sauvignon (BUT)
Klein Constantia Cabernet Sauvignon (AV)
Overgaauw Tria Corda (VIC)
1985
Zonnebloem Cabernet Sauvignon (BU)
1983
Zonnebloem Pinotage (BO)

£8.00 → £9.99
1994
★ Grangehurst Pinotage (BIB)
Hamilton Russell Pinot Noir (EY, TAN, PIP)
Kanonkop Pinotage (OD)
★ Uiterwyck Pinotage (LAY)
1993
Hamilton Russell Pinot Noir (CRO, AV, HAH)
Kanonkop Pinotage (ELL)
Neil Ellis Cabernet Sauvignon (MAJ)
1992
Neil Ellis Cabernet Sauvignon (ROB)
Thelema Cabernet Sauvignon (SOM, ELL, ENO, BEN, VIG)
Warwick Farm Cabernet Sauvignon (WS)

1991
Buitenverwachting Christine (NEZ)
Groot Constantia Cabernet Sauvignon (DAV)
Meerlust Cabernet Sauvignon (BU)
Meerlust Rubicon (BU)
Rustenberg Cabernet Sauvignon (WRI, CAP, LAY)
Rustenberg Gold (HOG)
Uitkyk Carlonet (CAP)
1990
Klein Constantia Cabernet Sauvignon (HAH, AD)
Klein Constantia Marlbrook (DI)
Meerlust Rubicon (POR)
Rust-en-Vrede Merlot (UB)
Rustenberg Gold (POR)
1989
Meerlust Merlot (BU)
Meerlust Rubicon (HOG, QUE)
Rustenberg Cabernet Sauvignon (AV)
Stellenryck Cabernet Sauvignon (CAP, POR)
Stellenryck Collection Cabernet Sauvignon (WRI)
Uitkyk Carlonet (HOG, BEN)
1988
Meerendal Pinotage (VIG)
Meerlust Cabernet Sauvignon (HOG)
Meerlust Merlot (ELL)
1986
Blaauwklippen Cabernet Sauvignon (BUT)
1985
Zonnebloem Pinotage (WRI)

£10.00 → £12.99
1994
Hamilton Russell Pinot Noir (UB)
Kanonkop Pinotage (PIP)
1992
Thelema Cabernet Sauvignon (NI)
1991
Buitenverwachting Christine (LAY)
Kanonkop Cabernet Sauvignon (QUE)
Meerlust Cabernet Sauvignon (CAP, WRI)
Meerlust Rubicon (CAP, ROB)
Rustenberg Gold (BER)

Please remember that
Webster's *is a price*
GUIDE and not a price
LIST. It is not meant to
replace up-to-date
merchants' lists.

1990
Rustenberg Gold (DI, AV, CAP)
1989
Meerlust Merlot (KA, BEN)
Meerlust Rubicon (KA, CRO, NI, WRI, BEN, VIG)
Warwick Farm Cabernet Sauvignon (VIG)
1986
Meerlust Cabernet Sauvignon (DI)

c. £18.00
1974
Zonnebloem Pinotage (GAU)

WHITE

Under £3.50
1995
KWV Chenin Blanc (MAR)
Van Loveren Blanc de Noir Red Muscadel (TES)

£3.50 → £3.99
1995
KWV Chenin Blanc (HOG, DAV, VIC, FUL)
KWV Roodeberg (VIC)
KWV Sauvignon Blanc (HOG)

CAPE PROVINCE WINES

South African Wine Specialists

- We have specialised in Quality Cape Wines since 1972
- Stocking over 130 Wines from Vineyards large and small throughout the Cape
- Prompt, efficient delivery service to any U.K. Mainland Address
- **Wine by Fax Service** (24hrs) Just fax your order with **VISA/ACCESS** details
- Selection of Rare Vintages Cape Wines
- Tasting Cases with notes available
- Shop Open 9.00am to 5.30pm. Monday-Saturday (Except Bank Holidays)

77, Laleham Road, Staines.
Middlesex. TW18 2EA
Tel: 01784 451860
Wine by Fax: 01784 469267
E.Mail capewines@msn.com

1994
KWV Chenin Blanc (THR, WR, BOT, UN)
1993
KWV Sauvignon Blanc (UN)

£4.00 → £5.99
Non-vintage
KWV Chenin Blanc (BO)
KWV Sauvignon Blanc (BO)
1996
Nederburg Chardonnay (CAP)
1995
Backsberg Sauvignon Blanc (HOG, CAP, WRI)
KWV Chenin Blanc (CAP, SAT)
KWV Sauvignon Blanc (FUL, VIC, DAV)
le Bonheur Sauvignon Blanc (CAP)
Nederburg Chardonnay (NEW, QUE)
Neil Ellis Sauvignon Blanc (SAI)
Rustenberg Chardonnay (HOG)
★ Vriesenhof Chardonnay (FOR)
de Wetshof Grey Label Chardonnay (SAI)
de Wetshof Rhine Riesling (TES, HOG)
1994
Backsberg Chardonnay (HOG)
Klein Constantia Chardonnay (HOG)
KWV Chenin Blanc (AUR)
KWV Sauvignon Blanc (CAP, THR, WR, BOT)
Nederburg Stein (HOG, CAP)
Rustenberg Chardonnay (PEN)
1993
De Leuwen Jagt Chardonnay (PEN)
Klein Constantia Chardonnay (WAI)
KWV Roodeberg (BY)
KWV Sauvignon Blanc (AUR, BY)
Nederburg Stein (QUE)
1992
KWV Chenin Blanc (PEN)
KWV Sauvignon Blanc (WHI)
1991
KWV Riesling (PEN)
1988
Rustenberg Chardonnay (PEN)
1986
KWV Steen Special Late Harvest (PEN)

£6.00 → £7.99
1996
de Wetshof Sauvignon Blanc (PIP)
1995
Boschendal Chardonnay (CAP)
Buitenverwachting Sauvignon Blanc (ELL, NEZ, LAY)
Groot Constantia Chardonnay (CAP)
Hamilton Russell Chardonnay (HOG)
Hilltop Chardonnay (PE)

★ Klein Constantia Chardonnay (CAP, UN)
Klein Constantia Sauvignon Blanc (CAP, AV)
le Bonheur Sauvignon Blanc (DI)
Neil Ellis Chardonnay (FUL)
★ Neil Ellis Sauvignon Blanc (FOR, FUL, ROB)
Rustenberg Chardonnay (CAP)
★ Steenberg Sauvignon Blanc (ARM)
Thelema Chardonnay (SOM)
Thelema Sauvignon Blanc (REI, SOM, ELL, SAI)
1994
Backsberg Chardonnay (BY)
Boschendal Chardonnay (SAI, SAF, YOU)
Hamilton Russell Chardonnay (GAU, AV, DI)
Klein Constantia Chardonnay (UN, DI)
Neil Ellis Sauvignon Blanc (AV)
l'Ormarins Sauvignon Blanc (WRI)
Rustenberg Chardonnay (AV)
Thelema Chardonnay (CO, HOG)
1993
Backsberg Chardonnay (WRI)
Klein Constantia Chardonnay (AV, WRI)
Thelema Chardonnay (LEA)
1991
Klein Constantia Sauvignon Blanc (GAU)
1989
Backsberg Sauvignon Blanc (BUT)
1988
Klein Constantia Sauvignon Blanc (BUT)

£8.00 → £9.99
1995
Hamilton Russell Chardonnay (CAP, TAN, WRI, LEA)
★ Mulderbosch Chardonnay (ARM)
Mulderbosch Sauvignon Blanc (ARM, LAY, CRO)
Neil Ellis Sauvignon Blanc (UB)
Thelema Sauvignon Blanc (BEN, ROB)
Zonnebloem Chardonnay (UB)
1994
Hamilton Russell Chardonnay (CRO)
Thelema Chardonnay (REI, ELL, SAI, ENO, TAN)
1993
Buitenverwachting Chardonnay (NEZ)

£11.00 → £13.99
1995
Mulderbosch Sauvignon Blanc (UB)
1989
Klein Constantia Vin de Constance ½ litre (AV, AD, ROB)
Nederburg Edelkeur ½ bottle (CAP)
1988
Klein Constantia Vin de Constance ½ litre (GAU)

ROSÉ

Under £5.00
1994
KWV Cabernet Sauvignon Blanc de Noir (CAP)
Nederburg Cabernet Sauvignon Blanc de Noir (CAP)
Nederburg Rosé (CAP)

SPARKLING

Under £6.00
Non-vintage
KWV Mousseux Blanc Cuvée Brut (CAP)
Nederburg Premiere Cuvée Brut (HOG)

£6.00 → £6.99
Non-vintage
Laborie Blanc de Noir (CAP)
Nederburg Premiere Cuvée Brut (CAP, QUE)

c. £10.50
1991
Boschendal Brut Vintage (CAP)

FORTIFIED

Under £4.50
Non-vintage
Mymering Pale Extra Dry (HOG)
Onzerust Medium (HOG)
Renasans Dry Amontillado (HOG)

£4.50 → £4.99
Non-vintage
Cavendish Fine Old Ruby (HOG)
Mymering Pale Extra Dry (CAP)
Onzerust Medium (CAP)
Renasans Pale Dry (CAP)

£5.00 → £6.99
Non-vintage
Cavendish Fine Old Ruby (CAP)
Mymering Pale Extra Dry (DI)
Onzerust Medium (DI)
Renasans Pale Dry (DI)
1979
Cavendish Vintage (HOG, CAP)

£7.00 → £8.99
1979
Cavendish Vintage (DI)
1963
Cavendish Vintage (PEN)

OTHER WINE REGIONS

Argentina could one day produce the finest reds in south America; Austria already has world-class whites, but we still don't drink many of them here. These countries could be the fashions of the future

ARGENTINA

There are those who predict that in the long run Argentina will produce finer wine than Chile. If this prediction comes true, it will be, I'd suggest, because Argentina has had a harder time of it. We all know how perfect Chile is for grapes; well, Argentina isn't perfect at all. And some of the areas now being tipped as sources of world-class wines are some of the last places on earth you'd choose to plant vines.

Take Salta. It's in the north of Argentina, which means it's nearer the Equator, which means it's hot. Unless, of course, you go 6000ft up the mountains. Then, with cool nights, lots of lots of sun and low humidity at your disposal, you can plant the white Torrontes to good effect. That is what Etchart has done, and so far it's Argentina's best white, clean, crisp and aromatic.

Mendoza, though, is Argentina's main wine region. Ninety per cent of Argentinian wines of export quality come from here, and there are two demarcated sub-regions, Lugán de Cuyo and San Rafael. And the grapes? Cabernet, Syrah, Sangiovese, Barbera, Semillon, Chenin Blanc, Torrontes, Chardonnay and Ugni Blanc. But my money's on Malbec, which seems more at home in Argentina than almost anywhere. Try *Catena* (and second label *Alamos Ridge*), *Trapiche, San Telmo, Navarro Correa, Cavas de Weinart, Etchart, Bodegas Norton, Santa Julia, Lurton*.

AUSTRIA

This is the great undiscovered wine country of Europe. There we are, all looking to Romania or Slovakia or heaven knows where to be the Next Big Thing, when there are superb, poised, beautifully made wines waiting for us a good deal nearer.

Every year Austria hopes that the world will realise what treasures it has; well, perhaps this year we really will find out.

Austria's vineyards are all in the east of the country, and although the grapes are pretty similar to those of Germany and Alsace, not to mention much of Central Europe – Riesling, Gewürztraminer, Welschriesling, Muskateller, Ruländer, Weissburgunder and some Chardonnay, plus the less usual Grüner Veltliner – the climate is warmer than most of Germany so the wines are fuller, and they're also made dry. If that makes them sound like Alsace wines – well, no, they're not quite like that, either. They have their own definite style, and they range from light and fresh and everyday – often grapes like Grüner Veltliner or Welschriesling, designed to be drunk by the half-litre without falling over afterwards – to richer and more vinous to sweet botrytized wines from Burgenland.

Austria has four wine regions: Niederösterreich (or Lower Austria), Burgenland, Steiermark (or Styria) and Vienna itself, which boasts vineyards actually within the city boundaries. Lower Austria's finest area is the Wachau, a place of steep slopes and terraces overlooking the Danube, and of wines from the Grüner Veltliner and Rhine Riesling which can be as good as anything in Austria and, in the case of Riesling, as good as in most of Germany too.

Kamptal and Donauland, also in Lower Austria, produce good Grüner Veltliner, and it is this grape that makes perhaps the most typical wine of Austria: light, dry and drunk within a year of the vintage at family-run inns known as Heurigen.

It is the Burgenland, though, that is becoming established as Austria's top area.

In the north there is a lake, the Neusiedler See, which is broad and shallow and obligingly spreads humidity over a wide area to the east; it's almost impossible not to make botrytized dessert wines there. On the western bank there is botrytis in a fairly narrow strip along the lake shore but also plenty of dry whites too, and further south there are some increasingly good reds.

The driest of the dry come from Steiermark. It's a beautiful, chilly, hilly area that borders Slovenia, and the fashion for dry wines that has gripped Austria for a decade has made Styria very trendy indeed. To an outside palate they can taste not merely dry but unripe, without enough body to balance the searing acidity. But the Austrians love them, and pay through the nose for them. Best producers in Austria include *Bründlmayer, Alois Kracher, Franz Hirtzberger, Josef Pöckl, Krutzler, Willi Opitz, Paul Achs, Robert Wenzel, Georg Stiegelmar, Feiler-Artinger, Lenz Moser, Prager, Erich Salomon, Umathum, Fritz Wieninger*. The majority of these names are now available in Britain.

CANADA

Hybrid grapes, which are most easily able to withstand the climate, used to be Canada's mainstay, but plantings of *vinifera* vines are increasing, new wineries are popping up all over, and experimentation is the order of the day. Cool Ontario's best bets are Riesling and Chardonnay; British Columbia, which is tiny in comparison, does well with Pinot Blanc, Pinot Gris, Riesling, Gewürztraminer and sometimes Merlot. Look out too for Icewines, made from Riesling or the hybrid Vidal. Best names include *Inniskillin, Henry of Pelham, Mission Hill, Cedar Creek, Calona Vineyards, Chateau des Charmes, Hillbrand, Gray Monk, Hainle, Sumac Ridge* and *Summerhill*.

CYPRUS

To describe many Cyprus wines as 'unexciting' is a compliment; all too often 'undrinkable' is the more appropriate term.

There's Cyprus fortified wine, of course, but it's not much good (it used to be called Cyprus 'sherry', but now the whole EU is in agreement: sherry comes only from Spain). The table wines we see over here are frequently tired, flabby and oxidized.

Thankfully, a few bright spots are appearing in this otherwise depressing picture. The Xynisteri grape is one of them. When grown in the cooler, mountainous centre of the island it can produce fresh, lively whites – if it is treated well. At present it accounts for some ten per cent of the vineyards, and is mostly not handled properly. *ETKO* makes a respectable version, called *Nefeli*, and *KEO* has a cool-fermented Xynisteri which is remarkably fragrant.

The other most widely planted native grape variety – in fact the most widely planted of all – is the Mavrodaphne, which so far makes better raisins than it does wine. There is a debate going on as to whether Cyprus should move whole-heartedly towards French varieties like Cabernet Sauvignon and Chardonnay, and the government's research station at Limassol grows these and more. If the pioneering work on grapes and wine-making being done there were taken up by the big producers, then Cyprus would at last begin to fulfil its potential.

GREECE

Greek wines are changing, though anybody who sticks to Retsina might be forgiven for doubting it. International wine-making techniques are gradually being applied to more and more wines, though as long as the vineyards aren't swamped with Cabernet and Chardonnay we're unlikely to see the end of a distinctly Greek style: the native grape varieties are too individual for that. Greece in fact has a wealth of vines found nowhere else, and while some of the red ones, like Agiortiko, can produce rich, earthy reds, there are some white vines that retain their acidity in spite of the heat of a Greek summer. All they want then is some decent wine-making in nice clean temperature controlled vats, and away they'll go.

The reds are still the best known. *Chateau Carras* is a reasonable shot at the classic Bordeaux blend, and is enthusiastically promoted and therefore quite expensive. *Tsantali* reds are also fairly reliable, and cheaper, and *Xinomavro Naoussa* is surprisingly good, with herby, slightly earthy fruit. *Gentilini* shows good international style, as does *Chateau Semili*. *Strofilia* Cabernet Sauvignons, both red and rosé, are very good. *Boutari* and *Achaia Clauss* are also worth a look.

For Retsina addicts (yes, they do exist), *Tsantali* and *Metaxa* have the authentic taste, and Sainsbury's own-label is good, with a little less resin.

INDIA

You can do anything if you're a millionaire; even make your very own Champagne lookalike. When Bombay millionaire Sham Chougule decided he wanted to produce wine, he asked Piper-Heidsieck to come and help; a state-of-the-art winery was built to process the grapes from high-altitude vineyards, and *Omar Khayyam* is the result. It's not as good now as when it was first launched.

ISRAEL

If a whole country's wine industry specializes in making a particular sort of wine (kosher) for a captive worldwide audience (observant Jews) then two things are likely to happen. First, it will produce that wine to impeccable kosher standards; Jews the world over will be able to rely on the rabbinical signature on the label and will be confident in the fact that the wine has been produced in accordance with the strictest rules. Second, it will probably taste awful. That captive audience will be far more interested in the purity (in kosher terms) of the wine than in what it tastes like. Taste, traditionally, is a secondary consideration.

Then, the worldwide wine revolution being what it is, two more things will happen – and indeed have happened. First, California wine-making techniques will be brought in to make kosher wines that taste good enough to tempt non-Jews, too. And second, the biggest wine-making company in Israel (*Carmel*) will be forced to follow suit and invest US$8m in new equipment. The most attractive wines in Israel are however still made by the *Golan Heights Winery*, whose Yarden wines are the best, followed by the Golan range. The *Golan Heights Winery* has recently invested $5m in new equipment. The region, however, is of great strategic importance and could one day be handed over as part of a peace agreement with Syria.

LEBANON

Lebanese wine is, to all intents and purposes for us in Britain, *Chateau Musar*. There are other vineyards, like *Chateau Kefraya*, but none is a patch on Musar.

Frost and rot, the causes of most growers' sleepless nights, are not a problem for Serge Hochar of Musar. Civil war, on the other hand, was, and in 1984 he was not able to make a wine at all: the front line ran between the vineyards and the winery, and the grape-laden lorries were not able to cross it.

Musar's style is, typically, big and powerful. For a time in the late 1960s Hochar turned to making lighter wines more reminiscent of Médoc, but now the wines are huge again, and age superbly – Hochar in fact reckons they should be drunk at 15 years, and will be even better at 30. The trouble is, they're often so wonderful at seven, when they are released, that keeping them that long requires an awful lot of willpower.

LUXEMBOURG

Luxembourg's wines, from the banks of the Mosel, are of little other than local interest. They lack the body, the interest and the aging potential of the best of their neighbours further down the river in Germany, but are perfectly acceptable, with light, delicate fruit. Most are made from Müller-Thurgau, here called Rivaner, which accounts for half the area under vine. Other grapes grown are Elbling, Riesling, Auxerrois, Gewürztraminer and Pinot Gris, with the last two making some of the most interesting wines.

NORTH AFRICA

Forget all those jokes about Algerian Burgundy: the march of Islamic fundamentalism in North Africa means that the vineyard area is shrinking and output is falling.

However, North Africa needs exports, and it needs to cater for its tourist industry – and it needs wine for both. There are faint signs that the wines might improve, the most optimistic of which is the involvement of western winemakers in Morocco. The Algerian fundamentalists are believed to support the production of wine for export, though not for domestic consumption.

A little North African wine is exported to Britain. Morocco makes some decent cheap reds, like *Domaine Cigogne*, *Domaine Mellil* and *Prestige du Menara*. Tunisia might have a name for its Muscats, if they were fresher and lighter, and Algeria, the biggest producer of the three in terms of quantity, can boast the Coteaux de Mascara, which makes heavy, rustic, rather coarse reds. All three countries have *appellation contrôlée* systems based on the French model. The term is *Appellation d'Origine Garantie* in Algeria and Morocco and *Appellation d'Origine Contrôlée* in Tunisia.

SWITZERLAND

Quality is improving in Switzerland, with an influx of imported wines helping to encourage Swiss growers towards lower yields and more concentrated flavours. Reds (mostly from Pinot Noir) can be good, but the stars are the whites. The most popular grape, the light, crisp Chasselas, changes its name to Dorin in the Vaud, Perlan in Geneva and Neuchâtel and Fendant in the Valais. All Swiss wine is hideously expensive, and not likely to get any cheaper.

TURKEY

Turkey's history of viticulture is rather more impressive than the wine itself. Although only three per cent of the total – huge – grape crop is made into wine, wine-making can be traced back some 4000 years – plenty of time in which to count the 1172 different grape varieties currently registered as being cultivated in the country.

It's hard positively to recommend Turkish wines or even any individual grape varieties, but *Buzbag* (red), *Villa Doluca* and *Doluca* (red and whites), *Hosbag* (red), *Villa Dona* (red and white) are brands to consider.

ZIMBABWE

There is some wine made here, and some is even exported to Britain, under the name of *Marondera*. You could try it, just to prove to your friends that it exists.

MERCHANTS SPECIALISING IN THESE COUNTRIES
see Merchant Directory (page 424) for details

Good merchants often stock a scattering of wines from these countries. The following have a slightly better choice: Argentina: Sommelier Wine Co (SOM); Austria: Adnams (AD), Enotria Winecellars (ENO), Lay & Wheeler (LAY), Christopher Piper Wines (PIP), T & W Wines (TW), Noel Young Wines (YOU); Canada: Averys of Bristol (AV), Corney & Barrow (CB), The Nadder Wine Co (NA), Terry Platt (PLA); Greece: Tanners (TAN); Israel: no actual specialists but Averys of Bristol (AV), Corney & Barrow (CB), Safeway (SAF); Lebanon: Château Musar is widely available. For older vintages try Chateaux Wines (CHA), Roberson (ROB)

OTHER WINE REGIONS

ARGENTINA

Under £4.00
1994
Etchart Torrontés (BOT, WR, THR)

£4.00 → £6.99
1993
Etchart Torrontés (UB)
1991
Etchart Cabernet Sauvignon (BOT, WR, THR)
Trapiche Cabernet Sauvignon Reserve (KA)
1990
Trapiche Cabernet Sauvignon Reserve (PLA)
1983
Cavas de Weinert Cabernet Sauvignon
  (BUT)

£9.00 → £11.99
1991
Cavas de Weinert Cabernet Sauvignon
  (LEA)
1989
Cavas de Weinert Cabernet Sauvignon
  (ARM)
1985
Cavas de Weinert Cabernet Sauvignon
  (QUE)

AUSTRIA

Under £4.00
1994
Grüner Veltliner Lenz Moser Selection
  (BOT, WR, THR)

c. £5.00
1994
Grüner Veltliner Lenz Moser Selection
  (PEN)

CANADA

Under £6.50
1993
Inniskillin Maréchal Foch Red (AV)

£7.00 → £9.99
1993
Inniskillin Chardonnay (AV)
1991
Inniskillin Pinot Noir Reserve (AV)

CYPRUS TABLE WINES

Under £4.00
Non-vintage
Aphrodite Keo White (TES)

£4.50 → £4.99
Non-vintage
Othello Keo Red (UN, DI)
St-Panteleimon Keo White (UN, DI)

CYPRUS FORTIFIED

Under £4.00
Non-vintage
Emva Cream (SAF, WAI, DAV)
1992
Emva Pale Cream (BO)

GREECE RED

Under £4.00
Non-vintage
Mavrodaphne Patras, Kourtaki (WAI)
1993
Naoussa Boutari (SAF)
1992
Nemea, Boutari (OD)

£4.00 → £5.99
Non-vintage
Demestica Achaia Clauss (DI)
1993
Nemea, Kouros (UN)

£6.00 → £6.99
1987
Château Carras (CRO, DI)

£8.00 → £9.99
1990
Château Carras (DI)
1989
Château Carras Côtes de Meliton (TAN)

GREECE WHITE

Under £3.00
Non-vintage
Retsina Kourtaki (WAI)
1995
Retsina Achaia Clauss (ASD)

£3.00 → £3.99

Non-vintage
Retsina Kourtaki (VIC, BO, THR, WR, OD, BOT)
Retsina Metaxas (DAV)
1994
Patras, Kouros (WAI)

£4.00 → £4.49

Non-vintage
Retsina Metaxas (AD)
Retsina Tsantali (TAN)

GREECE FORTIFIED

c. £4.50

Non-vintage
Mavrodaphne Patras (NO)

ISRAEL

Under £5.00

Non-vintage
Palwin No. 10 (SAF)
1995
Carmel Petite Sirah Shomron Israel (MAR)
1994
Carmel Cabernet Sauvignon (SAF)

1984
Carmel Cabernet Sauvignon (CRO)

£5.00 → £5.99

Non-vintage
Palwin No. 4 (SAF)
1993
Yarden Cabernet Sauvignon White
   Harvest (AV)
1991
Carmel Cabernet Sauvignon (SAF)

£7.00 → £7.99

1994
Yarden Cabernet Sauvignon White
   Harvest (WRI)
1993
Yarden Chardonnay (AV)
Yarden Mount Herman Dry White (BY)
1992
Golan Mount Hermon Dry White (WRI)
1990
Gamla Galilee Cabernet Sauvignon (WRI)

£9.00 → £9.49

1993
Yarden Chardonnay (WRI, BY)

LEBANON RED

Under £7.50

1988
Château Musar (REI)

£7.50 → £7.99

1988
Château Musar (CHA, FUL, UB, WAI, CO, BO, NI, MAJ)
1986
Château Musar (GAU)

£8.00 → £9.99

1989
Château Musar (DAV)
1988
Château Musar (PEN, YOU, WRI, CRO, WHI, TAN, BEN, GE, DI, AD, PLA, ROB, LEA)
1987
Château Musar (CHA, SO, BUT, WRI, WHI, YOU, BY, ROB)
1986
Château Musar (CHA, ELL, BUT, WRI, BEN, ROB)
1985
Château Musar (CHA, BUT)

£10.00 → £19.99

1988
Château Musar (AV)
1983
Château Musar (CHA)
1982
Château Musar (POR, YOU, QUE, NI, CRO, ROB)
1981
Château Musar (POR, CHA, YOU, QUE, WRI, BEN, ROB)
1980
Château Musar (CHA, YOU, POR, ROB)
1979
Château Musar (CHA, ROB)
1978
Château Musar (CHA)

> *Please remember that* **Webster's** *is a price GUIDE and not a price LIST. It is not meant to replace up-to-date merchants' lists.*

£20.00 → £29.99

1985
Château Musar (NI)
1983
Château Musar (NI)
1978
Château Musar (ROB)
1977
Château Musar (CHA, NI, ROB)
1975
Château Musar (GAU, CRO, CHA, POR, WRI)

c. £36.00

1970
Château Musar (GAU)

c. £52.00

1972
Château Musar (CHA)

c. £85.00

1964
Château Musar (ROB)

LEBANON WHITE

Under £7.00

1992
Château Musar Blanc (UB, DI, WRI)
1982
Château Musar Blanc (POR)

LUXEMBOURG

Under £8.00

Non-vintage
Cuvée de l'Ecusson Brut (EL)

MEXICO

Under £5.00

1993
L A Cetto Petit Sirah (CO, BOT, WR, THR, PLA, TAN)
1992
L A Cetto Cabernet Sauvignon (PLA, TAN)

£6.00 → £8.00

1993
L A Cetto Petit Sirah (CRO)
1988
L A Cetto Petit Sirah (CRO)

REGIONAL DIRECTORY

LONDON

John Armit	ARM
Berry Bros. & Rudd	BER
Bibendum	BIB
Bottoms Up	BOT
Bute Wines	BUT
Corney & Barrow	CB
Davisons	DAV
Enotria Winecellars	ENO
Farr Vintners	FA
Fine Wines of New Zealand	FIZ
Fullers	FUL
Goedhuis & Co	GOE
Haynes Hanson & Clark	HAH
Lea & Sandeman	LEA
London Wine	LO
Moreno Wines	MOR
Morris & Verdin	MV
Laytons	LAYT
Le Nez Rouge	NEZ
La Reserve	RES
Howard Ripley	RIP
Roberson	ROB
Summerlee Wines	SUM
Unwins	UN
La Vigneronne	VIG
Waterloo Wine Co	WAT

SOUTH-EAST AND HOME COUNTIES

Stéphane Auriol Wines	AUR
Australian Wine Centre	AUS
Berry Bros. & Rudd	BER
Bordeaux Direct	BOD
Bottoms Up	BOT
Butlers Wine Cellar	BU
Cape Province Wines	CAP
Ben Ellis	ELL
Philip Eyres	EY
Fuller's	FUL
Gallery Wines	GAL
Douglas Henn-Macrae	HE
High Breck Vintners	HIG
The Sunday Times	SUN
Wine Club	
Unwins	UN
Wine Society	WS

WEST AND SOUTH-WEST

Averys	AV
Bennetts	BEN
Bottoms Up	BOT
Châteaux Wines	CHA
Country Wine Merchant	—
Croque-en-Bouche	CRO
Eldridge, Pope & Co	EL
John Harvey & Sons	HA
Haynes Hanson & Clark	HAH
Hicks & Don	HIC
J C Karn	KA
The Nadder Wine Co	NA
The Nobody Inn	NO
Christopher Piper	PIP
Reid Wines (1992) Ltd	REI
Peter Wylie	WY
Yapp Brothers	YAP

EAST ANGLIA

Adnams	AD
Amey's Wines	AME
Anthony Byrne	BY
Corney & Barrow	CB
Roger Harris Wines	HAW
Hicks & Don	HIC
Lay & Wheeler	LAY
Thos. Peatling	PE
Satchells	SAT
Seckford Wines	SEC
T & W Wines	TW
Noel Young Wines	YOU

MIDLANDS

Gauntleys	GAU
Halves	HAL
Portland Wine Co	POR
Quellyn Roberts	QUE
Summerlee Wines	SUM
Tanners	TAN

Vintage Wines	VIN
Wines of Westhorpe	WIW

NORTH

Booths	BO
Penistone Court Wine Cellars	PEN
Whitesides of Clitheroe	WHI
Wright Wine Company	WRI

WALES

Ashley Scott	AS
Terry Platt	PLA

SCOTLAND

Bute Wines	BUT
Corney & Barrow	CB
Forth Wines	FOR
Gelston Castle	GE
J E Hogg	HOG
Raeburn Fine Wines	RAE
The Ubiquitous Chip	UB
Valvona & Crolla	VA

CHANNEL ISLANDS

Sommelier Wines	SOM

NORTHERN IRELAND

Direct Wine	DI
James Nicholson	NI

COUNTRYWIDE

ASDA	ASD
CWS	CO
Majestic	MAJ
Marks & Spencer	MAR
Oddbins	OD
Safeway	SAF
Sainsbury	SAI
Somerfield	SO
Tesco	TES
Thresher	THR
Victoria Wine	VIC
Waitrose	WAI
Wine Rack	WR

MERCHANT DIRECTORY

Abbreviations are as follows: **Credit cards** Access (AC), American Express (AE), Diners Club (DC), Switch (S), Visa/Barclaycard (V). The following services are available where indicated: **C** cellarage, **EP** en primeur offers, **G** glass hire/loan, **M** mail order, **T** tastings and talks. For key to codes, see page 29.

ADNAMS (AD)

(Head office & mail order) The Crown, High St, Southwold, Suffolk IP18 6DP, (01502) 727220, fax (01502) 727223;
Mail order: (01502) 727222;
The Cellar & Kitchen Store, Victoria St, Southwold, Suffolk IP18 6JW;
The Wine Shop, South Green, Southwold, Suffolk IP18 6EW;
The Grapevine, 109 Unthank Rd, Norwich NR2 2PE, (01603) 613998
Hours Mail order: Mon–Fri 9–5, Sat 9–12; Cellar & Kitchen Store: Mon–Sat 10–6.30; Wine Shop: Mon–Sat 10–7.15; The Grapevine: Mon–Sat 9–9.
Credit cards AC S V.
Discounts £3 per case off mail order price if collected.
Delivery £5 1 case, free 2 or more cases or over £100 mainland UK.
Minimum order 1 mixed case.
C EP G M T
The best wine lists are far more than just brief accounts of appellation, shipper and vintage; they are worth reading as journalism, and are infused with the merchant's knowlege and enthusiasm. Of course, it helps if they are literate (this one is) and if the wines are ones that you might want to drink (it would be hard to find any wines here of which you did not instantly crave a taste). The list also gives immensely helpful information on when to drink. The buyers here have been everywhere and know everybody, and they've got the grainy photographs to prove it. It's strong in all regions: fashionable French country wines, unfashionable Loire and Alsace, fine Bordeaux and Burgundy, Germany,

Italy, Australia, California… There's a particularly good list of spirits, including vintage early-landed Cognac, vintage Armagnac, potcheen from Co. Clare (not the illegal stuff) and unusual American Bourbons.

AMEY'S WINES (AME)

83 Melford Road, Sudbury, Suffolk CO10 6JT, (01787) 377144
Hours Tue–Sat 9.30–6.
Credit cards AC V.
Discounts 5% off 12 or more bottles.
Delivery Free within 20 miles of Sudbury, min order £50.
G
A varied and well-thought-out list; what is it about East Anglia that seems to attract so many good merchants? New this year are Barbera, Syrah and Malbec from Vistalba in Argentina, Newtonian from California, Domaine de la Soumade from the Rhône (including its Cabernet Sauvignon). And Montes from Chile is back.

JOHN ARMIT WINES (ARM)

5 Royalty Studios, 105 Lancaster Road, London W11 1QF, 0171-727 6846, fax 0171-727 7133
Hours Mon–Fri 9–6.
Credit cards AC V.
Delivery Free 3 or more cases.
Minimum order 1 unmixed case.
C EP M T
Another list that is a pleasure to read for its own sake. John Armit has positioned himself firmly at the top of the market, with outstanding selections from classic regions and an interesting sprinkling from elsewhere. New this year are the wines of Angelo Gaja, which haven't been easily available in Britain for some years. It's strongest in Bordeaux and Burgundy, where there are producers of the calibre of Domaine Roumier, Domaine Dujac and (of course) Domaine de la Romanée-Conti. The Rhône has been extended, but elsewhere the selections tend to be very good but decidedly short. It strikes

one as a list for lovers of classic wines, who will nevertheless try other regions if carefully tempted and reassured.

ASDA (ASD)

(Head office) Asda House, Southbank, Great Wilson Street, Leeds LS11 5AD, (01532) 435435, fax (01532) 418666
Hours Mon–Fri 9–8, Sat 8.30–8; open most bank hols; selected stores open Sunday.
Credit cards AC S V.
Discounts £1 off any 6 bottles; 6 for 5 bottles of Champagne or sparkling wine costing over £3.99.
G
Well, it's a varied list on the face of it, with all sorts of new wave stuff from Greece, Hungary and Argentina, as well as plenty from the classic regions. But when you taste them you get the impression that rather a lot have been bought to a price point; and that if that price point had been 50p or £1 higher the wine might have been more interesting. The whites are clean and fruity; the reds have a bit more personality. But there's plenty of sound drinking here.

ASHLEY SCOTT (AS)

PO Box 28, The Highway, Hawarden, Deeside, Flintshire CH5 3RY, tel & fax (01244) 520655
Hours 24-hr answerphone.
Discounts 5% unmixed case.
Delivery Free in North Wales, Cheshire, Merseyside.
Minimum order 1 mixed case.
G M T

This is a club, not a shop. It's quite strong on lesser clarets and on wines from the New World, and the Loires look worth investigating. Interesting names can pop up unexpectedly elsewhere, like Quintarelli's delicious Recioto della Valpolicella Amarone.

STÉPHANE AURIOL WINES (AUR)

High St, Hartley Wintney, Hampshire RG27 8NY, (01252) 843190, fax (01252) 844373
Hours Mon–Sat 9–9, Sun 11.30–2.
Credit Cards AC AE S V.
Discounts on half-cases.
Delivery Free locally and for over £150 central UK. Otherwise at cost.
G M T
The list makes the cardinal sin of not always listing producers, but that aside, the range is quite broad. Burgundy looks good, with Chablis from la Chablisienne and reds from Naigeon-Chauveau. Elsewhere the selections are short but quite good.

AUSTRALIAN WINE CENTRE (AUS)

Australian Wine Club, Freepost WC5500, Slough, Berks, SL3 9BH, freephone orderline (0800) 716893; 24-hr answerphone, fax (01753) 591369
Hours Mon–Fri 9–6, Sat 10–4.
Credit cards AC AE S V.
Delivery Free anywhere in UK 1 case or over.
M T
A club also supplying many top retailers with excellent wines, especially many of the most exciting creations of South Australia. But if you want to taste unadulterated press wine (Blaxland Shiraz Mourvedre Pressings) this could be your place.

*('Cellar it for as long as you can', they say, wisely.)
Other oddities: mature (1987) Ashton Hills Riesling
from the Adelaide Hills and the port-style 1992
Tim Adams Vintage, made from Shiraz. Buy now,
drink ten years' hence.*

AVERYS OF BRISTOL (AV)

Orchard House, Southfield Road, Nailsea,
Bristol BS19 1JD (01275) 811100, fax (01275)
811101
Hours Shop: 8 Park St, Bristol: Mon–Sat 10–6;
Wine Cellar: Culver St: Mon–Sat 9–7.
Credit cards AC V.
Discounts Monthly mail order offers, Bin Club
10% off most list prices.
Delivery Free 2 or more cases, otherwise
£5.50 per consignment.
C EP G M T
*Averys has a strong mail order side, and the knack
of succeeding at mail order (according to an ex-
director of Averys) is to price the wines fairly high on
the list, and then have regular discounted offers
through the post. But I'd hate to imply that they're
overpriced to start with, because they're not.
Everything's well chosen, with particularly strong
areas being Bordeaux, Germany and the New
World. Averys was a New World pioneer long
before everybody else got in on the act, and it has
some names that have since become classics here,
like Tyrrells and Sonoma-Cutrer. More recent are
wines from Canada and Argentina. There is a good
range of half-bottles and some big ones, like Averys
own-label Champagne in methusalah at £187.20,
for those evenings when a dozen friends just
happen to drop in.*

BENNETTS (BEN)

High Street, Chipping Campden, Glos GL55
6AG, 24-hr tel & fax (01386) 840392
Hours Mon–Fri 9–1 & 2–5.30, Sat 9–5.30.
Credit cards AC V.
Discounts On collected orders only.
Delivery Free 3 cases or more, England and
Wales.
Minimum order 1 case. Single bottles
available in shop.
E P G M T
*This isn't a coffee-table type list: instead of colour
illustrations and fancy type, umpteen first-class
wines are closely packed, usually without further
comment. There are inexpensive wines but quality
is the point here, not shaving off 50p. Bordeaux
and Burgundy are very good, as is the Loire. Alsace
comes mostly from the excellent house of
Schlumberger. Germany has been expanded and
upgraded as an experiment (so encourage them by
buying some) and Italy looks very interesting. The
California section is terrific, with top growers like
Kistler, Qupé, Bonny Doon, Il Podere dell'Olivos,
Calera, Ridge and Saintsbury, and unusual wines
like Vino Noceto Sangiovese (yes, from California).*

BERRY BROS. & RUDD (BER)

3 St James's St, London SW1A 1EG, 0171-396
9600, fax 0171-396 9611;
Berry's Wine Warehouse, Hamilton Close,
Houndmills, Basingstoke, Hants RG21 2YB,
(01256) 23566, fax (01256) 479558
Hours St James's St: Mon–Fri 9–5; Berry's Wine
Warehouse: Tues–Fri 9–5, Sat 9–4.

Credit cards AC DC S V.
Discounts 3–7.5% according to quantity.
Delivery Free 1 case.
C EP G M T

There's a 250-year-old shop in St James', a less romantic address in Basingstoke and a highly commercial duty-free branch at Heathrow's Terminal 3. You can order in advance, and collect before take-off. The list is a curious mix: it has lots of big names, as you'd expect, and most countries and regions are covered. But whereas in Europe the names tend to be tried and trusted rather than cutting edge (although some good new Burgundy growers are appearing), the New World wines are rather more adventurous.

BIBENDUM (BIB)

113 Regents Park Rd, London NW1 8UR, 0171-722 5577, fax 0171-722 7354
Hours Mon–Thur 10–6.30, Fri 10–8, Sat 9.30–5.
Credit cards AC AE S V.
Delivery Free mainland England, £10 per consignment Wales, Scotland.
Minimum order 1 mixed case.
C EP G M T

Another fat, glossy, classy list. Bibendum have made a name for intelligent, adventurous wine buying, and year after year the list is stuffed with wines that are almost irresistible. Burgundy, Bordeaux are first-rate, French country wines, Italy and the Rhône very good (look out for botrytized Petit Manseng from Jurançon, or white Raffiat de Moncade from Béarn), and the growers' Champagnes are justly famous. From Spain, take a look at the new white Rueda from Belontrade y Lurton. Selections from the New World are equally imaginative. There's a separate fine wine list, for when you win the lottery.

BOOTHS (BO)

4 Fishergate, Preston PR1 3LJ, (01772) 251701, fax (01772) 204316
Hours Office: Mon–Fri 9–5; shop hours vary.
Credit Cards AC S V.
Discounts 10% off mixed cases.
G T

A list with both depth and breadth. Look for claret and Burgundy at all levels, plus good Australians.

Alsace wines come from Turckheim at the cheaper level and Schlumberger for the more expensive ones, and you can't get much better than those. If you can wade through the Piesporters and Bereich Niersteins you'll find some good Germans, too. There's a sprinkling of prestigious wines, like Schlumberger's Gewürztraminer Cuvée Anne, Châteaux Latour and Pétrus, Sassicaia and Vega Sicilia, but somehow one assumes they're not necessarily stocked in absolutely every branch. You're more likely to find a more basic selection on the shelves, but Australia looks good. Eastern Europe is surely due for a major revamp, if it's to keep pace with the changes there.

BORDEAUX DIRECT (BOD)

New Aquitaine House, Paddock Rd, Reading, Berks RG4 5JY. (0118) 9481718, fax (0118) 9461493
Hours Mon–Fri 9–5.30 (Thur until 8), Sat 9–6; 24-hr answerphone;
Mail order: Mon–Fri 9–7, Sat–Sun 10–4.
Credit cards AC AE DC S V.
Discounts Special offers.
Delivery £3.99 per order.
G C EP M T

Mostly mail order, but there are five shops, and it is sister company to the Sunday Times Wine Club. Many of the wines here are not to be found elsewhere – Bordeaux Direct was shipping little country wines it had gone out and found itself long before most people started doing the same. These days, though, it's not looking quite as innovative as it was.

BOTTOMS UP (BOT)

(Head office) Sefton House, 42 Church Rd, Welwyn Garden City, Herts AL8 6PJ, (01707) 328244, fax (01707) 371398
Hours Mon–Sat 9–10, Sun 12–3 & 7–10.
Credit cards AC AE S V.
Discounts 10% mixed cases wine, 17.5% mixed cases Champagne.
Delivery Free locally (all shops). National delivery via Drinks Direct.
G T

The largest shops of the Thresher chain.

BUTE WINES (BUT)

2 Cottesmore Gardens, London W8 5PR, 0171-937 1629, fax 0171-361 0061
Delivery £9 for 1 case, £11 for 2, £13 for 3, £14 for 4, free for 5.
Minimum order 1 case.
EP M
Much emphasis on classic names, with half a dozen top Alsace producers are present in depth, and a few famous names from Italy. A decent sprinkling of New World, and Bordeaux and Burgundy are strongest of all. And that's very strong indeed.

BUTLERS WINE CELLAR (BU)

247 Queens Park Rd, Brighton BN2 2XJ, (01273) 698724, fax (01273) 622761
Hours Tue–Wed 10–6, Thu–Fri 10–7, Sat 10–7.
Credit cards AC AE S V.
Delivery Free locally 1 case or more, free mainland England and Wales, some parts of Scotland 3 or more cases; ring for further details.
G M T

Bin-ends are the speciality of this shop – and what bin-ends. A new list comes out every six weeks, which means that anything I say here is already long out of date. Never mind. A typical list has an ad hoc assortment of clarets going back to maybe 1923 (though not including every year between then and now). Burgundies, from all sorts of producers, might go back to the 1950s; there are Italians, a few from Australia, South Africa and Spain, and German wines might also go back to the '50s. There are often, too, a few bottles of Romanian dessert wine from the 1960s. By no means everything is fine and rare, and there are lots of interesting everyday bottles.

ANTHONY BYRNE (BY)

Ramsey Business Park, Stocking Fen Rd, Ramsey, Cambs PE17 1UR, (01487) 814555, fax (01487) 814962
Hours Mon–Fri 9–5.30.
Credit cards AC V.
Discounts available on cases.
Delivery £6 less than 5 cases, free 5 or more.
C M T
Anthony Byrne is a past master at digging out obscure little country wines which turn out to be delicious; he's also pretty good at capturing

high-quality big names. The net result is an extremely tempting list. Burgundy looks lovely, with producers of the calibre of Domaine de l'Arlot, Leflaive, la Pousse d'Or and many, many others; there's Didier Dageneau from Pouilly-Fumé, Roger Perrin, Alain Graillot and others from the Rhône, Château-Chalon from the Jura, Allegrini, Pieropan, Puiatti and others from Italy… I could go on, but I think you get the idea.

CAPE PROVINCE WINES (CAP)

77 Laleham Rd, Staines, Middx TW18 2EA, (01784) 451860/455244, fax (01784) 469267
Hours Mon–Sat 9–5.30.
Credit cards AC S V.
Delivery £6.50 locally and London, UK mainland varies with quantity.
Minimum order 6 bottles.
M T
South African wines are the be all and end all of this list. Cape Province have selected some lovely wines, like Meerlust Rubicon, or Rust-en-Vrede, but you'll have to do a lot of your own research as well because all this list does is arrange them alphabetically under grape variety, with no further information. Anyone who's interested in how South African wine is developing should try and get to the shop itself, particularly on a Saturday when there's often a tasting, because the list by itself is unlikely to make your mouth water.

CHÂTEAUX WINES (CHA)

Paddock House, Upper Tockington Rd, Tockington, Bristol BS12 4LQ, tel & fax (01454) 613959
Hours Mon–Fri 9–5.30, Sat 9–12.30.
Credit cards AC S V.
Discounts Negotiable.
Delivery Free UK mainland 2 cases or £100 (inc vat) in value.
Minimum order 1 case (unmixed).
C EP M T
Oh dear, Châteaux Wines really didn't like my last year's write-up. They also didn't like my description of their list as 'short'; they prefer 'carefully chosen'. Okay, carefully chosen it is – provided they promise always to describe me the same way. So how else

can I describe the list? Well, there are some tasty clarets, and Chablis from Simonnet-Febvre, but the rest of Burgundy is a bit sketchy. The only wines from outside France are vintages of Chateau Musar back to 1980.

CORNEY & BARROW (CB)

(Head office) 12 Helmet Row, London EC1V 3QJ, 0171-251 4051;
194 Kensington Park Rd, London W11, 0171-221 5122;
31 Rutland Sq, Edinburgh EH1 2BW, 0131-228 2233;
Belvoir House, High St, Newmarket CB8 8OH, (01638) 662068;
Corney & Barrow (Scotland) with Whighams of Ayr, 8 Academy Street, Ayr KA7 1HT, (01292) 267000
Hours Mon–Fri 9–6 (24-hr answerphone); Kensington Pk Rd: Mon–Sat 10.30–8; Newmarket: Mon–Sat 9–6; Ayr: Mon–Sat 9.30–5.30.
Credit cards AC AE V.
Delivery Free 2 or more cases within M25 boundary, elsewhere free 3 or more cases. Otherwise £8 + VAT per delivery.
C EP M T
Corney & Barrow is the sole UK importer of Château Pétrus from Bordeaux and Burgundy's Domaine de la Romanée-Conti, which gives you some clue as to the standard of the rest of the list. This is serious top-of-the-range stuff: all the Moueix wines are here, plus a range of petits châteaux. There's also a glittering cast of Burgundy producers; Australia is represented by Penfolds Grange and Parker Estate, Italy by Sassicaia. At the quirkier end there are a couple of Canadian wines but otherwise you'll find that it's an extremely serious list. For all the emphasis on quality, the big names are not treated as the be all and end all. Having said that, France is the main focus here, and other places can be represented rather briefly.

***Webster's** is an annual publication. We welcome your suggestions for next year's edition.*

COUNTRY WINE MERCHANT

The Ox House, Market Square, Northleach,
Cheltenham, Glos GL54 3EG, (01451) 860680,
fax (01451) 861166;
25 High Street, Hungerford, Berks RG17 0NF,
(01488) 686850;
85 High Street, Oxford OX1 4BG, (01865)
798085;
142 Old Brompton Road, London SW7 4NR,
0171-244 8118
Hours Northleach: Mon–Sat 9–6; Hungerford:
Mon–Sat 10–8; Oxford & London: Mon–Sat
8–10.
Credit cards AC S V.
Discounts In bond and ex-cellar terms available.
Delivery Free locally, elsewhere £6 for 1st case,
£2 each subsequent case, free for 5.
G M T
This is what used to be Windrush Wines – or at
least, at the time of going to press it looked as
though this would be Windrush's successor. A
management buy-out is going ahead even as I write,
and the new owners hope to maintain the old list.
But it wasn't sorted out in time for the new
company to feature in the price guides this year.

CROQUE-EN-BOUCHE (CRO)

221 Wells Road, Malvern Wells, Worcestershire
WR14 4HF, (01684 565612)
Hours No fixed hours; open by telephone
appointment 7 days a week.
Credit cards AC V.
Discounts 4% on 48 bottles +, if cash and
collected; 2.5% if paid by credit card.
Delivery Free locally or for orders over £280;
otherwise £8.50.
M T
Yes, I know the Croque-en-Bouche is a restaurant.
It's also a restaurant with a quite outstanding wine
list – and one that also sells wines retail, for around
£6 less than the restaurant price. It's a terrific list,
too, with California wines from Swanson, Kistler and
others, Albariño from Rias Baixas in Spain, lots of
good Alsace wines, the dry white from Château
Gilette in Bordeaux (the 1958 vintage, that is),
Rasteau Rancio from Domaine de la Soumade,
Anselmi's Recioto di Soave and others.

CWS (CO)

(Head office) New Century House, Manchester
M60 4ES, 0161-834 1212, fax 0161-827 5514
Hours Variable
Credit cards Variable
You'll know this as the Co-op. There's lots of good
basic stuff, and some distinctly interesting things like
Château Cissac 1983; Bad Tempered Cyril
Tempranillo-Syrah (possibly a suitable partner for
Long Slim Cabernet-Merlot); la Jaubertie Bergerac
Blanc; Viognier from the Pays d'Oc; Le Volte from
Ornellaia and L A Cetto's Petite Sirah from Mexico.

DAVISONS (DAV)

(Head office) 7 Aberdeen Road, Croydon,
Surrey CR0 1EQ, 0181-681 3222, fax 0181-760
0390; 76 shops around the south-east.
Hours Mon–Sat 10–2 & 5–10.
Credit cards AC S V.
Discounts 8.5% mixed case.
Delivery Free locally.
EP G T
Strong on claret, petits châteaux, Burgundy and
vintage ports. Davison's strengths have always been
in the classic areas, but these are now joined by
wines from Australia, Chile, Spain and Portugal.
Look, too, at the French country wines. Often very
good prices.

DIRECT WINE (DI)

5–7 Corporation Square, Belfast, Northern
Ireland BT1 3AJ, (01232) 243906, fax (01232)
240202
Hours Mon–Fri 9–6.30 (Thurs till 8), Sat 9.30–5.
Credit cards AC V S.
Discounts 10% discount, or 12% in free stock,
1 unmixed case.
Delivery Free in Northern Ireland 2 or more
cases.
C EP G M T
There's a nice balance here of good everyday wines
and some seriously fine ones from Bordeaux,
Burgundy, the Rhône and Alsace. Spain has masses
of Torres, but other goodies too, and the Germans
and Italians look interesting. DI is also taking an
increasing interest in the New World.

ELDRIDGE, POPE & CO (EL)

(Head office) Weymouth Ave, Dorchester,
Dorset DT1 1QT, (01305) 251251; Mail order:
(0800) 378757
Hours Mon–Sat 9–5.30.
Credit cards AC AE V.
Discounts On application.
Delivery £6 up to 2 cases, free 4 or more cases
or £120 in value.
C G M T
*The very comfortable and friendly feel of this list,
extends, too, to the company's Wine Libraries: wine
shops that turn into wine bars at lunchtime, where
you can buy wine at retail prices and drink them
with good and simple food. Nothing's pretentious,
and there's an air of enjoyment about it all. Having
said that, the list has plenty of first-class names, but
they're balanced with good, inexpensive everyday
stuff. All parts of France are well covered – as is
Luxembourg, for some reason. Germany could do
with a few new names, and Italy and Spain look
good. There's increasing emphasis on the New
World, partly as a reaction to the strong franc.*

BEN ELLIS WINES (ELL)

Brockham Wine Cellars, Wheelers Lane,
Brockham, Surrey RH3 3HJ, (01737) 842160, fax
(01737) 843210
Hours Mon–Fri 9–6, Sun 9.30–1.
Credit cards AC V.
Delivery Free 1 case Surrey and Surrey
borders and Central London, elsewhere free 5
cases or orders over £350, other orders £10
most of UK, otherwise at cost.
Minimum order 1 mixed case.
C G M T
*Ben Ellis has an excellent list, which makes it very
difficult to single any one thing out. Bordeaux, the
south of France, Burgundy and the Rhône all look
good – try in particular Domaine de Regusse's
Muscat Sec de Haut Provence and Viognier de
Haute Provence, and Albert Belle's Crozes-
Hermitage. There are good South Africans
(Warwick Trilogy and Cabernet Franc) and a couple
from England, including a Pinot Noir from Arundel
Vineyard. Olive oil freaks may like to try the one
from the excellent Quinta da la Rosa.*

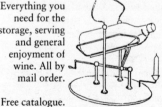

ENOTRIA WINECELLARS (ENO)

(Office) 4–8 Chandos Park Estate, Chandos Rd,
London NW10 6NF 0181-961 4411, fax 0181-
961 8773,
(Shop)153–155 Wandsworth High St, London
SW18 4JB, 0181-871 2668
Hours Mon–Sat 10–7.
Credit cards AC AE DC S V.
Discounts Various discounts on collection.
Delivery Free 1 case min within M25 boundary,
or 2 cases UK mainland. Otherwise £5.
Minimum order 1 bottle.
EP G M T
*A leading Italian specialist, with wines from top
producers in all regions. You want Brachetto del
Piemonte Passito? Or the Syrah from Isole e Olena?
Easy. About half the list is Italian, other half being
equally impressive, particularly Australia. The claret
section is quite small and doesn't go in for big
names – well, who needs them with so much else?*

PHILIP EYRES (EY)

The Cellars, Coleshill, Amersham, Bucks HP7
0LS, (01494) 433823, fax (01494) 431349
Hours Usually Mon–Fri 8–10, Sat–Sun variable;
answerphone out of hours.

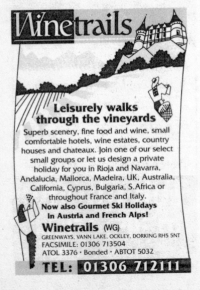
Credit cards AC V.
Delivery Free south Bucks, Windsor & Ascot,
Berkhamsted, Bicester, Highgate & Hampstead,
£6.50 central London 1 case, free 2 or more;
otherwise £10 UK mainland 1 case, £6.50 2–3
or free 4 or more. Delivery on special offers
charged separately.
Minimum order 1 case.
EP
*If you can't afford the Burgundy, go for the French
country wines. There's a brilliant selection of these,
even including a Pinot Noir from the Alpes de Haut
Provence. There's a Viognier from there, too. Clarets
look good, and there's a range of reasonably
affordable sweet white Bordeaux. Lovely Rhônes
and Loires, excellent Italians, good Australians, the
best of Argentina, plus a good selection from South
Africa. There's even sparkling red Burgundy, from
Chanson.*

FARR VINTNERS (FA)

19 Sussex St, London SW1V 4RR, 0171-828
1960, fax 0171-828 3500
Hours Mon–Fri 10–6.
Credit cards AC S V.
Discounts Orders over £2000.
Delivery £8.50 London; (per case) £3.75
Home Counties, minimum £11.25; £3.85 rest of
England and Wales, minimum £11.55; £5.80
Scotland, minimum £17.40 or give 48 hours
notice of collection.
Minimum order £500 plus vat.
C EP M T
*£500 may sound like a lot for a minimum order,
but we are talking about seriously fine wines here.
There are so many double magnums, jeroboams
and imperials that they have their own sections in
the red Bordeaux list, and vintages may go back to
the 1950s (or, in the case of Sauternes, the '20s).
Everything here is blue-chip, and apart from the
classic regions there are a few from Alsace, New
Zealand, Spain and Italy. Prices actually aren't
particularly high, so you get good value for your £500.*

FINE WINES OF NEW ZEALAND (FIZ)

PO Box 476, London NW5 2NZ, 0171-482
0093, fax 0171-267 8400

Hours Mon–Sat 9–5.
Credit cards AC V.
Discounts 2 or more cases.
Delivery £9 mixed case except for special offers.
Minimum order I mixed case.
M T
Small, quality-minded mail order outfit that pioneered many successful names here. It's run by a New Zealander, oddly enough. Look for Redwood Valley, Vidal, Te Motu, St Nesbit, Ata Rangi, Aotea, Stonyridge and others. There are lovely pudding wines in half-bottles, and there's even Chanel Chardonnay from Mission, for the designer freak with everything.

FORTH WINES LTD (FOR)

Crawford Place, Milnathort, Kinross-shire
KY13 7XF, (01577) 862513, fax (01577) 865296
Hours Mon–Fri 9–5.30.
Credit Cards AC V.
Delivery Free 3 or more cases.
Minimum Order I case.
M T
There's a strong, traditional red Bordeaux list here, plus lots of interesting country wines from France and some good Rhônes. South Africa also looks very appealing, and there are interesting, unusual wines from lots of places: Austrian red, for example, or Syrah from Washington State. If these don't tempt you there are oodles of whiskies, too, surprise surprise.

FULLER'S (FUL)

Griffin Brewery, Chiswick Lane South, Chiswick W4 2QB, 0181-996 2000, fax 0181-996 2087
Hours Mon–Sat 10–10, Sun 11–10.
Credit Cards AC S V.
Discounts I bottle free with every case and 10% on selected unmixed cases.
Delivery Free locally.
G T
An imaginative list of affordable wines, of which Bordeaux, Burgundy, the Rhône, Germany, Australia (Lindemans Botrytis-affected Semillon in half-bottles) look particularly appealing. But it's not all

everyday stuff, by any means. There are leading producers here, and they're not the obvious ones. Rhônes, for example, from Albert Belle and Jean-Luc Colombo.

GALLERY WINES (GAL)

Gomshall Cellars, The Gallery, Gomshall, Surrey GU5 9LB, (01483) 203795, fax (01483) 203282
Hours Mon–Sat 10–6.
Credit cards AC S V.
Discounts Wine Club members get 5% on all purchases and 10% on monthly offers.
Delivery Free 2 or more cases within local area, otherwise £7.50 for I case, £3.50 each additional case.
Minimum order I bottle.
C G M T
Not a very long list, but an interesting one. Bordeaux and the Loire look particularly good, and the South African and Australian sections have the virtue of not being the same as everybody else's. Some Burgundies are also very good, though I'm not sure that I share their view of Louis Latour's wines.

GAUNTLEYS (GAU)

4 High St, Exchange Arcade, Nottingham NG1 2ET, (01159) 417973, fax (01159) 509519
Hours Mon–Sat 9–5.30.
Credit cards AC S V.
Delivery Free within Nottingham area, otherwise £6.50 per case + VAT.
Minimum order I case.
C EP (not Bordeaux) **G M T**
A distinctly classy list of all the wines you'd most like to have: excellent French, Italian, Spanish, Australian, New Zealand and South African, plus port and sherry. There are also lots of French country wines, with the likes of Domaine l'Hortus in Coteaux du Languedoc and Domaine de la Rectorie from Collioure looking interesting.

GELSTON CASTLE FINE WINES (GE)

Castle Douglas, Scotland DG7 1QE, (01556) 503012, fax (01556) 504183; James King, 45 Warwick Square, London SW1V 2AJ, 0171-821 6841, fax 0171-821 6350

"BETTER BUY BULGARIAN"

It is still the wisest decision for the discerning wine buyer. The person seeking quality, choice and, above all, outstanding value.

Since Bulgarian Vintners launched Bulgarian wines in the UK back in 1980, sales have risen constantly, with millions enjoying our wines.

However, the emphasis is, as always, on quality – but still at highly affordable prices. During 1996 we are further expanding our range of distinctive white wines and our select range of top quality reds.

As the leading supplier of the best from Bulgaria's vineyards, we at Bulgarian Vintners know that "better buy Bulgarian" is a thought shared by more and more appreciative wine purchasers.

The Bulgarian Vintners

Hours Mon–Fri 9–6.
Credit Cards V.
Delivery Free within 25 miles of Castle
Douglas I case or more, £7 rest of mainland UK,
free for orders over £150.
Minimum order None, but mixed cases carry
a surcharge of £3 per case.

C EP G M T

*A real enthusiast's list, not terribly wide-ranging but
extremely discriminating. France is a major strength,
with lovely country wines – not necessarily the
cheapest you could buy, but then that's not the
point of Gelston Castle. There's Château Fabas, for
example, Mas Jullien and Domaine Tempier.
Beaujolais is so unfashionable at this merchant that
Chenas is under 'Odd backwaters of France'. Even
more unfashionable Germany is present in force,
and each wine has a useful indication of sweetness
or dryness. The New World wines are classy, but
you can tell their hearts are in France and Germany.*

GOEDHUIS & CO (GOE)

6 Rudolf Place, Miles Street, London SW8 IRP,
0171-793 7900, fax 0171-793 7170
Hours Mon–Fri 9–6.30.
Credit Cards AC V.
Delivery Free 3 or more cases in London, 5 or
more cases UK mainland.
Minimum order I case.

C EP G M T

*An unashamedly traditional merchant. They think
that Pauillac is more exciting than Coonawarra, and
they're not afraid to say so; not surprisingly, there's
a lot of serious Bordeaux and Burgundy here.
There's a sprinkling of wines from elsewhere, but*

*there's not much that's not French. But if that gives
the impression of a merchant bunging in token
wines, think again: there's Provence rosé from
Château St-Baillon, California wine from Bernardus,
and Tokaji from the revelatory Royal Tokaji Wine Co.*

HALVES (HAL)

Wood Yard, off Corve St, Ludlow, Shropshire
SY8 2PX, (01584) 877866, fax (01584)
877677
Hours Mail order only: Mon–Fri 9–6.
Credit cards AC AE S V.
Discounts Frequent mixed case offers.
Delivery Free to mainland UK,
£10 per case for off-shore islands and Northern
Ireland.
Minimum order I mixed case of 24 half-
bottles.

C EP M T

*Next time some restaurateur or merchant tells you
you can't have a half-bottle because the producers
won't bottle in halves, hand them a copy of this
price list – better still, keep it for yourself and order
from it. There's a bigger range here than many
merchants have of full bottles, and as well as
covering the wines you might guess would be easily
available in halves, like fino sherry or Champagne,
there is also oloroso, Chinon, Alsace Pinot Noir,
Meursault Charmes, Cahors, Condrieu, Montes
Cabernet Sauvignon from Chile, Rust-en-Vrede
Cabernet Sauvignon from South Africa and much,
much more. There are even half-bottle-sized
Screwpulls. And don't forget that a mixed case here
means you can have 24 different wines if you like –
a bit like letting a child loose in a sweet shop.*

ROGER HARRIS WINES (HAW)

Loke Farm, Weston Longville, Norfolk NR9
5LG, (01603) 880171/2, fax (01603) 880291
Hours Mon–Fri 9–5.
Credit cards AC AE V.
Delivery Free UK mainland, orders over £150.
Minimum order I mixed case.
M T
*'I have such an enduring love of Beaujolais that I
would from preference drink nothing else', says
Roger Harris. If your experience to date has been
such as to make you wonder why anybody would
ever buy a second bottle of the stuff, this is the
place to come. Roger Harris is only interested in the
more serious side of Beaujolais, and he's honest
about the problems the region is facing (though not
necessarily facing up to). He's picked wines from all
the cru villages – and they are seldom the best
known names – and to them he's added some
Pouilly, Coteaux du Lyonnais, vins de pays and
Champagne. There's also Fine de Gamay and Marc
de Gamay. And I bet you've never tasted that
before.*

JOHN HARVEY & SONS (HA)

12 Denmark St, Bristol BS1 5DQ, (01179)
275009, fax (01179) 275001
Hours Mon–Fri 9.30–6, Sat 9.30–1.
Credit cards AC AE DC S V.
Delivery Free 4 cases or more UK mainland,
no mixed cases.
C EP G M T
*You expect a classic list of fine wines from Harveys,
and that's what you get. In many regions and
countries there is a slightly unfashionable bias
towards négociants rather than growers themselves,
and personally I can't see the attraction of Louis
Latour red Burgundies. But then there's Gabriel
Meffre from the Rhône, and Chablis from J Moreau.
It's just that I get the feeling they're selling to a
clientele that likes to buy the names it's always
bought. And as long as they're happy with that,
then that's fine.*

HAYNES HANSON & CLARK (HAH)

Sheep St, Stow-on-the-Wold, Glos GL54 1AA,
(01451) 870808, fax (01451) 870508;
25 Eccleston St, London SW1 9NP, 0171-259
0102, fax 0171-259 0103
Hours Sheep St: Mon–Sat 9–6.
Eccleston St: Mon–Fri 9–7, Sat 10–6;
Credit cards AC S V.
Discounts 10% unsplit case.
Delivery Free central London and Glos,
elsewhere free for 5 or more cases.
EP G M T
*A first-class list built on tremendous knowledge and
experience, coupled with an awful lot of legwork.
Haynes Hanson & Clark is most famous for its
Burgundies, and for years it has been one of the
leading Burgundy merchants in the country. But the
list is strong in most other parts of France, as well –
the Rhône, in particular, looks excellent, and you
can also find the delicious wines of Christian Koehly
from Alsace here. HH&C's favoured Champagne,
Pierre Vaudon, is also very good value. The New
World section of the list is relatively short
(compared to all those Burgundies), but it's
interesting, nevertheless.*

DOUGLAS HENN-MACRAE (HE)

81 Mackenders Lane, Eccles, Aylesford, Kent
ME20 7JA, (01622) 710952, fax (01622) 791203
Hours Mail order & tel enquiries only, Mon–Sat
to 10pm.
Delivery Free UK mainland 10 cases, otherwise
£8 plus vat per order.
Minimum order 1 case.
M T
*This list looks less weird than it used to. From
Germany there are lots of good Rhines and Mosels,
plus oddities like pink Eiswein.*

HICKS & DON (HIC)

(Head office) Blandford St Mary, Dorset DT11
9LS, (01258) 456040, fax (01258) 450147;
Park House, Elmham, Dereham, Norfolk NR20
5JY, (01362) 668571/2, fax (01362) 668573;
The Old Bakehouse, Alfred St, Westbury,
Wiltshire BA13 3DY, (01373) 864723, fax
(01373) 858250
Hours Mon–Fri 9–5.
Credit cards AC S V.
Discounts Negotiable.
Delivery 1–2 cases £3 per case, 3 or more
cases free UK mainland.
Minimum order 1 mixed case.
C EP G M T
*A predominantly French list, at its most adventurous
perhaps in the Loire and (outside France) in New
Zealand. Hicks & Don is one of the most reliable
sources of Bordeaux en primeur; Burgundy is also
good, and there is sherry from the excellent
Sanlúcar house of Barbadillo. South Africa also looks
interesting. And if, under 'English wine', you see
something called Elmham Park, and you see that
the producer is one R S Don, you're right – Robin
Don is a poacher-turned-gamekeeper.*

HIGH BRECK VINTNERS (HIG)

Bentworth House, Bentworth, Nr Alton, Hants
GU34 5RB, (01420) 562218, fax (01420) 563827
Hours Mon–Fri 9.30–5.30, or by arrangement.
Delivery (south-east) £6 for 1 case, £4 for 2, 3
free; (rest of England) £9 for 1, £6 for 2, £4 for
3, 4 or more free.

Minimum order 1 mixed case.
E P G M T
*A very interesting list, stocked mainly with French
wines. High Breck ship a lot of these wines
themselves, from producers that you will often find
nowhere else. Take a particular look at Alsace and
the Loire; and the clarets cover the area efficiently.
There are the unbelievably good sherries from
Valdespino, but should you get fed up with wine
there is Alsace eau-de-vie and some old and rare
calvados.*

J E HOGG (HOG)

61 Cumberland St, Edinburgh EH3 6RA, 0131-
556 4025
Hours Mon–Tue, Thu–Fri 9–1 & 2.30–6; Wed,
Sat 9–1.
Credit cards S.
Delivery Free 12 or more bottles within
Edinburgh and East Lothian.
G T
*Now, here's a merchant who isn't led by fashion –
or has customers who can think for themselves, and
indeed drink for themselves, too. There are lots of
very good Alsace wines, some with plenty of bottle
age (does this suggest that they don't get drunk all
that fast after all? I hope not). There are also lots of
very good, and equally unfashionable, German
wines. If you stuck to just these two sections of the
list you could keep yourself in fine wine for a long
time. But don't miss the southern French selection,
nor the South Africans nor, in case you thought
things were getting just too trendy, the marvellous
sherries.*

J C KARN & SON LTD (KA)

7 Lansdown Place, Cheltenham, Glos GL50
2HU, (01242) 513265/250380
Hours Mon–Fri 9.30–6, Sat 9.30–1.30.
Credit cards AC V.
Discounts 5–10% per case.
Delivery Free in Gloucestershire.
G M T
*A decent, reliable list, of which the Loire is a
highlight. South Africa is also quite strong, with a
couple of Gewürztraminers among the whites.
There's a fair range of Riojas as well.*

LAY & WHEELER (LAY)

(Head office & shop) The Wine Market,
Gosbecks Road, Colchester CO2 9JT, (01206)
764446, fax (01206) 560002;
Hours Mon–Sat 9–7, Sun 10–4.
Credit cards AC AE S V.
Discounts 5% 5 or more mixed cases.
Delivery Free over £150.
C EP G M T
*Another fat, classy list. How to single out any area?
Well, the south of France looks good, Burgundy
shows thoughtful buying, and Chablis is from Daniel
Defaix, among others. There is also Aubert de
Villiane's Aligoté. Australia is brilliant, showing the
sort of variety the country is producing these days.
Germany is excellent, and Italy is outstanding.*

LAYTONS (LAYT)

20 Midland Road, London NW1 2AD, 0171-388
4567, fax 0171 383 7419;
50–52 Elizabeth Street, London SW1W 9PB,
0171-730 8108, fax 0171-730 9284;

21 Motcomb Street, London SW1X8LB, 0171-
235 3723, fax 0171-235 2062
Hours Mon–Sat 9–7.
Credit cards AC AE S V.
Delivery Free for orders of £130 ex-VAT,
otherwise £8.50 + VAT. Scotland and Cornwall:
free for orders of £250 ex-VAT, otherwise £20
+ VAT.
C EP G M T
*A long-established merchant with traditional
strengths in France, particularly Bordeaux, Burgundy
and the Rhône. Curiously, much of the list has the
air of having been translated into English by a
French waiter – 'Without contradiction we can
assure customers that Vino Cuore is a hearty wine'.
Or 'The tannins at the finish will enable reasonable
longevity to unravel'. That sort of thing. But never
mind: the wines are very good, and the house
Champagne is some of the best value around.*

LEA & SANDEMAN (LEA)

301 Fulham Road, London SW10 9QH, 0171-376
4767, fax 0171-351 0275;

211 Kensington Church Street, London W8 7LX, 0171-221 1982, fax 0171-221 1985
51 Barnes High Street, London SW13 9LN, 0181-878 8643, fax 0181-878 6522
Hours Mon–Fri 9–8.30, Sat 10–8.30.
Credit Cards AC AE S V.
Discounts 5–15% min 1 case.
Delivery Free to UK mainland south of Perth on orders over £150.
Minimum order None.
C G M T EP
Lea & Sandeman has taken over what was the Barnes Wine Shop, which explains the expansion to sunny SW13. France is the main focus, with very good Burgundies, Alsace and Languedoc. Italy is also excellent, and from Spain there is a full range of Valdespino sherries. The New World sections are short but good, and there are oddities like Polish rowan vodka (presumably not an oddity at all if you're Polish) and bison grass vodka. There are also (picnickers please take note) picnic glasses with spikes on them so you can push them into the ground. Clever, that.

MAJESTIC (MAJ)

(Head office) Odhams Trading Estate, St Albans Road, Watford, Herts WD2 5RE (01923) 816999, fax (01923) 819105
Hours Mon–Sat 10–8, Sun 10–6 (some stores may vary).
Credit cards AC AE DC S V.
Delivery Free locally.
Minimum order 1 mixed case.
G M T
Majestic goes in phases. It's rather good now, but you have to choose carefully: because it buys special parcels the list can change, and some things may be very high quality, while other things are there (I presume) because they are inexpensive. But the Rhône is strong, as is Germany, the USA, Champagne, much of Italy…actually, there's a lot here I'd be very happy to drink.

MARKS & SPENCER (MAR)

(Head office) Michael House, Baker Street, London W1A 1FDN, 0171-935 442; 290 licensed stores all over the country

Hours Variable.
Discounts 12 bottles for the price of 11.
M
Most things here are own-label, of course, but it does sell producers you will also find elsewhere. Everything is sound, quite a lot is very tasty, and some of the clarets (you won't find all these in your local store, unless you happen to live in somewhere like Marble Arch) are very high quality indeed. But there's a tendency to concentrate on commercial flavours, with nothing featured that is too quirky or out-of-the-way. 'Safe' is the word that immediately springs to mind.

MORENO WINES (MOR)

11 Marylands Road, London W9 2DU, 0171-286 0678, fax 0171-286 0513; 2 Norfolk Place, London W2 1QN, 0171-706 3055
Hours Marylands Road: Mon–Wed 12–10, Thurs–Sat 10–10.30, Sun 12–3; Norfolk Place: Mon–Sat 10–7.
Credit cards AC AE S V.
Discounts 5% mixed case.
Delivery Free locally.
G M T
Spanish specialist: there's Toro, Rueda, Somontano, Valencia and others, treats like Vega Sicilia, Bodegas Riojanas and CVNE, plus of course Spanish brandy.

MORRIS & VERDIN (MV)

10 The Leathermarket, Weston Street, London SE1 3ER, 0171-357 8866, fax 0171-357 8877
Hours Mon–Fri 8–6; closed bank hols.
Discounts 5 or more cases.
Delivery Free central London, elsewhere 5 or more cases.
Minimum order 1 mixed case.
C EP G M T
Excellent, really imaginative list, majoring on Burgundy: there are top names like Comte Lafon, Comte Armand, Roumier and many, many others. Since everything is good, it's almost invidious to pick anything out, but here goes. There's Domaine Ostertag from Alsace, with very good Sylvaner Vieilles Vignes, and barrique-aged Pinot Gris that

isn't allowed the Grand Cru designation because it is atypical. From California there is Au Bon Climat, Ca' del Solo, Il Podere dell'Olivos, Bonny Doon, Qupé and others. And now that Morris & Verdin is the agent for Bodegas Vega Sicilia in Spain, there's that as well. No, it's not cheap. About £50 a bottle and upwards, in fact.

THE NADDER WINE CO LTD (NA)

Hussars House, 2 Netherhampton Road, Harnham, Salisbury, Wiltshire SP2 8HE, (01722) 325418, fax (01722) 421617
Hours Mon–Fri 9–6, Sat 9–1.
Credit cards AC AE S V.
Discounts 5% on orders £100–£249, 7.5% on £250–£499, 10% on £500 plus.
Delivery Free Salisbury area & Central London on orders over £50; rest of UK mainland at carrier's cost. Ten cases or over free.
Minimum order 1 case.
G M T
There has always been plenty of decent drinking to be had at Nadder Wines, but they don't appear overmuch in the Price Guides this year (don't appear at all, in fact) because they are engaged in a major rethink of their list and nothing was finalised in time to give us details. However, by the time this Guide appears things should be settled and they'll have lots of new wines in stock once again. And that's good news for the folks of Salisbury.

NEW LONDON WINE (NEW)

1E Broughton Street, London SW18 3QJ, 0171-622 3000, Freefone order line (0800) 581266
Hours Mon–Fri 9–6.
Credit cards AC AE S V.
Delivery Free in central London, quotes available for national delivery.
Minimum order 1 case.
EP G M T
Choose carefully when picking from this list: there are some nice wines, but little to make one sit up and really take notice. Prices are quite good, though French wines look less competitive than the rest, since the strong franc has hit everybody, including this company.

LE NEZ ROUGE (NEZ)

12 Brewery Rd, London N7 9NH, 0171-609 4711;
Unit 456, St 7, Thorpe Arch Trading Estate, Wetherby, Yorkshire LS23 7BT, (01937) 844711
Hours Mon–Fri 9–5.30, (Sat 10–2 for occasional tasting); closed bank holiday weekends.
Credit cards AC V.
Discounts £3.50 per case collected. Other quantity discounts as well.
Delivery Included in price for mainland UK.
Minimum order 1 mixed case.
C EP G M T
A very strong list that looks mostly towards France: it is excellent in most areas, and Burgundy lovers will think they've gone to heaven. It has expanded its New World section, with Beringer from California, Bodega Norton from Argentina and Buitenverwachting from South Africa, and with all the pride of a new parent it seems keen to emphasize these and play down its traditional strengths. I can't think why, though – its New World list is fine and very welcome, but its French stuff is terrific.

JAMES NICHOLSON (NI)

27A Killyeagh St, Crossgar, Co. Down, Northern Ireland BT30 9DG, (01396) 830091, fax (01396) 830028
Hours Mon–Sat 10–7.
Credit cards AC AE S V.
Discounts 7–10% mixed case.
Delivery Free Northern Ireland for orders of £50 or 1 case, otherwise at cost.
C EP G M T
A comprehensive list of good names. Rhônes are the likes of Guigal, Beaucastel, Rostaing, Jaboulet and Colombo; Californians feature Kistler, Laurel Glen, Ridge, Newton and Saintsbury and Bordeaux has good middle-range names. There's also Drouhin's Oregon Pinot Noir. French country wines look good, as do clarets, and Germany and Italy are particularly strong. There are old vintages of Chateau Musar, Casablanca wines from Chile and Norton Bodegas from Argentina. All in all, a list that's looking better than ever this year.

THE NOBODY INN (NO)

Doddiscombsleigh, Nr Exeter, Devon EX6 7PS,
(01647) 252394, fax (01647) 252978
Hours Mon–Sat 12–2.30 & 6–11, Sun 12–3 &
7–10.30; or by appointment.
Credit Cards AC AE S V.
Discounts 5% per case.
Delivery Up to 2 cases £7.90; each additional
case £3.90.
G M T
*There's what's probably one of the best selections of
English wines around on this list, and it doesn't stop
there. The Nobody Inn's passion for sweet wines
pops up time and time again: there's a botrytis-
affected Mâcon-Clessé, sweet Pacherenc de Vic-Bihl,
sweet Jurançon, Muscats from Samos, the south of
France and Spain and of course oodles from
Sauternes, the Loire, Germany, Australia, California –
and that's before you get on to the dry whites and
the reds. You probably get the picture. And if you
want something to eat with it all, there is a wide
selection of British cheeses which now outnumber the
French varieties.*

ODDBINS (OD)

(Head office) 31–33 Weir Road, London SW19
8UG, 0181-944 4400; 214 shops.
Hours Generally Mon–Sat 10–10, Sun 10–8 in
England & Wales, 12.30–8 Scotland.
Credit cards AC AE S V.
Discounts 5% split case wine; 10% split case
tasting wines on day of tasting. 7 bottles of
Champagne and sparkling wine for the price of 6
(if £5.99 or above).
Delivery Available locally most shops.
*Still very, very good, and now there are six Fine
Wine shops as well. The New World is very strong
and there's good Alsace, German, Rhône, Bordeaux,
Spain, Italy… I could go on. The staff have a great
reputation for knowing the wines they're selling and
it's one of the most pleasant places to chew the cud.*

THOS. PEATLING (PE)

(Head office) Westgate House, Bury St
Edmunds, Suffolk IP33 1QS, (01284) 714466, fax
(01284) 705795

Hours Variable.
Credit cards AC AE S V.
Discounts 5% mixed case.
Delivery Free UK mainland 2 or more cases.
C EP G M T

Peatlings have always been known for their clarets, and the claret list is indeed strong here. But don't expect a mere recitation of those familiar top names: these are wines chosen on merit, not prestige, and you'll find lots of very good drinking for under a tenner. Burgundy is good, too: you'll find less in the selection under a tenner, but then that's the nature of the beast. The Rhône, Loire and Germany also look good, although the list has an irritating tendency to omit the producer's name. Italy, Spain, Australia and New Zealand also look interesting.

PENISTONE COURT WINE CELLARS (PEN)

The Railway Station, Penistone, Sheffield, South Yorkshire S30 6HG, (01226) 766037, fax (01226) 767310
Hours Mon–Fri 9–6, Sat 10–3.
Delivery Free locally, rest of UK mainland charged at cost 1 case or more.
G M

The producers you'll find in Penistone Court's list are on the whole sound but predictable (and not necessarily the worse for that). Austria has quite a wide range featured, and from the USA there are the excellent Rieslings of Renaissance as well as Sonoma-Cutrer Chardonnays, and Opus One at the seriously pricy end. There's a good range of Champagne, including the delicious Henriot and Dom Ruinart.

CHRISTOPHER PIPER WINES (PIP)

1 Silver St, Ottery St Mary, Devon EX11 1DB, (01404) 814139, fax (01404) 812100
Hours Mon–Sat 9–6.
Credit cards AC S V.
Discounts 5% mixed case, 10% 3 or more cases.
Delivery Free in south-west England for 4 cases, elsewhere free for 6 cases.
Minimum order 1 mixed case.
C EP G M T

Particularly strong in cru bourgeois and petit château clarets. Burgundy, the Loire and the Rhône are good, as is Italy. The New World has expanded, but the real strengths are still in Europe – there is a handful of lovely Austrians. A good, well-thought-out list with plenty of depth.

TERRY PLATT (PLA)

Ferndale Road, Llandudno Junction, Gwynedd LL31 9NT, (01492) 592971, fax (01492) 592196; World of Wine, 29 Mostyn Ave, Craig Y Don, (01492) 872997
Hours Ferndale Rd: Mon–Fri 8.30–5.30; Mostyn Ave: Mon–Sat 10–8, Sun 12–5.
Credit cards AC S V.
Delivery Free locally, or in mainland UK with minimum order of 3 cases.
Minimum order 1 mixed case.
G M T

The New World is looking rather sparky here, with Montes from Chile, Cetto from Mexico, Rockford from Australia and many others. Bordeaux looks good, and good value, as do the Loire, Rhône, Alsace and Midi. There are some nice Spanish wines, and there are Welsh wines, too – an even greater rarity on merchants' lists than English wines. Ports look attractive as well: there's the delicious Quinta do Ervamoira tawny and the equally delicious Quinta de Vargellas.

PORTLAND WINE CO (POR)

16 North Parade, off Norris Road, Sale, Cheshire M33 3JS, (0161) 962 8752, fax (0161) 905 1291; 152a Ashley Road, Hale WA15 9SA, (0161) 928 0357;

82 Chester Road, Macclesfield SK11 8DL,
(01625) 616147
Hours Mon–Sat 10–10, Sun 12–3 & 7–9.30.
Credit cards AC AE S V.
Discounts 10% off 1 mixed case, 5% off half a
mixed case.
Delivery Free locally.
G M T
*A long list of good, soundly chosen wines from just
about everywhere. Germany is weak, but in most
other countries there is very good drinking.
Bordeaux looks reliable, as does Burgundy, and
there are some nice Rhônes. The Loire includes
Moulin Touchais 1959, 1969 and 1976, as well as
good Savennières. Italians look very good, as do
California and Chile. And from the Australian range
there's my old favourite, Charles Melton Sparkling
Shiraz.*

QUELLYN ROBERTS (QUE)

15 Watergate Street, Chester CH1 2LB,
(01244) 310455, fax (01244) 346704
Hours Mon–Sat 8.45–5.45.
Credit cards AC AE S V.
Discounts 5% on a mixed case.
Delivery Free 2 cases or more, Chester and
surrounding districts.
G M T
*An interesting list, not enormously long, but with
some goodies. There's Morris' Liqueur Muscat from
Australia and old vintages of Chateau Musar; good
South Africans and Loires, and some nice New
Zealand wines. Germany could do with an upgrade,
but probably nobody would buy them.*

RAEBURN FINE WINES (RAE)

23 Comely Bank Rd, Edinburgh EH4 1DS, tel &
fax 0131-332 5166
Hours Mon–Sat 9–6, Sun 12.30–5.
Credit cards AC S V.
Discounts 5% unsplit case, 2.5% mixed.
Delivery Price negotiable, all areas.
EP G M T
*The Scots have always liked their claret, and this is
one of the places they come to buy it. Most of this
first-class list is French – Burgundies are from
producers of the quality of Michel Lafarge, Méo-*

*Camuzet and Jean-Marc Boillot, there are top
Rhônes and lovely wines from Alsace, and goodies
from south-west France like Gilbert Alquier's
Faugères, which is undoubtedly the best of the
region. And I haven't even mentioned the clarets,
but yes, they're excellent, too. Look out also for
Quintarelli's Recioto di Valpolicella and excellent
Californians.*

REID WINES (1992) LTD (REI)

The Mill, Marsh Lane, Hallatrow, Nr Bristol
BS18 5EB, (01761) 452645, fax (01761) 453642
Hours Mon–Fri 10.30–5.30.
Credit cards AC V (3% charge).
Delivery Free within 25 miles of Hallatrow
(Bristol), and in central London.
C G M T
*'A hard vintage, which is difficult to enjoy', say Reid
Wines of the 1937 clarets, before proceeding to
offer two. 'Brane Cantenac [1970] is one of the
worst wines we have ever tasted', they say; a snip,
no doubt, at £24.50. And 'Probably appalling, but
certainly cheap'. Yes, of course I'm quoting
selectively: how else should one quote? Most of the
wines sold by Reid are liked by them very much
indeed (viz. 'Yummo scrummo'). The net effect is to
make you want to rush over to Hallatrow and
become best friends with them. And you could do a
great deal worse: this is a first-class list. A lot of the
wines are only available in small quantities – indeed
there may only be a single bottle to be had – so it
changes rapidly. But clarets may go back to 1918
and Burgundies back to the 1930s; the Rhône back
to the '60s, and the Loire back to the '20s – you
get the picture. But this is far more than a cabinet
of curiosities, and Italy and Australia look
fascinating as well. Spirits-wise there is vintage
Armagnac, vintage and early-landed Cognac, Marc
Egrappé Hermitage from Paul Jaboulet Aîné and
Wooton Eau de Vie from Somerset. Oh, and a
single bottle of Cognac that was 'allegedly hidden in
a coalcellar during the last war'. Beat that.*

LA RESERVE (RES)

56 Walton St, London SW3 1RB, 0171-589
2020, fax 0171-581 0250
Hours Mon–Fri 9.30–9, Sat 9.30–6.

Credit Cards AC AE S V.
Discounts 5% per case except accounts.
Delivery Free 1 case or more Central London and orders over £200 UK mainland. Otherwise £7.50.
C EP G T
'We do not ship bland, commercial wines', say La Reserve proudly, and the result is a list that is by no means the cheapest around. But it is very, very good. Burgundy looks particularly attractive, with domaines of the standing of Etienne Sauzet and Patrick Javillier (and Patrick Bize's Bourgogne Blanc Cuvée Pinot Beurot – amaze your friends). The Loire, Alsace, Rhône, California and Australia all look tempting. There's also a separate Old and Rare list for anyone seeking – well, the old and the rare. La Reserve has three sister shops, all in London: The Heath Street Wine Company in Hampstead, Le Picoleur in W2 and Le Sac à Vin in SW6.

HOWARD RIPLEY (RIP)

35 Eversley Crescent, London N21 1EL, tel & fax 0181-360 8904
Hours Mon–Fri 9–10, Sat 9–1.
Delivery London free 5 cases or more, otherwise £8.50 plus vat, elsewhere at cost.
Minimum Order 1 mixed case.
EP G M T
A specialist Burgundy operation with an outstanding range of top names and vineyards. Look for names like Domaine de l'Arlot, Ramonet, Leroy, Michelot, Hudelot-Noëllat, Roumier, Dujac, Rousseau, Lafarge…

ROBERSON (ROB)

348 Kensington High St, London W14 8NS, 0171-371 2121, fax 0171-371 4010
Hours Mon–Sat 10–8.
Credit cards AC AE DC S V.
Delivery Free locally 1 case or more.
G M T
There's a terrific, if expensive, selection here – claret back to 1924, and depth and breadth in most other areas, too. Look particularly at Burgundy, the Rhône and the Loire – and at Italy, which looks stronger than ever. Europe is the main focus here, but South Africa, Australia and California are all well chosen. New Zealand is, well, short. Sherries and ports are very good, and there are eaux de vie from just about anything that grows, including eglantine and prunelle sauvage.

SAFEWAY (SAF)

(Head office) 6 Millington Road, Hayes, Middlesex UB3 4AY, 0181-848 8744, fax 0181-573 1865
Hours Mon–Sat 8–8 (Fri till 9), Sun 10–4 (selected stores).
Credit cards AC S V.
Discounts 5–10% on mixed cases.
G
There are vegetarian, organic and kosher wines here and some reasonable Burgundies. Spain and Portugal are interesting and they make quite a feature of Eastern Europe. There's a patriotically good range of English wines. The USA is distinctly unthrilling, yet South Africa's quite good. Australia looks standard.

SAINSBURY (SAI)

(Head office) Stamford House, Stamford St, London SE1 9LL, 0171-921 6000
Hours Variable, many open late.
Credit cards AC AE S V.
T M
This is still the country's largest wine retailer. The best areas are Bordeaux, Burgundy and the south of France, and the own-label Champagne is very good, and good value. As always with supermarkets, you have to go to a major branch to get the full range.

SATCHELLS (SAT)

North St, Burnham Market, Norfolk PE31 8HG, tel & fax (01328) 738 272
Hours Mon, Tues, Thurs, Fri 9.30–1 & 2–6; Wed 9.30–1; Sat 9.30–7.
Credit Cards AC S V.
Discounts 5% cases, larger orders negotiable.
Delivery Free locally, at cost nationally.
G M T

An attractive list of good appellations, but not necessarily featuring leading names. This may not be to its advantage in Burgundy, but the Portugal selection is mostly from Sogrape, and you can't go too far wrong with that. There are some nice Spanish wines, and pudding wines are interesting and varied. Look, in particular, for Vin de Paille from the Jura and Château Septy 1990 from Monbazillac.

SECKFORD WINES (SEC)

2 Betts Ave, Martlesham Heath, Ipswich, Suffolk IP5 7RH, (01473) 626681, fax (01473) 626004
Hours Tue–Sat 10–6.
Credit cards AC S V.
Delivery Free locally.
Minimum order 1 mixed case.
G M T
A well-balanced, well-chosen list from which one could happily stock quite a large cellar. Most things look interesting, but particularly those from the Rhône, the red Burgundies and French country wines. In particular look for Gilbert Alquier's marvellous Faugères, Henri Maire's Bonchalaz from the Jura and some nice rosés. Italy also looks strong, with Aldo Conterno, Vajra and Ascheri Giacomo all represented.

SOMERFIELD/GATEWAY (SO)

(Head office) Somerfield House, Hawkfield Business Park, Whitchurch Lane, Bristol BS14 0TJ, (0117) 359359
Hours Mon–Sat 9–8, variable late opening Friday all stores.
Credit cards AC S V.
T
Quality seems to be improving here, particularly if you want something tasty from the south of France. Names to look for here include Jacques Lurton's Terret, Vin de Pays d'Oc, Château de Caraguilhes from Corbières and wines from Val d'Orbieu and Jeanjean. There are also some Alsace wines from the Turckheim co-op. Otherwise there is some nice Spanish and Portuguese stuff and some reliable numbers like Crémant de Bourgogne and Chablis from la Chablisienne.

SOMMELIER WINE CO (SOM)

23 St George's Esplanade, St Peter Port, Guernsey, Channel Islands, GY1 2BG (01481) 721677, fax (01481) 716818
Hours Mon–Thu 10–5.30, Fri 10–6, Sat 9–5.30; answerphone out of hours.
Credit cards AC S V.
Discounts 5% 12 or more bottles.
Delivery Free 1 unmixed case.
G M (locally) **T**
At Sommelier Wine you can find the delicious Chateau Megyer Furmint and Tokaji from Hungary, as well as Pieropan's Recioto di Soave from Italy (perfect for bread-and-butter pud) and a very good selection of rosés. There are excellent and characterful wines at all price levels, but I'd go for my favourite, Charlie Melton's Sparkling Shiraz (from Australia, where else?), Guigal's Côtes du Rhône rosé and Allegrini's Amarone. And that's just for starters.

SUMMERLEE WINES (SUM)

Summerlee Rd, Finedon, Northhampton NN9 5LL, tel & fax (01933) 682221;
(London office) Freddy Price, 48 Castlebar Rd, London W5 2DD, 0181-997 7889, fax 0181-991 5178
Hours Mon–Fri 9.15–12.30 pm; answerphone out of hours.
Delivery Free England & Wales 5 or more cases, or Northants, Oxford, Cambridge & London 2 or more cases; otherwise £6.50 per consignment 1–4 cases.
EP G M
A fairly short but nevertheless very knowledgeable list consisting of excellent clarets and Alsace wines, plus good sherry, port, Loire, Burgundy, Faugères from Gilberg Alquier, wines from the New World and the Jura wines of Château d'Arlay. Freddy Price takes the trouble to seek out wines himself, and it shows in this selection. But it is the German wines that are the real stars of this show here. Summerlee themselves ship over wines from Max Ferd. Richter, Schloss Saarstein, Karthauserhof, Balthasar Ress, Paul Anheuser, Pfeffingen and Juliusspital, and those are some of the very best names in all Germany.

SUNDAY TIMES WINE CLUB (SUN)

New Aquitaine House, Paddock Road, Reading, Berks RG4 5JY, (0118) 9481713, fax (0118) 9461953

Hours Mail order, 24-hr answerphone.
Credit cards AC AE DC S V.
Discounts On special offers.
Delivery £3.99 per order.
C EP M T

The associate mail order company of Bordeaux Direct. The membership fee is £10 per annum. The club also runs tours and tastings and an annual festival in London, and does monthly promotions to its members.

T & W WINES (TW)

51 King St, Thetford, Norfolk IP24 2AU, (01842) 765646

Hours Mon–Fri 9.30–5.30, Sat 9.30–1.00.
Credit cards AC AE DC V.
Delivery Free UK mainland 2 or more cases.
C EP G M

An extraordinary selection of fine, old and rare wines – Burgundies (which are a speciality) and clarets dating back to 1949, and half-bottles of all sorts back to 1944. Terrific Rhônes, Australians, Californians and most other things as well, including lots of anniversary years. Oddities include André Clouet's Bouzy Rouge and Château la Borderie's Muscadelle, from Bergerac. They also stock Château Gilette from Sauternes, some sweet white Burgundy and Willi Opitz's stunning Austrian wines.

TANNERS (TAN)

26 Wyle Cop, Shrewsbury, Shropshire SY1 1XD, (01743) 232400, fax (01743) 344401;
4 St Peter's Square, Hereford HR1 2PJ (01432) 272044, fax (01432) 263316;
36 High Street, Bridgnorth WC16 4DB, (01746) 763148;
The Old Brewery, Brook St, Welshpool SY21 7LF, (01938) 552542, fax (01938) 556565

Hours Mon–Sat 9–6.
Credit cards AC AE S V.
Discounts 5% 1 mixed case (cash & collection);

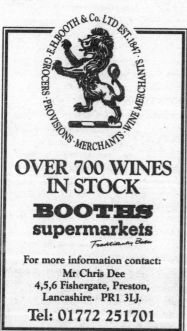

2.5% mixed case, 5% for 5, 7.5% for 10 cases (mail order).
Delivery Free 1 mixed case or more locally, or nationally over £75, otherwise £6.
C EP G M T
There's a terrific selection from the south of France at Tanners. It's a country wine merchant of the best sort: traditional and knowledgeable, but adventurous in its tastes and never, ever stuffy. So as well as the best of the classic regions of France, look for top Italians, deeply unfashionable Germans, beefy Mexicans and wonderful new Hungarians. The New World is well-chosen, and there are some delicate early landed vintage Cognacs, for when you feel like lashing out £60 or so.

TESCO (TES)

(Head office) Delamare Road, Cheshunt, Herts EN8 9SL, (01992) 632222, fax (01992) 630794; 526 licensed branches;
Mail order: (0800) 403403
Hours Variable (open Sunday).
Credit cards AC S V.
G M T
Wide range, and no longer regarded as runner-up to Sainsbury in quality terms. Lots of New World wines and good on Italy, Germany and French vins de pays too.

THRESHER (THR)

(Head office) Sefton House, 42 Church Street, Welwyn Garden City, Herts AL8 6PJ, (01707) 328244, fax (01707) 371398
Hours Mon–Sat 9–10 (some 10.30), Sun 12–3, 7–10; Scotland 12.30–10.30.
Credit cards AC S V.
Discounts Available on quantity.
Delivery Free locally, some branches. National delivery via Drinks Direct, 0800 232221.
G T
An extremely good list that can spring a number of surprises. Pleasant ones, of course. Champagnes are excellent, with good inexpensive ones (inexpensive for Champagne, that is) right up to Roederer Cristal. There's also Veuve Clicquot Demi-Sec and, for the brave, Piper Heidsieck Brut Sauvage. Bordeaux looks very good, though it's surprisingly heavily weighted towards the expensive end of the spectrum, and Burgundies also look attractive, though there's no pretence that Burgundy isn't expensive. French country wines are decidedly more affordable (and when you can get Mas de Daumas Gassac for the same price as Givry Premier Cru, I know which I'd rather have). Alsace is another region that Thresher does well, and there is quite a large selection from England. With the franc so strong, English wine is looking less expensive than it was in comparison. There are plenty of good single malts, too.

THE UBIQUITOUS CHIP (UB)

8 Ashton Lane, Glasgow G12 8SJ, 0141-334 5007, fax 0141-337 1302
Hours Mon–Fri 12–10, Sat 11–10.
Credit Cards AC AE DC V.
Discounts 5% cash or cheque purchases of cases.
Delivery Free Glasgow 3 cases or more, otherwise negotiable.
C G M T
What with the Burrell Collection and The Ubiquitous Chip, Glasgow must be a pretty good place to live. There's the sort of spread of growers here that betokens personal choice, wine by wine, rather than the acceptance of a whole range from a single producer (except in Beaujolais). The Rhône looks interesting, as do the Loire, Alsace and Italy. There are a few old vintages of Italian reds, like Gaja's Barbaresco 1982, or Caparzo's Brunello di Montalcino la Casa 1983. From Romania there's the excellent value sweet Tamaîïoasa, and California and New Zealand both look excellent. Germany is good, too. They helpfully recommend single malt whiskies as presents: 'It is often possible to match a bottle age to a birthday', they say. For the ten-year-old who has everything, presumably.

UNWINS (UN)

(Head office) Birchwood House, Victoria Road, Dartford, Kent DA1 5AJ, (01322) 272711/7; 310 specialist off-licences in south-east England
Hours Variable, usually Mon–Sat 9–10.30, Sun 12–10.
Credit cards AC AE DC S V.

Discounts 10% mixed case, 5% on six bottles.

G M T

French regional wines are good here, as is the Portuguese selection. There's an Eiswein from Austria and some nice Aussies. It's not a long list – not up to the standard of Thresher or Oddbins. Having said that, the wines that Unwins sent in to our Best Buys tasting this year were pretty interesting. So perhaps things are looking up. It's hard to see how Unwins can compete otherwise.

VALVONA & CROLLA (VA)

19 Elm Row, Edinburgh EH7 4AA, 0131-556 6066

Hours Mon–Wed 8.30–6, Thu–Fri 8.30–7.30, Sat 8.30–6.

Credit cards AC AE S V.

Discounts 5% mixed case, 10% unmixed case.

Delivery Free locally for orders over £30. Mail order £9.50 per case, £5.30 4 cases or more, free 10 or more.

G M T

An almost entirely Italian list that just about manages to squeeze in a few Champagnes and ports as concessions to the rest of the world. Practically all regions of Italy are represented, but not in equal numbers. There are the excellent wines of Jermann and Schioppetto from Friuli Venezia-Giulia, and yards and yards of goodies from Piedmont and Tuscany. The Veneto is also present in force; there's even a sparkling Recioto della Valpolicella, which should be worth a try. But wine is only part of the story here: it's also a specialist Italian food shop. Its list of olive oils is longer than some merchants' lists of Italian wines. If you happen to find yourself in Elm Row, and it happens to be lunchtime (as it so often is, I find), Valvona & Crolla now have an in-house café-bar, in which you can feast on food and wine from the shop. But the fizzy Recioto might be best left until dinner time. Best left altogether, perhaps? No, I didn't say that.

VICTORIA WINE (VIC)

(Head office) Dukes Court, Duke St, Woking, Surrey GU21 5XL, (01483) 715066; over 1550 branches throughout Great Britain (including Haddows and Victoria Wine Cellars)

Hours Variable, usually Mon–Sat 9–6 (high street), 10–10 (local shops), Sun 12–3 & 7–10.
Credit cards AC S V.
Discounts 5% mixed case (10% in Cellars), 7 bottles for the price of 6 on all Champagnes and fizz over £5.99 in Cellars.
Delivery Free locally (by arrangement only in shops).
G T
This habit off-licence chains have acquired, of splitting themselves into the ordinary sort of shop, and the better sort of shop with a slightly different name, is very confusing. Presumably it's good marketing, though they seem to come and go so rapidly that one wonders. Anyway, Victoria Wine's upmarket version is Victoria Wine Cellars (as opposed to Shops). They're bigger, they stock a bigger range (and 'adult snacks' as opposed to 'snacks' displayed, presumably, on the top shelf). The case discounts are bigger and they always have chilled Champagne. Actually the Victoria Wine list is very good, and you can order anything you want from the list, even if it's not on show in your local branch.

LA VIGNERONNE (VIG)

105 Old Brompton Rd, London SW7 3LE, 0171-589 6113, fax 0171-581 2983
Hours Mon–Fri 10–8, Sat 10–6.
Credit cards AC AE DC S V.
Discounts 5% mixed case (collected).
Delivery Free locally, £10 mainland England and Wales for orders under £100, £5 for £101–£200, free over £200; mainland Scotland £16 under £150, £8 £150–£300, free over £300.
C EP M T
Fascinating and very personal list, full of old vintages (1964 Alsace, 1969 Champagne) as well as the best of the new. It's not cheap, but everything is excellent.

VINTAGE WINES (VIN)

116/118 Derby Rd, Nottingham NG1 5FB, (0115) 9476565/9419614
Hours Mon–Fri 9–5.15, Sat 9–1.
Credit cards AC V S.
Discounts 10% mixed case.

Delivery Free within 60 miles.
G M T
Useful merchant with traditional taste who takes care with his house wines.

WAITROSE (WAI)

(Head office) Doncastle Rd, Southern Industrial Area, Bracknell, Berks RG12 8YA (01344) 424680; 115 licensed shops. (Mail order) 0181-543 0966, fax 0181-543 2415.
Hours Mon–Tue 8.30–6, Wed–Thurs 8.30–8, Fri 8.30–9, Sat 8.30–6.
Credit cards AC S V.
Discounts 5% whole cases of wine.
Delivery (From Waitrose Direct/Findlater Mackie Todd) Free 2 cases, or over £100 throughout mainland UK or Isle of Wight, otherwise £3.95.
G M
There's relatively little Waitrose own-label stuff here, and now the range has been expanded by a mail-order association with Findlater Mackie Todd. This is currently looking the best of the supermarkets, with a well-chosen range that is not as big as some, but is nevertheless much more interesting. Waitrose wines tend to have character; you won't find the sort of bland commercial flavours on which more than one supermarket chain seems to be relying at the moment. Their prices are competitive, too.

WATERLOO WINE CO (WAT)

6 Vine Yard, Borough, London SE1 1QL, 0171-403 7967, fax 0171-357 6976
Hours Mon–Fri 10–6.30, Sat 10–5.
Credit cards AC S V.
Delivery Free 5 cases or more.
G T
There's a passion for the Loire here, with wines of all colours and styles. The selection from Germany is also good, and there are generally some mature German wines to be had, since nobody else seems to buy them but the editor of this guide. Good Alsace wines come from Seltz, (umpteen different cuvées) and there are lovely New Zealand wines from Mark Rattray. You'll find some Valdespino sherries, too.

WHITESIDES OF CLITHEROE (WHI)

Shawbridge St, Clitheroe, Lancs BB7 1NA, (01200) 422281, fax (01200) 427129
Hours Mon–Fri 10–8, Sat 9–5.30.
Credit cards AC V.
Discounts 5% per case.
G M T
The Loire looks interesting here – there's nice Pouilly-Fumé and, for a curiosity, oak-aged Muscadet, though it's a pity the only Loire rosé Whitesides could find was an anonymous Cabernet d'Anjou. The Rhône looks worth sampling and there are some rather good Germans. There's also gluhwein, for those chilly Lancashire nights. The Italian section boasts such delights as Allegrini's Amarone della Valpolicella and Ca' del Pazzo from Caparzo. All in all, a very nice list.

WINE RACK (WR)

(Head office) Sefton House, 42 Church Street, Welwyn Garden City, Herts AL8 6PJ, (01707) 328244, fax (01707) 371398
Hours Mon–Sat 9–10 (some 10.30), Sun 12–3 & 7–10.
Credit cards AC AE S V.
Discounts 5% mixed cases wine, 12.5% mixed cases Champagne.
Delivery Free locally, all shops, and nationally via Drinks Direct, 0800 232221.
G T
This is part of Threshers; but it's the smarter end of the business, and with a wider, generally more upmarket range than the common-or-garden Thresher shops. There are 120 stores across the country.

WINE SOCIETY (WS)

(Head office) Gunnels Wood Rd, Stevenage, Herts SG1 2BG, (01438) 741177, fax (01438) 741392
Hours Mon–Fri 8.30–9; showroom: Mon–Fri 9–5.30, Sat 9–4.
Credit cards AC S V.
Discounts (per case) £1 for 5–9, £2 for 10 or more, £3 for collection.
Delivery Free 1 case or more UK mainland and Northern Ireland. Collection facility at Hesdin, France at French rates of duty and VAT.
C EP G M T
You have to be a member to buy wines from this non-profit-making co-operative, but lifetime membership is very reasonable at £20. They offer an outstanding range. France is the backbone, but there are also masses of good and adventurous wines from California, Germany, Italy, Portugal, Spain (including white from from the unpronounceable Basque coast) plus goodies like leek and almond relish, wood roasted piquillo peppers and rocket sauce. This is one of the country's most enterprising wine merchants, and every region has top growers and unexpected wines. Quoted prices include delivery, which makes them rather good value.

WINES OF WESTHORPE LTD (WIW)

Marchington, Staffs ST14 8NX, (01283) 820285, fax (01283) 820631
Hours Mon–Fri 8.30–6.30, Sat 8.30–1. These are minimum hours.
Credit cards AC S V.
Discounts (per case) £2.60 for 6–15, £3.60 for 16–25, 50p for Switch/debit cards.

Discover
a World *of* Wine

In pursuing excellence, look no further than ASDA.

Our wines are selected on a global scale; from familiar European classics to more enigmatic varieties and blends associated with the New World. The diverse flavours you'll encounter, together with unparalleled value, means

you are
tasting
wine
from

ASDA

Delivery Free UK mainland 2 or more cases.
Minimum order 1 mixed case.
M T
There are more Australians here than there used to be (from Karanga Hill and D'Arenberg), plus some Chileans and a Moldovan Cabernet, but the bulk of the list is from Bulgaria and Hungary. From the latter comes a sweet Cabernet Sauvignon, which the company recommends for strawberries and cream, plus Tokaji brandy, aged in barrels that were previously used for aging Tokaji Azsú. Beats adding caramel.

WRIGHT WINE CO (WRI)

The Old Smithy, Raikes Rd, Skipton, N. Yorks BD23 1NP, (01756) 700886
Hours Mon–Sat 9–6.
Credit cards AC S V.
Discounts Wholesale price unsplit case, 5% mixed case.
Delivery Free within 30 miles.
G
There are some pretty unusual wines here, tucked into a list that is anyway good. Sparkling red Burgundy? Pinot Beurot from the Hautes-Côtes de Nuits? This is the place. Chateau Musar from the Lebanon goes back to 1975, and sherry includes such treats as Valdespino. There are also more conventional goodies from Burgundy and Alsace in particular, and lots of half-bottles.

PETER WYLIE FINE WINES (WY)

Plymtree Manor, Plymtree, Cullompton, Devon EX15 2LE, (01884) 277555, fax (01884) 277557
Hours Mon–Fri 9–6.
Discounts Unsplit cases.
Delivery Free London 3 or more cases, UK mainland 1 case £122 cases £6.50 per case, 3 or more cases £4 per case.
C EP M
Looking for a present for a 90th birthday this year? Try Mouton-Rothschild 1907, a snip at £435. Deserving 21-year-olds are cheaper to buy for: a bottle of la Mission Haut-Brion comes in at £35. Peter Wylie doesn't stock every single year in between, but he's got a lot of them. Not everything here is old by any means, but we are definitely in fine and rare country here. There are a few Rhônes, and a handful of Loires and Californians; the other main emphases are port and Champagne, and there are some vintage Madeiras.

YAPP BROTHERS (YAP)

The Old Brewery, Mere, Wilts BA12 6DY, (01747) 860423, fax (01747) 860929
Hours Mon–Fri 9–5, Sat 9–1.
Credit cards AC V.
Discounts £3 per case on collection, quantity discount on 6 or more cases.
Delivery £5 single case or less.
C EP G M T
Rhône and Loire specialist of 25 years standing. The wines here are among the best of their kind, and the Yapps are always finding new ones. Côtes du Rhône-Brézème, for example – no, they'd never heard of it before, either. There are lots of everyday wines here, as well as serious ones for serious drinking. Provence and Alsace are also represented, and there are good Champagnes.

NOEL YOUNG WINES (YOU)

56 High Street, Trumpington, Cambridge CB2 2LS, (01223) 844744, fax (01223) 844736
Hours Mon–Sat 10–9, Sun 12–2
Credit cards DC V.
Discounts 5% 5–10 cases, 10% 10 cases or more.
Delivery £7.50 on orders up to £50, £6 on orders up to £100, £5 on orders up to £500, free over £500.
Minimum order 1 mixed case.
G M T
A newish merchant with a very good list. Noel Young ships some of Austria's top wines, so nobody could accuse him of pandering to fashion. Look for Wieninger, Kracher, Bründlmayer, Hirtzberger, Prager and Krutzler here. But Noel Young takes just about every region seriously. There's Hollick's lovely Ravenswood Cabernet from Coonawarra and D'Arenberg's Old Vine Shiraz from McLaren Vale; Navarro Correas from Argentina, and good Burgundies, Rhônes, French country wines and Bordeaux.

INDEX